Myth and the American Experience

Myth and the American Experience

Volume Two

Nicholas Cords & Patrick Gerster

Lakewood State Junior College
White Bear Lake, Minnesota

GLENCOE PRESS

A division of Benziger Bruce & Glencoe, Inc.
New York • Beverly Hills

GLENCOE PRESS
A division of Benziger Bruce & Glencoe, Inc.
8701 Wilshire Boulevard
Beverly Hills, California 90211
Collier-Macmillan Canada, Ltd., Toronto, Canada

Library of Congress catalog card number: 72-91271

Printed in the United States of America

First Printing, 1973

Second Printing, 1973

To
Maggie & Carole

Contents

Contents

Preface

It would be scarcely novel to suggest that America's historical past has been, at least in some measure, subject to distortion and myth. Comparatively, it appears that American history is more myth-laden than that of any other western nation. Indeed, Henry Steele Commager, in an article included in this work, demonstrates that during the period 1789–1860, at least, Americans set out with a vengeance to create a "usable past"—myths included.

Accuracy, it is said, must be the constant companion of the historian. It has been out of this constant concern for accuracy that one of the major thrusts of American historiography (at least in the twentieth century) has been the reinterpretation of America's historical myths, many of which were the products of historians themselves. Yet it seems equally true that such historical observations, though uttered consistently, have been expressed with a somewhat fragmented voice.

C. Vann Woodward, in a review article written in 1962 (also included in this work), challenged historians to face up to "the relationship between myth and history." Reminding us that "myth has more than pejorative usages and that it can be used to denote more than what one deems false about another man's beliefs," Professor Woodward goes on to suggest not the destruction of myths, but their serious critique. This collection of readings, focusing on the dichotomy of myth and reality in American history, is a partial reply to that challenge.

We do not intend here to supply a definitive answer as to why such a predisposition has intrigued professional historians and students of the American past, nor to suggest that this work supplies the final word as to what is myth and what is reality in American history. Realizing that one man's myth may well be another man's reality, we wish merely to bring together various myths that have been isolated and identified by members of the American historical community. Certainly we have selected the individual articles, but it is the individual historians represented in the selections who have identified the myths. Each article stands on its own arguments and its own merits, yet in some measure each seems to suggest the validity of studying the past within the framework of myth and reality.

In a more pragmatic sense, this work emanates from a course developed and taught by one of the editors, Patrick Gerster, which focused on the theme of myth and reality in American history. The course's marked success with lower division college students demonstrated the viability of the approach and the pervasiveness of myth, as well as its relevance to the study of America's past.

Perhaps we should make a further observation concerning the relationship between myth and reality: The black-and-white distinction between the two is used in this work as a tool for historical analysis. Remember that there is a point at which myth and reality intersect; thus, at given points, they can become one and the same thing. Myth becomes reality precisely when man reacts as if the myth were true and bases his beliefs and conduct upon it. Thus, the difficulty seems to lie not so much with the myth itself, but rather with the fact that myth often serves as the basis for mores and cultural attitudes—for canons and laws. All men, then, to a degree live in accordance with the norms and principles that have been drawn from myth. If one accepts the idea or perception of myth as an important ingredient in man's past and present, then the recognition and understanding of myth seems absolutely essential to the study of history.

As historians have continued to reinterpret and revise, and to demonstrate that history is more than a catalogue of great wars, crusading generals, and the decisions of presidents, increasingly they have discovered that discrepancies often exist between history as actuality and history as perceived. As a result of this process, history's scholarly practitioners have left ample and enviable commentary on America's myth-encrusted past. Significant examples of their findings comprise this work.

White Bear Lake, Minnesota
January 1973

NICHOLAS CORDS
PATRICK GERSTER

Acknowledgments

It is customary to acknowledge myriad debts—both intellectual and personal—to those who have contributed to publication. Often, the catalogue is sweeping: historians (from Herodotus to Handlin), sources (from *The Peloponnesian War* to *The Pentagon Papers*), teachers (from K through Ph.D.), students, colleagues, publishers, editors, research assistants (what are they?), typists, et al. Also included are wives, parents ("without whom this work would not have been possible"), children, in-laws and other sundry relatives and friends. Further sources of inspiration may well be represented. Having somewhat facetiously recited the litany, yet struck by the amount of truth therein, we selectively acknowledge our obligations to the above. More specifically, a word of thanks is extended to Clarke Chambers, Professor of History and Department Chairman, University of Minnesota, who has been aware of the project from its beginning, and who has strategically provided both constructive criticism and enthusiastic support as the occasion warranted. Finally, special thanks to those authors and publishers who have granted reprint privileges, particularly those who were financially considerate and those whose permissions were accompanied by notes of encouragement, interest and good will.

INTRODUCTION:
HISTORY AND MYTH

The Mythmakers of American History

Thomas A. Bailey

Thomas A. Bailey, long an established American diplomatic historian, and now Byrne Professor of American History, Emeritus, at
Stanford University, has been one of the most consistent and articulate spokesman on the topic of myth in American history. In an
expanded version of a presidential address given before the Organization of American Historians in 1968, Professor Bailey provides his
own definition of "historical myth" and highlights what he feels are
the major sources of America's historical myths—from poets and
presidents to historians themselves. Mr. Bailey's selection does
much to set both the tone and the perspective for the chapters that
follow.

False historical beliefs are so essential to our culture that if they did not exist,
like Voltaire's God, they would have to be invented. In this uncertain world
we crave certainties, and if an iconoclast were suddenly to shatter all myths,
our social structure would suffer a traumatic shock. We need only imagine
how different our national history would be if countless millions of our citizens had not been brought up to believe in the manifestly destined superiority
of the American people, in the supremacy of the white race, in the primacy
of the Nordics within the white race, in the safety-valve "free" land in the
West, in completely rugged individualism, and in the rags-to-riches dream of
a millionaire's blank check in every workingman's lunch box.[1]

Historical myths and legends are needful in establishing national identity and stimulating patriotic pride.[2] If Switzerland has its William Tell and
the arrowed apple, and if Scotland has its Robert Bruce and the persevering
spider, the United States has its George Washington and the chopped cherry
tree. The American colonials, having jettisoned George III, were under com-
pulsion to fabricate home-grown tales of their own in a hurry; and this perhaps explains why so many of our heroic legends are associated with the
"glorious" War of Independence.[3]

American children are indoctrinated with nonhistorical myths before
they are hardly out of the bassinet. Santa Claus keeps small fry better behaved
before Christmas, while the stork keeps them—or used to keep them—from
asking embarrassing questions between Christmases. The youngster also hears

From "The Mythmakers of American History," by Thomas A. Bailey, in *Journal of
American History*, Vol. LV (June 1968), pp. 5–21; reprinted by permission of the
author and publisher.

2

hero tales about Washington kneeling in the snow at Valley Forge and Abraham Lincoln reading by the light of a flickering fireplace. Yet there is no credible evidence that either did either.

Many elementary teachers of history and literature are not well enough informed to separate the legend from the truth. They are only too happy to keep the children entertained. Others, I find, know the facts but continue to tell the time-tested stories, including the Parson Weems tale about the cherry tree. Many teachers have discovered that the pupil does not remember the stories anyhow, so the end result does not make much difference. If the children are taught the debunked account, they might become unsettled. They might even repeat it in garbled form in a superpatriotic home, thereby stirring up trouble with the school authorities and jeopardizing their jobs. The safest course for the instructor is to perpetuate the hallowed myths and not rock the boat.[4]

The poets studied in school have also done their part in creating historical mythology. John Keats had poetical license on his side when he had Cortés rather than Balboa discover the Pacific, but this was carrying his license a bit too far. The stirring tale of Paul Revere's ride was a legend in search of a poet, and it found Henry Wadsworth Longfellow, who put the resolute rider on the wrong side of the river and had him thunder into Concord, which he failed to reach.[5] The playwrights, as cousins of the poets, have likewise sinned. Robert E. Sherwood's *Abe Lincoln in Illinois* (1938), whether on the stage or on the screen, has probably done more than any other single medium to implant the maudlin legend of Lincoln's grief-stricken love affair with Ann Rutledge.

Historical novels are among our most effective teachers, but they are naturally more concerned with dramatic effect than undramatic truth. Nathaniel Hawthorne's harsh image of the blue-nosed Puritan, as portrayed in *The Scarlet Letter*, persists in the face of recent scholarship. The fading picture that many high school graduates retain of the Civil War and Reconstruction from their dessicated textbooks is probably overshadowed by Margaret Mitchell's *Gone With The Wind*, which presents the story with a southern exposure and a rebel yell. Literature, including historical novels and novelized history, is often the continuation of war by other means.

Star-spangled history textbooks still dish up much mythology, shaped as they are in part by patriotic pressure groups. In our dealings with foreign countries, especially Britain, we are not only about one hundred percent right but one hundred percent righteous. (It is only fair to add that British versions of the two Anglo-American wars generally reverse the process.[6]) Professional patriots, like the Sons of the American Revolution and Texans for America, are still demanding that we teach patriotism above all. They would exalt the "Spirit of '76," restore Nathan Hale and his undying dying regret, and combat socialism or any other "ism" that foreshadows social change. The United

Daughters of the Confederacy are by no means mute more than a hundred years after the guns fell silent at Appomattox. The hyphenates are still vocal, especially the Italian-Americans, who insist on having Columbus, rather than the Norsemen, discover America.[7] The Italians are generally successful, except in Minnesota, where the Scandinavians, clinging to their questionable Kensington Stone, have more votes.

A newly formed hyphenate group, but not a new element, consists of African-Americans. Seeking a quasi-national identity, much as white America did after 1776, they are now understandably clamoring for historical recognition. For many generations they were the "invisible men" of American history—the dusky hoers of weeds and pluckers of cotton. Now, with black balloting power and portentous rioting power, they are insisting on visibility, if not overvisibility, in the textbooks. In at least two of our great cities—New York and Detroit—the school authorities have issued separate booklets, a hundred or so pages in length, detailing the contributions of the Negro.[8]

This belated recognition, though praiseworthy in many respects, is fraught with danger. Most non-militant Negroes would probably like to think of themselves as dark-skinned Americans, and this self-imposed Jim Crowism can be self-defeating. Pressure-group history of any kind is deplorable, especially when significant white men are bumped out to make room for much less significant black men in the interests of social harmony.[9] If this kind of distortion gets completely out of hand, we can visualize what will happen when the Negroes become the dominant group in all our largest cities, as they already are in Washington, D.C. Coexistence may end, and we may even have hard-backed Negro histories of the United States, with the white man's achievements relegated to a subsidiary treatment.

The apotheosis of Crispus Attucks is illuminating. He was a runaway Negro slave, we are told, whose blood was the first to be shed in the American struggle for independence. We have long known that he was fatally shot in the so-called Boston Massacre of March 5, 1770. But we do not know for a certainty whether he was a Negro or an Indian or even a runaway. He and his fellows were guilty of hooliganism that night; several other people had earlier lost their lives in the struggle against British authority since 1763; and the armed outburst at Lexington and Concord was a full five years in the offing.[10]

This determination to stand American history on its head, so characteristic of minority groups, may stimulate pride among Negroes, but it can win little support from true scholarship. The luckless African-Americans while in slavery were essentially in jail; and we certainly would not write the story of a nation in terms of its prison population. Yet the pressure is on to overstress Negro initiative in organizing revolts, in escaping from bondage, and in securing emancipation. President Andrew Johnson, who was once downgraded by James Ford Rhodes and John W. Burgess because he messed up Reconstruction for the southern whites, is again being downgraded, this time because he messed it up for the unfortunate blacks.[11]

Once the pupil, white or black, has escaped the tyranny of the timid teacher and timeserving textbook, he is at the mercy of the journalists. He scans the columns of his daily newspaper, probably unaware that dramatic historical tales are the stock-in-trade of the newsman, and that a good reporter never exaggerates unless he improves the story.[12] Mr. Drew Pearson, for example, has continued to give currency to the fabrication that the official purchase price of Alaska contained a secret payment for the costs of bringing the two Russian fleets to American waters during the Civil War.[13] Mr. Walter Lippmann, in a hands-across-the-seas book published during the war year 1943, falsely but patriotically described the Monroe Doctrine as a quasi-alliance with Britain.[14]

Pictorial history, including cartoons and faked photographs, also presents numerous pitfalls.[15] The artist, like the poet, is entitled to draw on his imagination for details, as did John Trumbull, the painter of the American Revolution. But Benjamin West's famous painting of Penn's Treaty with the Indians depicts a colorful scene which cannot be documented. The celebration which accompanied the dramatic "wedding of the rails," near Ogden, Utah, in 1869, was fortunately photographed. Yet the pasteurized painting of the scene, as later authorized by former Governor Leland Stanford of California, neatly eliminated the liquor bottles, included prominent men who had not been there, and excluded the numerous ladies of negotiable virtue who definitely were there.[16]

The television tube, in more ways than one, has helped to get the picture out of focus. We now discover Daniel Boone operating near West Point to rescue that key fortress from the treachery of Benedict Arnold. Television has turned murderous "hoods," like Jesse James and Billy the Kid, into veritable Robin Hoods. It has also contributed an additional encrustation of legend to such dubious frontier characters as Wyatt Earp and "Wild Bill" Hickok.[17]

Much of our historical mythology is created by the motion picture industry, which often spends enormous sums to get the facts straight and then proceeds to make them crooked. The pioneer cinema classic, *The Birth of a Nation* (1915), set back Reconstruction history by a generation or so by glorifying the hooded hoodlums of the old Ku Klux Klan and stimulating the besheeted bigots of the new.

The politician must also take high rank among the most prolific of mythmakers. His primary objective is to get into office and stay there, and his so-called history is apt to be hand tooled for these ends. I invariably cringe when a politician voices the sonorous "History teaches," because I know that he is going to make it teach whatever he wants it to teach.[18] Thomas Jefferson set an unfortunate example in the Declaration of Independence when he accused George III of many sins that the ill-starred monarch never dreamed of committing.

The worst history teachers of all in some respects are the Presidents of the United States, one of whose many roles is "Teacher-in-Chief." Only three of them could claim fairly solid credentials as historians—Theodore Roosevelt, Woodrow Wilson, and John F. Kennedy—and of these only Wilson had graduate training.[19] With tens of millions of listeners now in the living-room classroom, the President is keenly aware that he is making history, rather than writing it. A "credibility gap"—the phrase employed by journalists whose own credibility is often suspect—has existed since the days of George Washington. . . . President Lyndon B. Johnson's real problem was not so much misusing history as making statements that were obviously false. Perhaps he did not know enough about it to misuse it skillfully. The historian is a little disturbed to find him referring to the late President Diem (not Ho Chi Minh) as the Winston Churchill of Vietnam, to the Dominican intervention as "just like the Alamo," and to the Vietnam War as a hunt which must end, in Davy Crockett fashion, "with that coonskin on the wall."[20] The historical Big Lie is just as much a lie when it comes from the banks of the Potomac as from the beer halls of Munich.

It is easy enough for historians to pillory the politicians and the press while overlooking their own faults. Samuel Butler, the English essayist, is quoted as saying that since God himself cannot change the past, he is obliged to tolerate the existence of historians. Other cynics have wondered why history is so dull when so much of it is obviously fiction. The ugly fact is that the professional keeper of the record does not have a good public "image": Clio, wrote Arthur Schopenhauer, "is as permeated with lies as a street-whore with syphilis."[21]

Too many so-called historians are really "hysterians"; their thinking is often more visceral than cerebral. When their duties as citizens clash with their responsibilities as scholars, Clio frequently takes a back seat. How many of us can march in Mississippi one week and teach Negro history with reasonable objectivity the next? How many of us can be shining eggheads for Adlai Stevenson in the evening and sober spokesmen for scholarship the next morning? How many of us who are professional Southerners or New Englanders can deal fairly with other sections?[22] How many of us can forget that we are white or black when writing about whites or blacks? How many of us can avoid the academic homosexuality of falling in love with our own hero? We recall with scholarly shame that for some twenty-five years the only reasonably respectable one-volume biography of Woodrow Wilson was written with sticky adulation by an eminent American historian.[23]

How many of us can forget that we are Americans, presumably loyal Americans? To be sure, we have ample, if not admirable precedent, in the patriotic effusions of George Bancroft, whose every page seemingly voted for Andrew Jackson or American democracy or both. We remember without pride how certain prominent historians sprang to the colors in 1917 and prostituted their art in an effort to hamstring the Hun and make the world safe for normalcy.[24] The conduct of scholars during World War II was more commendable. Both they and the American people were more sophisticated, and, with Hitler on the loose, the issues were clearer cut. But even today our history texts suffer from being too America-centered, as though we were the hub of the universe and all other nations were barbarians dwelling in outer darkness.[25]

How many of us, seeking an instant reputation at the expense of some towering figure, have embarked upon dubious revisionism for the sake of sensationalism or in response to faddism? No one will deny that fresh interpretations are desirable, or that history becomes more meaningful when rewritten by succeeding generations in the light of their own experience, as it invariably is. But much of our revisionism comes about as a result of a flair for novelty or a reaction against the monotony of repeating the eternal verities year after year. And let us not forget that revisionists, like evangelists, universally overstate their case in their effort to get a hearing.

Sometimes revisionism comes from a conspiratorial complex, for which mankind has a natural affinity, as recently demonstrated anew by the Kennedy assassination case. The eminent historian who warned us most emphatically against the Devil Theory of history, ironically enough, stumbled into his own well-described trap. Near the end of a memorable career, he published two books that portrayed Franklin D. Roosevelt as a veritable Mephistopheles, bent on having war at almost any price, including the destruction of our Pacific fleet.[26]

The scholar often falls into the error of failing to understand the mentality of the masses, who obviously are not all fellow historians. Ensconced in his book-lined study, a century or two after the event, he betrays a species of arrogance when he assumes that men living in a bygone era did not have the fuzziest idea of what was going on about them or what they wanted. This assumption has led to what may be called "the flight from the obvious." We should take heed of Ralph Waldo Emerson's warning in 1836, "In analysing history do not be too profound, for often the causes are quite superficial."[27]

Let us look at America's wars. The men of 1776 thought they were fighting for liberty; the revisionists of the twentieth century played up economic motivations. Now, in something of a back-to-Bancroft movement, we are again stressing liberty. The men of 1812 believed they were fighting for a free sea; the revisionists of the 1920s had them fighting for Canada. Now we have left Tippecanoe Creek and are back again on the bounding main. The men of 1861, including Lincoln, assumed that slavery was the principal villain in the coming of the war. In the 1920s Beard and others shifted emphasis to the North's alleged industrial imperialism—a thesis which the Southerners happily embraced as taking a load off their consciences. Now we think that slavery, directly or indirectly, had much to do with the guns of April. The men of 1917 concluded that the submarine plunged us into hostilities with imperial Germany. The revisionists of the 1930s blamed the financiers, the "munitioneers," the "propagandeers," and the "sloganeers."[28] Now, scores of volumes and millions of casualties later, we are back, at the risk of some oversimplification, with the submarine.

Much of our revisionism has come from premature and half-baked hypotheses, launched, in Carl Becker's immortal phrase, "without fear and without research." New hypotheses should certainly be encouraged, but if the evidence is lacking or scanty, they should be advanced with the utmost tentativeness. Charles A. Beard, in his pathbreaking study of the Constitution, modestly acknowledged in his preface that his research was "frankly fragmentary," and he implied that he was advancing views which would be more firmly established by later evidence. His modesty was fully justified by the revelations of subsequent hatchet-wielders.

Sometimes historians degenerate into polemicists, as did Harry Elmer Barnes, with an inevitable distortion of the record. Their diatribes can become so shrill that they cannot secure reputable publishers, whereupon they raise pained cries of "Court History" or "historical blackout."[29] David Starr Jordan once observed that no man can shout and at the same time tell the truth.

Some scholars run to the other extreme. They are so afraid of being labeled debunkers that they cling like barnacles to the tried and true bunk. Anatole France, in a classic passage in the preface of *Penguin Island*, points out that people do not like to be jolted but prefer the comfort of the old sillinesses (*les sottises*). The mythmaker simplifies and soothes; the critic complicates and agitates. The word "debunker," evidently coined by W. E. Woodward in 1923, has unfortunate overtones.[30] We certainly cannot get at the solid timber of truth unless we first clear away the underbrush of myth and legend. But the historian who spends his life hacking at underbrush in search of shockers is misapplying his talents. This Weemsianism-in-reverse runs the risk of "rebunking"—that is, substituting new bunk for old. And if the debunker manages to dig up dirt about our national heroes, say Lincoln, he is not likely to get a Book-of-the-Month Club adoption or even a *Reader's Digest* abridgment.[31] He who strikes at patriotic myths strikes at the foundations of our society; he is deemed guilty of sacrilege, at least by the anti-revolutionary Daughters of the American Revolution.

Too many historical writers are the votaries of cults, which, by definition, are dedicated to whitewashing warts and hanging halos. Many of us have developed a warping bias for or against Jefferson, Andrew Jackson, Lincoln, Wilson, or the Roosevelts. The overnight birth in this city of a Kennedy cult, complete with an eternal flame, should provide a poignant reminder of the pitfalls of apotheosis. We recall that Kennedy's Secretary of the Navy, Fred Korth, was accused of involvement in a conflict-of-interest scandal, which led to his hush-hush resignation. By a tasteful coincidence this episode is not even mentioned in either of the lengthy books by Sorensen and Schlesinger, two of the President's close associates and admirers.[32]

Presidents of the American Historical Association, no less than those of the United States, are exposed to cultism, as evidenced by the embarrassing adoration of impressionable disciples. Frederick Jackson Turner, Beard, and Herbert Eugene Bolton were among those historians so honored. Their devotees have not only defended the mistakes of the master but have sometimes carried his theories beyond all reasonable bounds.

Special dangers lurk in a vested interest in a given interpretation, whether by the master or his students. The temptation is almost overpowering to ignore negative evidence or to manipulate positive evidence, in the Procrustean-bed fashion of an Arnold Toynbee. A case in point came to my attention some twenty-five years ago. A well-known defender of southern slavery urged a colleague to be on the alert, in his related researches, for as many instances as he could find of northern husbands beating their wives.

A close cousin of cultism is monocausationism. Turner was by no means a monocausationist, but many of his followers tended to view the entire spectrum through the chinks of a log cabin. Karl Marx's lucubrations have led to an overemphasis on economic factors, as presently exemplified by some younger writers of the so-called New Left.[33] Beard's block-busting book on the Constitution was an attempt to deal with one set of causes—the economic. Narrowing the problem in this way is a perfectly legitimate historical exercise, given one's interest and available time. But such an approach invariably leads to distortion, no matter how emphatically the author sets forth his intentions in the preface, which all too often is skipped.[34]

Monocausation has also led the unwary to confuse causes with objectives. The major military goal of the Americans in the War of 1812 was Canada, because that was the only place where Britain was getatable. But the battle cry "On to Canada" has deceived short-sighted observers, then as now, into concluding that we went to war primarily because we lusted after the timbered lands of our semi-defenseless northern neighbor, rather than the right to sail the high seas unhindered.

Dexter Perkins has spoken eloquently of the scholarly joy of revising one's conclusions in the light of more information or reflection. Not all historians experience this praiseworthy thrill. Loyalty to one's errors is one of the lowest forms of loyalty, and repetition in the classroom for thirty-five years does not make truths of untruths or half-truths. Rigidity is a major vice in the historian, be he a teacher, writer, or editor. Some twenty years ago I was puzzled by an eminent Lincoln scholar who flatly refused to accept new evidence that reflected unfavorably on Wilson. I began to wonder what he did with new evidence that reflected unfavorably on Lincoln. I later found the answer—he suppressed it.

The historian, despite his training in historical method and his presumed objectivity, is often unjustifiably emotional or gullible.[35] The diary of William E. Dodd, published under dubious auspices, is still too highly respected as a primary source.[36] After some humbling experience, I have concluded that most, if not all, of the pretty little stories of history are in some degree false, if pursued to their smallest details. In the absence of expert shorthand or mechanical recording, I would question all or most of the stirring utterances that have come down to us from John Paul Jones to Ronald Reagan. The text of Patrick Henry's famous "liberty-or-death" speech, for example, was pieced together some forty years after the event with the help of old men who contributed their motheaten recollections.[37] I now have less confidence than I had forty-five years ago in the memories of elderly men.

"Presentitis" is another cardinal sin of the myth-making writer of history. Coupling historical events with current events can be most useful in stimulating classroom discussion and clarifying thought, but this practice may be carried to extremes, especially in strained analogies. The historian who attempts to interpret the past to the present in terms of present-day values often undertakes the almost impossible task of serving two masters—of trying to be both a chronicler and a chameleon. Surely we misuse the evidence when we read back into the Jackson era the beginnings of the New Deal, or when we apply to the so-called "Robber Barons" of the nineteenth century the same ethical standards that were finally sanctified in 1914 by the Federal Trade Commission Act. Recent scholarship tends to regard the "Robber Barons" as industrial statesmen, more baronial than piratical.[38]

Textbook writers, from McGuffey on up, have been among the most active preservers of hoary myths. If they do not know any better, they are in beyond their depth. But if they deliberately falsify the record to secure lucrative state adoptions, they are prostitutes. Publishers have perhaps been more guilty than authors, for they have different ethical standards. But we can only look with shame upon the numerous textbooks dealing with the Negro and the Civil War that have been published in two editions: one for the North and one for the South, as though there could be a northern truth and a southern truth, on a take-your-pick basis.[39]

Perhaps the most fruitful contributor to historical mythology is sheer ignorance. Wilson once wondered how the conscientious scholar could sleep nights. The historian should be more than cautious in using such treacherous words as "the only," "always," "the first," and "never before"; and especially the superlatives "oldest," "best," "richest," and "greatest." For many years I told my students that Eli Whitney invented the cotton gin in 1793, and then I discovered that a successful gin was employed on a considerable scale by the French in San Domingo as early as the 1740s.[40] For many years I assured my classes that the American Civil War was the bloodiest thus far in history, with a loss of some 600,000 lives. I changed my tune somewhat when I finally learned that the contemporaneous Taiping Rebellion in China (c. 1850–1864) lasted about fourteen years and cost some 20,000,000 lives.

The rising flood of books and articles is such a mighty torrent that there is an acute "Digestion Gap." The teacher of history simply cannot keep on top of all this material. Those of us who write books do not have time to read books—or at least not all the books and journals we should. In 1939 I published a lengthy article in the *American Historical Review* based on manuscript materials from the archives of three nations. It demonstrated that the British did *not* save George Dewey's fleet from the German fleet at Manila Bay in August 1898. Yet the myth lives merrily on in works by distinguished scholars, including a brilliant survey by a onetime president of the American Historical Association who has shown unusual interest in ship movements. Aside from the "Digestion Gap," this particular tale endures, like other myths that endure, largely because it serves or has served a useful purpose: hands-across-the-sea for the British and fists-across-the-Rhine for the Germans.[41] One is tempted to say that old myths never die; they just become embedded in the textbooks.

Every year dozens of articles of a myth-shattering nature appear in the two hundred or so American magazines, often in journals so obscure that the overburdened teacher never heard of them. I herewith propose, in all earnestness, that the Organization of American Historians and the American Historical Association jointly set up in an appropriate place a centralized Myth Registry, for both articles and books. Abstracts of discredited myths can be recorded, much as dissertation titles are registered, either by the author or by an appropriate abstracting agency.[42] Then, with the marvelous data-recovery processes now being perfected, the requisite information can be made speedily available on request. Such an agency should be a gold mine for teachers, researchers, and especially textbook writers, who have a heavy obligation to keep abreast of this verbal Niagara.

Most historical myths, I suppose, are not dangerous. The cherry tree yarn does no real harm, except perhaps to make young George an insufferable prig. It may even do some good in building youthful character by telling a lie to discourage lie telling. But a little history, to paraphrase Alexander Pope, can be a dangerous thing, and certain historical myths are infinitely mischievous, especially in the area of foreign relations.[43] As John F. Kennedy remarked in 1961 "Domestic policy can only defeat us, but foreign policy can kill us."[44]

The *Herrenvolk* myth, American style, has been with us since the early days of Massachusetts Bay. The conviction that we were God's chosen people, and that we had a divine mandate to spread our ennobling democratic institutions over the rest of the benighted globe, encouraged us to shoulder the White Man's Burden in the Philippines and elsewhere at the turn of the century. We Americans continue to believe that we are a mighty nation, not primarily because we were endowed with magnificent natural resources, but because there was something inherent in our genes that enabled us to become great. This superiority complex has strengthened the conviction that we can impose our democracy on illiterate peasants in faraway rice paddies, including those of Vietnam.

The myth of American omnipotence has led us into some strange and steamy jungles. We find in our America-centered textbooks that we won all our wars, although we certainly did not win the War of 1812 or the Korean War, second phase; neither did we lose them. The pride of unbroken victory —a false pride—pushed us ever deeper into the vortex of Vietnam at a time when face-saving negotiations held some promise of success. President Johnson, with his Alamo complex, has been charged with not wanting to be known as the first President of the United States who failed to win a war for which he was responsible.[45]

The myth that we won all our wars, in spite of being unready for them, has repeatedly caused us to skate to the brink of disaster. This was painfully true in 1916–1917 and later in the pre-Pearl Harbor years, when we clung to the minuteman policy of not preparing until we saw the whites of the enemy's eyes. The myth of unlimited American might has also seduced our policy makers into assuming that we can halt Communist aggression all over the world, including Vietnam.[46] Many hawkish Americans still feel that we could have saved China with American troops in the mid-1940s. The recent costly experience in relatively tiny Vietnam should silence some of the criticism in that quarter.

The myth of permanent victory, fortified by the illusion of invariable "unconditional surrender," has resulted in some expensive but ill-learned lessons. We Americans seem not to realize that impermanence is one of the most permanent features of history, and that victory does not keep. We whipped the Kaiser in 1918 and then brought the doughboys home before the fire was out. We repeated the same process in 1945, when the "I Wanna Go Home" movement reached mutinous proportions. Some wag has said that history repeats itself because no one was listening the first time.

The myth of American righteousness has resulted in some glaring inconsistencies. Our nationalistic textbooks tend to stress the view that there are two sides to every international dispute: our side and the wrong side. We excuse our sins, if excuse them we must, by pointing the accusing finger at other nations, as was notably true of our countercharges when the U–2 spy plane went down in 1960, along with America's holier-than-thou reputation. When the Cuban crunch came in 1962, relatively few Americans, including some near the throne, saw anything inconsistent about encircling the Soviet Union with missiles, while denying Moscow the right to emplace missiles in Cuba.[47]

The Munich myth has likewise borne a lush harvest of evil fruit. Before 1938 the word "appeasement" was in reasonably good odor; after Munich it became a dirty word. The Munich agreement was a compromise, although lopsided and morally vulnerable. Peacetime negotiation, as we know, is normally impossible without mutual compromise and concession. But after Munich countless two-fisted Americans inevitably branded all compromise as appeasement. One basic reason why we refused to sign the Geneva Accords of 1954 regarding Vietnam was that cries of base surrender were being raised in the United States. Bad though the Munich sellout was, the misapplication of its so-called lessons since then may already have caused even greater damage.[48]

Perhaps more harmful has been the myth of the Communist monolith, which has flourished not only in patriotic textbooks but among the planners on the Potomac. Fearful of this Kremlin-directed behemoth, we have fought two undeclared wars and disbursed over 100 billion dollars in foreign aid. But international communism was never a monolith, and most of the time not even communistic. Lenin, Trotsky, and Stalin were never in complete accord, and Trotsky paid for his dissent with exile and a smashed skull. But after China fell to the Reds in 1949, the monolith seemed all the more menacing. The next year, in May 1950, President Harry S. Truman committed the United States to support the French in Vietnam with dollars and military hardware, and since then we have sunk ever deeper into the bottomless bed of snakes.

The irony is that the absence of a monolith was noisily advertised when Red China openly split with Red Russia in the 1960s. The men of Moscow had every reason to believe that they had reared up a nuclear Frankenstein's monster. "Who lost China?" was a question that could be more appropriately asked in the Kremlin than in Congress. The Sino-Soviet split removed the basic reason for our being in Vietnam, yet by this time we were too heavily bemired in the monsoon mud to pull out and had to stress other reasons for remaining. The crack in the so-called monolith presented Washington with a heaven-sent opportunity, yet our Vietnam policies, based in part on false assumptions, tended to narrow, rather than widen, the split between the once-intimate ideological bedfellows.

This by no means exhausts the list of costly or dangerous myths in the field of foreign affairs. Their persistence is a pointed reminder that the historian is involved in much more than art for art's sake. History *does* repeat itself, with variations, and the price seems to go up each time. As trustees of the nation's past, we historians have a special obligation to set the record straight and keep it straight. We cannot muzzle the poets, the playwrights, the pedagogues, the "patrioteers," the press, the politicians, and other muddiers of historical waters; but we can, if we will, control ourselves. The Republic has wrought so many mighty deeds since independence that our people no longer need to be proud of history that never happened.

Notes

1. A historical myth is here defined as an account or belief that is demonstrably untrue, in whole or substantial part. I here exclude fantasies, like Coronado's Seven Cities of Cibola, or the fabrications of hoaxers and charlatans.

2. See Henry Steele Commager, *The Search for a Usable Past and Other Essays in Historiography* (New York, 1967), 3–27.

3. The numerous immigrants also needed the cohesion of legends; many newcomers had little in common except a miserable crossing of the Atlantic Ocean.

4. I am indebted to Dr. Norman E. Tutorow for a number of personal interviews with teachers at various levels in the San Jose area of California.

5. Esther Forbes, *Paul Revere & the World He Lived In* (Boston, 1942), 461, 472. Henry Wadsworth Longfellow also popularized the legends of Miles Standish, Evangeline, and Hiawatha, as John Greenleaf Whittier did the legend of Barbara Fritchie. Ballads have also played an important role in myth-making. The popular song, "The Hunters of Kentucky," for example, left the impression that the riflemen rather than the cannoneers inflicted the heaviest losses at the battle of New Orleans.

6. See Ray Allen Billington and others, *The Historian's Contribution to Anglo-American Misunderstanding* (New York, 1966); Arthur Walworth, *School Histories at War* (Cambridge, 1938).

7. The publication by the Yale University Press in 1965 of a book containing a pre-Columbian map of America stirred up the Italians. See R. A. Skelton and others, *The Vinland Map and the Tartar Relation* (New Haven, 1965).

8. Board of Education, City of New York, *The Negro in American History* (New York, 1964); The Board of Education of the City of Detroit, *The Struggle for Freedom and Rights: Basic Facts about the Negro in American History* (Detroit, 1964).

9. See Kenneth M. Stampp and others, "The Negro in American History Textbooks," *Integrated Education*, II (October–November 1964), 9–13; Howard N. Meyer, "Overcoming the White Man's History," *Massachusetts Review*, VII (Summer 1966), 569–78.

10. E. K. Alden, "Crispus Attucks," Allen Johnson and Dumas Malone, eds., *Dictionary of American Biography* (20 vols., New York, 1928–1936), I, 415. A recent pro-Attucks version is an editorial, "The Boston Massacre and the Martyrdom of Crispus Attucks," *Negro History Bulletin*, XXX (March 1967), 4.

11. See Albert Castel, "Andrew Johnson: His Historiographical Rise and Fall," *Mid-America*, XLV (July 1963), 175–84.

12. This category includes radio and television commentators. Mankind evidently has a natural affinity for both exaggeration and error. Contrary to legend, the Salem witches were hanged (not burned); little George Washington (in the Weems version) only *barked* the tree; and the Liberty Bell was fatally cracked in 1835 (not while proclaiming independence).

13. Drew Pearson and Jack Anderson, *U.S.A.—Second-Class Power?* (New York, 1958), 303.

14. Walter Lippmann, *U.S. Foreign Policy: Shield of the Republic* (Boston, 1943), 17. I was informed by a Harvard historian in 1943 that he had prepared a lengthy critique of the Lippmann manuscript for the publishers, but evidently little heed was taken of his list of errors.

15. Homer Davenport's cartoons of little "Willie" McKinley as a puppet of blowsy Mark Hanna implanted the picture of a wishy-washy President which to this day has not been fully corrected.

16. Lucius Beebe, "Pandemonium at Promontory," *American Heritage*, IX (February 1958), 21.

17. R. F. Adams, *Burrs under the Saddle: A Second Look at Books and Histories of the West* (Norman, 1964); Kent Ladd Steckmesser, *The Western Hero in History and Legend* (Norman, 1965).

18. A related expression is "The verdict of history will be. . . ." History is dead and speechless. Interpreters of history, including historians, return the verdicts.

19. The discredited legend that Marcus Whitman saved Oregon from the British by a hurry-up trip on horseback (or foot) to Washington appealed to President Warren G. Harding as a stirring hero tale, and he preferred to cherish it on the grounds that "it ought to be true." He also endorsed the poetical version of Paul Revere and Barbara Fritchie. *Speeches and Addresses of Warren G. Harding, President of the United States: Delivered During the Course of His Tour from Washington, D.C., to Alaska and Return to San Francisco, June 20 to August 2, 1923* (Washington, D.C., 1923), 256–57.

20. New York *Times*, May 13, 1961; Philip Geyelin, *Lyndon B. Johnson and the World* (New York, 1966), 237; Arthur M. Schlesinger, Jr., *The Bitter Heritage* (Boston, 1967), 32n. President Franklin D. Roosevelt was a frequent user of "managed history." In urging a repeal of the arms embargo upon Congress in 1939, he alleged that Thomas Jefferson's embargo, followed by limited sanctions, had been "the major cause" of the War of 1812. The evidence is strong that such economic pressures came within a few weeks of averting it. See *Department of State Bulletin*, I (September 23, 1939), 277.

21. Quoted in Egon Friedell, *A Cultural History of the Modern Age* (3 vols., New York, 1932), III, 7.

22. The New Englander Edward Channing did not even mention Captain John Smith of Virginia in his six-volume history of the United States. Perhaps he was unduly influenced by Henry Adams' famous attack, which is a classic example of a young historian striving for quick fame by attacking a big name. See Henry Adams, *Historical Essays* (New York, 1891), 42–79. In the light of recent evidence Smith seems somewhat more trustworthy than scholars previously assumed. Consult Philip L. Barbour, *The Three Worlds of Captain John Smith* (Boston, 1964).

23. William E. Dodd, *Woodrow Wilson and His Work* (Garden City, 1920).

24. James R. Mock and Cedric Larson, *Words That Won The War: The Story of the Committee on Public Information, 1917–1919* (Princeton, 1939), 158–86. I knew several of these scholars who, during the 1930s and 1940s, seemed to have a defensive guilt complex regarding their participation.

25. The efforts of the United Nations Educational, Scientific and Cultural Organization (UNESCO) to rewrite national history from the viewpoint of the man on Mars has evoked violent outcries from right-wing patriotic groups in the United States. On the other hand, there is the self-flagellation school of historical writers which evidently takes pleasure in finding the United States preponderantly in the wrong in its international dealings. An example is D. F. Fleming, *The Cold War and Its Origins, 1917–1960* (2 vols., Garden City, 1961).

26. Charles A. Beard, *American Foreign Policy in the Making, 1932–1940: A Study in Responsibilities* (New Haven, 1946); Charles A. Beard, *President Roosevelt and the Coming of the War, 1941: A Study in Appearances and Realities* (New Haven, 1948).

27. Edward Waldo Emerson and Waldo Emerson Forbes, eds., *Journals of Ralph Waldo Emerson, with Annotations, 1820–1872* (10 vols., Boston, 1909–1914), IV, 160.

28. Slogans have contributed richly to the mythology of American history. "He Kept Us Out of War" is often cited as a pledge by Wilson in 1916. He did not devise it, did not use it, and did not really approve of its use as a tacit promise.

29. See Harry Elmer Barnes, ed., *Perpetual War for Perpetual Peace: A Critical Examination of the Foreign Policy of Franklin Delano Roosevelt and Its Aftermath* (Caldwell, Idaho, 1953), 1–78.

30. W. E. Woodward and Rupert Hughes (the novelist) were in the forefront of a move to debunk Washington. Hughes' unfinished work stopped with volume three (1930), and reveals the conversion of a man who came to scoff and remained to worship.

31. Edgar Lee Masters, the poet, wrote a debunking life of Abraham Lincoln, *Lincoln, the Man* (New York, 1931); but it fell flat. For evidence that the editors of the *Encyclopaedia Britannica* softened an exposure of the Weemsian cherry tree myth, presumably in response to patriotic pressure, see Harvey Einbinder, *The Myth of the Britannica* (New York, 1964), 173–74.

32. Arthur M. Schlesinger, Jr., in his pre-publication series in *Life*, gives an account of John F. Kennedy's tearful breakdown after the Bay of Pigs botch. More tastefully, it does not appear in his later book, *Life*, 59 (July 23, 1965), 75; Arthur M. Schlesinger, Jr., *A Thousand Days* (Boston, 1965). For a revelation of some of the pressures brought to bear on William Manchester—*The Death of a President* (New York, 1967)—to put the Kennedys in a better light, see John Corry, *The Manchester Affair* (New York, 1967).

33. See Irwin Unger, "The 'New Left' and American History: Some Recent Trends in United States Historiography," *American Historical Review*, LXXII (July 1967), 1237–63.

34. Julius W. Pratt's *Expansionists of 1812* (New York, 1925) quite legitimately focused on the West, but Marxists have out-Pratted Pratt in their emphasis on economic determinism.

35. After observing the conduct of trained historians in two world wars, I fear that they do not keep their heads much better than other scholars in times of great emotional stress.

36. William E. Dodd, Jr., and Martha Dodd, eds., *Ambassador Dodd's Diary, 1933–1938* (New York, 1941). Internal and circumstantial evidence suggests that the Dodd diary was largely put together in some fashion by Dodd's son and daughter, the joint editors. Charles A. Beard was asked to write the introduction, and Martha Dodd inserted some hyperbole on her own. When Beard saw the galley proofs, he insisted on restoring his own prose, and demanded not only the page proofs but also the plate proofs. Declaring that he had seen only a typescript copy of what purported to be the original diary, he insisted that, in view of this experience, he would not believe a word of it. From the author's notes of a conversation with Beard at The Johns Hopkins University, in the spring of 1941.

37. Bernard Mayo, *Myths and Men: Patrick Henry, George Washington, Thomas Jefferson* (Athens, Ga., 1959), 4.

38. Thomas C. Cochran, "The Legend of the Robber Barons," *Pennsylvania Magazine of History and Biography*, LXXIV (July 1950), 307–21; Edward C. Kirkland, "The Robber Barons Revisited," *American Historical Review*, LXVI (October 1960), 68–73.

39. Following the desegregation decision of the Supreme Court in 1954, some publishers brought out editions of books with integrated or non-integrated pictures, in an effort to cater to local prejudices.

40. Daniel H. Thomas, "Pre-Whitney Cotton Gins in French Louisiana," *Journal of Southern History*, XXXI (May 1965), 135–48.

41. Thomas A. Bailey, "Dewey and the Germans at Manila Bay," *American Historical Review*, XLV (October 1939), 59–81. The Russian fleet myth of 1863 has also been useful during those periods when Americans were interested in promoting a hands-across-the-Volga policy. See Thomas A. Bailey, "The Russian Fleet Myth Re-Examined," *Mississippi Valley Historical Review*, XXXVIII (June 1951), 81–90.

42. A promising beginning in abstracting has been made by the American Bibliographical Center, Santa Barbara, California, in its quarterly publication, launched in 1964, and entitled *America, History and Life: A Guide to Periodical Literature*.

43. In addition to those hereinafter discussed, one may mention the Lafayette myth (that nations help others primarily for sentimental reasons); the immutability myth (that a policy enunciated by Washington is good for all circumstances and ages); the Yalta myth (we cannot negotiate with the Russians); and the Marshall Plan myth (what will work industrially in sophisticated Europe will work in backward Latin America or Vietnam). For the dangers inherent in myths like the Jewish stab in the back, see Dietrich Orlow, "The Conversion of Myths into Political Power: The Case of the Nazi Party," *American Historical Review*, LXXII (April 1967), 906–24.

44. Robert D. Heinl, Jr., comp., *Dictionary of Military and Naval Quotations* (Annapolis, Md., 1966), 240.

45. Mr. James Reston reported this statement on the basis of hearsay testimony, but it is in character. New York *Times*, Oct. 1, 1967. Related to the myth of invincibility is that of "free security," which allegedly was provided in the nineteenth century by the oceans and defense in depth. "Free security" is like free love, which can be extremely costly in the end. This concept proved to be expensive in wars that we might have avoided with adequate preparedness, and in wasteful expenditures involved in trying to prepare, after war was declared. Moreover, many Americans felt quite insecure during much of the nineteenth century, especially during the recurrent Anglo-American crises, which posed the threat of the British navy. For a contrary view, see C. Vann Woodward, "The Age of Reinterpretation," *American Historical Review*, LXVI (October 1960), 1–19.

46. The history of the United States is one of the great success stories of all time, and Americans have let success go to their heads. A slogan in World War II used by a branch of the United States forces was: "The difficult we do immediately. The impossible takes a little longer."

47. This inconsistency seems all the more curious in view of President Kennedy's willingness to risk a nuclear holocaust rather than agree to withdraw from Turkey the obsolescent Jupiter missiles which he had ordered removed some two months earlier. Elie Abel, *The Missile Crisis* (Philadelphia, 1966), 191. The withdrawal had been recommended in 1961 by both the Congressional Committee on Atomic Energy and the Secretary of Defense. Schlesinger, *A Thousand Days*, 807. The Jupiter missiles were removed from Turkey, April 15–26, 1963, some six months later. Assistant Secretary of Defense Warnke to Representative Charles S. Gubser, January 8, 1968 (letter in possession of author).

48. Secretary of State Dean Rusk, publicly defending his Vietnam policy, repeated in classic form the Hitler appeasement analogy. New York *Times*, December 9, 1967.

A great literature will yet arise out of the era of those four [Civil War] years, those scenes—era compressing centuries of native passion, first-class pictures, tempests of life and death—an inexhaustible mine for the histories, drama, romance, and even philosophy, of peoples to come—indeed the verteber of poetry and art (of personal character too) for all future America—far more grand, in my opinion, to the hands capable of it, than Homer's siege of Troy, or the French wars to Shakespeare.

Walt Whitman, 1879

1

MYTHS OF THE CIVIL WAR
AND RECONSTRUCTION

The Glorious and the Terrible
Allan Nevins

The Civil War and the Modern World
David M. Potter

The Folklore Lincoln
David Donald

The Tragic Legend of Reconstruction
Kenneth M. Stampp

Did the Civil War Retard Industrialization?
Thomas C. Cochran

The Glorious: John A. Logan in action.

The Terrible: Union dead after Gettysburg.

Introduction

Today the Civil War remains central to America's national historical experience. For many Americans the War between the States represents the greatest single event in their history. From the epic struggle emerges a gallery of heroic figures and memorable episodes—Lincoln and Lee, Shiloh and Gettysburg. *The War* enjoys the status of an American *Iliad*. As novelist and poet Robert Penn Warren suggested, the Civil War marked America's "Homeric Age." To Warren, the War between the States quickly became the great synthesis of the American experience and the inexhaustible reservoir of American symbol and myth:

> From the first, Americans had a strong tendency to think of their land as the Galahad among nations, and the Civil War, with its happy marriage of victory and virtue, has converted this tendency into an article of faith nearly as sacrosanct as the Declaration of Independence.

As Warren implies, ideas concerning the past often combine with emotion. Because of this, time, which is supposed to bring detachment and objectivity to one's historical understanding, very often has the opposite effect. The American Civil War proves an interesting case in point. Images of either the heroic (as with the war itself) or the tragic (as with the period of reconstruction that followed) have supplanted a proportioned view. Civil War and reconstruction history has been an exceptionally fertile breeding ground for distortion and myth.

The importance of recognizing what people think happened as against what did—the discrepancies between history as perceived and history as actuality—holds particular significance, then, to our historical judgments concerning the war and its aftermath. A proper view of our "Homeric Age" requires that the American penchant for overemphasizing both the heroic and tragic elements of history be challenged. A proper understanding of the era of the Civil War must yield much more than the pageantry and legend of the martyred Lincoln and the Christlike Lee. It must supply more than the tragic legend of the war's aftermath. One can begin to appreciate the entire era in its proper historical perspective only by noting the war's multiple causes, the complexity of Lincoln as politician, the conflict in both its glorious and terrible aspects, the war's importance as a stage in the development of modern nationalism and its significance to American industrial development, and reconstruction's subsequent importance to the course of American race relations. In the end, the Civil War and its heritage can indeed remain central to our national historical experience, but for reasons other than those which we might previously have imagined.

The Glorious and the Terrible

Allan Nevins

It was the American Civil War General William Tecumseh Sherman
who was purported to have said "War is Hell"; yet it seems that few
have truly taken his words to heart. War's pageantry and splendor,
the fascination of its drama, have most often resulted in historical
myopia. The slaughter and destruction which all know to be the
desserts of warfare are buried as quickly as its casualties. Perhaps
in no instance is this truer than with the classic confrontation between the Blue and the Gray. But the lustrous veneer, says the late
Allan Nevins of the Huntington Library in San Marino, California,
must be stripped away for sound historical judgment to proceed.
The Civil War was not, in the words of the military historian Bruce
Catton, "Glory Road." Rather, it was the testing of the character of
an entire civilization. Though we are inclined to remember the
glorious and forget the terrible, historical integrity requires we recognize both in order to eliminate the myth of the American Civil
War.

Every great war has two sides, the glorious and the terrible. The glorious is
perpetuated in multitudinous pictures, poems, novels, statues: in Meissonier's
canvases of Friedland and Austerlitz, Byron's stanzas on Waterloo and Ten-
nyson's on the Light and Heavy brigades, St. Gaudens's Sherman riding
forward victory-crowned, Freeman's "Lee." The terrible is given us in a much
slighter body of memorabilia: Jacques Callot's gruesome etchings of the
Thirty Years War, Goya's paintings of French atrocities in Spain, Zola's
"The Debacle," Walt Whitman's hospital sketches, and the thousand-page
novels that drearily emerged from the Second World War.

The two aspects do exist side by side. Every student of war comes upon
hundreds of veracious descriptions of its pomp and pageantry, innumerable
tales of devotion and heroism. They exalt the spirit. Yet every such student
falls back from this exaltation upon a sombre remembrance of the butchery,
the bereavement, and the long bequest of poverty, exhaustion, and despair. In
observing the centenary of the Civil War, every sensible man should keep in
mind that the conflict was a terrible reproach to American civilization and a
source of poison and debilities still to be felt.

If it were not true that its debits far outweighed its credits, we might
conclude that the republic would profit by a civil war in every generation,
and that we should have commemorated Bull Run last July by again setting

Yankee boys and Southern boys to killing each other. The mind recoils from the thought. But as the Civil War histories, novels, and motion pictures continue to pour forth, we shall be fortunate if we escape two very erroneous views.

The first view is that the war can somehow be detached from its context and studied as if it stood alone, without reference to causes or effects. War in fact, as Clausewitz long ago insisted, does not stand apart from and opposed to peace. It is simply a transfer of the normal inescapable conflicts of men from the realm of adjustment to that of violence. It represents not a complete transformation of national policy, but a continuance of policy by sanguinary means. That is, it cannot be understood without regarding both its causes and its results. Our Civil War, as Walt Whitman insisted, grew peculiarly out of national character. The other erroneous view is that the Civil War was, in the phrase of that graphic military historian Bruce Catton, a "Glory Road."

"Consider it not so deeply," Lady Macbeth says to her husband, stricken by the thought of red-handed murder; and "Consider it not so deeply," people instinctively say to those who remind them of war's inhuman massacre. Who wishes to while away an idle hour by looking at the harrowing pictures in the "Medical and Surgical History" of the war? It is a trick of human memories to forget, little by little, what is painful, and remember what is pleasant, and that tendency appertains to the folk memory as well. One of the finest descriptive pieces of the war was written by the true-hearted Theodore Winthrop, novelist and poet, just after his regiment crossed the Potomac on a spring night in 1861 to encamp on the Virginia side. It is rapturous in its depiction of the golden moon lighting a path over the river, the merry files of soldiers, the white tents being pitched in the dewy dawn. But ere long Winthrop was slain at Big Bethel in an engagement too blundering, shabby and piteous for any pen. We remember the happy march but forget the death.

Or take two contrasting scenes later in the war, of the same day—the day of Malvern Hill, July 1, 1862. That battle of Lee and McClellan reached its climax in the gathering dusk of a lustrous summer evening, no breath of wind stirring the air. The Union army had placed its ranks and its artillery on the slope of a great hill, a natural amphitheatre, which the Southerners assaulted. Participants never forgot the magnificence of the spectacle. From the Confederate and Union guns stately columns of black smoke towered high in the blue sky. The crash of musketry and deeper thud of artillery; the thunder of gunboat mortars from the James River, their shells curving in fiery golden lines; the cavalry on either flank, galloping to attack; the foaming horses flying from point to point with aides carrying dispatches; the steady advance of the Confederate columns and the unyielding resistance of the dense Union lines; then as darkness gathered, the varicolored signal lights flashing back and forth their messages—all this made an unforgettable panorama.

But the sequel! The troops on both sides sank exhausted on their arms. From the field the shrieking and moaning of the wounded were heart-rending, yet nothing could be done to succor them. The sky grew overcast; intense darkness shut down; and at dawn came a fierce downpour. "Such rain, and such howling set up by the wounded," wrote one Southern soldier; "such ugly wounds, sickening to the sight even of the most hardened as the rain beat upon them, washing them to a pale purple; such long-fingered corpses, and in piles, too, like cordwood—may I never see the like again!"

Both novelist and poet almost instinctively turn to the heroic aspects and picturesque incidents of war. Lowell's "Commemoration Ode," one of the half-dozen finest pieces of literature born from the conflict, necessarily eulogizes the heroes; Mary Johnston's "The Long Roll," perhaps the best Southern war novel, celebrates the ardors, not the anguishes, of Stonewall Jackson's foot-cavalry; St. Gaudens's monument on Boston Common to Robert Gould Shaw and his black infantry—the men whose dauntless hearts beat a charge right up the red rampart's slippery swell—shows the fighters, not the fallen. The historian assists in falsifying the picture. Cold, objective, he assumes that both the glorious and horrible sides exist, and need no special emphasis. He thus tends to equate the two, although the pains and penalties of war far outweigh its gleams of grandeur.

Then, too, a problem of expression impedes the realistic writer. It is not difficult to describe the pageantry of Pickett's charge. But when we come to the costs, what can we say except that the casualties were 3,000 killed, 5,000 wounded? It is impossible to describe the agony of even one soldier dying of a gangrened wound, or the heartache of one mother losing her first born; what of 10,000 such soldiers and mothers? Moreover, most historians, like the novelists and poets, have an instinctive preference for the bright side of the coin. Henry Steele Commager's otherwise fine introduction to his valuable compilation "The Blue and The Gray" has much to say about gallantry and bravery, but nothing about the squalor, the stench, and the agony.

If we protest against the prettification of the Civil War, the thoughtless glorification of what was essentially a temporary breakdown of American civilization, we must do so with an acknowledgement that it did call forth many manifestations of an admirable spirit. The pomp and circumstance, the parade and pageantry, we may dismiss as essentially empty. The valor of the host of young men who streamed to the colors we may deeply admire, but as valor we may fortunately take it for granted, for most men are brave. The patriotic ardor displayed in the first months of the war may also be taken for granted. What was highly impressive was the serious, sustained conviction, the long-enduring dedication, of countless thousands on both sides for their chosen cause. This went far beyond the transient enthusiasms of Sumter and Bull Run; far beyond ordinary battlefield courage. Lecky was correct in writing: "That which invests war with a certain grandeur is the heroic self-sacrifice which it elicits." All life is in a real sense a conflict between good and evil, in which every man or woman plays a part. A host of young Americans felt that they were enlisted in this larger struggle, and regarded their service to the North or South as part of a lifetime service to the right.

Those who seek examples of this dedication can find them scattered throughout the war records. Lincoln specially admired his young friend Elmer Ellsworth, who had endured poverty and hardship with monastic devotion to train himself for service; Lee specially admired John Pelham, the daring artillerist. Both gave their lives. Some fine illustrations of the consecrated spirit can be found in the two volumes of the "Harvard Memorial Biographies" edited by Thomas Wentworth Higginson just after the war. The ninety-eight Harvard dead were no better than the farm lads from Iowa or Alabama, the clerks from New Orleans or New York, but some of them had special gifts of self-expression. Hearken, for example, to Colonel Peter A. Porter, who wrote in his last will and testament:

> I can say, with truth, that I have entered on the course of danger with no ambitious aspirations, nor with the idea that I am fitted, by nature, or experience, to be of any important service to the government; but in obedience to the call of duty, demanding every citizen to contribute what he could, in means, labor, or life, to sustain the government of his country—a sacrifice made the more willingly by me when I consider how singularly benefitted I have been, by the institutions of the land. . . .

As we distinguish between the shining glory of the war—this readiness of countless thousands to die for an enduring moral conviction—and the false or unimportant glories, so we must distinguish between the major and the lesser debits of the conflict. Some evils and mischiefs which seemed tremendous at the time have grown less in the perspective of years; some which at first appeared small now loom large.

It was one of the bloodiest of all wars; the total deaths in the Union and Confederate armies have been computed at about 620,000; and one of the facts which appalls any careful student is the enormous amount of suffering on the field and in the hospitals. The evidence of this, while not within the view of general readers, is incontrovertible. Armies the world over in 1860 were *worse* provided with medical and surgical facilities than in Napoleon's day. The United States, after its long peace, began the war with practically no medical service whatever. Surgical application of the ideas of Pasteur and Lister lay in the future. Almost every abdominal wound meant death. Any severe laceration of a limb entailed amputation, with a good chance of mortal gangrene or erysipelas. The North systematically prevented shipments of drugs and surgical instruments to the South, a measure which did not shorten the conflict by a day, but cost the Southern troops untold agony. Had it not been for the Sanitary Commission, a body privately organized and supported, Northern armies would have duplicated the experience of British forces in the Crimea; yet Secretary of War Stanton at first deliberately impeded the Commission's work.

The story of battle after battle was the same. Night descended on a field ringing with cries of agony: Water! Water! Help!—if in winter, Blankets! Cover! All too frequently no help whatever was forthcoming. After some great conflicts the wounded lay for days, and sometimes a week, without rescue. Shiloh was fought on a Sunday and Monday. Rain set in on Sunday night, and the cold April drizzle continued through Tuesday night. On Tuesday morning nine-tenths of the wounded still lay where they fell; many had been there forty-eight hours without attention; numbers had died of shock or exhaustion; some had even drowned as the rain filled depressions from which they could not crawl. Every house in the area was converted into a hospital, where the floors were covered with wretches heavily wounded, sometimes with arms or legs torn off, who after the first bandages, got no nursing, medical care, or even nourishment. "The first day or two," wrote a newspaper reporter, "the air was filled with groans, sobs, and frenzied curses, but now the sufferers are quiet; not from cessation of pain, but mere exhaustion." Yet at this time the war was a year old.

Still more poignant versions of the same story might be given. Lee and Pope fought Second Manassas on the last Friday and Saturday in August, 1862, so near Washington that groups standing on housetops in the capital heard the rumble of artillery. The battleground, five miles long and three wide, was thickly strewn with dead and wounded. Pope retreated in confusion; many in Washington feared the city might be taken. In these circumstances, as late as the following Wednesday one member of the inadequate body of surgeons estimated that 2,000 wounded had received no attention. Many had not tasted food for four days; some were dying of hunger and thirst. A reporter for the Washington *Republican* wrote on Thursday that some dying men could yet be saved by prompt help. And on Friday, a week after the battle began, a correspondent of the New York *Tribune* told of heart-rending scenes as the doctors searched among heaps of putrefying dead men for men yet clinging to life—men who, when anyone approached, would cry, "Doctor, come to *me*; you look like a kind man; for God's sake come to *me*."

Anyone who is tempted to think of Gettysburg only in terms of its heroic episodes, its color and drama, should turn to the pages in "Battles and Leaders" in which General John D. Imboden describes the transport of the Confederate wounded, after their defeat, back into Maryland. He was ordered to ride to the head of the long wagon column as, in darkness and storm, it moved south:

> For four hours I hurried forward on my way to the front, and in all that time I was never out of hearing of the groans and cries of the wounded and dying. Scarcely one in a hundred had received adequate surgical aid, owing to the demands on the hard-working surgeons from still worse cases that had to be left behind. Many of the wounded in their wagons had been without food for thirty-six hours. Their torn and bloody clothing, matted and hardened, was rasping the tender, inflamed, and still oozing wounds. Very few of the wagons had even a layer of straw in them, and all were without springs. The road was rough and rocky from the heavy washings of the preceding day. The jolting was enough to have killed strong men, if long exposed to it. From nearly every wagon as the teams trotted on, urged by whip and shout, came such cries and shrieks as these:
> "My God! Why can't I die?"
> "My God! Will no one have mercy and kill me?"
> "Stop! Oh, for God's sake stop just for one minute; take me out and leave me to die on the roadside."
> Occasionally a wagon would be passed from which only low, deep moans could be heard. No help could be rendered to any of the sufferers. No heed could be given to any of their appeals. Mercy and duty to the many forbade the loss of a moment in the vain effort then and there to comply with the prayers of the few. On! On! We must move on. The storm continued and the darkness was appalling. There was no time even to fill a canteen with water for a dying man; for, except the drivers and the guards, all were wounded and utterly helpless in that vast procession of misery. During this one night I realized more of the horrors of war than I had in all the preceding two years.

After such a description, we can understand why a radical Northern Senator, looking across the battlefield of the Wilderness as fighting ended, told Hugh McCulloch that if in 1861 he had been given one glimpse of the agonies he there beheld, he would have said to the South: "Erring sisters, go in peace." John Esten Cooke was right in his elegy for Pelham; the living were brave and noble, but the dead were the bravest of all.

Yet *this* was far from being the ugliest side of war. Nor was the suffering in the huge prison camps, South and North, part of the worst side of war; the suffering which MacKinlay Kantor describes in his novel and to which Benét briefly adverts in "John Brown's Body":

> The triple stockade of Andersonville the damned,
> Where men corrupted like flies in their own dung
> And the gangrened sick were black with smoke and their filth.

What maims the bodies of men is less significant than what maims their spirit.

One ugly aspect of the Civil War too generally ignored is the devastation, more and more systematic, that accompanied it. For three reasons too little has been said of this devastation; the facts were kept out of official reports, the tale is too painful, and the recital easily becomes monotonous. Yet by 1862 the war in the South had become one of general depredation; by 1863, of wanton destruction; and by 1864, of an organized devastation which in terms of property anticipated the worst chapters of the two world wars. Georgia and the Shenandoah suffered in 1864 almost precisely as Belgium and Serbia suffered in 1914—the executions omitted. It was barbaric, and the only excuse to be made is that war is barbarism.

The turning point in the attitude of Northern military men was reached when General John Pope on July 18, 1862, issued from Washington headquarters a set of Draconian general orders. Order No. 5 directed that the army should subsist as far as practicable upon the country, giving vouchers for supplies seized. Order No. 7 decreed the summary execution of persons caught firing upon Union troops from houses. Order No. 11 (five days later) required officers to arrest immediately all disloyal males within reach, to make them take the oath of allegiance or go South, and to shoot all who violated their oath or who returned from the Confederacy. The order for living on the country, widely publicized East and West, changed the attitude of troops, and inspired private looting as well as public seizures of property. Pope was soon ousted, but the moral effect of his orders persisted.

Though most of the facts were excluded from official reports, their sum total, insofar as one shrewd observer could arrive at it, may be found in John T. Trowbridge's graphic volume written in 1866, "A Picture of the Desolated States." In his preface Trowbridge speaks of the Union forces not as our heroic armies but our destroying armies. Even this practiced reporter is less graphic, however, than the people who suffered under the onslaught and wrote while their emotions, like their property, still burned. Hear a lady of Louisiana tell what occurred when N. P. Banks's army passed:

> I was watching from my window the apparently orderly march of the first Yankees that appeared in view and passed up the road, when, suddenly, as if by magic, the whole plantation was covered with men, like bees from an overthrown hive; and, as far as my vision extended, an inextricable medley of men and animals met my eye. In one place, excited troopers were firing into the flock of sheep; in another, officers and men were in pursuit of the boys' ponies, and in another, a crowd were in excited chase of the work animals. The kitchen was soon filled with some, carrying off the cooking utensils and the provisions of the day; the yard with others, pursuing the poultry.... They penetrated under the house, into the outbuildings, and into the garden, stripping it in a moment of all its vegetables.... This continued during the day ... and amid a bewildering sound of oaths and imprecations.... When the army had passed, we were left destitute.

Sherman believed in total war; that is, in waging war not only against the Southern armies, but the Southern people. His theory was that every man, woman, and child was "armed and at war." He wrote his wife in the summer of 1862 that the North might fall into bankruptcy, "but if they can hold on the war will soon assume a turn to extermination, not of soldiers alone, but the people." He denied, in effect, that Southerners had a right to resist invasion. When Union steamers were fired on near Randolph, Mississippi, in the fall of 1862, he destroyed Randolph, and a little later had all houses, farms, and cornfields devastated for fifteen miles along the banks.

When he drove his red plowshare across Georgia and the Carolinas, his object was to leave only scorched earth behind. He had already written of his Western operations: "Not a man is to be seen; nothing but women with houses plundered, fields open to the cattle and horses, pickets lounging on every porch, and desolation sown broadcast; servants all gone, and women and children bred in luxury . . . begging . . . for soldiers' rations." His aim was that which Phil Sheridan avowed: to leave them nothing but their eyes to weep with.

The final devastation of half the South was horrible to behold, and it was distressing to think that these savage losses had been inflicted by Americans upon fellow Americans. Yet this was far from being the worst aspect of the conflict, or the least easily reparable. Damages on which we can fix the dollar sign are important not in themselves, but as they become translated into cultural and spiritual losses; into the intellectual retardation caused by poverty, for example. The physical recovery of the South was rapid. As it was primarily an agricultural section, a few good crops at fair prices did much to restore it; and the swiftness with which housing, railroads, bridges, and public facilities were rebuilt astonished observers of the 1870s just as the swift postwar recovery of Germany and Poland has astonished observers of our day.

Infinitely worse were the biological losses—the radical hurts—inflicted by the Civil War. The killing of between 600,000 and 700,000 young men in a nation of 33,000,000 and the maiming or permanent debilitation of as many more had evil consequences projected into the far-distant future. We lost not only these men, but their children, and their children's children. Here, indeed, was a loss that proved highly cumulative. During the First World War, Lord Dunsany wrote a slender volume called "Tales of War." One of his apologues showed the Kaiser, as the embodiment of German militarism, commanded by a spirit to come on a tour. They crossed the German plain to a neat garden. Look, said the spirit:

> The Kaiser looked; and saw a window shining and a neat room in a cottage; there was nothing dreadful there, thank the good German God for that; it was all right, after all. The Kaiser had had a fright, but it was all right; there was only a woman with a baby sitting before a fire, and two small children and a man. And it was quite a jolly room. And

the man was a young soldier; and, why, he was a Prussian Guardsman —there was a helmet hanging on the wall—so everything was all right. They were jolly German children; that was well. How nice and homely the room was. . . . The firelight flickered, and the lamp shone on, and the children played on the floor, and the man was smoking out of a china pipe; he was strong and able and young, one of the wealth-winners of Germany.

"Have you seen?" asked the phantom.

"Yes," said the Kaiser. . . .

At once the fire went out and the lamp faded away, the room fell sombrely into neglect and squalor, and the soldier and the children faded away with the room; all disappeared phantasmally, and nothing remained but the helmet in a kind of glow on the wall, and the woman sitting all by herself in the darkness.

"It has all gone," said the Kaiser.

"It has never been," said the phantom.

The Kaiser looked again. Yes, there was nothing there, it was just a vision. . . .

"It might have been," said the phantom.

Just so, we can say that the multitude of Civil War dead represent hundreds of thousands of homes, and hundreds of thousands of families, that might have been, and never were. They represent millions of people who might have been part of our population today and are not. We have lost the books they might have written, the scientific discoveries they might have made, the inventions they might have perfected. Such a loss defies measurement.

The only noteworthy attempt to measure the biological losses was made by David Starr Jordan and his son Harvey in a volume called "War's Aftermath" (1914). The authors circulated carefully drawn questionnaires in Spottsylvania and Rockbridge Counties in Virginia, and in Cobb County in Georgia, inquiring particularly into the eugenic effects of the conflict. One of their queries brought out evidence that by no means all casualties were among the men; numerous girls and women succumbed to the hardships and anxieties of the conflict in the South. Another question elicited unanimous agreement that "the flower of the people" went into the war at the beginning, and of these a large part died before the end. President Jordan, weighing all the responses, reached two conclusions: first, that the evidence "leaves a decided evidence in favor of grave racial hurt," and second, that "the war has seriously impoverished this country of its best human values."

Even the terrible loss of young, productive lives, the grave biological injury to the nation, however, did not constitute the worst side of the war. One aspect of the conflict was still more serious. It was the aspect to which Lowell referred in lines written a few years after Appomattox:

> I looked to see an ampler atmosphere
> By that electric passion-gust blown clear
> I looked for this; consider what I hear. . . .

> Murmur of many voices in the air
> Denounces us degenerate,
> Unfaithful guardians of a noble fate. . . .

The war, as Walt Whitman truly said, had grown out of defects in the American character; of American faults it cured few, accentuated a number, and gave some a violently dangerous trend. Far behind the lines, it added to the already discreditable total of violence in American life. Applying to industry a great forcing-draft, the bellows of huge wartime appropriations, it strengthened the materialistic forces in our civilization. Its state and federal contracts, its bounty system, its innumerable opportunities for battening on the nation's woes, made speculation fashionable, and corruption almost too common for comment. Its inflation bred extravagance and dissipation.

Every month heightened the intolerance of war; it began with mobs in New York threatening newspaper offices, a mob in Philadelphia trying to lynch Senator James A. Bayard, and mobs in the South flogging and exiling Union men; as it went on, freedom of speech almost disappeared over broad areas. The atmosphere of war fostered immorality; Richmond and Washington alike became filled with saloons, brothels, and gambling dens, and such occupied cities as Memphis and Nashville were sinks of iniquity. For every knightly martyr like James Wadsworth or Albert Sidney Johnston there arose two such coarse, aggressive, selfish careerists as Ben Butler and Dan Sickles. Wadsworth and Johnston died in battle, but Butler and Sickles remained to follow postwar political careers. Seen in perspective, the war was a gigantic engine for coarsening and lowering the American character even while it quickened certain of our energies.

Parson Brownlow, a Tennessee Unionist, went from city to city in the North in 1862 demanding "grape for the Rebel masses, and hemp for their leaders"; saying that he himself would tie the rope about the necks of some rebel generals; calling for the confiscation of all Southern property; proclaiming that he would be glad to arm every wolf, bear, catamount, and crocodile, every devil in hell, to defeat the South; and declaring he would put down the rebellion "if it exterminates from God's green earth every man, woman, and child south of Mason and Dixon's Line."

In the South two famous leaders, Robert Toombs and Howell Cobb, united that year in an address to their people just as vitriolic. "The foot of the oppressor is on the soil of Georgia," it began. "He comes with lust in his eye, poverty in his purse, and hell in his heart. How shall you meet him? . . . With death for him or for yourself!" Better the charnel house for every Southerner, they continued, than "loathsome vassalage to a nation already sunk below the contempt of the civilized world." Thaddeus Stevens nursed his hatred until he spoke of "exterminating" or driving into exile all Southerners, just as Sherman declared he would "slay millions" to assure the safety of the Mississippi. Women of the South meanwhile expressed the most vindictive detestation of all Yankees. "I hate them," wrote one Mississippi woman after a raid on her community, "more now than I did the evening I saw them sneaking off with all we cared for, and so it will be every day I live."

Hatred was seen in its most naked form in those communities divided against themselves and racked by guerrilla war; in Missouri, Arkansas, parts of Kentucky, and east Tennessee. Writes Charles D. Drake, a distinguished Missouri leader, of his state: "Falsehood, treachery, and perjury pervaded the whole social fabric." He went on: "Could there be written a full account of all the crimes of the rebels of Missouri, and the outrages and wrongs inflicted by them upon her loyal inhabitants, during the four years of the rebellion, the world would shrink aghast from a picture which has no parallel in the previous history of any portion of the Anglo-Saxon race." Confederate sympathizers in Missouri would have said the same of Union irregulars. One atrocity provoked another. These hatreds long survived the conflict, and indeed in some spots the embers still smoulder. Typifying the whole range of spiritual injuries wrought by the war, they justify the poet Blake's cry:

> The soldier, armed with sword and gun,
> Palsied strikes the summer sun.

The historian Mendelssohn Bartholdy, in his volume entitled "War and German Society," written as part of the Carnegie Endowment's huge economic history of World War I, concluded that the moral effects of war are much worse than the material effects. He also concluded that they are radically bad, for they strike at the very heart of a country's character; "modern war, with its robot-like disregard of individual values, is bound to make the peculiar virtue of a nation an object of attack." As respects the Civil War, we can agree. If it was necessary for preserving the Union and extinguishing slavery, it was of course worth more than it cost; but should it have been necessary? Could not better leadership from 1830 to 1860 have averted it? This is a bootless question. But it is certain that the conflict, so much the greatest convulsion in our history, so tremendous in its impact on our national life, so fascinating in its drama, was in spite of all compensating elements, all the heroism, all the high example we find in Lee's character and Lincoln's wisdom, materially a disaster and morally a tragedy.

It is unfortunate that of the flood of books on the war ninety-nine in a hundred are on military topics and leaders, and that a great majority fasten attention on the floating banners, the high-ringing cheers, the humors of the camp, the ardors of the charge; the whole undeniable fascination and romance of the first true *volkskrieg* in history. It is right, within measure, to let them lift our hearts. But the long commemoration will pass essentially unimproved if it does not give us a deeper, sterner, more scientific study of the collision of two creeds and two ways of life as related to an examination of war in general.

We should probe more deeply into its roots, a process that will expose some of the weaknesses of our social fabric and governmental system. We should pay fuller attention to its darker aspects, and examine more honestly such misrepresentations as the statement it was distinguished by its generosity of spirit, the magnanimity with which the combatants treated each other; a statement absurd on its face, for no war which lasts four years and costs 600,000 lives leaves much magnanimity in its later phases. We should above all examine more closely the effects of the great and terrible war not on the nation's politics—we know that; not on its economy—we also know that; but on its character, the vital element of national life.

This examination will lead into unpleasant paths, and bring us to unhappy conclusions; but it will profit us far more than stirring battle canvases. All nations must be schooled in such studies if the world is ever to find an answer to a question uttered just after World War I by William E. Borah, a question that still rings in men's ears: "When shall we escape from war? When shall we loosen the grip of the monster?"

The Civil War and the Modern World

David M. Potter

Few historians possess the late David M. Potter's ability to convey the "feel" and texture of historical reality. In one of his most important essays, Potter, whose tenure within the profession included distinguished terms at both Yale and Stanford, questions the parochialism of Americans as regards their Civil War. In the interest of supplying a new dimension of understanding, he suggests the rather basic importance of the conflict to the fusion of nationalism and liberalism on an international scale. A view of the American Civil War that takes into account the various nineteenth-century movements toward national unification—as for example in Italy and Germany—makes the Civil War experience more intelligible to us as it asserts its broader meaning to the political life of the Western world.

It has been the curious fate of the United States to exert immense influence in the modern world, without itself quite understanding the nature of this influence. Major trends of the modern world—both constructive trends and socially injurious ones—have repeatedly become apparent in the United States before they became evident elsewhere. But though the United States has often been a step ahead in the process of social change, it has frequently been a step behind in its awareness of the meaning of new developments. The shape of things to come often became visible in America earlier than it did elsewhere, but American preconceptions about the frontier, the classless society, and the agrarian basis of democracy prevented Americans from perceiving this shape as realistically as it was perceived by social thinkers in other countries. If Americans have failed effectively to interpret their experience to people in other societies, it is in part because they have not always been able to explain it to themselves. Further, the distinctive qualities of life in America have caused a good many forces which were generically universal to take forms which seemed more restrictively peculiar to the New World than they really were.

Thus in the late eighteenth century, America executed the first democratic political revolution of a democratic age, but American society was already so equalitarian that the revolutionary implication was muted. Without any great social overturn, the American War of Independence seemed conservative when compared with the socially cataclysmic forces released in

From "Civil War," by David M. Potter, Chapter 10 in *The Comparative Approach to American History*, edited by C. Vann Woodward. © 1968 by C. Vann Woodward. Basic Books, Inc., Publishers, New York.

France a decade later. In the twentieth century the United States developed what was perhaps the first mass society, but the American cult of equality and individualism prevented Americans from analyzing their mass society in realistic terms. Often they treated it as if it were simply an infinite aggregation of Main Streets in Zenith, Ohio. America has witnessed episodes of extreme industrial conflict, but these have not been interpreted in the class terms which a Marxist society would invoke. America has experienced a sweeping revolution in sex behavior, but has not incorporated this change into the system of values by which it explains itself. Ironically, the United States has cherished a belief in its mission to spread a democracy for which it has had difficulty in finding converts, while it has led the world in technological changes which produced social transformations that it had no especial desire to bring about.

The reader need not be astonished, therefore, if the Civil War has been interpreted in terms which disguised its broader meaning. If, as some Americans asserted, its chief importance was in putting an end to chattel slavery, this could hardly be regarded as a leading development in the history of Western civilization; for slavery had disappeared from western Europe, except vestigially, while it still flourished in the Americas, and it had disappeared from most of Latin America, except Cuba and Brazil, while it still persisted in the United States. The American republic was almost destroyed therefore in a struggle over an institution which world opinion regarded as an anachronism.

If, on the other hand, the Civil War was, as some other Americans asserted, important chiefly because it preserved the American Union, this statement also was framed in restrictive terms which failed to reveal its broader implications. Beginning with the mystic phrase, *E pluribus unum*, the republic had not been able for two generations to resolve the question whether it was, in the last analysis, *pluribus* or *unum*. The Civil War gave *unum* the upper hand, and the importance of this fact became visible in world history in 1917 and again in 1941 when the strength of a consolidated American republic impinged decisively on two world wars. But at the time, in a literal sense, there was not much significance for other nations in the fact that the United States waited for fourscore years and ten to settle a question which other nations settled at their inception. There seemed little universality of significance in a war fought to find, or at least determine, a clear meaning for a cryptic federal system such as no other nation had ever had, and such as was deliberately made ambiguous in the first place in order not to lose the support which it certainly would have lost if its meaning had been clarified.

While the war was in progress, European policy makers tended to think of it simply in terms of whether it would leave the United States weaker or stronger than before. After it was over, the only people who examined it closely were military historians, looking for the lessons of strategy and tactics that might be derived from the first major conflict in which repeating arms, ironclad vessels, trench warfare, and railroads as supply lines were used on a significant scale.

Thus, while the campaigns of Lee and Grant have fascinated English and European readers, just as the campaigns of Napoleon have fascinated Americans, and while the personality of Lincoln has held an appeal for men everywhere, writers have scarcely asked the question: what was the role of the American Civil War in the history of the modern world? Did it have historical significance for anyone except Americans?

If we are seeking an answer to this question, it may be useful to begin by asking ourselves, simply, what were the prevalent tendencies of the nineteenth century, and what did the Civil War contribute in causing these tendencies to prevail? Historians have neglected the latter part of this question, but have repeatedly given an answer to the first part. They tell us, over and over, that the nineteenth century was an era of liberalism and nationalism. The basis for the generalization is obvious. Nationalism, as we know it in its modern form, scarcely existed before the French Revolution; but by the end of the nineteenth century Britain, France, Germany, Italy, and Japan had become prototypes for modern nationality, sometimes after great travail. Nationalistic forces were fermenting throughout other parts of Europe, and even in the colonial world of Asia and Africa the premonitory stirrings of a latent nationalism could already be detected. The Monroe Doctrine had done its bit to make the Western Hemisphere safe for nationalism, and the Latin Americans had responded by erecting eighteen separate nationalistic republics. Likewise with liberalism. It was scarcely more than an ideology in the minds of British and French rationalists before the French Revolution, but by the beginning of the twentieth-century representative government and other liberal institutions prevailed in Britain, France, and Italy, and to some extent even in Germany and Austria-Hungary. The Hapsburgs, the Hohenzollerns, and the Romanoffs were still on their thrones, but they stood on the defensive before the onslaughts of Social Democrats, Social Revolutionaries, and other militant reformers.

All these facts are familiar to the point of triteness and it would be parochial to exaggerate the importance of the American Civil War in connection with them. But if we are to define the place of this war in terms of world history, rather than merely of American history, there are two aspects in which it exercised a crucial effect in shaping the tendencies of world history. These aspects may or may not have served the long-range welfare of human society, and it may be argued that, ultimately, their effect was pernicious. But for good or ill, here are two things which the Civil War did: first, it turned the tide which had been running against nationalism for forty years, or ever since Waterloo; and second, it forged a bond between nationalism and liberalism at a time when it appeared that the two might draw apart and move in opposite directions.

Because of the ultimate triumph of nationalism as a worldwide force by 1900, it is easy to forget how seriously nationalism appeared to have failed at the time when the Civil War occurred. After establishing firm bridgeheads in Britain and France, it had met with disaster after disaster in its efforts to spread into southern and central Europe. Britain had moved successfully to suppress nationalism in Ireland, and Russia had taken the most repressive measures in 1830 to crush it out in Poland. After the galaxy of nationalist revolutions of 1848 the dreams of a United Italy had ended with disaster at Custozza, those of a United Germany with the anticlimax of the Frankfurt Parliament, those of Czechoslovakia with the overthrow of the Pan-Slavic Congress, and those of Hungary with the defeat of Louis Kossuth. Simultaneously, in America, the steadily rising tensions between North and South seemed increasingly likely to destroy the feeling of national unity which had appeared completely triumphant during the first two decades of the century. The forces of nationalism reasserted themselves successfully in the Italian peninsula in the two years preceding the American Civil War, but otherwise nationalism and especially liberal nationalism in Europe seemed a lost cause. Louis Napoleon had made himself emperor of France in 1852, and within another decade was busily planting a Hapsburg imperialist regime in Mexico.

Viewed from the standpoint of appearances only, the forces which opposed nationalism in Europe were entirely unlike those which opposed it in America. In Europe, one might say, the forces which thwarted nationalism were those of universalism—of the Catholic Church and of the Hapsburg and Romanoff empires, for which the nationalist impulse seemed too localizing and disruptive. In America, one might say, the forces which thwarted it were those of localism and of sectionalism, for which the nationalist impulse seemed too consolidating and centralizing. In Europe, imperial forces sought to stamp out nationalism from above; in America, particularistic forces sought to resist it from below. It is perhaps because the opposition was centripetal in Europe and centrifugal in America that historians have tended to overlook the parallel triumphs of national unification, all within a period of twelve short years, in Italy, the United States, and Germany.

But the contrast between universalism and localism, as the forces which opposed nationalism, is perhaps more apparent than real. In both Europe and America, the forces of tradition and privilege tended to be arrayed against nationalism, while the forces of liberalism and democracy tended to support it. In America, the succession of the Southern states has been accurately described as a conservative revolt—a revolution by men who were not revolutionists, and who justified their revolution less by a philosophical defense of the right of the self-determination of peoples than by refined, legalistic arguments upon the intent of the Constitution of 1787. These "Rebels," instead of advocating change, were rebelling against it and were the champions of a traditional, relatively static, hierarchical society. They feared, with some reason, as we may now conclude, the transformations that might be wrought by an industrial society. They feared the destruction of a familiar social order and defended the evil institution of slavery less because they believed in human bondage as such than because they could not conceive of their social order without slavery.

In a certain sense, then, the landed planters of the South who opposed American nationalism were not unlike the landed proprietors in central Europe who opposed German or Polish or Italian or Hungarian or Bohemian nationalism. All of them were traditionalists. All feared that nationalism was linked with a democracy which they distrusted. All feared to release from the bottle the genii of manhood suffrage, of democratic equality, of social mobility, of universal education—and in the South, of emancipation for almost four million slaves. In this sense, European and American conservatism shared much in common, and the issue in the war between North and South carried implications considerably beyond the mere question as to whether the American states should form one republic or two.

The uprising of the North in 1861, and its decision to wage a war to preserve the American Federal Union, coming in the same year in which Victor Emmanuel was crowned king of a united Italy, marked a turning of the tide which had been running against nationalism for the preceding forty-five years. For better or worse, the course was set toward a world of sovereign nation-states, subject to no ultimate control in their conduct toward one another. The process of forging additional nations would reach out, within another century, from Europe and the Americas to Asia and Africa until by 1966 there would be more than 130. As the number of "nations" increased, the beneficial effects of nationalism became increasingly uncertain, for all too many of the new sovereignties regarded the possession of nuclear destructive power as the crowning sanction of their nationhood.

Nationalism today seems something of a curse because of the paradox that while the people of the earth have been growing more and more functionally interdependent socially and economically, they have also simultaneously grown more and more irresponsibly independent of one another politically. The fragmentation of empires and other forms of supranational political authority has proceeded in ironic parallelism with increases in the cohesion of the peoples whose political relationships are being fragmented. At the same time, nationalism has shown that it can have a hideous side, undreamed of by such idealistic nationalists as Mazzini, and Lamartine, and Daniel Webster. Hitler is the supreme example, but even at the present moment a number of tyrants whose authority would command no more respect than that of a gangster if it were not sanctified by the mystique of national inviolability—a number of such tyrants have given us cause to doubt that the advancement of nationalism is necessarily a contribution to human progress. Suppose Lincoln did save the American Union, did his success in keeping

one strong nation where there might have been two weaker ones really entitle him to a claim to greatness? Did it really contribute any constructive
values for the modern world?

To answer these questions, it may be necessary to recognize not only that
Lincoln sought to save American nationalism, but also why he sought to
save it. To him, as to other idealistic nationalists, the Union—that is, the
nation—was not an end in itself but a means to an end. He might affirm that
"my paramount object . . . is to save the Union," and he might wage one of
the most deadly wars ever fought up to that time to achieve his object. But
he thought of the Union primarily as a context within which freedom might
be preserved and extended. Moreover, he thought that survival of a liberal
nation in America was vital as a test of the survival capacity of liberal
nationalism anywhere. Thus, although personally he was distinctively and
uniquely and even restrictively American—the only one of the great presidents who never went outside the United States—he thought of American
democracy in the least restrictive of terms. Many years before his Presidency,
he eulogized Henry Clay as one who "loved his country partly because it was
his own country but mostly because it was a free country." When the Civil
War came, he asserted that it involved "more than the fate of these United
States" and was of concern "to the whole family of man." The Union mattered to him not because of the question of authority at Washington, but
because of the "necessity that is upon us of proving that popular government
is not an absurdity." In his supreme moment at Gettysburg, this American
nationalist did not once use the word American, or United States. He spoke,
to be sure, of the nation "which our fathers brought forth," but this one nation
conceived in liberty and dedicated to equality was linked in his thought with
"any other nation so conceived and so dedicated." He wanted the war to
result, for his own nation, in a "new birth of freedom," but this goal was
not for America alone; it was to assure "men everywhere" that "government
of the people, by the people, and for the people shall not perish from the earth."

It has been well said that Lincoln fused the cause of Union with the
cause of freedom, which is equivalent to saying that he fused the cause of
nationalism with the cause of liberalism. A number of idealistic nationalists
of the nineteenth century made this same equation, and impressed it upon
the public mind so vigorously that, even a century later, when we have had
fairly numerous as well as traumatic illustrations of how completely antagonistic liberalism and nationalism can sometimes be, most of us respond affirmatively to claims made in the name of national integrity. We do so because
our own thought still moves in the grooves cut by the great liberal nationalists
of the nineteenth century.

This equation of liberalism and nationalism is not, of course, without
logical foundations. Nationalism and liberalism both share certain common
assumptions. Both depend upon the awakening self-consciousness of the individual—in the one case awakening to his membership in the political com-

munity, in the other awakening to his rights to participate in the decisions of the community and to enjoy its advantages. But while logic might impel nationalism and liberalism to go hand in hand, history often violates logic, and today we have copious proof that nationalism can flourish in separation from any liberal counterpart. It did so in Fascist Italy and Nazi Germany. It does so in Red China, and in Soviet Russia (though these countries theoretically reject nationalism), and it is doing so in various dictatorships in the "emerging" nations. But if one kind of logic would prove nationalism and liberalism to be twin offspring of the idea of the free individual as patriot and as citizen, there is another logic which declares liberalism and nationalism to be opposites, since liberalism regards the state as existing for the individual and nationalism regards the individual as existing for the state.

This is only to say that the nineteenth-century conjunction of nationalism and liberalism was by no means inevitable. To regard it as inevitable is to lose the larger meaning of the Civil War, for the war was one of the important historic developments contributing to a conjunction which, in other circumstances, might never have occurred. Lincoln's dedication of nationalistic means to liberal ends went far to produce this conjunction in the cosmos of American values. But at the same time when Lincoln was fusing nationalism with liberalism in America, another of the great figures who made the nineteenth century a century of nationalism, Count Otto von Bismarck, was carefully disassociating liberalism from nationalism in Germany. Having watched how the debacle of liberalism wrecked all hopes of German unification at Frankfurt in 1848, Bismarck wedded his nationalism to a concept of power and not to ideas of freedom or popular government. He signalized this position by publicly embracing a policy of "blood and iron" when he came to the head of the Prussian ministry in the year of Lincoln's Emancipation Proclamation. Nine years and three wars later, while President Grant, as the head of an imperfectly reunited nation, was struggling to reconcile the liberal principle of home rule for the South with the liberal principle of citizenship rights for the Negro, Bismarck made his monarch emperor of a Germany which was at last firmly united under authoritarian controls.

Bismarck and Lincoln were, perhaps, the two foremost exponents of nineteenth-century nationalism, after Napoleon. No two exemplars of the same force could have been more dissimilar, and no dramatist could have designed two figures better suited to point up contrasting styles of nationalism. The Gettysburg Address would have been as foreign to Bismarck as a policy of "blood and iron" would have been to Lincoln.

The contrast, perhaps, points the way to what was significant, in world perspective, about the American Civil War. The significance lay not in the fact that it was a triumph for nationalism (though the war forged the North as well as the South into a nation larger than any in western Europe), not in the fact that it was a triumph of liberalism (though Lincoln vindicated government of the people, by the people, and for the people, and proved that democracy, with all its weaknesses, can withstand the shocks of war). The significance lay rather in the fact that the Civil War, more perhaps than any event in Europe, fused the two great forces of the nineteenth century—liberalism and nationalism. It fused them so thoroughly that their potential separateness was lost from view. The fusion gave to nationalism a sanction which, frequently since then, it has failed to deserve, and gave to liberalism a strength which, since then, it has frequently not known how to use.

Meanwhile, Americans remained in confusion as to what their war had signified for the world. Some thought they had proved the strength of democracy, forgetting that the Confederacy which they defeated was also democratic and shared democracy's weaknesses. Others thought that they had vindicated the principle of nationalism, forgetting that the loyalty which Southerners gave to the Confederacy was no less nationalistic than the loyalty which Yankees gave to the Union. Few perceived that one of the most sweeping consequences of the war was to identify with one another these two forces which were not necessarily linked. This partially fictitious identification may, in the final analysis, have done great harm by giving a spurious sanction to modern nationalism, with all its potential dangers for the larger human society. But in a more immediate sense, it was perhaps the most constructive identification made during the nineteenth century, for it gave significant moral purpose to the force of nationalism, which, without such purpose, was always in danger of degenerating into mere group egocentrism or chauvinism. At the same time, it also gave significant institutional support to the principle of freedom, which without such support would have had only the ideals of reformers to sustain it.

The Folklore Lincoln

David Donald

As Richard Hofstadter has suggested, important elements of the "Lincoln myth" were consciously sustained by Abraham Lincoln himself. But one must take into account as well the proliferation of myth after Lincoln, for it was chiefly in the postwar decades that the images of the Great Emancipator and the Great Martyr became usable material in a developing American folklore. From self-made origins emerged a national savior "with malice toward none." Though committed to objective criticism of the Lincoln lore, David Donald, Director of the Institute of Southern History at Johns Hopkins University, contends that Lincoln was in important ways one of the chief custodians of the democratic spirit. Our "reconstruction" of Abraham Lincoln should not be carried to the extreme, Donald says, for the Lincoln legends offer ready access to the workings of the American mind. "The student can use these myths for an understanding of what plain Americans wished their leaders to be."

I

The Lincoln cult is almost an American religion. It has its high priests in the form of Lincoln "authorities" and its worshippers in the thousands of "fans" who think, talk, and read Lincoln every day. The very name of its founder possesses magical significance—witness its use in advertising everything from automobiles to barbershops. Lincoln's birthday is a national holiday, commemorated with solemn ceremonies. In 1909, the centennial of his birth, Illinois teachers were directed to devote at least half of the day of February 12 to "public exercises . . . patriotic music, recitations of sayings and verses . . . and speeches." The schoolchildren were to conclude the celebration by chanting in unison, with their faces turned toward Springfield, the following ritual:

> A blend of mirth and sadness, smiles and tears;
> A quaint knight errant of the pioneers;
> A homely hero, born of star and sod;
> A Peasant Prince; a masterpiece of God.

The Lincoln birthplace in Kentucky, the memorial in Washington, and the tomb in Illinois have become national shrines visited by thousands each week.

It was probably inevitable that Lincoln should have, as Emerson said, "become mythological in a very few years." America was badly in need of a hero. By 1865 George Washington seemed so dignified and remote that it

From *Lincoln Reconsidered*, by David Donald, Vintage Books, 1961 Edition. Reprinted by permission of the author and the *Journal of the Illinois State Historical Society.*

was hard to think of him as a man, much less as a boy; he was a portrait by Peale or a Houdon bust. Davy Crockett had degenerated from frontier hero into comic legend. Andrew Jackson, Henry Clay, and Daniel Webster were already slipping into the limbo of lost souls, the history books.

The times and events of the Civil War had made a great popular leader necessary. There had been the emotional strain of war, the taut peril of defeat, the thrill of battles won, the release of peace. Then had come the calamitous, disastrous assassination. The people's grief was immediate and it was immense. Properly to describe it one would need the eloquence of a Whitman or a Sandburg. Men had a lost feeling. "The news of his going," mourned William H. Herndon, "struck me dumb, the deed being so infernally wicked . . . so huge in consequences, that it was too large to enter my brain. Hence it was incomprehensible, leaving a misty distant doubt of its truth. It *yet* does not appear like a worldly reality."

Mourning intensified grief. The trappings of death—the black-draped catafalque, the silent train that moved by a circuitous route over the land, the white-robed choirs that wailed a dirge, the crepe-veiled women, the stone-faced men—made Lincoln's passing seem even more calamitous. Over a million persons took a last sad look at the face in the casket and went away treasuring an unforgettable memory. They became of that select group who had seen Lincoln plain.

II

In those dark postwar decades there was keen interest in the Great Emancipator and Great Martyr—those two phrases, always in capitals, keep cropping up in nearly all the correspondence of the period. There were those who speculated on what Lincoln would have done had he lived, and there were more who tried to recall what he had done while alive. An avid audience looked forward eagerly to the memoirs and reminiscences that began to flood the country. Jay Monaghan's *Lincoln Bibliography* lists over four hundred and fifty speeches, sermons, and histories of Lincoln which appeared in the year of his death.

To this urgent demand for details on Lincoln's life, few would answer as did George Spears, a friend from New Salem days, who explained the brevity of his recollections by declaring: "At that time I had no idea of his ever being President therefore I did not notice his course as close as I should of." Not only persons who knew Lincoln retailed "facts" to the eager world, but also those who had merely met the President, or those who thought they had met him, or those who wished to have met him. Stories, sometimes without the slightest shadow of factual foundation, were spread by word of mouth, and by mere repetition gained authenticity. Then they appeared in Lincoln biographies and have been handed down ever since as indubitably accurate.

At the time of Lincoln's death there was no single pattern into which the stories and anecdotes about him could fit. In the blurred memories of former slaves there was the shadowy outline of a preternaturally shrewd Lincoln, half Moses, half Yankee. "I think Abe Lincoln was next to the Lord," said one ex-slave. "He done all he could for the slaves; he set 'em free." Then the aged Negro went on to "reminisce":

> 'Fore the election he [Lincoln] traveled all over the South, and he come to our house and slept in Old Mistress' bed. Didn't nobody know who he was. . . . He come to our house and he watched close. . . . When he got back up North he writ Old Master a letter and told him that he was going to have to free his slaves, that everybody was going to have to. . . . He also told him that he had visited at his house and if he doubted it to go in the room he slept in and look on the bedstead at the head and he'd see where he'd writ his name. Sure enough, there was his name: A. Lincoln.

Gradually the Negro built up a more emotional image of Lincoln, a perfect man and, in a peculiarly individual way, a personal emancipator. In Negro houses all over the nation one could find "many old pictures of Lincoln pasted on the walls of the sitting room over the mantelpiece. . . . They just had to have Lincoln near them," explains their chronicler, John E. Washington; "they loved him so." "His life to these humble people was a miracle, and his memory has become a benediction," Dr. Washington adds. "To the deeply emotional and religious slave, Lincoln was an earthly incarnation of the Savior of mankind."

At the other extreme were the stories spread by Lincoln's political enemies, legends that still persist in some parts of the South. To these the sixteenth President was only "a man of coarse nature, a self-seeking politician, who craved high office . . . to satisfy his own burning desire for distinction." ". . . his real name is Abraham Hanks," one political opponent charged. "He is the illegitimate son by an [sic] man named Inlow—from a Negress named Hanna Hanks." His presumptive parents were immoral, shiftless poor white trash. Unscrupulous as a lawyer, he was unprincipled as a politician. He was a man of low morality, and his "inordinate love of the lascivious, of smut," it was whispered, was "something nearly akin to lunacy."

III

Naturally the strongest growth of Lincoln legends has occurred in the North. There have been, in general, two opposing schools of tradition. One, essentially literary in character and often of New England or Eastern sponsorship, presented a prettified Lincoln, a combination of George Washington and Christ. Occasionally there were difficulties of reconciling the two ideas, and the resulting portrait looks somewhat like a Gilbert Stuart painting with a halo dubbed in by later, less skillful hands. The problem was to reconcile the standards of democracy in the gilded age with the familiar pattern of the Christ story. Fortunately for authors, consistency is not an essential in folklore.

In eulogies, sermons, birthday speeches, Republican campaign addresses, orations before the G.A.R., and in poems too numerous to count and too tedious to read, one gets a glimpse of the pattern. This Lincoln has the outlines of a mythological hero; he is a demi-god. Born in obscure circumstances, he rose over hardships, became President, was lawgiver to the Negro people, won a tremendous victory, and was killed at the height of his power. By his death he expiated the sins of his country. After one makes the obvious concessions required by mid-century morality and by the exigencies of a republican form of government, this Lincoln conforms very closely to the type of ideal hero in classical mythology.

The eulogists had some doubts as to how Lincoln's ancestry should be presented. A mythological hero should spring from unknown parentage (or at least it is concealed even from himself), sent by the gods to save his tribe. There are a number of Lincoln poets and biographers who ask: "Whence came this man?" and answer: "As if on the wings of the winds of God that blew!" On the other hand, it comported more with American notions of respectability that the hero should have at least some family connections. The Lincolns have, therefore, been traced in elaborate monographs back to the early Massachusetts settlers and even to the English family of that name. The Hankses have been "proved" to derive their name from an Egyptian dynasty, or, as an alternative explanation, they were relatives of the Lees of Virginia.

Regardless of origins, the biographers were sure of one thing. Lincoln loved his angel-mother. It is characteristic of the American attitude toward family life and of the extreme veneration for the maternal principle that the utterly unknown Nancy Hanks should be described as "a whole-hearted Christian," "a woman of marked natural abilities," of "strong mental powers and deep-toned piety," whose rigid observance of the Sabbath became a byword in frontier Kentucky—in short, "a remarkable woman." "A great man," asserted J. G. Holland in his widely circulated *Life of Abraham Lincoln*, "never drew his infant life from a purer or more womanly bosom than her own; and Mr. Lincoln always looked back to her with an unspeakable affection."

Lincoln's early life became, to this school of biography, an illustration of how determination and energy could triumph over circumstances; this Lincoln was the transcendent rail-splitter. It was a carefully manipulated symbolism that had begun at the Illinois state Republican convention of 1860 when rails that Lincoln might have split were introduced to elicit applause. The theme was drummed and piped and bugled all through the campaigns of 1860 and 1864, and the tale of Lincoln's "life of labor" that "brought forth his kingly qualities of soul" has become a part of the American tradition. Lincoln was never to escape; his Civil War administration would be appraised in terms of his early struggles:

> Out yonder splitting rails his mind had fed
> On Freedom—now he put her foes to rout.

46

From these origins he rose to become President of the United States, and, surprisingly enough, a successful President. There must have been, a great many people believed, some supernatural force, some divine guidance behind his rise. "Out of the unknown, and by ways that even he knew not," orated one centennial speaker, becoming more mystical with each phrase, "came to this place of power, Abraham Lincoln. He came mysteriously chosen . . . by the instinctive voice of a predestined people. Called because he was chosen; chosen, because he was already choice."

There were elements in Lincoln's personality and career which did not blend well in this portrait of a demigod. He was indubitably homely—not a major difficulty, to be sure, yet if a hero is not handsome he should at least be impressive. Rhymesters went to great length to explain the truth. Was Lincoln "ungainly, plain"? Not at all. "Grave was his visage," it was admitted, "but no cloud could dull the radiance from within that made it beautiful." A more serious obstacle was Lincoln's levity. He told jokes—a thing unprecedented in the record of mythology. Writers were more familiar with the idea of "one who knew no play, nor ever tasted rest." How could a man of sadness and tears laugh at Artemus Ward? One poet suggested that Lincoln's laughter was really a sort of anodyne "to cease his ceaseless dole." Thus Lincoln became the laughing man of sorrows.

Another difficulty was Lincoln's religion. It was embarrassing that this "soldier of his Captain Christ" belonged to no Christian church. Shortly after Lincoln's death there began to appear a veritable flood of affidavits and statements to prove, as Holland put it, that "Lincoln's power" had been the "power of a true-hearted Christian man." Reminiscences on this point probably include more nonsense than can be found anywhere else in the whole tiresome mass of spurious Lincoln recollections. To him are attributed the most improbable statements. Lincoln was supposed to have had a secret conference with Newton Bateman, Illinois superintendent of public instruction, during which he pulled a Testament from his bosom and pointed to it as *"this rock* on which I stand." "I know," he is alleged to have confided, "that liberty is right, for Christ teaches it and Christ is God."

Countless similar statements were given wide newspaper circulation. Lincoln reportedly ran upon one Benjamin B. Smith, a minister of Canton, Missouri, in a railway station, brought him into his office, and begged from the willing pastor a private, hour-long discourse upon "foreordination, election and predestination." During the darkest hours of the war Lincoln was supposed to have left his post in Washington in order to pray with Henry Ward Beecher in Brooklyn. So it went. There were those who could demonstrate that Lincoln was a Catholic, a Congregationalist, a Methodist, a Presbyterian, a Universalist, or a Spiritualist. Conflicting claims became so amusing that the editor of the Springfield *Illinois State Register* rejected them as "all wrong." "We are," he remarked whimsically, "prepared to prove by indisputable documentary evidence that he was a Mormon, and the boon companion of Joe Smith."

For these minor defects Lincoln amply compensated by the manner of his passing. His assassination at once brought to mind the tender, familiar outlines of the Christ story. Lincoln as "Savior of his country" was by his death expiating the sins of the nation. The idea had universal appeal. One has only to leaf through the pages of Lloyd Lewis's *Myths after Lincoln* to discover how frequently the idea of vicarious sacrifice recurred to Northern preachers on that dread Black Easter of 1865. Some pointed to the significance of Lincoln's martyrdom on Good Friday. "It is no blasphemy against the Son of God," asserted a Connecticut parson, "that we declare the fitness of the slaying of the second Father of our Republic on the anniversary of the day on which He was slain. Jesus Christ died for the world, Abraham Lincoln died for his country." Even so early the pattern of apotheosis was complete. America had a martyr hero, a perfect man, born to do great things, pure in heart, noble in action, and constant in principle. This was Lincoln, "President, savior of the republic, emancipator of a race, true Christian, true man."

IV

Lincoln was saved from this kind of deification by a different stream of tradition, frequently Western in origin and more truly folkloristic in quality. The grotesque hero—the Gargantua or the Till Eulenspiegel—is one of the oldest and most familiar patterns in folk literature. In America the type had been already exemplified by such favorites as Davy Crockett, Mike Fink, and Paul Bunyan. Of a like cut was the myth of Lincoln as frontier hero. This Lincoln of "folk say" was the practical joker, the teller of tall and lusty tales. Stupendously strong, he was also marvelously lazy. A true romantic, he pined over the grave of Ann Rutledge, but he also lampooned one woman who refused him and jilted another who accepted. He was Old Abe, a Westerner, and his long flapping arms were not the wings of an angel.

This folk pattern of Lincoln as frontier hero had been sketched in outline before his death. After his assassination the details were filled in. Many of the stories in the strong Western tradition can be traced back to Herndon, Lincoln's law partner, who has been called the "master myth-maker" of Lincoln folklore. Herndon did not invent the legends, but his singular personality made him peculiarly receptive to this type of Western mythology. Herndon was born in Kentucky, and, as an early German traveler put it, "the Kentuckian is a peculiar man." Moody, erratic, loquacious, addicted to high-flown "philosophical" language, but with a fondness for earthy stories, Herndon had shortly after his partner's death decided to write a biography of Lincoln. From the very outset he had in mind showing Lincoln as a Western character, shaped by the "power of mud, flowers, & mind" which he had encountered in the pioneer Northwest. Deliberately he sought to emphasize those factors which would distinguish Lincoln as a Westerner from his Eastern contemporaries. He proposed to exhibit "the type" of the "original western and south-western pioneer— . . . at times . . . somewhat open, candid, sincere, energetic, spontaneous, trusting, tolerant, brave and generous."

Seeking information about Lincoln, Herndon interviewed older settlers in central Illinois and southern Indiana at just the time when the outlines of the folk portrait were becoming firmly established. From his notes emerged the essentially fictitious picture of a semilegendary frontier hero. The stories Herndon collected fall into patterns familiar to the student of American folk-lore. Some remembered Lincoln as a ring-tailed roarer of the Davy Crockett type, who would wave a whisky bottle over his head to drive back his foes, shouting that "he was the big buck at the lick." There were tales of the Paul Bunyan variety, describing how Lincoln would "frequently take a barrel of whiskey by the chimes and lift it up to his face as if to drink out of the bunghole," a feat that "he could accomplish with greatest ease."

This was the Lincoln who chastely wooed Ann Rutledge and, when she died, pined sadly over her grave. "My heart," he was supposed to have said, "lies buried there." More in the frontier tradition was his courtship of Mary Owens, a well-educated Kentucky lady who refused his hand. Afterward Lincoln described her as "weather-beaten," "oversize," and lacking teeth. Of a like pattern were the tales Herndon accumulated of Lincoln's domestic un-happiness with Mary Todd, for the henpecked husband is one of the oldest comic types and was a favorite in the Western joke books of the day. Herndon also collected irreligious or, as he called them, "infidel" statements attributed to Lincoln; the folk hero is frequently anticlerical.

Many of these tales probably had a grain of historical truth, and their evolution exhibits the familiar development of folk literature. "If a man has been well known for special powers," Robert Price has pointed out in his examination of the Johnny Appleseed traditions, "folk fancies soon seize upon particular instances of these powers, begin to enhance them into facts of re-markable quality, and then proceed, as the desire for greater color grows, to invent still others that will markedly emphasize the quality admired." As the historical personage becomes absorbed in the myth, "the whole cycle of his birth, youth, education, loves, mating, maturity, and death becomes sig-nificant and grows increasingly in color and particular detail." On a rather sophisticated plane, the Lincoln of Western legend represented a true folk-hero type.

The folkloristic quality of these stories is sometimes overlooked. When Herndon visited in Indiana, he was told of verses that Lincoln had written to celebrate the wedding of his sister:

> When Adam was created
> He dwelt in Eden's shade,
> As Moses has recorded,
> And soon a bride was made.

(The poem continues for seven additional stanzas.) Dr. Milo M. Quaife has traced this ballad back to early English folk verse and has shown that it was introduced into America before the Revolutionary War. In the process of being handed down, it somehow became identified in the minds of backwoods Hoosiers with Lincoln; it was related to Herndon as such; he published the verses in his Lincoln biography; and the poem is not infrequently cited as Lincoln's original composition. Of the making of myths there is no end.

The process of evolving Western legends about Lincoln neither began nor ended with Herndon. Gossip, imagination, delayed recollection, and hearsay have all continued to multiply "Lincoln" stories. Sometimes the results of this accumulation of "folk say" are amusing. One can take, for example, a less familiar episode in Lincoln's early career—his projected duel with James Shields. The actual facts of the affair are easily ascertained. In 1842 Mary Todd and Julia Jayne published anonymously in the *Sangamo Journal* some satirical verses about Shields, then Illinois state auditor. That hot-tempered Irishman demanded of the editor the names of the writers, and Lincoln, to protect the ladies, offered to take the blame. After some stilted correspondence and much dashing back and forth of seconds, a duel with broadswords was arranged. Ultimately, however, explanations and apologies were made, and actual combat was averted. The affair remained a sore memory to Lincoln, and he disliked hearing the episode referred to. The whole affair is summarized in any good Lincoln biography.

As this same tale comes down in folklore, the whole emphasis is altered. It becomes an illustration of Lincoln the humorist and the practical joker. The duel had an amusing origin, according to one old settler who had heard another old-timer tell the story:

> Lawyer Shields and Julia Jayne were seated together at the supper table. Across the table from them sat Abe and Mary Todd. By and by the lawyer squeezed Julia's hand. In those days, you know, a pin was a woman's weapon. Julia used it when Shields squeezed her hand. And that made him scream. . . . Lincoln, who was a laughing fellow, haw-hawed right out loud, much to the embarrassment of Shields. Well to make a long story short, Shield[s] issued a duel challenge to Abe.

Another version gives a play-by-play account of the duel that never happened. "Shields fired and missed," says this "eyewitness," speaking of an encounter that was to have been fought with broadswords. "Lincoln then took steady aim and fired. A blotch of read [sic] appeared on the breast of Shields who fell to the ground thinking he was mortally wounded, but in fact was unhurt. Lincoln's gun was loaded with pokeberries."

To treat such statements simply as exaggerated reminiscences is to miss their significance. They are really folk stories. Seldom do they have an identifiable author, for the narrator is recounting what "they said." The very pattern of the statement is significant; "to make a long story short" is a frequent formula to conclude a folk tale. The Shields episode is only one less widely known incident about which a surprisingly large amount of folklore has accumulated. The body of tradition concerning Lincoln's courtship, his marriage, or his law practice is much more voluminous. And there is an extensive cycle of ribald and Rabelaisian stories attributed to Lincoln, for the most part unprintable and now almost forgotten.

V

Few Negroes have written books about their Great Emancipator, and the viciously anti-Lincoln publications are nearly forgotten, but the other two major currents of tradition have produced a mountainous pile of Lincoln literature. Writers who fitted Lincoln into the pattern of a mythological demigod had the early start at the printing presses. A series of widely read and often quoted biographies began to appear shortly after Lincoln's death, starting with the Arnold and the Holland lives and running without interruption through the work of Nicolay and Hay and that of Ida M. Tarbell. All were characterized by a highly laudatory tone and all presented Lincoln in an aura of great respectability.

Those who thought of Lincoln as the archetype of the frontiersman were outraged. Herndon was especially bitter at the "Finical fools," the "nice sweet smelling gentlemen" who tried to "handle things with silken gloves & 'a cammel [sic] hair pencil,' " but for personal reasons his own book about Lincoln was delayed for many years. The publication in 1872 of Ward Hill Lamon's biography, ghost-written from Herndonian sources, marked the first widespread circulation in print of the Western version of Lincoln's career. It was greeted as "a national misfortune." When *Herndon's Lincoln* appeared seventeen years later, it, too, met with shrill disapproval, and some shocked souls appealed to Anthony Comstock to suppress this indecent book. This food was too coarse for sensitive stomachs.

It is a mistake to consider these two opposing currents of Lincoln tradition as representing respectively the "ideal" and the "real" Lincoln. Each was legendary in character. The conflict in Lincoln biography between the Holland-Hay-Tarbell faction and the Herndon-Lamon-Weik contingent was not essentially a battle over factual differences; it was more like a religious war. One school portrayed a mythological patron saint; the other, an equally mythological frontier hero. Not all the Lincoln stories related by either school were false, but the facts were at most a secondary consideration. Acceptance or rejection of any Lincoln anecdote depended upon what was fundamentally a religious conviction. Even today this attitude is sometimes found. A recent writer has attacked certain legends that he asserts "libel" Lincoln on two grounds—first, because they "do not create a truer or finer image of him" and, second, because the myths are "unsupported by trustworthy evidence." The order of the reasons deserves notice.

It is widely recognized that the biographies of the Holland school are remote from reality. They present a conventionalized hero who is discussed from a "frankly eulogistic point of view." The temptation has naturally been to treat their opponents—such as Herndon, Lamon, and Weik—as realists, intent on giving a "true" picture of Lincoln. If there is any meaning left in the word "realism," which is rapidly becoming semantically obsolete, *Herndon's Lincoln* (a biography typical of this latter school) is realistic neither in literary style nor in biographical approach. Herndon's book was dedicated to proving a thesis—that Lincoln had his origin in a "stagnant, putrid pool" and rose through adversity to "the topmost round of the ladder." All of its contents Herndon deliberately arranged to support this contention and to enlist readers' sympathies in behalf of his protagonist. Rough and coarse elements were introduced into the biography, not primarily from conviction that these were vital aspects of human existence, but principally to serve the same function as the villain in the contemporary melodrama. Unlike the true realists, Herndon was concerned with the unusual and the sensational. It is difficult to see how anyone can find in Herndon's emotionalized treatment of the Ann Rutledge legend the work of a biographical or literary realist. Actually the biographies of the Herndon school are stylized presentations of Western folklore. Herndon's own book recounts the epic of the frontier hero, transmogrified into the pattern of the sentimental novel.

Toward the end of the century the two conceptions of Lincoln—as mythological demigod and as legendary frontier hero—began to blend, sometimes with amusing results. John T. Morse's *Abraham Lincoln*, one of the better early biographies, made no effort to reconcile the two concepts, but accepted both. For Lincoln's early years Morse followed Herndon, and for the period of the Presidency, Nicolay and Hay. The result, he admitted, tended to show that Lincoln was "physically one creature, morally and mentally two beings." In the huge file of newspaper reminiscences in the Lincoln National Life Foundation one can trace the process by which demigod and hero became inextricably scrambled. By the centennial year of Lincoln's birth the frontier stories that had been considered gamy and rough by an earlier generation had been accepted as typical Lincolnisms; and on the other side, the harshness of the Herndonian outlines was smoothed by the acceptance of many traits from the idealized Lincoln. The result was a "composite American ideal," whose "appeal is stronger than that of other heroes because on him converge so many dear traditions." The current popular conception of Lincoln is "a folk-hero who to the common folk-virtues of shrewdness and kindness adds essential wit and eloquence and loftiness of soul."

VI

One may question the value of studying these legendary accounts of Lincoln. A more conventional procedure is to assault these air castles of contemporary mythology, to use the sharp tools of historical criticism to raze the imaginary structures, to purify the ground by a liberal sprinkling of holy water in the form of footnotes, and to erect a new and "authentic" edifice. Such an approach has its merits. One cannot overestimate the importance of thorough-going historical investigation of Lincoln's career; far too little of the huge bibliography of Lincolniana is based upon scholarly, scientific research.

But there is also room for investigation of another sort. Referring to the debunking of historical myths and legends, W. A. Dunning, in his presidential address before the American Historical Association, reminded his hearers that in many cases "influence on the sequence of human affairs has been exercised, not by what really happened, but by what men erroneously believed to have happened." In turning to history for guidance, he observed, men have acted upon "the error that passes as history at the time, not from the truth that becomes known long after." He concluded by pointing out that "for very, very much history there is more importance in the ancient error than in the new-found truth."

His warning applies in the field of Lincoln biography. As J. Frank Dobie has put it, "The history of any public character involves not only the facts about him but what the public has taken to be facts." It is important to examine the Lincoln legends as expressing a collective wish-fulfillment of the American people. This is no psychological jargon; it is simply a way of saying that "heroes embody the qualities that we most admire or desire in ourselves." Fully realizing their general inaccuracy and almost universal distortion, the student can use these myths for an understanding of what plain Americans have wished their leaders to be. "If the folk aspiration is worthy, its dreams of great men will be worthy too."

Unless one conceives of time as ending with 1865, the Lincoln of folklore is more significant than the Lincoln of actuality. The historian may prove that the Emancipation actually freed a negligible number of slaves, yet Lincoln continues to live in men's minds as the emancipator of the Negroes. It is this folklore Lincoln who has become the central symbol in American democratic thought; he embodies what ordinary, inarticulate Americans have cherished as ideals. As Ralph H. Gabriel says, he is "first among the folk heroes of the American people." From a study of the Lincoln legends the historian can gain a more balanced insight into the workings of the American mind. As it is now written, intellectual history is too often based on printed sources—sermons, speeches, commencement addresses, books, and newspapers. The result is inevitably a distortion. The men who write books or edit papers are not average citizens. It is much as though the Gallup poll were to interrogate only college presidents. To understand the thinking of ordinary men and women, the historian must delve into their beliefs, their superstitions, their gossip, and their folklore.

The Lincoln ideal offers an excellent starting-point for the investigation. As the pattern has gradually become standardized, the folklore Lincoln is as American as the Mississippi River. Essentially national, the myth is not nationalistic. It reveals the people's faith in the democratic dogma that a poor boy can make good. It demonstrates the incurable romanticism of the American spirit. There is much in the legend which is unpleasant—Lincoln's preternatural cunning, his fondness for Rabelaisian anecdote, his difficulties with his wife—yet these traits seem to be attributed to every real folk hero. The fundamental qualities of the legendary Lincoln emphasize the essential dignity and humanity of our nation's everyday thinking. It speaks well for Americans that to the central hero in their history their folklore has attributed all the decent qualities of civilized man: patience, tolerance, humor, sympathy, kindliness, and sagacity.

The Tragic Legend of Reconstruction

Kenneth M. Stampp

Perhaps legend and myth become most debilitating when they directly affect a society's overt social and political behavior. If this is so, the legend of reconstruction qualifies as particularly tragic. Kenneth M. Stampp, an historical scholar at the University of California, Berkeley, applies a revisionist lens to the era of reconstruction in the interest of explaining American racial attitudes, past and present. Through his revisionist view of the reconstruction "radicals," Stampp brings much weight to bear against the mythology of northern postwar brutality. It was a mythology that was largely the product of the historical community itself, but one that nonetheless found an especially receptive audience both North and South.

In much serious history, as well as in a durable popular legend, two American epochs—the Civil War and the reconstruction that followed—bear an odd relationship to one another. The Civil War, though admittedly a tragedy, is nevertheless often described as a glorious time of gallantry, noble self-sacrifice, and high idealism. Even historians who have considered the war "needless" and have condemned the politicians of the 1850's for blundering into it, once they passed the firing on Fort Sumter, have usually written with reverence about Civil War heroes—the martyred Lincoln, the Christlike Lee, the intrepid Stonewall Jackson, and many others in this galaxy of demigods.

Few, of course, are so innocent as not to know that the Civil War had its seamy side. One can hardly ignore the political opportunism, the graft and profiteering in the filling of war contracts, the military blundering and needless loss of lives, the horrors of army hospitals and prison camps, and the ugly depths as well as the nobility of human nature that the war exposed with a fine impartiality. These things cannot be ignored, but they can be, and frequently are, dismissed as something alien to the essence of the war years. What was real and fundamental was the idealism and the nobility of the two contending forces: the Yankees struggling to save the Union, dying to make men free; the Confederates fighting for great constitutional principles, defending their homes from invasion. Here, indeed, is one of the secrets of the spell the Civil War has cast: it involved high-minded Americans on both sides, and there was glory enough to go around. This, in fact, is the supreme sythesis of Civil War historiography and the great balm that has healed the nation's wounds: Yankees and Confederates alike fought bravely for what they believed to be just causes. There were few villains in the drama.

But when the historian reaches the year 1865, he must take leave of the war and turn to another epoch, reconstruction, when the task was, in Lincoln's words, "to bind up the nation's wounds" and "to do all which may achieve and cherish a just and lasting peace." How, until recently, reconstruction was portrayed in both history and legend, how sharply it was believed to contrast with the years of the Civil War, is evident in the terms that were used to identify it. Various historians have called this phase of American history "The Tragic Era," "The Dreadful Decade," "The Age of Hate," and "The Blackout of Honest Government." Reconstruction represented the ultimate shame of the American people—as one historian phrased it, "the nadir of national disgrace." It was the epoch that most Americans wanted to forget.

Claude Bowers, who divided his time between politics and history, has been the chief disseminator of the traditional picture of reconstruction, for his book, *The Tragic Era*, published in 1929, has attracted more readers than any other dealing with this period. For Bowers reconstruction was a time of almost unrelieved sordidness in public and private life; whole regiments of villains march through his pages; the corrupt politicians who dominated the administration of Ulysses S. Grant; the crafty, scheming northern carpetbaggers who invaded the South after the war for political and economic plunder; the degraded and depraved southern scalawags who betrayed their own people and collaborated with the enemy; and the ignorant, barbarous, sensual Negroes who threatened to Africanize the South and destroy its Caucasian civilization.

Most of Bowers's key generalizations can be found in his preface. The years of reconstruction, he wrote, "were years of revolutionary turmoil, with the elemental passions predominant. . . . The prevailing note was one of tragedy. . . . Never have American public men in responsible positions, directing the destiny of the nation, been so brutal, hypocritical, and corrupt. The constitution was treated as a doormat on which politicians and army officers wiped their feet after wading in the muck. . . . The southern people literally were put to the torture . . . [by] rugged conspirators . . . [who] assumed the pose of philanthropists and patriots." The popularity of Bowers's book stems in part from the simplicity of his characters. None are etched in shades of gray; none are confronted with complex moral decisions. Like characters in a Victorian romance, the Republican leaders of the reconstruction era were evil through and through, and the helpless, innocent white men of the South were totally noble and pure.

If Bowers's prose is more vivid and his anger more intense, his general interpretation of reconstruction is only a slight exaggeration of a point of view shared by most serious American historians from the late nineteenth century until very recently. Writing in the 1890's, James Ford Rhodes, author of a multi-volumed history of the United States since the Compromise of

1850, branded the Republican scheme of reconstruction as "repressive" and "uncivilized," one that "pandered to the ignorant negroes, the knavish white natives and the vulturous adventurers who flocked from the North." About the same time Professor John W. Burgess, of Columbia University, called reconstruction the "most soul-sickening spectacle that Americans had ever been called upon to behold."[1] Early in the twentieth century Professor William A. Dunning, also of Columbia University, and a group of talented graduate students wrote a series of monographs that presented a crushing indictment of the Republican reconstruction program in the South—a series that made a deep and lasting impression on American historians. In the 1930's, Professor James G. Randall, of the University of Illinois, still writing in the spirit of the Dunningites, described the reconstruction era "as a time of party abuse, of corruption, of vindictive bigotry." "To use a modern phrase," wrote Randall, "government under Radical Republican rule in the South had become a kind of 'racket.'" As late as 1947, Professor E. Merton Coulter, of the University of Georgia, reminded critics of the traditional interpretation that no "amount of revision can write away the grievous mistakes made in this abnormal period of American history."[2] Thus, from Rhodes and Burgess and Dunning to Randall and Coulter the central emphasis of most historical writing about reconstruction has been upon sordid motives and human depravity. Somehow, during the summer of 1865, the nobility and idealism of the war years had died.

A synopsis of the Dunning School's version of reconstruction would run something like this: Abraham Lincoln, while the Civil War was still in progress, turned his thoughts to the great problem of reconciliation; and, "with malice toward none and charity for all," this gentle and compassionate man devised a plan that would restore the South to the Union with minimum humiliation and maximum speed. But there had already emerged in Congress a faction of radical Republicans, sometimes called Jacobins or Vindictives, who sought to defeat Lincoln's generous program. Motivated by hatred of the South, by selfish political ambitions, and by crass economic interests, the radicals tried to make the process of reconstruction as humiliating, as difficult, and as prolonged as they possibly could. Until Lincoln's tragic death, they poured their scorn upon him—and then used his coffin as a political stump to arouse the passions of the northern electorate.

The second chapter of the Dunning version begins with Andrew Johnson's succession to the presidency. Johnson, the old Jacksonian Unionist from Tennessee, took advantage of the adjournment of Congress to put Lincoln's mild plan of reconstruction into operation, and it was a striking success. In the summer and fall of 1865, Southerners organized loyal state governments, showed a willingness to deal fairly with their former slaves, and in general accepted the outcome of the Civil War in good faith. In December, when Congress assembled, President Johnson reported that the process of reconstruction was nearly completed and that the old Union had been restored. But the radicals unfortunately had their own sinister purposes: they repudiated the governments Johnson had established in the South, refused to seat southern Senators and Representatives, and then directed their fury against the new President. After a year of bitter controversy and political stalemate, the radicals, resorting to shamefully demagogic tactics, won an overwhelming victory in the congressional elections of 1866.

Now, the third chapter and the final tragedy. Riding rough-shod over presidential vetoes and federal courts, the radicals put the South under military occupation, gave the ballot to Negroes, and formed new southern state governments dominated by base and corrupt men, black and white. Not satisfied with reducing the South to political slavery and financial bankruptcy, the radicals even laid their obscene hands on the pure fabric of the federal Constitution. They impeached President Johnson and came within one vote of removing him from office, though they had no legal grounds for such action. Next, they elected Ulysses S. Grant President, and during his two administrations they indulged in such an orgy of corruption and so prostituted the civil service as to make Grantism an enduring symbol of political immorality.

The last chapter is the story of ultimate redemption. Decent southern white Democrats, their patience exhausted, organized to drive the Negroes, carpetbaggers, and scalawags from power, peacefully if possible, forcefully if necessary. One by one the southern states were redeemed, honesty and virtue triumphed, and the South's natural leaders returned to power. In the spring of 1877, the Tragic Era finally came to an end when President Hayes withdrew the federal troops from the South and restored home rule. But the legacy of radical reconstruction remained in the form of a solidly Democratic South and embittered relations between the races.

This point of view was rarely challenged until the 1930's, when a small group of revisionist historians began to give new life and a new direction to the study of reconstruction. The revisionists are a curious lot who sometimes quarrel with each other as much as they quarrel with the disciples of Dunning. At various times they have counted in their ranks Marxists of various degrees of orthodoxy, Negroes seeking historical vindication, skeptical white Southerners, and latter-day northern abolitionists. But among them are numerous scholars who have the wisdom to know that the history of an age is seldom simple and clear-cut, seldom without its tragic aspects, seldom without its redeeming virtues.

Few revisionists would claim that the Dunning interpretation of reconstruction is a pure fabrication. They recognize the shabby aspects of this era: the corruption was real, the failures obvious, the tragedy undeniable. Grant is not their idea of a model President, nor were the southern carpetbag governments worthy of their unqualified praise. They understand that the radical Republicans were not all selfless patriots, and that southern white men were not all Negro-hating rebels. In short, they have not turned history on its head, but rather, they recognize that much of what Dunning's disciples have said about reconstruction is true.

Revisionists, however, have discovered that the Dunningites overlooked a great deal, and they doubt that nobility and idealism suddenly died in 1865. They are neither surprised nor disillusioned to find that the Civil War, for all its nobility, revealed some of the ugliness of human nature as well. And they approach reconstruction with the confident expectation that here, too, every facet of human nature will be exposed. They are not satisfied with the two-dimensional characters that Dunning's disciples have painted.

What is perhaps most puzzling in the legend of reconstruction is the notion that the white people of the South were treated with unprecedented brutality, that their conquerors, in Bowers's colorful phrase, literally put them to the torture. How, in fact, *were* they treated after the failure of their rebellion against the authority of the federal government? The great mass of ordinary Southerners who voluntarily took up arms, or in other ways supported the Confederacy, were required simply to take an oath of allegiance to obtain pardon and to regain their right to vote and hold public office. But what of the Confederate leaders—the men who held high civil offices, often after resigning similar federal offices; the military leaders who had graduated from West Point and had resigned commissions in the United States Army to take commissions in the Confederate Army? Were there mass arrests, indictments for treason or conspiracy, trials and convictions, executions or imprisonments? Nothing of the sort. Officers of the Confederate Army were paroled and sent home with their men. After surrendering at Appomattox, General Lee bid farewell to his troops and rode home to live his remaining years undisturbed. Only one officer, a Captain Henry Wirtz, was arrested; and he was tried, convicted, and executed, not for treason or conspiracy, but for "war crimes." Wirtz's alleged offense, for which the evidence was rather flimsy, was the mistreatment of prisoners of war in the military prison at Andersonville, Georgia.

Of the Confederate civil officers, a handful were arrested at the close of the war, and there was talk for a time of trying a few for treason. But none, actually, was ever brought to trial, and all but Jefferson Davis were released within a few months. The former Confederate President was held in prison for nearly two years, but in 1867 he too was released. With a few exceptions, even the property of Confederate leaders was untouched, save, of course, for the emancipation of their slaves. Indeed, the only penalty imposed on most Confederate leaders was a temporary political disability provided in the Fourteenth Amendment. But in 1872 Congress pardoned all but a handful of Southerners; and soon former Confederate civil and military leaders were serving as state governors, as members of Congress, and even as Cabinet advisers of Presidents.

What, then, constituted the alleged brutality that white Southerners endured? First, the freeing of their slaves; second, the brief incarceration of a few Confederate leaders; third, a political disability imposed for a few years on most Confederate leaders; fourth, a relatively weak military occupation terminated in 1877; and, last, an attempt to extend the rights and privileges of citizenship to southern Negroes. Mistakes there were in the implementation of these measures—some of them serious—but brutality almost none. In fact, it can be said that rarely in history have the participants in an unsuccessful rebellion endured penalties as mild as those Congress imposed upon the people of the South, and particularly upon their leaders. After four years of bitter struggle costing hundreds of thousands of lives, the generosity of the federal government's terms was quite remarkable.

If northern brutality is a myth, the scandals of the Grant administration and the peculations of some of the southern reconstruction governments are sordid facts. Yet even here the Dunningites are guilty of distortion by exaggeration, by a lack of perspective, by superficial analysis, and by overemphasis. They make corruption a central theme of their narratives, but they overlook constructive accomplishments. They give insufficient attention to the men who transcended the greed of an age when, to be sure, self-serving politicians and irresponsible entrepreneurs were all too plentiful. Among these men were the humanitarians who organized Freedmen's Aid Societies to help four million southern Negroes make the difficult transition from slavery to freedom, and the missionaries and teachers who went into the South on slender budgets to build churches and schools for the freedmen. Under their auspices the Negroes first began to learn the responsibilities and obligations of freedom. Thus the training of Negroes for citizenship had its successful beginnings in the years of reconstruction.

In the nineteenth century most white Americans, North and South, had reservations about the Negro's potentialities—doubted that he had the innate intellectual capacity and moral fiber of the white man and assumed that after emancipation he would be relegated to an inferior caste. But some of the radical Republicans refused to believe that the Negroes were innately inferior and hoped passionately that they would confound their critics. The radicals then had little empirical evidence and no scientific evidence to support their belief—nothing, in fact, but faith. Their faith was derived mostly from their religion: all men, they said, are the sons of Adam and equal in the sight of God. And if Negroes are equal to white men in the sight of God, it is morally wrong for white men to withhold from Negroes the liberties and rights that white men enjoy. Here, surely, was a projection into the reconstruction era of the idealism of the abolitionist crusade and of the Civil War.

Radical idealism was in part responsible for two of the most momentous enactments of the reconstruction years: the Fourteenth Amendment to the federal Constitution which gave Negroes citizenship and promised them equal protection of the laws, and the Fifteenth Amendment which gave them the right to vote. The fact that these amendments could not have been adopted under any other circumstances, or at any other time, before or since, may suggest the crucial importance of the reconstruction era in American history. Indeed, without radical reconstruction, it would be impossible to this day for the federal government to protect Negroes from legal and political discrimination.

If all of this is true, or even part of it, why was the Dunning legend born, and why has it been so durable? Southerners, of course, have contributed much to the legend of reconstruction, but most Northerners have found the legend quite acceptable. Many of the historians who helped to create it were Northerners, among them James Ford Rhodes, William A. Dunning, Claude Bowers, and James G. Randall. Thus the legend cannot be explained simply in terms of a southern literary or historiographical conspiracy, satisfying as the legend has been to most white Southerners. What we need to know is why it also satisfies Northerners—how it became part of the intellectual baggage of so many northern historians. Why, in short, was there for so many years a kind of national, or inter-sectional, consensus that the Civil War was America's glory and reconstruction her disgrace?

The Civil War won its place in the hearts of the American people because, by the end of the nineteenth century, Northerners were willing to concede that Southerners had fought bravely for a cause that they believed to be just; whereas Southerners, with few exceptions, were willing to concede that the outcome of the war was probably best for all concerned. In an era of intense nationalism, both Northerners and Southerners agreed that the preservation of the federal Union was essential to the future power of the American people. Southerners could even say now that the abolition of slavery was one of the war's great blessings—not so much, they insisted, because slavery was an injustice to the Negroes but because it was a grievous burden upon the whites. By 1886, Henry W. Grady, the great Georgia editor and spokesman for a New South, could confess to a New York audience: "I am glad that the omniscient God held the balance of battle in His Almighty hand, and that human slavery was swept forever from American soil—the American Union saved from the wreck of war." Soon Union and Confederate veterans were holding joint reunions, exchanging anecdotes, and sharing their sentimental memories of those glorious war years. The Civil War thus took its position in the center of American folk mythology.

That the reconstruction era elicits neither pride nor sentimentality is due only in part to its moral delinquencies—remember, those of the Civil War years can be overlooked. It is also due to the white American's ambivalent attitude toward race and toward the steps that radical Republicans took to protect the Negroes. Southern white men accepted the Thirteenth Amendment to the Constitution, which abolished slavery, with a minimum of complaint, but they expected federal intervention to proceed no further than that. They assumed that the regulation of the freedmen would be left to the individual states; and clearly most of them intended to replace slavery with a caste system that would keep the Negroes perpetually subordinate to the whites.

Negroes were to remain a dependent laboring class; they were to be governed by a separate code of laws; they were to play no active part in the South's political life; and they were to be segregated socially. When radical Republicans used federal power to interfere in these matters, the majority of southern white men formed a resistance movement to fight the radical-dominated state governments until they were overthrown, after which southern whites established a caste system in defiance of federal statutes and constitutional amendments. For many decades thereafter the federal government simply admitted defeat and acquiesced; but the South refused to forget or forgive those years of humiliation when Negroes came close to winning equality. In southern mythology, then, reconstruction was a horrid nightmare.

As for the majority of northern white men, it is hard to tell how deeply they were concerned about the welfare of the American Negro after the abolition of slavery. If one were to judge from the way they treated the small number of free Negroes who resided in the northern states, one might conclude that they were, at best, indifferent to the problem—and that a considerable number of them shared the racial attitudes of the South and preferred to keep Negroes in a subordinate caste. For a time after the Civil War the radical Republicans, who were always a minority group, persuaded the northern electorate that the ultimate purpose of southern white men was to rob the North of the fruits of victory and to re-establish slavery and that federal intervention was therefore essential. In this manner radicals won approval of, or acquiescence in, their program to give civil rights and the ballot to southern Negroes. Popular support for the radical program waned rapidly, however, and by the middle of the 1870's it had all but vanished. In 1875 a Republican politician confessed that northern voters were tired of the "wornout cry of 'southern outrages,' " and they wished that "the 'nigger' the 'everlasting nigger' were in—Africa." As Northerners ceased to worry about the possibility of another southern rebellion, they became increasingly receptive to criticism of radical reconstruction.

The eventual disintegration of the radical phalanx, those root-and-branch men who, for a time, seemed bent on engineering a sweeping reformation of southern society, was another important reason for the denigration of reconstruction in American historiography. To be sure, some of the radicals, especially those who had been abolitionists before the war, never lost faith in the Negro, and in the years after reconstruction they stood by him as he struggled to break the intellectual and psychological fetters he had brought with him out of slavery. Other radicals, however, lost interest in the cause— tired of reform and spent their declining years writing their memoirs. Still others retained their crusading zeal but became disenchanted with radical reconstruction and found other crusades more attractive: civil service reform, or tariff reform, or defense of the gold standard. In 1872 they repudiated Grant and joined the Liberal Republicans; in subsequent years they considered themselves to be political independents.

This latter group had been an important element in the original radical coalition. Most of them were respectable, middle-class people in comfortable economic circumstances, well educated and highly articulate, and acutely conscious of their obligation to perform disinterested public service. They had looked upon Senator Charles Sumner of Massachusetts as their political spokesman, and upon Edwin L. Godkin of the New York *Nation* as their editorial spokesman. Like most radicals they had believed that the Negro was what slavery had made him; give the Negro equal rights and he would be quickly transformed into an industrious and responsible citizen. With the radical reconstruction program fairly launched, they had looked forward to swift and dramatic results.

But reconstruction was not as orderly and the Negro's progress was not nearly as swift and dramatic as these reformers had seemed to expect. The first signs of doubt came soon after the radicals won control of reconstruction policy, when the *Nation* warned the Negroes that the government had already done all it could for them. They were now, said the *Nation*, "on the dusty and rugged highway of competition"; henceforth "the removal of white prejudice against the Negro depends almost entirely on the Negro himself." By 1870 this bellwether of the reformers viewed with alarm the disorders and irregularities in the states governed by Negroes and carpetbaggers; by 1871 it proclaimed: "The experiment has totally failed. . . . We owe it to human nature to say that worse governments have seldom been seen in a civilized country." And three years later, looking at South Carolina, the *Nation* pronounced the ultimate epithet: "This is . . . socialism." Among the former radicals associated with the *Nation* in these years of tragic disillusionment were three prewar abolitionists: Edmund Quincy of Massachusetts, James Miller McKim of Pennsylvania, and the Reverend O. B. Frothingham of New York.

Finally, in 1890, many years after the reconstruction governments had collapsed, the *Nation*, still accurately reflecting the state of mind of the disenchanted reformers, made a full confession of its past errors. "There is," said the *Nation*, "a rapidly growing sympathy at the North with Southern perplexity over the negro problem. . . . Even those who were not shocked by the carpet-bag experiment . . . are beginning to 'view with alarm' the political prospect created by the increase of the negro population, and by the continued inability of southern society to absorb or assimilate them in any sense, physical, social, or political. . . . The sudden admission to the suffrage of a million of the recently emancipated slaves belonging to the least civilized race in the world . . . was a great leap in the dark, the ultimate consequences of which no man now living can foresee. No nation has ever done this, or anything like this for the benefit of aliens of any race or creed. Who or what is . . . [the Negro] that we should put the interests of the 55,000,000 whites on this continent in peril for his sake?" Editor Godkin answered his own question in a letter to another one-time radical: "I do not see . . . how the negro is ever to be worked into a system of government for which you and I would have much respect."

Actually, neither the obvious shortcomings of reconstruction nor an objective view of the Negro's progress in the years after emancipation can wholly explain the disillusionment of so many former radicals. Rather, their changed attitude toward the Negro and the hostile historical interpretation of reconstruction that won their favor were in part the product of social trends that severely affected the old American middle classes with whom most of them were identified. These trends had their origin in the industrial revolution; they were evident in the early nineteenth century but were enormously accelerated after the Civil War. Their institutional symbols were the giant manufacturing and railroad corporations.

In the new age of industrial enterprise there seemed to be no place for the old families with their genteel culture and strong traditions of disinterested public service. On the one hand, they were overshadowed by new and powerful industrial capitalists whose economic strength brought with it vast political influence. Legislative bodies became arenas in which the political vassals of oil, steel, and railroad barons struggled for special favors, while the interests of the public—and the old middle classes liked to think of themselves as *the public*—counted for nothing. On the other hand, they were threatened by the immigrants who came to America to work in the mines and mills and on the railroads—Italians, Slavs, and Jews from Poland and Russia. The immigrants crowded into the tenements of eastern cities, responded to the friendly overtures of urban political bosses, and used their ballots to evict the old middle-class families from power. Here was a threat to the traditional America that these families had loved—and dominated—to that once vigorous American nationality that was Protestant, Anglo-Saxon, and pure. Henry James commented bitterly about the people he met on Boston Common during a stroll one Sunday afternoon: "No sound of English, in a single instance escaped their lips; the greater number spoke a rude form of Italian, the others some outland dialect unknown to me. . . . The types and faces bore them out; the people before me were gross aliens to a man, and they were in serene and triumphant possession."

Soon the new immigrant groups had become the victims of cruel racial stereotypes. Taken collectively it would appear that they were, among other things, innately inferior to the Anglo-Saxons in their intellectual and physical traits, dirty and immoral in their habits, inclined toward criminality, receptive to dangerous political beliefs, and shiftless and irresponsible.

In due time, those who repeated these stereotypes awoke to the realization that what they were saying was not really very original—that, as a matter of fact, these generalizations were *precisely* the ones that southern white men had been making about Negroes for years. And, in their extremity, the old middle classes of the North looked with new understanding upon the problems of the beleaguered white men of the South. Perhaps all along Southerners had understood the problem better than they. Here, then, was a crucial part of the intellectual climate in which the Dunning interpretation of reconstruction was written. It was written at a time when xenophobia had become almost a national disease, when the immigration restriction movement was getting into high gear, when numerous northern cities (among them Philadelphia and Chicago) were seriously considering the establishment of racially segregated schools, and when Negroes and immigrants were being lumped together in the category of unassimilable aliens.

Several other attitudes, prevalent in the late nineteenth century, encouraged an interpretation of reconstruction that condemned radical Republicans for meddling in southern race relations. The vogue of social Darwinism discouraged governmental intervention in behalf of Negroes as well as other underprivileged groups; it encouraged the belief that a solution to the race problem could only evolve slowly as the Negroes gradually improved themselves. A rising spirit of nationalism stimulated a desire for sectional reconciliation, and part of the price was a virtual abdication of federal responsibility for the protection of the Negro's civil and political rights. An outburst of imperialism, manifested in the Spanish-American War and the annexation of the Hawaiian Islands, found one of its principal justifications in the notion that Anglo-Saxons were superior to other peoples, especially when it came to politics. In the words of Senator Albert J. Beveridge of Indiana: "God has not been preparing the English-speaking and Teutonic people for a thousand years for nothing but vain and idle self-admiration. No! He has made us the master organizers of the world to establish system where chaos reigns. . . . He has made us adept in government that we may administer government among savages and senile peoples." What folly, then, to expect Italians and Slavs to behave like Anglo-Saxons—or to accept the sentimental doctrine that Negroes deserve to be given the same political rights as white men!

Finally, at this critical juncture, sociologists, anthropologists, and psychologists presented what they regarded as convincing evidence of innate racial traits—evidence indicating that Negroes were intellectually inferior to whites and had distinctive emotional characteristics. The social scientists thus supplied the racists of the late nineteenth and early twentieth centuries with something that antebellum pro-slavery writers had always lacked: a respectable scientific argument. When, in 1916, Madison Grant, an amateur cultural anthropologist, published *The Passing of the Great Race*, his racism was only a mild caricature of a point of view shared by numerous social scientists. Examining the history of the United States, Grant easily detected her tragic blunder:

> Race consciousness . . . in the United States, down to and including the Mexican War, seems to have been very strongly developed among native Americans, and it still remains in full vigor today in the South,

where the presence of a large negro population forces this question upon the daily attention of the whites. . . . In New England, however . . . there appeared early in the last century a wave of sentimentalism, which at that time took up the cause of the negro, and in so doing apparently destroyed, to a large extent, pride and consciousness of race in the North. The agitation over slavery was inimical to the Nordic race, because it thrust aside all national opposition to the intrusion of hordes of immigrants of inferior racial value, and prevented the fixing of a definite American type. . . . The native American by the middle of the nineteenth century was rapidly becoming a distinct type. . . . The Civil War, however, put a severe, perhaps fatal, check to the development and expansion of this splendid type, by destroying great numbers of the best breeding stock on both sides, and by breaking up the home ties of many more. If the war had not occurred these same men with their descendants would have populated the Western States instead of the racial nondescripts who are now flocking there.[3]

In this social atmosphere, armed with the knowledge of race that the social scientists had given them, historians exposed the folly of radical reconstruction. At the turn of the century, James Ford Rhodes, that intimate friend of New England Brahmins, gave his verdict on Negro suffrage—one that the Dunningites would soon develop into the central assumption, the controlling generalization, of the reconstruction legend. "No large policy in our country," concluded Rhodes, "has ever been so conspicuous a failure as that of forcing universal negro suffrage upon the South. . . . From the Republican policy came no real good to the negroes. Most of them developed no political capacity, and the few who raised themselves above the mass did not reach a high order of intelligence. . . . The negro's political activity is rarely of a nature to identify him with any movement on a high plane. . . . [He] has been politically a failure and he could not have been otherwise."[4]

In the course of time the social scientists drastically revised their notions about race, and in recent years most of them have been striving to destroy the errors in whose creation their predecessors played so crucial a part. As ideas about race have changed, historians have become increasingly critical of the Dunning interpretation of reconstruction. These changes, together with a great deal of painstaking research, have produced the revisionist writing of the past generation. It is dangerous, of course, for an historian to label himself as a revisionist, for his ultimate and inevitable fate is one day to have his own revisions revised.

But that has never discouraged revisionists, and we may hope that it never will, especially those who have been rewriting the history of the reconstruction era. One need not be disturbed about the romantic nonsense that still fills the minds of many Americans about their Civil War. This folklore is essentially harmless. But the legend of reconstruction is another matter. It has had serious consequences, because it has exerted a powerful influence upon the political behavior of many white men, North and South.

Notes

1. James Ford Rhodes: *History of the United States from the Compromise of 1850 . . .*, 7 vols. (New York, 1893–1906), Vol. VII, p. 168; John W. Burgess: *Reconstruction and the Constitution* (New York, 1902), p. 263.
2. James G. Randall: *Civil War and Reconstruction* (Boston, 1937), pp. 689, 852; E. Merton Coulter: *The South during Reconstruction, 1865–1877* (Baton Rouge, 1947), p. xi.
3. Madison Grant: *The Passing of the Great Race* (New York, 1916), pp. 77–9.
4. Rhodes: *History of the United States*, Vol. VII, pp. 168–70.

Did the Civil War
Retard Industrialization?

Thomas C. Cochran

Nations in the twentieth century tend to define their existence largely in economic terms. We as Americans see our status and fate invariably interpreted in terms of the continued viability of "capitalism" as both an economic and political way of life. Thus it is not surprising that, historically speaking, we have come to attach considerable importance to the development of the American economy. In the traditional view, the Civil War was always considered basic to American economic development. It served as the convenient dividing line between limited economic growth and massive industrial expansion. In the selection here reprinted, however, Thomas C. Cochran, economic historian from the University of Pennsylvania, poses the possibility that the Civil War, rather than generating economic growth, actually retarded its development.

In most textbooks and interpretative histories of the United States the Civil War has been assigned a major role in bringing about the American Industrial Revolution. Colorful business developments in the North—adoption of new machines, the quick spread of war contracting, the boost given to profits by inflation, and the creation of a group of war millionaires—make the war years seem not only a period of rapid economic change but also one that created important forces for future growth. The superficial qualitative evidence is so persuasive that apparently few writers have examined the available long-run statistical series before adding their endorsement to the conventional interpretation. The following quotations taken from the books of two generations of leading scholars illustrate the popular view.

"The so-called Civil War," wrote Charles A. and Mary R. Beard in 1927, "... was a social war ... making *vast changes* in the arrangement of classes, in the accumulation and distribution of wealth, *in the course of industrial development*." Midway between 1927 and the present, Arthur M. Schlesinger, Sr., wrote: "On these tender industrial growths the Civil War *had the effect of a hothouse*. For reasons already clear ... nearly every branch of industry grew lustily." Harold U. Faulkner, whose textbook sales have ranked near or at the top, said in 1954: "In the economic history of the United States the Civil War was extremely important.... In the North *it speeded the Industrial Revolution* and the development of capitalism by the

From "Did the Civil War Retard Industrialization?" by Thomas C. Cochran. *Mississippi Valley Historical Review* (September 1961). Reprinted by permission of *The Journal of American History*.

prosperity which it brought to industry." The leading new text of 1957, by Richard Hofstadter, William Miller, and Daniel Aaron, showed no weakening of this interpretation: "The growing demand for farm machinery as well as for the 'sinews of war' led to American industrial expansion. . . . Of necessity, *iron, coal, and copper* production boomed during the war years." A sophisticated but still essentially misleading view is presented by Gilbert C. Fite and Jim E. Reese in a text of 1959: "The Civil War proved to be a boon to Northern economic development. . . . Industry, for example, was not created by the war, but wartime demands *greatly stimulated and encouraged industrial development* which already had a good start." In a reappraisal of the Civil War, in *Harper's Magazine* for April, 1960, Denis W. Brogan, a specialist in American institutions, wrote: "It may have been only a catalyst but the War *precipitated the entry* of the United States *into the modern industrial world*, made 'the take-off' (to use Professor W. W. Rostow's brilliant metaphor) come sooner."

In all of these reiterations of the effect of the Civil War on industrialism, statistical series seem to have been largely neglected. None of the authors cited reinforce their interpretations by setting the war period in the context of important long-run indexes of industrial growth. Since 1949, series of the period 1840 to 1890 that would cast doubt on the conventional generalizations have been available in *Historical Statistics of the United States, 1789–1945*. In 1960 a new edition of *Historical Statistics* and the report of the Conference on Research in Income and Wealth on *Trends in the American Economy in the Nineteenth Century* have provided additional material to support the argument that the Civil War retarded American industrial development. These volumes give data for many growth curves for the two decades before and after the war decade—in other words, the long-run trends before and after the event in question. The pattern of these trends is a mixed one which shows no uniform type of change during the Civil War decade, but on balance for the more important series the trend is toward retardation in *rates* of growth rather than toward acceleration. This fact is evident in many series which economists would regard as basic to economic growth, but in order to keep the discussion within reasonable limits only a few can be considered here.

Robert E. Gallman has compiled new and more accurate series for both "total commodity output," including agriculture, and "value added by manufacture," the two most general measures of economic growth available for this period. He writes: "Between 1839 and 1899 total commodity output increased elevenfold, or at an average decade rate of slightly less than 50 percent. . . . Actual rates varied fairly widely, high rates appearing during the decades ending with 1854 and 1884, and a very low rate during the decade ending with 1869." From the over-all standpoint this statement indicates the immediately retarding effect of the Civil War on American economic growth, but since most of the misleading statements are made in regard to industrial growth, or particular elements in industrial growth, it is necessary to look in more detail at "value added by manufacture" and some special series. Gallman's series for value added in constant dollars of the purchasing power of 1879 shows a rise of 157 percent from 1839 to 1849; 76 percent from 1849 to 1859; and only 25 percent from 1859 to 1869. By the 1870's the more favorable prewar rates were resumed, with an increase of 82 percent for 1869–1879, and 112 percent for 1879–1889. Thus two decades of very rapid advance, the 1840's and the 1880's, are separated by thirty years of slower growth which falls to the lowest level in the decade that embraces the Civil War.

Pig-iron production in tons, perhaps the most significant commodity index of nineteenth-century American industrial growth, is available year-by-year from 1854 on. Taking total production for five-year periods, output increased 9 percent between the block of years from 1856 to 1860 and the block from 1861 to 1865. That even this slight increase might not have been registered except for the fact that 1857 to 1860 were years of intermittent depression is indicated by an 81 percent increase over the war years in the block of years from 1866 to 1870. If annual production is taken at five-year intervals, starting in 1850, the increase is 24 percent from 1850 to 1855; 17 percent from 1855 to 1860; 1 percent from 1860 to 1865; and 100 percent from 1865 to 1870. While there is no figure available for 1845, the period from 1840 to 1850 shows 97 percent increase in shipments, while for the period 1870 to 1880 the increase was 130 percent. To sum up, depression and war appear to have retarded a curve of production that was tending to rise at a high rate.

Bituminous coal production may be regarded as the next most essential commodity series. After a gain of 199 percent from 1840 to 1850 this series shows a rather steady pattern of increase at rates varying from 119 to 148 percent each decade from 1850 to 1890. The war does not appear to have markedly affected the rate of growth.

In the mid-nineteenth century copper production was not a basic series for recording American growth, but since three distinguished authors have singled it out as one of the indexes of the effect of the war on industry it is best to cite the statistics. Before 1845 production of domestic copper was negligible. By 1850 the "annual recoverable content" of copper from United States mines was 728 tons, by 1860 it was 8,064 tons, by 1865 it was 9,520 tons, and by 1870 it was 14,112 tons. In this series of very small quantities, therefore, the increase from 1850 to 1860 was just over 1,000 percent, from 1860 to 1865 it was 18 percent, and from 1865 to 1870 it was 48 percent.

Railroad track, particularly in the United States, was an essential for industrialization. Here both the depression and the war retarded the rate of growth. From 1851 through 1855 a total of 11,627 miles of new track was laid, from 1856 through 1860, only 8,721 miles, and from 1861 through 1865, only 4,076 miles. After the war the rate of growth of the early 1850's was resumed, with 16,174 miles constructed from 1866 through 1870. Looked at by decades, a rate of over 200 percent increase per decade in the twenty years before the war was slowed to 70 percent for the period from 1860 to 1870, with only a 15 percent increase during the war years. In the next two decades the rate averaged about 75 percent.

Next to food, cotton textiles may be taken as the most representative consumer-goods industry in the nineteenth century. Interference with the flow of southern cotton had a depressing effect. The number of bales of cotton consumed in United States manufacturing rose 143 percent from 1840 to 1850 and 47 percent from 1850 to 1860, but *fell* by 6 percent from 1860 to 1870. From then on consumption increased at a little higher rate than in the 1850's.

While woolen textile production is not an important series in the overall picture of industrial growth, it should be noted that, helped by protection and military needs, consumption of wool for manufacturing more than doubled during the war, and then *fell* somewhat from 1865 to 1870. But Arthur H. Cole, the historian of the woolen industry, characterizes the years from 1830 to 1870 as a period of growth "not so striking as in the decades before or afterwards."

Immigration to a nation essentially short of labor was unquestionably a stimulant to economic growth. Another country had paid for the immigrant's unproductive youthful years, and he came to the United States ready to contribute his labor at a low cost. The pattern of the curve for annual immigration shows the retarding effect of both depression and war. In the first five years of the 1850's an average of 349,685 immigrants a year came to the United States. From 1856 through 1860 the annual average fell to 169,-958, and for the war years of 1861 to 1865 it fell further to 160,345. In the first five postwar years the average rose to 302,620, but not until the first half of the 1870's did the rate equal that of the early 1850's. Had there been a return to prosperity instead of war in 1861, it seems reasonable to suppose that several hundred thousand additional immigrants would have arrived before 1865.

In the case of farm mechanization the same type of error occurs as in the annual series on copper production. "Random" statistics such as the manufacture of 90,000 reapers in 1864 are frequently cited without putting them in the proper perspective of the total number in use and the continuing trends. Reaper and mower sales started upward in the early 1850's and were large from 1856 on, in spite of the depression. William T. Hutchinson estimates that most of the 125,000 reapers and mowers in use in 1861 had been sold during the previous five years. While the business, without regard to the accidental coming of the war, was obviously in a stage of very rapid growth, the war years presented many difficulties and may actually have retarded the rate of increase. Total sales of reapers for the period 1861–1865 are estimated at 250,000—a quite ordinary increase for a young industry—but the 90,000 figure for 1864, if it is correct, reinforces the evidence from the McCormick correspondence that this was the one particularly good year of the period. During these years William S. McCormick was often of the opinion that the "uncertainties of the times" made advisable a suspension of manufacturing until the close of the war.

For a broader view of agricultural mechanization the series "value of farm implements and machinery" has special interest. Here the census gives a picture which, if correct, is explicable only on the basis of wartime destruction. Based on constant dollars the dollar value of all loans was more than 15 percent lower than just before the war. If instead of examining loans one looks at total assets of all banks the decline in constant dollars from 1860 to 1870 is reduced to 10 percent, the difference arising from a larger cash position and more investment in government bonds.

Net capital formation would be a more proper index of economic growth than bank loans or assets. Unfortunately, neither the teams of the National Bureau of Economic Research nor those of the Census Bureau have been able to carry any reliable series back of 1868. From colonial times to 1960, however, the chief single form of American capital formation has undoubtedly been building construction. Farm houses, city homes, public buildings, stores, warehouses, and factories have year-by-year constituted, in monetary value, the leading type of capital growth. Gallman has drawn up series for such construction based on estimating the flow of construction materials and adding what appear to be appropriate markups. Admittedly the process is inexact, but because of the importance of construction in reflecting general trends in capital formation it is interesting to see the results. The rate of change for the ten-year period ending in 1854 is about 140 percent; for the one ending in 1859 it is 90 percent; for 1869 it is 40 percent; and for 1879 it is 46 percent. Taking a long view, from 1839 to 1859 the average decennial rate of increase was about 70 percent, and from 1869 to 1899 it was about 40 percent. The *rate* of advance in construction was declining and the war decade added a further dip to the decline.

Since the decline in rate is for the decade, the exact effect of the war years can only be estimated, but the logic of the situation, reinforced by the record of sharp cut-backs in railroad building, seems inescapable: the Civil War, like all modern wars, checked civilian construction. The first year of war was a period of depression and tight credit in the Middle West, which checked residential and farm construction in the area that grew most rapidly before and after the war. In both the East and the West the last two years of the war were a period of rapid inflation which was regarded by businessmen as a temporary wartime phenomenon. The logical result would be to postpone construction for long-term use until after the anticipated deflation. The decline in private railroad construction to a small fraction of the normal rate exemplifies the situation.

Lavish expenditure and speculation by a small group of war contractors and market operators gambling on the inflation seem to have created a legend of high prosperity during the war years. But the general series on fluctuations in the volume of business do not bear this out. Leonard P. Ayres's estimates of business activity place the average for 1861 through 1865 below normal, and Norman J. Silberling's business index is below its normal line for all years of the war. Silberling also has an intermediate trend line for business, which smooths out annual fluctuations. This line falls steadily from 1860 to 1869. Much of Silberling's discussion in his chapter "Business Activity, Prices, and Wars" is in answer to his question: "Why does it seem to be true that despite a temporary stimulating effect of war upon some industries, wars are generally associated with a long-term retarding of business growth . . .?" He puts the Civil War in this general category.

Collectively these statistical estimates support a conclusion that the Civil War retarded American industrial growth. Presentation of this view has been the chief purpose of this article. To try to judge the non-measurable or indirect effects of the war is extremely difficult. But since further discussion of the conventional qualitative factors may help to explain the prevailing evaluation in American texts, it seems appropriate to add some conjectural obiter dicta.

Experience with the apparently stimulating effects of twentieth-century wars on production makes the conclusion that victorious war may retard the growth of an industrial state seem paradoxical, and no doubt accounts in part for the use of detached bits of quantitative data to emphasize the Civil War's industrial importance. The resolution of the paradox may be found in contemporary conditions in the United States and in the nature of the wartime demand. The essential wastefulness of war from the standpoint of economic growth was obscured by the accident that both of the great European wars of the twentieth century began when the United States had a high level of unemployment. The immediate effect of each, therefore, was to put men to work, to increase the national product, and to create an aura of prosperity. Presumably, the United States of the mid-nineteenth century tended to operate close enough to full employment in average years that any wasteful labor-consuming activities were a burden rather than a stimulant.

By modern standards the Civil War was still unmechanized. It was fought with rifles, bayonets, and sabers by men on foot or horseback. Artillery was more used than in previous wars, but was still a relatively minor consumer of iron and steel. The railroad was also brought into use, but the building of military lines offset only a small percentage of the overall drop from the prewar level of civilian railroad construction. Had all of these things not been true, the Confederacy with its small industrial development could never have fought through four years of increasingly effective blockade.

In spite of the failure of direct quantitative evidence to show accelerating effects of the war on rates of economic growth, there could be long-run effects of a qualitative type that would gradually foster a more rapid rate of economic growth. The most obvious place to look for such indirect effects would be in the results of freeing the slaves. Marxists contended that elimination of slavery was a necessary precursor of the bourgeois industrialism which would lead to the socialist revolution. The creation of a free Negro labor force was, of course, of great long-run importance. In the twentieth century it has led to readjustment of Negro population between the deep South and the northern industrial areas, and to changes in the use of southern land.

But economically the effects of war and emancipation over the period 1840 to 1880 were negative. Richard A. Easterlin writes: "In every southern state, the 1880 level of per capita income originating in commodity production and distribution was below, or at best only slightly above that of 1840. . . . [This] attests strikingly to the impact of that war and the subsequent disruption on the southern economy." In general the Negroes became sharecroppers or wage laborers, often cultivating the same land and the same crops as before the war. In qualification of the argument that free Negro labor led to more rapid industrialization it should be noted that the South did not keep up with the national pace in the growth of non-agricultural wealth until after 1900.

Two indirect effects of the war aided industrial growth to degrees that cannot accurately be measured. These were, first, a more satisfactory money market, and, secondly, more security for entrepreneurial activity than in the prewar period. The sharp wartime inflation had the usual effect of transferring income from wage, salary, and interest receivers to those making profits. This meant concentration of savings in the hands of entrepreneurs who would invest in new activities; and this no doubt helps to explain the speculative booms of the last half of the 1860's and first two years of the 1870's which have been treated as the prosperity resulting from the war. Inflation also eased the burdens of those railroads which had excessive mortgage debts. But a great deal of new research would be needed to establish causal connections between the inflationary reallocation of wealth, 1863 to 1865, and the high rate of industrial progress in the late 1870's and the 1880's.

The National Banking Act, providing a more reliable currency for interstate operations, has been hailed as a great aid to business expansion although it would be hard to demonstrate, aside from a few weeks during panics, that plentiful but occasionally unsound currency had seriously interfered with earlier industrial growth. The existence of two and a half billion dollars in federal bonds also provided a basis for credit that was larger than before the war. This led to broader and more active security markets as well as to easier personal borrowing. But two qualifications must be kept in mind. First, local bank lending to favored borrowers had probably tended to be too liberal before the war and was now put on a somewhat firmer basis. In other words, since 1800 a multiplication of banks had made credit relatively easy to obtain in the United States, and in the North this continued to be the situation. Second, the southern banking system was largely destroyed by the war and had to be rebuilt in the subsequent decades. It should also be remembered that by 1875 some 40 percent of the banks were outside the national banking system.

Because of a few colorful speculators like Jay Gould, Daniel Drew, and Jim Fisk, and the immortality conferred on them, initially by the literary ability of the Adams brothers, the New York stock exchange in the postwar decade appears to have mirrored a new era of predatory wealth. But one has only to study the scandals of the London and New York stock exchanges in 1854 to see that there was little growth in the sophistication or boldness of stock operators during these fifteen years. In any case, the exploits of market operators were seldom related in a positive way to economic growth. Even a record of new issues of securities, which is lacking for this period, would chiefly reflect the flow of capital into railroads, banks, and public utilities rather than into manufacturing. Very few "industrial" shares were publicly marketed before the decade of the 1880's; such enterprises grew chiefly from the reinvestment of earnings.

There was strong government encouragement to entrepreneurial activity during the Civil War, but to ascribe to it unusual importance for economic growth requires both analysis of the results and comparison with other periods. Government in the United States has almost always encouraged entrepreneurs. The federal and state administrations preceding the Civil War could certainly be regarded as friendly to business. They subsidized railroads by land grants, subscribed to corporate bond issues, and remitted taxes on new enterprise. Tariffs were low, but railroad men and many bankers were happy with the situation. Whether or not American industrialism was significantly accelerated by the high protection that commenced with the war is a question that economists will probably never settle.

The building of a subsidized transcontinental railroad, held back by sectional controversies in the 1850's, was authorized along a northern route with the help of federal loans and land grants when the southerners excluded themselves from Congress. Putting more than a hundred million dollars into this project in the latter half of the 1860's, however, may have had an adverse effect on industrial growth. In general, the far western roads were built for speculative and strategic purposes uneconomically ahead of demand. They may for a decade, or even two, have consumed more capital than their transportation services were then worth to the economy.

To sum up this part of the obiter dictum, those who write of the war creating a national market tied together by railroads underestimate both the achievements of the two decades before the war and the ongoing trends of the economy. The nation's business in 1855 was nearly as intersectional as in 1870. Regional animosities did not interfere with trade, nor did these feelings diminish after the war. By the late 1850's the United States was a rapidly maturing industrial state with its major cities connected by rail, its major industries selling in a national market, and blessed or cursed with financiers, security flotations, stock markets, and all the other appurtenances of industrial capitalism.

But when all specific factors of change attributable to the war have been deflated, there is still the possibility that northern victory had enhanced the capitalist spirit, that as a consequence the atmosphere of government in Washington among members of both parties was more friendly to industrial enterprise and to northern-based national business operations than had formerly been the rule. It can be argued that in spite of Greenbackers and discontented farmers legislation presumably favorable to industry could be more readily enacted. The Fourteenth Amendment, for example, had as a by-product greater security for interstate business against state regulation, although it was to be almost two decades before the Supreme Court would give force to this protection. By 1876, a year of deep depression, the two major parties were trying to outdo each other in promises of stimulating economic growth. This highly generalized type of argument is difficult to evaluate, but in qualification of any theory of a sharp change in attitude we should remember that industrialism was growing rapidly from general causes and that by the 1870's it was to be expected that major-party politics would be conforming to this change in American life.

Massive changes in physical environment such as those accompanying the rise of trade at the close of the Middle Ages or the gradual growth of industrialism from the seventeenth century on do not lend themselves readily to exact or brief periodization. If factory industry and mechanized transportation be taken as the chief indexes of early industrialism, its spread in the United States was continuous and rapid during the entire nineteenth century, but in general, advance was greater during periods of prosperity than in depressions. The first long period without a major depression, after railroads, canals, and steamboats had opened a national market, was from 1843 to 1857. Many economic historians interested in quantitative calculations would regard these years as marking the appearance of an integrated industrial society. Walter W. Rostow, incidentally, starts his "take-off" period in the 1840's and calls it completed by 1860. Others might prefer to avoid any narrow span of years. Few, however, would see a major stimulation to economic growth in the events of the Civil War.

Finally, one may speculate as to why this exaggerated conception of the role of the Civil War in industrialization gained so firm a place in American historiography. The idea fits, of course, into the Marxian frame of revolutionary changes, but it seems initially to have gained acceptance quite independently of Marxian influences. More concentrated study of the war years than of any other four-year span in the nineteenth century called attention to technological and business events usually overlooked. Isolated facts were seized upon without comparing them with similar data for other decades.

The desire of teachers for neat periodization was probably a strong factor in quickly placing the interpretation in textbooks; thus, up to 1860 the nation was agricultural, after 1865 it was industrial. Recent study of American cultural themes suggests still another reason. From most standpoints the Civil War was a national disaster, but Americans like to see their history in terms of optimism and progress. Perhaps the war was put in a perspective suited to the culture by seeing it as good because in addition to achieving freedom for the Negro it brought about industrial progress.

Suggested Further Reading for Chapter 1

Thomas A. Bailey, "The Russian Fleet Myth Re-examined," *Mississippi Valley Historical Review*, 38 (1951).

Henry Blumenthal, "Confederate Diplomacy: Popular Notions and International Realities," *Journal of Southern History*, 32 (1966).

Richard Current, *The Lincoln Nobody Knows* (New York: Hill & Wang, 1963).

Edwin Fishel, "The Mythology of Civil War Intelligence," *Civil War History*, 10 (1964).

Mark M. Krug, "On Rewriting of the Story of Reconstruction in the U.S. History Textbooks," *The Journal of Negro History*, 46 (1961).

Lloyd Lewis, *Myths After Lincoln* (New York: Grosset & Dunlap, Inc., 1957).

D. O'Flaherty, "The Blockade that Failed," *American Heritage*, 6 (1955).

Thomas J. Pressley, *Americans Interpret their Civil War* (New York: The Free Press, 1966).

Robert Penn Warren, *The Legacy of the Civil War* (New York: Vintage Books, 1964).

Bernard A. Weisberger, "The Dark and Bloody Ground of Reconstruction Historiography," *Journal of Southern History*, 5 (1939).

Arnold Whitridge, "The John Brown Legend," *History Today*, 7 (1957).

It is a glorious history our God has bestowed upon His chosen people; a history whose keynote was struck by Liberty Bell; a history heroic with faith in our mission and our future; a history of statesmen, who flung the boundaries of the Republic out into unexplored lands and savage wildernesses; a history of soldiers, who carried the flag across blazing deserts and through the ranks of hostile mountains, even to the gates of sunset; a history of a multiplying people, who overran a continent in half a century; a history divinely logical, in the process of whose tremendous reasoning we find ourselves today . . . it is ours to execute the purpose of a fate that has driven us to be greater than our small intentions.

Senator Albert Beveridge
"The March of the Flag," 1898

2

AMERICAN MYTHS
AT CENTURY'S END

Ten-Gallon Hero
David Brion Davis

The Myth of the Happy Yeoman
Richard Hofstadter

From Rags to Respectability: Horatio Alger
John G. Cawelti

Social Darwinism and the Businessman
Irvin G. Wyllie

The Myth of the Melting Pot
Nathan Glazer and Daniel P. Moynihan

America's Emergence as a World Power: The Myth and the Verity
Thomas A. Bailey

The pleasures of the country: home sweet home.

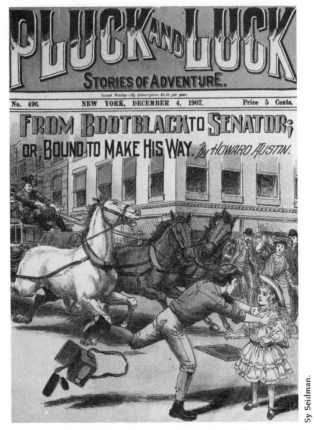

From bootblack to senator: an American dream.

The pleasures of the country: home sweet home. Nebraska, ca. 1889.

"Tipple Boy"—the bitter cry of the children: an American reality.

Introduction

According to Henry Steele Commager's seminal book *The American Mind,* the 1890s were especially significant to the development of American institutions and traditions. The span of the nineties, Commager contends, marked the transition from the "old" to the "new" America. It was at this "watershed" in American historical consciousness that the two faces of America stood exposed:

> On the one side [Commager says] lies an America predominantly agricultural; concerned with domestic problems . . . an America still in the making, physically and socially; an America on the whole self-confident, self-contained, self-reliant, and conscious of its unique character and of a unique destiny. On the other side lies the modern America, predominantly urban and industrial; inextricably involved in world economy and politics . . . experiencing profound changes in population, social institutions, economy, and technology; and trying to accommodate its traditions and institutions and habits of thought to conditions new and in part alien.

Thus, as America reached the conclusion of one century and the beginning of another, new forces were astir in all areas of American life—forces that were to produce a period of trauma and urgent readjustment for the American mind.

At century's end, America's self-image was being strongly conditioned by a curious mixture of anticipation and nostalgia. It was at once an age of confidence and an age of doubt. Such conditions served to create an environment conducive to the myth-building of both contemporaries and future historians. Thus, the cluster of myths that appears in the late nineteenth century speaks clearly not only to America's confrontation with the new, but also, perhaps as importantly, to her desire to secure that which she felt she was about to lose. It was as the frontier was ending, for example, that Americans began to picture it as something it had rarely been, and the frontiersman became an obvious candidate for national hero worship. The cowboy in particular symbolized the golden past and a pre-industrial age, and the West now came to rival the South as a major source of American symbol and myth. It was of little concern that this inflated image did not conform to reality. Similarly, it was as America's agricultural past was being challenged and the rural life was becoming increasingly subject to business practices and mechanization that it too became an inexhaustible resource for the American romantic imagination. The American novelist Hamlin Garland reflected this state of mind in recalling an element of his own rural experience:

It all lies in the unchanging realm of the past——this land of my child-hood. Its charm, its strange domination cannot return save in the poet's reminiscent dream. No money, no railway train can take us back to it. It did not in truth exist——it was a magical world, born of the vibrant union of youth and firelight, of music and the voice of moaning winds.

In such fashion did America repress the tragic and cruel elements of her rural-agricultural heritage in favor of an idealized Jeffersonian version of the yeoman farmer.

Ten-Gallon Hero

David Brion Davis

The cowboy-as-folk-hero, the product of commercial convention and psychological need, has enjoyed sustained vitality in American mythology since the end of the nineteenth century. Indeed, ever since the solidification of the myth of the "ten-gallon hero," America has responded to it with a poignant impulse. To David Brion Davis of Yale University, the haunting nostalgia the cowboy elicits is a synthesis of two American traditions—the myths of the Western scout and the antebellum South. Though the portrait of the cowboy-hero has been incompletely drawn, and although he therefore represents in many ways an essentially false tradition, when compared with other folk-heros the cowboy is perhaps the least obnoxious of the lot.

In 1900 it seemed that the significance of the cowboy era would decline along with other brief but romantic episodes in American history. The Long Drive lingered only in the memories and imaginations of old cowhands. The "hoe-men" occupied former range land while Mennonites and professional dry farmers had sown their Turkey Red winter wheat on the Kansas prairies. To be sure, a cattle industry still flourished, but the cowboy was more like an employee of a corporation than the free-lance cowboy of old.[1] The myth of the cowboy lived on in the Beadle and Adams paperback novels, with the followers of Ned Buntline and the prolific Colonel Prentiss Ingraham. But this seemed merely a substitution of the more up-to-date cowboy in a tradition which began with Leatherstocking and Daniel Boone.[2] If the mountain man had replaced Boone and the forest scouts, if the cowboy had succeeded the mountain man, and if the legends of Mike Fink and Crockett were slipping into the past, it would seem probable that the cowboy would follow, to become a quaint character of antiquity, overshadowed by newer heroes.

Yet more than a half-century after the passing of the actual wild and woolly cowboy, we find a unique phenomenon in American mythology. Gaudy-covered Western or cowboy magazines decorate stands, windows, and shelves in "drug" stores, bookstores, grocery stores and supermarkets from Miami to Seattle. Hundreds of cowboy movies and television shows are watched and lived through by millions of Americans. Nearly every little boy demands a cowboy suit and a Western six-shooter cap pistol. Cowboys gaze out at you with steely eye and cocked revolver from cereal packages and television screens. Jukeboxes in Bennington, Vermont, as well as Globe, Arizona, moan and warble the latest cowboy songs. Middle-age folk who had once thought of William S. Hart, Harry Carey, and Tom Mix as a passing phase, have lived to see several Hopalong Cassidy revivals, the Lone Ranger, Tim McCoy, Gene Autry, and Roy Rogers. Adolescents and even grown men in Maine and Florida can be seen affecting cowboy, or at least modified cowboy garb, while in the new airplane plants in Kansas, workers don their cowboy boots and wide-brimmed hats, go to work whistling a cowboy song, and are defiantly proud that they live in the land of lassos and sixguns.

When recognized at all, this remarkable cowboy complex is usually defined as the distortion of once-colorful legends by a commercial society.[3] The obvious divergence between the real West and the idealized version, the standardization of plot and characters, and the ridiculous incongruities of cowboys with automobiles and airplanes, all go to substantiate this conclusion.

However, there is more than the cowboy costume and stage setting in even the wildest of these adventures. Despite the incongruities, the cowboy myth exists in fact, and as such is probably a more influential social force than the actual cowboy ever was. It provides the framework for an expression of common ideals of morality and behavior. And while a commercial success, the hero cowboy must satisfy some basic want in American culture, or there could never be such a tremendous market. It is true that the market has been exploited by magazine, song, and scenario writers, but it is important to ask why similar myths have not been equally profitable, such as the lumbermen of the early northwest, the whale fishermen of New Bedford, the early railroad builders, or the fur traders. There have been romances written and movies produced idealizing these phases of American history, but little boys do not dress up like Paul Bunyan and you do not see harpooners on cereal packages. Yet America has had many episodes fully as colorful and of longer duration than the actual cowboy era.

The cowboy hero and his setting are a unique synthesis of two American traditions, and echoes of this past can be discerned in even the wildest of the modern horse operas. On the one hand, the line of descent is a direct evolution from the Western scout of Cooper and the Dime Novel; on the other, there has been a recasting of the golden myth of the antebellum South.[4] The two were fused sometime in the 1880's. Perhaps there was actually some basis for such a union. While the West was economically tied to the North as soon as the early canals and railroads broke the river-centered traffic, social ties endured longer. Many Southerners emigrated West and went into the cattle business, and of course, the Long Drive originated in Texas.[5] The literary synthesis of two traditions only followed the two social movements. It was on the Great Plains that the descendants of Daniel Boone met the drawling Texas cowboy.

Henry Nash Smith has described two paradoxical aspects of the legendary Western scout, typified in Boone himself.[6] This woodsman, this buckskin-clad wilderness hunter is a pioneer, breaking trails for his countrymen to follow, reducing the savage wilderness for civilization. Nevertheless, he is also represented as escaping civilization, turning his back on the petty materialism of the world, on the hypocritical and self-conscious manners of community life, and seeking the unsullied, true values of nature.

These seemingly conflicting points of view have counterparts in the woodsman's descendant, the cowboy. The ideal cowboy fights for justice, risks his life to make the dismal little cowtown safe for law-abiding, respectable citizens, but in so doing he destroys the very environment which made him a heroic figure. This paradox is common with all ideals, and the cowboy legend is certainly the embodiment of a social ideal. Thus the minister or social reformer who rises to heroism in his fight against a sin-infested community would logically become a mere figurehead once the community is reformed. There can be no true ideal or hero in a utopia. And the civilization for which the cowboy or trailblazer struggles is utopian in character.

But there is a further consideration in the case of the cowboy. In our mythology, the cowboy era is timeless. The ranch may own a modern station wagon, but the distinguishing attributes of cowboy and environment remain. There is, it is true, a nostalgic sense that this is the last great drama, a sad knowledge that the cowboy is passing and that civilization is approaching. But it never comes. This strange, wistful sense of the coming end of an epoch is not something outside our experience. It is a faithful reflection of the sense of approaching adulthood. The appeal of the cowboy, in this sense, is similar to the appeal of Boone, Leatherstocking, and the later Mountain Man. We know that adulthood, civilization, is inevitable, but we are living toward the end of childhood, and at that point "childness" seems eternal; it is a whole lifetime. But suddenly we find it is not eternal, the forests disappear, the mountains are settled, and we have new responsibilities. When we shut our eyes and try to remember, the last image of a carefree life appears. For the nation, this last image is the cowboy.

The reborn myth of the antebellum South also involves nostalgia; not so much nostalgia for something that actually existed as for dreams and ideals. When the Southern myth reappeared on the rolling prairies, it was purified and regenerated by the casting off of apologies for slavery. It could focus all energies on its former rôle of opposing the peculiar social and economic philosophy of the Northeast. This took the form of something more fundamental than mere agrarianism or primitivism. Asserting the importance of values beyond the utilitarian and material, this transplanted Southern philosophy challenged the doctrine of enlightened self-interest and the belief that leisure time is sin.

Like the barons and knights of Southern feudalism, the large ranch owners and itinerant cowboys knew how to have a good time. If there was a time for work, there was a time for play, and the early rodeos, horse races, and wild nights at a cowtown were not occasions for reserve. In this respect, the cowboy West was more in the tradition of fun-loving New Orleans than of the Northeast. Furthermore, the ranch was a remarkable duplication of the plantation, minus slaves. It was a hospitable social unit, where travelers were welcome even when the owner was absent. As opposed to the hard-working, thrifty, and sober ideal of the East, the actual cowboy was overly cheerful at times, generous to the point of waste, and inclined to value friendly comradeship above prestige.[7]

The mythical New England Yankee developed a code of action which always triumphed over the more sophisticated city slicker, because the Yankee's down-to-earth shrewdness, common sense, and reserved humor embodied values which Americans considered as pragmatically effective. The ideal cowboy also had a code of action, but it involved neither material nor social success. The cowboy avoided actions which "just weren't done" because he placed a value on doing things "right," on managing difficult problems and situations with ease, skill, and modesty. The cowboy's code was a Western and democratic version of the Southern gentleman's "honor."

In the early years of the twentieth century, a Philadelphia lawyer, who affected a careless, loose-tied bow instead of the traditional black ribbon and who liked to appear in his shirt sleeves, wrote: "The nomadic bachelor west is over, the housed, married west is established."[8] In a book published in 1902 he had, more than any other man, established an idealized version of the former, unifying the Southern and Western hero myths in a formula which was not to be forgotten. Owen Wister had, in fact, liberated the cowboy hero from the Dime Novels and provided a synthetic tradition suitable for a new century. *The Virginian* became a key document in popular American culture, a romance which defined the cowboy character and thus the ideal American character in terms of courage, sex, religion, and humor. The novel served as a model for hundreds of Western books and movies for half a century. In the recent popular movie "High Noon" a Hollywood star, who won his fame dramatizing Wister's novel, reenacted the same basic plot of hero rejecting heroine's pleas and threats, to uphold his honor against the villain Trampas. While this theme is probably at least a thousand years old, it was Owen Wister who gave it a specifically American content and thus explicated and popularized the modern cowboy ideal, with its traditions, informality, and all-important code.

Of course, Wister's West is not the realistic, boisterous, sometimes monotonous West of Charlie Siringo and Andy Adams. The cowboy, after all, drove cattle. He worked. There was much loneliness and monotony on the range, which has faded like mist under a desert sun in the reminiscences of old cow hands and the fiction of idealizers. The Virginian runs some errands now and then, but there are no cattle-driving scenes, no monotony, no hard work. Fictional cowboys are never bored. Real cowboys were often so bored that they memorized the labels on tin cans and then played games to see how well they could recite them.[9] The cowboys in books and movies are far too busy making love and chasing bandits to work at such a dreary task as driving cattle. But then the Southern plantation owner did no work. The befringed hero of the forests did not work. And if any ideal is to be accepted by adolescent America, monotonous work must be subordinated to more exciting pastimes. The fact that the cowboy hero has more important things to do is only in keeping with his tradition and audience. He is only a natural reaction against a civilization which demands increasingly monotonous work, against the approaching adulthood when playtime ends.

And if the cowboy romance banishes work and monotony, their very opposites are found in the immensity of the Western environment. To be sure, the deserts and prairies can be bleak, but they are never dull when used as setting for the cowboy myth. There is always an element of the unexpected, of surprise, of variety. The tremendous distances either seclude or elevate the particular and significant. There are mirages, hidden springs, dust storms, hidden identities, and secret ranches. In one of his early Western novels William MacLeod Raine used both devices of a secret ranch and hidden identity, while Hoffman Birney combined a hidden ranch, a secret trail, and two hidden identities.[10] In such an environment of uncertainty and change men of true genius stand out from the rest. The evil or good in an individual is quickly revealed in cowboy land. A man familiar with the actual cowboy wrote that "brains, moral and physical courage, strength of character, native gentlemanliness, proficiency in riding or shooting—every quality of leadership tended to raise its owner from the common level.[11]

The hazing which cowboys gave the tenderfoot was only preliminary. It was a symbol of the true test which anyone must undergo in the West. After the final winnowing of men, there emerge the heroes, the villains, and the clowns. The latter live in a purgatory and usually attach themselves to the hero group. Often, after the stress of an extreme emergency, they burst out of their caste and are accepted in the élite.

While the Western environment, according to the myth, sorts men into their true places, it does not determine men. It brings out the best in heroes and the worst in villains, but it does not add qualities to the man who has none. The cowboy is a superman and is adorable for his own sake. It is here that he is the descendant of supernatural folk heroes. Harry Hawkeye, the creator of an early cowboy hero, Calvin Yancey, described him as:

> ... straight as an arrow, fair and ruddy as a Viking, with long, flowing golden hair, which rippled over his massive shoulders, falling nearly to his waist; a high, broad forehead beneath which sparkled a pair of violet blue eyes, tender and soulful in repose, but firm and determined under excitement. His entire face was a study for a sculptor with its delicate aquiline nose, straight in outline as though chiselled from Parian marble, and its generous manly mouth, with full crimson and

arched lips, surmounted by a long, silken blonde mustache, through which a beautiful set of even white teeth gleamed like rows of lustrous pearls.[12]

While the Virginian is not quite the blond, Nordic hero, he is just as beautiful to behold. His black, curly locks, his lean, athletic figure, his quiet, unassuming manner, all go to make him the most physically attractive man Owen Wister could describe. Later cowboy heroes have shaved their mustaches, but the great majority have beautiful curly hair, usually blond or red, square jaws, cleft chins, broad shoulders, deep chests, and wasp-like waists. Like the Virginian, they are perfect men, absolutely incapable of doing the wrong thing unless deceived.[13]

Many writers familiar with the real cowboy have criticized Wister for his concentration on the Virginian's love interest and, of course, they deplore the present degeneration of the cowboy plot, where love is supreme. There were few women in the West in the Chisholm Trail days and those few in Dodge City, Abilene, and Wichita were of dubious morality. The cowboy's sex life was intermittent, to say the least. He had to carry his thirst long distances, like a camel, and in the oases the orgies were hardly on a spiritual plane.[14] Since earlier heroes, like the woodsman, led celibate lives, it is important to ask why the cowboy depends on love interest.

At first glance, there would seem to be an inconsistency here. The cowboy is happiest with a group of buddies, playing poker, chasing horse thieves, riding in masculine company. He is contemptuous of farmers, has no interest in children, and considers men who have lived among women as effete. Usually he left his own family at a tender age and rebelled against the restrictions of mothers and older sisters. Neither the Virginian nor the actual cowboys were family men, nor did they have much interest in the homes they left behind. Thus it would seem that courting a young schoolteacher from Vermont would be self-destruction. At no place is the idealized cowboy further from reality than in his love for the tender woman from the East. Like the law and order he fights for, she will destroy his way of life.

But this paradox is solved when one considers the hero cowboy, not the plot, as the center of all attention. Molly Wood in *The Virginian*, like all her successors, is a literary device, a *dea ex machina* with a special purpose. Along with the Western environment, she serves to throw a stronger light on the hero, to make him stand out in relief, to complete the picture of an ideal. In the first place, she brings out qualities in him which we could not see otherwise. Without her, he would be too much the brute for a real folk hero, at least in a modern age. If Molly Wood were not in *The Virginian*, the hero might seem too raucous, too wild. Of course, his affair with a blonde in town is handled genteelly; his boyish pranks such as mixing up the babies at a party are treated as good, clean fun. But still, there is nothing to bring out his qualities of masculine tenderness, there is nothing to show his conscience until Molly Wood arrives. A cowboy's tenderness is usually revealed through his kindness to horses, and in this sense, the Eastern belle's rôle is that of a glorified horse. A woman in the Western drama is somebody to rescue, somebody to protect. In her presence, the cowboy shows that, in his own way, he is a cultural ideal. The nomadic, bachelor cowboys described by Andy Adams and Charles Siringo are a little too masculine, a little too isolated from civilization to become the ideal for a settled community.

While the Western heroine brings out a new aspect of the cowboy's character, she also serves the external purpose of registering our attitudes toward him. The cowboy ideal is an adorable figure and the heroine is the vehicle of adoration. Female characters enable the author to make observations about cowboys which would be impossible with an all-male cast.[15] This rôle would lose its value if the heroine surrendered to the cowboy immediately. So the more she struggles with herself, the more she conquers her Eastern reservations and surmounts difficulties before capitulating, the more it enhances the hero.

Again, *The Virginian* is the perfect example. We do not meet Molly Wood in the first part of the book. Instead, the author, the I, who is an Easterner, goes to Wyoming and meets the Virginian. It is love at first sight, not in the sexual sense, of course (this was 1902), but there is no mistaking it for anything other than love. This young man's love for the Virginian is not important in itself; it heightens our worship of the hero. The sex of the worshiper is irrelevant. At first the young man is disconsolate, because he cannot win the Virginian's friendship. He must go through the ordeal of not knowing the Virginian's opinion of him. But as he learns the ways of the West, the Virginian's sublime goodness is unveiled. Though increasing knowledge of the hero's character only serves to widen the impossible gulf between the finite Easterner and the infinite, pure virtue of the cowboy, the latter, out of his own free grace and goodness recognizes the lowly visitor, who adores him all the more for it. But this little episode is only a preface, a symbol of the drama to come. As soon as the Virginian bestows his grace on the male adorer, Molly Wood arrives. The same passion is reenacted, though on a much larger frame. In this rôle, the sex of Molly *is* important, and the traditional romance plot is only superficial form. Molly's coyness, her reserve, her involved heritage of Vermont tradition, all go to build an insurmountable barrier. Yet she loves the Virginian. And Owen Wister and his audience love the Virginian through Molly Wood's love. With the male adorer, they had gone about as far as they could go. But Molly offers a new height from which to love the Virginian. There are many exciting possibilities. Molly can save his life and nurse him back to health. She can threaten to break off their wedding if he goes out to fight his rival, and then forgive him when he disobeys her plea. The Virginian marries Molly in the end and most of his descendants either marry or are about to marry their lovely ladies. But this does not mean a physical marriage, children, and a home. That would be building up a hero only to destroy him. The love climax at the end of the cowboy drama raises the hero to a supreme height, the audience achieves an emotional union with its ideal. In the next book or movie the cowboy will be the care-free bachelor again.

The classic hero, Hopalong Cassidy, has saved hundreds of heroines, protected them, and has been adored by them. But in 1910 Hopalong, "remembering a former experience of his own, smiled in knowing cynicism when told that he again would fall under the feminine spell."[16] In 1950 he expressed the same resistance to actual marriage:

> "But you can't always move on, Hoppy!" Lenny protested. "Some-day you must settle down! Don't you ever think of marriage?" "Uh-huh, and whenever I think of it I saddle Topper and ride. I'm not a marrying man, Lenny. Sometimes I get to thinkin' about that poem a feller wrote, about how a woman is only a woman but—" "The open road is my Fate!" she finished. "That's it. But can you imagine any woman raised outside a tepee livin' in the same house with a restless man?"[17]

The cowboy hero is the hero of the pre-adolescent, either chronologically or mentally. It is the stage of revolt against femininity and feminine standards. It is also the age of hero worship. If the cowboy romance were sexual, if it implied settling down with a real *girl*, there would be little interest. One recent cowboy hero summarized this attitude in terms which should appeal strongly to any ten-year-old: "I'd as soon fight a she-lion barehanded as have any truck with a gal."[18] The usual cowboy movie idol has about as much social presence in front of the leading lady as a very bashful boy. He is most certainly not the lover-type. That makes him lovable to both male and female Americans. There can be no doubt that Owen Wister identified himself, not with the Virginian, but with Molly Wood.

While some glorifiers of the actual cowboy have maintained that his closeness to nature made him a deeply religious being, thus echoing the devoutness of the earlier woodsman hero who found God in nature, this tradition has never carried over to the heroic cowboy. Undoubtedly some of the real cowboys were religious, though the consensus of most of the writers on the subject seems to indicate that indifference was more common.[19] Intellectualized religion obviously had no appeal and though the cowboy was often deeply sentimental, he did not seem prone to the emotional and frenzied religion of backwoods farmers and squatters. Perhaps his freedom from family conflicts, from smoldering hatreds and entangled jealousies and loves, had something to do with this. Despite the hard work, the violent physical conflicts, and the occasional debaucheries, the cowboy's life must have had a certain innocent, Homeric quality. Even when witnessing a lynching or murder, the cowboy must have felt further removed from total depravity or original sin than the farmer in a squalid frontier town, with his nagging wife and thirteen children.

At any rate, the cowboy hero of our mythology is too much of a god himself to feel humility. His very creation is a denial of any kind of sin. The cowboy is an enunciation of the goodness of man and the glory which he can achieve by himself. The Western environment strips off the artifice, the social veneer, and instead of a cringing sinner, we behold a dazzling superman. He is a figure of friendly justice, full of self-reliance, a very tower of strength. What need has he of a god?

Of course, the cowboy is not positively anti-religious. He is a respecter of traditions as long as they do not threaten his freedom. The Virginian is polite enough to the orthodox minister who visits his employer's ranch. He listens respectfully to the long sermon, but the ranting and raving about his evil nature are more than he can stand. He knows that his cowboy friends are good men. He loves the beauty of the natural world and feels that the Creator of such a world must be a good and just God. Beyond that, the most ignorant cowboy knows as much as this sinister-voiced preacher. So like a young Greek god leaving Mount Olympus for a practical joke in the interest of justice, the Virginian leaves his rôle of calm and straightforward dignity, and engages in some humorous guile and deceit. The minister is sleeping in the next room and the Virginian calls him and complains that the devil is clutching him. After numerous sessions of wrestling with his conscience, the sleepy minister acting as referee, morning comes before the divine finds he has been tricked. He leaves the ranch in a rage, much to the delight of all the cowboys. The moral, observes Wister, is that men who are obsessed with evil and morbid ideas of human nature, had better stay away from the cowboy West. As Alfred Henry Lewis put it, describing a Western town the year *The Virginian* was published, "Wolfville's a hard practical outfit, what you might call a heap obdurate, an' it's goin' to take more than them fitful an' o'casional sermons I aloodes to,—to reach the roots of its soul."[20] The cowboy is too good and has too much horse sense to be deluded by such brooding theology. Tex Burns could have been describing the Virginian when he wrote that his characters "had the cow hand's rough sense of humor and a zest for practical jokes no cow hand ever outgrows."[21]

Coming as it did at the end of the nineteenth century, the cowboy ideal registered both a protest against orthodox creeds and a faith that man needs no formal religion, once he finds a pure and natural environment. It is the extreme end of a long evolution of individualism. Even the individualistic forest scout was dependent on his surroundings, and he exhibited a sort of pantheistic piety when he beheld the wilderness. The mighty captain of industry, while not accountable to anyone in this world, gave lip-service to the generous God who had made him a steward of wealth. But the cowboy hero stood out on the lonely prairie, dependent on neither man nor God. He was willing to take whatever risks lay along his road and would gladly make fun of any man who took life too seriously. Speaking of his mother's death, a real cowboy is supposed to have said:

With almost her last breath, she begged me to make my peace with God, while the making was good. I have been too busy to heed her last advice. Being a just God, I feel that He will overlook my neglect. If not, I will have to take my medicine, with Satan holding the spoon.[22]

While the cowboy hero has a respect for property, he does not seek personal wealth and is generous to the point of carelessness. He gives money to his friends, to people in distress, and blows the rest when he hits town on Saturday night. He owns no land and, in fact, has only contempt for farmers, with their ploughed fields and weather-beaten buildings. He hates the slick professional gambler, the grasping Eastern speculator, and railroad man. How are these traits to be reconciled with his regard for property rights? The answer lies in a single possession—his horse. The cowboy's horse is what separates him from vagabondage and migratory labor. It is his link with the cavalier and plumed knight. More and more, in our increasingly property-conscious society, the cowboy's horse has gained in importance. A horse thief becomes a symbol of concentrated evil, a projection of all crime against property and, concomitantly, against social status. Zane Grey was adhering to this tradition when he wrote, "in those days, a horse meant all the world to a man. A lucky strike of grassy upland and good water . . . made him rich in all that he cared to own." On the other hand, "a horse thief was meaner than a poisoned coyote."[23]

When a cowboy is willing to sell his horse, as one actually does in *The Virginian*, he has sold his dignity and self-identity. It is the tragic mistake which will inevitably bring its nemesis. His love for and close relationship with his horse not only make a cowboy seem more human, they also show his respect for propriety and order. He may drift from ranch to ranch, but his horse ties him down to respectability. Yet the cowboy hero is not an ambitious man. He lacks the concern for hard work and practical results which typifies the Horatio Alger ideal. Despite his fine horse and expensive saddle and boots, he values his code of honor and his friends more than possessions. Because the cowboy era is timeless, the hero has little drive or push toward a new and better life. He fights for law and order and this implies civilization, but the cowboy has no visions of empires, industrial or agrarian.

One of the American traits which foreign visitors most frequently described was the inability to have a good time. Americans constantly appear in European journals as ill-at-ease socially, as feeling they must work every spare moment. Certainly it was part of the American Protestant capitalistic ethic, the Poor Richard, Horatio Alger ideal, that spare time, frivolous play, and relaxation were sins which would bring only poverty, disease, and other misfortunes. If a youth would study the wise sayings of great men, if he worked hard and made valuable friends but no really confidential ones, if he never let his hair down or became too intimate with any person, wife included, if he stolidly kept his emotions to himself and watched for his chance in the world, then he would be sure to succeed. But the cowboy hero is mainly concerned with doing things skillfully and conforming to his moral code for its own sake. When he plays poker, treats the town to a drink, or raises a thousand dollars to buy off the evil mortgage, he is not aiming at personal success. Most cowboy heroes have at least one friend who knows them intimately, and they are seldom reserved, except in the presence of a villain or nosey stranger.

Both the hero and real cowboy appear to be easy-going and informal. In dress, speech, and social manner, the cowboy sets a new ideal. Every cowboy knows how to relax. If the villains are sometimes tense and nervous, the hero sits placidly at a card game, never ruffled, never disturbed, even when his arch rival is behind him at the bar, hot with rage and whisky. The ideal cowboy is the kind of man who turns around slowly when a pistol goes off and drawls, "Ah'd put thet up, if Ah were yew." William MacLeod Raine's Sheriff Collins chats humorously with some train robbers and maintains a calm, unconcerned air which amuses the passengers, though he is actually pumping the bandits for useful information.[24] Previously, he had displayed typical cowboy individualism by flagging the train down and climbing aboard, despite the protests of the conductor. Instead of the eager, aspiring youth, the cowboy hero is like a young tomcat, calm and relaxed, but always ready to spring into action. An early description of one of the most persistent of the cowboy heroes summarizes the ideal characteristics which appeal to a wide audience:

> Hopalong Cassidy had the most striking personality of all the men in his outfit; humorous, courageous to the point of foolishness, eager for fight or frolic, nonchalant when one would expect him to be quite otherwise, curious, loyal to a fault, and the best man with a Colt in the Southwest, he was a paradox, and a puzzle even to his most intimate friends. With him life was a humorous recurrence of sensations, a huge pleasant joke instinctively tolerated, but not worth the price cowards pay to keep it. He had come onto the range when a boy and since that time he had laughingly carried his life in his open hand, and . . . still carried it there, and just as recklessly.[25]

Of course, most cowboy books and movies bristle with violence. Wild fist fights, brawls with chairs and bottles, gun play and mass battles with crashing windows, fires, and the final racing skirmish on horseback, are all as much a part of the cowboy drama as the boots and spurs. These bloody escapades are necessary and are simply explained. They provide the stage for the hero to show his heroism, and since the cowboy is the hero to the pre-adolescent, he must prove himself by their standards. Physical prowess is the most important thing for the ten- or twelve-year-old mind. They are constantly plagued by fear, doubt, and insecurity, in short, by evil, and they lack the power to crush it. The cowboy provides the instrument for their aggressive impulses, while the villain symbolizes all evil. The ethics of the cowboy band are the ethics of the boy's gang, where each member has a rôle determined by his physical skills and his past performance. As with any group of boys, an individual cowboy who had been "taken down a peg" was forever ridiculed and teased about his loss in status.[26]

The volume of cowboy magazines, radio programs and motion pictures would indicate a national hero for at least a certain age group, a national hero who could hardly help but reflect specific attitudes. The cowboy myth has been chosen by this audience because it combines a complex of traits, a way of life, which they consider the proper ideal for America. The actual drama and setting are subordinate to the grand figure of the cowboy hero, and the love affairs, the exciting plots, and the climactic physical struggles present opportunities for the definition of the cowboy code and character. Through the superficial action, the heroism of the cowboy is revealed, and each repetition of the drama, like the repetition of a sacrament, reaffirms the cowboy public's faith in their ideal.

Perhaps the outstanding cowboy trait, above even honor, courage, and generosity, is the relaxed, calm attitude toward life. Though he lives intensely, he has a calm self-assurance, a knowledge that he can handle anything. He is good-humored and jovial.[27] He never takes women too seriously. He can take a joke or laugh at himself. Yet the cowboy is usually anti-intellectual and anti-school, another attitude which appeals to a younger audience.[28]

Above all, the cowboy is a "good joe." He personifies a code of personal dignity, personal liberty, and personal honesty. Most writers on the actual cowboy represented him as having these traits.[29] While many of these men obviously glorify him as much as any fiction writers, there must have been some basis for their judgment. As far as his light-hearted, calm attitude is concerned, it is amazing how similar cowboys appear, both in romances and non-fiction.[30] Millions of American youth subscribed to the new ideal and yearned for the clear, Western atmosphere of "unswerving loyalty, the true, deep affection, and good-natured banter that left no sting."[31] For a few thrilling hours they could roughly toss conventions aside and share the fellowship of ranch life and adore the kind of hero who was never bored and never afraid.

Whether these traits of self-confidence, a relaxed attitude toward life and good humor, have actually increased in the United States during the past fifty years is like asking whether men love their wives more now than in 1900. Certainly the effective influence of the cowboy myth can never be determined. It is significant, however, that the cowboy ideal has emerged above all others. And while the standardization of plot and character seems to follow other commercial conventions, the very popularity of this standard cowboy is important and is an overlooked aspect of the American character. It is true that this hero is infantile, that he is silly, overdone, and unreal. But when we think of many past ideals and heroes, myths and ethics; when we compare our placid cowboy with, say, the eager, cold, serious hero of Nazi Germany (the high-cheekboned, blond lad who appeared on the Reichsmarks); or if we compare the cowboy with the gangster heroes of the thirties, or with the serious, self-righteous and brutal series of Supermen, Batmen, and Human Torches;

when, in an age of violence and questioned public and private morality, if we think of the many possible heroes we might have had—then we can be thankful for our silly cowboy. We could have chosen worse.

Notes

1. Edward Douglas Branch, *The Cowboy and His Interpreters* (New York: D. Appleton & Company, 1926), p. 69.
2. Henry Nash Smith, *Virgin Land* (Cambridge: Harvard University Press, 1950), pp. v, vi.
3. Smith, *Virgin Land*, p. 111.
4. Emerson Hough, *The Story of the Cowboy* (New York: D. Appleton & Company, 1901), p. 200.
5. Edward E. Dale, *Cow Country* (Norman, Okla.: University of Oklahoma Press, 1942), p. 15.
6. Smith, *Virgin Land*, p. v.
7. Alfred Henry Lewis, *Wolfville Days* (New York: Stokes, 1902), p. 24.
8. Branch, *The Cowboy and His Interpreters*, pp. 190 ff.
9. Philip Ashton Rollins, *The Cowboy* (New York: Charles Scribner's Sons, 1922), p. 185.
10. William MacLeod Raine, *Bucky O'Connor* (New York: Grosset & Dunlap, 1907); Hoffman Birney, *The Masked Rider* (New York: Penn, 1928).
11. Rollins, *The Cowboy*, p. 352.
12. Branch, *The Cowboy and His Interpreters*, p. 191.
13. A Zane Grey hero is typical and is also seen through the eyes of a woman: "She saw a bronzed, strong-jawed, eagle-eyed man, stalwart, superb of height." Zane Grey, *The Light of Western Stars* (New York: Harper & Brothers, 1914), pp. 29–30.
14. Charles A. Siringo, *A Lone Star Cowboy* (Santa Fe: C. A. Siringo, 1919), p. 64.
15. No male character could observe that, " 'Cowboys play like they work or fight,' she added. 'They give their whole souls to it. They are great big simple boys.' " Grey, *The Light of Western Stars*, p. 187.
16. Clarence E. Mulford, *Hopalong Cassidy* (Chicago: A. C. McClurg & Company, 1910), p. 11.
17. Tex Burns, pseud. (Louis L'Amour), *Hopalong Cassidy and the Trail to Seven Pines* (New York: Doubleday, 1951), p. 187.
18. Davis Dresser, *The Hangmen of Sleepy Valley* (New York: Jefferson House, 1950), p. 77.
19. Hough, *The Story of the Cowboy*, p. 199; Branch, *The Cowboy and His Interpreters*, p. 160; Rollins, *The Cowboy*, p. 84; Lewis, *Wolfville Days*, p. 216.
20. Lewis, *Wolfville Days*, p. 216.
21. Burns, *Hopalong Cassidy*, p. 130.
22. Siringo, *A Lone Star Cowboy*, p. 37.
23. Zane Grey, *Wildfire* (New York: Harper & Brothers, 1917), pp. 10, 7.
24. Raine, *Bucky O'Connor*, p. 22.
25. Mulford, *Hopalong Cassidy*, p. 65.
26. Sam P. Ridings, *The Chisholm Trail* (Medford, Okla.: S. P. Ridings, 1936), p. 297.

27. The cowboy hero was judged to be "out of sorts when he could not vent his peculiar humor on somebody or something." Grey, *The Light of Western Stars*, pp. 118–19.

28. This anti-intellectualism in the Western myth is at least as old as Cooper's parody of the scientist, Obed Bat, in *The Prairie*. More recently, Will James took pride in his son's poor attitude and performance in school. Will James, *The American Cowboy* (New York: Charles Scribner's Sons, 1942), p. 107.

29. Ridings, *The Chisholm Trail*, pp. 278–94; Rollins, *The Cowboy*, p. 67; Dale, *Cow Country*, pp. 122, 153.

30. According to Alfred Henry Lewis, surly and contentious people were just as unpopular in Wolfville as they appear to be in fiction. Lewis, *Wolfville Days*, p. 217.

31. Mulford, *Hopalong Cassidy*, p. 155.

The Myth of the Happy Yeoman

Richard Hofstadter

For centuries man has cherished the notion that agriculture is the most basic of industries and the yeoman farmer the most virtuous of men. Though certainly not alone in viewing the farmer-as-folk-hero, Americans have perhaps been the most persistent in articulating their support for this romantic vision. A commitment to the yeoman farmer as ideal man and ideal citizen can be found in the views of such diversified Americans as Benjamin Franklin, Thomas Jefferson, Alexander Hamilton, and Calvin Coolidge. Richard Hofstadter, until his recent death Dewitt Clinton Professor of American History at Columbia University, here comments on the yeoman myth as it evolved from a literary to a popular ideal.

The United States was born in the country and has moved to the city. From the beginning its political values as well as ideas were of necessity shaped by country life. The early American politician, the country editor, who wished to address himself to the common man, had to draw upon a rhetoric that would touch the tillers of the soil; and even the spokesman of city people knew that his audience had been in very large part reared upon the farm.

But what the articulate people who talked and wrote about farmers and farming—the preachers, poets, philosophers, writers, and statesmen—liked about American farming was not, in every respect, what the typical working farmer liked. For the articulate people were drawn irresistibly to the noncommercial, non-pecuniary, self-sufficient aspect of American farm life. To them it was an ideal.

Writers like Thomas Jefferson and Hector St. John de Crèvecoeur admired the yeoman farmer not for his capacity to exploit opportunities and make money but for his honest industry, his independence, his frank spirit of equality, his ability to produce and enjoy a simple abundance. The farmer himself, in most cases, was in fact inspired to make money, and such self-sufficiency as he actually had was usually forced upon him by a lack of transportation or markets, or by the necessity to save cash to expand his operations.

For while early American society was an agrarian society, it was fast becoming more commercial, and commercial goals made their way among its agricultural classes almost as rapidly as elsewhere. The more commercial this society became, however, the more reason it found to cling in imagination to the noncommercial agrarian values. The more farming as a self-sufficient way

From "The Myth of the Happy Yeoman," by Richard Hofstadter, in *American Heritage* Magazine (April 1956). Reprinted by permission of Beatrice K. Hofstadter.

of life was abandoned for farming as a business, the more merit men found in what was being left behind. And the more rapidly the farmers' sons moved into the towns, the more nostalgic the whole culture became about its rural past. Throughout the nineteenth and even in the twentieth century, the American was taught that rural life and farming as a vocation were something sacred.

This sentimental attachment to the rural way of life is a kind of homage that Americans have paid to the fancied innocence of their origins. To call it a "myth" is not to imply that the idea is simply false. Rather the "myth" so effectively embodies men's values that it profoundly influences their way of perceiving reality and hence their behavior.

Like any complex of ideas, the agrarian myth cannot be defined in a phrase, but its component themes form a clear pattern. Its hero was the yeoman farmer, its central conception the notion that he is the ideal man and the ideal citizen. Unstinted praise of the special virtues of the farmer and the special values of rural life was coupled with the assertion that agriculture, as a calling uniquely productive and uniquely important to society, had a special right to the concern and protection of government. The yeoman, who owned a small farm and worked it with the aid of his family, was the incarnation of the simple, honest, independent, healthy, happy human being. Because he lived in close communion with beneficent nature, his life was believed to have a wholesomeness and integrity impossible for the depraved populations of cities.

His well-being was not merely physical, it was moral; it was not merely personal, it was the central source of civic virtue; it was not merely secular but religious, for God had made the land and called man to cultivate it. Since the yeoman was believed to be both happy and honest, and since he had a secure propertied stake in society in the form of his own land, he was held to be the best and most reliable sort of citizen. To this conviction Jefferson appealed when he wrote: "The small land holders are the most precious part of a state."

In origin the agrarian myth was not a popular but a literary idea, a preoccupation of the upper classes, of those who enjoyed a classical education, read pastoral poetry, experimented with breeding stock, and owned plantations or country estates. It was clearly formulated and almost universally accepted in America during the last half of the eighteenth century. As it took shape both in Europe and America, its promulgators drew heavily upon the authority and the rhetoric of classical writers—Hesiod, Xenophon, Cato, Cicero, Virgil, Horace, and others—whose works were the staples of a good education. A learned agricultural gentry, coming into conflict with the industrial classes, welcomed the moral strength that a rich classical ancestry brought to the praise of husbandry.

Chiefly through English experience, and from English and classical writers, the agrarian myth came to America, where, like so many other cultural importations, it eventually took on altogether new dimensions in its new setting. So appealing were the symbols of the myth that even an arch-opponent of the agrarian interest like Alexander Hamilton found it politic to concede in his *Report on Manufactures* that "the cultivation of the earth, as the primary and most certain source of national supply . . . has intrinsically a strong claim to pre-eminence over every other kind of industry." And Benjamin Franklin, urban cosmopolite though he was, once said that agriculture was "the only *honest way*" for a nation to acquire wealth, "wherein man receives a real increase of the seed thrown into the ground, a kind of continuous miracle, wrought by the hand of God in his favour, as a reward for his innocent life and virtuous industry."

Among the intellectual classes in the eighteenth century the agrarian myth had virtually universal appeal. Some writers used it to give simple, direct, and emotional expression to their feelings about life and nature; others linked agrarianism with a formal philosophy of natural rights. The application of the natural rights philosophy to land tenure became especially popular in America. Since the time of Locke it had been a standard argument that the land is the common stock of society to which every man has a right—what Jefferson called "the fundamental right to labour the earth"; that since the occupancy and use of land are the true criteria of valid ownership, labor expended in cultivating the earth confers title to it; that since government was created to protect property, the property of working land-holders has a special claim to be fostered and protected by the state.

At first the agrarian myth was a notion of the educated classes, but by the early nineteenth century it had become a mass creed, a part of the country's political folklore and its nationalist ideology. The roots of this change may be found as far back as the American Revolution, which, appearing to many Americans as the victory of a band of embattled farmers over an empire, seemed to confirm the moral and civic superiority of the yeoman, made the farmer a symbol of the new nation, and wove the agrarian myth into his patriotic sentiments and idealism.

Still more important, the myth played a role in the first party battles under the Constitution. The Jeffersonians appealed again and again to the moral primacy of the yeoman farmer in their attacks on the Federalists. The family farm and American democracy became indissolubly connected in Jeffersonian thought, and by 1840 even the more conservative party, the Whigs, took over the rhetorical appeal to the common man, and elected a President in good part on the strength of the fiction that he lived in a log cabin.

The Jeffersonians, moreover, made the agrarian myth the basis of a strategy of continental development. Many of them expected that the great empty inland regions would guarantee the preponderance of the yeoman— and therefore the dominance of Jeffersonianism and the health of the state —for an unlimited future. The opening of the trans-Allegheny region, its protection from slavery, and the purchase of the Louisiana Territory were the first great steps in a continental strategy designed to establish an internal empire of small farms. Much later the Homestead Act was meant to carry to its completion the process of continental settlement by small homeowners. The failure of the Homestead Act "to enact by statute the fee-simple empire" was one of the original sources of Populist grievances, and one of the central points at which the agrarian myth was overrun by the commercial realities.

Above all, however, the myth was powerful because the United States in the first half of the nineteenth century consisted predominantly of literate and politically enfranchised farmers. Offering what seemed harmless flattery to this numerically dominant class, the myth suggested a standard vocabulary to rural editors and politicians. Although farmers may not have been much impressed by what was said about the merits of a noncommercial way of life, they could only enjoy learning about their special virtues and their unique services to the nation. Moreover, the editors and politicians who so flattered them need not in most cases have been insincere. More often than not they too were likely to have begun life in little villages or on farms, and what they had to say stirred in their own breasts, as it did in the breasts of a great many townspeople, nostalgia for their early years and perhaps relieved some residual feelings of guilt at having deserted parental homes and childhood attachments. They also had the satisfaction in the early days of knowing that in so far as it was based upon the life of the largely self-sufficient yeoman the agrarian myth was a depiction of reality as well as the assertion of an ideal.

Oddly enough, the agrarian myth came to be believed more widely and tenaciously as it became more fictional. At first it was propagated with a kind of genial candor, and only later did it acquire overtones of insincerity. There survives from the Jackson era a painting that shows Governor Joseph Ritner of Pennsylvania standing by a primitive plow at the end of a furrow. There is no pretense that the Governor has actually been plowing—he wears broadcloth pants and a silk vest, and his tall black beaver hat has been carefully laid in the grass beside him—but the picture is meant as a reminder of both his rustic origin and his present high station in life. By contrast, Calvin Coolidge posed almost a century later for a series of photographs that represented him as haying in Vermont. In one of them the President sits on the edge of a hay rig in a white shirt, collar detached, wearing highly polished black shoes and a fresh pair of overalls; in the background stands his Pierce Arrow, a secret service man on the running board, plainly waiting to hurry the President away from his bogus rural labors. That the second picture is so much more pretentious and disingenuous than the first is a measure of the increasing hollowness of the myth as it became more and more remote from the realities of agriculture.

Throughout the nineteenth century hundreds upon hundreds of thousands of farm-born youths sought their careers in the towns and cities. Particularly after 1840, which marked the beginning of a long cycle of heavy country-to-city migration, farm children repudiated their parents' way of life and took off for the cities where, in agrarian theory if not in fact, they were sure to succumb to vice and poverty.

When a correspondent of the *Prairie Farmer* in 1849 made the mistake of praising the luxuries, the "polished society," and the economic opportunities of the city, he was rebuked for overlooking the fact that city life *"crushes, enslaves,* and *ruins so many thousands of our young men* who are insensibly made the victims of *dissipation,* of *reckless speculation,* and of *ultimate crime."* Such warnings, of course, were futile. "Thousands of young men," wrote the New York agriculturist Jesse Buel, "who annually forsake the plough, and the honest profession of their fathers, if not to win the fair, at least form an opinion, too often confirmed by mistaken parents, that agriculture is not the road to wealth, to honor, nor to happiness. And such will continue to be the case, until our agriculturists become qualified to assume that rank in society to which the importance of their calling, and their numbers, entitle them, and which intelligence and self-respect can alone give them."

Rank in society! That was close to the heart of the matter, for the farmer was beginning to realize acutely not merely that the best of the world's goods were to be had in the cities and that the urban middle and upper classes had much more of them than he did but also that he was losing in status and respect as compared with them. He became aware that the official respect paid to the farmer masked a certain disdain felt by many city people. "There has . . . a certain class of individuals grown up in our land," complained a farm writer in 1835, "who treat the cultivators of the soil as an inferior caste . . . whose utmost abilities are confined to the merit of being able to discuss a boiled potato and a rasher of bacon." The city was symbolized as the home of loan sharks, dandies, fops, and aristocrats with European ideas who despised farmers as hayseeds.

The growth of the urban market intensified this antagonism. In areas like colonial New England, where an intimate connection had existed between the small town and the adjacent countryside, where a community of interests and even of occupations cut across the town line, the rural-urban hostility had not developed so sharply as in the newer areas where the township plan was never instituted and where isolated farmsteads were more common. As settlement moved west, as urban markets grew, as self-sufficient farmers became rarer, as farmers pushed into commercial production for the cities they feared and distrusted, they quite correctly thought of themselves as a vocational and economic group rather than as members of a neighborhood. In the Populist era the city was totally alien territory to many farmers, and the primacy of agriculture as a source of wealth was reasserted with much bitterness. "The great cities rest upon our broad and fertile prairies," declared Bryan in his "Cross of Gold" speech. "Burn down your cities and leave our farms, and your cities will spring up again as if by magic; but destroy our farms, and the grass will grow in the streets of every city in the country."

Out of the beliefs nourished by the agrarian myth there had arisen the notion that the city was a parasitical growth on the country. Bryan spoke for a people raised for generations on the idea that the farmer was a very special creature, blessed by God, and that in a country consisting largely of farmers the voice of the farmer was the voice of democracy and of virtue itself.

The agrarian myth encouraged farmers to believe that they were not themselves an organic part of the whole order of business enterprise and speculation that flourished in the city, partaking of its character and sharing in its risks, but rather the innocent pastoral victims of a conspiracy hatched in the distance. The notion of an innocent and victimized populace colors the whole history of agrarian controversy.

For the farmer it was bewildering, and irritating too, to think of the great contrast between the verbal deference paid him by almost everyone and the real economic position in which he found himself. Improving his economic position was always possible, though this was often done too little and too late; but it was not within anyone's power to stem the decline in the rural values and pieties, the gradual rejection of the moral commitments that had been expressed in the early exaltations of agrarianism.

It was the fate of the farmer himself to contribute to this decline. Like almost all good Americans he had innocently sought progress from the very beginning, and thus hastened the decline of many of his own values. Elsewhere the rural classes had usually looked to the past, had been bearers of tradition and upholders of stability. The American farmer looked to the future alone, and the story of the American land became a study in futures.

In the very hours of its birth as a nation Crèvecoeur had congratulated America for having, in effect, no feudal past and no industrial present, for having no royal, aristocratic, ecclesiastical, or monarchial power, and no manufacturing class, and had rapturously concluded: "We are the most perfect society now existing in the world." Here was the irony from which the farmer suffered above all others: the United States was the only country in the world that began with perfection and aspired to progress.

To what extent was the agrarian myth actually false? During the colonial period, and even well down into the nineteenth century, there were in fact large numbers of farmers who were very much like the yeomen idealized in the myth. They were independent and self-sufficient, and they bequeathed to their children a strong love of craftsmanlike improvisation and a firm tradition of household industry. These yeomen were all too often yeomen by force of circumstance. They could not become commercial farmers because they were too far from the rivers or the towns, because the roads were too poor for bulky traffic, because the domestic market for agricultural produce was too small and the overseas markets were out of reach. At the beginning of the nineteenth century, when the American population was still living largely in the forests and most of it was east of the Appalachians, the yeoman farmer did exist in large numbers, living much as the theorists of the agrarian myth portrayed him.

But when the yeoman practiced the self-sufficient economy that was expected of him, he usually did so not because he wanted to stay out of the market but because he wanted to get into it. "My farm," said a farmer of Jefferson's time, "gave me and my family a good living on the produce of it; and left me, one year with another, one hundred and fifty dollars, for I have never spent more than ten dollars a year, which was for salt, nails, and the like. Nothing to wear, eat, or drink was purchased, as my farm provided all. With this saving, I put money to interest, bought cattle, fatted and sold them, and made great profit." Great profit! Here was the significance of self-sufficiency for the characteristic family farmer. Commercialism had already begun to enter the American Arcadia.

For, whatever the spokesman of the agrarian myth might have told him, the farmer almost anywhere in early America knew that all around him there were examples of commercial success in agriculture—the tobacco, rice, and indigo, and later the cotton planters of the South, the grain, meat, and cattle exporters of the middle states.

The farmer knew that without cash he could never rise above the hardships and squalor of pioneering and log-cabin life. So the savings from his self-sufficiency went into improvements—into the purchase of more land, of herds and flocks, of better tools; they went into the building of barns and silos and better dwellings. Self-sufficiency, in short, was adopted for a time in order that it would eventually be unnecessary.

Between 1815 and 1860 the character of American agriculture was transformed. The rise of native industry created a home market for agriculture, while demands arose abroad for American cotton and foodstuffs, and a great network of turnpikes, canals, and railroads helped link the planter and the advancing western farmer to the new markets. As the farmer moved out of the forests onto the flat, rich prairies, he found possibilities for machinery that did not exist in the forest. Before long he was cultivating the prairies with horse-drawn mechanical reapers, steel plows, wheat and corn drills, and threshers.

The farmer was still a hardworking man, and he still owned his own land in the old tradition. But no longer did he grow or manufacture almost everything he needed. He concentrated on the cash crop, bought more and more of his supplies from the country store. To take full advantage of the possibilities of mechanization, he engrossed as much land as he could and borrowed money for his land and machinery. The shift from self-sufficient to commercial farming varied in time throughout the West and cannot be dated with precision, but it was complete in Ohio by about 1830 and twenty years later in Indiana, Illinois, and Michigan. All through the great Northwest, farmers whose fathers might have lived in isolation and self-sufficiency were surrounded by jobbers, banks, stores, middlemen, horses, and machinery.

This transformation affected not only what the farmer did but how he felt. The ideals of the agrarian myth were competing in his breast, and gradually losing ground, to another, even stronger ideal, the notion of opportunity, of career, of the self-made man. Agrarian sentiment sanctified labor in the soil and the simple life; but the prevailing Calvinist atmosphere of rural life implied that virtue was rewarded with success and material goods. Even farm boys were taught to strive for achievement in one form or another, and when this did not take them away from the farms altogether, it impelled them to follow farming not as a way of life but as a *career*—that is, as a way of achieving substantial success.

The sheer abundance of the land—that very internal empire that had been expected to insure the predominance of the yeoman in American life for centuries—gave the *coup de grâce* to the yeomanlike way of life. For it made of the farmer a speculator. Cheap land invited extensive and careless cultivation. Rising land values in areas of new settlement tempted early liquidation and frequent moves. Frequent and sensational rises in land values bred a boom psychology in the American farmer and caused him to rely for his margin of profit more on the appreciation in the value of his land than on the sale of crops. It took a strong man to resist the temptation to ride skyward on lands that might easily triple or quadruple their value in one decade and then double in the next.

What developed in America, then, was an agricultural society whose real attachment was not, like the yeoman's, to the land but to land values. The characteristic product of American rural society, as it developed on the prairies and the plains, was not a yeoman or a villager, but a harassed little country businessman who worked very hard, moved all too often, gambled with his land, and made his way alone.

While the farmer had long since ceased to act like a yeoman, he was somewhat slower in ceasing to think like one. He became a businessman in fact long before he began to regard himself in this light. As the nineteenth century drew to a close, however, various things were changing him. He was becoming increasingly an employer of labor, and though he still worked with his hands, he began to look with suspicion upon the working classes of the cities, especially those organized in trade unions, as he had once done upon the urban fops and aristocrats. Moreover, when good times returned after the Populist revolt of the 1890's, businessmen and bankers and the agricultural colleges began to woo the farmer, to make efforts to persuade him to take the businesslike view of himself that was warranted by the nature of his farm operations. "The object of farming," declared a writer in the *Cornell Countryman* in 1904, "is not primarily to make a living, but it is to make money. To this end it is to be conducted on the same business basis as any other producing industry."

The final change, which came only with a succession of changes in the twentieth century, wiped out the last traces of the yeoman of old, as the coming first of good roads and rural free delivery, and mail order catalogues, then the telephone, the automobile, and the tractor, and at length radio, movies, and television largely eliminated the difference between urban and rural experience in so many important areas of life. The city luxuries, once so derided by farmers, are now what they aspire to give to their wives and daughters.

In 1860 a farm journal satirized the imagined refinements and affectations of a city girl in the following picture:

> Slowly she rises from her couch. . . . Languidly she gains her feet, and oh! what vision of human perfection appears before us: Skinny, bony, sickly, hipless, thighless, formless, hairless, teethless. What a radiant belle! . . . The ceremony of enrobing commences. In goes the dentist's naturalization efforts; next the witching curls are fashioned to her "classically molded head." Then the womanly proportions are properly adjusted; hoops, bustles, and so forth, follow in succession, then a profuse quantity of whitewash, together with a "permanent rose tint" is applied to a sallow complexion; and lastly the "killing" wrapper is arranged on her systematical and matchless form.

But compare this with these beauty hints for farmers' wives from the *Idaho Farmer*, April, 1935:

> Hands should be soft enough to flatter the most delicate of the new fabrics. They must be carefully manicured, with none of the hot, brilliant shades of nail polish. The lighter and more delicate tones are in keeping with the spirit of freshness. Keep the tint of your fingertips friendly to the red of your lips, and check both your powder and your rouge to see that they best suit the tone of your skin in the bold light of summer.

Nothing can tell us with greater finality of the passing of the yeoman ideal than these light and delicate tones of nail polish.

From Rags to Respectability:
Horatio Alger

John G. Cawelti

The notion that through hard work, luck, and moral rectitude one
can become President of the United States remains one of the
sacred dogmas of the American Creed. To think that the idea of the
self-made man was born in America is, itself, a myth; yet, the concept has enjoyed surprising durability within our social and political
folklore. The myth of rags to riches is of course a reflection of truth.
Upward mobility—the rise of men to higher social and economic
station—has occurred in America, but perhaps not with the frequency or in the manner generally presumed. John G. Cawelti, a
professor of English and humanities at the University of Chicago,
here explains how the myth of "rags to respectability" is related to
the myths surrounding Horatio Alger's writings—a myth upon a
myth, if you will.

> Luke Walton is not puffed up by his unexpected and remarkable
> success. He never fails to recognize kindly, and help, if there is need,
> the old associates of his humbler days, and never tries to conceal the
> fact that he was once a Chicago Newsboy.
>
> *Horatio Alger,*
> *Luke Walton*

Today his books are read more often by cultural historians than by children,
and such erstwhile classics as *Struggling Upward* and *Mark, The Matchboy*
are no longer on the shelves of libraries, but the name of Horatio Alger has
become synonymous with the self-made man. American businessmen who
commission brief biographies often are described in the following manner:

> The Horatio Alger quality of William J. Stebler's rise to the presi-
> dency of General American Transportation Corporation makes one
> almost pause for breath.

There is even a Horatio Alger award presented annually by the American
Schools and Colleges Association to eight Americans who have reached posi-
tions of prominence from humble beginnings. In recent years, this award, a
bronze desk plaque, has been presented to such leading industrialists and
financiers as Benjamin F. Fairless, retired chairman of the United States Steel
Corporation; James H. Carmichael, chairman of Capital Airlines; and Milton
G. Hulme, president and chairman of a large investment banking firm in
Pittsburgh. The creator of *Ragged Dick* has become a familiar idol to Ameri-

From *Apostles of the Self-Made Man,* by John G. Cawelti; pp. 101–123. Reprinted
by permission of the author and the University of Chicago Press. Copyright 1965
by The University of Chicago. All rights reserved.

cans concerned about the decline of what they refer to as "individualistic free enterprise." *Advertising Age* in December, 1947, tired of "government interference" in business, begged for a new Horatio Alger to inspire American youth with the independence and enterprise of their fathers.

Many of those who parade under Alger's mantle know little about their hero beyond the fact that he wrote books about success. They would probably be startled if they read one, for Alger was not a partisan of "rugged individualism," and only within limits an admirer of pecuniary success. For a patron saint of success, his life was rather obscure. Born in 1832 in Revere, Massachusetts, he was trained for the ministry at the insistence of his domineering father. He soon gave this up when he found he could support himself by writing children's books. He published a collection of sentimental tales in 1856, and his first widely popular juvenile, *Ragged Dick*, was published serially in Oliver Optic's (William T. Adams) *Student and Schoolmate* magazine, and as a book, in 1867. Alger moved to New York about 1866 and, aside from an occasional trip West and to Europe, spent most of his life in and around the Newsboys' Lodging House, an institution which figures in many of his stories. Its superintendent, Charles O'Connor, was one of his few close friends. Alger, whose books made fortunes for several publishers, died a relatively poor man. He sold most of his books outright for small sums, and spent what money he received in acts of spontaneous and unflagging charity to help almost anyone who applied to him. His amazingly rapid composition of books like *Grit, the Young Boatman of Pine Point* and *Jed, the Poorhouse Boy* was interspersed with occasional efforts at a serious novel, desultory participation in various reform movements—New York Mayor A. Oakey Hall, member of the Tweed ring, once named him chairman of an anti-vice commission—and brief forays into education (he sometimes tutored boys in Greek and Latin to supplement the income from his books).

Alger's death in 1899 did not put an end to the publication of Alger books. Publishers hired ghosts like Edward Stratemeyer, later the author of the Rover Boys series, to capitalize on Alger's popularity. Inevitably, there were signs of a reaction. Parents began to protest against what they considered the false values and unreality of the Alger stories, and a number of libraries removed his books from the shelves. They were republished less often in the second decade of the twentieth century, and, after World War I, sales declined rapidly. At the centennial of Alger's birth, in 1932, a survey of New York working children showed that less than 20 percent of the "juvenile proletariat" had ever heard of Alger; only 14 percent had read an Alger book; and, even more threatening, a "large number" dismissed the theory of "work and win" as "a lot of bunk." A similar survey taken in the forties revealed that only 1 percent of 20,000 children had read an Alger book.

Alger and His Predecessors

There was a marked difference between Alger's work and that of his most important predecessor in the field of juvenile fiction. Jacob Abbott, author of the "Rollo" and "Caleb" books, began his extremely successful career as a writer of children's books in the early 1830's with a long, rather heavily theological, tome discussing the Christian duties of young boys and girls. A strong emphasis on evangelical Protestantism remained the central element in his work. Alger, on the other hand, was not so concerned with the role of religion in the lives of his young heroes. There were other important differences between the Abbott boy and the Alger boy. A firm believer in the ethic of industry, frugality, integrity, and piety, Abbott rarely made ambition itself a significant element in his stories. Rollo and Caleb were not poor boys but the scions of well-to-do middle-class families. The typical Abbott book concerns everyday events from which Rollo or Caleb learns an important moral lesson. In *Rollo at Work*, for example, the hero learns how to work through a Lockean course of instruction which instills in him a progressively greater capacity for sustained effort.

Unlike Alger, Abbott chose to write about younger boys from well-established families for whom social mobility was not a significant problem, and his stories reflect the more conservative social views of the upper middle-class audience for which he wrote. As he presents American life, there are rightful and fundamental class distinctions, each class has its particular role, and there is relatively little movement between classes. At the same time, there is no conception of a leisure class in the Abbott books, and, in terms of worldly luxuries, the gulf between the higher and lower ranks is not great. According to Abbott, since every rank has its proper work, there should be no idlers.

In Alger's stories, on the other hand, rising and falling in society are characteristic phenomena. This is not the first appearance in American children's literature of the idea of mobility. Even in the period of Abbott's dominance, some juvenile authors began to write tales anticipating those of Alger. An interesting halfway house can be seen in the works of Mrs. Louisa M. Tuthill in the period 1830–50. Like Abbott, Mrs. Tuthill generally wrote about boys from well-established families, not the street boys who were Alger's favorite subjects. As an adherent of the Jeffersonian ideal of natural aristocracy, Mrs. Tuthill believed that American institutions properly encouraged the rise of talented and virtuous young men to whatever positions of eminence their merits entitled them. In her *I Will Be a Gentleman*, for example, she attacks the idea of hereditary distinction:

> Having no hereditary titles in the United States, there can be no higher distinction than that which belongs to moral worth, intellectual superiority, and refined politeness. A republican gentleman, therefore need acknowledge no superior; he is a companion for nobles and kings, or, what is better, for the polite, the talented, the good. Since such are an American's only claims to distinction, it becomes the more important for him to cultivate all those graces which elevate and dignify humanity. No high ancestral claims can he urge for his position in society. Wealth he may possess, and there are those who will acknowledge that claim; but if the possessor have not intelligence and taste to teach him how

to use his wealth, it will only make him a more conspicuous mark for ridicule. Those glorious institutions of New England, common schools, afford to every boy the opportunity to acquire that intelligence and taste, and his associates there are from every class of society. There is no unsurmountable obstacle in any boy's way; his position in society must depend mainly upon himself.

Mrs. Tuthill puts the same limits on rising in society as the didactic novelists of the same period. The candidate for distinction must be talented, virtuous, and refined, although he need not spring from an aristocratic family tradition. This emphasis on gentility and refinement, however acquired, also has an important role in the Alger books. Alger constantly emphasizes neatness, good manners, and the proper clothes, and yet his conception of gentility is far less elevated than Mrs. Tuthill's. In spite of her frequent protestations that the way was open to all, Mrs. Tuthill's heroes spring from respectable families who have the means to educate their children.

Most of the children's literature of the pre-Civil War period deals with the offspring of secure, middle-class families, but the orphaned boy of the city streets is not without his bards. As early as 1834, a putative autobiography of a bootblack who rose from poverty to be a member of Congress was published with the delightful title *A Spur to Youth; or, Davy Crockett Beaten*. In the following year, Charles F. Barnard published *The Life of Collin Reynolds, the Orphan Boy and Young Merchant*. In this tearful tale, dedicated to the pupils of the Hollis Street Sunday School in Boston, the hero is orphaned when his mother dies and his father goes to sea. Undaunted, he determines to support himself by peddling candy, peanuts, and sundries on the New York ferries. In good Alger fashion, he soon meets the wealthy Mr. J., who is impressed by the boy's history, his industry, and his enterprise and adopts him. Entering Mr. J.'s store, Collin is doing well when the opportunity to sigh forth a highly sentimental deathbed scene proves more attractive to his creator than the fulfilment of material promise. Poor Collin is disposed of in a fall from a horse.

Even closer to the Alger formula is J. H. Ingraham's *Jemmy Daily: or, The Little News Vender*, published in 1843. Ingraham, a hack writer of astonishing fertility, made sentimental romance out of almost any subject. Ingraham's treatment of the newsboy foreshadowed both Alger's characteristic material and his method of treating it. Jemmy Daily and his noble mother, reduced to starvation by a drunken father, are saved when, in a chance encounter, the lovely daughter of a wealthy merchant gives Jemmy food and a sixpence. As a newsboy, Jemmy manages to support his mother. When father becomes intolerable, Jemmy and his mother leave him, a shock which happily reforms the drunkard. The rest of the story concerns Jemmy's fight with a bully and his foiling of the quack Dr. Wellington Smoot's lascivious designs on his mother. Once reformed, the father is granted a convenient death, and Jemmy takes over the family, becoming a clerk under the benevolent tutelage of Mr. Weldon. Jemmy's reward is the promise of a junior partnership and the hand of Mr. Weldon's daughter, the girl who had originally befriended him.

The difference between Ingraham's tale and the typical Alger story is largely a matter of emphasis. The plot and characters are essentially the same, but Ingraham stresses religious conversion and "the great moral temperance reform, which is without question one of the agents of God in ameliorating the condition of fallen man." Jemmy Daily's rise in society and his gradual acquisition of respectability are not as important to him as they were to Alger.

In the 1850's, as urban phenomena became of increasing interest and concern, newsboys and bootblacks were common figures in popular fiction. A. L. Stimson's *Easy Nat* includes an Alger-like street boy adopted by a benevolent farmer, and Seba Smith's wife, a sentimental novelist of considerable popularity, published a long novel, *The Newsboy*, in 1854. This is a typical romantic adventure, containing as one of its many plots the narrative of a poor newsboy's rise to some prominence, through, as usual, the patronage of a benevolent merchant. One writer in the 1850's went so far as to proclaim the newsboy the symbol of a new age:

> Our clarion now, more potent than the Fontabrian horn, is the shrill voice of the news-boy, that modern Minerva, who leaped full blown from the o'erfraught head of journalism; and, as the news-boy is in some respects the type of the time—an incarnation of the spirit of the day,—a few words devoted to his consideration may not be deemed amiss. [Joseph C. Neal, *Peter Ploddy*]

Alger had considerable precedent for his dramatization of the street boy's rise to social respectability. Nor was he the only writer of his time to employ this subject. In fact, Alger neither created the Alger hero nor was he his only exponent. A flood of children's books by such authors as Oliver Optic, Mrs. Sarah Stuart Robbins, Mrs. Madeline Leslie, and the Rev. Elijah Kellog dealt with the rise to moderate security of a poor boy. Alger, however, outsold them all. Somehow he was able to seize upon just those combinations of characters and plot situations that most engrossed adolescent American boys of the nineteenth century.

Alger's Message

Alger's contemporary position as a symbol of individualistic free enterprise has obscured the actual characteristics of his stories. A number of misconceptions must be cleared away before we can get to the heart of the Alger version of what constitutes success. Here, for example, is a typical interpretation of the Alger hero in a recent book:

> Alone, unaided, the ragged boy is plunged into the maelstrom of city life, but by his own pluck and luck he capitalizes on one of the myriad opportunities available to him and rises to the top of the economic heap. Here, in a nutshell, is the plot of every novel Alger ever

wrote; here, too, is the quintessence of the myth. Like many simple formulations which nevertheless convey a heavy intellectual and emotional charge to vast numbers of people, the Alger hero represents a triumphant combination—and reduction to the lowest common denominator—of the most widely accepted concepts in nineteenth-century American society. The belief in the potential greatness of the common man, the glorification of individual effort and accomplishment, the equation of the pursuit of money with the pursuit of happiness and of business success with spiritual grace: simply to mention these concepts is to comprehend the brilliance of Alger's synthesis.

This passage illustrates several important misconceptions concerning Alger's books. In the first place, Alger's heroes are rarely "alone and unaided," and do not win their success entirely through individual effort and accomplishment. From the very beginning of his career, the Alger boy demonstrates an astounding propensity for chance encounters with benevolent and useful friends, and his success is largely due to their patronage and assistance. In the course of his duties Fred Fenton, the hero of *The Erie Train Boy*, meets a wealthy young girl named Isabel Archer—presumably named in homage to Alger's literary idol, Henry James—who gives him money to pay his mother's rent. In addition, he encounters an eccentric miner, who later helps him sell some land belonging to his late father, and the uncle of a wealthy broker, who gives young Fred his chance in business. Alger's heroes are well aware of their indebtedness to these patrons, and modestly make no pretense of success through their own efforts, although Alger assures his readers that they deserve their advancement. Ragged Dick, congratulated on his achievement by one of the innumerable wealthy men who befriended him, replies: " 'I was lucky,' said Dick, modestly. 'I found some good friends who helped me along.' " [*Mark, the Match Boy*]

Nor did the Alger hero rise "to the top of the economic heap." Some years ago a writer for *Time*, in a mathematical mood, calculated that the average Alger hero's fortune is only $10,000. Usually the hero is established in a secure white-collar position, either as a clerk with the promise of a junior partnership or as a junior member of a successful mercantile establishment. None achieve anything resembling economic or political prominence. Moderate economic security would best summarize the pecuniary achievements of the typical Alger hero, in spite of such tantalizing titles as *Fame and Fortune*, *Striving for Fortune*, and *From Farm to Fortune*. For example, at the end of *Fame and Fortune*, the hero is in possession of a magnificent income of $1,400 a year, plus the interest on about $2,000 in savings. In Alger's mind, this was "fame and fortune."

We may admit that Alger's representation of economic reality was highly sentimentalized, but it is unfair to call him an uninhibited adulator of wealth who equated spiritual grace with business success. The true aim of the Alger hero is respectability, a happy state only partially defined by economic repute. Nor was Alger unaware that many men were successful as the result of questionable practices. He may have lacked knowledge of these practices, but Alger frequently reminded his readers that many wealthy and successful men were undeserving of their fortunes. One of his favorite villains is the wealthy, unscrupulous banker who accumulates wealth by cheating widows and orphans. On the whole, Alger's formula is more accurately stated as middle-class respectability equals spiritual grace.

Alger was no more an unrestrained advocate of the "potential greatness" of the common man than he was of the uninhibited pursuit of financial success. His heroes are ordinary boys only in the sense of their lowly origin. In ability and personal character they are far above average. Many boys in the Alger books are unable, in spite of their earnest efforts, to rise above a lowly position. Micky McGuire, a young slum boy who is a secondary character in the *Ragged Dick* series, is reformed at last through the efforts of Dick and his patron Mr. Rockwell. But the old maxim "No Irish Need Apply" still held for Alger.

> Micky has already turned out much better than was expected, but he is hardly likely to rise much higher than the subordinate position he now occupies. In capacity and education he is far inferior to his old associate, Richard Hunter, who is destined to rise much higher than at present. *[Mark, the Match Boy]*

Who, then, is the Alger hero, and what is the nature of the adventures in which he is involved? Alger has two types of heroes. The first, and probably the more popular, is the poor, uneducated street boy—sometimes an orphan, more frequently the son of a widowed mother—who rises to moderate affluence. The second is a well-born and well-educated middle-class youth whose father dies, leaving the son to fend for himself. In some cases a villainous squire or distant relative attempts to cheat the hero out of his rightful legacy, but, in the end, the hero is restored to his inheritance or succeeds in rising to his proper place.

Alger made desultory attempts to vary the character of his hero in each story, but such an achievement was beyond his skill, and the reader could be certain that, whatever the situation, and whether the hero smokes or uses slangy language, the same solid core of virtue is present. Alger's heroes, who range in age from around twelve to eighteen, are in the tradition of the didactic novels of self-improvement. One must give Alger some credit for making his young paragons a little less earnest and more lively than the placid prigs of T. S. Arthur. The Alger hero might begin as an intemperate spendthrift like Ragged Dick, but soon he becomes a master of the traditional virtues of industry, economy, integrity, and piety. He is manly and self-reliant—two of Alger's favorite words—and, in addition, kind and generous. Never a genius, he is usually a boy of above-average intelligence, particularly in the area of mathematics, and is also a strenuous devotee of self-culture. The Alger hero is never snobbish or condescending; indeed, he is the veritable apotheosis of modesty. Thoroughly democratic in his tastes, he befriends other poor boys and is uniformly courteous to people of all classes. The Alger hero demonstrates to a high degree those traits that might be called the employee virtues: fidelity, punctuality, and courteous deference. It is upon these latter traits that Alger places the greatest stress.

Against his hero, Alger sets three types of boys who serve as foils to the hero's sterling qualities. One of these may be called the lesser hero. He is usually a slightly younger and less vigorous edition of the major figure. The lesser hero often has greater advantages than his friend, but he lacks the enterprise, the courage, and the self-reliance of the hero, and frequently depends on him for protection against the harsh urban world, enabling the hero to demonstrate his courage and generosity. Another boy who appears in almost all the Alger books is the snob. Insisting that he is a gentleman's son, the snob looks down his nose at the hero's willingness to work at such lowly trades as that of bootblack or newsboy. Sometimes the snob is the son of a rich but grasping relative of the hero's, envious of his greater capabilities and endeavoring to get him into trouble. The young snob shows the obverse of all the hero's virtues: he is lazy, ignorant, arrogant, and unwilling to work because he considers it beneath his station. He is overtly contemptuous and secretly envious of the hero's successes. Alger delights in foiling this little monster, usually by arranging for his father to fail in business, thereby forcing the snob to go to work at a salary lower than the hero's.

Another type appearing somewhat less frequently in the Alger books is the poor boy who lacks the intelligence and ability of the hero and is more susceptible to the corruption of his environment. Often he becomes involved in plots against the hero, but is usually won over when he recognizes his true manliness and forgiving character. Although sometimes reformed through the hero's efforts, the Micky McGuire type is doomed to remain in a subordinate but respectable position by his lack of intelligence and enterprise. Curiously enough, these dim-minded characters are Alger's most interesting and vivid creations, and foreshadow the "bad boy" heroes of later juvenile books. In addition, they frequently represent immigrant groups—Irish, Italians, Germans—who, not all bad, play a distinctly inferior role in Alger's version of America.

The adult characters vary no more than the boys in the typical Alger book. The central adult figure is the benevolent businessman whose chance encounter with the hero gives him his big opportunity. Like all adults in Alger, this figure is thinly characterized, his major traits being the ability to recognize and reward the hero's potentialities. He is called upon to deliver long homilies on the virtues requisite to success. Generally, he is a merchant or a highly reputable stockbroker. In his business dealings he is honest and upright, scorning all but the most elevated commercial practices. In effect his role is to serve as an ideal adoptive father for the hero.

The second most important male adult in the Alger books is the villain, who usually has some important hold over the hero. Sometimes he is a mean stepfather, more often a grasping uncle or cousin who becomes the hero's guardian, and frequently a cruel, miserly squire who holds a mortgage on the family property. Whatever his mask, he invariably attempts to assert his tyrannical authority over the hero, and fails. One is tempted to describe him in Freudian terms as the overbearing father-figure whose authority the adolescent hero rejects and overthrows.

Few of the Alger heroes are orphans; the majority have a widowed mother dependent upon them for support. Here Alger differs appreciably from his predecessors. The Alger mother stands in a very different relationship to her doughty young offspring than do the mothers in the novels of T. S. Arthur. The "Arthurian" mother is pre-eminently a source of moral authority, an instructor and preceptor, whose gentle commands the young hero is expected to obey. In Alger, the mother rarely commands or instructs; although she presumably has some hand in her son's development, her authoritative function is mentioned only rarely. On the contrary, she is both a dependent and an admiring onlooker. Always gentle and supremely confident in her son's ability, she never criticizes or disciplines. Indeed, occasionally she is weak and indecisive, qualities which might lead the family into difficulty were it not for the manly self-reliance of her son. Characteristic of the Alger version of maternity is this interchange between Paul the peddler and his mother:

> "You see, mother, Phil would be sure of a beating if he went home without his fiddle. Now he doesn't like to be beaten, and the padrone gives harder beatings than you do, mother."
> "I presume so," said Mrs. Hoffman, smiling. "I do not think I am very severe."
> "No, you spoil the rod and spare the child."   [Phil, the Fiddler]

The benevolent merchant, the villainous father-figure, and the gentle and appreciative mother are at the center of most Alger books. They are joined by a variety of minor figures, all of whom can be traced to the traditional stereotypes of the sentimental novel: the warm-hearted Irish woman, poor and crude, kind and generous, who helps the hero escape from the villain; the snobbish female with aristocratic pretensions; the "stage Yankee" who appears in an occasional novel as a friend of the hero; and a variety of minor villains, such as the miserly moneylender, the petty swindler, and, in the Western stories, the stagecoach robber.

From such material, together with carefully accumulated local color—the books are filled with detailed descriptions of New York City—Alger constructed his tales. Almost invariably, they follow the same formula: by an amazing series of coincidences, and a few acts of personal heroism and generosity, the hero escapes from the plots laid by his enemies—usually an unholy alliance between the snobbish boy and the villainous father-figure—and attains the patronage of the benevolent merchant. In generating the action, chance and luck play a dominant role. Alger was apparently aware that the unbelievable tissue of coincidences which ran through his stories put some strain on the tolerance of his youthful readers. In *Struggling Upward*, for example, Linton Tomkins, the lesser hero, chances upon practically every other character in the book in the course of a twenty-minute promenade. Somewhat amazed at this feat, Alger can only remark that "Linton was destined to meet plenty of acquaintances." At the book's conclusion he confesses:

> So closes an eventful passage in the life of Luke Larkin. He has struggled upward from a boyhood of privation and self-denial into a youth and manhood of prosperity and honor. There has been some luck about it, I admit, but after all he is indebted for most of his good fortune to his own good qualities.

However much the hero's good qualities may have been involved, and they often seem incidental, Alger is obsessed with luck. The chapter which contains the crucial turning point of the book is invariably entitled ———'s *Luck*, and every accession to the hero's fortunes stems from a coincidence: the land thought to be worthless suddenly becomes valuable because a town has been built around it; the strongbox which the hero saves from thieves turns out to belong to an eccentric and wealthy old man who rewards the hero; the dead father's seemingly worthless speculation in mining stock is in fact a bonanza.

Alger's emphasis on luck resembles that found in the stories of T. S. Arthur and other apostles of the self-made man in the pre-Civil War era. Like them, he represents American society as an environment in which sudden and unaccountable prosperity frequently comes to the deserving like manna from heaven. To some extent, this reliance on luck or Providence is a literary shortcoming. Both Alger and Arthur turned out books at a tremendous rate; sloppiness and inadequacies in plotting and motivation could be concealed in part by defending coincidence. Furthermore, accident, luck, and chance have always played a large role in folk and popular literature, for they allow for exciting plot manipulation and the maintenance of suspense. It is equally true that the form which the accidental takes in a given work is some indication of the beliefs of an author and his intended audience.

In the case of Arthur and his contemporaries, the accidental assumes the form of the more or less direct intervention of Divine Providence. God acts to reward the deserving, punish the evil, and convert the doubting to a faith in his powers. Alger ignores the religious implications of the accidental. In his stories, luck is seemingly independent of the divine, inhering in the particular social environment of America, with its absence of hereditary class distinctions and the freedom it allows. Because most of the great merchants had been poor boys themselves, they were always on the lookout for deserving young men to assist. If the hero has the daring and self-assurance to seize one of his many opportunities to come to the attention of a benevolent patron, and is also blessed with the virtues of industry, fidelity, and good manners, he is certain to get ahead.

Religion itself does not play a major role in the life of the Alger hero. His heroes pray and go to Sunday School willingly enough, but Alger places greater stress on their obligations to others—loyalty to family and employer, and personal assistance to the less fortunate. His books encourage humanitarianism in their emphasis on practical good works and frequent insistence that Americans extend opportunities for worldly success to the juvenile proletariat of the cities. Although, like most writers in the tradition of self-improvement, Alger attributes success and failure to qualities within the individual, he occasionally points out to his young readers that a stifling and corrupting environment can be a major cause of vice and failure. An important factor in the rise of his streetboy heroes is their removal from the streets, where, if they remain, moral decay and poverty are certain. Alger can hardly be granted a profound understanding of the contemporary scene, but sympathy for the underprivileged is strong in his books. Judging from the prominence of his themes, there is as much evidence that Alger was an important influence on future reformers as a popular model for incipient robber barons.

Luck is not the only element in the success of the Alger hero. He has to deserve his luck by manifesting certain important traits which show him to be a fit candidate for a higher place in society. He carries the full complement of middle-class virtues, but these are not solely industry, frugality, and piety. Far more important are those qualities of character and intellect which make the hero a good employee and a reputable member of middle-class society. To his hero's cultivation of these qualities Alger devotes much of his attention. The hero has to learn how to dress neatly and modestly, to eliminate slang and colloquialisms from his speech, and to develop a facility with the stilted and pretentious language that Alger took to be the proper medium of verbal intercourse among respectable Americans. In addition, he has to educate himself. Alger's conception of the liberally educated man is also closely tied to social respectability. It is particularly desirable for the hero to have a neat hand and mathematical ability, but it is also important that he show a smattering of traditional culture. A foreign language is usually the prescribed curriculum. Ragged Dick studies French, for example. Since a foreign language plays no part in the hero's economic life, it is apparently intended by Alger as a certificate of a certain kind of respectability. The ability to learn French or Latin, although he might never have an opportunity to use such a skill, shows that the hero has a respect for learning as an end in itself and is no mere materialist. Thus, the Alger hero is a pale reflection of the ideal of self-culture as well as a devotee of rising in society.

Inner attainments are marked by characteristic external signs. The most crucial event in the hero's life is his acquisition of a good suit. The good suit, which is usually presented to the hero by his patron, marks the initial step in his advancement, his escape from the dirty and ragged classes and his entry upon respectability. It immediately differentiates the hero from the other bootblacks, and often leads to a quarrel with such dedicated proletarians as Micky McGuire. A second important event follows on the first: he is given a watch. The new watch marks the hero's attainment of a more elevated position, and is a symbol of punctuality and his respect for time as well as a sign of the attainment of young manhood. Alger makes much of the scene in which his hero receives from his patron a pocket watch suitably engraved.

Perhaps the most important group of qualities which operate in the hero's favor are those which make him the ideal employee: fidelity, dependability, and a burning desire to make himself useful. In a common Algerine situation, the hero, entrusted with some of his employer's money, is confronted by a villainous robber. At great risk to his own life, he defends his employer's property, preferring to lose his own money, or even his life, rather than betray his patron's trust. Under lesser stress, the hero demonstrates his superiority over the snobs by showing his willingness to perform any duties useful to his employer, and by going out of his way to give cheerful and uncomplaining service without haggling over wages. In *Fame and Fortune*, Roswell Crawford, a snob, is fired from his position as errand boy in a dry goods store when he not only complains of being required to carry packages—work too low for a "gentleman's son"—but has the additional temerity to ask for a raise. Ragged Dick, on the other hand, generously offers to carry Roswell's packages for him. Needless to say, Dick receives a raise without asking for it, because his patron recognizes his fidelity and insists on a suitable reward.

Emphasis on fidelity to the employer's interests is perhaps the worst advice Alger could have given his young readers if financial success was of major interest to them. Contrast the Alger hero's relations with his employers and Benjamin Franklin's as described in the *Memoirs*. Franklin keeps his eyes on his own interests when he works for his brother, and for the Philadelphia printers, Bradford and Keimer; indeed, he shows considerable satisfaction at his ability to turn Keimer's faults to his own benefit. By studying the inadequacies of his former employer he is able to make his own business a success. The Alger hero would never resort to such a self-serving device.

Placed against Emerson and his philosophy of self-reliance, Alger is simply another exponent of the idealized version of the self-made man found in the novels of T. S. Arthur, Sylvester Judd, and other sentimentalists of the 1840's and 1850's. His understanding of social mobility is on the same level of abstraction and idealization. Emerson, in comparison, has a much more profound understanding of the implications of social mobility and the actual characteristics likely to lead to economic and social advancement, as well as a broader ideal of self-culture. It is as true of Alger as of Arthur that he presents the mobile society through the rose-colored glasses of the middle-class ethical tradition of industry, frugality, and integrity, and the sentimental Christian version of a benevolent Providence.

The great attainment of Alger's hero is to leave the ranks of the "working class" and become an owner or partner in a business of his own. Yet few of Alger's heroes have any connection with such enterprises as mining, manufacturing, or construction, the industries in which most of the large fortunes of the late nineteenth century were made. Alger's favorite reward is a junior partnership in a respectable mercantile house. This emphasis is a throwback to the economic life of an earlier period, when American business was still dominated by merchants whose economic behavior in retrospect seemed refined and benevolent in comparison to the devastating strategies of transcontinental railroad builders, iron and steel manufacturers, and other corporate giants. Alger's version of success is, in effect, a reassertion of the values of a bygone era in an age of dramatic change and expansion.

Alger's Popularity

Today one would hardly expect adolescent boys to respond to Alger's vision of a dying past. His popularity with many older Americans—a phenomenon that continues into the present time—is certainly nostalgic. Alger is a teacher of traditional manners and morals rather than an exponent of free enterprise. His fictions embody the values that middle-class Americans have been taught to revere: honesty, hard work, familial loyalty; good manners, cleanliness, and neatness of appearance; kindness and generosity to the less fortunate; loyalty and deference on the part of employees, and consideration and personal interest on the part of employers. These "bourgeois virtues" are strenuously displayed by the Alger hero and his benevolent patron, along with that strong respect for education and self-culture which is a considerable part of the middle-class heritage. On the other hand, the Alger villains represent those vices particularly reprehensible to many nineteenth-century Americans: they have aristocratic pretensions and try to adopt the airs of the leisure-class; they frequent theaters and gaming houses and are intemperate; they are disloyal to their families and often try to cheat their relatives; they are avaricious, miserly, and usurious; and they lack integrity and are unscrupulous in business affairs. The conflict between middle-class virtues and vices is played out against a background of unlimited opportunities in which the virtues ultimately show themselves to be indispensable and the vices trip up their possessors.

At the time when Alger wrote, traditional commercial practices and ethics had been undermined by economic expansion. A lifetime of hard work often left a man worse off than when he began. The growing gulf between millionaire and employee and the increasing development of complex economic hierarchies were so circumscribing individual ownership and control that a clerk was better off working for others than attempting to found and operate his own business. Alger reasserts an older economic model, one that had begun to be out of date as early as 1830, but which still lingered in the minds of Americans as the ideal form of economic organization: a multiplicity of small individual businesses or partnerships. He certainly had little idea of the actuality of business enterprise in his day—nowhere in his novels do industrial corporations or the character types they produce appear—but he does have enough personal knowledge of New York City to give a certain plausibility and contemporaneity to his representation of American life. He is able to present the traditional pattern of middle-class economic ideals in late nineteenth-century dress and fill the bustling streets and thoroughfares of a nineteenth-century industrial metropolis with a nostalgic reincarnation of the ideal *eighteenth-century* merchant and his noble young apprentice. This moral and economic anachronism is an important source of Alger's popularity with adults. When, a generation or so later, the accumulation of social and economic change made it no longer tenable, even in fantasy, the books began to come down from the library shelves, classed as unrealistic and misleading, perhaps even dangerous, fairy tales.

Although parents encouraged their children to read Alger because he seemed to reassert the validity of hard work, economy, integrity, and family loyalty, this is probably not the source of his popularity with young boys. There were a great many reasons why children liked Alger. He writes of places that they were interested in. In these locales he places a set of characters whose activities have enough of the fantastic and unusual to be exciting, yet always retain enough connection with the ordinary activities of American boys to encourage an emotionally satisfying empathy. Alger's glorification of financial success has been overemphasized by commentators, but many of his young readers enjoyed dreaming of the day when they would be rich enough to buy gold watches, good clothes, and have others dependent on their beneficences. Furthermore, Alger has a simple and unsophisticated sense of justice, which punishes the enemies of boyhood. The snobs, the bullies, the uncles and spinster aunts who do not like boys get their comeuppances in ways that must have appealed to a juvenile audience. Alger is hardly a master stylist, but his narrative and dialogue are simple, clear, and relatively fast-moving; and his diction, if formal and stilted, is not arcane or difficult.

These elements were undoubtedly important factors in Alger's popularity with his juvenile audience; and there was a further dimension to the Alger formula. Legion are the dangers of Freudian interpretation of literary works, but Alger cries out for this kind of treatment. Consider the following brief summary, which can apply with variations to almost any of the Alger books: an adolescent boy, the support of a gentle, loving, and admiring mother, is threatened by a male figure of authority and discipline. Through personal heroism he succeeds in subverting the authority of this figure and in finding a new male supporter who makes no threats to his relationship with the mother and does not seek to circumscribe his independence. The pattern is too obvious to require extended comment. When we recall that the late nineteenth century was an era of relatively strict paternal discipline and control, it does not seem farfetched to suggest that the Alger books may have been appreciated as phantasies of father-elimination. The rapid decline in the popularity of Alger books after World War I probably resulted in part from the changing character of familial relationships in the twenties and thirties. When new ideals of parent-child relationship became generally accepted, the Alger hero's victory over the villainous father-figure must have lost much of its bite.

Social Darwinism and the Businessman

Irvin G. Wyllie

One of the revered stereotypes of turn-of-the-century America, given credibility through both historical studies and literature, is that of the businessman as industrial tycoon. Supporting this view is the notion that the writings of Charles Darwin (more particularly their application to society by Herbert Spencer and William Graham Sumner) served the important role of justifying such an exploitive system. The "Robber Baron Generation," it has been said, found the ideas of "survival of the fittest" and "natural selection" both comfortable and convenient. Irvin G. Wyllie, President of the University of Wisconsin, Parkside Campus, contends that the impact of social Darwinism on American business thought has been overplayed. The establishment of trusts, businessmen's excursions into philanthropy and their obvious lack of intellectual sophistication as to Darwinian principles, along with other evidence, seem to suggest that intellectual commitments to social Darwinism were the exception rather than the rule among the Captains of Industry.

The American humorist Mark Twain, when asked to explain why he wore a white suit, replied that clothes make the man, that naked people have little or no influence in society. Unlike Mark Twain, or his fellow countryman Alec Guinness, Charles Darwin was no man in a white suit. But he was a man who exerted a far-reaching influence in society. If Darwin had done no more than change the methods and assumptions of the biological sciences, and contribute to the general store of scientific knowledge, he would still be an important figure in world history. The impact of his ideas was by no means limited to the sciences, however. His theory of evolution touched off a general intellectual revolution that altered the course of religious thought, re-directed the social sciences, and contributed new insights and slogans to the popular and academic varieties of social theory.

The changes that flowed from the Darwinian revolution were so impressive as to suggest that it had unlimited transforming power. In the words of Bert J. Loewenberg, a pioneer student of this subject, "Evolution germinated ideas wherever it penetrated, and it penetrated everywhere." Just as historians of the American and French and Russian revolutions sometimes overestimated the extent to which these upheavals transformed the societies in which they occurred, so historians of the Darwinian intellectual revolution have sometimes misjudged the outer limits of its influence and overestimated

From "Social Darwinism and the Businessman," by Irvin G. Wyllie, in *Proceedings of the American Philosophical Society*, Vol. 103, No. 5 (1959); pp. 629–635. Reprinted by permission of the author and the American Philosophical Society.

the completeness of its sway. The tendency to exaggerate the impact of Darwinism, especially on popular thought, is nowhere better illustrated than in the claim that American businessmen in the post-Civil War decades rationalized their personal careers and justified their business operations in terms of Herbert Spencer's competitive social version of Darwin's theory of evolution.

Even the most casual examination of American historical writing in the last twenty years reveals the prevalence of the assumption that entrepreneurs of the Gilded Age were not only practicing social Darwinists, but philosophical social Darwinists as well. Intellectual historians who treat ideas in their social contexts suggest that Darwinism served as an ideological shield and buckler for the Robber Baron generation of businessmen. In his Pulitzer prize-winning book, *The Growth of American Thought*, Merle Curti argued that defenders of rugged individualism, both inside and outside the business community, invoked Darwin to justify the struggles of the market place. Herbert Spencer became the oracle of the age, displacing Adam Smith and John Stuart Mill in the defense of *laissez-faire*. In Curti's view social Darwinist doctrine "admirably suited the needs of the great captains of industry who were crushing the little fellows when these vainly tried to compete with them." In his study of *The American Mind* Henry S. Commager not only conceded the usefulness of social Darwinism to dominant business interests, but also claimed for the Spencerian system an imperial sway over the minds of most middle-class people in the half-century after Appomatox. "Between them," wrote Commager, "Darwin and Spencer exercised such sovereignty over America as George III had never enjoyed."

Richard Hofstadter's perceptive treatise on *Social Darwinism in American Thought* offered the most systematic statement by an intellectual historian of the case for the businessman as a Darwinist. "With its rapid expansion, its exploitative methods, its desperate competition, and its peremptory rejection of failure," Hofstadter wrote, "post-bellum America was like a vast human caricature of the Darwinian struggle for existence and survival of the fittest." In this circumstance businessmen accepted Darwinian terminology "almost by instinct," and discovered that the plausible analogies of social selection were most congenial to their ways of thinking. Hofstadter quoted leading entrepreneurs, among them John D. Rockefeller, Andrew Carnegie, James J. Hill, and Chauncey Depew, to establish the Darwinian cast of their minds. Depew testified that the guests at the great banquets in New York City in the Gilded Age represented the survival of the fittest, men who had come through the fierce competitions of the great city because of their superior ability, foresight, and adaptability. James J. Hill's career in the railroad industry led him to observe that the fortunes of railroad companies were determined by the law of the survival of the fittest, a conclusion that John D. Rockefeller also allegedly reached as a result of his operations in the oil industry. When Hofstadter cited Andrew Carnegie's assertion that competition is "best for the race, because it insures the survival of the fittest in every department," this bit of evidence seemed almost superfluous in light of the case that he had already built for the captain of industry as a disciple of Herbert Spencer.

Business historians, economists, anthropologists and journalists have likewise portrayed Herbert Spencer as the patron saint of the late nineteenth-century entrepreneur. In the *Age of Enterprise* Thomas C. Cochran and William Miller argued that men of affairs in post-Civil War America found a much-needed philosophy for industrial progress in the Spencerian system. "To a generation singularly engrossed in the competitive pursuit of industrial wealth," they wrote,

> it gave cosmic sanction to free competition. In an age of science, it "scientifically" justified ceaseless exploitation. Precisely attuned to the aspirations of American businessmen, it afforded them a guide to faith and thought perfectly in keeping with the pattern of their worka-day lives. . . . Their cupidity, it defended as part of the universal struggle for existence; their wealth, it hallowed as a sign of the "fittest." Business America in the Gilded Age had supreme faith in itself; no wonder it embraced Spencer's philosophy, which sanctified business activities.

So well did this rationale serve the businessman's purpose, according to Cochran and Miller, that he was reluctant to abandon it even after business practices made Spencerianism obsolete. Joseph J. Spengler, an economist who examined the impact of Darwin's theory on economics, shared the Cochran-Miller view that social Darwinism exactly suited the business temper of the Gilded Age. "An outstandingly successful business man," Spengler observed, "was hard put to find a philosophical basis for his *apologia* . . . more satisfactory than this essentially perverted form of Darwinism."

Others who have looked upon competitive social Darwinism as a perversion, such as Ashley Montagu, the anthropologist, have insisted that it was a perversion freely indulged in by the business community. Even though in his little book on *Darwin, Competition & Cooperation* Montagu attributed the Spencerian aberration to the impact of social thought and social conditions on Darwinian biology, rather than the other way around, he accepted the idea that Spencer and Darwin supplied nineteenth-century industrialists with a welcome pseudo-scientific sanction for free competition. In *The Age of the Moguls* Stewart Holbrook, a journalist, suggested that business barons purged their consciences by accepting Darwinism. "It was welcome balm to their impaired consciences," Holbrook declared, "to be told they enjoyed their riches simply because of the working of natural laws over which neither they nor anyone else had control." In accounting for the decline of the moguls in the twentieth century Holbrook wrote,

> They became extinct because they were too stupid to comprehend the danger from the changes of the jungle environment which their business methods and their ways of living had helped to bring about. It was full circle. Darwin had explained their origin and prophesied their end. . . .

The fact that the social Darwinist businessman has made his way into American history textbooks is but another indication of the consensus that scholars have reached on this question. The novice who discovers the Gilded Age through Henry Bamford Parkes, *The United States of America*, will learn that Spencer "provided the big businessmen of America with exactly the justification they needed," and that industrialists "learned from him to apply phrases like 'survival of the fittest' to the formation of trusts and monopolies and to regard the millionaire as the finest flower of evolution." In *A History of the United States*, only recently off the press, three leading historians declare that Darwinism explained for many businessmen both their own success and the nature of the society in which they operated.

> The weak went down, the strong endured and became stronger, and society was benefited because the unfit were eliminated and the fit survived. Men who had risen to dominance by crushing their competitors were intrigued and comforted by a doctrine that justified any method that succeeded and proclaimed that wealth was a reward of competence. [*A History of the United States* 2: 58, New York, Alfred A. Knopf, 1959]

The clear implication of the foregoing statements is that the captain of industry was a conscious, philosophical social Darwinist, and not just a tough competitor. The world has known many businessmen, before Darwin's time as well as after, who were sharp in tooth and claw. To put such men down as social Darwinists, in the absence of evidence that their thinking reflected the influence of Darwin or Spencer, would be to deprive the term of meaning. Those who represent the entrepreneur as a Darwinist portray a man who had a conscious Darwinian perspective on his personal success, his business activities, and his general social role. He was a man who not only recited Spencer's phrases, but understood their implications, and perhaps even their intellectual derivation. He was, in other words, a man of the type of Andrew Carnegie. An avid reader of Spencer, Carnegie was converted to social Darwinism at an early age. "Few men have wished to know another man more strongly than I to know Herbert Spencer," Carnegie testified in his *Autobiography*, "for seldom has one been more deeply indebted than I to him and to Darwin." He came to know Spencer extremely well, and during Spencer's memorable visit to the United States in 1882 had the satisfaction of having Spencer single him out publicly as one of his two best American friends. Carnegie's addresses, essays, and books are so full of Spencerian allusions, of references to men like himself who came into the business world as "athletes trained for the contest, with sinews braced, indomitable wills, resolved to do or die," that it would be impossible to deny his Darwinist orientation. Because Carnegie supplied such clear evidence of his intellectual indebtedness he is invariably cited to prove the case for the entrepreneur as a social Darwinist.

What is puzzling, especially in light of the claim that businessmen generally took their cues from Spencer, is that so few others have testified so clearly on this point as Carnegie. If men of affairs explained their personal success and justified their business operations in terms of natural selection and the survival of the fittest we should have abundant evidence on this point. It would be folly to deny that such evidence exists, but it is accurate to say that so far it has not been adduced. The men that historians have called to succeed Carnegie on the witness stand have not only been few in number, but on the whole incompetent as well. In support of their case Cochran and Miller cite only one businessman in addition to Carnegie, the publisher Henry Holt. Holt, like Carnegie, was as much an intellectual as a businessman. A graduate of Yale, he was an author and a scholar as well as a publisher, and therefore not truly representative of the business community in his intellectual sensitivity. Furthermore, he did not testify that he was a social Darwinist, but rather that Spencer had considerable vogue among informed people in England and America in the years between 1870 and 1900. What appears to be a case for the businessman as a disciple of Darwin is in *The Age of Enterprise* merely an elaboration of Holt's point, a demonstration that intellectually sophisticated men like Edward Livingston Youmans, John Fiske, Charles W. Eliot, Henry Cabot Lodge, and Nicholas Murray Butler did read Darwin and Spencer.

Hofstadter's case, though it relies more directly on business testimony, also leaves room for doubt. Even if we were to accept all of his evidence without question, we would still be accepting a case based on the statements of only four businessmen. Part of the evidence must be questioned, however. The statement attributed to John D. Rockefeller is one he never made, namely that "The growth of a large business is merely a survival of the fittest. . . . The American beauty rose can be produced . . . only by sacrificing the early buds which grow up around it." This sentiment, uttered by John D. Rockefeller, Jr. in 1902 in an address to the YMCA at his alma mater, Brown University, may prove that the university-trained son knew how to use Darwinian phraseology, but it does not prove that his Bible-reading father was a Spencerian in the Gilded Age. Chauncey Depew's observation that the guests at the great banquets in New York represented the survival of the fittest is likewise open to objection. Since he recorded this observation in 1922, when, thanks to William Jennings Bryan, the air was filled with evolutionary discussion, we may ask how reliably this statement reflected Depew's thinking forty years before. Even if it mirrored his early thought perfectly, the fact remains that in his intellectual awareness he was no more representative of the business community than Henry Holt. A bookish man, and a Yale graduate in 1856, he was a lifelong intimate of Andrew Dixon White, the historian-president of Cornell University. He also served as a regent of the University of the State of New York from 1877 to 1904. Unlike most post-Civil War men of affairs he moved in intellectual circles, and therefore had ample opportunity to master Spencerian clichés. James J. Hill's observation that the fortunes of railroads were determined by the law of the survival of the fittest is likewise open to the objection that a statement made in 1910 does not necessarily prove that its author took his cues from Spencer in the 1870's and 1880's. To make the case for the post-Civil War businessman as a social Darwinist we need direct testimony out of the Gilded Age.

Such testimony may be available, but so far it seems to be in short supply. In 1888 Henry Clews resorted to Darwinian analysis to explain the displacement of Wall Street's conservative old guard by a young, imaginative group of financiers after the Panic of 1857. "The change was a fine exemplification of the survival of the fittest," Clews declared, "and proved that there was a law of natural selection in financial affairs that superseded old conservatism and sealed its doom." In June of 1899 Henry O. Havemeyer, President of the American Sugar Refining Company, replied affirmatively when a member of the United States Industrial Commission asked him if he believed that a trust or combine represented the survival of the fittest in business. Havemeyer testified that he rested his whole political philosophy on this proposition. Nathan A. Taylor, an independent tin-plate manufacturer, also explained failures in his industry in terms of the survival of the fittest. If Gilded Age businessmen were social Darwinists, they could be expected to give evidence of this fact in their discussions of industrial concentration. Yet in the mountain of testimony piled up by the Congressional investigations of 1889 and 1899, talk of the survival of the fittest is exceptional, not common. And sometimes this talk originated with merchants of ideas, rather than with captains of industry. It was a newspaperman, Patrick C. Boyle of the *Oil City Derrick*, and not an official of Standard Oil, who told the United States Industrial Commission in 1899 that "Darwin's theory of survival of the fittest was never better illustrated than in the organization of the Standard Oil Company; it represents the best element in all branches of the trade."

Sometimes the direct testimony of businessmen revealed only that they were religious evolutionists, not social Darwinists. In the year 1900 the banker Roeliff Brinkerhoff reported that "I am an evolutionist of the Herbert Spencer type, and have been so from the earliest announcement of that theory, and with me it has been a power for good, and not for evil." In context Brinkerhoff's testimony indicated that evolution had influenced his religious thinking, but not his social views. In an autobiography published in the year 1885 Thomas Mellon, founder of the Mellon banking fortune, devoted fifteen pages to a discussion of evolution, all dealing with the impact of the theory on religion. He revealed himself to be a Christian and an evolutionist, but not a social Darwinist. Though Mellon believed in competition and *laissez-faire*, he found his sanction in classical economics, not in Spencer's *Social Statics*.

The testimony of other businessmen before Congressional committees also revealed the persistent influence of pre-Darwinian economic ideas in the late nineteenth century. When Benjamin Brewster, president of the National Transit Company, told the House Committee on Manufactures in 1889 that there were natural laws of commerce as well as of science, he did not refer to evolution, but rather to the law of gravitation and the law of supply and demand. John E. Parsons, a trustee of the Sugar Refineries Company, invoked John Stuart Mill to defend his views in the same investigation. It was Jeremy Bentham, not Spencer, who was cited as authority for attorney John R. Dos Passos' observation to the United States Industrial Commission that "Society is so constituted that some must suffer. It is the sacrifice that the few are forced to make for the good of the whole." Such usages require that we reconsider prevailing assumptions concerning the extent to which Herbert Spencer and William Graham Sumner displaced the classical economists as the high priests of *laissez-faire*. Even more, they require that we exercise caution in attributing to Darwin and Spencer ultimate responsibility for the competitive social ideas of the businessman in the Gilded Age.

Too often, after an uncooperative captain of industry has refused to identify himself as a social Darwinist, he has been asked to step down from the witness stand, so that a sociologist or economist might take his place. Richard Hofstadter, convinced that businessmen "are not the most articulate social philosophers," called upon a reform-minded University of Chicago sociologist, Charles R. Henderson, to testify to the Darwinian cast of the entrepreneurial mind. "It would be strange if the 'captain of industry' did not sometimes manifest a militant spirit," Henderson wrote in 1896, "for he has risen from the ranks largely because he was a better fighter than most of us. Competitive commercial life is not a flower bed of ease, but a battle field where the 'struggle for existence' is defining the industrially fittest to survive." All this statement proved was that Henderson, an intellectual, had the ability to see Darwinian meaning in the struggles of the business world. He did not pretend that the businessman saw his activities in the same light. In fact he deplored the ideological gulf that separated the entrepreneur from the social theorist, and acknowledged that businessmen did not hold the intellectual in high esteem. "They say, with some touch of contemptuous sarcasm and cynicism," Henderson wrote, "that they can hire talkers and buy books."

Gilded Age businessmen were not sufficiently bookish, or sufficiently well educated, to keep up with the changing world of ideas. As late as 1900, 84 percent of the businessmen listed in *Who's Who in America* had not been educated beyond high school. Though college men in business increased steadily in the last decades of the nineteenth century, they were always a minority. The uneducated majority had little time for books. Cornelius Vanderbilt, who read only one book in his life, *Pilgrim's Progress*, after he was seventy years of age, once remarked that if he had taken time to learn education he would not have had time to learn anything else. Many an unlettered businessman undoubtedly shared this view, and also subscribed to Daniel Drew's opinion that "Book learning is something, but thirteen million dollars is also something, and a mighty sight more." Since in the late nineteenth century Darwin's adherents were for the most part scientists, social scientists, philosophers, clergymen, editors, and other educationally advantaged persons, it would be surprising to find a really large contingent of businessmen in his camp. The minority of college graduates and devotees of self-culture may be found there, but the untutored majority probably will not.

Scholars whose work requires them to deal with ideas in a systematic way, and to keep abreast of changing modes of thought, are generally reluctant to concede that other men may be far behind the times, and philosophically disorganized and inconsistent as well. To them it is unthinkable that any influential body of men in the Gilded Age should have failed to embrace the most advanced idea of that age, and that businessmen in particular could have ignored a formulation like that of Spencer, which seemed to explain so many hard facts of business life. However, there is considerable wisdom in the observation that "It must not be thought that Social Darwinism made brutal misanthropists of the Great Entrepreneurs and the Finance Capitalists. They were, by and large, too simple-minded for that; it was only an intellectual like W. G. Sumner who became a misanthropist." Though John D. Rockefeller might transact business according to the law of the jungle, he was a pious Christian who looked upon his wealth as a God-given reward for virtue. Railroad executives, who by certain reckonings were social Darwinists, sometimes violated Spencerian efficiency by decreeing that in slack times single men should be fired first, to be followed by men with the least seniority. Andrew Carnegie, a secular-minded man and a tough-minded Darwinian, was also a generous philanthropist who gave a practical demonstration of the social utility of the old Christian doctrine of the stewardship of wealth. Robert Harris, whose job as president of the Chicago, Burlington, and Quincy Railroad might have been expected to put him on the side of the survival of the fittest, testified that "As a general proposition, it seems to me that the strong should help the weak, now by one course and now by another; and in exercising authority to do it as we would wish it done to ourselves."

Anyone who examines the voluminous nineteenth-century literature of business success cannot fail to be impressed that businessmen who talked about success and failure took their texts from Christian moralists, not from Darwin and Spencer. In the race for wealth they attributed little influence to native intelligence, physical strength, or any other endowment of nature, and paramount influence to industry, frugality, and sobriety—simple moral virtues that any man could cultivate. They urged young men to seek the business way of life in the Bible, not in *The Descent of Man* or *The Principles of Sociology*. The problem of success was not that of grinding down one's competitors, but of elevating one's self—and the two were not equivalent. Business practice may have suggested a Darwinian struggle for existence, but self-help advisers of the Gilded Age suggested that the only struggle of consequence was the struggle for good character. Failure was likewise attributed to defective character rather than to deficiencies of endowment or opportunity. Opportunities for success, like opportunities for salvation, were limitless; heaven could receive as many as were worthy. Because American businessmen operated in a land blessed with an abundance of resources they rejected the Malthusian idea that chances were so limited that one man's rise meant the fall of many others. Theirs was a more optimistic view, that every triumph opened the way for more. Advanced thinkers might explain both success and failure in terms of social Darwinism, but most businessmen were probably inclined to follow the lead of the *Commercial and Financial Chronicle* in permitting "this fashionable philosophy . . . to spin its shining web and to apply its specious theories where it can."

In order to deprive the captain of industry of the public relations advantage he enjoyed when he passed himself off as a model of virtue, critics of business in the late nineteenth and early twentieth centuries represented that the great barons were robber barons who knew no moral law except that of the jungle. They inverted the businessman's moral pyramid and tried to demonstrate that he owed his success not to simple Christian virtues, but to brutality, rapacity, dishonesty, and cunning. Augustus Tack, a petroleum refiner who had been squeezed out by Standard Oil, gained a measure of revenge in 1889 when he described Rockefeller as a heartless Darwinist to the House Committee on Manufactures. Tack testified that he had gone to Rockefeller, hoping for a reprieve, but that he had been sent away with the brutal comment, "There is no hope. . . . The weakest must go first." Henry Demarest Lloyd, that erstwhile critic of Rockefeller and student of Standard Oil, observed in *Wealth Against Commonwealth* that "The man who should apply in his family or his citizenship this 'survival of the fittest theory' as it is practically professed and operated in business would be a monster, and would be speedily made extinct, as we do with monsters." When John D. Rockefeller, Jr. made his unfortunate remarks about the American Beauty rose in 1902 he discovered that he had played into the hands of his father's enemies as well as his own. Critics who denounced him as "a young scion of wealth and greed, possessed of more dollars than ideas," forgot that the title of his talk had been "Christianity in Business," and that he had entered a plea for more Christian virtue in the transaction of business. In the spring of 1905, at the height of the "tainted money" controversy, his father's enemies depicted the senior Rockefeller, pruning shears in hand, cutting away the buds that had grown up around the finest flower of the oil industry.

Rockefeller was not the only businessman to be tarred with the brush of social Darwinism in the era of the muckrakers. In his criticism of the men who organized the Beef Trust, Charles Edward Russell explained that "They have merely followed to its logical conclusion the idea of the survival of the fittest, the right of the strong to annihilate the weak, the theory that in business any advantage is fair—the accepted creed of inordinate gain." All the leading muckrakers sensed that there was no better way to discredit a businessman than to portray him as a renegade of the jungle. In light of the eagerness of early twentieth-century critics to condemn the entrepreneur as a Spencerian, it is ironic that sympathetic students of business in our own time have tried so hard to link the businessman to social Darwinism.

There is reason to believe that this mode of interpretation is changing. In his 1953 study of *Railroad Leaders, 1845–1890*, Thomas C. Cochran stated the case for social Darwinism more cautiously, and with greater awareness of exceptions and complexities than in his earlier *Age of Enterprise*. Though he still argued that railroad executives more or less consciously subscribed to Spencerian ideas, he conceded that few of them read Spencer, and indicated instances in which they violated Darwinist precepts in word and deed. My own *Self-Made Man in America*, published in 1954, directly challenged prevailing assumptions on this question. In *Dream and Thought in the Business Community*, published three years ago, Edward C. Kirkland suggested that Darwinism may have done no more than furnish new terms for old ideas in the years after Appomattox, and that businessmen may have derived their ideas of competition and survival from experience and observation, rather than from Spencer.

In the years ahead we can look forward to a more complete and discriminating appraisal of the businessman's acceptance of social Darwinism. Greater awareness of the weaknesses of the old assessment will contribute to the strengthening of the new. In the future historians will distinguish between representative and unrepresentative views, between the ideas of an intellectually unsophisticated majority and those of an educated, bookish minority. They will also discriminate between positive social Darwinists and mere biological or religious evolutionists. They will ask whether competitive social Darwinism did fit the businessman like a glove, whether it served all of his interests and satisfied his every aspiration. Was he a Spencerian when he cooperated with other businessmen in pools and trusts that throttled competition? What did he contribute to the survival of the fittest when he practiced philanthropy? From a public relations point of view, who profited more from the claim that he was a social Darwinist, the businessman or his critics? As historians undertake to explain what the businessman actually thought about social Darwinism they will recognize that their greatest single need is a need for more direct, reliable evidence on all the points at issue. This means evidence out of the Gilded Age, and evidence supplied by businessmen themselves, not by outside observers. It also means testimony that leaves little or nothing to inference, testimony that ties ideas to their actual and not their assumed sources. My prediction is that such evidence will force us to revise downward our estimate of the impact of social Darwinism on American business thought. The businessman drew his ideas and social values from many sources, not just one. He would not have been ideologically naked without the Spencerian formulation.

The Myth of the Melting Pot

Nathan Glazer and Daniel P. Moynihan

Historically, the idea of America as a melting pot has had a wide currency. One of the early sources for this belief was the famous solution-within-a-question by Hector St. John de Crèvecoeur: *"What then is the American, this new man?"* Assuming, then, that the American was a new man, de Crèvecoeur went on to differentiate him from others. Nathan Glazer and Daniel P. Moynihan, of Harvard University, have examined the melting pot idea, using New York City as a test case. Looking at that city in the 1960s, a half-century after the great impact of the "new immigration," they find the idea of the melting pot to be a myth—at least to that point in time. According to the study, many elements—history, family, interests, formal organizational life—have operated and continue to operate to "keep much of New York life channeled within the bounds of the Ethnic Group."

In 1660 William Kieft, the Dutch governor of New Netherland, remarked to the French Jesuit Isaac Jogues that there were eighteen languages spoken at or near Fort Amsterdam at the tip of Manhattan Island. There still are: not necessarily the same languages, but at least as many; nor has the number ever declined in the intervening three centuries. This is an essential fact of New York: a merchant metropolis with an extraordinarily heterogeneous population. The first shipload of settlers sent out by the Dutch was made up largely of French-speaking Protestants. British, Germans, Finns, Jews, Swedes, Africans, Italians, Irish followed, beginning a stream that has never yet stopped.

The consequences of this confusion, soon to be compounded by the enormous size of the city itself, have been many. Not least has been the virtual impossibility ever of describing New York City or even the state in simple terms. By preference, but also in some degree by necessity, America has turned elsewhere for its images and traditions. Colonial America is preserved for us in terms of the Doric simplicity of New England, or the pastoral symmetry of the Virginia countryside. Even Philadelphia is manageable. But who can summon an image of eighteenth-century New York that will hold still in the mind? A third of the battles of the Revolution were fought on

New York soil, but Bunker Hill and Yorktown come easiest to memory, as do Paul Revere and Patrick Henry.

History, or perhaps historians, keep passing New York by. During the Civil War "New York [State] provided the greatest number of soldiers, the greatest quantity of supplies, and the largest amount of money. In addition, New York's citizens paid the most taxes, bought the greatest number of war bonds, and gave the most to relief organizations." Yet it is recalled as a war between Yankees and Southerners. The Union preserved, the American mind roams westward with the cowboys, returning, if at all, to the Main Streets of the Midwest. The only New York image that has permanently impressed itself on the national mind is that of Wall Street—a street on which nobody lives. Paris may be France, London may be England, but New York, we continue to reassure ourselves, is *not* America.

But, of course, it *is* America: not all of America, or even most, but surely the most important single part. As time passes, the nation comes more under the influence of the city—consider the effect of television in the past fifteen years. As time passes, the nation comes more to resemble the city: urban, heterogeneous, materialist, tough; also, perhaps, ungovernable, except that somehow it is governed, and not so badly, and with a considerable measure of democracy.

With all this, our feeling for the city is at best remote. Even New Yorkers seem to avoid too direct an involvement. The taverns of the West Side of New York boast tunes as old and as good as many gleaned in Appalachian hollows, but when the latter-day folk singers of Morrisania and Greenpoint take to the night clubs, they give forth with "Barbree Allen" and the "Ballad of the Boll Weevil." Even the sociologists, wedded to complexity and eager for fresh subjects, have tended to shy away from the city. Chicago has been far more thoroughly studied, in part because of the accident of the existence of a great department of sociology at the University of Chicago. But it is no accident that a department of equal distinction at Columbia University during the 1940's and 1950's had almost nothing to do with New York. Big as it was, Chicago still offered a structure and scale that could be more easily comprehended.

When magazines on occasion devote issues to San Francisco or Chicago or Houston, and publish pictures of well-dressed and distinguished people in elegant settings, and tell us that these are the important people in this city, it is easy to believe them. When the same magazines get to New York and do the same, the informed reader cannot help but think they are indulging in a game. True, there *must* be important people in New York, but are they this banker, this publisher, this playwright, this society leader? The head of a huge corporation or financial complex in Chicago or Pittsburgh or Boston does play an important role in his city. He will be a central figure in a great movement to reform city government or rebuild the city center. In New York, the man who heads an institution or corporation of equal size is only one of many. The men who can sit around a table and settle things in smaller cities would here fill an auditorium. Indeed, in New York one can fill an auditorium with people of many kinds, who in other cities can sit around a room—high school principals, or educational reformers and thinkers and leaders, police captains and experts on crime and law enforcement, housing project managers and experts on housing and urban renewal, hospital directors and specialists in any field of medicine, directors of societies that help the poor and organizations that raise money from the rich, professors of sociology and owners of art galleries.

Of course there are important people in New York. But they have been men like Robert Moses, who has no equivalent in any other city in the United States, and whose major virtue was that he was well enough connected with enough of the centers of power to get something done, to get things moving. Everyone was so astonished at this fact that for a long time it hardly mattered that what he was getting done on a scale appropriate to the city's size was brutal and ugly, and only exacerbated its problems. The Rockefellers are also important in New York City. Perhaps only their combination of wealth and energy and political skill makes it possible for them to approximate the role that the Mellons play in Pittsburgh. But really there is no comparison. The Mellons can be a moving force in remaking the center of Pittsburgh, and in reshaping the image of that city. But all the wealth and skill of the Rockefellers, wedded to the power of Robert Moses, produce a smaller impact on New York. Robert Wagner, the mayor of New York, is an important man. He probably has never met, and never consults, men who in cities of a million or two million people would be movers of city affairs.

We must begin with this image of the city. New York is more than ten times as large as San Francisco, and twice as large as Chicago, but this does not suggest how much more complicated it is. For in the affairs of men, twice as large means four or eight times as complicated. Twice as large means that the man on top is perhaps four or eight times away from what happens on the bottom. But attempts at calculation understate the complexity. When you have 24,000 policemen in a city, it not only means that you need a few additional levels of authorities to deal with them—those over hundreds, and five hundreds, and thousands, and five thousands—but it also means (for example) that there are enough Jewish or Negro policemen to form an organization. And they too can fill a hall.

The interweaving of complexity that necessarily follows from its size with the complexity added by the origins of its population, drawn from a staggering number of countries and from every race, makes New York one of the most difficult cities in the world to understand, and helps us understand why so few books try in any serious way to understand it. . . .

Let us introduce some order into this huge buzzing confusion. The best way to do so is historically. English stock has apparently never been in a clear majority in New York City. In 1775 one-half of the white population of the state was of English origin, but this proportion was probably lower in New York City, with its Dutch and other non-English groups, and with its large Negro population. After the Revolution and the resumption of immigration, English and Scottish immigrants as well as migrants from New England and upstate New York probably maintained the British-descent group as the largest in the city through the first half of the nineteenth century.

In the 1840's Irish and Germans, who had of course been present in the city in some numbers before this time, began to enter in much larger numbers, and soon became dominant. By 1855 the Irish-born made up 28 percent of the city, the German-born 16 percent of the city; with their children they certainly formed a majority of the city, and they maintained this dominance until the end of the century. In 1890 Irish-born and German-born and their children made up 52 percent of the population of New York and Brooklyn (then separate cities).

In the 1880's Jews and Italians began to come in large numbers (there were of course sizable communities of both groups in the city before this time), and this heavy immigration continued until 1924, and on a reduced scale after that.

The Negroes began to enter the city in great numbers after World War I, the Puerto Ricans after World War II.

Thus six great groups have entered the city two by two, in subsequent epochs; and to these we must add as a seventh group the "old stock," or the "white Anglo-Saxon Protestants." The two terms are of course not identical, but the overlap among those they comprise is great. The "old stock" includes those New Yorkers who descend from families that were here before the Revolution. They were largely of English, Scottish, and Welsh origin, but also included Dutch, French, and other settlers from Northwestern Europe. It has been relatively easy for later immigrants of the same ethnic and religious background—from Canada and from Europe—to assimilate to this "old stock" group if they were in occupations of high status and of at least moderate affluence.

What is the relative size of these seven groups in the city today? For all except the Negroes and the Puerto Ricans, who are listed separately in the census, it is difficult to give more than a very general guess. The accepted religious breakdown of the city population, based on sample surveys and estimates by various religious groups, indicates that less than a quarter of the population is Protestant, and more than half of that is Negro. The white Protestants of course include many of German, Scandinavian, Czech, and Hungarian origins. It is thus not likely that more than about one-twentieth of the population of the city is "old stock," or "WASP." Public opinion polls which ask for "national origin" suggest that about a tenth of the population is Irish, another tenth German. The same sources suggest that about a sixth is Italian. Jewish organizations estimate that one-quarter of the population is Jewish. The census reports that Negroes form 14 percent of the population, Puerto Ricans 8 percent. We have accounted for about 90 percent of the population of the city. . . . These figures, aside from being inexact (except for Puerto Rican and Negro), also assume that everyone in the city can be neatly assigned to an ethnic category. Of course this is in large measure myth; many of the people in the city, as in the nation, have parents and grand-parents of two or three or four groups.

Despite the immigration laws, old groups grow and new groups form in the city. Thus, Batista and Castro, as well as the growing size of the Spanish-speaking population, have encouraged the growth of a large Cuban community of 50,000. For despite the stringent immigration laws, the United States is still the chief country of immigration in the world, and 2,500,000 were able to enter this country as immigrants between 1950–1959. Very large numbers of these immigrants settle in New York and its region, where large communities of their compatriots make life easier and pleasanter. Buried in this vast population of the city are new groups (such as 18,000 Israelis) that in any other city would be marked and receive attention. In New York their coffee shops and bars and meeting places and political disputes and amusements and problems are of interest only to themselves. Only when an immigrant group reaches the enormous size of the Puerto Ricans does it become a subject of interest, attention, and concern.

New York cannot be read out of America because of its heterogeneity; but it is true its heterogeneity is to some extent extreme, even among the heterogeneous cities of the Northeast. The cities of the South, except for the presence of Negroes, are far more homogeneous. They are largely inhabited by white Protestants whose ancestors came from the British Isles. The cities of the Great Plain—from Indianapolis to Kansas City—are also somewhat less mixed. Their largest ethnic element is generally German; and Germans have also found it easiest to assimilate to the white Anglo-Saxon Protestant culture that is still the norm in American life. The cities of the Far West, too, are in their ethnic aspect somewhat different from the cities of the Northeast. Their populations, if we trace them back far enough, are as diverse as the populations of Northeastern cities. But these immigrants have come from the East, Midwest, and South of the United States, rather than from Europe. This second immigration to the Far West has made them more alike. If you ask people there, "Where did you come from?," the answer is Illinois or Iowa, Oklahoma or New York. In the Northeast, the answer is more likely to be Germany or Sweden, Russia or Italy. In terms of immediate origins, the populations of Far Western cities consist of Iowans and Illinoisans and New Yorkers, rather than Germans, Jews, and Italians.

But now what does it mean for New York that most of its population is composed of people who think of themselves—at least at some times, for some purposes—as Jews, Italians, Negroes, Germans, Irishmen, Puerto Ricans? Is New York different, because of this fact, from London, Paris, Moscow, Tokyo?

Do we not, in every great city, meet people from all over the world? We do; but we should not confuse the heterogeneity of most of the great cities of the world with that of New York. The classic heterogeneity of great cities has been limited to the elite part of the population. It is the small numbers of the wealthy and exceptional who represent in those other cities the variety of the countries of the world, not, as in the United States, the masses. This for the most part is still true of the great cities of Europe, even though large numbers of Irishmen and colored people now form part of the working class of London, large numbers of Algerians part of the working class of Paris. Those with very special skills and talents have always been drawn from all over the world into its great cities. Thus, the specialized trading peoples—Phoenicians, Syrians, Greeks, Jews—have formed, for thousands of years, part of the specialized commercial and trading classes of the Mediterranean cities. And even today, trade with foreign countries is still in large measure carried on by nationals of the countries involved, who have special knowledge of language and conditions and local laws and regulations. There is also to be found in all great cities the diplomatic corps, now enormously swollen by international agencies of all sorts. There are the people involved in cultural and artistic activities, who may be of any part of the world. These elites, commercial, political, cultural, today give such cities as London, Paris, and Tokyo an international flavor. It is these people we think of when we say that people from all over the world flock to its great cities; they do, but they are relatively few in numbers.

The heterogeneity of New York is of the masses—numbers so great that Negroes are not exotic, as they are in Paris, Puerto Ricans not glamorous representatives of Latin American culture, as they might be in London, Italians not rare representatives of a great nation, as they are in Tokyo. Here the numbers of each group are so great, so steady and heavy a presence, that it takes an effort of mind to see that all these group names describe a double aspect: those one sees around one, and those in some other country, on some other continent, with a different culture.

Admittedly, even this heterogeneity of the masses is not unique to the cities of the United States. The cities of Canada and Latin America have also drawn their populations from varied groups (though none equals New York in its variety). Even in the great cities of the past one could find sizable differences among the masses. In Athens one might presumably find countrymen from every deme, in Paris workers from every province. There was probably a tendency for them to cluster together. Even though all spoke the same language, they spoke different dialects. Even though they were all of the same religion, they may have preferred to worship among friends and relatives. Even though they all participated in some forms of a growing national culture, they must have preferred their own provincial specialties in food, folk music, and dancing.

But in New York the masses that make up the city have come not from different provinces but different countries. Their languages have been mutually unintelligible, their religion radically different, their family structures, values, ideals, cultural patterns have been as distinct as those of the Irish and the Southern Negro, of urban Jews and peasant Italians.

This is the way it was, but will it be relevant for New York City much longer? The foreign-language press declines rapidly in circulation; the old immigrant quarters now hold only some of the old-timers. The immigrant societies play little role in the city's politics. The American descendants of immigrants diverge markedly from the people of the old country. American descendants of Germans seem no more committed to the unity of Germany and the defense of Berlin than other Americans, the foreign policy of the American Irish seems to have nothing in common any more with the foreign policy of a neutral Eire, and the political outlook and culture of Americans of Italian descent seem to have little in common with what one can see in Italy. (New Italian movies exploring the limits of modern sensibility are as incomprehensible to Italian immigrants as to other immigrants.) And perhaps the Jewish commitment to Israel is best explained by the recency of the establishment of the state and the permanent danger surrounding it. American culture seems to be as attractive to the children of immigrants as the descendants of pioneers (and indeed, as attractive to Indonesians or Russians as to Americans). The powerful assimilatory influences of American society operate on all who come into it, making the children of immigrants and even immigrants themselves a very different people from those they left behind. In what sense, then, can we put immigrants, their children, their grandchildren, and even further descendants into one group and speak of, for example, "the" Irish? Must we not speak of the middle-class Irish and the working-class Irish, the big-city Irish and the small-town Irish, the recent immigrants and the second and third and fourth generation, the Democrats and the Republicans; and when we do, is there any content left to the group name?

Perhaps the meaning of ethnic labels will yet be erased in America. But it has not yet worked out this way in New York. It is true that immigrants to this country were rapidly transformed, in comparison with immigrants to other countries, that they lost their language and altered their culture. It was reasonable to believe that a new American type would emerge, a new nationality in which it would be a matter of indifference whether a man was of Anglo-Saxon or German or Italian or Jewish origin, and in which indeed, because of the diffusion of populations through all parts of the country and all levels of the social order, and because of the consequent close contact and intermarriage, it would be impossible to make such distinctions. This may still be the most likely result in the long run. After all, in 1960 almost half of New York City's population was still foreign-born or the children of foreign-born. Yet it is also true that it is forty years since the end of mass immigration, and new processes, scarcely visible when our chief concern was with the great masses of immigrants and the problems of their "Americanization," now emerge to surprise us. The initial notion of an American melting pot did not, it seems, quite grasp what would happen in America. At least it did not grasp what would happen in the short run, and since this short run encompasses at least the length of a normal lifetime, it is not something we can ignore. . . .

America's Emergence as a World Power: The Myth and the Verity

Thomas A. Bailey

In the interest of forging a measure of order out of chaos, of organizing thinking on a particular subject, the intellectual community
—historians included—often formulates labels, categories, and
"periods." Although such generalizations always imply definite intellectual reservations, to those less familiar with their usage, they convey the sense of certitude and fact. Thomas A. Bailey, diplomatic
historian at Stanford, advances the controversial interpretation that
our "organized" thinking on the date of America's emergence as a
"world power" has been largely mistaken. Bailey notes the "formidable phalanx of error" that has led us to date America's assumption of world leadership at 1898. With a convincing array of evidence
Professor Bailey suggests July 2, 1776 as a more accurate date.

Every American schoolboy knows—or would know if he bothered to read
his textbook—that the United States did not become a world power until
1898. Commodore Dewey, according to the traditional tale, staged our
memorable coming-out party at Manila Bay on May Day of that year. At
the risk of arousing the United Spanish War Veterans, I venture to take
issue with this melodramatic interpretation and to suggest that the United
States became a world power 122 years earlier, on the day of its official birth,
July 2—not July 4—1776.

I have collected the titles or subtitles of more than a dozen books that
associate America's so-called spectacular eruption with the era of the Spanish-
American War. This formidable phalanx of error does not include the scores
of chapter titles or subtitles or magazine articles that reaffirm the May Day
myth. I shall not name names, lest I redden the faces of certain scholars
present, while magnifying my own sin. The embarrassing truth is that for
eighteen years I further misled the youth of this land with a chapter title
which I have since then unobtrusively corrected.

I cannot exculpate myself completely by pleading that at a tender age
I was misled by my elders and betters, or that I later erred in distinguished
company. By the time I became a graduate student I should have realized
that cataclysmic changes, especially in the power position of a nation, seldom
or never occur overnight. I should also have known that the very first

From "America as a World Power: The Myth and the Verity," by Thomas A.
Bailey. © 1961 by the Pacific Coast Branch, American Historical Association.
Reprinted from *Pacific Historical Review*, Volume 30, Number 1, pp. 1–16, by
permission of the Branch and the author.

obligation of the scholar is to examine critically all basic assumptions—the more basic the more critically. The majority is often wrong, and repetition does not make things so.

The pitfalls of periodization have no doubt contributed richly to our misunderstanding. Watershed dates like 1898 are useful as pedagogical landmarks, and although the careful historian has mental reservations while using them, the rote-minded student is likely to accept them as gospel.

More misleading is the singular indifference of many scholars to precision in terminology. Unabridged lexicons exist for standardizing the language, and we historians would do well to thumb them occasionally. The least unsatisfactory definition of a "world power" that I have uncovered is given by Webster as follows: "A state or organization powerful enough to affect world politics by its influence or actions." This concept is obviously too broad, and I therefore propose to narrow it to exclude "nuisance value" power, such as that exerted by Serbia in 1914. My rewriting reads: "A nation with sufficient power in being, or capable of being mobilized, to affect world politics positively and over a period of time."[1] The term "great power," as distinguished from the less exalted "world power," will be considered later.

Did the United States in 1776 measure up to the world-power formula that I have just propounded? The answer, in my judgment, is an emphatic affirmative.

First of all, what are the components of national power? I have made up a detailed list of about one hundred items, major and minor, tangible and intangible, but I shall not inflict them all on you. Let us examine a few of the more noteworthy with reference to the United States during the era of the American Revolution.

In territory, we exceeded all the European states, except Russia. In population, we outranked many of the European nations, and possibly excelled them all in birth rate. In quality of population, we could boast what was perhaps the most literate people in the world, and certainly one of the more ingenious. In moral force we were from the outset probably the most influential power of all—the lodestar of liberals and the mecca of the masses. In statecraft and diplomacy we could point pridefully to Franklin, Washington, Adams, Jay, and Jefferson, to name only a corporal's guard of the Founding Fathers. In military strength we could muster adequate militia for defense, though shunning large professional armies. In the capacity to attract allies we could offer economic concessions and diversionary or additive military strength. In richness of soil, salubrity of climate, abundance of natural resources, and general self-sufficiency we were almost certainly the most blessed of all peoples.

Finally, in merchant shipping we were from the beginning a leader, ranking in the same top bracket with Britain, France, Spain, and Holland. In the days of the windjammer and smoothbore cannon an amphibious nation could so easily improvise a navy that a great maritime power could hardly escape being a world power.[2] Privateers played a devastating role in our two wars with Britain, and although we lost about as many ships as we captured, we bloodied our enemy's nose while getting our own bloodied. The menace of more privateers gave Downing Street nightmares during every Anglo-American crisis of the nineteenth century.

The power position of the United States, already formidable, was immensely strengthened by six fortunate circumstances. First, we had between us and Europe the watery vastness of the Atlantic Ocean—America's greatest liquid asset. Second, we had defense in depth, as the footsore British redcoats learned to their dismay in two frustrating wars. Third, we had the precarious European balance of power, which caused our potential adversaries to fear the dagger thrust of an envious neighbor. Fourth, we had an imbalance of power in the Americas, with the United States enjoying the top-dog position from the outset, and with our weak neighbors dreading us rather than our people dreading them. Fifth, we had Canada under the muzzles of our muskets, as a hostage unwittingly given to us by the British for their good behavior. Finally, we had mountainous surpluses of foodstuffs, cotton, and other raw materials, upon which our most redoubtable diplomatic rivals, notably Britain, developed a dangerous dependence. Every time the British faced up to the prospect of again fighting the Yankees, they had to reckon with the sobering consequences of cutting their own economic throats. All this adds up to the conclusion that from its birth the United States has been incomparably the luckiest of all the great nations—so far.

I have said that the United Colonies became a world power in July, 1776, when the Continental Congress solemnly severed the umbilical cord. I might start even earlier and assert that in a broad sense we had become a power before we became a nation.[3] Charles and Mary Beard dated America's birth as a "world power" from Edmund Burke's masterly speech of 1775 on conciliation—an appeal in which the orator revealed that the resources of the colonies were so boundless as to render them unconquerable.[4] I do not accept this particular date, primarily because Burke's views did not prevail with Parliament, and because his speech neither added to nor subtracted from our power potential.

But America's strength was already considerable by 1775. Her trade, as Burke revealed, was nearly equal to that of England's with the entire world in 1700. Her manufacturing, despite the frowns of the Mother Country, was prospering; in fact, her iron foundries, though smaller, were more numerous than those of England. Her economic coercive power was such as to force Parliament to repeal the detested Stamp Act in 1766. Her nautical biceps were bulging. Benjamin Franklin noted that the total tonnage, gunnage, and manpower of the colonial privateering fleets in the war with France ending in 1748 equaled the entire English navy which had defeated the Spanish Armada in 1588.

In manpower and military strength—the conventional criteria of world power—the homespun colonials were far from contemptible. Thomas Paine, referring in *Common Sense* (1776) to the veterans of the recent French and Indian War, numbering about 25,000, could state with some exaggeration that we had "the largest body of armed and disciplined men of any power under Heaven." After Lexington, Washington commanded an army of some 20,000 men that trapped the British in Boston and finally ejected them. In the winter of 1775–1776, some seven months before independence, the brash Americans, not content with purely defensive operations against the world's greatest power, launched a two-pronged invasion of Canada which narrowly missed capturing the Fourteenth Colony.

In my view the most satisfying date for emergence is July, 1776, when the United States proclaimed a clean break with Britain. The Founding Fathers themselves believed that they were launching a new world power on the turbulent sea of international politics. The proud preamble of the Declaration of Independence proclaimed an intention "to assume among the Powers of the earth the separate and *equal* station to which the Laws of Nature and of Nature's God entitle them." John Adams, who quarreled in Paris with Foreign Minister Vergennes, informed him in 1780, "The United States of America are a great and powerful people, whatever European statesmen may think of them."[5]

But actions speak louder than verbs. The strength of the upstart colonials was so apparent that France, seeking to redress the world balance of power, undertook to wean them away from their imperial apron strings and embrace them as allies. This move, the French reasoned, would have a double-barreled impact. It would not only add to the strength of France but it would subtract correspondingly from that of Britain. The French consequently provided secret aid for about three years, and in 1778 finally came out into the open with twin treaties of alliance and commerce. One of the most striking features of these pacts was that in tone and terminology they implied an agreement between two equal and long-established powers.

The British, unwilling to lose their most prized overseas possessions, had countered belatedly with an offer of home rule. The two most powerful nations of the world were thus openly bidding for the favor of the robust young republic. The anxiety of both rivals indicates that America's strength was regarded as sufficient to tip the balance.

But the embattled British, outbid in 1778, turned the tables in 1782. Fighting desperately against a fearsome coalition, they in effect seduced America from the French alliance—a counter-seduction if you will—by offering incredibly generous terms of peace. These concessions were both the measure of Britain's desperation and of America's substantial weight in the world balance of power.

Yet many historians, awed by the magnitude of open French aid, are apt to downgrade the basic strength of the Americans. The truth is that the ex-colonials carried the burden of battle alone for three years—and against two nations. So tough was the colonial nut that the British were forced to seek assistance abroad, and in hiring some 30,000 so-called Hessians made what amounted to a military alliance with a second power. American privateers, whitening the seas, established a partial blockade of the British Isles during the three years before France threw off the mask of neutrality. After Lexington, the raw colonials pinned down tens of thousands of British troops, and in 1777, at Saratoga, compelled the surrender of the largest force that Britain had yet yielded to a foreign foe.

I would be the last to discount the French role during the American Revolution, especially secret aid and the naval contribution at Yorktown. But the United States could conceivably have won its independence without open assistance from France. After the signing of the alliance of 1778, a kind of let-François-do-it attitude began to prevail, and American enlistments declined in a ratio roughly corresponding to the size of the French expeditionary forces. If we gained from the alliance, so did the French. If they had not calculated that we would be of about as much value to them as they would be to us, they almost certainly would not have struck the perilous bargain.

More than a century later, when the Philippines fell as a gift from Heaven—or was it Heaven?—American imperialists insisted that we had to keep the islands to prove that we were a world power. To this argument the anti-imperialist Carl Schurz replied early in 1899: "Well, we *are* a world power now, and have been for many years."[6] William Jennings Bryan, in his acceptance speech of 1900, was more specific: "The forcible annexation of the Philippine Islands is not necessary to make the United States a world power. For over ten decades our Nation has been a world power."[7] But both Schurz and Bryan, the one a professional calamity howler and the other a hardy quadrennial, were voices crying in the cornfields.

Of different stature was Professor A. B. Hart of Harvard, who published a challenging article in *Harper's Magazine* in February, 1899.[8] He cogently argued that the United States had been a world power from 1776 on, and he may have conveyed this notion dimly to Bryan. But the idea apparently wilted in the feverish imperialistic atmosphere of the era, and Professor Hart himself evidently weakened in the faith. In 1907, eight years later, he edited as one of the volumes of the *American Nation Series* a contribution by Professor John H. Latané, entitled, *America as a World Power, 1897–1907*. Professor Latané himself declared cautiously (p. 318) that "the United States has always been a world power *in a sense*." He then went on to discuss our influence in shaping civil liberties and international law the world over.[9] But Professor Hart is the only spokesman whom I have found, historian or layman, who unreservedly dates our birth as a world power from the declaring of independence.

Try as I may, I cannot escape the unflattering conclusion that we historians are largely responsible for the perpetuation of the Manila Bay hallucination. Certainly the Fourth of July orator never doubted for one moment that we were not only the greatest power of all time from the very beginning, but had twice whipped the next greatest power.[10] How did the trained scholar —the professional custodian of our traditions—get so far off the track?

First of all, we historians have been unduly swayed by the smallness of our army and navy.[11] We tend to judge national power by the size of armed forces *in being*. Until the present century the United States relied heavily on land militia and sea militia, and although amateurs rarely do as well as professionals, we somehow managed to muddle through with a minimum of disaster. Huge military establishments, contrary to popular fancy, are a source of weakness rather than of strength. They reduce productive employment, burden the taxpayer, and unless assembled for blatantly aggressive purposes, are an almost infallible symptom of insecurity and fear.

The United States was the only first-rate nation that until recent times could afford the luxury of a third-rate army. In 1812 Madison invaded Canada with some 6,000 men; simultaneously Napoleon invaded Russia with some 600,000 men. The erroneous assumption is that France was one hundred times stronger than the United States. The fact is that we may not have had much of an army but what we had we had here, and Napoleon was powerless to come to grips with us. He was more than one hundred times stronger than we were in Europe, but we were stronger than he was in America.[12]

A two-way provincialism thus continues to curse American historiography. If American historians are too America-centered, many European historians are too Europe-centered. A true perspective lies between these extremes.

Certain historians have also misinterpreted our early isolationism. We did not want to become one of the great powers of Europe, not so much because we were weak as because we thought it prudent to take full advantage of our unique geographical location and our phenomenal fecundity. Lord Castlereagh was quoted as saying that the fortunate Americans won their victories not on the battle field but in the bedchamber. Certainly to play for time, to avoid unnecessary entanglements, to fatten as feeders while the Europeans famished as fighters—all this was statesmanship rather than timidity.[13]

The Monroe Doctrine has further muddied the waters. Some writers have hailed it as a virtual alliance with England, which it emphatically was not—quite the reverse.[14] In 1823 the British and the Americans, both intent on keeping inviolate the newly opened trade of Latin America, were pursuing a parallel policy. This meant that the mighty British navy, yardarm-to-yardarm with the modest American navy, was prepared to thwart possible intervention by the so-called Holy Alliance. The legend has therefore taken root that the Monroe Doctrine was upheld by the British navy throughout the nineteenth century and beyond. We thus have a mental image of the Yankee cringing behind the oaken petticoats of the Mother Country—a posture that hardly suggests world power.

The disillusioning truth is that the British navy upheld the Monroe Doctrine only when the policies of Downing Street and Washington ran parallel, as they definitely did not during much of the nineteenth century. The sacred dictum of Monroe was flouted—or allegedly flouted—a score or so of times before 1904; and the British were involved in many of these infractions, either actively or passively. Beyond a doubt, the Royal Navy could have hamstrung or halted all such encroachments, had it been the protector-in-chief of the Monroe Doctrine. And as far as defending the United States was concerned, during the dozen or so Anglo-American crises between 1823 and 1898, we rightly regarded the British navy as our most formidable single adversary.[15]

Still another source of misunderstanding was the alleged absence of a far-flung American colonial empire until 1898. An authentic world power seemingly had to be burdened with overseas liabilities, as well as huge armies, navies, and national debts. The point is often missed that during the nineteenth century the United States practiced internal colonialism and imperialism on a continental scale. When the Western European nations expanded, they had to go overseas; when we expanded, we had to go west.[16] We self-righteously preened ourselves on not becoming an imperialistic power until 1898, when we acquired Spanish real estate in the Philippines, Guam, and Puerto Rico. Yet hundreds of Spanish place names pepper the land from California to Texas, all of which, curiously enough, somehow managed to come under our nonimperialistic flag a half century earlier. As for the claim that the Philippines added to our national strength, the troublesome islands proved to be a perennial liability—militarily, economically, politically, and morally.

Another misleading cliché of the nineteenth century was that the United States, though still a lusty adolescent, loomed as *the* great power of the future. British editors condescendingly conceded that in the fullness of time —and thanks largely to our British blood and breeding—we would arrive.[17] Long after we had indubitably "arrived," the misleading habit persisted of referring cheerfully to America as the nation of the future.

Additional confusion came from British travelers and others who harped on the youthfulness of America. We started as the youngest of modern republics, and we revealed a boyishness of spirit as we proceeded to crystallize our dreams into realities. But as the nineteenth century lengthened, as dozens of new nations sprang into existence, and as we developed a continental spread, critics continued to comment on our youth. Oscar Wilde, writing in 1893, had one of his characters quip, "The youth of America is their oldest tradition. It has been going on now for three hundred years." The juvenile behavior of some Americans, especially when abroad, still gives support to this illusion.

A false estimate of our power position has also contributed lushly to the legend of 1898. I have already said that the United States, from the very day of its legal birth, was the strongest nation in the Western Hemisphere—a basic fact often overlooked.[18] In the pubescent period of the republic, France, Britain, Russia, Prussia, Austria, Spain—to name no others—could all marshall larger armed forces *in Europe*, but not effectively against us. As for the other sister republics of the Americas, the epithet "Colossus of the North" carries its own melancholy implications.

The United States from the outset was a European power—on those infrequent occasions when it chose to exert its power in Europe.[19] The panic-inspiring raids of John Paul Jones on the British coasts, to say nothing of the ravages of American privateers in British waters during two Anglo-American wars, are twice-told tales. Less familiar was the damaging effect of the American Embargo Act and the Non-intercourse Act, which together forced the British to suspend their infuriating orders in council before we declared war on them in 1812. The simple fact is that in the years before the Civil War the coercive power of King Cotton on British textile manufacturers was so potent that in an economic sense alone America was a world power.

The United States was also an African power in the nineteenth century, when it chose to be one. Most Americans have forgotten, if they ever knew, that William Eaton, the incredible Connecticut Yankee, led a motley army of some 500 men across the desert from Egypt to Tripoli and captured Derne in 1805. Most Americans have forgotten, if they ever knew, that the United States was the nation that chastised the cutthroats of Morocco, Algiers, Tunis, and Tripoli in naval campaigns extending from 1801 to 1815. Most Americans have forgotten, if they ever knew, that the United States launched Liberia in the 1820's, and in 1884, following the spectacular explorations of the American journalist Henry M. Stanley, joined the other great powers by invitation at the Berlin Conference on the Congo.

The United States was a Far Eastern power in the nineteenth century— fifty years or so before our ill-informed expansionists clamored for the Philippines so as to make America an active force in the Eastern Hemisphere. It was Commodore Perry, who with seven warships and the velvet glove, forced open the bamboo portals of Japan in 1854. It was "Blood-is-thicker-than-water" Tattnall who went to the rescue of the British off the Chinese forts in 1859. It was an American warship, in the midst of our own Civil War, that helped punish the Japanese feudal lord at Shimonoseki in 1864. It was a fleet of five American warships that demolished five Korean forts and killed some two hundred Koreans in 1871. And it was Commodore Shufeldt who initiated our diplomatic relations with Korea in 1882.[20] On the other side of Asia, it was an American man-of-war in Turkish waters that forced an Austrian warship to release the Hungarian refugee Martin Koszta in 1853. Nor does this catalogue take into account the moral influence of America through educational and missionary establishments, ranging all the way from the missions of China and Japan to Robert College at Constantinople.

In short, critics have often failed to recognize our three-ply policies in the nineteenth century: voluntary abstentionism, as a rule, in Europe; unilateral intervention in the Americas and Africa; and unilateral or joint-power intervention in the Far East. One reason for associating our advent as a world power with 1898 is the popular but erroneous assumption that the acquisition of the Philippines marked a complete break with the past. We are told that hitherto we had shunned colonizing (which is untrue), that we had formerly been isolated (which is untrue), and that thereafter we were internationalist (which is also untrue).

The May Day misconception can further be traced to the testimony of contemporary Americans and Britons—our esteemed primary sources. In 1898 a number of editors, further proving that propinquity often dulls perception, hailed America's sudden and sensational advent as a world power.[21] Americans are notoriously afflicted with "hurryupitis," and the concept of emerging in a hurry chimed in with the national psychology. President McKinley himself remarked in 1899 that "in a few short months we have become a world power."[22] But let us bear in mind that McKinley, to put it charitably, was slightly confused. Ex-President Benjamin Harrison, writing in 1901, and thinking of our unchallenged primacy in the Americas, declared that before 1898 we had been half a world power—as though world power could be divided and compartmented.[23]

If my reasoning is sound, the United States became a world power in 1776 and has never fallen below that exalted status, except for the six-year hiatus of the so-called Critical Period following the Revolution. A nation that was militarily impotent, diplomatically despised, financially bankrupt, and politically fragmented ceased to be a power, much less a world power. We almost ceased to be a nation, for British and Spanish forces held or controlled about one half of our territory. The Constitution of 1787 was in part designed —and successfully so—to restore and strengthen American prestige.[24]

The next question is: When did we step up a rung and become a great power? Webster, apparently the only lexicographer to spell out this distinction, defines the great powers as "The most powerful nations of the world, especially in political influence, resources, and military and naval strength." The "Great Powers of Europe," as the pat phrase went, formed a kind of exclusive club, and by the 1890's included Britain, France, Russia, Germany, Italy, and Austria-Hungary. When did the United States deserve the status of a great power in its own right, rather than as an influential counterweight in the world balance?

A possible date is 1803, when we dramatically doubled our original birthright by the windfall of Louisiana. "From this day," exulted Minister Livingston in Paris, "the United States take their place among the powers of the *first* rank.[25] But this self-congratulatory assessment seems unduly optimistic.

I likewise reject the miserable little War of 1812, from which we were lucky to escape with a relatively whole skin. Yet forty-seven years ago the historian Charles Francis Adams, Jr., published an article strangely entitled: "Wednesday, August 19, 1812, 6:30 P.M.: The Birth of a World Power."[26] He referred, of course, to the first frigate duel of the War of 1812, in which "Old Ironsides" partially restored American self-esteem by smashing the aged and overmatched *Guerrière*. But the tiny United States Navy, despite heroic individual efforts on the high seas, was ultimately wiped out. The Americans did manage to win a grudging degree of diplomatic and naval respect, particularly for their postwar chastisement of the Barbary states, yet on balance the War of 1812 added little, if anything, to our overall strength.

I also reject the enunciation of the Monroe Doctrine, which likewise added nothing substantial to our national power. Much as it tickled our own fancy in 1823, it annoyed rather than alarmed Europeans. In their eyes, we seemed to be shaking our fists behind the stout wooden walls of the British navy.

A good case can be made out for the Mexican War as marking the emergence of the United States as a great power—and an imperialistic power at that. We impressed European skeptics, but we impressed ourselves even more. Henry David Thoreau ceased communion with the woodchucks long enough to mention in *Walden* the current discussion of America's being "a first rate power."[27] In an imperialistic coup worthy of the Romans, we sheared away one-half of Mexico, assumed sway over thousands of Spanish-speaking peoples, added one-third again to our continental domain, won a panoramic Pacific frontage, and further validated our claims to being both a Pacific and a Far Eastern power. While still one month deep in the war with Mexico, we stared the British down over the issue of the Oregon boundary, and forced them to yield the disputed triangle north of the Columbia River. This in itself was no mean feat, especially when one considers the booming broadsides of the British navy. But again the European balance of power and the might of the rival French fleet strengthened our hand.[28]

The end of the Civil War, in my judgment, marks the arrival of the United States as a great power. We were now the third most populous white nation, ranking behind only Russia and France. We had achieved peaceful coexistence among the sections by the greatest constitutional decision of them all: that handed down by Grant at Appomattox Court House. We had washed away the moral incubus of slavery in a bath of blood. We had attained a staggering agricultural productivity, while our smokestacks ranked second only to Britain's. We had an immense navy of about 500 ships, with numerous ironclads, and we boasted the largest standing army in the world—a battle-singed army at that. When Secretary of State Seward demanded that the French clear out of Mexico, he spoke with the voice of one million bayonets—and Napoleon III, for reasons both foreign and domestic, took French leave of his ill-starred puppet Maximilian.

The Civil War had presented both Britain and France with the opportunity of the century. They had long distrusted our explosive power in this hemisphere, they had since 1783 pursued a policy of containment, and they had prayed for the day when they could engage in the hoary game of divide and dominate. But such was the strength of the United States—even a disunited United States locked in the throes of fratricidal conflict—that the two greatest powers of Europe, individually and collectively, shrank from the bloody consequences of armed intervention.[29]

After the Civil War, America turned inward. The navy fell prey to worms and decay. Not until the end of the century did we have a modern steel fleet that had forged into about sixth place.[30] The standing army had dwindled to some 28,000 men by 1890, and ranked about thirteenth, below the armies of Belgium, Bulgaria, and Sweden. The usual over-reliance of Europe-centered scholars on military force recently prompted a gifted young diplomatic historian to write for the Voice of America, "Before 1890 the United States was at most a second-rate power."[31]

Let us take a hard look at this "second-rate power" in the eight or so years before the Spanish-American War. By 1890 we were the number two white nation in population, still trying to catch up with the Russians. We had bounded into first place in total manufacturing, including top rank in iron and steel—the standard indices of military potential. In addition, we held either first or second place in railroads, telegraphs, telephones, merchant marine, and in the production of cattle, coal, gold, copper, lead, petroleum, cotton, corn, wheat, and rye. The armies and navies were not there, but we had the means of creating them when we needed them—and did.

The diplomatic box score is most revealing. In a series of breathtaking crises, we forced our adversaries—three of them "great powers"—to come to terms or knuckle under: Germany over the Samoa scramble in 1889; Italy over the New Orleans lynching bee of 1891; Chile over the *Baltimore* brawl in 1891; Britain over the Venezuela boundary imbroglio in 1896.[32] Spain capitulated diplomatically over Cuba in 1898, but we picked a fight with her anyhow and forced her to capitulate militarily.

The flash of Dewey's guns merely spotlighted a maturation that had long since taken place. The irony is that we finally won belated acceptance into the great power "club" by thrashing a second-rate power in two naval engagements that cost us only one life.[33]

I fear that some critics will regard my remarks this evening as academic hairsplitting. Power, world power, great power, superpower—what difference does it all make?

First of all, a failure to read and heed our history contributed to our costly overseas aberration in 1898. If enough of our historians—and their former students—had been able to say at the time that we had been a world power since 1776, that we had always been a colonizing nation, and that we did not have to wallow in the cesspool of overseas imperialism to prove our stature, we might have spared ourselves the tribulations of keeping up with the imperialistic Joneses.

A misreading of our history likewise accelerated the deadly isolationist drift of the 1920's and 1930's. With uncharacteristic modesty, we Americans confessed that we were greenhorns at the poker table of world politics. We were content to let the white-spatted British and French, old hands at the diplomatic game, breathe life into the stillborn League of Nations. If we had only realized how long, and in what varied areas, we had in fact been a great power, we probably would have been more willing to play a role commensurate with our monstrous strength.

A further misreading of our history has caused us to forget that national power is moral as well as physical. In the formative years of the republic, the three most feared "isms" in the world were probably American republicanism, constitutionalism, and liberalism. They no longer are. Unless we can rekindle some of the dynamic faith in our democracy that we displayed in the nineteenth century, our adversaries will bury us.

Finally, many Americans—including some in high places—evidently have not examined our past with sufficient care to appreciate the extent to which national power is relative. In 1789 we were absolutely weak but relatively strong. Today we are absolutely strong but relatively vulnerable. We can blow up more people than ever before, yet we were never in such mortal danger of annihilation. If we are a supercolossal power under these terrifying conditions, one can hardly avoid a degree of nostalgic respect for the United States of 1776. We were then only a newcomer in the family of nations, but we were, I submit, a world power, and within less than a century we were destined to become a great power.

Notes

1. The *New Standard Dictionary of the English Language* (Funk and Wagnalls) defines a world power as "A state whose policy and action are of world-wide influence or concern." Professor A. C. Coolidge defined the world powers in 1908 as "powers which are directly interested in all parts of the world and whose voices must be listened to everywhere." *The United States as a World Power* (New York, 1908), 7. A literal application of this definition would have disqualified all nations.
2. President John Adams told Congress in 1797, on the eve of the crisis with France: "However we may consider ourselves, the maritime and commercial powers of the world will consider the United States of America as forming a weight in that balance of power in Europe which never can be forgotten or

neglected." J. D. Richardson, comp., *Messages and Papers of the Presidents* (Washington, 1896), I, 238.

3. Colonial military and naval contributions in the Seven Years' War indirectly affected the fall of both India and the Philippines to the British.

4. Charles A. and Mary R. Beard, *History of the United States* (New York, 1921), 477. The Beards asserted that the United States (even during the Critical Period) was continuously a world power from March, 1775, "to the settlement at Versailles in 1919." The curious implication is that the United States ceased to be a world power after 1919.

5. The passage continues: "If we take into our estimate the numbers and the character of her people, the extent, variety, and fertility of her soil, her commerce, and her skill and materials for ship-building, and her seamen, excepting France, Spain, England, Germany [?] and Russia, there is not a state in Europe so powerful." C. F. Adams, ed., *The Works of John Adams* (Boston, 1852), VII, 226–227 (July 13, 1780).

6. Carl Schurz, *American Imperialism* (n.p., 1899), 28.

7. W. J. Bryan, ed., *Speeches of William Jennings Bryan* (New York, 1909), II, 14.

8. Later published in expanded form as chap. 1 of A. B. Hart, *The Foundations of American Foreign Policy* (New York, 1901).

9. Italics inserted. Seth Low, former president of Columbia University, wrote two years earlier with similar qualifications: "From the beginning of its history the United States has been a world power, *in the sense* that it has profoundly affected the movements of thought and of action outside of itself." He refers to our influence on the French Revolution, our stand for neutral rights and arbitration, our example of fair dealing with neighbors, our reception of immigrants, and our contributions to education. *Annals of the American Academy of Political and Social Science*, XXVI (1905), 6. Italics inserted.

10. Col. A. L. Snowden, in an Independence Day address delivered in 1895 before Independence Hall, attributed American superiority largely to a superior national character. "The Foremost Nation of the World." *American Historical Register*, III (1895), 65–70.

11. Even so acute an observer as James Bryce, writing in 1901, could refer to the United States in 1834 as follows: "Already a great nation, it could become a great power as soon as it cared to spend money on fleets and armies." James Bryce, *Studies in History and Jurisprudence* (Oxford, 1901), I, 395. An unwillingness to recognize the power position of the United States did not negate that power, as Mexico learned to her sorrow in the war of 1846–1848.

12. Such a concept inspired this piece of extravagance in a speech by young Abraham Lincoln in 1838: "Shall we expect some transatlantic military giant to step the Ocean and crush us at a blow? Never! All the armies of Europe, Asia and Africa combined, with all the treasure of the earth (our own excepted) in their military chest; with a Buonaparte for a commander, could not by force, take a drink from the Ohio, or make a track on the Blue Ridge, in a trial of a thousand years." R. P. Basler, ed., *The Collected Works of Abraham Lincoln* (New Brunswick, 1953), I, 109.

13. Washington's Farewell Address, in urging the desirability of staying out of European embroilments, tended to overemphasize the weakness of the United States.

14. See Walter Lippmann, *U. S. Foreign Policy: Shield of the Republic* (Boston, 1943), 16–22, for a full statement of the legend. Secretary Adams' famous remark about a "cockboat" coming in "in the wake of the British man-of-war" was obviously designed to stress not so much our weakness as the

desirability of pursuing an independent course. C. F. Adams, ed., *Memoirs of John Quincy Adams* (Philadelphia, 1875), VI, 179.

15. On this point see Theodore Roosevelt's remarkable letter of November 30, 1918, in E. F. Morison, ed., *The Letters of Theodore Roosevelt* (Cambridge, 1954), VIII, 1407–1409. A writer in the Manchester *Guardian Weekly* recently stated that "American security was, in fact, a by-product of the strength of the British fleet." LXXXII, 10 (June 30, 1960). It is true that Britain helped preserve the balance of power in Europe, to our incidental advantage, but if there had been no British navy, the balance would presumably have been redressed by other navies, or by a stronger American navy. Similarly, if there had been no United States navy to back the Monroe Doctrine, the Latin American republics would have had to maintain larger navies.

16. Tariffs to protect our domestic market were in some degree the equivalent of European imperialism for establishing overseas markets. Both American tariffs and European imperialism affected foreign peoples adversely.

17. For examples of British opinion see *Scots Magazine*, LXXVII (1815), 63; *Edinburgh Review*, XXIV (1814), 262; *ibid.*, LXXXVI (1847), 395–396. Whig, rather than Tory, journals were disposed to play up the actual or potential power of the United States. See Richard S. Cramer, "British Magazines and the United States, 1815–1848" (unpublished doctoral dissertation, Stanford University). In 1765, eleven years before independence, the London *Gazette* remarked: "Little doubt can be entertained that America will in time be the greatest and most prosperous empire that perhaps the world has ever seen." Quoted in Hart, *Foundations of American Foreign Policy*, 12.

18. In 1856 a writer in *Blackwood's Edinburgh Magazine* thus described the United States: "The dominant power of the New World, and with three thousand miles of sea separating it from the great military states of Europe, the Union has found on its own continent no power which unaided can check its aggressions, and as yet no European state but Great Britain has had either an interest or the power to enter the lists against it." LXXX (1856), 116-117.

19. The Czar of Russia thought well enough of the United States to invite it to join the Holy Alliance in 1819.

20. As far as the nineteenth century as a whole was concerned, Britain, and possibly Russia and France, were the only powers that exerted more influence than the United States in the Far East. Germany, Italy, and Austria-Hungary, the other three great powers of Europe, certainly exerted less.

21. See *Public Opinions* XXIV, 580 (May 12, 1898); *ibid.*, 615 (May 19, 1898); *Westminster Review*, CL (1898), 168; *Nineteenth Century*, XLIV (1898), 194. A British comment ran: "Unless all signs deceive, the American Republic breaks from her old moorings, and sails out to be a 'world power'." *Blackwood's Edinburgh Magazine*, CLXIII (1898), 703.

22. Cortelyou's Diary, Aug. 17, 1899, quoted in Margaret Leech, *In the Days of McKinley*, (New York, 1959), 464.

23. *North American Review*, CLXXII (1901), 177–190.

24. Modern scholarship has undertaken to show that domestic conditions under the Articles of Confederation were not so bad as traditionally pictured, but the nation's posture in foreign affairs was still weak.

25. François Barbé-Marbois, *The History of Louisiana* (Philadelphia, 1830), 310–311. Italics inserted.

26. *American Historical Review*, XVIII (1913), 513–521. Adams, oddly enough, refers to the United States in 1812 as "a power of the third class," ranking below Portugal and "more nearly on the level of Algiers" (p. 514).

27. Henry David Thoreau, *Walden* (Mt. Vernon, N. Y., [1956]), 317. The British scientist Alexander Mackay wrote in 1850 of the United States as being in "the first rank amongst the powers of the earth." *The Western World, or, Travels in the United States in 1846–1847* (London, 1849), II, 284. A British consul in Japan in the late 1850's informed the Japanese that "there were five great nations, viz. France, the Germanic Confederation, Great Britain, Russia, and the United States." C. P. Hodgson, *A Residence at Nagasaki and Hakodate in 1859–1860* (London, 1861), 308.

28. British statesmen feared that hostilities with America might prompt the French, whose new steam navy was about as strong as Britain's, to invade England with a powerful steamer-borne army. John S. Galbraith, "France as a Factor in the Oregon Negotiations," *Pacific Northwest Quarterly*, XLIV (1953), 69–73.

29. A writer in the London *Spectator* (March 16, 1861) conceded that the North alone would have enough strength left to "be entitled to rank as a first-class power." XXXIV, 273. Richard Cobden wrote to Charles Sumner in March, 1865, that it was "nothing but your great *power* that has kept the hands of Europe off you." *American Historical Review*, II (1897), 318. The *Spectator* declared in February, 1866, "Nobody doubts any more that the Union is a power of the first class, a nation which it is very dangerous to offend and almost impossible to attack." XXXIX, 177. The same journal conceded in February, 1869, that America was "the greatest power in the whole world." *Ibid.*, XLII, 250. Ignorance of such facts prompted the German General Friedrich von Bernhardi to condemn Britain's "unpardonable blunder" in not supporting the South. *Germany and the Next War* (trans. by A. H. Powles, London, 1914), 94.

30. Such estimates can be only approximations, owing to differences in types of ships, guns, armor, crews, bases, and other factors. Many European warships were built for short-range operations, and consequently lacked the bunker capacity to cross the Atlantic and engage the American navy.

31. Program of October 15, 1959. Ex-Secretary of State Richard Olney, writing in the *Atlantic Monthly* of May, 1898 (and presumably shortly before Dewey's victory), declared "The United States is certainly now entitled to rank among the great Powers of the world." LXXXI, 578.

32. As early as 1879 the London *Saturday Review* had referred to the United States as "A power of the first rank." XLVIII (1879), 226. Five years later it bracketed America with "all other great Powers." *Ibid.*, LVII (1884), 333. See also the *Nineteenth Century*, XXI (1887), 799; *Spectator*, LXVII (1889), 532; *Westminster Review*, CXXXI (1889), 508; *Public Opinion*, VII, 229 (June 22, 1889). For an unfavorable view of America's power position, see *Nineteenth Century*, XXXIX (1896), 906–913.

33. In 1909 Professor F. A. Ogg discerned three schools of thought: (1) we had always been a world power, (2) we became a world power with the Spanish-American War, (3) we had never become a world power. *Dial*, XLVI (1909), 44. Some scholars, mostly European, or Europe-centered, would not accord the United States great-power status until 1917–1918, if then. They have been misled by the reluctance of American isolationist elements to face up to the responsibilities of world leadership.

Suggested Further Reading for Chapter 2

James A. Barnes, "Myths of the Bryan Campaign," *The Mississippi Valley Historical Review*, 34 (1947).

Thomas C. Cochran, "The Legend of the Robber Barons," *Pennsylvania Magazine of History and Biography*, 74 (1950).

Henry Steele Commager, *The American Mind* (New Haven: Yale University Press, 1950).

Ruth M. Elson, *Guardians of Tradition: American Schoolbooks in the Nineteenth Century* (Lincoln, Neb.: University of Nebraska Press, 1964).

John K. Fairbank, " 'American China Policy' to 1898: A Misconception," *Pacific Historical Review*, 39 (1970).

Joe B. Frantz and Julian E. Choate, *The American Cowboy: The Myth and Reality* (Norman, Okla.: University of Oklahoma Press, 1955).

Robert S. Henry, "The Railroad Land-Grant Legend in American History Texts," *The Mississippi Valley Historical Review*, 32 (1945).

Grady McWhiney and Francis Simkins, "The Ghostly Legend of the KKK," *Negro History Bulletin*, 14 (1951).

Norman Pollack, "The Myth of Populist Anti-Semitism," *American Historical Review*, 68 (1962).

Peter J. Schmitt, *Back to Nature: The Arcadian Myth in Urban America* (New York: Oxford University Press, 1969).

Henry Nash Smith, *Virgin Land: The American West as Symbol and Myth* (New York: Vintage Books, 1962).

Kent Steckmesser, "The Frontier Hero in History and Legend," *Wisconsin Magazine of History*, 83 (1963).

Keith Sward, *The Legend of Henry Ford* (New York: Atheneum Publishers, 1968).

Paul A. Varg, *The Making of a Myth: The United States and China, 1897–1912* (East Lansing, Mich.: Michigan State University Press, 1968).

C. Vann Woodward, *The Strange Career of Jim Crow* (New York: Oxford University Press, 1966).

Irvin G. Wyllie, *The Self-Made Man in America: The Myth of Rags to Riches* (New York: The Free Press, 1954).

Our country—this great republic—means nothing unless it means the triumph of a real democracy, the triumph of popular government, and, in the long run, of an economic system under which each man shall be guaranteed the opportunity to show the best that there is in him. That is why the history of America is now the central feature of the history of the world; for the world has set its face hopefully toward our democracy; and, O my fellow citizens, each one of you carries on your shoulders not only the burden of doing well for the sake of your own country, but the burden of doing well and of seeing that this nation does well for the sake of mankind.

Theodore Roosevelt
Speech at Osawatomie,
Kansas, August 31, 1910

MYTHS OF PROGRESSIVISM
AND THE 1920s

Teddy Roosevelt: the "Progressive" pioneer.

Courtesy Houghton Mifflin Company from Hermann Hagedorn, *Roosevelt in the Badlands* (Boston, 1921).

From the depths: the "Progressive" paradox.

Introduction

The study of United States history is in a constant state of revision. Those ubiquitous revisionists among American historians have been particularly active since the end of World War II. Almost every historical personage, event, topic, or chronological period has come in for some sort of reinterpretation; many revisionists have lived to be revised—sometimes by themselves.

One of the major twentieth-century revisions deals with the subject of progressivism. Once considered rather easily definable, "progressives" were simply all those who, philosophically or actively, sought reform during the early part of the twentieth century. Within the last twenty-five years, however, historians have seen the necessity of reworking this entire definition. Perhaps the earlier definition was too simplistic, too all-inclusive; perhaps not all progressives supported every reform. Thus a southern progressive might not get exercised over civil rights reform; a midwest rural progressive might lack a burning impulse to involve himself in ghetto reform on New York's Lower East Side. Perhaps the historian should approach the subject with a little more caution, recognize the diversity and complexity of progressivism, delineate and analyze the various progressive groups, and still be prepared for much irony and paradox.

Partially as a result of its complexity, irony, and paradox, the progressive period is richly laden with myth. One of the chief reasons is that during the progressive era, more than any previous period in American history, the development of myth was aided and abetted by professional historians themselves. At times, one might argue, they acted as the movement's high priests—at intervals announcing total victory for their ideology. Indeed at one point, many historians supported the announcement of the arrival of a "New Republic" by their contributions to a nascent magazine of that name.

The study of the progressive period deeply involves one with myth as he attempts to find out who the progressives really were and to focus on the central area of action. One must attempt to understand and demythologize the two major brands of progressivism—the New Nationalism and the New Freedom—along with their chief proponents, Theodore Roosevelt and Woodrow Wilson. And one must come to grips with the issue of progressivism as a movement reformist or conservative in nature. A body of myths has also grown up concerning the progressives and their relation to imperialism, and certainly around Woodrow Wilson, the President who is thought to have arrived at a synthesis of the New Nationalism and the New Freedom. Issues surrounding United States' entry into World

War I and Wilson's role in it have also provided fertile ground for distortion and myth. In addition, the life span of progressivism has been a popular subject for mythmakers. Did the idea die with the close of the Great War or did it live on into the 1920s, albeit in a somewhat altered form? How complete was our isolation in the 1920s? Is it possible to see the decade as one of more, rather than less involvement in foreign affairs?

Answers to these questions, which take into account the body of myths surrounding them, will lead to a clearer understanding of the progressive period and the 1920s.

The Progressive Profile

George E. Mowry

A writer of history is always tempted to make his rendition a story of élites in which only the most visible, the most articulate, or the most powerful are given adequate representation. Of course, such a tendency provides a climate ripe for the development of myth and a one-dimensional view of the past in which simplicity supplants complexity. It remains the province of the historian, then, to counter myth and to draw a fair representational view of the past. Such an unbiased cross-sectional treatment is afforded by George E. Mowry's progressive profile. Professor Mowry, of the University of North Carolina, is perhaps the best known historian of progressivism. Here, he isolates the essential ideas and assumptions of progressivism, yet demonstrates its ambivalence and paradox. Progressivism was not an exercise in conformity. Its essence was its great complexity.

As a group, the reform mayors and governors, their prominent supporters, and the muckrakers were an interesting lot. Considering the positions they held, they were very young. Joseph W. Folk was only thirty-five when elected governor, Theodore Roosevelt forty, Charles Evans Hughes and Hiram Johnson forty-four, and Robert La Follette forty-five. The average age of the important progressive leaders who upset the Southern Pacific Railroad machine in California was a little over thirty-eight. The tale of a rather typical young reformer was that of Joseph Medill Patterson of the Chicago *Tribune* family. Patterson's grandfather founded the *Tribune*, his father was general manager of the paper, and his cousin was Robert Mc-Cormick, who controlled the paper for over thirty years. Patterson sharply reacted against the reigning conservatism by winning a seat in the Illinois legislature at the age of twenty-four on a platform advocating the municipal ownership of all city utilities in the state. Two years later he resigned from the Chicago Commission of Public Works to become a Socialist because, he announced, it was impossible to reform the city and the country under capitalism. In 1906 he published a diatribe against wealth in the *Independent* entitled "The Confessions of a Drone," and followed it two years later with a book of similar tone.[1] Obviously, this was a period, like the ones after the War of 1812 and in the 1850's, when energetic and incautious youth took command. And in each instance the departure of the elder statesmen portended great changes.

Some of these reformers, like Golden Rule Jones, Charles Evans Hughes, and Tom Johnson, were self-made men, although Hughes's father was a minister, and Johnson's, a Confederate colonel, had come from the upper stratum of Kentucky society. A surprising number of them came from very wealthy families, with names like du Pont, Crane, Spreckels, Dodge, Morgenthau, Pinchot, Perkins, McCormick, and Patterson. The quip was made that this was a "millionaire's reform movement." But the great majority of the reformers came from the "solid middle class," as it then was called with some pride. That their families had been of the economically secure is indicated by the fact that most of them had had a college education in a day when a degree stamped a person as coming from a special economic group. It is interesting to note that most of the women reformers and social workers had gone to college. Occupationally also the reformers came from a very narrow base in society. Of a sample of over four hundred a majority was lawyers, as might be expected of politicians, and nearly 20 percent of them newspaper editors or publishers. The next largest group was from the independent manufacturers or merchants, with the rest scattered among varied occupations, including medicine, banking, and real estate. A statistical study of sixty of the wealthier reformers reveals that the largest single group of twenty-one was manufacturers or merchants, ten lawyers, six newspaper publishers, while nineteen more had inherited their wealth. Quite a few among the latter group had no definite occupation save that of preserving their family fortune and indulging in reform. Of the sixty only about half attended college, a figure much lower than that for the entire group of reformers. Of this number just 50 percent came from three institutions, Harvard, Princeton, and Yale.[2]

If names mean anything, an overwhelming proportion of this reform group came from old American stock with British origins consistently indicated. Except for the women, who were predominantly Midwestern, the reformers' places of origin were scattered over the country roughly in proportion to population densities. Practically all of them by 1900, however, lived in northern cities, most of the Southerners having left their section during early manhood. Religious affiliations were surprisingly difficult to get, and no really trustworthy national sample was obtained. The figures collected were not at all consonant with national church membership statistics. Representatives of the Quaker faith bulked large among the women reformers, as did members of the Jewish religion among the very wealthy. But for the group as a whole the religious descendants of Calvin and Knox predominated, with the Congregationalists, Unitarians, and Presbyterians in the vast majority. Thus it seems likely that the intellectual and religious influence of New England was again dominating the land.

Whether Democrats or Republicans, the overwhelming number of this group of twentieth-century reformers had been conservatives in the nineties. If Republican, they had almost to a man followed the way of Theodore

Roosevelt, Robert La Follette, Lincoln Steffens, and William Allen White to support William McKinley. Most of the progressive Democrats had not been supporters of Bryan, but, like Woodrow Wilson, John Johnson, and Hoke Smith of Georgia, had either followed the Gold Democratic ticket or had remained silent during the election of 1896. Yet from four to six years later most of these men were ardent advocates of municipal gas and water socialism, and were opposed to their regular party machines to the extent of leading either nonpartisan movements in the municipalities or rebellious splinter groups in the states. Moreover, the new century found most of them, except on the currency issue, supporting many of the 1896 Populist and Bryanite demands. Before the Progressive years were finished they and their kind had not only secured the inception of a host of the Populists' reforms, but had contributed a few of their own.

Obviously, a good many questions arise about the motivation of this economically secure, well-educated, middle-class group. On the surface it looked as if the progressive movement was simply a continuation, under different leadership, of the Populist cause. According to William Allen White, Populism had "shaved its whiskers, washed its shirt, put on a derby, and moved up into the middle class. . . ." But White's remark scarcely probed beneath the surface. Populism arose from farmer distress in a period of acute depression. Its reforms were belly reforms. The movement was led by angry men and women not too far removed from the Grange hall. Except for the western silver men, they were incensed at the mounting figures of farm foreclosures and a withering countryside. To the contrary, progressivism arose in a period of relative prosperity. Its reforms were more the results of the heart and the head than of the stomach. Its leaders were largely recruited from the professional and business classes of the city. A good many were wealthy men; more were college graduates. As a group they were indignant at times, but scarcely ever angry. What caused them to act in the peculiar way they did? A part of the answer lies in the peculiar economic and social position in which this middle-class group found itself at about the turn of the century, a part in the intellectual and ethical climate of the age, a part in the significant cluster of prejudices and biases that marked the progressive mind.

"The world wants men, great, strong, harsh, brutal men—men with purpose who let nothing, nothing, nothing stand in their way," Frank Norris wrote in one of his novels. This worship of the strong man, so characteristic of the age, produced a cult of political leadership with ominous overtones for later years. Tempered at this time with the ethics of the social gospel, the cult produced an image far less frightening: an image of men dedicated to the social good, an image approximating the hope of Plato for his guardians. These strong good men, "the changemakers," Harold Frederic wrote, were the protectors of morality, the originators of progress. They were ambitious men and ruthless, but only ruthless in their zeal for human advancement. They were supremely alone, the causative individuals. Far from being disturbed when isolated, David Graham Phillips's hero Scarborough was only concerned when he was "propped up" by something other than his own will and intelligence. "I propose," he commented, "never to 'belong' to anything or anybody."[3]

In 1872 a future progressive, Henry Demarest Lloyd, confessed that he wanted power above all things, but "power unpoisoned by the presence of obligation." That worship of the unfettered individual, the strong pride of self, the strain of ambition, and the almost compulsive desire for power ran through progressive rhetoric like a theme in a symphony. From Frank Norris's strong-minded heroes to Richard Harding Davis's men of almost pure muscle these feelings were a badge of a restless, sensitive, and troubled class. They were never far below the surface in the character of Theodore Roosevelt. Robert La Follette knew them, and Woodrow Wilson had more than his share of them. While still a scholar and teacher, Wilson poured out his frustration with the contemplative life: "I have no patience with the tedious world of what is known as 'research,'" he wrote to a friend. "I should be complete if I could inspire a great movement of opinion. . . ."[4]

A few progressive leaders like William Jennings Bryan and Golden Rule Jones really thought of themselves as servants of the people,[5] and almost completely identified themselves with their constituents. But most progressives set themselves apart from the crowd. Mankind was basically good and capable of progress, but benign change scarcely issued from the masses. Rather it was only accomplished through the instrumentality of a few great and good men. Woodrow Wilson believed that efficient government could come only from "an educated elite," William Kent thought that progress never came from the bottom, and Roosevelt often spoke of government as the process of "giving justice from above." Occasionally, when the electorate disagreed with them, the progressives contented themselves with the thought that truth "was always in the minority" and a possession alone of the "few who see." In 1912 Walter Lippmann wrote that since men could do anything but govern themselves, they were constantly looking for some "benevolent guardian." To the progressive politician that guardian, of course, was patterned after his image of himself.[6]

"I am so sick of fraud and filth and lies," David Graham Phillips plaintively wrote to Senator Beveridge in 1902, "so tired of stern realities. I grasp at myths like a child." The myths Phillips reached for were the supposed realities of an older day, a day when the individual presumably had been able to make his way to the top by the strength of his abilities, and yet a day when there was enough opportunity left at the bottom so that mass poverty, slums, and crime were never evident enough to assault either the eye or the conscience of the successful. Things were different now even in the Valley of Democracy.

The Indiana town where Booth Tarkington's Magnificent Ambersons had benevolently ruled from their big house on Amberson Boulevard had now become a city. In the process of growth spanning the lives of just one generation, the fortunes of the Ambersons had declined until the grandson George was working as a clerk in a factory. As all the young George Ambersons set about to reassert their rightful power and prestige, they were confronted both by enormous and monopolizing wealth and by the rising labor unions. The United States, it seemed, had become almost what Bellamy's historian in *Equality* called it, a world of organized degraded serfs run by a plundering and tightly knit plutocracy. The continual clash between the serfs and the plutocrats engulfed almost everyone. It was enough to disenchant the bystander whose loyalties were neither to the plunderers nor the plundered, but rather to an older America where such social extremes, it was felt, had not existed. Morosely, Professor Barett Wendell observed that America had sold her democratic, equalitarian birthright and was becoming "just another part of the world." Europe no longer learned at America's feet, Walter Weyl, the economist and publicist, wrote with an air of nostalgia, but rather in some respects had become "our teacher." Obviously something needed to be done. Should it be the "return or reversion . . . to certain elementary doctrines of common sense" and the simple rural institutions of the past, as some progressives hoped, or a going forward to something approaching Howells's utopia, which combined the new urban industrialism and a concern for human values in a new type of ethical socialism?[7]

A small reform-minded minority in 1900 was outspoken in defense of the large industrial and commercial city as the creator of the good life. Some of them saw the city as a place of refuge from an ugly countryside and from a hostile natural environment. Remembering his own bleak and lonely boyhood on an upstate New York farm, the novelist Harold Frederic condemned a daily communion with nature that starved the mind and dwarfed the soul. Theodore Dreiser bluntly described the natural processes as inimical to man as a species. Others felt the fascination of the city, a place of excitement and of opportunity. Lincoln Steffens recalled that he felt about the concrete canyons of New York as other youths felt about the wild West. For people like Jane Addams, Jacob Riis, and Hutchins Hapgood the city offered a place to work and an avenue to opportunity.

For the great majority of the new century's reformers, however, the city contained almost the sum of their dislikes. It was a "devilsburg of crime" sucking into its corrupt vortex the "young, genuine, strong and simple men from the farm." There, if successful, they became "financial wreckers" who made their money strangling legitimate enterprises and other human beings. If they were failures—that is, if they remained factory workers—they gradually became like the machine they tended, "huge, hard, brutal, strung with a crude blind strength, stupid, unreasoning." At the worst such unfortunates became the flotsam of the slums, making the saloon their church and the dive their home. The native American lost not only his morals in the city but also his talent for creative work and his sense of beauty. "Sometimes, I think, they'se poison in th' life in a big city," Mr. Dooley remarked, "the flowers won't grow there...." If a man stayed in the city long enough, one of David Graham Phillips's characters remarked, he would almost inevitably lose those qualities that made him an American: one had to go West to see a "real American, a man or a woman who looks as if he or she would do something honest or valuable...."[8]

With such intense anti-urban feeling, it is small wonder that the United States began to romanticize its pioneer past and its agrarian background. Following the Spanish War historical novels fairly poured from the publishers. The public appetite for western stories had one of its periodic increases, and the virtues of the countryside were extolled in even the best literature. In one of Ellen Glasgow's first novels the country, "with its ecstatic insight into the sacred plan of things," is contrasted with the city's "tainted atmosphere." Almost repeating William Jennings Bryan in 1896, Miss Glasgow wrote that the country was the world as God had planned it, the city as man had made it. The cult of the frontier, first introduced into historical scholarship by Frederic Jackson Turner in 1890, and the new emphasis upon agrarian virtues were zealously reflected by the more sensitive politicians. William Jennings Bryan, Theodore Roosevelt, Robert La Follette, and Woodrow Wilson all showed to varying degrees this national nostalgia, this reactionary impulse. Roosevelt in particular saw the great city as the creator of national weakness and possible disintegration, and the countryside as the nation's savior. It was the man on the farm, he wrote, who had consistently done the nation the "best service in governing himself in time of peace and also in fighting in time of war." Dangerous elements to the commonwealth lurked in every large city, but among the western farmers of the West "there was not room for an anarchist or a communist in the whole lot." What Professor Richard Hofstadter has called the agrarian myth, but which might better be called the agrarian bias, was one of the more important elements that went into the making of the progressive mind.[9]

A part of the progressive's romantic attraction to the countryside at this particular time can be explained by the alien character of the urban population. In 1903 the Commissioner of Immigration reported that the past year had witnessed the greatest influx of immigrants in the nation's history. But far from being pleased, the Commissioner was plainly worried. An increasing percentage of these newcomers, he pointed out, belonged to an "undesirable foreign element," the "indigestible" aliens from south Europe. The public was neither surprised at the figures of the report nor shocked by its adjectives. It had been made increasingly sensitive to the changing patterns of immigration by numerous periodical articles and newspaper items calling attention to the alien nature of the eastern seaboard cities. As the immigrant tide welled stronger each year, the nativist spirit that had been so obviously a part of the mental complex leading to the Spanish War increased in intensity. Throughout the decade editors, novelists, and politicians competed with each other in singing the praises of the "big-boned, blond, long-haired" Anglo-Saxon with the blood of the berserkers in his veins, and in denigrating Jack London's "dark pigmented things, the half castes, the mongrel bloods, and the dregs of long conquered races. . . ." In Frank Norris's novels the really despicable characters run all to a type. Braun, the diamond expert in *Vandover*; Zerkow, the junk dealer in *McTeague*; the flannel-shirted Grossman in *The Pit*; and Behrman in *The Octopus* were all of the same religion and approximately from the same regions in Europe. One of the themes in Homer Lea's *The Vermillion Pencil* was the extranational loyalty of the Catholic bishop who intrigued endlessly for the Church and against the State. Although Chester Rowell frankly admitted that California needed "a class of servile labor," he was adamantly opposed to the admission of Orientals, who were dangerous to the state and to "the blood of the next generation."[10]

The progressives, of course, had no monopoly of this racism. Such conservatives as Elihu Root, Henry Cabot Lodge, and Chauncey Depew, and even radicals like Debs, shared their views to a degree. But for one reason or another neither conservative nor radical was as vocal or as specific in his racism as was the reformer. No more eloquent testimony to the power of racism over the progressive mind is evident than in the writings of the kindly, tolerant Middle Westerner William Allen White. In a book published in 1910 White explained nearly all of America's past greatness, including its will to reform, in terms of the nation's "race life" and its racial institutions, "the home and the folk moot." Nor would this genius, this "clean Aryan blood," White promised, be subjected to a debilitating admixture in the future despite the incoming hordes. "We are separated by two oceans from the inferior races and by an instinctive race revulsion to cross breeding that marks the American wherever he is found."[11] Such diverse reformers as Theodore Roosevelt, Albert J. Beveridge, Chester Rowell, Frank Parsons, Hoke Smith, Richard W. Gilder, and Ray Stannard Baker, with more or less emphasis, echoed White's sentiments.

The attitude of the progressive toward race, religion, and color, and his attending views of the great city, was to have profound effects on both internal and external policy. Its consequences were already obvious by 1905 in the South; it was to provoke an international storm in California, and it was to keep alive and possibly nourish a strain of bigotry that was to bear bitter fruit for the United States after the First World War and for the entire world in post-depression Germany. But this is far from saying that the progressive was a spiritual father of either the Ku-Klux Klan of the twenties or the Nazi of the thirties. He might well have been anti-immigrant, anti-Catholic, and anti-Jewish, and he might have thought of himself as one of the racial lords of creation, but he was also extremely responsive to the Christian ethic and to the democratic tradition. It was just not in his character to be ruthless toward a helpless minority, especially when the minority was one of his own. The progressive's response to the big-city slum was the settlement-house movement and housing, fire, and sanitary regulations, not the concentration camp. It was probably not entirely politics that prompted Theodore Roosevelt to invite the first Negro to lunch in the White House or to appoint people of Jewish or of Catholic faith to the Cabinet. Roosevelt thoroughly sympathized with California's Oriental problem. But he insisted that the state live up to the nation's international agreements and to the Constitution in its treatment of American Orientals. True, he was worried about Japan's reaction, but elsewhere in international politics he was not so careful of the sensibilities of other nations.

The progressive had reasons beyond racial ones for disliking the big city. For him the metropolis was the home of great wealth, and excessive wealth was as much an enemy to civilization as excessive poverty. A surprising number of very wealthy men supported the progressive cause, and their feelings toward their wealth produced a most interesting psychic state. Taken together, their statements sounded something like those in a confessional session of an early Puritan congregation. Explaining that he had acquired his wealth by "special privilege," Joseph Fels sought expiation by proposing "to spend the damnable money to wipe out the system by which I made it." Medill Patterson and William Kent produced similar variations on the same theme, and Tom Johnson repeatedly used coups from his own career of money-making to illustrate the social viciousness of the system he was contending against in Cleveland. Professor Hofstadter has ascribed this sense of guilt to the Protestant mind as it made the transit from rural and village life to the urban world where great extremes of economic circumstance were the common condition. It is also probable that as the Protestant upper middle class lost its mystical religion, it compensated by more fiercely adhering to Protestant ethic. It may be of note that the very wealthy who maintained their belief in a mystical religion were never as earnest in social well-doing as their erring brothers. If no one is as zealous as a convert, then perhaps no one conserves what is left of his ideological inheritance more than the man who has lost part of it.[12]

The less well-circumstanced progressive was just as critical of great wealth as his more fortunate colleague. Theodore Roosevelt, who had been left a comfortable but not a great fortune, disliked the American multimillionaire and felt that a society that created an ideal of him was in a very "rotten condition." Bryan once declared that great wealth and personal goodness was something of a paradox. And a reforming journalist from the midlands raised the question whether a man could honestly earn more than a few million dollars in one lifetime. By 1913 Walter Lippmann noted that great wealth, along with "the economic man of the theorists," was in public disrepute.[13]

The reasons for this antimaterialistic crusade of the progressive are an interesting study in complex human motivation. Some of the sentiment undoubtedly came from personal frustration and personal envy. Perhaps to the point is Lincoln Steffens's experience with the stock market. In 1900 he wrote his father that the boom in stocks had made him considerable profits and that he was joining the Republican organization in his district. A year later, after some reverses, he insisted that character was the important desideratum for a young man and not wealth, which often meant the loss of character. The rising intensity of competition for the small merchants and industrialists also played a part in the attack on great wealth. Occasionally one found a reformer who had lost his business. But more often than not in the new century such men were moderately prosperous. Their resentment, if it arose from economic causes, came not from despair but from other feelings, from their sense of lessened power, perhaps, from their regard for their good name, from their sensitivity to the opinion of their fellows. Their relative status and power in society had been going down consistently since the rise of the economic moguls following the Civil War. The gap between them and the Morgans and the Rockefellers had been steadily increasing, and their hopes for attaining the top of the economic heap were progressively dimming. As one commentator noted, the ambitious middle classes in society had "suffered a reduction less in income than in outlook."[14]

This reduction in outlook that Walter Weyl perceived was even more acute for another class, the old American elite whose wealth, family, name, and social power had been secure long before the rise of the relatively new multimillionaires. The Adamses, the Lodges, the Roosevelts, the Bonapartes, and their local counterparts in the hinterlands were a self-consciously proud group. Although Theodore Roosevelt was well down academically in his 1880 Harvard class, he observed that "only one gentleman stands ahead of me." The turbulent and revolutionary waves of the new industrialism and finance had washed up on such polished shores some exceedingly rough gravel. The Rockefellers, the Hannas, and the Harrimans, to say nothing of the Jay Goulds, had not importuned for power in either industry or politics; they had seized it. As their names dominated the newspaper headlines and their ladies laid violent siege to formal society, old families and old ways seemed to have been forgotten. To the recent plutocrats, Henry Cabot Lodge acidly observed from the historic shores of Nahant, "the old American family" and society's long-tested "laws and customs" meant nothing. And far to the west in Cincinnati, it was reported, a social war had broken out between "the stick-ems" and "the stuck-ems." The first group was a "barbarous new class" of millionaires, just risen from the packing industry, who had assaulted an older class of "thousandaires," who had inherited their wealth made two generations before in the same industry.[15]

In the nineties New England's Brooks Adams had written a book about the fall of Rome. The volume contributed little to historical scholarship, but it revealed with remarkable clarity one facet of the American patrician mind at the end of the century. Fundamental to the work was a hypothesis that human history moved in a two-staged evolutionary scheme. The first stage was one reminiscent of the early days of the Republic, of an expanding progressive society dominated by a military, religious, and artistic mind with an emphasis upon loyalty to the state and containing a superstitious strain, which led the adventurous spirit to the creative act. A second stage of decay, clearly identified with Adams's own day, was characterized by an acquisitive, greedy, and feminine personality which resulted in a static and defensive upper class and a sullen, idle mass below, whose loyalty to the state was as uncertain as its livelihood.[16]

In 1905 a young hunchbacked Californian, Homer Lea, decided that a local Los Angeles reform movement was too tame for his impetuous, adventurous spirit. Lea dropped politics to sail to the Orient, where he eventually became a general in the Chinese revolutionary armies and military adviser to Sun Yat-sen. During his short, incredible career Lea wrote two books, the first of which indicted commercialism as "the natural enemy" of national militancy. Pure industrialism Lea approved of as "incidental to national progress." But industrialism as a vehicle of "individual avarice" was a national cancer because it tended to destroy "the aspirations and world-wide career open to the nation." Herbert Croly, sometimes described as the theorist of the progressive movement, echoed Lea's sentiments a few years later. Modern democracy, unlike economic individualism, he argued, impelled men to forget their self-interest and to transfer their devotion away from acquisitiveness toward "a special object," the nation-state and its "historic mission." This distrust of materialism and emphasis upon romantic nationalism were reflected in a good many progressives, especially those with more collectivist inclinations. It was almost completely absent in the thinking of such Midwesterners as Robert La Follette and George W. Norris. But something of the same spirit had sent Theodore Roosevelt to the Cuban shores in 1898 and something akin to it perhaps was to lead Woodrow Wilson into his great crusade for international idealism in 1917.[17]

The idea that value was created only by the production of things or in rendering service, and that there was something dishonest in making money on other men's products, was an old American one. In part it stemmed from religious origins, in part from an unsophisticated system of agrarian economics. It was implicit in the thought of Henry George; it was basic to the progressive attitude toward great wealth. In apologizing to his constituents for his wealth, the progressive Congressman William Kent admitted that he was not entitled to the money he had made out of speculation. Andrew Carnegie, who late in life became something of a progressive, agreed with the attitude. It was time, he felt, that the honest businessman, who made money "legitimately," should refuse to recognize those of his fellows who made money and rendered no value for it. Speculators, to the progressive, were immoralists, men with fat hands sitting in mahogany offices who had acquired the dishonest art of taking money away from the earth's real producers. They believed, said the hero of one of Winston Churchill's novels, that "the acquisition of wealth was exempt from the practice of morality."[18]

In reviewing Professor Seligman's *The Economic Interpretation of History*, the editors of *The Outlook* vehemently denied that progress primarily depended upon materialist forces. The history of society, they argued, was like the history of individuals, composed of a struggle between the moral and the material forces, and "only through the subordination of material ends to moral ends has humanity advanced." There was something corrosive about great wealth, the progressive believed, and in acquiring it a man usually had to sacrifice moral values to overriding material ambitions. In the world of progressive fiction this sloughing off of morality usually produced the hero's economic collapse and his return to morality. But in the less well-ordered practical world the progressive was sure that the multimillionaire remained unredeemed, trapped by the very ethics he had used to acquire his fortune. The world of the great rich was usually an idle one, a sensuous one, and often a vicious one. The lives of its people, Theodore Roosevelt observed, often "vary from rotten frivolity to rotten vice." The way to rescue them from their state of moral degradation, a Midwest editor wrote, was "to put them to work."[19]

Since the progressive usually came from a comfortable part of society and a general attack upon property was usually furthest from his mind, this assault upon great wealth put him in a rather ambiguous position. The one way out of the paradox was to draw a line between good and bad wealth. For some the limit of private fortunes was the total that man could "justly acquire." For others the measurement was made in terms of service to society. Tom Johnson, for example, believed that the law could be so drawn that men would be able "to get" only the amount "they earned." Still others argued that there must be a point where additional money ceased to be salubrious for a man's character and became instead a positive evil force. Wayne MacVeagh, Garfield's Attorney General, suggested that all people could be divided into three classes: those who had more money than was good for them, those who had just enough, and those who had much less than was morally desirable. Just where the exact lines should be drawn, most progressives would not say. But the imputation that the state ought to redivide wealth on a morally desirable basis found a receptive audience. To George F. Baer's claim that coal prices should be the sum of "all the traffic will bear," the editors of *The Outlook* replied that property was private not by any natural right but by an "artificial arrangement made by the community." "If under those artificial arrangements," the editorial continued, "the community is made to suffer, the same power that made them will find a way to unmake them." Thus in the progressive mind the classical economic laws repeatedly described in the past as natural had become artificial arrangements to be rearranged at any time the community found it morally or socially desirable. Admittedly the formulations of new ethical standards for a division of national wealth were to be extremely difficult. But once the progressive had destroyed the popular sanction behind the "laws" of rent, prices, and wages, there was to be no complete turning back. A revolution in human thought had occurred. Man, it was hoped, would now become the master and not the creature of his economy. And the phrases punctuating the next fifty years of history—the "square deal," the New Deal, the Fair Deal, the just wage, the fair price—attested to his efforts to make the reality square with his ambitions.[20]

After revisiting the United States in 1905, James Bryce, the one-time ambassador from Great Britain, noted that of all the questions before the public the ones bearing on capital and labor were the most insistent and the most discussed. Certainly for many a progressive the rise of the labor union was as frightening as the rise of trusts. True, he talked about them less because nationally they were obviously not as powerful as were the combines of capital. But emotionally he was, if anything, more opposed to this collectivism from below than he was to the collectivism above him in the economic ladder.[21]

"There is nothing ethical about the labor movement. It is coercion from start to finish. In every aspect it is a driver and not a leader. It is simply a war movement, and must be judged by the analogues of belligerence and not by industrial principles." This statement by a Democratic progressive illustrates the ire of the small and uncertain employer who was being challenged daily by a power he often could not match. In their lawlessness and in their violence, remarked another, unions were "a menace not only to the employer but to the entire community."[22] To the small employer and to many middle-class professionals unions were just another kind of monopoly created for the same reasons and having the same results as industrial monopoly. Unions, they charged, restricted production, narrowed the available labor market, and raised wages artificially in the same manner that trusts were restricting production, narrowing competition, and raising their own profits. "Every step in trade unionism has followed the steps that organized capital has laid down before it," Clarence Darrow observed in a speech before the Chicago Henry George Association. The ultimate direction of the two monopolies was as clear to the individual entrepreneur as it was to Darrow. Either trade unionism would break down, a Midwestern editor argued, or it would culminate in "a dangerously oppressive partnership" with the stronger industrial trusts. The end result was equally obvious to such men: a steady decrease in opportunity for the individual operating as an individual, an economy of statics, an end to the open society. The burden of the industrial evolution, Darrow said in concluding his speech, "falls upon the middle class."[23] And Howells's traveler from Altruria put the case even more graphically: "the struggle for life has changed from a free fight to an encounter of disciplined forces, and the free fighters that are left get ground to pieces between organized labor and organized capital."

On the whole, the average progressive preferred to talk in moral rather than in economic terms. Orally, at least, he reacted more quickly to appeals based upon abstractions than the usual ones connected with day-to-day liveli-hood. Characteristically, he denounced more vehemently the philosophic overtones of unionism than its pragmatic economic gains. He was almost obsessed with the class consciousness implicit in unionism and flaunted by the more radical parties of the left. Almost to a man the progressive fervently agreed with one of Harold Frederic's heroes that "the abominable word 'class' could be wiped out of the English language as it is spoken in Amer-ica."[24] Sociologists, economists, preachers, politicians, and publishers all joined the chorus. Economic classes, according to the sociologist Cooley, were characterized by a "complacent ignorance." Other progressives regarded them as "greedy," "arrogant," "insolent," "ruthless," "unsocial," and "tyranni-cal." Morality did not know them, declared one editor, because morality could only come from the individual who had not succumbed to "the eco-nomic temptation" manifested by the class. But the ultimate in the way of devastating criticism of the class spirit came from Ray Stannard Baker. Although sympathetic with the economic plight of the garment workers, Baker observed that in devotion to their class they were "almost more union-ists than Americans."

"'I am for labor,' or 'I am for capital,' substitutes something else for the immutable laws of righteousness," Theodore Roosevelt was quoted as saying in 1904. "The one and the other would let the class man in, and letting him in is the one thing that will most quickly eat out the heart of the Republic." Roosevelt, of course, was referring to class parties in politics. Most progressives agreed with Herbert Croly that a "profound antagonism" existed between the political system and a government controlled by a labor party.[25] In San Francisco in 1901, in Chicago in 1905, and in Los Angeles in 1911, when labor used or threatened direct political action, the progressive reacted as if touched by fire. Chicago was a "class-ridden" city, remarked one progressive journal, which would not redeem itself until the evil pretensions of both organized capital and labor had been suppressed. In Los Angeles, where a Socialist labor group came within a hair's breadth of controlling the city, the progressives combined with their old enemies, the corporation-dominated machine, to fight off the challenge, and as a result never again exerted the power they once had in the city. Apropos of that struggle punctu-ated by a near general strike, dynamite, and death, the leading California progressive theorist, Chester Rowell, expostulated that no class as a class was fit to rule a democracy; that progress came only from activities of good citi-zens acting as individuals. Class prejudice and class pride excused bribery, mass selfishness, lawlessness, and disorder. This class spirit emanating from both business and labor was "destroying American liberty." When it became predominant, Rowell concluded, American institutions would be dead, for peaceful reform would no longer be possible, and "nothing but revolution" would remain.[26]

At various times and places the progressive politician invited the support of organized labor, but such co-operation was almost invariably a one-way street. Somewhat reminiscent of the early relations between the British Liberal and Labor parties, it worked only if the progressive rather than the labor politician was in the driver's seat. In Maine, for example, when labor attempted to lead a campaign for the initiative and referendum, it was defeated in part by progressives, who two years later led a successful campaign on the same issues.[27] In the progressive literature the terms "captain of industry" and "labor boss" were standard, while "labor statesman" was practically unknown. Roosevelt's inclination to try labor lawbreakers in a criminal court is well known; his administration's failure to indict criminally one corporation executive is eloquent of the limits of his prejudice. Progressive literature contained many proposals for permitting corporations to develop until they had achieved quasi-monopoly status, at which time federal regulation would be imposed. No such development was forecast for labor. Unions were grudgingly recognized as a necessary evil, but the monopolistic closed shop was an abomination not to be tolerated with or without government regulation. In the Chicago teamsters' strike of 1905 Mayor Dunne ordered the city police to be "absolutely impartial" toward both capital and labor. But he also insisted that the strikers not be allowed to block the teams of nonunion men or the delivery of nonunion-marked goods.[28]

A few progressives, of course, hailed the rise of labor unions as an advance in democracy. But the majority, while sincerely desirous of improving the plight of the individual workingman, was perhaps basically more hostile to the union than to corporate monopoly. If the progressive attention was mostly centered on the corporation during the decade, it was largely because the sheer social power of the corporation vastly overshadowed that of the rising but still relatively weak unions. When confronted with a bleak either-or situation, progressive loyalties significantly shifted up and not down the economic ladder.

Emotionally attached to the individual as a causative force and to an older America where he saw his group supreme, assaulted economically and socially from above and below, and yet eager for the wealth and the power that flowed from the new collectivism, the progressive was at once nostalgic, envious, fearful, and yet confident about the future. Fear and confidence together for a time inspired this middle-class group of supremely independent individuals with a class consciousness that perhaps exceeded that of any other group in the nation. This synthesis had been a long time developing. Back in the early 1890's Henry George had remarked that the two dangerous classes to the state were "the very rich" and "the very poor." Some years afterward a Populist paper referred to the "upper and lower scum" of society. At about the same time the acknowledged dean of American letters had inquired just where the great inventions, the good books, the beautiful pictures, and the just laws had come from in American society. Not from the "uppermost" or "lowermost" classes, Howells replied. They had come mostly from the middle-class man. In the first decade of the twentieth century the progressive never questioned where ability and righteousness resided. Nor was he uncertain of the sources of the nation's evils. "From above," one wrote, "come the problems of predatory wealth. . . . From below come the problems of poverty and pigheaded and brutish criminality."[29]

As the progressive looked at the sharply differentiated America of 1900, he saw "pyramids of money in a desert of want." For William Allen White the world was full of "big crooks" and the "underprivileged." The polar conditions of society assaulted the progressive conscience and threatened progressive security. Supremely individualistic, the progressive could not impute class consciousness, or, as he would have phrased it, class selfishness, to himself. His talk was therefore full of moral self-judgments, of phrases like "the good men," "the better element," "the moral crowd." From the Old Source, he paraphrased, "Thou shalt not respect the person of the poor, nor honor the person of the great; in righteousness shalt thou judge thy neighbor." His self-image was that of a "kind-hearted man" dealing in justice. William Kent publicly stated that he could not believe in the class struggle because every great reform of the past had been wrought by men who were not "selfishly interested." "I believe," he concluded, "altruism is a bigger force in the world than selfishness."[30]

Since the progressive was not organized economically as was the capitalist and the laborer, he chose to fight his battles where he had the most power—in the political arena. And in large terms his political program was first that of the most basic urge of all nature, to preserve himself, and secondly to refashion the world after his own image. What the nation needed most, wrote a Midwestern clergyman, was an increase in the number of "large-hearted men" to counteract the class organization of both capital and labor. "Solidarity," Herbert Croly stated, "must be restored." The point of reconcentration around which the hoped-for solidarity was to take place, of course, was the middle class. It was to "absorb" all other classes, thought Henry Demarest Lloyd. It was to be both the sum and substance of the classless state of the future.[31]

The progressive mentality was a compound of many curious elements. It contained a reactionary as well as a reform impulse. It was imbued with a burning ethical strain which at times approached a missionary desire to create a heaven on earth. It had in it intense feelings of moral superiority over both elements of society above and below it economically. It emphasized individual dynamism and leadership. One part of it looked backward to an intensely democratic small America; another looked forward to a highly centralized nationalistic state. And both elements contained a rather ugly strain of racism.

The progressive mentality was generated in part from both a fear of the loss of group status and a confidence in man's ability to order the future. Had progressive militancy come in a more despondent intellectual and ethical climate and in a bleaker economic day, group fear might have won over group hope. Its more benign social ends might then have been transmuted into something more malignant. But in the warm and sunny atmosphere of 1900 the optimistic mood prevailed. For the year marking the beginning of the new century was a year of progressive success in the cities and the states. And within another year, by the ugly agent of an assassin's gun, Theodore Roosevelt had become President. With the shot in Buffalo, progressivism achieved a spokesman in the White House.

Notes

1. George E. Mowry, *The California Progressives* (Berkeley and Los Angeles, 1952), p. 87; *The Public*, April 8, 1905; *Independent*, LXI (1906), 493–495; Joseph Medill Patterson, *Little Brother of the Rich* (Chicago, 1908).
2. These statistics and the ones following came from a series of studies in the writer's seminar. The figures were rechecked and are in the author's possession.
3. Frank Norris, *A Man's Woman* (New York, 1900), p. 71; David Graham Phillips (Indianapolis, 1904), *The Cost*, p. 17.
4. Quoted in Daniel Aaron, *Men of Good Hope* (New York, 1951), p. 139; Richard Hofstadter, *The American Political Tradition and the Men Who Made It* (New York, 1948), p. 243.
5. Frances G. Newlands, *Public Papers* (New York, 1932), p. 311.
6. Theodore Roosevelt, "Who is a Progressive?" *The Outlook*, C (1912), 2; *The Public*, April 18, 1903; Walter Lippmann, *Drift and Mastery* (New York, 1914), p. 189.
7. Walter Weyl, *The New Democracy* (New York, 1912), p. 2; Colin P. Goodykoontz, *The Papers of Edward P. Costigan Relating to the Progressive Movement in Colorado, 1902–1917* (Boulder, Colo., 1941), p. 17.
8. For varied expressions of this antiurbanism, see Irving Bacheller, *Eben Holden* (Boston, 1900), p. 336; Alice H. Rice, *Mrs. Wiggs of the Cabbage Patch* (New York, 1901), p. 29; Winston Churchill, *The Dwelling-Place of Light* (New York, 1917), p. 79; Finley Peter Dunne, *Mr. Dooley in Peace and War* (Boston, 1898), p. 125; D. G. Phillips, *Golden Fleece* (New York, 1903), pp. 57–58.
9. Ellen Glasgow, *The Descendant* (New York, 1897), p. 254; Roosevelt to George Otto Trevelyan, March 9, 1905, and to Kermit Roosevelt, January 1, 1907, Roosevelt MSS.; *The Public*, November 14, 1903.
10. *Literary Digest*, XXVII (1903), 158; Jack London, *The Mutiny of the Elsinore* (New York, 1914), pp. 197–198. See also John Higham, *Strangers in the Land, Patterns of American Nativism, 1860–1925* (New Brunswick, N.J., 1955), pp. 131 ff.
11. William Allen White, *The Old Order Changeth* (New York, 1910), pp. 128, 197, 253.
12. Joseph Fels, "Mr. Fels' Own Story," *World's Work*, XXIII (1912), 566; *San Francisco Bulletin*, January 14, 1910; Joseph M. Patterson, *A Little Brother of the Rich* (New York, 1906); Richard Hofstadter, *The Age of Reform* (New York, 1955), pp. 203–206.
13. Roosevelt to Cecil Arthur Spring-Rice, March 19, 1904, Roosevelt MSS.; *The Public,* February 4, 1905; Lippmann, *Drift and Mastery*, pp. 28–30.
14. Lincoln Steffens to Joseph Steffens, November 11, 1900, Steffens to William F. Neeley, January 14, 1901, in Ella Winter and Granville Hicks (eds.), *The Letters of Lincoln Steffens* (2 vols., New York, 1938), I, 1, 136, 143; Weyl, *The New Democracy*, p. 249.

15. Theodore Roosevelt, quoted in Arthur Mann, *Yankee Reformers in the Urban Age* (Cambridge, 1954), p. 103; John A. Garraty, *Henry Cabot Lodge* (New York, 1953), p. 226; Weyl, *The New Democracy*, p. 242.

16. Brooks Adams, *The Law of Civilization and Decay* (Boston, 1895).

17. Homer Lea, *The Valor of Ignorance* (New York, 1909), pp. 26–27; Croly, *The Promise of American Life*, p. 418.

18. William Kent, quoted in the San Francisco *Bulletin*, June 14, 1910; *The Public*, April 13, 1907. For literary expressions of the view, see Churchill, *The Crisis* (New York, 1901), p. 345, and *Mr. Crewe's Career* (New York, 1908), p. 392; Robert Grant, *Unleavened Bread* (New York, 1900), p. 392.

19. *The Outlook*, LXXIII (1903), 216; Roosevelt to Cecil Arthur Spring-Rice, July 30, 1901, Roosevelt MSS.; Girard (Kansas), *The Appeal to Reason*, March 3, 1906.

20. *The Public*, September 23, 1905, and February 3, 1906; Wayne MacVeagh, "An Appeal to Our Millionaires," *North American Review*, June, 1906; *The Outlook*, LXXVI (1904), 240.

21. James Bryce, "America Revisited," *The Outlook*, LXXIX (1905), 848.

22. *The Public*, June 13, 1903; *The Outlook*, LXVIII (1901), 683.

23. Chicago *Record Herald*, June 26, 1903; *The Public*, June 11, 1903.

24. Harold Frederic, *The Lawton Girl* (New York, 1890), p. 444.

25. Charles H. Cooley, *Human Nature and the Social Order* (New York, 1902), p. 72; Ray Stannard Baker, "The Rise of the Tailors," *McClure's*, XXIV (1904), 14. For other expressions of the same spirit, see Simon Patten, *The New Basis of Civilization* (New York, 1907), p. 84; John N. McCormick, *The Litany and the Life* (Milwaukee, 1904), p. 93; H. B. Brown, "Twentieth Century," *Forum* XIX (1895), 641; *The Public*, November 26, 1914; Jacob A. Riis, "Theodore Roosevelt, The Citizen," *The Outlook*, LXXVI (1904), 649; Croly, *Promise*, p. 129.

26. *The Public*, May 13, 1905, and June 17, 1905; Fresno *Republican*, November 20, 1911.

27. J. William Black, "Maine's Experience with the Initiative and Referendum," *Annals of the American Academy of Political Science*, XLII, 164–165.

28. *The Public*, April 15, 1905.

29. Aaron, *Men of Good Hope*, pp. 84, 193; Jackson (Michigan) *Industrial News*, March 8, 1894; *California Weekly*, December 18, 1908.

30. William Allen White to Henry J. Allen, July 28, 1934, in Walter Johnson (ed.), *Selected Letters of William Allen White, 1899–1943* (New York, 1947), p. 348; San Francisco *Bulletin*, September 8, 1911.

31. William J. McCaughan, *Love, Faith and Joy* (Chicago, 1904), p. 206; Croly, *Promise of American Life*, p. 139; Aaron, *Men of Good Hope*, p. 160.

Theodore Roosevelt's New Nationalism: Myths and Realities

William E. Leuchtenburg

Theodore Roosevelt was many things to many men—ornithologist, historian, cowboy, pugilist, language expert, legislator, police commissioner, naval expert, rough rider, governor, vice-president, President, and all-around character. A cartoonist's delight, he was also a tempting target for mythmakers. In this article, William E. Leuchtenburg, Professor of History at Columbia University, attacks a general and a specific myth. Generally, he disagrees both with progressive historians who saw Teddy as the champion of the common man, and with the position held by many "new leftists," that Roosevelt acted on behalf of big business. More specifically, Leuchtenburg argues that Theodore Roosevelt was basically a nationalist. He goes on to destroy the myth that the progressive Roosevelt of 1910-12 "got religion" after reading Herbert Croly's *The Promise of American Life*. In fact, Teddy clearly had outlined The New Nationalism as early as 1907-08; his 1912 position had deeper roots than has previously been thought.

Much of the confusion about Roosevelt's position came from a misguided attempt to classify him either as a progressive or a business-oriented conservative when Roosevelt, in fact, was neither. He approached the political problems of the day with quite different assumptions from the humanitarian reformer, committed to advancing the interests of the underprivileged, or from the business-minded conservative, opposed to any change that might jeopardize the interests of the propertied classes.

Roosevelt believed that the country faced the most serious crisis since the eve of the Civil War. Over and over again in his letters in 1910, he returned to the analogy between the division in the Republican party and the troubles which had destroyed the pre-war Whigs. As the occasion to introduce the New Nationalism, he chose the dedication ceremonies of John Brown's battlefield at Osawatomie. He held up to both factions the ideal of Abraham Lincoln, the Lincoln who was the saint of American nationalism, the man who had risked bloody civil strife to preserve the nation, and who, on the eve of triumph in a war to unite the nation, had been martyred on Good Friday. Americans of Roosevelt's generation came close to transforming the Lincoln legend into a secular cult; the California progressive leader William Kent's only religious affiliation was with the Abraham Lincoln Center of Chicago.

William E. Leuchtenburg, ed., *The New Nationalism*, by Theodore Roosevelt. © 1961. Reprinted by permission of Prentice-Hall, Inc., Englewood Cliffs, New Jersey.

Roosevelt traced the source of the new crisis facing the country to the fact that men lacked a sense of national unity. The nation was still much too parochial in its outlook, too sectionally-minded in its attitude toward American politics, too provincial in its view of the world. More serious even than this parochialism were the actions of two warring classes, capital and labor, both of which pursued their private advantages heedless of the national interest. Roosevelt had the deep contempt of the patrician for the greedy businessman who lacked even a primitive sense of justice. He felt at the same time a horror of mob violence; he saw in each new labor leader, in each new tribune of the people, a potential Robespierre. Throughout his western trip, he warned that the Scylla of demagogism was as much to be dreaded as the Charybdis of conservatism; the reckless agitator and the unscrupulous reactionary both stood "on the same plane of obnoxiousness."

The factions which threatened to divide the nation were the very factions whose extreme members threatened to disrupt the Republican party, Roosevelt believed. The conservatives who fawned on business, he wrote Lodge in mid-September, were "really the heirs of the cotton Whigs, and not of the Republicanism of Lincoln." On the other hand, the radical wing of the insurgents posed the same threat to sane politics that John Brown once had. A few weeks before he went to Osawatomie, he explained: "At the moment, I am endeavoring to prevent the John Browns among the insurgents getting themselves in a position from which the Abraham Lincolns cannot extricate them." In December after the state campaigns had been fought and lost to the Democrats, a weary and melancholy Roosevelt made one more attempt to explain his position: "I wish to be radical, as Lincoln was radical compared to Buchanan and Fillmore, and conservative as he was conservative compared to Wendell Phillips and John Brown."

As the Lincoln who would reunite a fragmented nation, Roosevelt insisted that the national interest was prior to any individual right. At Osawatomie, he had made the bold assertion: "The man who wrongly holds that every human right is secondary to his profit must now give way to the advocate of human welfare, who rightly maintains that every man holds his property subject to the general right of the community to regulate its use to whatever degree the public welfare may require it." The rights of the community, greater than any individual rights, would best be advanced, Roosevelt argued, by a powerful central government. Since business had been nationalized, states and localities were no longer able to cope with "lawbreakers of great wealth"; only the federal government could do so. It should have power to complete its tasks, unfettered by the casuistries of judges who would shackle it. The hope of the people lay not in the courts but in a vigorous Chief Executive who would be "the steward of the public welfare."

Roosevelt had a peculiarly European concern with the health of the state. The great menace to the health of the nation, Roosevelt believed, lay in the utilitarianism of a business civilization, insensible to national honor, and that popular pursuit of ease which placed rights above duties, pleasures above the national interest. A people unwilling to sacrifice for the good of the state was a decadent people; the New Nationalism would seek, by teaching and by action, to reinvigorate American society. "Social efficiency," Roosevelt thought, derived from "love of order, ability to fight well and breed well, capacity to subordinate the interests of the individual to the interests of the community."

Many of Roosevelt's contemporaries believed that Roosevelt had drawn the doctrines of the New Nationalism directly from the American political philosopher, Herbert Croly. In the 1912 campaign, for example, the *American Magazine* described Croly as "the man from whom Colonel Roosevelt got his 'New Nationalism.'" Roosevelt had had his attention called to Croly's *The Promise of American Life*, published in 1909, by both Learned Hand and Henry Cabot Lodge, not in Africa, as is sometimes said, but on his tour of Europe as he headed home for America. Sometime in the late spring or early summer of 1910, Roosevelt read Croly's study. In late July, at a time when the Colonel was preparing his speeches for his western tour, he wrote Croly: "I do not know when I have read a book which I felt profited me as much as your book on American life." Roosevelt added: "I shall use your ideas freely in speeches I intend to make."

Such direct evidence of the influence of a writer on a public man is more than most historians ever hope to find, and it is little wonder that they have made so much of the impact of Croly on Roosevelt. They have not only suggested that he influenced the New Nationalism but have gone still further to argue that Croly converted Roosevelt from the conservatism of his White House years to the advanced progressivism of the Bull Moose campaign of 1912. Such a view of Croly's influence arises from the mistaken conviction that Roosevelt as President was a fraud, a conservative masquerading as a reformer. Since no one could deny that the Colonel made a radical appeal in 1912, historians who conceive of Roosevelt as a pseudo-progressive as President have felt compelled to explain the "change" in Roosevelt and to attribute it to some external agent.

The notion that the Colonel changed the views of a lifetime as the result of reading one book betrays a wistful faith in the power of the pen, but little else. There is scarcely a theme or a recommendation of the New Nationalism which Roosevelt had not already enunciated before Croly wrote his book. In three messages to Congress in 1907 and 1908, Roosevelt had spelled out almost the entire program of the New Nationalism: federal regulation of business, legislation to benefit labor, the inheritance and income taxes, and instrumentalities like postal savings banks. He had accused individual business leaders of "rottenness," of "flagrant dishonesty," and of "bitter and unscrupulous craft." He had urged that workers be guaranteed "a larger share of the wealth." He had assaulted the judiciary, and especially the federal courts, and had suggested that some judges were "incompetent." Well before 1907, in private letters and in some public acts, he had foreshadowed the main outlines of New Nationalist thought: nationalism, love of order, alarm at both corporation and union power, fear of revolution, distrust of the Jeffersonian tradition of reform, faith in a strong state and a powerful Chief Executive—the list could be extended to embrace every important tenet of the New Nationalism.

This is not to say Croly had no importance at all. The book could hardly have helped but have a great appeal to Roosevelt not only because it mirrored his own thinking but also because the Colonel was the hero of the book. It probably prodded Roosevelt to clarify his thoughts in the summer of 1910, and he may even, as many writers have suggested, have taken the very phrase "New Nationalism" from Croly, although this seems unlikely. Some of the words Roosevelt spoke at Osawatomie seemed to be a direct response to Croly's urging that he carry his thinking to its logical conclusion. But *The Promise of American Life* is less important for the impact Croly had on Roosevelt than as evidence of the impact Roosevelt had on Croly. In Croly's work, we can find a more systematic statement of Roosevelt's New National-ism than Roosevelt himself ever found time to set down, and for this reason it commands our attention.

The central argument of *The Promise of American Life* rests on the premise that the ills of American society can be traced to the persistence of Jeffersonian thinking. Croly believed that Jefferson, a man of "intellectual superficiality and insincerity," had started the country off on the wrong foot. Jefferson's "cant" about equal rights for all and special privileges for none had licensed greed and the pursuit of self-interest without regard to the na-tional interest. Instead of seeking to create and sustain fluid elites, Jefferson had prattled about the equality of all men. By his suspicion of concentrated power, he had obscured the need for a strong central government which would direct the fortunes of the nation with a coherent sense of national purpose.

The familiar cliché about Croly is that he favored the achievement of Jeffersonian ends by Hamiltonian means. To say this is to misunderstand Croly altogether. Jefferson is the villain of *The Promise of American Life*, and Croly condemns Jeffersonian ends as well as Jeffersonian means. A truck-ler to the masses, Jefferson, Croly declared, wanted "a government of and by the people," when he should have sought "a government for the people by popular but responsible leaders." The gross error of Jeffersonianism was that it supposed that "the people were to guide their leaders, not their leaders the people."

Jefferson's "fatal policy of drift," Croly argued, fixed the course of American history for the next century. Jackson perpetuated the Jeffersonian errors, especially the equal rights fetishism and the suspicion of the expert. In the Jacksonian era, "Americans of intelligence" were subjected to "social equalitarianism." For a time, under Lincoln, when all of the resources of the nation were mobilized to wipe out slavery, the country did achieve a sense of national purpose. Lincoln rallied the nation to a sense of its responsibilities by refusing to allow local and individual rights to stand in his way; the war itself "began to emancipate the American national idea from an obscurantist individualism and provincialism." Unhappily, as soon as the war ended, the country slipped back into an aimless policy of drift.

In the years since the Civil War, Croly continued, the industrialization of the country had destroyed the homogeneous society of the early republic. Jefferson's ideas had been mischievous even then, but in the world of the early twentieth century, they were downright dangerous. The doctrine of equal rights had resulted, paradoxically, in the concentration of wealth and power in the hands of a few. The founding fathers had imagined neither such concentration of financial power nor the growth of special interests like labor unions; to cope with them, America needed to develop both a body of opinion and instrumentalities strong enough to discipline both in the national interest. To replace the instinctive homogeneity of 1800, the nation had to reconstruct a new "democratic social ideal." But every attempt to achieve "a national purpose" broke against the fatalistic faith in progress, the irresponsible optimism of a people who thought that, despite the revolutionary changes in American society, they could afford to drift along without taking conscious action in pursuit of a national ideal.

To be sure, there had been countless efforts at reform, Croly conceded, but the reform movement had been cursed by the old Jeffersonian emphases. The reformer's faith in individualism and equal rights had led him to reject the need for a stratified society and to embrace the folly of trust busting. A reformer like Bryan who was a Democrat started out with a fatal handicap, for his party distrusted the concentration of power in the state. Moreover, Bryan's idealization of the common man and his suspicion of the exceptional man meant that he stood for "the sacrifice of the individual to the popular average; and the perpetuation of such a sacrifice would mean ultimate democratic degeneration." An even greater danger came from Jacobins like William Randolph Hearst who abused businessmen by holding them up to public scorn instead of recognizing that politics must be grounded in "mutual confidence and fair dealing."

Fortunately, Croly wrote, there was one reformer "whose work has tended to give reform the dignity of a constructive mission": Theodore Roosevelt. Roosevelt's strength arose from the fact that he was even more a nationalist than a reformer. He had nationalized the reform movement by reviving "the Hamiltonian ideal of constructive national legislation," while at the same time being, as Hamilton was not, a democrat. Roosevelt, with his sense of the national interest, his faith in a strong state, and his willingness to give power to exceptional men, had served "to emancipate American democracy from its Jeffersonian bondage." He had given the Republican party, which had slipped back into the ineffectiveness of the old Whig party, some sense of "its historic mission."

But Roosevelt was not yet the perfect reformer, Croly observed, for he was not yet the perfect nationalist. He continued, at times, to talk the language of Jeffersonianism. What was "the square deal" but an unhappy revival of the assumptions of equal rights, including the demagogic assumption that businessmen had been acting like dishonest sharpers? Fortunately, Roosevelt was building better than he knew or would admit. He was, in fact, a thoroughgoing nationalist whose actions pointed him toward a complete break with the Jeffersonian tradition. Nevertheless, Croly concluded, the danger remained that, so long as Roosevelt refused to acknowledge this fact, the reform movement with which he was associated might go astray.

In his western tour in 1910, Roosevelt did not altogether come to terms with Croly's strictures. Yet he did take another step along the path he had been moving away from the old reform tradition which emphasized natural rights, egalitarianism, and the limited state. His 1910 speeches anticipated the Progressive Party program of 1912. That year, in contrast to Woodrow Wilson's "New Freedom," with its emphasis on a return to the maxims of a nineteenth-century society, Roosevelt would advocate a great augmentation of power of the federal government. In 1912, he would say more than he had in 1910 about permitting the trusts to develop, rather than breaking them up; readers of *The New Nationalism* are often astonished to find that there is only a single passage about the trusts, that it is not at all a book about trusts. In 1912, too, he would come out for welfare measures that he had not yet come to advocate in 1910. But all the main features of the Bull Moose program had been sketched in 1910.

The New Nationalism would be the most fruitful doctrine of the Progressive era, for it stated the underlying assumptions of much of what was later to be known as the Welfare State. Liberated from the fear of centralized authority, political leaders could, for the first time, use the powers of the federal government to make an industrial society more humane. Freed from the unrealistic assumption that every worker was a potential entrepreneur, the government began to take steps to recognize rights of workingmen which previously had been denied. No longer bound by the view that the state should be, at most, an umpire, government officials could embark on bold new programs of regional planning, slum clearance, and public power development.

Yet the New Nationalism too raised disturbing questions about the relation of progressive values to the omnicompetent state. Roosevelt minimized the danger in unrestrained exercise of power by the Executive, yet he himself had demonstrated on many occasions the perils of the lawless use of power by a President who confused his own obsessions with the "national interest." He saw little danger in the cartelization of American society, yet the concentration of decision-making in the hands of a few government and corporation leaders raised a decided threat to individual liberties, quite apart from the question of whether corporations so powerful would not soon control the state.

Even more doubtful was the conception of Roosevelt and Croly that man should find fulfillment in service to the state, the nation-state which Croly insisted had an individuality of its own. Although Croly saw an important role for voluntaristic organization, he based most of his hopes on the state. The Promise of American Life was to be fulfilled not by a maximum grant of freedom, or by the abundant satisfaction of wants, "but by a large measure of individual subordination and self-denial . . . to the fulfillment of a national purpose." Instead of speaking simply for a collectivity of individuals, the New Nationalists' state, Croly explained, would act for "the nation of yesterday and tomorrow, organized for its national historical mission." Both leaders and people would subordinate their desires to "a morally authoritative Sovereign will."

Much as in Bismarck's Germany, Roosevelt and many of the progressives who followed him used as their touchstone the health of the state and its mystical sense of national mission. The same state which promised new social benefits could also embark on nationalistic wars and crush out dissent, also in the name of patriotic ideals. The New Nationalism, Croly explained, was to be "unscrupulously" nationalistic. In 1916, the Progressive Party, which helped give birth to the idea of a positive state dedicated to social welfare, would be destroyed in the name of a positive state dedicated to chauvinism and military preparedness. In the end, as many had always feared, Roosevelt's nationalism ran deeper than his progressivism.

The Lost Democracy

Gabriel Kolko

Gabriel Kolko—for a time Professor of History at the University of Pennsylvania, and more recently an expatriate scholar at York University in Toronto, Canada—is representative of "New Left" historical attitudes toward American progressivism. Challenging the generally accepted interpretation of the progressive era as a stage of liberalism in America, Kolko suggests that it was but another case of conservative consolidation. More specifically, rather than marking an age of "trust busting" and consumer-oriented governmental intervention, the business community consciously sought governmental regulation in the interests of greater predictability and control of the economy for themselves. In the end, progressivism marked but another attempt to "save" the capitalistic system.

The American political experience during the Progressive Era was conservative and this conservatism profoundly influenced American society's response to the problems of industrialism. The nature of the economic process in the United States, and the peculiar cast within which industrialism was molded, can only be understood by examining the political structure. Progressive politics is complex when studied in all of its aspects, but its dominant tendency on the federal level was to functionally create, in a piecemeal and haphazard way that was later made more comprehensive, the synthesis of politics and economics I have labeled "political capitalism."

The varieties of rhetoric associated with progressivism were as diverse as its followers, and one form of this rhetoric involved attacks on businessmen—attacks that were often framed in a fashion that has been misunderstood by historians as being radical. But at no point did any major political tendency dealing with the problem of big business in modern society ever try to go beyond the level of high generalization and translate theory into concrete economic programs that would conflict in a fundamental way with business supremacy over the control of wealth. It was not a coincidence that the results of progressivism were precisely what many major business interests desired.

Ultimately businessmen defined the limits of political intervention, and specified its major form and thrust. They were able to do so not merely because they were among the major initiators of federal intervention in the economy, but primarily because no politically significant group during the

Progressive Era really challenged their conception of political intervention. The basic fact of the Progressive Era was the large area of consensus and unity among key business leaders and most political factions on the role of the federal government in the economy. There were disagreements, of course, but not on fundamentals. The overwhelming majorities on votes for basic progressive legislation is testimony to the near unanimity in Congress on basic issues.

Indeed, an evaluation of the Progressive Era must concede a much larger importance to the role of Congress than has hitherto been granted by historians who have focused primarily on the more dramatic Presidents. Congress was the pivot of agitation for banking reform while Roosevelt tried to evade the issue, and it was considering trade commissions well before Wilson was elected. Meat and pure food agitation concentrated on Congress, and most of the various reform proposals originated there. More often than not, the various Presidents evaded a serious consideration of issues until Congressional initiatives forced them to articulate a position. And businessmen seeking reforms often found a sympathetic response among the members of the House and Senate long before Presidents would listen to them. This was particularly true of Roosevelt, who would have done much less than he did were it not for the prodding of Congress. Presidents are preoccupied with patronage to an extent unappreciated by anyone who has not read their letters.

The Presidents, considered—as they must be—as actors rather than ideologists, hardly threatened to undermine the existing controllers of economic power. With the possible exception of Taft's Wickersham, none of the major appointees to key executive posts dealing with economic affairs were men likely to frustrate business in its desire to use the federal government to strengthen its economic position. Garfield, Root, Knox, Straus—these men were important and sympathetic pipelines to the President, and gave additional security to businessmen who did not misread what Roosevelt was trying to say in his public utterances. Taft, of course, broke the continuity between the Roosevelt and Wilson Administrations because of political decisions that had nothing to do with his acceptance of the same economic theory that Roosevelt believed in. The elaborate relationship between business and the Executive created under Roosevelt was unintentionally destroyed because of Taft's desire to control the Republican Party. Wilson's appointees were quite as satisfactory as Roosevelt's, so far as big business was concerned, and in his concrete implementation of the fruits of their political agitation—the Federal Reserve Act and the Federal Trade Commission Act—Wilson proved himself to be perhaps the most responsive and desirable to business of the three Presidents. Certainly it must be concluded that historians have overemphasized the basic differences between the Presidents of the Progressive Era, and ignored their much more important similarities. In 1912 the specific utterances and programs of all three were identical on fundamentals, and party platforms reflected this common agreement.

This essential unanimity extended to the area of ideologies and values, where differences between the Presidents were largely of the sort contrived by politicians in search of votes, or seeking to create useful images. None of the Presidents had a distinct consciousness of any fundamental conflict between their political goals and those of business. Roosevelt and Wilson especially appreciated the significant support business gave to their reforms, but it was left to Wilson to culminate the decade or more of agitation by providing precise direction to the administration of political capitalism's most important consequences in the Progressive Era. Wilson had a small but articulate band of followers who seriously desired to reverse the process of industrial centralization—Bryan and the Midwestern agrarians reflected this tradition more than any other group. Yet ultimately he relegated such dissidents to a secondary position—indeed, Wilson himself represented the triumph of Eastern Democracy over Bryanism—and they were able to influence only a clause or amendment, here and there, in the basic legislative structure of political capitalism.

But even had they been more powerful, it is debatable how different Bryanism would have been. Bryan saw the incompatibility between giant corporate capitalism and political democracy, but he sought to save democracy by saving, or restoring, a sort of idealized competitive capitalist economy which was by this time incapable of realization or restoration, and was in any event not advocated by capitalists or political leaders with more power than the agrarians could marshal. Brandeis, for his part, was bound by enigmas in this period. Big Business, to him, was something to be ultimately rejected or justified on the basis of efficiency rather than power accumulation. He tried to apply such technical criteria where none was really relevant, and he overlooked the fact that even where efficient or competitive, business could still pose irreconcilable challenges to the political and social fabric of a democratic community. Indeed, he failed to appreciate the extent to which it was competition that was leading to business agitation for federal regulation, and finally he was unable to do much more than sanction Wilson's actions as they were defined and directed by others.

There was no conspiracy during the Progressive Era. It is, of course, a fact that people and agencies acted out of public sight, and that official statements frequently had little to do with operational realities. But the imputation of a conspiracy would sidetrack a serious consideration of progressivism. There was a basic consensus among political and business leaders as to what was the public good, and no one had to be cajoled in a sinister manner. If détentes, private understandings, and the like were not publicly proclaimed it was merely because such agreements were exceptional and, generally known, could not have been denied to other business interests also desiring the security they provided. Such activities required a delicate sense of public relations, since there was always a public ready to oppose preferential treatment for special businesses, if not the basic assumptions behind such arrangements.

Certainly there was nothing surreptitious about the desire of certain businessmen for reforms, a desire that was frequently and publicly proclaimed, although the motives behind it were not appreciated by historians and although most contemporaries were unaware of how reforms were implemented after they were enacted. The fact that federal regulation of the economy was conservative in its effect in preserving existing power and economic relations in society should not obscure the fact that federal intervention in the economy was conservative in purpose as well. This ambition was publicly proclaimed by the interested business forces, and was hardly conspiratorial.

It is the intent of crucial business groups, and the structural circumstances within the economy that motivated them, that were the truly significant and unique aspects of the Progressive Era. The effects of the legislation were only the logical conclusion of the intentions behind it. The ideological consensus among key business and political leaders fed into a stream of common action, action that was sometimes stimulated by different specific goals but which nevertheless achieved the same results. Political leaders, such as Roosevelt, Wilson, and their key appointees, held that it was proper for an industry to have a decisive voice or veto over the regulatory process within its sphere of interest, and such assumptions filled many key businessmen with confidence in the essential reliability of the federal political mechanism, especially when it was contrasted to the unpredictability of state legislatures.

Business opposition to various federal legislative proposals and measures did exist, of course, especially if one focuses on opposition to particular clauses in specific bills. Such opposition, as in the case of the Federal Reserve Bill, was frequently designed to obtain special concessions. It should not be allowed to obscure the more important fact that the essential purpose and goal of any measure of importance in the Progressive Era was not merely endorsed by key representatives of businesses involved; rather such bills were first proposed by them.

One can always find some businessman, of course, who opposed federal regulation at any point, including within his own industry. Historians have relished in detailing such opposition, and, indeed, their larger analysis of the period has encouraged such revelations. But the finding of division in the ranks of business can be significant only if one makes the false assumption of a monolithic common interest among all capitalists, but, worse yet, assumes that there is no power center among capitalists, and that small-town bankers or hardware dealers can be equated with the leaders of the top industrial, financial, and railroad corporations. They can be equated, of course, if all one studies is the bulk of printed words. But in the political as well as in the economic competition between small and big business, the larger interests always managed to prevail in any specific contest. The rise of the National Association of Manufacturers in the Progressive Era is due to its antilabor position, and not to its opposition to federal regulation, which it voiced only after the First World War. In fact, crucial big business support could be found for every major federal regulatory movement, and frequent small business support could be found for any variety of proposals to their benefit, such as price-fixing and legalized trade associations. Progressivism was not the triumph of small business over the trusts, as has often been suggested, but the victory of big businesses in achieving the rationalization of the economy that only the federal government could provide.

Still, the rise of the N.A.M. among businessmen in both pro- and anti-regulation camps only reinforces the fact that the relationship of capitalists to the remainder of society was essentially unaltered by their divisions on federal intervention in the economy. In terms of the basic class structure, and the conditions of interclass relationships, big and small business alike were hostile to a labor movement interested in something more than paternalism and inequality. In this respect, and in their opposition or indifference to the very minimal social welfare reforms of the Progressive Era (nearly all of which were enacted in the states), American capitalism in the Progressive Era acted in the conservative fashion traditionally ascribed to it. The result was federal regulation in the context of a class society. Indeed, because the national political leadership of the Progressive Period shared this *noblesse oblige* and conservatism toward workers and farmers, it can be really said that there was federal regulation because there *was* a class society, and political leaders identified with the values and supremacy of business.

This identification of political and key business leaders with the same set of social values—ultimately class values—was hardly accidental, for had such a consensus not existed the creation of political capitalism would have been most unlikely. Political capitalism was based on the functional unity of major political and business leaders. The business and political élites knew each other, went to the same schools, belonged to the same clubs, married into the same families, shared the same values—in reality, formed that phenomenon which has lately been dubbed The Establishment. Garfield and Stetson met at Williams alumni functions, Rockefeller, Jr. married Aldrich's daughter, the Harvard clubmen always found the White House door open to them when Roosevelt was there, and so on. Indeed, no one who reads Jonathan Daniels' remarkable autobiography, *The End of Innocence*, can fail to realize the significance of an interlocking social, economic, and political élite in American history in this century.

The existence of an Establishment during the Progressive Era was convenient, even essential, to the functional attainment of political capitalism, but it certainly was not altogether new in American history, and certainly had antecedents in the 1890's. The basic causal factor behind national progressivism was the needs of business and financial elements. To some extent, however, the more benign character of many leading business leaders, especially those with safe fortunes, was due to the more secure, mellowed characteristics and paternalism frequently associated with the social élite. Any number of successful capitalists had long family traditions of social graces and refinement which they privately doubted were fully compatible with their role as capitalists. The desire for a stabilized, rationalized political capitalism was fed by this current in big business ideology, and gave many businessmen that air of responsibility and conservatism so admired by Roosevelt and Wilson. And, from a practical viewpoint, the cruder economic conditions could also lead to substantial losses. Men who were making fortunes with existing shares of the market preferred holding on to what they had rather than establishing control over an industry, or risking much of what they already possessed. Political stabilization seemed proper for this reason as well. It allowed men to relax, to hope that crises might be avoided, to enjoy the bountiful fortunes they had already made.

Not only were economic losses possible in an unregulated capitalism, but political destruction also appeared quite possible. There were disturbing gropings ever since the end of the Civil War: agrarian discontent, violence and strikes, a Populist movement, the rise of a Socialist Party that seemed, for a time, to have an unlimited growth potential. Above all, there was a labor movement seriously divided as to its proper course, and threatening to follow in the seemingly radical footsteps of European labor. The political capitalism of the Progressive Era was designed to meet these potential threats, as well as the immediate expressions of democratic discontent in the states. National progressivism was able to short-circuit state progressivism, to hold nascent radicalism in check by feeding the illusions of its leaders—leaders who could not tell the difference between federal regulation *of* business and federal regulation *for* business.

Political capitalism in America redirected the radical potential of mass grievances and aspirations—of genuine progressivism—and to a limited extent colored much of the intellectual ferment of the period, even though the amorphous nature of mass aspirations frequently made the goals of business and the rest of the public nearly synonymous. Many well-intentioned writers and academicians worked for the same legislative goals as businessmen, but their innocence did not alter the fact that such measures were frequently designed by businessmen to serve business ends, and that business ultimately reaped the harvest of positive results. Such innocence was possible because of a naïve, axiomatic view that government economic regulation, *per se*, was desirable, and also because many ignored crucial business support for such measures by focusing on the less important business opposition that existed. The fetish of government regulation of the economy as a positive social good was one that sidetracked a substantial portion of European socialism as well, and was not unique to the American experience. Such axiomatic and simplistic assumptions of what federal regulation would bring did not take into account problems of democratic control and participation, and in effect assumed that the power of government was neutral and socially beneficent. Yet many of the leading muckrakers and academics of the period were more than naïve but ultimately conservative in their intentions as well. They sought the paternalism and stability which they expected political capitalism to bring, since only in this way could the basic virtues of capitalism be maintained. The betrayal of liberalism that has preoccupied some intellectual historians did not result from irrelevant utopianism or philosophical pragmatism, but from the lack of a truly radical, articulated alternative economic and political program capable of synthesizing political democracy with industrial reality. Such a program was never formulated in this period either in America or Europe.

Historians have continually·tried to explain the seemingly sudden collapse of progressivism after the First World War, and have offered reasons that varied from moral exhaustion to the repression of nonconformity. On the whole, all explanations suffer because they really fail to examine progressivism beyond the favorable conventional interpretation. Progressive goals, on the concrete, legislative level, were articulated by various business interests. These goals were, for the most part, achieved, and no one formulated others that big business was also interested in attaining. Yet a synthesis of business and politics on the federal level was created during the war, in various administrative and emergency agencies, that continued throughout the following decade. Indeed, the war period represents the triumph of business in the most emphatic manner possible. With the exception of a brief interlude in the history of the Federal Trade Commission, big business gained total support from the various regulatory agencies and the Executive. It was during the war that effective, working oligopoly and price and market agreements became operational in the dominant sectors of the American economy. The rapid diffusion of power in the economy and relatively easy entry virtually ceased. Despite the cessation of important new legislative enactments, the unity of business and the federal government continued throughout the 1920's and thereafter, using the foundations laid in the Progressive Era to stabilize and consolidate conditions within various industries. And, on the same progressive foundations and exploiting the experience with the war agencies, Herbert Hoover and Franklin Roosevelt later formulated·programs for saving American capitalism. The principle of utilizing the federal government to stabilize the economy, established in the context of modern industrialism during the Progressive Era, became the basis of political capitalism in its many later ramifications.

In this sense progressivism did not die in the 1920's, but became a part of the basic fabric of American society. The different shapes political capitalism has taken since 1916 deserve a separate treatment, but suffice it to say that even Calvin Coolidge did not mind evoking the heritage of Theodore Roosevelt, and Hoover was, if anything, deeply devoted to the Wilsonian tradition in which Franklin Roosevelt gained his first political experience.

. . . Any reasonable generalization on the phenomenon of progressivism must necessarily take into account the economic realities and problems of the period, and the responses that were set in motion. Yet the crucial factor in the American experience was the nature of economic power which required political tools to rationalize the economic process, and that resulted in a synthesis of politics and economics. This integration is the dominant fact of American society in the twentieth century, although once political capitalism is created a dissection of causes and effects becomes extraordinarily difficult. The economy had its own problems, dictated by technological innovation, underconsumption, crises, and competition. But these difficulties were increasingly controlled by political means to the extent that the consideration of economic problems outside their political context is meaningless. The "laws of capitalist development" were not self-contained imperatives in the technological, economic, or political sphere, but an inseparable unification of all three elements.

The object of such a combination was not merely capital accumulation, although it was that as well, but a desire to defend and exercise power through new media more appropriate to the structural conditions of the new century: the destructive potential of growing competition and the dangerous possibilities of a formal political democracy that might lead to a radical alteration of the distribution of wealth or even its total expropriation. Politics and the state become the means of attaining order in the economic sphere and security in the political arena. And they were accessible tools because the major political parties and leaders of the period were also conservative in the sense that they believed in the basic value of capitalist social relations—of some variation of the status quo. The resilience of capitalism, under these circumstances, becomes something that cannot be evaluated in isolated economic terms. Behind the economy, resting on new foundations in which effective collusion and price stability is now the rule, stands the organized power of the national government. The stability and future of the economy is grounded, in the last analysis, on the power of the state to act to preserve it. Such support does not end crises, nor does it eliminate antagonisms inherent in the very nature of the economy, but it does assure the ability of the existing social order to overcome, or survive, the consequences of its own deficiencies. The theory of the national government as a neutral intermediary in its intervention into the economic process is a convenient ideological myth, but such a contention will not survive a serious inquiry into the origins and consequences of such intervention. The rhetoric of reform is invariably different than its structural results. Such mythology is based on the assumption that those who control the state will not use it for their own welfare.

It is important to stress that under conditions of political capitalism the form of the industrialization process, and of the political machinery of society, take on those characteristics necessary to fulfill the peculiar values, attributes, and goals of the ascendant class of that society. The rationalized, dominated, and essentially totalitarian decision-making process is not a consequence of forces inherent in industrialism, but in political capitalism in all its components. The organization of industry is based on the decisions of men whose motives have nothing whatsoever to do with inexorable destiny. Mergers, the scale of effective production, the nature of the production itself, and the direction given to the fruits of technology—all these were decisions made by men whose motives, interests, and weaknesses were peculiar to the basic capitalist assumptions upon which they operated. Their errors were many, as were the possibilities for their failure; but the national government stood behind them so that the consequences of their mistakes would not be calamitous. Perhaps industrialization would not have permitted democratic control and direct participation in the work process under any circumstances. All one can do is point to the large extent to which the concentration of industry in this period had nothing to do with considerations of efficient technology, and suggest that no effort whatsoever was ever made to democratize the work situation and industrial control, much less consider the desirability of reducing technological efficiency, if necessary, in such a way as to make decentralization or workers' control possible.

Nor is there any evidence to suggest that the bureaucratization of the political machinery of society, to the extent it took place, was as inevitable as the concentration of industry. It was perfectly logical for men who had spent years solving their economic problems or making their fortunes through political means to also welcome the intervention of a centralized state power to meet problems they could not solve themselves. Social forces, dynamic institutional factors, were the cause of bureaucratic developments in the form of new political agencies and the strengthening of many of the older ones. American capitalism was not merely interested in having law that operated like a piece of machinery, as Weber suggested, but in utilizing the state on terms and conditions which made bureaucratic functions class functions. Bureaucracy, in itself, needed a power base in order to operate in a roughly continuous, systematic fashion. Since it had no economic power itself, it had to support, and hence be supported by, powerful economic groups. This was especially true in a situation where the conditions of political activity were defined by political parties which in turn reflected economic interests, or where the idea of the bureaucracy originated with those operating in the very area in which the bureaucracy was to function.

The skeptical reader may ask whether political capitalism changed after 1916, or perhaps whether capitalism was made more socially responsible by virtue of the stability and rationalization it attained through political means. The question is a moot one, and would take at least one more volume to answer properly. All one can do is point to the continuity in the nature of the political parties and their key leaders, but, more important, to the perpetuation of the same distribution of wealth and the same social relations over the larger part of this century. The solution of economic problems has continued to take place in the political sphere, and the strength of the status quo is based ultimately on the synthesis of politics and economics. Crises have been overcome, or frozen, as much by the power of the state as by internal economic resources applied by business in isolation.

The question remains: Could the American political experience, and the nature of our economic institutions, have been radically different than they are today? It is possible to answer affirmatively, although only in a hypothetical, unreal manner, for there was nothing inevitable or predetermined in the peculiar character given to industrialism in America. And, abstractly regarding all of the extraneous and artificial measures that provided shape and direction to American political and economic life, and their ultimate class function, it would be possible to make a case for a positive reply to the question. Yet ultimately the answer must be a reluctant "No."

There can be no alternatives so long as none are seriously proposed, and to propose a relevant measure of fundamental opposition one must understand what is going on in society, and the relationship of present actions to desired goals. To have been successful, a movement of fundamental change would have had to develop a specific diagnosis of existing social dynamics and, in particular, the variable nature and consequences of political intervention in the economy. It would have, in short, required a set of operating premises radically different than any that were formulated in the Progressive Era or later. Populism rejected, on the whole, the values of business even as it was unable to articulate a viable alternative. Intellectually it left a vacuum, and, more important, the movement was dead by 1900. The Socialist Party suffered from the fetishistic belief in the necessity of centralization that has characterized all socialist groups that interpreted Marx too literally, and it had a totally inaccurate estimate of the nature of progressivism, eventually losing most of its followers to the Democrats. The two major political parties, as always, differed on politically unimportant and frequently contrived details, but both were firmly wedded to the status quo, and the workers were generally their captives or accomplices. No socially or politically significant group tried to articulate an alternative means of organizing industrial technology in a fashion that permitted democratic control over centralized power, or participation in routine, much less crucial, decisions in the industrial process. No party tried to develop a program that suggested democracy could be created only by continuous mass involvement in the decisions that affected their lives, if the concentration of actual power in the hands of an élite was to be avoided. In brief, the Progressive Era was characterized by a paucity of alternatives to the status quo, a vacuum that permitted political capitalism to direct the growth of industrialism in America, to shape its politics, to determine the ground rules for American civilization in the twentieth century, and to set the stage for what was to follow.

Progressivism and Imperialism: The Progressive Movement and American Foreign Policy, 1898-1916

William E. Leuchtenburg

One of the early "sacred tenets" of progressivism, concerning the subject of imperialism, suggested a rather strict separation between domestic and foreign affairs. When the latter was discussed, most progressives were described as anti-imperialist and in favor of very limited foreign activity on the part of the government. William E. Leuchtenburg, Professor of History at Columbia University, attacks this whole proposition head on. For him, the progressives, with but a few exceptions such as Jane Addams, "ardently supported the imperialist surge or, at the very least, proved agreeably acquiescent." Leuchtenburg goes on to argue that the progressives' advocacy of a "strong" foreign policy, inherent in the writings of Herbert Croly, contributed heavily to the demise of the party.

No distinction is more revered by the American historian than that between domestic and foreign affairs and in few periods of our history has that distinction been more religiously observed than in the Progressive era. The Theodore Roosevelt who fought the trusts, defied the special interests, and stood at Armageddon to battle for the Lord, and the Theodore Roosevelt who preached jingoism and "took" Panama have been divorced on grounds of incompatibility.[1]

The leaders of the Progressive movement, we are given to understand, welcomed Roosevelt's aid in fighting the railway kings and the coal barons, but dissented vigorously from his imperialism and chauvinism. The Progressives were deeply disturbed by Roosevelt's racism, and even more by such episodes as the acquisition of the Canal Zone, but accepted his leadership because of his avowed hostility to corporation control of American life. George Norris' biographer represents the prevailing attitude in asserting that "Western progressives . . . had never adhered to the big-stick doctrines of Roosevelt."[2]

The thesis of this article is that the Progressives, contrary to the orthodox accounts, did not oppose imperialism but, with few exceptions, ardently supported the imperialist surge or, at the very least, proved agreeably acquiescent. The majority of the Progressive members of Congress voted for increased naval expenditures and for Caribbean adventures in imperialism. At

From "Progressivism and Imperialism: The Progressive Movement and American Foreign Policy, 1898–1916," by William E. Leuchtenburg, in *Mississippi Valley Historical Review* (December 1962). Reprinted by permission of the publisher.

no time did the Republican insurgents in the Taft administration take issue with Dollar Diplomacy, even when the Progressives were searching for campaign issues in 1912. Not until after the 1912 elections did they concern themselves actively with foreign affairs and then it was not to combat imperialism but to urge the use of American force in Mexico and an increase in armaments. By 1916 the Progressive party had forsaken its program of domestic reform to condemn the foreign policy of the Wilson administration, and a fondness for a "strong" foreign policy was an important cause of the death of the party. Moreover, the ideological content and the motivation of imperialism and progressivism had much in common, a relationship made explicit in the writings of Herbert Croly.

Senator Albert J. Beveridge of Indiana epitomized the two interlocking forces, although his imperialistic views were unquestionably more fervently held than those of the average Progressive. One of the most eloquent orators of the period, he made the keynote speech at the Progressive convention of 1912 in Chicago. Beveridge's fame as an orator started with his declamatory avowal of American imperialism in the Spanish-American War, and he maintained this enthusiasm for imperialism throughout the Progressive era. " 'The opposition tells us we ought not to rule a people without their consent. I answer, the rule of liberty, that all just governments derive their authority from the consent of the governed, applies only to those who are capable of self-government,' " he told an enthusiastic Indianapolis meeting in 1898.

> The proposition of the opposition makes the Declaration of Independence preposterous, like the reading of Job's lamentations would be at a wedding, or an Altgeld speech on the Fourth of July. . . . Cuba not contiguous? Porto Rico not contiguous? The Philippines not contiguous? Our navy will make them contiguous! . . . Dewey and Sampson and Schley have made them contiguous, and American speed, American guns, American heart and brain and nerve will keep them contiguous forever.[3]

No member of the Senate in the first decade of this century contributed more to the Progressive movement than Senator Beveridge. He sponsored the bill for federal meat inspection and carried the fight against the bitter opposition of the slaughterhouses. He fought a long, courageous, abortive campaign to end child labor in America. In the 1910 campaign in Indiana he urged federal control of railways, the eight-hour day, and the regulation of trust capitalization. It was Beveridge who managed the insurgent revolt against the Payne-Aldrich tariff. He walked out of the Republican party with the Progressives in 1912, and he fought against the drift toward reconciliation after the election, even accepting the hopeless assignment of Progressive candidate for the Senate in 1914.

Yet his faith in America's imperialist mission continued to be just as strong as his belief in economic reform, and Beveridge's imperialism ultimately proved his undoing as a Progressive. Many of the reforms dearest to Beveridge, which the Republican party had opposed and Roosevelt had shunned, were pushed through Congress by Woodrow Wilson, and Beveridge could have little quarrel with the President's domestic program, but by 1914 he was bitterly opposed to him. Wilson should have recognized Huerta, for Mexico needed a strong man, and the repeal of the Panama tolls was a "fatal blunder." "The Progressive Party in Congress will be solid against the repeal." [4] In 1916 he lashed into Wilson for refusing to use arms to support American investments in China, for his proposal to withdraw from the Philippines, and, strangely, for not increasing the tariff to meet new European competition. Beveridge, faced with the necessity to choose between progressivism and imperialism for the first time, chose the latter. By 1920 he was crying out against " 'Organized labor's assault on American institutions!' " interspersing speeches against the League of Nations with demands for the repeal of the excess profits tax. Inflation was caused by the draining of money to Europe through foreign propaganda and the unreasonable demands of labor unions for higher wages. [5] Once more Beveridge's views on domestic and foreign policy had merged, and this new outlook persisted until his death.

At the outbreak of the Spanish-American War few men saw any conflict between social reform and democratic striving at home and the new imperialist mission; indeed, the war seemed nothing so much as an extension of democracy to new parts of the world, and few political figures exceeded the enthusiasm of William Jennings Bryan for the Spanish war. [6] As the war continued and its consequences were realized, as the dream of *Cuba libre* gave way to the realities of Aguinaldo's insurrection, a few of the Progressives, like Hazen Pingree and Jane Addams, joined the anti-imperialist forces, but, first and last, it was the conservatives who bore the burden of the anti-imperialist campaign.

In late March, 1899, William Allen White explained the Emporia *Gazette's* support of the war. " 'Only Anglo-Saxons can govern themselves. . . . It is the Anglo-Saxon's manifest destiny to go forth as a world conqueror,' " [7] he observed. Years later he wrote of this time:

> And we in Emporia, and "Our Charley" in Washington, thought we were free to spout and jower and jangle about the atrocities of the "brute Weyler" without in the slightest affecting the reality of our lives. We were as little boys making snoots across the fence, throwing rocks into the next yard, but innocent of the fact that we were starting wars that would last far into the next century, threaten all that we loved and wreck much that we cherished. [8]

"Though I hate war *per se*," wrote Elizabeth Cady Stanton, "I am glad that it has come in this instance. I would like to see Spain . . . swept from the face of the earth." [9]

A few of the Progressives, and many of the older generation of radicals like Henry Demarest Lloyd, joined forces with the anti-imperialists, but it was conservative Republicans like Thomas B. Reed, Democrats like Grover Cleveland and Bryan, frequently for partisan ends, businessmen like Andrew Carnegie, and Mugwumps like Carl Schurz who provided the bulk of the leadership. "The Republicans who joined the anti-imperialist movement were, almost without exception, Republicans of the older generation. . . . The anti-imperialists made great efforts to attract labor support, but, on the whole, were unsuccessful." [10] The one important political figure who persistently linked the fight for progressivism with the struggle against imperialism was the ineffective Silver Republican, Senator Richard Pettigrew of South Dakota, and he was retired from office in 1900, partly because of his anti-imperialist views.[11]

Theodore Roosevelt's accession to the presidency brought the new imperialist movement to full flower, and, in all of his foreign ventures, in Santo Domingo, Panama, the Far East, in building a greater American fleet, Roosevelt had the support of a majority of the Progressives. "I confess that the half-hearted criticism I hear of the way of the administration with Panama provokes in me a desire to laugh," Jacob Riis noted. "I am not a jingo; but when some things happen I just have to get up and cheer. The way our modern American diplomacy goes about things is one of them." [12] Gifford Pinchot warmly admired Roosevelt's policy in Panama,[13] while Oscar Straus, the Progressive candidate for governor of New York in 1912, helped prepare the dubious legal defense of Roosevelt's course with Panama, with his concept of a " 'covenant running with the land.' " As John Bassett Moore observed cynically to Straus, it was "indifferently, a question of the 'covenant running with the land' or a question of the 'covenant running (*away!*) with the land!!' " [14] When Bryan negotiated a treaty of indemnity and apology with Colombia, the Progressives were outraged. The Colombians, said Senator Joseph L. Bristow heatedly, were "a lot of blackmailers." As for the contention that Roosevelt had acted immorally in Panama, "there could be no greater slander pronounced against the Government and nothing more unjust, and in my opinion it borders on treason." [15] The final word on the Progressive position on Panama was had by George Norris over forty years later, when he ruefully observed:

> Often those years I followed him [Roosevelt] when I had some doubts as to the righteousness of his course. . . . Yet he built the Panama Canal after other governments and a great corporation had spent a vast amount of money and had failed in their efforts. He threw his heart into the construction of this waterway, whose long useful service has caused the struggle for it to be forgotten; but during its progress the means by which the Panama Canal was accomplished in some respects seem doubtful to me. *I followed him step by step in that fight.* Doubts assailed me at the time, and I have since reached the conclusion that our government's decision to establish the new republic of Panama, which in reality prevented Colombia from defending her own territory with her army, was open to argument.[16]

The Progressives were scarcely less cooperative in promoting American hegemony in the Caribbean and defending Roosevelt's big stick diplomacy there. On the Platt amendment Senators Beveridge and Jonathan P. Dolliver voted with the majority, and the Silver Republicans, Pettigrew and Henry M. Teller, cast the only dissenting Republican votes.[17] Roosevelt's action in taking over the customhouse of the Dominican Republic received the approval of Senators Beveridge, Moses E. Clapp, Dolliver, and Robert M. La Follette, with not a single Progressive senator voting against the treaty.[18] By March, 1907, Charles Joseph Bonaparte, who prosecuted the trusts under Roosevelt and was to be a bitter foe of George W. Perkins in 1916, could sound a popular note in praising the President's skill in "promoting the peace of Central America, in staying civil strife in Cuba, in discouraging rebellion in Santo Domingo." [19]

Bonaparte also shared with a great many Progressives Roosevelt's enthusiasm for a big navy, a viewpoint of inestimable advantage for a secretary of the navy. When Roosevelt appointed him to this post in 1905, Bonaparte assured him: "It is perhaps proper to say, in this connection, that I am in hearty sympathy with your frequently expressed views as to the importance and, indeed, necessity of a very strong and very efficient Navy to the United States." [20] The anti-navy bloc in Congress was led not by the Progressives but by the conservative Eugene Hale in the Senate and the conservative Theodore Burton in the House, and their main supporters were likewise conservatives.[21]

The first uprising of the insurgents against Nelson W. Aldrich occurred not over the Payne-Aldrich tariff, but on behalf of Roosevelt's request for four new battleships in 1908 against the outspoken opposition of the Old Guard. Led by Senator Beveridge, two fifths of the Republicans deserted Aldrich in a debate featuring repeated attacks on the leadership of the Old Guard. The debate, which ended in a compromise on two battleships, badly shook Aldrich's domination of the Senate. "The Senate oligarchy is in a bad way," reported the *Saturday Evening Post*. "It is tottery and wobbly at the knees. Its members do not know just what it was that hit them, but they do know that they have been hit hard." [22] On the final vote on the Piles amendment for four battleships, which was defeated 50 to 23, Beveridge, William E. Borah, and Jonathan Bourne voted with the big navy minority against Aldrich, W. Murray Crane, Thomas C. Platt, and other Old Guard leaders. Senator Weldon B. Heyburn expressed the general sentiment of the debate in observing: "I care nothing for the poetic idea of turning swords into plowshares and spears into pruning hooks. This is a business proposition." On this occasion two of the Progressives, Clapp and Joseph M. Dixon, voted against navalism, and Clapp launched a brilliant, bitter attack on Beveridge for raising false issues "that the public might be prejudiced." [23]

The degree to which the majority of the Progressives were bound to Roosevelt's foreign policy is indicated in a letter of Brand Whitlock's:

I have your note asking me if I could help you with a letter against wasting $32,000,000 on two more useless battleships. I am not sure that anything I can say on that subject will be of any use in stopping the construction of battleships; if it would I would say a great deal, for, of course, it is all but a part of the vast and amazing superstition of war. . . . I suppose that as long as there are some nations in the world who want to go to war, and so long as there are commercial interests that will keep up revolutions in Mexico and Central and South America, we shall need a navy and army to do police duty and keep the peace in this hemisphere, for which, under the Monroe Doctrine, I suppose we are responsible; but I know of no reason for going beyond this need.[24]

Whitlock was an intelligent, eloquent critic of Roosevelt's foreign policy who once observed that "Thayer can see the megalomania which afflicted Garibaldi but cannot see it when the same symptoms are repeated in Roosevelt." [25] Yet even the hostile Whitlock accepted reluctantly the obligations of "police duty" and the Monroe Doctrine, and from these premises much could follow.

In March, 1909, Theodore Roosevelt gave way to his heir apparent, William Howard Taft, and for the next four years the Progressives were confronted by the phenomenon of Dollar Diplomacy. Philander C. Knox, who had prosecuted the Northern Securities case, directed the new Caribbean policy, while Willard D. Straight, who in 1914 was to found the *New Republic* "to explore and develop and apply the ideas which had been advertised by Theodore Roosevelt when he was the leader of the Progressive party,"[26] fostered Dollar Diplomacy in the Orient. The liberal character of Straight's Oriental diplomacy, which attempted to force American capital to go into China where it did not care to enter, rests on the nice distinction between territorial integrity and economic hegemony, and the dubious assumption that the investments of Edward H. Harriman, who allegedly asserted he could buy Congress and, if need be, the judiciary, would be more beneficial to the Chinese people than French and Russian capital. Ultimately Straight ended up attempting to raise a foreign loan to crush the Chinese revolution, on the assumption that what China needed was a dictator. The British and Germans were unsympathetic, and Straight was forced to allow the Chinese people to determine their own political destiny.[27]

From the days of the Payne-Aldrich tariff dispute, the rift between the insurgents and Taft grew wider, and Taft was beleaguered by a Progressive bloc which at times opposed him on purely ideological grounds, on occasion out of personal spite, but at no time because of disagreement with Taft's Dollar Diplomacy. While the Progressives were meeting in Chicago in 1912 to establish their third party, Taft was landing American marines in Nicaragua, but no word of condemnation for Taft's foreign policy appears in the Progressive platform of 1912. Instead, the platform stated:

It is imperative to the welfare of our people that we enlarge and extend our foreign commerce. In every way possible our federal government should co-operate in this important matter. Germany's policy of co-operation between government and business has in comparatively few years made that nation a leading competitor for the commerce of the world. . . . The Panama Canal, built and paid for by the American people, must be used primarily for their benefit. . . . American ships engaged in coastwise trade shall pay no tolls.

Roosevelt's speech to the Progressive convention called for building a larger navy,[28] and Frank Munsey assured his readers that "The new Progressive party believes in a navy that will insure peace, that will give us a rightful position among the powers of the world, and that will make the Monroe Doctrine an actuality." [29]

The two issues of foreign policy which did affect the Progressive bolt of 1912 were the arbitration treaties and Taft's Mexican policy, both of which earned the ire of Theodore Roosevelt, and with Taft's prosecution of United States Steel, brought about the final break between Roosevelt and Taft. "Describing the treaties as an outrage, born of some very 'sloppy thinking,' Roosevelt furiously set about to destroy them. He wrote innumerable letters to [Henry Cabot] Lodge, chairman of the Senate Foreign Relations Committee, corresponded with [Elihu] Root, and indirectly reached [Albert B.] Cummins and Borah." [30] In a series of articles in the *Outlook*, starting on May 20, 1911, Roosevelt lashed out at the arbitration treaties with thinly veiled references to Taft. We should not indulge in "amiable sentimentality"; it is "our duty not to indulge in shams, not to make believe we are getting peace by some patent contrivance which sensible men ought to know cannot work"; "to speak of it as silly comes far short of saying what should be said." [31] When the treaties reached the Senate floor, the Progressive forces were divided, Borah, Bourne, Bristow, and Cummins voting for the crippling amendment to exclude from arbitration questions affecting the admission of aliens to the United States or any question involving the Monroe Doctrine, while Clapp and John D. Works voted against it, a courageous act on the part of Senator Works, who came from the alien-conscious state of California.[32] Roosevelt denounced as "flabby" Taft's firm action in refusing to intervene on behalf of American oil interests in Mexico.[33] "Of all the misconduct of the Administration," Roosevelt concluded, "no misconduct had been greater than that relating to foreign affairs." [34]

The campaign of 1912 offered the Progressives another excellent opportunity to attack Taft's Dollar Diplomacy, but they were strangely silent. Scarcely had the election returns of November, 1912, been counted, however, than they began their attack on Woodrow Wilson and a movement started within the Progressive party to return to the Republican fold at almost any price. The Progressives were embarrassed by Wilson's commendable record in domestic affairs, and as Wilson drove through one reform after another in 1913 it became clear that their only choice was between joining forces with Wilson or maintaining their party organization intact with a more radical approach to domestic problems; there were no grounds for choosing the Republicans over the Wilson administration. Instead, they chose to fight it out with the administration on foreign policy. For the first time in the history of the Progressive movement foreign affairs determined the line of direction, and by 1916 the Progressives were completely absorbed with foreign policy issues and their movement was moribund.

On July 11, 1914, Roosevelt announced the new direction of the party when he resigned as contributing editor to the *Outlook* to devote his time to opposing the Wilson administration for its foreign policy which had "meant the abandonment of the interest and honor of America."[35] In later years Roosevelt indicated that his violent turn against the administration was over Wilson's indifference to the plight of Belgium, but in September, 1914, Roosevelt was urging American neutrality with respect to Belgium. "Of course it would be folly to jump into the gulf ourselves to no good purpose; and very probably nothing that we could have done would have helped Belgium."[36] The main grievances of Roosevelt and the Progressives with Wilson were originally not over the European war at all, but over the treaty of apology and indemnity with Colombia, Bryan's cooling off treaties, and the "mushy amiability" of Wilson in withdrawing from Mexico and agreeing to arbitration by the ABC powers.[37]

Borah announced a "last ditch" fight against Wilson's bill to repeal the Panama Canal tolls, and on the vote for final passage, Borah, Bristow, Clapp, Cummins, La Follette, Miles Poindexter, and Works all voted in opposition, with only Asle J. Gronna and Norris voting with the Wilson administration.[38] Mexico was an even hotter issue. In March, 1915, Walter A. Johnson, New York state chairman of the Progressive party, asserted in an interview in the New York *Sun* that Wilson, instead of following the policy of "watchful waiting" in Mexico, should follow the sterling example of Theodore Roosevelt in the Perdicaris case in Morocco by sending warships and issuing an ultimatum.[39] A few months later Dr. H. Nelson Jackson, chairman of the Progressive party of Vermont, issued a statement to the Burlington *Free Press*:

> While hundreds of Americans were being murdered, their wives and daughters outraged, their property destroyed, and have received no protection from our spineless, psalm-singing administration, thousands of our citizens thought that President Wilson was locked in his study praying and planning for peace and good will to this beloved country of ours, but in the past few weeks they suddenly realized that his time had been taken up otherwise, with courting. . . . Oh! God give us a leader that will keep our country in the exalted position made possible by such leaders as Washington and Abraham Lincoln and that will make Americans feel no matter where they go, no matter where they invest their capital, that they, their families, and their properties will be respected and protected, and above all that our dear flag will be honored among all nations.[40]

In December, 1914, the Progressives issued a statement completely omitting the progressive planks of the 1912 platform and concentrating on demands for a higher protective tariff, a far cry from the insurgency of 1909 and a clear bid for amalgamation with the Republican party. By the fall of 1915 domestic issues had almost completely disappeared from the Progressive program, and the one issue that was hammered home in Progressive publications and meetings was the need for military preparedness. On September 25, 1915, Victor Murdock, the Kansas radical who was chairman of the National Committee of the Progressive party, wrote Walter Johnson:

> I was greatly gratified to find this view [the necessity for maintaining the Progressive party] confirmed at a dinner given by Mr. Perkins to me at the Manhattan Hotel here on Wednesday evening. . . . There was straight-out, complete candor in the addresses made by all of them, and an absence of boast and fustian. They were in favor of holding the line, facing forward and throwing themselves into the campaign of 1916 with uncompromising aggression, behind a ticket and platform which will challenge the sense and patriotism of the nation.
>
> The strong notes sounded were for military and economic preparedness. The men present favored insuring peace for the nation by placing us in a position to command respect and for an adjustment of the tariff under the Progressive plan of a tariff commission to meet the abnormal selling campaign by Europe which will follow inevitably the cessation of hostilities abroad.[41]

Not only had foreign policy become a key issue, but it had been linked by now with the need for high tariff walls, a prophecy of the economic policy of Warren G. Harding and Herbert Hoover.

In December Chairman Murdock issued a statement emphasizing the main points of the Progressive party program:

> The Progressive Party proposes to bring, first of all, a constructive program for business ills, the proposal of a sane protective tariff policy and a demand for social justice and for straight-out preparedness both on the military side and the industrial and economic sides. The Progressive Party's policy of 1912 for a tariff commission with broad powers has already the endorsement of the whole country and must be enacted into law if the industrial invasion from Europe after the war is to be forestalled.[42]

On January 11, 1916, the Progressive National Committee, meeting in Chicago, issued a statement, adopted unanimously, condemning the Wilson administration for its failure "to deal adequately with National honor and industrial welfare."

> The Wilson administration has repudiated the faith of our forefathers which made the American flag the sufficient protection of an American citizen around the world. It has suffered American men, women and children to be slaughtered in Mexico and on the high seas, American property to be destroyed and American liberty to travel and

trade to be subject to the arbitrary and lawless coercion of foreign belligerents. . . . We need a reawakening of our elder Americanism, of our belief in those things that our country and our flag stand for.

At their national convention in 1916 the Progressive party, which had had only a few sentences on foreign policy in its 1912 platform, devoted almost its entire platform to preparedness, Americanism, and the excoriation of the Wilson program on Mexico and the European war. The Progressives demanded a regular army of 250,000 men, compulsory universal military training, and "a navy restored to at least second rank in battle efficiency." When Roosevelt refused the nomination, the party turned to Charles E. Hughes, who Roosevelt told them stood for "clean-cut, straightout Americanism," and the party decided to support him, because only he could "serve the two vital causes of Americanism and Preparedness."[43]

For many it was a hard choice. The Republican platform of 1916, as the *New Republic* observed, was a "stupidly, defiantly and cynically reactionary document." "The Republican party of 1916 does not differ in any essential respect from that portion of the party which nominated Mr. Taft. . . . They have revised none of their professed principles; they have dismissed none of their objectionable leaders; they have not by a single act or declaration betrayed a leaning towards liberalism, such as would make an honest Progressive welcome reunion."[44] When Raymond Robins of Illinois, chairman of the national convention, heard Roosevelt tell him that "Mr. Hughes would answer the preparedness, Americanism and progressive demands of our party," Robins dissented. On June 26, at a meeting of the Progressive National Committee, Robins announced: "At this hour, if I had to vote or declare my sentiments, I should declare for Woodrow Wilson and vote for him."

Robins sounded out the other Progressive leaders. Hiram W. Johnson, Gifford Pinchot, and James R. Garfield all told him that the only hope was to go back to the Republican party and support Hughes, Pinchot explaining it was necessary because of "this national crisis." Soon Robins was announcing his support of Hughes, in part because "we must develop a national mind that will comprehend our social, industrial and military unpreparedness. It must appreciate the domestic injury and national danger that lies in our lack of a definite foreign policy." He further asserted his warm support of compulsory military training, the Oriental Exclusion acts, and "our obligations under the Monroe Doctrine."[45]

In the campaign of 1916 the Progressive party frankly announced its abandonment of its earlier political ideals. On June 26, 1916, the National Committee, after listing recent important gains in progressive legislation, which it termed "national advance," observed that the war had brought

an issue deeper than national advance, the issue of national unity and the nation's existence, of Americanism and of Preparedness. The Progressive Platform of 1916, therefore, placed foremost as our immediate need preparedness in arms, industry and spirit. . . . The Pro-

gressive National Committee recognizes that such are now the issues
that immediately confront the country and *looks only to the duty that
arises therefrom.*[46]

The Republican and Progressive platforms of 1916 were almost identical,
except that Lodge could not get the Republicans to accept the provision for
universal service.[47] Partly out of political desperation, partly out of loyalty
to Roosevelt, in large part because of their views on foreign affairs, the mass
of the Progressives supported Hughes, although the Republicans made no
pretense of progressivism and Wilson had enacted much of the Progressive
platform. The 1916 campaign was the last presidential election the Progressive party entered; imperialism and militarism had replaced the old liberal
formulas of protest, and within a year the party was dead.

How does one account for the wide divergence between Progressive
principle and practice, between a concern for democratic processes at home
and a disregard of them abroad, for antagonism to financial empires in America and encouragement of them overseas, for the destruction of American
progressivism in the interest of imperialism, militarism, and Americanism?

In the first place, many Progressives were able to convince themselves
that there was no conflict at all, that their domestic and foreign policies were
two sides of the same coin. The Spanish-American War was not merely a
struggle to bring freedom to Cuba and end Spanish tyranny but a crusade
for principle against the greed of Wall Street interests opposed to the war.
"Cuba is free and she thanks President Roosevelt for her freedom," wrote
Jacob Riis. "But for his insistence that the nation's honor was bound up in
the completion of the work his Rough-Riders began at Las Guasimas and on
San Juan Hill, a cold conspiracy of business greed would have left her in the
lurch, to fall by and by reluctantly into our arms, bankrupt and helpless,
while the sneer of the cynics that we were plucking that plum for ourselves
would have been justified."[48] "We will have this war for the freedom of
Cuba in spite of the timidity of the commercial interests," Roosevelt told a
Gridiron dinner.[49] We must save the "wretched Cubans" from Spain, Roosevelt averred, and then noted, "It would be a splendid thing for the Navy,
too."[50]

Compulsory military training was likewise a phase of progressivism.
"The proposed continental army is utterly undemocratic; it denies to the
patriotic man of small means the chance to train which it gives to his well-
to-do brother," Roosevelt asserted.[51] Compulsory universal military training,
agreed Raymond Robins, "will do more in one generation to break down
class and section prejudice, develop disciplined, vigorous and efficient citizenship, and to unify the diverse groups of our national life in a vital Americanism than all other forces combined." As opposed to this Progressive program,
Robins added, the Democrats, in opposing universal training, offer only "a
state-dominated militia with its menace of shiftless incompetence, spoils
politics and organized snobbery as a national defense force, at a time of
world peril."[52]

Secondly, it is impossible to understand the acquiescence of any Progressives in the imperialist movement without realizing the remarkable hold that Theodore Roosevelt had on his followers. Norris' testimony that "often those years I followed him when I had some doubts as to the righteousness of his course" is not an isolated instance. To many American liberals "Roosevelt was . . . [by 1912] something more than a revered political leader. He was gradually becoming a minor deity."[53] Years later, William Allen White described his first meeting with Roosevelt:

> I met Theodore Roosevelt. He sounded in my heart the first trumpet call of the new time that was to be. . . . I had never known such a man as he, and never shall again. He overcame me. And in the hour or two we spent that day at lunch, and in a walk down F Street, he poured into my heart such visions, such ideals, such hopes, such a new attitude toward life and patriotism and the meaning of things, as I had never dreamed men had.[54]

Even after Roosevelt had deserted the Progressives and helped disrupt the movement, even after he had had the obtuseness to suggest Lodge as the standardbearer, Harold Ickes could see only George Perkins as the Iago of the movement and had no harsh words for Roosevelt.[55]

Thirdly, the attitude of the Progressives toward the American Negro made them more receptive to American imperialism. They readily accepted the notion that the little brown brother was a ward of the United States, not fit for self-government, because they regarded the southern Negro as a ward when they did not think of him as a corrupt politician attempting to sell his vote to the highest bidder at Republican conventions. The Progressive party plan with respect to the Negro, wrote Roosevelt, was "to try for the gradual re-enfranchisement of the worthy colored man of the South by frankly giving the leadership of our movement to the wisest and justest white men of the South."[56] Despite the fact that the Negro vote in Maryland was credited with giving Roosevelt his margin of victory over Taft in the 1912 primaries, he persisted in his aim to make the Progressive party a lily white party in the South, with Senator Dixon, his national campaign manager, publicly disavowing a Progressive organization in South Carolina because of its Negro membership and the convention refusing to seat any southern Negro delegates, despite the dissent of Jane Addams.[57] W. A. D. Venerable, head of the Colored Men's National Progressive Association, denounced the Progressive party for holding the Negro unfit for suffrage in the South, and, immediately after the convention, his organization announced for Wilson in the 1912 elections.[58]

Nor was this policy limited to the Progressive party. At the American Socialist Congress in 1910, over a third of the delegates led by Victor Berger, favored legislation against Asiatic immigration. Ernest Untermann, the Socialist candidate for governor of Idaho, asserted: "The question as to what race shall dominate the globe must be met as surely as the question of what class shall own the world. We should neglect our duty to the coming generation of Aryan peoples if we did not do everything in our power, even today, to insure the final race victory of our own people." Both Robert Hunter of the National Executive Committee of the Socialist party and Adolph Germer of the Miners' Union attacked foreign and Negro labor as hostile to unionism, and Untermann stated, " 'we should be false to our Socialist agitation if we insisted first on doing away with the race prejudice.' " [59]

Hostility toward and contempt for Oriental labor, in particular, was an avowed part of the Progressive campaign of 1912, a legacy of its trade union support and the sectional attitudes of the west coast which made an unsympathetic attitude toward Oriental nations a concomitant part of the outlook of many Progressives. The *Progressive Bulletin*, the official organ of the party, attacked Wilson in 1912 because he "prefers Chinese immigrants to white," and inquired whether "the Chinese are more desirable immigrants than the white people who dig our ground?" The first two points listed on Roosevelt's "labor record" in the 1912 campaign were "renewing the Chinese Exclusion Act and extending its provisions to the island territory of the United States," and "prohibiting the employment of Mongolian labor on irrigation works." [60] Nor did the Progressives always view southern European labor with favor. "These hearty 'hunkies' and 'dagoes' feel that they are working to make America rich and that their services should be appreciated, but are they?" asked the leading Progressive magazine on the west coast. "Are they not rather displacing the American of forty-five to fifty, when otherwise, he would work on until sixty without showing the white feather?" [61]

Most important, imperialism and progressivism flourished together because they were both expressions of the same philosophy of government, a tendency to judge any action not by the means employed but by the results achieved, a worship of definitive action for action's sake, as John Dewey has pointed out, [62] and an almost religious faith in the democratic mission of America. The results of the Spanish-American War were heartily approved not merely because the war freed subject peoples from tyranny, but because, since the United States was the land of free institutions, any extension of its domain was *per se* an extension of freedom and democracy. It was an age that admired results, that was not too concerned with fine distinctions and nice theories. The Progressives, quite apart from sharing in the general excitement of middle-class America in the rise of the United States as a world power and the sense of identity with the nation which imperialism afforded in a time of national stress, admired anyone who could clean up the slaughterhouses or link two great oceans, who could get a job done without months of tedious debate and deference to legal precedents.

The Progressives believed in the Hamiltonian concept of positive government, of a national government directing the destinies of the nation at home and abroad. They had little but contempt for the strict construction of the Constitution by conservative judges, who would restrict the power of the national government to act against social evils and to extend the blessings of democracy to less favored lands. The real enemy was particularism, state rights, limited government, which would mean the reign of plutocracy at home and a narrow, isolationist concept of national destiny abroad, which would deny the democratic mission of America and leave the brown peoples pawns of dynastic wars and colonial exploitation.

No writer better demonstrates the close link between progressivism and imperialism, with the concept of the Hamiltonian state and the democratic mission, than Herbert Croly, whose *The Promise of American Life* (1909) influenced the Progressive movement more profoundly than any other work. Roosevelt was more deeply moved by Croly's book than by anything he had read since the early Alfred T. Mahan. A few months after his return from Africa, Roosevelt was preaching the "New Nationalism" of Croly in his Osawatomie address and the war against the Old Guard was on in earnest.

"The American nation, just in so far as it believes in its nationality and is ready to become more of a nation, must assume a more definite and a more responsible place in the international system," wrote Croly. ". . . In spite of 'old-fashioned democratic' scruples and prejudices, the will to play that part for all it was worth would constitute a beneficial and a necessary stimulus to the better realization of the Promise of our domestic life."[63] We should shun the Jefferson administration's policy of basing "its international policy not upon the firm ground of national interest, but on the treacherous sands of international democratic propagandism."[64]

The first task of a truly national foreign policy was to develop hemispheric solidarity, and Croly left no doubt of what he meant by "a stable American international system."

> In all probability no American international system will ever be established without the forcible pacification of one or more centers of disorder. . . . In short, any international American political system might have to undertake a task in states like Venezuela, similar to that which the United States is now performing in Cuba. . . . The United States has already made an effective beginning in this great work, both by the pacification of Cuba and by the attempt to introduce a little order in the affairs of the turbulent Central American republics.[65]

Our work was greatly simplified by the fact that the political condition of Mexico, under the dictatorship of Diaz, had "become more stable and more wholesome," and "any recrudescence of revolutionary upheavals in Mexico would enormously increase the difficulties and perils of the attempt."[66]

The Spanish-American War was a great boon to the American people for it ushered in the Progressive era.

> Not until the end of the Spanish War was a condition of public feeling created, which made it possible to revive Hamiltonianism. That war and its resulting policy of extra-territorial expansion, so far from hindering the process of domestic amelioration, availed, from the sheer

force of the national aspirations it aroused, to give a tremendous impulse to the work of national reform . . . and it indirectly helped to
place in the Presidential chair the man who, as I have said, represented
both the national idea and the spirit of reform. The sincere and intelligent combination of those two ideas is bound to issue in the Hamiltonian practice of constructive national legislation.[67]

Bryan's campaign of 1900, on the other hand, Croly continued, was composed of two disastrous mistakes. "In seeking to prevent his countrymen
from asserting their national interest beyond their own continent, he was
also opposing in effect the resolute assertion of the national interest in
domestic affairs. He stamped himself, that is, as an anti-nationalist, and his
anti-nationalism has disqualified him for effective leadership of the party
of reform."[68]

Far from being isolated movements, our international mission and our
domestic reform program were interlocking forces, and frequently one and
the same thing. Croly concluded, for "it is entirely possible that hereafter the
United States will be forced into the adoption of a really national domestic
policy because of the dangers and duties incurred through her relations with
foreign countries."[69]

As Felix Frankfurter observed, "Unlike almost all American prewar
writers on politics (with the notable exception of Captain Mahan, because of
his special interest in navalism) Croly saw the American situation with its
international implications."[70] He did more than that. He provided an intelligible rationale for the union of progressivism and imperialism, ordering the
apparently unrelated events of the Roosevelt administration into a coherent
political system and contending that imperial ventures were an important
phase of the new religion of national reform, steps toward the fulfillment
of the promise of American life.

The attitude of the Progressives toward imperialism explains much
about the basic character of the Progressive movement. Despite the evangelical aura about the 1912 convention, the movement was not an attempt to
remold the world anew, to discard the old system for a new society. The
Progressives were completely a part of American life, accepting the traditional values and ideals, cherishing the aspirations of middle-class America,
including the new sense of delight in the rise of the United States as a world
power. Although a few leaders like Jane Addams saw the movement as an
aspect of a broad humanitarian philosophy, the most influential spokesman
thought not in terms of universals but of providing remedies for certain
specific political abuses and economic ills. Insofar as they thought in more
general terms, they were concerned less with the rights of *all* men, with universal brotherhood, than with the promise of *American* life. They were interested not only in a more equitable division of the pie but in a larger pie to
divide, and consequently saw nothing incongruous in supporting American
investments abroad in the interest of expanded markets while condemning
the same businesses at home for excessive profits and substandard wages.

The same group of men who could tear the Republican party asunder because of a discriminatory tariff in 1909 could outdo the Old Guard in arguing for protectionism in 1916 when they feared foreign goods would undercut the home market.

In the final analysis the Progressive movement suffered from a contradiction between humanistic values and nationalist aspirations, which, if not inherent, had certainly beset other democracies from the time of the wars of the French Revolution. In arguing for a positive national government, the followers of Croly ultimately lost sight of the distinction between the state as an instrument and the state as an end. The consequences were not only the endorsement of an imperialistic foreign policy but the death of the Progressive party in the interest of their nationalist zeal.

Notes

1. Insofar as any link has been made between the domestic and foreign aspects of the Progressive period, it has been to present a tableau of Theodore Roosevelt, the warrior, brandishing a big stick at American corporations on the one hand and foreign potentates on the other.
2. Alfred Lief, *Democracy's Norris* (New York, 1939), 155.
3. Claude G. Bowers, *Beveridge and the Progressive Era* (Boston, 1932), 73–76.
4. *Ibid.*, 448.
5. *Ibid.*, 511–12.
6. Merle Curti, *Bryan and World Peace*, Smith College *Studies in History* (Northampton), XVI, Nos. 3–4 (1931), 117 ff.
7. Walter Johnson, *William Allen White's America* (New York, 1947), 111.
8. *The Autobiography of William Allen White* (New York, 1946), 305–306.
9. Merle Curti, *Peace or War: The American Struggle, 1636–1936* (New York, 1936), 171.
10. Fred H. Harrington, "The Anti-Imperialist Movement in the United States, 1898–1900," *Mississippi Valley Historical Review* (Cedar Rapids), XXII (September, 1935), 218–19. See also Fred H. Harrington, "Literary Aspects of American Anti-Imperialism, 1898–1902," *New England Quarterly* (Baltimore, Portland), X (December, 1937), 650–67. The support given by organized labor to various imperialist ventures may be traced in John C. Appel, "The Relationship of American Labor to United States Imperialism, 1895–1905" (Ph.D. dissertation, University of Wisconsin, 1950).
11. Cf. Richard Pettigrew, *Imperial Washington* (Chicago, 1922); William G. Carleton, "Isolationism and the Middle West," *Mississippi Valley Historical Review*, XXXIII (December, 1946), 379. Even Senator Pettigrew favored war with Spain, "because I believe it will put us on a silver basis." Arthur W. Dunn, *From Harrison to Harding . . . 1888–1921*, 2 vols. (New York, 1922), I, 232. There was a close tie, in fact, between the jingoes and the silverites. Julius W. Pratt, *Expansionists of 1898* (Baltimore, 1936), 242 ff.
12. Jacob A. Riis, *Theodore Roosevelt, The Citizen* (New York, 1903), 384, 385.
13. Cf. Gifford Pinchot, *Breaking New Ground* (New York, 1947).
14. Oscar S. Straus, *Under Four Administrations; From Cleveland to Taft* (Boston, 1922), 175, 176.
15. New York *Times*, October 14, 1914, p. 10; Claudius O. Johnson, *Borah of Idaho* (New York, 1936), 191 ff.

16. *Fighting Liberal: The Autobiography of George W. Norris* (New York, 1945), 145–47 (italics supplied).
17. *Congressional Record,* 56 Cong., 2 Sess., 3151–52.
18. *Ibid.,* 59 Cong., 2 Sess., 3917.
19. Charles J. Bonaparte, "Two Years of a Government That Does Things," *Outlook* (New York), LXXXV (March 16, 1907), 600.
20. Joseph B. Bishop, *Charles Joseph Bonaparte* (New York, 1922), 100.
21. Curti, *Peace or War,* 220.
22. *Saturday Evening Post* (Philadelphia), CLXXX (May 23, 1908), 18–19.
23. *Congressional Record,* 60 Cong., 1 Sess., 5291, 5284, 5274.
24. Brand Whitlock to General Isaac R. Sherwood, February 26, 1913, Allan Nevins (ed.), *The Letters and Journal of Brand Whitlock,* 2 vols. (New York, 1936), I, 158–59.
25. Whitlock to Albert J. Nock, June 14, 1916, *ibid.,* 195.
26. Walter Lippmann, "Notes for a Biography," *New Republic* (New York), LXIII (July 16, 1930), 250.
27. Herbert Croly, *Willard Straight* (New York, 1924), 422 ff.
28. Chicago *Record-Herald,* August 7, 1912, p. 5.
29. Frank A. Munsey, "The New Progressive Party—What It Is and Why It Is," *Munsey's Magazine* (New York), XLVII (August, 1912), 678.
30. George E. Mowry, *Theodore Roosevelt and the Progressive Movement* (Madison, 1946), 187 ff.
31. See particularly Theodore Roosevelt, "The Peace of Righteousness," *Outlook,* XCIX (September 9, 1911), 66 ff.
32. *Congressional Record,* 62 Cong., 2 Sess., 2954–55.
33. Mowry, *Theodore Roosevelt and the Progressive Movement,* 307.
34. *Ibid.,* 187 ff.
35. *Outlook,* CVII (July 11, 1914), 569.
36. Theodore Roosevelt, "The World War: Its Tragedies and Its Lessons," *ibid.,* CVIII (September 23, 1914), 169–78.
37. New York *Times,* June 25, 1914, p. 2.
38. *Congressional Record,* 63 Cong., 2 Sess., 10247—48. This is not to say that the Wilson administration was free from imperialist manifestations. Indeed, the degree to which Woodrow Wilson was involved with American imperialist aspirations makes the attitude of the Progressives all the more remarkable. The relation of the New Freedom to American foreign policy merits further study, but it necessarily lies outside the scope of this short paper.
39. *Progressive Opinion* (New York), I (March 27, 1915), 7.
40. *Ibid.,* II (January, 1916), 3.
41. *Ibid.,* II (October 2, 1915), 2.
42. *Ibid.,* II (December 4, 1915), 3.
43. Progressive Party, National Committee, *The Progressive Party; Its Record From January to July, 1916* (New York, n.d.), 6 ff.
44. *New Republic,* VII (June 17, 1916), 160.
45. Progressive Party, National Committee, *The Progressive Party; Its Record From January to July, 1916,* pp. 102 ff.
46. *Ibid.,* 112 ff.
47. Mowry, *Theodore Roosevelt and the Progressive Movement,* 348.
48. Riis, *Theodore Roosevelt, The Citizen,* 383.
49. Arthur W. Dunn, *Gridiron Nights* (New York, 1915), 70 ff.
50. Theodore Roosevelt to Henry C. Lodge, August 3, 1897, Henry C. Lodge (ed.), *Selections from the Correspondence of Theodore Roosevelt and Henry Cabot Lodge, 1884–1918,* 2 vols. (New York, 1925), I, 268.

51. *Progressive Opinion*, II (December 4, 1915), 6.
52. Progressive Party, National Committee, *The Progressive Party; Its Record From January to July, 1916*, pp. 121 ff.
53. Mowry, *Theodore Roosevelt and the Progressive Movement*, 243.
54. *Autobiography of William Allen White*, 297.
55. Harold L. Ickes, "Who Killed the Progressive Party?" *American Historical Review* (New York), XLVI (January, 1941), 306–37.
56. Theodore Roosevelt, "The Progressives and the Colored Man," *Outlook*, CI (August 24, 1912), 911.
57. "Official Minutes of the (Provisional) Progressive National Committee," Theodore Roosevelt Collection (Widener Library, Harvard University, Cambridge); George E. Mowry, "The South and the Progressive Lily White Party of 1912," *Journal of Southern History* (Baton Rouge, Lexington), VI (May, 1940), 237–47.
58. *Chicago Record-Herald*, August 6, 1912, p. 1; August 9, 1912, p. 2. See also the attack on the action of the convention in "No Square Deal," *Independent* (New York), LXXIII (August 15, 1912), 391–93.
59. William E. Walling, *Progressivism—And After (New York, 1914)*, 377–81.
60. *Progressive Bulletin* (New York), I (September 16, 1912), 5. At the same time, however, the *Bulletin* attacked the nativism of the Republican party.
61. *California Outlook* (Los Angeles and San Francisco), XII (February 10, 1912), 5. William Allen White recalled that "of course, I read the popular pseudo-sciences of the day, such as 'Anglo-Saxon Superiority,' by Edmond Demolins." *Autobiography of William Allen White*, 326.
62. John Dewey, *Characters and Events*, 2 vols. (New York, 1929), I, 91.
63. Herbert Croly, *The Promise of American Life* (New York, 1909), 289.
64. *Ibid.*, 290.
65. *Ibid.*, 302-303.
66. *Ibid.*, 301, 303.
67. *Ibid.*, 169.
68. *Ibid.*, 157.
69. *Ibid.*, 310.
70. Felix Frankfurter, "Herbert Croly and American Political Opinion," *New Republic*, LXIII (July 16, 1930), 248.

Woodrow Wilson: A Profile

Arthur S. Link

Woodrow Wilson, like other great American Presidents, has attracted many biographers, some of whom have contributed myths in reconstructing his "life and times." The Wilson mystique, however, seems to have drawn a wider spectrum of biographer-types—thus resulting, if not in more myths, at least in an increased variety. For example, Wilson has been analyzed by none other than the great Sigmund Freud himself. Arthur S. Link, Professor of History at Princeton University and America's premier Wilson scholar, attacks several of the myth-builders, including Ray Stannard Baker, Robert Lansing, and Colonel House; he even fires a salvo at the Bullitt-Freud study. Link argues that it is possible to know the real Wilson, perhaps even better than he knew himself, if one cultivates detachment and makes use of the large and growing amount of information available on the subject.

It is by no means impossible for a dilligent researcher to discover the public facts about most important individuals, but it is always extraordinarily difficult to get behind the facade and to study, describe, and re-create verbally the personality of a subject. It requires several years of intense analysis for a psychiatrist to probe into the psyche of a live subject. How much more difficult it is for the scholar who has to rely only upon the written word!

Ordinary difficulties aside, it is little wonder that the personality of Woodrow Wilson has so long remained a mystery or been only imperfectly understood. Ray Stannard Baker, Wilson's authorized biographer, was originally partially responsible for the mystification. Baker had exclusive possession of what were thought to be the entire body of the Wilson Papers until he completed his biography in the late 1930's. His eight-volume *Woodrow Wilson: Life and Letters* (1927–1939) was for many years the only full-scale biography available. Indispensable though it was, Baker's work embodied a portrait of the Wilsonian personality that was something of a caricature.

Baker labored under some obvious handicaps. First, his long acquaintance with and intense admiration of Wilson not only influenced him in obvious ways but also profoundly affected his reading of the documentary evidence. Second, Baker *was* writing the authorized biography, and writing it under Mrs. Wilson's watchful eye. Third, Baker, because of his own limitations, was never fully sensitive to the subtleties and changes in Wilson's religious thought and their manifestations in Wilson's personal and public conduct. Finally, as Robert Bannister's acute study *Ray Stannard Baker: The Mind and Thought of a Progressive* has recently shown, Baker to a large degree imposed his own personality profile upon Wilson.

Whatever the cause, the result was a portrait that was scarcely credible to critical readers. The Wilson of the Baker biography is too good to be true— or human. By robbing Wilson of his humanity, Baker unconsciously created a less interesting as well as a less credible character. For example, Baker was so intent upon protecting Wilson's reputation against contemporary slanderers that he ended by portraying his subject as being mainly feminine in personality, if not virtually a sexual neuter. Perhaps this statement is too strong. In any event, Baker refused either to come to grips with or to describe the strong masculine drive that was one of the great sources of Wilson's life power.

It was very difficult for biographers to get a clear view of the Wilsonian personality for years after the completion of Baker's biography simply because the essential biographical materials were either missing or unavailable. Such absolutely indispensable collections as the letters between Wilson and his first and second wives, Ellen Axson Wilson and Edith Bolling Wilson, and Wilson's letters to his friend and intimate correspondent, Mary Allen Hulbert, were closed to all scholars until the 1960's. Even worse, the great body of the Wilson Papers for the first forty years of Wilson's life were hidden in trunks in the Wilson house on S Street in Washington. Only after the discovery of this collection was it possible, for example, to understand the relationship between Wilson and his father, the Reverend Dr. Joseph Ruggles Wilson. Enough was known for all biographers to affirm that this relationship was indubitably the most important force during the formative years of Woodrow Wilson's life. And yet all biographers, Baker included, had never seen the relationship with anything but very imperfect and distorted vision.

Biographers and historians in pursuit of truth necessarily have to use whatever evidence is at hand. In Wilson's case, the unavailability of the most elementary personal documents forced historians and biographers to rely heavily upon the letters, diaries, etc., of his contemporaries. These sources are of course indispensable: without them, we could never see many facets of Wilson's personality. However, the light from these sources is distorted by the prisms of the contemporary's own prejudices, varying ability to understand personality, and above all his purpose in writing a letter, memorandum, or diary entry. There is distortion both ways, to be sure. Contemporaries who ardently admired Wilson tended to leave documentary evidence just as distorted as that left by individuals who had strong feelings against Wilson.

There are numerous examples of the dangers of relying too much on the testimony left by Wilson's close associates. One such example among the serious works is a psychological study of Wilson by Alexander L. and Juliette

L. George, *Woodrow Wilson and Colonel House*, published in 1956. This study, like many others of the Wilson era, is based heavily on the diary of Colonel Edward M. House, Wilson's intimate adviser. This massive diary is one of the most important sources of Wilsonian biography. Yet we are only now beginning to see the degree to which Colonel House wrote for the specific purpose of creating his own version of the historical record. Portions of the House diary are simply unreliable, and the truth about any particular episode can be determined only when one is able to compare House's account with accounts left by other participants. It is more important to say that House's numerous comments on Wilson's actions and personality have to be read in light of House's unrelenting effort to defend, through his diary, the superiority of his own mind, intellect, and policies against Wilson's.

One has to be equally careful in using the various memoranda left by Wilson's Secretary of State from 1915 to 1920, Robert Lansing—the papers usually referred to as the Lansing diary. I quoted one of these memoranda— a personality profile—at length in my *Wilson: The New Freedom* (1956). Were I rewriting that book, I would probably use the extract again. But I would be careful to point out that it was the testimony of a bitter man, and that the bitterness that Lansing felt was not by any means justified by Wilson's treatment of his Secretary of State.

Is it possible really to know Woodrow Wilson? And is it possible to construct a full and accurate profile of his personality?

One has to begin the answer to the first question by saying that many of the major contours of Wilson's personality have been long known and written about. Virtually all contemporaries and historical writers, friendly and hostile, have agreed that Wilson was different from the run of ordinary men. His personality was, in short, strong, aggressive, dominant, and, to many persons, compelling. He had the power to command loyalty, to charm, and also to repel. The testimony of his contemporaries, from his student days to the end of his life, is so unanimous on this point as to be conclusive.

In addition, all observers, contemporary and historical, agree that Wilson was an extraordinarily intense person. He was not merely a well-disciplined and hard worker, but a person who was always driving, never satisfied with momentary achievements and triumphs. Psychologists have attributed this inner drive to Wilson's highly developed superego, derived particularly from the demands and expectations of his father.

The great majority of Wilson's contemporaries also agree that he had a first-class mind, though one more adept at synthesizing ideas than originating them. He was, as Gamaliel Bradford, Jr., put it, a "creature of brains." But, as Bradford and other writers have made clear, Wilson was interested in ideas for the practical use to which they might be put, and hardly at all in abstract speculation.

All observers strongly affirm that Wilson was an idealist, and all his close friends agree that he had a strong conscience, a highly developed ethical system, and deep Christian faith. However, very few of Wilson's

216

contemporaries understood the nature of Wilson's idealism, and some sec-ondary writers have followed them in incorrectly interpreting it as being largely moralism and slavish obedience to an ethical system. Recent research has put this whole matter in a new perspective. Wilson, at least in his mature years, was not, technically, an idealist, even though he continued to use the language of idealism. On the contrary, he had little use for ethical abstractions or ideals as these terms have been defined by philosophers. Having discovered the meaning of justification by faith in about 1905 and 1906, Wilson became increasingly afterward a Christian realist whose ethics were very much affected by the context and circumstances of any particular situation demanding a moral decision.

Most contemporaries and biographers also agree that Wilson was by nature headstrong, opinionated, and combative. Some critics have asserted that he had no capacity for self-criticism or understanding, would brook no opposition, and cut off friends who disagreed with him.

Finally, views of Wilson the man in day-to-day relationships have varied according to the subjective reactions of contemporaries and biographers. To persons who did not like him, Wilson seemed cold, even capable of some personal cruelty. To members of his family and to his friends, on the other hand, Wilson was outgoing, warmhearted, and generously capable of friendship.

The foregoing generalizations summarize a fairly extensive and intimate understanding of Wilson's personality—a much better understanding, indeed, than we possess about most historic personages. Is it possible to know Wilson even better? Is it possible to define sharply what is now described imprecisely in talking about various aspects of his personality? Can we probe behind the facade of behavior to the wellsprings of motivation? Or is what Wilson once said about Lincoln also true of himself? "That brooding spirit had no real familiars. I get the impression that it never spoke out in complete self-revelation, and that it could not reveal itself completely to anyone."

Wilson was not describing himself. We are now in a position to know him better than probably any other important individual in history. We are in a position to know him better than any of his contemporaries did, even members of his family. We can now probably know him better than he knew himself.

From his student days onward, Wilson wrote constantly—in letters, lectures, articles, editorials, essays, and diaries. He never held anything back because he was incapable of successful dissimulation. He poured out his thoughts in torrents of words. The form did not particularly matter. To be sure, he expressed himself more fully and frankly in diaries and in letters to members of his family and to intimate friends. As he once put it in a letter, "I am apt to let my thoughts and feelings slip more readily from the end of my pen than from the end of my tongue." He revealed himself differently but perhaps just as importantly in essays in literary criticism, lectures on the Reformation, diplomatic notes, sermons, and political speeches.

Wilson rarely threw anything away. He saved not only letters and the things that one usually finds in personal papers, but also thousands of envelopes, loose pages, scraps of paper, etc., as well as his books. On many of these he jotted down thoughts as they came from his mind. Even though he did not usually keep copies of his personal letters, many of his correspondents did save them, and it has been possible to reconstruct virtually a complete Wilsonian archive.

The present writer and his colleagues at Princeton University are now deep into this vast collection, and the early fruits of their work, the first three volumes of *The Papers of Woodrow Wilson*, are in print. In addition, four other volumes in various stages of production cover Wilson's life to 1893.

It would require a fairly sizable volume adequately to relate what the documents in these first volumes of *The Papers* tell us about the formation and maturing of Wilson's personality. One can say in summary that it is evident that:

1. The relationship between Wilson and his father was very determinative. The letters show plainly enough why Wilson later called his father "the best instructor, the most inspiring companion . . . that a youngster ever had." The relationship during its early stages was of course that of father and son, master and pupil. Dr. Wilson had exacting standards and gave the most extraordinary attention to his son's intellectual and literary development. However the extant letters indicate very strongly that Dr. Wilson was more intent upon drawing out his son's own talent than upon imposing ideas and techniques upon him, and that he evoked these talents with measured encouragement and love. This relationship was, actually, liberating and creative for both partners. It had become a relationship between equals by the time of Woodrow Wilson's maturity, and from this time forward the father increasingly drew strength and ideas from his son.

2. Wilson's mother, Janet Woodrow Wilson, was in her own quiet way a much greater influence upon her son than we had ever known. Indeed, it is clear that Wilson derived his ideal of womanhood in large measure from the example set by his mother.

3. Dr. and Mrs. Wilson were proud, sensitive, and quick to resent alleged slights. Midwesterners who had moved to the South before the Civil War, they had warmly embraced the Southern cause. Even so, they were obviously never fully accepted by the extremists called "Southrons" and "unreconstructed rebels," and this antagonism, if not hostility, accentuated the Wilsons' sensitivity and caused them to find self-protection in family clannishness and pride. Woodrow Wilson came by his own pride and sensitivity quite naturally.

4. Wilson was a precocious child. Family tradition had it that he was a slow starter—this tradition says, for example, that he did not learn to read until he was nine. This may or may not be correct. But Wilson learned rapidly enough once he began, and by his eighteenth year he had acquired the funda-

mental habits of hard work and incredible self-discipline that were to characterize everything that he did from his undergraduate days at Princeton onward.

5. Wilson's education in ancient history and ancient and modern languages, modern history, political science, economics, legal studies, and literature was much more extensive and profound than we had ever imagined. To be sure, much of his undergraduate education was self-motivated and self-acquired, and this fact is another early evidence of his iron self-discipline. But at The Johns Hopkins University he acquired what was probably as good an education in the social sciences as it was possible to acquire at the time, the 1880's.

6. During the formative years of his life, Wilson had a keen capacity for self-criticism and seems to have suffered from insecurity on account of his inability to achieve as rapidly as he thought he should. However, he seems to have come to full self-realization—and to terms with himself, at least temporarily—by 1890. Wilson's self-realization, incidentally, did not do full justice to his intellectual powers.

7. Normal insecurity during his early years drove Wilson to depend upon the love of his family and friends, but he also clearly developed a high capacity for wholehearted friendship. His own numerous comments about his inability to give himself in friendship are to be taken with some large grains of salt.

8. Wilson was from his youth onward, as I have said, extraordinarily intense; that is to say, he worked with unrelenting efforts to achieve his self-appointed goals. His superego undoubtedly set these goals, but power came from his own life force, and one can only conclude that the genes combined with family influences and environment to make him what he was.

9. The incidence and intensity of Wilson's psychosomatic illnesses during these formative years have been much exaggerated by Baker, and particularly by Sigmund Freud and William C. Bullitt in their *Thomas Woodrow Wilson, A Psychological Study* (1967). Ironically, insufficient attention has been paid to the exact nature and effects of Wilson's strokes in 1906 and 1919. Edwin A. Weinstein, M.D., of the Washington School of Psychiatry, has begun what promises to be a thorough investigation. His tentative conclusions to date are that Wilson suffered a severe stroke with accompanying brain damage in 1906, that he achieved substantial and almost miraculous recovery through sheer determination, and that he suffered a massive stroke with considerable damage to the brain in 1919. We know that subtle but very important changes occurred in Wilson's personality in 1906; that, for example, he became less tractable than he had been before and more intense than ever in pursuing goals. It seems likely that Wilson's almost self-destructive behavior during the controversies at Princeton from 1907 to 1910 and over ratification of the Treaty of Versailles from 1919 to 1920 was profoundly if not decisively influenced by certain brain damage. But we will

not be able to speak authoritatively on this matter until Dr. Weinstein and other medical experts have completed their work.

10. His personal advantages and precocity aside, Wilson seems to have been a remarkably normal person during the first forty years of his life. His childhood was serene in spite of growing up in the South during the Civil War and Reconstruction. He may or may not have been robust as a boy —we simply have no good evidence on this point—but he knew most of the pleasures of boyhood. He played baseball, and football to a lesser degree, and maintained an avid interest in sports. He dreamed of building great warships and of commanding large armies in the field. Like most boys from the same kind of families in the Victorian era, he was something of a prig, at least by our own standards. He fell deeply in love and knew all the joys of romance and courtship. He had numerous male friends.

Students of personality, and particularly of Wilson's personality, will be able to make their own analyses and form their own conclusions as the evidence becomes available in *The Papers of Woodrow Wilson*. Indeed, we will soon have the evidence in print for a detailed study of Wilson's mature personality. . . .

American Intervention: 1917

Ernest R. May

This article dealing with the United States' entry into World War I is historiographical in nature. Ernest R. May, distinguished diplomatic historian from Harvard University, speaks to the great debate between pro-administration authors such as Walter H. Page and Colonel House and isolationists such as Walter Millis and Charles C. Tansill. This confrontation resulted in considerable myth-building. May himself represents a more "Realistic" school of historians who seek to avoid the probably insoluble question as to whether intervention was good or bad, and simply attempt to "set forth the tragic dilemmas in which the men of 1917 found themselves."

For Marxists, only socialist states can be "peace-loving." "Aggressive capitalist-imperialist" countries cannot. On the historical record, however, America deserves such a label at least as much as any other nation. Having led most modern peace movements, including those for arbitration and disarmament, and having insisted until very recently that their government pursue isolationist foreign policies and maintain only minimal military forces, Americans could be said not only to love peace but to have been infatuated with it.

Not least among evidences of this romance is their remorse over departures from peaceful ways. Bitter self-recrimination followed the Mexican War, the Civil War, the Spanish American War, and especially the two world wars.

In historical writing, it is true, the reaction usually developed slowly. After World War I, according to most observers, disillusionment quickly settled over the public. Books dealing with the war continued nevertheless to express pride and satisfaction in American intervention. The most widely read were two semiautobiographies: *The Life and Letters of Walter H. Page* (3 volumes; Garden City, New York: Doubleday, Page, & Company, 1922–26), edited by Burton J. Hendrick, and *The Intimate Papers of Colonel House* (4 volumes: Boston, Massachusetts: Houghton Mifflin, 1926–28), edited by Charles Seymour. According to the extracts from diaries and letters published in these volumes, Page, who had been American ambassador in London, and House, who had been President Wilson's confidant and unofficial ambassador at large, both had advocated intervention and rejoiced that it had taken place. Though the collections consisted more of raw materials for history than of

Reprinted by the permission of the American Historical Association, from Ernest R. May, *American Intervention: 1917 and 1941*, Washington, D.C., 1969, pp. 1–13 and 25–26.

narrative and analysis, they set forth one interpretation of Wilson's diplomacy.

Both works divided the years 1914–1917 into two periods, broken by the *Lusitania* crisis of May–June 1915. In the first period, according to both Page and House, the United States did not yet face a moral imperative to intervene. The issue was simply whether or not to obstruct the Allies. Wilson and his official aids, Secretary of State William Jennings Bryan and State Department Counselor Robert Lansing, inclined to be overly legalistic. They pressed, in particular, for acceptance by the belligerents of the unratified Declaration of London of 1909, a code of rules for naval warfare, which, by protecting American trade with continental Europe, would seriously limit the Allies' ability to cut off food and supplies for Germany. Page fought such a policy with all his resources. On one occasion he visited the Foreign Secretary, Sir Edward Grey, read him a formal note from the State Department, and then said, "I have now read the dispatch, but I do not agree with it; let us consider how it should be answered!" House, meanwhile, carried on the same battle in Washington, quietly advising Wilson and going behind the back of the State Department to work out a compromise with the British ambassador. The United States eventually ceased to press for acceptance of the Declaration of London and declared that it would simply stand by the traditional rule of international law. This gave Britain greater freedom to block German imports, and both Page and House celebrate this victory as the first among many that kept the United States from obstructing the Allies.

In the second phase, after the sinking of the *Lusitania*, according to both works, benevolent neutrality ceased to be enough. Page actually had become convinced earlier that German militarism represented a threat to American democracy; House on occasion had the same conviction. After the spring of 1915, Page rarely doubted that it was his country's duty to get into the war as soon as possible. House urged breaking relations with Germany. When Wilson allowed the issue of the *Lusitania* to cool, House advised that the next submarine incident, the sinking of the *Arabic* in August 1915, be made the occasion for the break. He made the same plea after an attack on the Channel steamer *Sussex* in the spring of 1916. At moments of crisis, House and Page stood together in urging that opportunity be seized for a rupture in relations or a declaration of war.

House meanwhile recommended that Wilson plan for possible intervention. In the winter of 1915–1916 he induced the President to send him to Europe on an extraordinary mission. He sought an agreement with the Allies under which Wilson would make a public appeal for peace negotiations. If the Germans either refused or declined to meet conditions satisfactory to the Allies, the United States would then intervene. Though actually initialed by House and Grey in February 1916 and endorsed conditionally by Wilson, this agreement never went into effect. When Wilson made a public appeal for peace in December 1916, he regarded the agreement out of date. To House, this appeal seemed a mistake; it fortunately came to nought. And in

1917 the President finally yielded, broke diplomatic relations, and asked Congress to declare war on Germany.

Through both the Page and House accounts ran a contention that American intervention had been the right course, at least after the sinking of the *Lusitania*. This contention rested in part on an assumption that the Allies had morality on their side and that Germany, absolutist and aggressively militarist, represented principles antithetic to those of the United States and the Western Allies. Page and House judged that the war had tested which code, which set of political abstractions, would prevail, and the United States had to join in preventing a German victory in order to defend representative government and individual freedom. Indeed, defeat of Imperial Germany, a malignant survival of feudalism, had been necessary if the world were to be made safe for democracy.

But the Page and House view drew on another line of reasoning, occasionally in evidence at the time, but best articulated later by Walter Lippmann in *U.S. Foreign Policy: Shield of the Republic* (Boston, Massachusetts: Little, Brown, 1943). In this argument the security of the United States depended on there being no dominant power in Europe. Wilhelmine Germany, like Napoleonic France, threatened to master all the Continent's immense war potential. If that occurred, the United States would confront an enemy stronger than itself, not only capable of challenging its hemispheric supremacy but of jeopardizing its very existence. As Page and House hinted and Lippmann, among others, said explicitly, the United States had a vital security interest in helping the Allies to prevent German triumph.

Only toward the end of the 1920's did another version of American intervention begin to gain currency. It grew out of the revisionism of Americans, Englishmen, and Germans who re-examined the wartime assumption that Germany had been responsible for starting the war. Drawing on the forty volumes of *Diplomatischen Akten des Auswärtigen Amtes, 1871–1914,* better known as *Die Grosse Politik,* these writers portrayed Imperial Germany as no worse than its opponents. Bickering among erstwhile allies, coupled with the consolidation of Soviet power and the rise of Fascism in Italy, meanwhile, made it seem doubtful if the war had in fact made democracy more secure in the world. As Warren I. Cohen shows in *The American Revisionists* (Chicago, Illinois: University of Chicago Press, 1967), these new perceptions led to the questioning of moral premises so confidently accepted by Page and House.

In the late 'twenties C. Hartley Grattan published a detailed indictment of Wilson's diplomacy entitled *Why We Fought* (New York: Vanguard Press, 1929). Contending that neither the United States nor the world had gained anything from the war, he asked how and why America had given up its policy of neutrality. He found Wilson's abandonment of the Declaration of London and retreat from an initial ban on private loans to belligerent governments explicable only as reflecting, first, the sentimental Anglophilism of Page, House, and Wilson and, second, the influence of capitalists, financiers, and munitions makers who profited from supplying the Allies. Wilson had taken a stand against German submarine warfare more because it menaced trade than because it threatened neutral rights, Grattan argued, and had pressed his case to the point of war in order to protect America's investment in the Allied cause. Citing a senile congressman's tendentious testimony that Wilson had called a "sunrise conference" early in 1916 to tell congressional leaders that he wanted war, Grattan charged the President with having planned this step long in advance. The final prod to action he found in a telegram of 1917 from Page warning that Britain faced economic collapse if America did not enter the war. And the public followed, Grattan reasoned, because it had been subjected to a barrage of English propaganda and frightened by tales contrived by the administration of German espionage and sabotage. Though this crude summary does not do justice to Grattan's skillfully argued indictment, it suffices to indicate his themes—that the administration worked in the interest of munitions makers and bankers and that the people had been tricked into an irrational and almost hysterical frame of mind.

Such views won wide credence during the Great Depression. In 1936 and 1937 Ray Stannard Baker, who had worked with Wilson at Versailles and later, reached the years of neutrality in Volumes V and VI of his eight-volume authorized biography. Despite his continuing reverence for Wilson, Baker assailed the follies of Page and House, deplored the abandonment of the Declaration of London, ridiculed the House-Grey understanding, and lamented the final decision to intervene. Walter Millis of the New York *Herald Tribune* meanwhile devoted his lively pen and studious mind to a one-volume account of the background of intervention, *Road to War, 1914–1917* (Boston, Massachusetts: Houghton Mifflin, 1935). A popular bestseller, Millis' book also ridiculed the illusions of the interventionists and suggested that American intervention had been due to a combination of folly, sentimentalism, and greed. In 1936 the United States Senate set up a special committee under the chairmanship of Senator Gerald P. Nye of North Dakota to investigate the influence of munitions makers on foreign policy. The committee interrogated representatives of such firms as J. P. Morgan and Company and the National City Bank of New York and ransacked the files of the State and Treasury Departments. International lawyers, such as Edwin M. Borchard of Yale University and the elderly John Bassett Moore, meanwhile assailed the legal theories upon which Wilson had acted. Borchard and William P. Lage published *Neutrality for the United States* (New Haven, Connecticut: Yale University Press, 1937), denouncing any and all efforts to safeguard "freedom of the seas." In the midst of this climate of opinion, Congress passed Neutrality Acts, designed, as someone said, to prevent any future President from getting the United States into the war of 1914–1918.

Scholars also joined in the clamor. Joseph V. Fuller, a historian for the Department of State and the author of a monograph on Bismarckian diplomacy, published an article asking why the Germans had not abandoned submarine warfare and thus deprived Wilson of his excuse for intervention ("The Genesis of the Munitions Traffic," *Journal of Modern History*, VI [1934]). He answered that Germany had to stop munitions from reaching the Allies and that the provocation was therefore Wilson's refusal to heed pleas for an embargo on arms. In the late 'thirties H. C. Peterson of the University of Oklahoma wrote *Propaganda for War* (Norman: University of Oklahoma Press, 1939), a lengthy monograph on how Sir Gilbert Parker and agencies in Wellington House entrapped the American public. Among other such articles and monographs, Charles Callan Tansill's *America Goes to War* (Boston, Massachusetts: Little, Brown, 1938) was foremost. Eventually a professor at Fordham University and then at Georgetown University, Tansill previously had published monographs on American relations with Santo Domingo and on the acquisition of the Virgin Islands. Though not allowed to use the Wilson manuscripts, which Baker still hoarded, he had seen parts of the unpublished House diaries and had been given free access to the information gathered by the Nye Committee. Correspondence from an obliging officer in the Berlin *Marine-Archiv* enabled him to sketch the German side. His bibliography, though including some items not actually used, was full and impressive.

Tansill's volume stressed the enormous growth of American trade in munitions and other war supplies and the extent of American private loans to the Allies. Portraying House, Page, and even Lansing as influenced by these interests and moved by blind hatred for Germany, he showed how they frustrated true neutrality, as he conceived it, persuading the President to abandon the Declaration of London, give up his early opposition to loans, resist pressure for an embargo on arms, and take an unjustifiable stand against German submarine warfare. Some of the chapter titles indicate the thread of his argument: "War Profits Beckon to 'Big Business,' " "England Looks upon the Declaration of London as a 'Mere Scrap of Paper,' " "Mr. Lansing Leads the President along the Road to War," "Colonel House Blocks a Path to Peace," "The Kaiser Chooses Peace with America Rather than Victory at Verdun." Though reviewers in scholarly journals did not call his book dispassionate, most found it solid and convincing.

The interpretation popularized by Grattan and Millis and footnoted by Tansill had, of course, its own foundation in faith. It rested on the premise that the United States had no reason, moral or material, for opposing Germany or helping the Allies. Some members of this school assumed that if the United States had remained neutral a negotiated peace would have resulted, with happier results than those of the Versailles *Diktat*. Even if Germany had been absolutist, militaristic, and imperialistic, which these writers doubted, and even if it had been on the edge of triumph, still they felt that the outcome of the war should have remained a matter of indifference to Americans. As many writers asserted, among them Charles A. Beard in his eloquent *Open Door at Home* (New York: Macmillan, 1934), the United

States was strong precisely because it did not involve itself in European diplomatic chicanery and waste its substance in preparations for war. From this premise it followed that the intervention of 1917 had been at least a blunder and probably a crime.

Though most writing on 1914–1917 in the twenty years after Versailles resembled either that in Page's *Letters* and the House *Papers* or Grattan and Tansill, a third approach already had been discovered. In 1923 Malbone W. Graham published a University of Texas Ph.D. dissertation entitled *The Controversy between the United States and Allied Governments Respecting Neutral Rights and Commerce during the Period of American Neutrality, 1914–1917* (Austin: University of Texas Press, 1923). It neither glorified American policy nor recriminated against its architects. Graham found that with slight departures in one direction or another the United States had tried to follow the applicable rules of international law. Another scholar, Richard Van Alstyne, writing in the *Journal of Modern History* (VII [November 1935], 434–47), reached much the same conclusion about the abandonment of the Declaration of London. But, curiously enough, it was Seymour, the editor of the House *Papers*, who published the first book-length study dealing with intervention as a historical episode rather than a question of moral doctrine.

In *American Diplomacy during the World War* (Baltimore, Maryland: Johns Hopkins University Press, 1934), the Albert Shaw Lectures for 1933, and in supplementary essays published as *American Neutrality, 1914–1917* (New Haven, Connecticut: Yale University Press, 1935), Seymour analyzed Wilson's policies toward the Allies, his efforts to mediate, and his opposition to submarine warfare. He reported that the President and his advisers, while influenced by belief in the moral superiority of the English and French, had adhered to international law as they understood it and, indeed, had taken risks to prevent inroads upon it. In the interval between the *Sussex* pledge and the coming of war, when German submarines were under control, Seymour pointed out, American relations with Britain had become so troubled that Wilson talked vexedly of employing economic sanctions against the Allies.

The submarine issue alone, Seymour contended, brought intervention. Wilson saw German undersea warfare as a challenge that could not be ignored. If a belligerent could extend its operations anywhere, interfere with the trade of neutral states, and imperil the lives of neutral citizens, then neither neutrality nor international law had meaning. The President felt compelled in conscience to oppose the Germans on this issue and, paradoxically, to risk neutrality for the sake of neutrality. He was not entirely altruistic, for American lives and property were at stake. Though the German government respected Wilson's wishes for a time, it eventually ceased to do so. At Spa on January 7, 1917, the Kaiser and his advisers decided to launch a campaign of unrestricted submarine warfare in defiance of the United States and in conscious certainty that war would result. The decisive roles were played by these German leaders, not by Page, House, Lansing, or even Wilson.

Much the same view of intervention appeared in a bulkier study, Harley F. Notter's *The Origins of the Foreign Policy of Woodrow Wilson* (Baltimore, Maryland: Johns Hopkins University Press, 1937). Setting Wilson's diplomacy in the context of his earlier life and thought, Notter's volume tended to highlight Wilson's preoccupation with moral issues. But Notter's work was more diffuse, less studied, and less incisive than Seymour's volumes.

When World War II called attention to more immediate problems of neutrality, debate tended to diminish. After Pearl Harbor the parallels of 1919 seemed more relevant than those of 1917, and scholarly work centered on the armistice, the Peace Conference, and the fight over the League of Nations.

After World War II a generation with different attitudes and preoccupations began to restudy problems of World War I. Lippmann already had provided one new point of departure by suggesting that intervention had been necessary for the rescue of the balance of power and the protection of American security. In various popular and scholarly periodicals and in a book, *In Defense of the National Interest* (New York: Alfred A. Knopf, 1951), a University of Chicago political scientist, Hans J. Morgenthau, attacked the Wilson administration for having failed to concentrate on realistic goals. In lectures printed as *American Diplomacy, 1900–1950* (Chicago, Illinois: University of Chicago Press, 1950), the erudite and sophisticated career diplomat George Frost Kennan put the same charge into captivating phrases. He accused Wilson and other American leaders of excessive moralism and legalism. Taking a position halfway between the major prewar schools, he argued that while intervention might have been justified by the national interest, the overlay of other excuses had ruined its purpose. As a result, the United States became

> uncomfortably similar to one of those prehistoric monsters with a body as long as this room and a brain the size of a pin; he lies there in his comfortable primeval mud and pays little attention to his environment; he is slow to wrath—in fact, you practically have to whack his tail off to make him aware that his interests are being disturbed; but, once he grasps this, he lays about him with such blind determination that he not only destroys his adversary but largely wrecks his native habitat.

While prewar writers had argued over whether intervention had been right or wrong, Morgenthau and Kennan suggested instead that it had been right, but for the wrong reasons.

This hypothesis intrigued a number of young scholars. Robert E. Osgood, a political scientist in Morgenthau's Chicago Center for the Study of American Foreign Policy, investigated it in *Ideals and Self-Interest in America's Foreign Relations* (Chicago, Illinois: University of Chicago Press, 1953).

In several chapters devoted to World War I, he amplified the theses that Morgenthau and Kennan had sketched. Another political scientist, Edward H. Buehrig of the University of Indiana, in *Woodrow Wilson and the Balance of Power* (Bloomington: Indiana University Press, 1955), assessed these criticisms as not altogether fair. The submarine issue symbolized a clash of national interests, he said, and while American leaders did concern themselves with legal and moral issues, Wilson, House, and especially Lansing showed acute awareness of the balance of power. Daniel M. Smith in *Robert Lansing and American Neutrality, 1914–1917* (Berkeley and Los Angeles: University of California Press, 1958), detailed the evidence regarding Lansing, stressing that Lansing's opinions derived from a mixture of political, economic, and moral considerations. In a subsequent article, "National Interest and American Intervention, 1917: An Historiographical Appraisal" (*Journal of American History*, LIX [June 1965]), Smith carefully weighed the support for the balance of power thesis to be found in known evidence; he concluded that it neglected much and therefore belonged among the "more simplistic" interpretations.

Like the tortoise competing with the hare, the separate line of scholarship started by Graham, Van Alstyne, and Seymour meanwhile kept up its plodding pace. Arthur S. Link, professor of history at Princeton University, Northwestern University, and then Princeton again, launched a magisterial biography of Wilson. In a shorter work, *Woodrow Wilson and the Progressive Era* (New York: Harper, 1954), and in *Wilson, the Diplomatist* (Baltimore, Maryland: Johns Hopkins University Press, 1957), the Albert Shaw Lectures for 1956, Link sketched his tentative findings about the period 1914–1917. By 1965 he had finally completed the fifth volume of *Wilson* (Princeton, N. J.: Princeton University Press, 1947–   ) carrying the narrative to the declaration of war. By that time, my own *The World War and American Isolation* (Cambridge, Massachusetts: Harvard University Press, 1959) had appeared. In that book, I argued that in nearly every case requiring a decision by the President, considerations of law, morality, power, national prestige, and domestic politics all had to be taken into account. Neither Wilson nor his advisers could ever see clearly the probable results of their decisions. In each instance, the weight of argument seemed to commend the course finally adopted. Each time, however, the decision tended to close out one or more alternatives until in 1917 there seemed no real option except war. The Germans, whom I tried to study in some detail, found themselves similarly driven into a corner from which they too could see no exit. Karl E. Birnbaum, a Swedish scholar, in *Peace Moves and U-Boat Warfare, 1916–1917* (Stockholm: Almquist & Wiksell, 1958), more fully described German diplomatic maneuvers in the crucial final stage, suggesting that there might have been moments when better communications between Berlin and Washington could have altered the outcome. But the necessary understanding of the other side simply did not exist within the Kaiser's councils or, equally importantly, among leaders in the *Reichstag*. The German decision to force a crisis, compelling Wilson either to make war or to concede that he had bluffed, therefore had a quality of tragic inevitability.

The central themes of Link's vast and nearly definite biographical volumes proved not to differ markedly from those foreshadowed in his shorter works and set forth in my own book. By meticulous analysis of data, some of which was uniquely available to him (notably French diplomatic archives that remain officially closed), he set the record straight on a number of points where others, including myself, had been in doubt or in error. Thus, for example, he proved that the House-Grey agreement merited less attention than it received. Playing a devious game, House misled Wilson as to what he was seeking, misrepresented the President's views when speaking to the Allies, and then misrepresented their views to Washington. In accepting the document, Wilson had no sense of committing himself to intervention. Link also showed that a public letter sent to Senator William J. Stone by Wilson in 1916, seemingly stating a dogmatic moral position with regard to submarine warfare, was actually a hastily drafted document tailored to fit a particular challenge to presidential leadership of the legislative branch. It neither expressed Wilson's private thoughts nor mirrored the policy he was pursuing. Link showed what a flexible and conciliatory course Wilson actually followed, backing away between 1915 and 1917 from the perilous ground taken in the *Lusitania* correspondence and standing instead on the proposition that submarine operations would become cause for war only in the event of willful attacks on American citizens or ships. Link described better than anyone else the domestic problems that Wilson faced, the difficulties made for him by, on the one hand, near-pacifist Democrats, German-Americans, and Irish-Americans who opposed any resolute defense of American interests or rights against Germany, and, on the other hand, by Roosevelt Republicans, Anglophiles, Francophiles, and chauvinists who clamored against any compromises whatever. The Wilson one sees in Link's biography is many sided, moved by conscience and by deeply felt religious ideas, by a sense of responsibility for the economic welfare of his country and for its international standing, credit, and influence, and by an additional sense of responsibility as leader of a party and sponsor of domestic reforms, the success of which seemed to depend on his party's continuance in power. The range of alternatives open to him in regard to the European war appears narrower than either the Page and House, the isolationist, or the Morgenthau and Kennan school would concede; Wilson's choices seem the best that, in the circumstances, any prudent man could have made.

It is perhaps significant that most who continue to debate whether intervention in World War I was right or wrong describe themselves as political scientists. Historians by and large now deal with that war much as with the Punic or Napoleonic Wars, seeking rather to achieve some kind of empathy than to assign praise or blame. The chief exceptions, as yet few in number, have some association with what is called the New Left.

Because the New Left accords much attention to businessmen and bankers, it is sometimes confused with an older school of economic interpretation. It is, in fact, quite different. The older group took the view that businessmen constituted a special class. Through force, corruption, and chicanery, this class used government to serve its special interests at the expense of the interests of other classes. Thus, bankers and munitions makers brought about American intervention in order to protect their investment and profits. Although the thought of the New Left owes much to Marxist class struggle analysis, from which most economic interpretation derived, it is also indebted to Louis Hartz, John Higham, and others who challenged traditional assumptions by marshaling evidence that American history had been characterized less by conflict among interest groups or ideologies than by broad consensus. The New Left argues that, from the late nineteenth century onward, America has had a single dominant system of values in which the protection of private property, opportunity for individual enrichment, increase in production, and expansion of markets have been goals above all others. The New Left regards this capitalist system of values as wrong and productive of evil. It leads inevitably, they contend, to varieties of imperialism designed to ensure access to markets and, as a corollary, to conflict with revolutionary movements that espouse other than free market forms of economic and political organization. But the New Left does not, like the "Old Left," charge these outcomes to conspiracies. Its members blame instead the whole society's failure to think objectively and critically about fundamental assumptions. Those who have touched on American intervention in World War I, notably William Appleman Williams in *The Tragedy of American Diplomacy* (revised and enlarged edition; New York: Dell, 1962) and N. Gordon Levin, Jr., in *Woodrow Wilson and World Politics* (New York: Oxford University Press, 1968), concede that each move by the American government was, in the circumstances, logical and understandable. Indeed, they agree that Wilson's actions had a quality of inevitability, given the values accepted by him and by the largest part of the American public. They raise the philosophical question—one that might be raised with regard to Republican Rome or Napoleonic France—of whether the results might not have been otherwise if these values had been radically different. . . .

That some new debate will develop seems a safe prediction. Historians still dispute, after all, about the Persian and Peloponnesian Wars. Like Little Billie Potts in Robert Penn Warren's poem, all men try to remember when they lost whatever it was they lost and try to retrace their steps from that point. The date 1917 . . . will long remain [a point] at which Americans pause in such a search, and historians will keep going back to [it], seeking at least to understand what was, and sometimes speculating about what might have been.

What Happened to the
Progressive Movement in the 1920s?

Arthur S. Link

The conventional view of the decade of the 1920s holds that the
period witnessed the death of idealism, a termination of the progressive spirit, and the triumph of crass materialism and special privilege. Such a rendering of progressivism tends to neglect the fact
that the progressive movement never existed at any time as a recognizable organization with common goals. The popular view also ignores the continued importance of progressive sentiment, represented by the congressional Farm Bloc, supporters of TVA, and other
"progressive" achievements such as immigration restriction and
prohibition. In this spirit, Princeton historian Arthur S. Link attempts
to counter the governing hypotheses of the period which, to his
mind, had been offered "without fear or much research."

If the day has not yet arrived when we can make a definite synthesis of political developments between the Armistice and the Great Depression, it is
surely high time for historians to begin to clear away the accumulated heap
of mistaken and half-mistaken hypotheses about this important transitional
period. Writing often without fear or much research (to paraphrase Carl
Becker's remark), we recent American historians have gone on indefatigably
to perpetuate hypotheses that either reflected the disillusionment and despair
of contemporaries, or once served their purpose in exposing the alleged hiatus
in the great continuum of twentieth-century reform.

Stated briefly, the following are what might be called the governing
hypotheses of the period under discussion: The 1920's were a period made
almost unique by an extraordinary reaction against idealism and reform. They
were a time when the political representatives of big business and Wall Street
executed a relentless and successful campaign in state and nation to subvert
the regulatory structure that had been built at the cost of so much toil and
sweat since the 1870's, and to restore a Hanna-like reign of special privilege
to benefit business, industry, and finance. The surging tides of nationalism
and mass hatreds generated by World War I continued to engulf the land
and were manifested, among other things, in fear of communism, suppression
of civil liberties, revival of nativism and anti-Semitism most crudely exemplified by the Ku Klux Klan, and in the triumph of racism and prejudice in
immigration legislation. The 1920's were an era when great traditions and

ideals were repudiated or forgotten, when the American people, propelled by a crass materialism in their scramble for wealth, uttered a curse on twenty-five years of reform endeavor. As a result, progressives were stunned and everywhere in retreat along the entire political front, their forces disorganized and leaderless, their movement shattered, their dreams of a new America turned into agonizing nightmares.

To be sure, the total picture that emerges from these generalizations is overdrawn. Yet it seems fair to say that leading historians have advanced each of these generalizations, that the total picture is the one that most of us younger historians saw during the years of our training, and that these hypotheses to a greater or lesser degree still control the way in which we write and teach about the 1920's, as a reading of textbooks and general works will quickly show.

This paper has not been written, however, to quarrel with anyone or to make an indictment. Its purposes are, first, to attempt to determine the degree to which the governing hypotheses, as stated, are adequate or inadequate to explain the political phenomena of the period, and, second, to discover whether any new and sounder hypotheses might be suggested. Such an effort, of course, must be tentative and above all imperfect in view of the absence of sufficient foundations for a synthesis.

Happily, however, we do not have to proceed entirely in the dark. Historians young and old, but mostly young, have already discovered that the period of the 1920's is the exciting new frontier of American historical research and that its opportunities are almost limitless in view of the mass of manuscript materials that are becoming available. Thus we have (the following examples are mentioned only at random) excellent recent studies of agrarian discontent and farm movements by Theodore Saloutos, John D. Hicks, Gilbert C. Fite, Robert L. Morlan, and James H. Shideler; of nativism and problems of immigration and assimilation by John Higham, Oscar Handlin, Robert A. Devine, and Edmund D. Cronon; of intellectual currents, the social gospel, and religious controversies by Henry F. May, Paul A. Carter, Robert M. Miller, and Norman F. Furniss; of left-wing politics and labor developments by Theodore Draper, David A. Shannon, Daniel Bell, Paul M. Angle, and Matthew Josephson; of the campaign of 1928 by Edmund A. Moore; and of political and judicial leaders by Alpheus T. Mason, Frank Freidel, Arthur M. Schlesinger, Jr., Merlo J. Pusey, and Joel F. Paschal. Moreover, we can look forward to the early publication of studies that will be equally illuminating for the period, like the biographies of George W. Norris, Thomas J. Walsh, and Albert B. Fall now being prepared by Richard Lowitt, Leonard Bates, and David Stratton, respectively, and the recently completed study of the campaign and election of 1920 by Wesley M. Bagby.

Obviously, we are not only at a point in the progress of our research into the political history of the 1920's when we can begin to generalize, but we have reached the time when we should attempt to find some consensus, however tentative it must now be, concerning the larger political dimensions and meanings of the period.

In answering the question of what happened to the progressive movement in the 1920's, we should begin looking briefly at some fundamental facts about the movement before 1918, facts that in large measure predetermined its fate in the 1920's, given the political climate and circumstances that prevailed.

The first of these was the elementary fact that the progressive movement never really existed as a recognizable organization with common goals and a political machinery geared to achieve them. Generally speaking (and for the purposes of this paper), progressivism might be defined as the popular effort, which began convulsively in the 1890's and waxed and waned afterward to our own time, to insure the survival of democracy in the United States by the enlargement of governmental power to control and offset the power of private economic groups over the nation's institutions and life. Actually, of course, from the 1890's on there were many "progressive" movements on many levels seeking sometimes contradictory objectives. Not all, but most of these campaigns were the work of special interest groups or classes seeking greater political status and economic security. This was true from the beginning of the progressive movement in the 1890's; by 1913 it was that movement's most important characteristic.

The second fundamental fact—that the progressive movements were often largely middle class in constituency and orientation—is of course well known, but an important corollary has often been ignored. It was that several of the most important reform movements were inspired, staffed, and led by businessmen with very specific or special-interest objectives in view. Because they hated waste, mismanagement, and high taxes, they, together with their friends in the legal profession, often furnished the leadership of good government campaigns. Because they feared industrial monopoly, abuse of power by railroads, and the growth of financial oligarchy, they were the backbone of the movements that culminated in the adoption of the Hepburn and later acts for railroad regulation, the Federal Reserve Act, and the Federal Trade Commission Act. Among the many consequences of their participation in the progressive movement, two should be mentioned because of their significance for developments in the 1920's; First, the strong identification of businessmen with good government and economic reforms for which the general public also had a lively concern helped preserve the good reputation of the middle-class business community (as opposed to its alleged natural enemies, monopolists, malefactors of great wealth, and railroad barons) and helped to direct the energies of the progressive movement toward the strengthening instead of the shackling of the business community. Second, their activities and influence served to intensify the tensions within the broad reform movement, because they often opposed the demands of farm groups, labor unions, and advocates of social justice.

The third remark to be made about the progressive movement before 1918 is that despite its actual diversity and inner tensions it did seem to have unity; that is, it seemed to share common ideals and objectives. This was true in part because much of the motivation even of the special-interest groups was altruistic (at least they succeeded in convincing themselves that they sought the welfare of society rather than their own interests primarily); in part because political leadership generally succeeded in subordinating inner tensions. It was true, above all, because there were in fact important idealistic elements in the progressive ranks—social gospel leaders, social justice elements, and intellectuals and philosophers—who worked hard at the task of defining and elevating common principles and goals.

Fourth and finally, the substantial progressive achievements before 1918 had been gained, at least on the federal level, only because of the temporary dislocations of the national political structure caused by successive popular uprisings, not because progressives had found or created a viable organization for perpetuating their control. Or, to put the matter another way, before 1918 the various progressive elements had failed to destroy the existing party structure by organizing a national party of their own that could survive. They, or at least many of them, tried in 1912; and it seemed for a time in 1916 that Woodrow Wilson had succeeded in drawing the important progressive groups permanently into the Democratic party. But Wilson's accomplishment did not survive even to the end of the war, and by 1920 traditional partisan loyalties were reasserting themselves with extraordinary vigor.

With this introduction, we can now ask what happened to the progressive movement or movements in the 1920's. Surely no one would contend that after 1916 the political scene did not change significantly, both on the state and national levels. There was the seemingly obvious fact that the Wilsonian coalition had been wrecked by the election of 1920, and that the progressive elements were divided and afterward unable to agree upon a program or to control the national government. There was the even more "obvious" fact that conservative Republican presidents and their cabinets controlled the executive branch throughout the period. There was Congress, as Eric F. Goldman had said, allegedly whooping through procorporation legislation, and the Supreme Court interpreting the New Freedom laws in a way that harassed unions and encouraged trusts. There were, to outraged idealists and intellectuals, the more disgusting spectacles of Red hunts, mass arrests and deportations, the survival deep into the 1920's of arrogant nationalism, crusades against the teaching of evolution, the attempted suppression of the right to drink, and myriad other manifestations of what would now be called a repressive reaction.

Like the hypotheses suggested at the beginning, this picture is overdrawn in some particulars. But it is accurate in part, for progressivism was certainly on the downgrade if not in decay after 1918. This is an obvious fact that needs explanation and understanding rather than elaborate proof. We can go a long way toward answering our question if we can explain, at least partially, the extraordinary complex developments that converge to produce the "obvious" result.

For this explanation we must begin by looking at the several progressive elements and their relation to each other and to the two major parties after 1916. Since national progressivism was never an organized or independent movement (except imperfectly and then only temporarily in 1912), it could succeed only when its constituent elements formed a coalition strong enough to control one of the major parties. This had happened in 1916, when southern and western farmers, organized labor, the social justice elements, and a large part of the independent radicals who had heretofore voted the Socialist ticket coalesced to continue the control of Wilson and the Democratic party.

The important fact about the progressive coalition of 1916, however, was not its strength but its weakness. It was not a new party but a temporary alliance, welded in the heat of the most extraordinary domestic and external events. To be sure, it functioned for the most part successfully during the war, in providing the necessary support for a program of heavy taxation, relatively stringent controls over business and industry, and extensive new benefits to labor. Surviving in a crippled way even in the months following the Armistice, it put across a program that constituted a sizable triumph for the progressive movement—continued heavy taxation, the Transportation Act of 1920, the culmination of the long fight for railroad regulation, a new child labor act, amendments for prohibition and woman suffrage, immigration restriction, and water power and conservation legislation.

Even so, the progressive coalition of 1916 was inherently unstable. Indeed, it was so wracked by inner tensions that it could not survive, and destruction came inexorably, it seemed systematically, from 1917 to 1920. Why was this true?

First, the independent radicals and antiwar agrarians were alienated by the war declaration and the government's suppression of dissent and civil liberties during the war and the Red scare. Organized labor was disaffected by the administration's coercion of the coal miners in 1919, its lukewarm if not hostile attitude during the great strikes of 1919 and 1920, and its failure to support the Plumb Plan for nationalization of the railroads. Isolationists and idealists were outraged by what they thought was the President's betrayal of American traditions or the liberal peace program at Paris. These tensions were strong enough to disrupt the coalition, but a final one would have been fatal even if the others had never existed. This was the alienation of farmers in the Plains and western states produced by the administration's refusal to impose price controls on cotton while it maintained ceilings on the prices of other agricultural commodities, and especially by the administration's failure to do anything decisive to stem the downward plunge of farm prices that began in the summer of 1920. Under the impact of all these stresses, the Wilsonian coalition gradually disintegrated from 1917 to 1920 and disappeared entirely during the campaign of 1920.

The progressive coalition was thus destroyed, but the components of a potential movement remained. As we will see, these elements were neither inactive nor entirely unsuccessful in the 1920's. But they obviously failed to find common principles and a program, much less to unite effectively for political action on a national scale. I suggest that this was true, in part at least, for the following reasons:

First, the progressive elements could never create or gain control of a political organization capable of carrying them into national office. The Republican party was patently an impossible instrument because control of the GOP was too much in the hands of the eastern and midwestern industrial, oil, and financial interests, as it had been since about 1910. There was always the hope of a third party. Several progressive groups—insurgent midwestern Republicans, the railroad brotherhoods, a segment of the AF of L, and the moderate Socialists under Robert M. La Follette—tried to realize this goal in 1924, only to discover that third party movements in the United States are doomed to failure except in periods of enormous national turmoil, and that the 1920's were not such a time. Thus the Democratic party remained the only vehicle that conceivably could have been used by a new progressive coalition. But that party was simply not capable of such service in the 1920's. It was so torn by conflicts between its eastern, big city wing and its southern and western rural majority that it literally ceased to be a national party. It remained strong in its sectional and metropolitan components, but it was so divided that it barely succeeded in nominating a presidential candidate at all in 1924 and nominated one in 1928 only at the cost of temporary disruption.

Progressivism declined in the 1920's, in the second place, because, as has been suggested, the tensions that had wrecked the coalition of 1916 not only persisted but actually grew in number and intensity. The two most numerous progressive elements, the southern and western farmers, strongly supported the Eighteenth Amendment, were heavily tinged with nativism and therefore supported immigration restriction, were either members of, friendly to, or politically afraid of the Ku Klux Klan, and demanded as the principal plank in their platform legislation to guarantee them a larger share of the national income. On all these points and issues the lower and lower middle classes in the large cities stood in direct and often violent opposition to their potential allies in the rural areas. Moreover, the liaison between the farm groups and organized labor, which had been productive of much significant legislation during the Wilson period, virtually ceased to exist in the 1920's. There were many reasons for this development, and I mention only one—the fact that the preeminent spokesmen of farmers in the 1920's, the new Farm Bureau Federation, represented the larger commercial farmers who (in contrast to the members of the leading farm organization in Wilson's day, the National Farmers' Union) were often employers themselves and felt no identification with the rank and file of labor.

It was little wonder, therefore (and this is a third reason for the weakness of progressivism in the 1920's), that the tension-ridden progressive groups were never able to agree upon a program that, like the Democratic platform of 1916, could provide the basis for a revived coalition. So long as progressive groups fought one another more fiercely than they fought their natural opponents, such agreement was impossible; and so long as common goals were impossible to achieve, a national progressive movement could not take effective form. Nothing illustrates this better than the failure of the Democratic conventions of 1924 and 1928 to adopt platforms that could rally and unite the discontented elements. One result, among others, was that southern farmers voted as Democrats and western farmers as Republicans. And, as Professor Frank Freidel once commented to the author, much of the failure of progressivism in the 1920's can be explained by this elementary fact.

A deeper reason for the failure of progressives to unite ideologically in the 1920's was what might be called a substantial paralysis of the progressive mind. This was partly the result of the repudiation of progressive ideals by many intellectuals and the defection from the progressive movement of the urban middle classes and professional groups, as will be demonstrated. It was the result, even more importantly, of the fact that progressivism as an organized body of political thought found itself at a crossroads in the 1920's, like progressivism today, and did not know which way to turn. The major objectives of the progressive movement of the prewar years had in fact been largely achieved by 1920. In what direction should progressivism now move? Should it remain in the channels already deeply cut by its own traditions, and, while giving sincere allegiance to the ideal of democratic capitalism, work for more comprehensive programs of business regulation and assistance to disadvantaged classes like farmers and submerged industrial workers? Should it abandon these traditions and, like most similar European movements, take the road toward a moderate socialism with a predominantly labor orientation? Should it attempt merely to revive the goals of more democracy through changes in the political machinery? Or should it become mainly an agrarian movement with purely agrarian goals?

These were real dilemmas, not academic ones, and one can see numerous examples of how they confused and almost paralyzed progressives in the 1920's. The platform of La Follette's Progressive party of 1924 offers one revealing illustration. It embodied much that was old and meaningless by this time (the direct election of the President and a national referendum before the adoption of a war resolution, for example) and little that had any real significance for the future. And yet it was the best that a vigorous and idealistic movement could offer. A second example was the plight of the agrarians and insurgents in Congress who fought so hard all through the 1920's against Andrew Mellon's proposals to abolish the inheritance tax and to make drastic reductions in the taxes on large incomes. In view of the rapid reduction of the federal debt, the progressives were hard pressed to justify the continuation of nearly confiscatory tax levels, simply because few of them realized the wide social and economic uses to which the income tax could be put. Lacking any programs for the redistribution of the national income (except to farmers), they were plagued and overwhelmed by the surpluses in the federal Treasury until, for want of any good arguments, they finally gave Secretary Andrew Mellon the legislation he had been demanding. A third and final example of this virtual paralysis of the progressive mind was perhaps the most revealing of all. It was the attempt that Woodrow Wilson, Louis D. Brandeis, and other Democratic leaders made from 1921 to 1924 to draft a new charter for progressivism. Except for its inevitable proposals for an idealistic world leadership, the document that emerged from this interchange included little or nothing that would have sounded new to a western progressive in 1912.

A fourth reason for the disintegration and decline of the progressive movement in the 1920's was the lack of any effective leadership. Given the political temper and circumstances of the 1920's, it is possible that such leadership could not have operated successfully in any event. Perhaps the various progressive elements were so mutually hostile and so self-centered in interests and objectives that even a Theodore Roosevelt or a Woodrow Wilson, had they been at the zenith of their powers in the 1920's, could not have drawn them together in a common front. We will never know what a strong national leader might have done because by a trick of fate no such leader emerged before Franklin D. Roosevelt.

Four factors, then, contributed to the failure of the progressive components to unite successfully after 1918 and, as things turned out, before 1932: the lack of a suitable political vehicle, the severity of the tensions that kept progressives apart, the failure of progressives to agree upon a common program, and the absence of a national leadership, without which a united movement could never be created and sustained. These were all weaknesses that stemmed to a large degree from the instability and failures of the progressive movement itself.

There were, besides, a number of what might be called external causes for the movement's decline. In considering them one must begin with what was seemingly the most important—the alleged fact that the 1920's were a very unpropitious time for any new progressive revolt because of the ever-increasing level of economic prosperity, the materialism, and the general contentment of the decade 1919 to 1929. Part of this generalization is valid when applied to specific elements in the population. For example, the rapid rise in the real wages of industrial workers, coupled with generally full employment and the spread of so-called welfare practices among management, certainly did much to weaken and avert the further spread of organized labor, and thus to debilitate one of the important progressive components. But to say that it was prosperity *per se* that created a climate unfriendly to progressive ideals would be inaccurate. There was little prosperity and much depression during the 1920's for the single largest economic group, the farmers, as well as for numerous other groups. Progressivism, moreover, can flourish as much during periods of prosperity as during periods of discontent, as the history of the development of the progressive movement from 1901 to 1917 and of its triumph from 1945 to 1956 prove.

Vastly more important among the external factors in the decline of progressivism was the widespread, almost wholesale, defection from its ranks of the middle classes—the middling businessmen, bankers, and manufacturers, and the professional people closely associated with them in ideals and habits —in American cities large and small. For an understanding of this phenomenon no simple explanations like "prosperity" or the "temper of the times" will suffice, although they give some insight. The important fact was that these groups found a new economic and social status as a consequence of the flowering of American enterprise under the impact of the technological, financial, and other revolutions of the 1920's. If, as Professor Richard Hofstadter had claimed, the urban middle classes were progressive (that is, they demanded governmental relief from various anxieties) in the early 1900's because they resented their loss of social prestige to the *nouveaux riches* and feared being ground under by monopolists in industry, banking, and labor— if this is true, then the urban middle classes were not progressive in the 1920's for inverse reasons. Their temper was dynamic, expansive, and supremely confident. They knew that they were building a new America, a business civilization based not upon monopoly and restriction but upon a whole new set of business values—mass production and consumption, short hours and high wages, full employment, welfare capitalism. And what was more important, virtually the entire country (at least the journalists, writers in popular magazines, and many preachers and professors) acknowledged that the nation's destiny was in good hands. It was little wonder, therefore, that the whole complex of groups constituting the urban middle classes, whether in New York, Zenith, or Middletown, had little interest in rebellion or even in mild reform proposals that seemed to imperil their leadership and control.

Other important factors, of course, contributed to the contentment of the urban middle classes. The professionalization of business and the full-blown emergence of a large managerial class had a profound impact upon social and political ideals. The acceleration of mass advertising played its role, as did also the beginning disintegration of the great cities with the spread of middle- and upper-class suburbs, a factor that diffused the remaining reform energies among the urban leaders.

A second external factor in the decline of the progressive movement after 1918 was the desertion from its ranks of a good part of the intellectual leadership of the country. Indeed, more than simple desertion was involved here; it was often a matter of a cynical repudiation of the ideals from which progressivism derived its strength. I do not mean to imply too much by this generalization. I know that what has been called intellectual progressivism not only survived in the 1920's but actually flourished in many fields. I know that the intellectual foundations of our present quasi-welfare state were either being laid or reinforced during the decade. Even so, one cannot evade the conclusion that the intellectual-political climate of the 1920's was vastly different from the one that had prevailed in the preceding two decades.

During the years of the great progressive revolt, intellectuals—novelists, journalists, political thinkers, social scientists, historians, and the like—had made a deeply personal commitment to the cause of democracy, first in domestic and then in foreign affairs. Their leadership in and impact on many phases of the progressive movement had been profound. By contrast, in the 1920's a large body of this intellectual phalanx turned against the very ideals they had once deified. One could cite, for example, the reaction of the idealists against the Versailles settlement; the disenchantment of the intellectuals with the extension of government authority when it could be used to justify the Eighteenth Amendment or the suppression of free speech; or the inevitable loss of faith in the "people" when en masse they hounded so-called radicals, joined Bryan's crusade against evolution, or regaled themselves as Knights of the Ku Klux Klan. Whatever the cause, many alienated intellectuals simply withdrew or repudiated any identification with the groups they had once helped to lead. The result was not fatal to progressivism, but it was serious. The spark plugs had been removed from the engine of reform.

The progressive movement, then, unquestionably declined, but was it defunct in the 1920's? Much, of course, depends upon the definition of terms. If we accept the usual definition for "defunct" as "dead" or "ceasing to have any life or strength," we must recognize that the progressive movement was certainly not defunct in the 1920's; that on the contrary at least important parts of it were very much alive; and that it is just as important to know how and why progressivism survived as it is to know how and why it declined.

To state the matter briefly, progressivism survived in the 1920's because several important elements of the movement remained either in full vigor or in only slightly diminished strength. These were the farmers, after 1918 better organized and more powerful than during the high tide of the progressive revolt; the politically conscious elements among organized labor, particularly the railroad brotherhoods, who wielded a power all out of proportion to their numbers; the Democratic organizations in the large cities, usually vitally concerned with the welfare of the so-called lower classes; a remnant of independent radicals, social workers, and social gospel writers and preachers; and finally, an emerging new vocal element, the champions of public power and regional developments.

Although they never united effectively enough to capture a major party and the national government before 1932, these progressive elements controlled Congress from 1921 to about 1927 and continued to exercise a near control during the period of their greatest weakness in the legislative branch, from 1927 to about 1930.

Indeed, the single most powerful and consistently successful group in Congress during the entire decade from 1919 to 1929 were the spokesmen of the farmers. Spurred by an unrest in the country areas more intense than at any time since the 1890's, in 1920 and 1921 southern Democrats and midwestern and western insurgents, nominally Republican, joined forces in an alliance called the Farm Bloc. By maintaining a common front from 1921 to 1924 they succeeded in enacting the most advanced agricultural legislation to that date, legislation that completed the program begun under Wilsonian auspices. It included measures for high tariffs on agricultural products, thoroughgoing federal regulation of stockyards, packing houses, and grain exchanges, the exemption of agricultural cooperatives from the application of the antitrust laws, stimulation of the export of agricultural commodities, and the establishment of an entirely new federal system of intermediate rural credit.

When prosperity failed to return to the countryside, rural leaders in Congress espoused a new and bolder plan for relief—the proposal made by George N. Peek and Hugh S. Johnson in 1922 to use the federal power to obtain "fair exchange" or "parity" prices for farm products. Embodied in the McNary-Haugen bill in 1924, this measure was approved by Congress in 1927 and 1928, only to encounter vetoes by President Calvin Coolidge.

In spite of its momentary failure, the McNary-Haugen bill had a momentous significance for the American progressive movement. Its wholesale espousal by the great mass of farm leaders and spokesmen meant that the politically most powerful class in the country had come full scale to the conviction that the taxing power should be used directly and specifically for the purpose of underwriting (some persons called it subsidizing) agriculture. It was a milestone in the development of a comprehensive political doctrine that it was government's duty to protect the economic security of all classes and particularly depressed ones. McNary-Haugenism can be seen in its proper perspective if it is remembered that it would have been considered almost absurd in the Wilson period, that it was regarded as radical by nonfarm elements in the 1920's, and that it, or at any rate its fundamental objective, was incorporated almost as a matter of course into basic federal policy in the 1930's.

A second significant manifestation of the survival of progressivism in the 1920's came during the long controversy over public ownership or regulation of the burgeoning electric power industry. In this, as in most of the conflicts that eventually culminated on Capitol Hill, the agrarian element constituted the core of progressive strength. At the same time a sizable and well-organized independent movement developed that emanated from urban centers and was vigorous on the municipal and state levels. Throughout the decade this relatively new progressive group fought with mounting success to expose the propaganda of the private utilities, to strengthen state and federal regulatory agencies, and to win municipal ownership for distributive facilities. Like the advocates of railroad regulation in an earlier period, these proponents of regulation or ownership of a great new natural monopoly failed almost as much as they had succeeded in the 1920's. But their activities and exposures (the Federal Trade Commission's devastating investigation of the electric power industry in the late 1920's and early 1930's was the prime example) laid secure foundations for movements that in the 1930's would reach various culminations.

Even more significant for the future of American progressivism was the emergence in the 1920's of a new objective, that of committing the federal government to plans for large hydroelectric projects in the Tennessee Valley, the Columbia River watershed, the Southwest, and the St. Lawrence Valley for the purpose, some progressives said, of establishing "yardsticks" for rates, or for the further purpose, as other progressives declared, of beginning a movement for the eventual nationalization of the entire electric power industry. The development of this movement in its emerging stages affords a good case study in the natural history of American progressivism. It began when the Harding and Coolidge administrations attempted to dispose of the government's hydroelectric and nitrate facilities at Muscle Shoals, Alabama, to private interests. In the first stage of the controversy, the progressive objective was merely federal operation of these facilities for the production of cheap fertilizer—a reflection of its exclusive special-interest orientation. Then, as new groups joined the fight to save Muscle Shoals, the objective of public production of cheap electric power came to the fore. Finally, by the end of the 1920's, the objective of a multipurpose regional development in the Tennessee Valley and in other areas as well had taken firm shape.

In addition, by 1928 the agrarians in Congress, led by Senator George W. Norris, had found enough allies in the two houses and enough support in the country at large to adopt a bill for limited federal development of the Tennessee Valley. Thwarted by President Coolidge's pocket veto, the progressives tried again in 1931, only to meet a second rebuff at the hands of President Herbert Hoover.

All this might be regarded as another milestone in the maturing of American progressivism. It signified a deviation from the older traditions of mere regulation, as President Hoover had said in his veto of the second Muscle Shoals bill, and the triumph of new concepts of direct federal leadership in large-scale development of resources. If progressives had not won their goal by the end of the 1920's, they had at least succeeded in writing what would become perhaps the most important plank in their program for the future.

The maturing of an advanced farm program and the formulation of plans for public power and regional developments may be termed the two most significant progressive achievements on the national level in the 1920's. Others merit only brief consideration. One was the final winning of the old progressive goal of immigration restriction through limited and selective admission. The fact that this movement was motivated in part by racism, nativism, and anti-Semitism (with which, incidentally, a great many if not a majority of progressives were imbued in the 1920's) should not blind us to the fact that it was also progressive. It sought to substitute a so-called scientific and a planned policy for a policy of *laissez-faire*. Its purpose was admittedly to disturb the free operation of the international labor market. Organized labor and social workers had long supported it against the opposition of large employers. And there was prohibition, the most ambitious and revealing progressive experiment of the twentieth century. Even the contemned antievolution crusade of Bryan and the fundamentalists and the surging drives for conformity of thought and action in other fields should be mentioned. All these movements stemmed from the conviction that organized public power could and should be used purposefully to achieve fundamental social and so-called moral change. The fact that they were potentially or actively repressive does not mean that they were not progressive. On the contrary, they superbly illustrated the repressive tendencies that inhered in progressivism precisely because it was grounded so much upon majoritarian principles.

Three other developments on the national level that have often been cited as evidences of the failure of progressivism in the 1920's appear in a somewhat different light at second glance. The first was the reversal of the tariff-for-revenue-only tendencies of the Underwood Act with the enactment of the Emergency Tariff Act of 1921 and the Fordney-McCumber Act of 1922. Actually, the adoption of these measures signified, on the whole, not a repudiation but a revival of progressive principles in the realm of federal fiscal policy. A revenue tariff had never been an authentic progressive objective. Indeed, at least by 1913, many progressives, except for some southern agrarians, had concluded that it was retrogressive and had agreed that the tariff laws should be used deliberately to achieve certain national objectives—for example, the crippling of noncompetitive big business by the free admission of articles manufactured by so-called trusts, or benefits to farmers by the free entry of farm implements. Wilson himself had been at least partially converted to these principles by 1916, as his insistence upon the creation of the Federal Tariff Commission and his promise of protection to the domestic chemical industry revealed. As for the tariff legislation of the early 1920's, its only important changes were increased protection for aluminum, chemical products, and agricultural commodities. It left the Underwood rates on the great mass of raw materials and manufactured goods largely undisturbed. It may have been economically shortsighted and a bad example for the rest of the world, but for the most part it was progressive in principle and was the handiwork of the progressive coalition in Congress.

Another development that has often been misunderstood in its relation to the progressive movement was the policies of consistent support that the Harding and Coolidge administrations adopted for business enterprise, particularly the policy of the Federal Trade Commission in encouraging the formation of trade associations and the diminution of certain traditional competitive practices. The significance of all this can easily be overrated. Such policies as these two administrations executed had substantial justification in progressive theory and in precedents clearly established by the Wilson administration.

A third challenge to usual interpretations concerns implications to be drawn from the election of Harding and Coolidge in 1920 and 1924. These

243

elections seem to indicate the triumph of reaction among the mass of American voters. Yet one could argue that both Harding and Coolidge were political accidents, the beneficiaries of grave defects in the American political and constitutional systems. The rank and file of Republican voters demonstrated during the preconvention campaign that they wanted vigorous leadership and a moderately progressive candidate in 1920. They got Harding instead, not because they wanted him, but because unusual circumstances permitted a small clique to thwart the will of the majority. They took Coolidge as their candidate in 1924 simply because Harding died in the middle of his term and there seemed to be no alternative to nominating the man who had succeeded him in the White House. Further, an analysis of the election returns in 1920 and 1924 will show that the really decisive factor in the victories of Harding and Coolidge was the fragmentation of the progressive movement and the fact that an opposition strong enough to rally and unite the progressive majority simply did not exist.

There remains, finally, a vast area of progressive activity about which we yet know very little. One could mention the continuation of old reform movements and the development of new ones in the cities and states during the years following the Armistice: For example, the steady spread of the city manager form of government, the beginning of zoning and planning movements, and the efforts of the great cities to keep abreast of the transportation revolution then in full swing. Throughout the country the educational and welfare activities of the cities and states steadily increased. Factory legislation matured, while social insurance had its experimental beginnings. Whether such reform impulses were generally weak or strong, one cannot say; but what we do know about developments in cities like Cincinnati and states like New York, Wisconsin, and Louisiana justifies a challenge to the assumption that municipal and state reform energies were dead after 1918 and, incidentally, a plea to young scholars to plow this unworked field of recent American history.

Let us, then, suggest a tentative synthesis as an explanation of what happened to the progressive movement after 1918:

First, the national progressive movement, which had found its most effective embodiment in the coalition of forces that reelected Woodrow Wilson in 1916, was shattered by certain policies that the administration pursued from 1917 to 1920, and by some developments over which the administration had no or only slight control. The collapse that occurred in 1920 was not inevitable and cannot be explained by merely saying that "the war killed the progressive movement."

Second, large and aggressive components of a potential new progressive coalition remained after 1920. These elements never succeeded in uniting effectively before the end of the decade, not because they did not exist, but because they were divided by conflicts among themselves. National leadership, which in any event did not emerge in the 1920's, perhaps could not have succeeded in subduing these tensions and in creating a new common front.

Third, as a result of the foregoing, progressivism as an organized national force suffered a serious decline in the 1920's. This decline was heightened by the defection of large elements among the urban middle classes and the intellectuals, a desertion induced by technological, economic, and demographic changes, and by the outcropping of certain repressive tendencies in progressivism after 1917.

Fourth, in spite of reversals and failures, important components of the national progressive movement survived in considerable vigor and succeeded to a varying degree, not merely in keeping the movement alive, but even in broadening its horizons. This was true particularly of the farm groups and of the coalition concerned with public regulation or ownership of electric power resources. These two groups laid the groundwork in the 1920's for significant new programs in the 1930's and beyond.

Fifth, various progressive coalitions controlled Congress for the greater part of the 1920's and were always a serious threat to the conservative administrations that controlled the executive branch. Because this was true, most of the legislation adopted by Congress during this period, including many measures that historians have inaccurately called reactionary, was progressive in character.

Sixth, the progressive movement in the cities and states was far from dead in the 1920's, although we do not have sufficient evidence to justify any generalizations about the degree of its vigor.

If this tentative and imperfect synthesis has any value, perhaps it is high time that we discard the sweeping generalizations, false hypotheses, and clichés that we have so often used in explaining and characterizing political developments from 1918 to 1929. Perhaps we should try to see these developments for what they were—the normal and ordinary political behavior of groups and classes caught up in a swirl of social and economic change. When we do this we will no longer ask whether the progressive movement was defunct in the 1920's. We will ask only what happened to it and why.

The Legend of Isolationism in the 1920s

William Appleman Williams

The myth of the 1920s as the "Jazz Age," a decade of "booze, bobbed hair and the blues," had its origins when the era was indeed "only yesterday." That this view is mostly myth, at least to the extent that it described only certain domestic aspects of the age, has been emphasized so much that we may be coming to believe it. One of the aspects of the "Jazz Age" myth which has maintained its tenacity is that which characterizes U.S. foreign policy of the period as isolationist. In this article, William Appleman Williams, Professor of History at the University of Oregon, and one of the early "new leftists," attacks this stance as completely mythological—a reflection of "the folklore of American foreign relations." He sees America's approach to foreign affairs during the 1920s as related to other so-called isolationist periods in American history when the country, led by the business community and supported by the government, was in fact very much expansionist.

The widely accepted assumption that the United States was isolationist from 1920 through 1932 is no more than a legend. Sir Francis Bacon might have classed this myth of isolation as one of his Idols of the Market-Place. An "ill and unfit choice of words," he cautioned, "leads men away into innumerable and inane controversies and fancies." And certainly the application of the terms *isolation* and *isolationism* to a period and a policy that were characterized by vigorous involvement in the affairs of the world with consciousness of purpose qualifies as an "ill and unfit choice of words." Thus the purpose of this essay: on the basis of an investigation of the record to suggest that, far from isolation, the foreign relations of the United States from 1920 through 1932 were marked by express and extended involvement with—and intervention in the affairs of—other nations of the world.

It is both more accurate and more helpful to consider the twenties as contiguous with the present instead of viewing those years as a quixotic interlude of low-down jazz and lower-grade gin, fluttering flappers and Faulkner's fiction, and bootlegging millionaires and millionaire bootleggers. For in foreign policy there is far less of a sharp break between 1923 and 1953 than generally is acknowledged. A closer examination of the so-called isolationists of the twenties reveals that many of them were in fact busily engaged in extending American power. Those individuals and groups have not dramatically changed their outlook on foreign affairs. Their policies and objectives may differ with those of others (including professors), but they have never sought to isolate the United States.

This interpretation runs counter to the folklore of American foreign relations. Harvard places isolationism "in the saddle." Columbia sees "Americans retiring within their own shell." Yale judges that policy "degenerated" into isolation—among other things. Others, less picturesque but equally positive, refer to a "marked increase of isolationist sentiment" and to "those years of isolationism." Another group diagnoses the populace as having "ingrained isolationism," analyzes it as "sullen and selfish" in consequence, and characterizes it as doing "its best to forget international subjects." Related verdicts describe the Republican party as "predominantly isolationist" and as an organization that "fostered a policy of deliberate isolation."

Most pointed of these specifications is a terse two-word summary of the diplomacy of the period: "Isolation Perfected." Popularizers have transcribed this theme into a burlesque. Their articles and books convey the impression that the Secretaries of State were in semi-retirement and that the citizenry wished to do away with the Department itself. Columnists and commentators have made the concept an eerie example of George Orwell's double-think. They label as isolationists the most vigorous interventionists.

The case would seem to be closed and judgment given if it were not for the ambivalence of some observers and the brief dissents filed by a few others. The scholar who used the phrase "those years of isolationism," for example, remarks elsewhere in the same book that "expansionism . . . really was long a major expression of isolationism." Another writes of the "return to an earlier policy of isolation," and on the next page notes a "shift in policy during the twenties amounting almost to a 'diplomatic revolution'." A recent biographer states that Henry Cabot Lodge "did not propose . . . an isolationist attitude," but then proceeds to characterize the Monroe Doctrine—upon which Lodge stood in his fight against the League of Nations treaty—as a philosophy of "isolation." And in the last volume of his trilogy, the late Professor Frederick L. Paxton summed up a long review of the many diplomatic activities of the years 1919–1923 with the remark that this was a foreign policy of "avoidance rather than of action."

But a few scholars, toying with the Idol of the Market-Place, have made bold to rock the image. Yet Professor Richard Van Alstyne was doing more than playing the iconoclast when he observed that the "militant manifest destiny men were the isolationists of the nineteenth century." For with this insight we can translate those who maintain that Lodge "led the movement to perpetuate the traditional policy of isolation." Perhaps William G. Carleton was even more forthright. In 1946 he pointed out that the fight over the League treaty was not between isolationists and internationalists, and added that many of the mislabeled isolationists were actually "nationalists and imperialists." Equally discerning was Charles Beard's comment in 1933 that the twenties were marked by a "return to the more aggressive ways . . . [used] to protect and advance the claims of American business enterprise." All these interpretations were based on facts that prompted another scholar to change his earlier conclusion and declare in 1953 that "the thought was all of keeping American freedom of action."

These are perceptive comments. Additional help has recently been supplied by two other students of the period. One of these is Robert E. Osgood, who approached the problem in terms of *Ideals and Self-Interest in American Foreign Relations*. Though primarily concerned with the argument that Americans should cease being naïve, Osgood suggests that certain stereotypes are misleading. One might differ with his analysis of the struggle over the Treaty of Versailles, but not with his insistence that there were fundamental differences between Senators Lodge and William E. Borah—as well as between those two and President Woodrow Wilson. Osgood likewise raises questions about the reputed withdrawal of the American public. Over a thousand organizations for the study of international relations existed in 1926, to say nothing of the groups that sought constantly to make or modify foreign policy.

Osgood gives little attention to this latter aspect of foreign relations, a surprising omission on the part of a realist. But the underlying assumption of his inquiry cannot be challenged. The foreign policy issue of the twenties was never isolationism. The controversy and competition were waged between those who entertained different concepts of the national interest and disagreed over the means to be employed to secure that objective. Secretary of State Charles Evans Hughes was merely more eloquent, not less explicit. "Foreign policies," he explained in 1923, "are not built upon abstractions. They are the result of practical conceptions of national interest arising from some immediate exigency or standing out vividly in historical perspective."

Historian George L. Grassmuck used this old-fashioned premise of the politician as a tool with which to probe the *Sectional Biases in Congress on Foreign Policy*. Disciplining himself more rigorously in the search for primary facts than did Osgood, Grassmuck's findings prompted him to conclude that "the 'sheep and goats' technique" of historical research is eminently unproductive. From 1921 to 1933, for example, the Republicans in both houses of Congress were "more favorable to both Army and Navy measures than . . . Democrats." Eighty-five percent of the same Republicans supported international economic measures and agreements. As for the Middle West, that much condemned section did not reveal any "extraordinary indication of a . . . tendency to withdraw." Nor was there "an intense 'isolationism' on the part of [its] legislators with regard to membership in a world organization." And what opposition there was seems to have been as much the consequence of dust bowls and depression as the product of disillusioned scholars in ivory towers.

These investigations and correlations have two implications. First, the United States was neither isolated nor did it pursue a policy of isolationism from 1920 to 1933. Second, if the policy of that era, so generally accepted as the product of traditional isolationist sentiment, proves non-isolationist, then the validity and usefulness of the concept when applied to earlier or later periods may seriously be challenged.

Indeed, it would seem more probable that the central theme of American foreign relations has been the expansion of the United States. Alexander Hamilton made astute use of the phrase "no entangling alliances" during the negotiation of Jay's Treaty in 1794, but his object was a *de facto* affiliation with the British Fleet—not isolation. Nor was Thomas Jefferson seeking to withdraw when he made of Monticello a counselling center for those seeking to emulate the success of the American Revolution. A century later Senator Lodge sought to revise the Treaty of Versailles and the Covenant of the League of Nations with reservations that seemed no more than a restatement of Hamilton's remarks. Yet the maneuvers of Lodge were no more isolationist in character and purpose than Hamilton's earlier action. And while surely no latter-day Jefferson, Senator Borah was anything but an isolationist in his concept of the power of economics and ideas. Borah not only favored the recognition of the Soviet Union in order to influence the development of the Bolshevik Revolution and as a check against Japanese expansion in Asia, but also argued that American economic policies were intimately connected with foreign political crises. All those men were concerned with the extension of one or more aspects of American influence, power, and authority.

Approached in this manner, the record of American foreign policy in the twenties verifies the judgments of two remarkably dissimilar students: historian Richard W. Leopold and Senator Lodge. The professor warns that the era was "more complex than most glib generalizations . . . would suggest"; and the scholastic politician concludes that, excepting wars, there "never [was] a period when the United States [was] more active and its influence more felt internationally than between 1921 and 1924." The admonition about perplexity was offered as helpful advice, not as an invitation to anti-intellectualism. For, as the remarks of the Senator implied, recognition that a problem is involved does not mean that it cannot be resolved.

Paradox and complexity can often be clarified by rearranging the data around a new focal point that is common to all aspects of the apparent contradiction. The confusion of certainty and ambiguity that characterizes most accounts of American foreign policy in the twenties stems from the fact that they are centered on the issue of membership in the League of Nations. Those Americans who wanted to join are called internationalists. Opponents of that move became isolationists. But the subsequent action of most of those who fought participation in the League belies this simple classification. And the later policies of many who favored adherence to the League casts serious doubts upon the assumption that they were willing to negotiate or arbitrate questions that they defined as involving the national interest. More pertinent is an examination of why certain groups and individuals favored or disapproved of the League, coupled with a review of the programs they supported after that question was decided.

Yet such a re-study of the League fight is in itself insufficient. Equally important is a close analysis of the American reaction to the Bolshevik Revolution. Both the League Covenant and the Treaty of Versailles were written on a table shaken by that upheaval. The argument over the ratification of the combined documents was waged in a context determined as much by Nikolai Lenin's *Appeal to the Toiling, Oppressed, and Exhausted Peoples of Europe* and the Soviet *Declaration to the Chinese People* as by George Washington's Farewell Address.

Considered within the setting of the Bolshevik Revolution, the basic question was far greater than whether or not to enter the League. At issue was what response was to be made to the domestic and international division of labor that had accompanied the Industrial Revolution. Challenges from organized urban labor, dissatisfied farmers, frightened men of property, searching intellectual critics, and colonial peoples rudely interrupted almost every meeting of the Big Four in Paris and were echoed in many Senate debates over the treaty. And those who determined American policy through the decade of the twenties were consciously concerned with the same problem.

An inquiry into this controversy over the broad question of how to end the war reveals certain divisions within American society. These groupings were composed of individuals and organizations whose position on the League of Nations was coincident with and part of their response to the Bolsheviks; or, in a wider sense, with their answer to that general unrest, described by Woodrow Wilson as a "feeling of revolt against the large vested interests which influenced the world both in the economic and the political sphere." Once this breakdown has been made it is then possible to follow the ideas and actions of these various associations of influence and power through the years 1920 to 1933.

At the core of the American reaction to the League and the Bolshevik Revolution was the quandary between fidelity to ideals and the urge to power. Jefferson faced a less acute version of the same predicament in terms of whether to force citizenship on settlers west of the Mississippi who were reluctant to be absorbed in the Louisiana Purchase. A century later the anti-imperialists posed the same issue in the more sharply defined circumstances of the Spanish-American War. The League and the Bolsheviks raised the question in its most dramatic context and in unavoidable terms.

There were four broad responses to this reopening of the age-old dilemma. At one pole stood the pure idealists and pacifists, led by William Jennings Bryan. A tiny minority in themselves, they were joined, in terms of general consequences if not in action, by those Americans who were preoccupied with their own solutions to the problem. Many American business men, for example, were concerned primarily with the expansion of trade and were apathetic toward or impatient with the hullabaloo over the League. Diametrically opposed to the idealists were the vigorous expansionists. All these exponents of the main chance did not insist upon an overt crusade to run the world, but they were united on Senator Lodge's proposition that the United States should dominate world politics. Association with other nations they accepted, but not equality of membership or mutuality of decision.

Caught in the middle were those Americans who declined to support either extreme. A large number of these people clustered around Woodrow Wilson, and can be called the Wilsonites. Though aware of the dangers and temptations involved, Wilson declared his intention to extend American power for the purpose of strengthening the ideals. However noble that effort, it failed for two reasons. Wilson delegated power and initiative to men and organizations that did not share his objectives, and on his own part the President ultimately "cast in his lot" with the defenders of the *status quo.*

Led by the Sons of the Wild Jackass, the remaining group usually followed Senator Borah in foreign relations. These men had few illusions about the importance of power in human affairs or concerning the authority of the United States in international politics. Prior to the world war they supported—either positively or passively—such vigorous expansionists as Theodore Roosevelt, who led their Progressive Party. But the war and the Bolshevik Revolution jarred some of these Progressives into a closer examination of their assumptions. These reflections and new conclusions widened the breach with those of their old comrades who had moved toward a conservative position on domestic issues. Some of those earlier allies, like Senator Albert J. Beveridge, continued to agitate for an American century. Others, such as Bainbridge Colby, sided with Wilson in 1916 and went along with the President on foreign policy.

But a handful had become firm anti-expansionists by 1919. No attempt was made by these men to deny the power of the United States. Nor did they think that the nation could become self-sufficient and impregnable in its strength. Borah, for example, insisted that America must stand with Russia if Japan and Germany were to be checked. And Johnson constantly pointed out that the question was not whether to withdraw, but at what time and under what circumstances to use the country's influence. What these men did maintain was that any effort to run the world by establishing an American system comparable to the British Empire was both futile and un-American.

In this they agreed with Henry Adams, who debated the same issue with his brother Brooks Adams, Theodore Roosevelt, and Henry Cabot Lodge in the years after 1898. "I incline now to anti-imperialism, and very strongly to anti-militarism," Henry warned. "If we try to rule politically, we take the chances against us." By the end of the first world war another generation of expansionists tended to agree with Henry Adams about ruling politically, but planned to build and maintain a similar pattern of control through the use of America's economic might. Replying to these later expansionists, Borah and other anti-expansionists of the nineteen-twenties argued that if Washington's influence was to be effective it would have to be used to support the movements of reform and colonial nationalism rather than deployed in an effort to dam up and dominate those forces.

For these reasons they opposed Wilson's reorganization of the international banking consortium, fearing that the financiers would either influence strongly or veto—as they did—American foreign policies. With Senator Albert B. Cummins of Iowa they voted against the Wilson-approved Webb-Pomerene Act, which repealed the anti-trust laws for export associations. In the same vein they tried to prevent passage of the Edge Act, an amendment to the Federal Reserve Act that authorized foreign banking corporations. Led by Borah, they bitterly attacked the Versailles Treaty because, in their view, it committed the United States to oppose colonial movements for self-government and to support an unjust and indefensible *status quo*. From the same perspective they criticized and fought to end intervention in Russia and the suppression of civil liberties at home.

Contrary to the standard criticism of their actions, however, these anti-expansionists were not just negative die-hards. Senator Cummins maintained from the first that American loans to the allies should be considered gifts. Borah spoke out on the same issue, hammered away against armed intervention in Latin America, played a key role in securing the appointment of Dwight Morrow as Ambassador to Mexico, and sought to align the United States with, instead of against, the Chinese Revolution. On these and other issues the anti-expansionists were not always of one mind, but as in the case of the Washington Conference Treaties the majority of them were far more positive in their actions than has been acknowledged.

Within this framework the key to the defeat of the League treaty was the defection from the Wilsonites of a group who declined to accept the restrictions that Article X of the League Covenant threatened to impose upon the United States. A morally binding guarantee of the "territorial integrity and existing political integrity of all members of the League" was too much for these men. First they tried to modify that limitation. Failing there, they followed Elihu Root and William Howard Taft, both old time expansionists, to a new position behind Senator Lodge. Among those who abandoned Wilson on this issue were Herbert Hoover, Calvin Coolidge, Charles Evans Hughes, and Henry L. Stimson.

Not all these men were at ease with the vigorous expansionists. Stimson, for one, thought the Lodge reservations "harsh and unpleasant," and later adjusted other of his views. Hoover and Hughes tried to revive their version of the League after the Republicans returned to power in 1920. But at the time all of them were more uneasy about what one writer has termed Wilson's "moral imperialism." They were not eager to identify themselves with the memories of that blatant imperialism of the years 1895 to 1905, but neither did they like Article X. That proviso caught them from both sides, it illegalized changes initiated by the United States, and obligated America to restore a *status quo* to some aspects of which they were either indifferent or antagonistic. But least of all were they anxious to run the risk that the Wilsonian rhetoric of freedom and liberty might be taken seriously in an age of revolution. Either by choice or default they supported the idea of a community of interest among the industrialized powers of the world led by an American-British *entente* as against the colonial areas and the Soviet Union.

This postwar concept of the community of interest was the first generation intellectual offspring of Herbert Croly's *Promise of American Life* and Herbert Hoover's *American Individualism.* Croly's opportunistic nationalism provided direction for Hoover's "greater mutuality of interest." The latter was to be expressed in an alliance between the government and the "great trade associations and the powerful corporations." Pushed by the Croly-Hoover wing of the old Progressive Party, the idea enjoyed great prestige during the twenties. Among its most ardent exponents were Samuel Gompers and Matthew Woll of the labor movement, Owen D. Young of management, and Bernard Baruch of finance.

What emerged was an American corporatism. The avowed goals were order, stability, and social peace. The means to those objectives were labor-management co-operation, arbitration, and the elimination of waste and inefficiency by closing out unrestrained competition. State intervention was to be firm, but moderated through the cultivation and legalization of trade associations which would, in turn, advise the national government and supply leaders for the federal bureaucracy. The ideal was union in place of diversity and conflict.

Other than Hoover, the chief spokesmen of this new community of interest as applied to foreign affairs were Secretaries of State Hughes and Stimson. In the late months of 1931 Stimson was to shift his ground, but until that time he supported the principle. All three men agreed that American economic power should be used to build, strengthen, and maintain the co-operation they sought. As a condition for his entry into the cabinet, Hoover demanded—and received—a major voice in "all important economic policies of the administration." With the energetic assistance of Julius Klein, lauded by the National Foreign Trade Council as the "international business go-getter of Uncle Sam," Hoover changed the Department of Commerce from an agency primarily concerned with interstate commerce to one that concentrated on foreign markets and loans, and control of import sources. Hughes and Stimson handled the political aspects of establishing a "community of ideals, interests and purposes."

These men were not imperialists in the traditional sense of that much abused term. All agreed with Klein that the object was to eliminate "the old imperialistic trappings of politico-economic exploitation." They sought instead the "internationalization of business." Through the use of economic power they wanted to establish a common bond, forged of similar assumptions and purposes, with both the industrialized nations and the native business community in the colonial areas of the world. Their deployment of America's material strength is unquestioned. President Calvin Coolidge reviewed their success, and indicated the political implications thereof, on Memorial Day, 1928. "Our investments and trade relations are such," he summarized, "that it is almost impossible to conceive of any conflict anywhere on earth which would not affect us injuriously."

Internationalization through the avoidance of conflict was the key objective. This did not mean a negative foreign policy. Positive action was the basic theme. The transposition of corporatist principles to the area of foreign relations produced a parallel policy. American leadership and intervention would build a world community regulated by agreement among the industrialized nations. The prevention of revolution and the preservation of the sanctity of private property were vital objectives. Hughes was very clear when he formulated the idea for Latin America. "We are seeking to establish a *Pax Americana* maintained not by arms but by mutual respect and good will and the tranquillizing processes of reason." There would be, he admitted, "interpositions of a temporary character"—the Secretary did not like the connotations of the word intervention—but only to facilitate the establishment of the United States as the "exemplar of justice."

Extension to the world of this pattern developed in Latin America was more involved. There were five main difficulties, four in the realm of foreign relations and one in domestic affairs. The internal problem was to establish and integrate a concert of decision between the government and private economic groups. Abroad the objectives were more sharply defined: circumscribe the impact of the Soviet Union, forestall and control potential resistance of colonial areas, pamper and cajole Germany and Japan into acceptance of the basic proposition, and secure from Great Britain practical recognition of the fact that Washington had become the center of Anglo-Saxon collaboration. Several examples will serve to illustrate the general outline of this diplomacy, and to indicate the friction between the office holders and the office dwellers.

Wilson's Administration left the incoming Republicans a plurality of tools designed for the purpose of extending American power. The Webb-Pomerene Law, the Edge Act, and the banking consortium were but three of the more obvious and important of these. Certain polishing and sharpening remained to be done, as exemplified by Hoover's generous interpretation of the Webb-Pomerene legislation, but this was a minor problem. Hoover and Hughes added to these implements with such laws as the one designed to give American customs officials diplomatic immunity so that they could do cost accounting surveys of foreign firms. This procedure was part of the plan to provide equal opportunity abroad, under which circumstances Secretary

Hughes was confident that "American business men would take care of themselves."

It was harder to deal with the British, who persisted in annoying indications that they considered themselves equal partners in the enterprise. Bainbridge Colby, Wilson's last Secretary of State, ran into the same trouble. Unless England came "to our way of thinking," Colby feared that "agreement [would] be impossible." A bit later Hughes told the British Ambassador that the time had come for London's expressions of cordial sentiment to be "translated into something definite." After many harangues about oil, access to mandated areas, and trade with Russia, it was with great relief that Stimson spoke of the United States and Great Britain "working together like two old shoes."

Deep concern over revolutionary ferment produced great anxiety. Hughes quite agreed with Colby that the problem was to prevent revolutions without making martyrs of the leaders of colonial or other dissident movements. The dispatches of the period are filled with such expressions as "very grave concern," "further depressed," and "deeply regret," in connection with revolutionary activity in China, Latin America, and Europe. American foreign service personnel abroad were constantly reminded to report all indications of such unrest. This sensitivity reached a high point when one representative telegraphed as "an example of the failure to assure public safety . . . the throwing of a rock yesterday into the state hospital here." Quite in keeping with this pattern was Washington's conclusion that it would support "any provisional government which gave satisfactory evidence of an intention to re-establish constitutional order."

Central to American diplomacy of the twenties was the issue of Germany and Japan. And it was in this area that the government ran into trouble with its partners, the large associations of capital. The snag was to convince the bankers of the validity of the long range view. Hoover, Hughes and Stimson all agreed that it was vital to integrate Germany and Japan into the American community. Thus Hughes opposed the French diplomacy of force on the Rhine, and for his own part initiated the Dawes Plan. But the delegation of so much authority to the financiers backfired in 1931. The depression scared the House of Morgan and it refused to extend further credits to Germany. Stimson "blew up." He angrily told the Morgan representative in Paris that this strengthened France and thereby undercut the American program. Interrupted in the midst of this argument by a trans-Atlantic phone call from Hoover, Stimson explained to the President that "if you want to help the cause you are speaking of you will not do it by calling me up, but by calling Tom Lamont." Stimson then turned back to Lamont's agent in Europe and, using "unregulated language," told the man to abandon his "narrow banking axioms."

Similar difficulties faced the government in dealing with Japan and China. The main problem was to convince Japan, by persuasion, concession, and the delicate use of diplomatic force, to join the United States in an application of its Latin American policy to China. Washington argued that the era of the crude exploitation of, and the exercise of direct political sovereignty over, backward peoples was past. Instead, the interested powers should agree to develop and exercise a system of absentee authority while increasing the productive capacity and administrative efficiency of China. Japan seemed amenable to the proposal, and at the Washington Conference, Secretary Hughes went a great distance to convince Tokyo of American sincerity. Some writers, such as George Frost Kennan and Adolf A. Berle, claim that the United States did not go far enough. This is something of a mystery. For in his efforts to establish "cooperation in the Far East," as Hughes termed it, the Secretary consciously gave Japan "an extraordinarily favorable position."

Perhaps what Kennan and Berle have in mind is the attitude of Thomas Lamont. In contrast to their perspective on Europe, the bankers took an extremely long range view of Asia. Accepting the implications of the Four and Nine Power Treaties, Lamont began to finance Japan's penetration of the mainland. Hughes and Stimson were trapped. They continued to think in terms of American business men taking care of themselves if given an opportunity, and thus strengthening Washington's position in the world community. Hughes wrote Morgan that he hoped the consortium would become an "important instrumentality of our 'open door' policy." But the American members of the banking group refused to antagonize their Japanese and British colleagues, and so vetoed Washington's hope to finance the Chinese Eastern Railway and its efforts to support the Federal Telegraph Company in China.

In this context it is easy to sympathize with Stimson's discomfort when the Japanese Army roared across Manchuria. As he constantly reiterated to the Japanese Ambassador in Washington, Tokyo had come far along the road "of bringing itself into alignment with the methods and opinion of the Western World." Stimson not only wanted to, but did in fact give Japan every chance to continue along that path. So too did President Hoover, whose concern with revolution was so great that he was inclined to view Japanese sovereignty in Manchuria as the best solution. Key men in the State Department shared the President's conclusion.

Stimson's insight was not so limited. He realized that his predecessor, Secretary of State Frank B. Kellogg, had been right: the community of interest that America should seek was with the Chinese. The Secretary acknowledged his error to Senator Borah, who had argued just such a thesis since 1917. Stimson's letter to Borah of February 23, 1932, did not say that America should abandon her isolationism, but rather that she had gone too far with the wrong friends. The long and painful process of America's great awakening had begun. But in the meantime President Hoover's insistence that no move should be made toward the Soviet Union, and that the non-recognition of Manchuko should be considered as a formula looking toward conciliation, had opened the door to appeasement.

Suggested Further Reading for Chapter 3

Charles A. Beard, *The Myth of Rugged American Individualism* (New York: John Day Co., 1932).

Paul A. Carter, "The Campaign of 1928 Re-examined: A Study in Political Folklore," *Wisconsin Magazine of History*, 46 (1963).

John Chamberlain, *Farewell to Reform: The Rise, Life and Decay of the Progressive Mind in America* (Chicago: Quadrangle Press, 1965).

Clarke Chambers, *Seedtime of Reform: American Social Service and Social Action, 1918–1933* (Minneapolis: University of Minnesota Press, 1963).

Samuel P. Hays, "The Politics of Reform in Municipal Government in the Progressive Era," *The Pacific Northwest Quarterly*, 55 (1964).

Frederick Hoffman, *The Twenties: American Writing in the Postwar Decade* (New York: The Viking Press, Inc., 1955).

Richard Hofstadter, *Age of Reform: From Bryan to F.D.R.* (New York: Vintage Books, 1955).

Richard Hofstadter, "Herbert Hoover and the Crisis of American Individualism," in *The American Political Tradition and the Men Who Made It* (New York: Vintage Books, 1961).

George Kennan, *American Diplomacy, 1900–1950* (Chicago: University of Chicago Press, 1967).

Arthur Mann (ed.), *The Progressive Era* (New York: Holt, Rinehart & Winston, Inc., 1963).

Ernest May, "Shifting Perspectives on the 1920's," *The Mississippi Valley Historical Review*, 43 (1956).

Robert K. Murray, *Red Scare: A Study in National Hysteria, 1919–1920* (New York: McGraw-Hill Book Company, 1955).

David W. Noble, "The Paradox of Progressive Thought," *American Quarterly*, 5 (1953).

Robert E. Osgood, *Ideals and Self-Interest in American Foreign Relations: The Great Transformation of the Twentieth Century* (Chicago: University of Chicago Press, 1953).

John William Ward, "The Meaning of Lindbergh's Flight," *American Quarterly*, 10 (1958).

William Appleman Williams, *The Tragedy of American Diplomacy* (New York: Dell Publishing Co., Inc., 1962).

In our day these economic truths have been accepted as self-evident. We have accepted, so to speak, a second Bill of Rights under which a new basis of security and prosperity can be established for all—regardless of station, race, or creed.

Among these are:

The right to a useful and remunerative job in the industries or shops or farms or mines of the Nation;

The right to earn enough to provide adequate food and clothing and recreation;

The right of every farmer to raise and sell his products at a return which will give him and his family a decent living;

The right of every businessman, large and small, to trade in an atmosphere of freedom from unfair competition and domination by monopolies at home or abroad;

The right of every family to a decent home;

The right to adequate medical care and the opportunity to achieve and enjoy good health;

The right to protection from the economic fears of old age, sickness, accident, and unemployment;

The right to a good education.

All of these rights spell security. And after this war is won, we must be prepared to move forward, in the implementation of these rights, to new goals of human happiness and well being.

America's own rightful place in the world depends in large part upon how fully these and similar rights have been carried into practice for our citizens. For unless there is security here at home there cannot be lasting peace in the world.

Franklin D. Roosevelt
State of the Union Message, January 11, 1944

4

MYTHOLOGY OF ROOSEVELT, THE NEW DEAL, AND BEYOND

Franklin D. Roosevelt: A Profile
William E. Leuchtenburg

The Legendary Roosevelt
Edgar E. Robinson

Roosevelt: The Liberal Myth
Howard Zinn

American Entry into World War II: A Historiographical Appraisal
Wayne S. Cole

The Liberals, Truman, and FDR as Symbol and Myth
Alonzo L. Hamby

J.F.K.: The Stained-Glass Image
Andy Logan

America as Peaceful Belligerent: A Myth Revisited
J. William Fulbright

Image and Reality in Indochina
Harrison E. Salisbury

East meets West: Torgau, 1945.

OURS...to fight for

FREEDOM FROM WANT

Freedom from want.

East confronts West: Berlin, 1968.

Freedom from want?

Introduction

Much that was said in the preceding chapter introduction concerning the healthy climate for myth-building during the progressive era might also be applied to the Age of Roosevelt and beyond. But perhaps there are some differences which bear notice, particularly since many of the period's results still directly affect present-day America.

Most people, supporters and detractors alike, agree that Franklin Delano Roosevelt was more central to his age than either Theodore Roosevelt or Woodrow Wilson had been to theirs. In any assessment of the New Deal, laymen as well as scholars are compelled to deal with FDR's rather elusive personal style; indeed, for many this is the key. The farther observers move to either the conservative or radical end of the interpretive spectrum, the more marked their myths about the man and his age seem to become. This held true in foreign as well as domestic affairs.

Roosevelt, after a significant setback following the "quarantine speech" at Chicago in 1937, slowly came to dominate foreign affairs. Though remaining somewhat tenuous for a time, FDR's leadership toward an internationalist posture became increasingly evident after the outbreak of the European war in 1939 and America's involvement became imminent. These developments occurred in the midst of great controversy, typified on the one extreme by the America First Committee, on the other by the Committee to Defend America by Aiding the Allies. Such a climate acted as a breeding ground for myths concerning our ultimate involvement and President Roosevelt's role in it. Correspondingly, many of these myths are reflected in historians' works on FDR and the United States' entry into World War II.

FDR's influence, conditioned by myths, continued into the postwar decades. Eric Goldman's *The Crucial Decade—And After: America, 1945–1960*, in fact argues that the economic and social revolution of the New Deal era continued into the 1960s, along with the policies of containment and co-existence which resulted from the World War II period. Not surprisingly, FDR's successor, President Truman, fell victim to the liberal Roosevelt myth—evidenced in the presidential campaign of 1948.

Indeed, constructing presidential myths remains a minor industry; cases in point are those following the assassination of the popular and promising John F. Kennedy. More recently, many of the J.F.K. myths have been mitigated as growing numbers of Americans have come to question the basic philosophy behind the historical conduct of our foreign affairs, particularly as a result of the long and severely debilitating war in Vietnam. Critics from many diverse sectors—scholars, clergymen, journalists, congressmen and senators—have largely come to agree that myth has and continues to dominate American foreign policy. While one should be aware that those who attempt to destroy myths often only succeed in substitution rather than destruction, to this point at least, a myth-oriented approach to the area of foreign affairs has proven both popular and viable.

Franklin D. Roosevelt: A Profile

It has been said that historical studies often tell as much about the authors as they do about the subject. Such is undoubtedly true of studies written of Franklin D. Roosevelt, who has generated his share of both love and hate. He is one of our "hero-Presidents," and interpretations of his historical import too often have been characterized by either enthusiastic support or outright condemnation. The tendency has been either to debunk or to engage in what has been called "academic homosexuality"—falling in love with one's historical heroes. William E. Leuchtenburg, Roosevelt scholar and Columbia Professor of History, here senses the difficulty of achieving the truly delicate balance of detachment and sympathy that sound historical scholarship demands.

Of the making of controversies about Franklin Delano Roosevelt there is no end. In his lifetime, he was literally worshiped by many Americans. One Congressman compared him to Jesus Christ and in a poll of New York schoolchildren God ran him a poor second. Yet he was just as strongly detested by others who, as one historian has noted, depicted him "as a liar, a thief, a madman, a syphilitic, and a communist." Since his death, scholars have kept the coals of disputation live. Some, like Basil Rauch, have contended that the "study of Roosevelt's words and of all his actions will confirm the instinct of the younger generation that another hero-President has lately been added to the company of George Washington, Thomas Jefferson, Andrew Jackson, Abraham Lincoln, Theodore Roosevelt, and Woodrow Wilson." Others, like Edgar Eugene Robinson, have asserted that Roosevelt's reign resulted "in a weakened Constitutional system, in imperiled national security, in diminished national morale, in deteriorated political morality, and in an overburdened economy."

Roosevelt's admirers argue that he was a creative leader not only of the United States but of the Western world at a time when democracy was in peril. They point out that he inspirited the nation in the dark weeks of March, 1933, and that by the end of the Hundred Days the country had regained much of its self-confidence. Roosevelt, they note, inspired faith in man's ability to master events instead of being victimized by them; he saw the world as an unfinished universe in which men must act to shape their destiny. At the same time, he offered fatherly reassurance of his own capacity

Reprinted by permission of Hill and Wang, A division of Farrar, Straus & Giroux, from *Franklin D. Roosevelt: A Profile*, edited by William E. Leuchtenburg. Copyright © 1967 by William E. Leuchtenburg.

to make the world more secure. He combined courage in the face of hardship with openness to ideas, he raised public issues that had long been submerged, and he showed skeptics that government could be efficient and still democratic. Elected for an unprecedented four terms, he led the country through the Great Depression, expanded the responsibility of the national government, took giant strides toward the achievement of social justice, guided the country through a victorious war against the Fascist powers, and laid the groundwork for America's entrance into the United Nations.

Roosevelt's critics, however, raise doubts as to whether he was truly a history-making man. They argue that nothing fundamental was altered in the Age of Roosevelt, that the United States at the end of the era remained pretty much what it had been in the beginning, a capitalist nation that rewarded the acquisitive instinct and tolerated a wide range of social injustice. Moreover, they assert that whatever changes did occur were the result less of Roosevelt than of impersonal forces that the President only dimly understood. His conservative campaign in 1932 has been cited to show that he did not intend to be a change maker, and the contradictory character of New Deal measures has been adduced as evidence that Roosevelt lacked a clear sense of direction.

Writers have differed too about whether Roosevelt was a conservative or a liberal. Although most perceive him as a reformer, some view him as an enlightened Tory who preserved capitalism and who never revealed more than "a-basket-for-the-poor-family-down-the-lane approach to social problems." Radicals have complained that he missed an opportunity to nationalize the banks, that he failed to discipline the nation in collectivism, and that he gave indifferent support to the planners like Rexford Tugwell. They see him, at best, as a broker who mediated among interests and who moved only as far as the pressures exerted on him required. They note that groups like the sharecroppers who could not articulate their demands got short shrift in the broker state, and that Roosevelt agreed to measures like insurance of bank deposits and the Wagner Act only because Congress compelled him to do so.

Yet others are convinced that FDR was the paladin of social reform. "He takes his place," writes Henry Steele Commager, "in the great tradition of American liberalism, along with Jefferson, Jackson, Lincoln, Theodore Roosevelt and Wilson." Roosevelt, it has been pointed out, often showed his concern for unrepresented groups, as in his sponsorship of the Federal Arts Project, and frequently drove liberal legislation through a hostile Congress, as in his persistent fight for the death sentence on holding companies. Richard Rovere has written:

> He led us, I think, magnificently. In the early years, to be sure, he was called upon merely to lead us back to where we had been—to keep the ship of state afloat and head it back to its moorings in the snug harbor of 1929. But that is almost always the way statesmen prove themselves. What more did Lincoln do? No more—and yet, in the doing, a great deal more. For the Union restored was not the *status quo* ante-

bellum but something very different. And while there was vastly less misery and danger in the late thirties than in the early thirties, the late thirties were very different from the late twenties. It has taken daring and imagination and high intelligence to hold this society together, and the exercise of these virtues proved in itself creative.

Some writers, indeed, have protested not that the New Deal was too conservative but that Roosevelt was a radical who overturned venerated American institutions and even fostered a Communist conspiracy. When in the 1950's Senator Joseph McCarthy asserted that the recognition of Soviet Russia in 1933 had ushered in "twenty years of treason," he was voicing a common suspicion. "Roosevelt's leadership," Edgar Eugene Robinson has written, "was the facade behind which a less understanding but profoundly convinced revolutionary leadership was provided in Congress, in administrative departments, in the press, on the radio, and in the colleges and schools." Yet many writers have observed that if Roosevelt had the squire's contempt for business, he also had the squire's sense of tradition and his conservative instinct to safeguard property rights. Like Lord Grey, who was also damned as a traitor to his class, FDR sought to avert serious class conflict by timely concessions. As a consequence of New Deal measures, it has been argued, capitalism was resuscitated and the Socialist movement all but destroyed. "What cut the ground out pretty completely from under us," observed the Socialist leader, Norman Thomas, "was Roosevelt in a word. You don't need anything more."

Roosevelt has often been portrayed as the founder of the Welfare State in America. Sir Isaiah Berlin has even written that he was "the greatest leader of democracy, the greatest champion of social progress, in the twentieth century." For the first time, it has been said, the United States government recognized that men have inherent social rights and that the government must be responsible for guaranteeing at least a minimal livelihood. Yet FDR's critics have asserted that the Social Security Act was an appallingly limited piece of legislation which compared unfavorably with that adopted in European countries decades before. Moreover, they deny that the United States has achieved even today the rudiments of a Welfare State.

Political scientists and historians have quarreled about Roosevelt's performance as a party builder. FDR's champions contend that he put together a new coalition that ended a period of Republican supremacy that dated back to the Civil War and inaugurated a new era of Democratic preponderance. They point out that FDR was the only victorious Democratic Presidential candidate in a century to win more than fifty percent of the vote. They credit the "Roosevelt coalition" with a successful appeal to the masses in the great cities, and note in particular that in the 1930's the Negro broke his historic tie to the Republican party. Other writers dispute these claims. They state that the real builder of the metropolitan coalition was not Roosevelt but Al Smith. Analysts like James MacGregor Burns argue that the President missed an exceptional opportunity to reshape the party by failing to encourage progressive dissidents in states like Wisconsin. Furthermore, Roosevelt, it has been said, was too concerned with advancing his own political interests. As a consequence, at his death, the Democratic party was left divided and leaderless and the prey of entrenched Southern oligarchs and Northern machine bosses.

An even livelier controversy has centered on Roosevelt's economic policies. Critics have pointed out that recovery in the United States was tardier than in almost any other major country. They note that as late as 1939 ten million Americans were still jobless and they argue that only war pulled the nation out of the Depression. They contend that Roosevelt moved in the wrong direction by adopting restrictionist economics in the National Recovery Administration (N.R.A.) and the Agricultural Adjustment Administration (A.A.A.) and by embarking on the gold-buying fiasco. Conservatives claim that government meddling impaired business confidence and thus slowed recovery, while Keynesians lament the fact that Roosevelt proved unwilling to embrace massive deficit spending. On the other hand, FDR's partisans allege that he inherited from his predecessor an economy so badly impaired that it would inevitably take some years before recovery could be achieved. They insist that significant gains were made under FDR, and some believe that prosperity would have been restored even if war had not come. Roosevelt's willingness to break taboos about budget balancing has seemed more remarkable than his reluctance to subscribe to Keynes's unorthodoxy. Most important, it has been said, the New Deal provided a series of underpinnings for the economy that make another depression unlikely.

Almost all commentators have agreed that FDR's approach was untheoretical, but they have differed about whether this was a virtue or a defect. Roosevelt's critics have emphasized that he was untutored, especially about economics, and that his intellectual interests were superficial. They deplore his preference for puttering with ship models and stamp collections to reading and reflection. It was Roosevelt himself, they note, who said that he was "the least introspective man in the world." They recall his reply when his wife asked him whether their children should go to church: "I really never thought about it. It is just as well not to think about things like that too much." His shallowness and lack of learning, it has been asserted, meant that, as President, he was required to live beyond his intellectual means and that he was reduced in policy making to "catch-penny opportunism."

Those who have been impressed by Roosevelt's record, however, deny that he was ill-informed. Daniel R. Fusfeld has claimed that Roosevelt got a good grounding in economics at Harvard, and had demonstrated his competence in economic matters long before he entered the White House. Others have been astonished by FDR's grasp of detail in a wide spectrum of subjects. The publisher J. David Stern recalled an occasion when the President recited the average price of ten commodities in 1933 and ten years before and was correct on ninety percent of them. In June, 1940, *Time* reported:

For three weeks he had discussed battlefield contours in military detail with U.S. experts; again and again they have whistled respectfully at his apparent knowledge of Flanders—hills, creeks, towns, bridges. The President's particular forte is islands; he is said to know every one in the world, its peoples, habits, population, geography, economic life. When a ship sank off Scotland several months ago, experts argued: Had the ship hit a rock or had it been torpedoed? The President pondered latitude and longitude, said: "It hit a rock. They ought to have seen that rock." Naval Aide Daniel J. Callaghan recalled the rock, disagreed. "At high tide, Mr. President, that rock is submerged." No such thing, said the President, even at high tide that rock is 20 feet out of the water.

Roosevelt's sympathizers claim that his "untheoretical" methods made possible a "pragmatic" approach that liberated government from the prison of orthodoxy. Uncommitted to dogma, Roosevelt was free to break traditions and to encourage experimentation. Disrespectful of the classic taboos, he showed a hospitality to new ideas that made the 1930's such a remarkable decade. Yet, they add, for all the improvisation and innovation, New Deal thought was more coherent than has often been recognized, for his administration, as Roosevelt said, had "a consistency and continuity of broad purpose."

Historians have also disagreed about whether Roosevelt should be hailed as a master of the art of compromise or faulted as a vacillator. Roosevelt, it has been said, alertly recognized the necessity of heeding the demands of a great many divergent interests and working out arrangements that would reconcile them. His critics, however, see FDR as too often the fox rather than the lion, too unwilling to impose the national interest on parochial groups, too much a temporizer rather than a leader. Such disapprobation has been voiced both by radicals, who believe the President should have scourged businessmen, and conservatives, who castigate him as a demagogue who truckled to labor.

Judgments about whether Roosevelt was a dynamic leader or a time-server have frequently hinged on a writer's assessment of the President's character. Some have seen him as a deeply moral man, as a Christian and a Democrat motivated by idealism and a sense of social responsibility. Others have viewed him as a Catiline willing to cater to any demand that would serve his lust for power. H. L. Mencken said of FDR: "If he became convinced tomorrow that coming out for cannibalism would get him the votes he so sorely needs, he would begin fattening a missionary in the White House backyard come Wednesday." To some, Roosevelt's buoyant optimism has seemed admirable; others have deplored it as "Eagle Scout" superficiality and as the insouciance of a man unaware of his own limitations. Not a few of his admirers would concede that Roosevelt had been a rather superficial, supercilious man in his youth but claim that he underwent a "spiritual transformation" after he was crippled by poliomyelitis; he emerged, in Will Durant's words, "softened and cleansed and illumined with pain." Other writers, however, deny that his paralysis resulted in an emotional *crise.*

Both those who esteem Roosevelt and those who abhor him have found it difficult to penetrate his reserve. Roosevelt rarely revealed himself even to intimates. Not even to his minister would he speak of sorrows or disappointments. He seldom confided even in his own family. "You are a wonderful person but you are one of the most difficult men to work with that I have ever known," Harold Ickes told the President bluntly one day. "Because I get too hard at times?" Roosevelt parried. "No, you never get too hard but you won't talk frankly even with people who are loyal to you and of whose loyalty you are fully convinced. You keep your cards close up against your belly." After years of study, many historians have remained puzzled about what kind of man was hidden behind Roosevelt's mask of amiable gregariousness.

Questions about Roosevelt's character have also influenced the whole current of discussion about the President's foreign policy. Collective-security advocates have stigmatized FDR as weak-willed while nationalists have execrated him as deceitful. Internationalists have charged that Roosevelt bowed to the isolationists in scuttling the London Economic Conference, agreeing to neutrality legislation, blocking aid to Loyalist Spain, and delaying too long in intervening in World War II. On the other hand, isolationists have arraigned Roosevelt as a big-navy man who seized on every opportunity to meddle in foreign affairs and who ultimately led the United States into a needless war to cover up his domestic failures. His supporters, however, respond that the President sought both to preserve peace and to mount resistance to fascist expansion and that war came only when these two goals proved irreconcilable. Once again, disputes over Roosevelt's character are significant. Isolationist critics claim that by deceptive statements such as his "again-and-again-and-again" speech in the 1940 campaign and his misrepresentation of the Battle of the Atlantic Roosevelt attempted to lead the country into war with Germany and that when this failed, he provoked the Japanese assault at Pearl Harbor even though it required sacrificing the men and ships at the base. In meeting these charges, Roosevelt's supporters are sometimes divided; some argue that the President's conduct was straightforward while others state that Roosevelt did good by stealth, that only by a degree of misrepresentation could he have led a nation deceived by the isolationists into a necessary war against the Axis. All of them agree, however, that the allegations about Pearl Harbor are bizarre.

World War II hatched a new flock of controversies about Roosevelt. Rexford Tugwell has written that in war he was "a very different kind of Roosevelt." Some writers have credited the President with many of the achievements of the war years: the victory over the Axis, the unanticipated social gains, the creation of the United Nations. Others have contended that America's war aims were compromised by the means employed: the internment of Japanese-Americans and the deals with collaborationists in North Africa and Italy. Above all, historians have quarreled about the diplomacy of the war. They have disagreed about whether Roosevelt was a skillful statesman who succeeded, where Wilson had failed, in leading the United States into an international association of nations, or was a blunderer who threw away the sacrifices of the war at Yalta and other conference tables.

Finally, writers have differed about the legacy Roosevelt left. A new generation of radicals, distrustful of centralized power, looks back at the New Deal achievements with suspicion. A new generation of conservatives rehearses the old arguments against the New Deal and claims that the attempt to create a Welfare State has produced a Poorhouse State with a permanent class of reliefers. To these arguments, Roosevelt's admirers make two replies. One is that he reigned at a time of perpetual crisis, that if he could only see six months ahead, he almost always had a six-month answer ready. The other is that Roosevelt was, in John M. Blum's words, "the most daring democrat of his time." He made the American government more responsive to the needs of the people than had any other man who had ever held the office of President.

Less than two years after the President's death, Hamilton Basso wrote: "When the historian of the future gets around to evaluating the character and influence of Franklin Delano Roosevelt, he is going to have a man-sized job on his hands." The student who wishes to develop his own interpretation of Roosevelt faces no easy task. He will quite probably find that just at the point when he feels reasonably certain that he knows how to assess Roosevelt he will come upon a new insight that will jar his conviction of certitude. Yet there are rewards, too, in the attempt to decide FDR's place in history, for few men have so dominated their times as he did. To come to terms with the significance of the protagonist of the Age of Roosevelt is to move a long way toward comprehending the meaning of both domestic and foreign affairs in the twentieth century.

The Legendary Roosevelt

Edgar E. Robinson

In this article, Edgar E. Robinson, Margaret Byrne Professor of American History at Stanford University, sees the liberal interpretation of the New Deal as mostly myth—a response to a crisis situation and a popular demand. Displaying constitutional concerns and admitting the existence of a crisis, Professor Robinson denies that there was massive public support for New Deal reforms. He also registers alarm at the directions in which the Roosevelt leadership was steering the American people. Robinson sees Roosevelt's as an alien influence, away from traditional American values—down an "unaccustomed and dimly-discerned road to the future."

The leadership of Franklin Delano Roosevelt is an outstanding fact of modern history. Others have seized power and dominated millions. Others have swayed the imagination of their fellow men for a longer time. Roosevelt was chosen by the people, repeatedly, against continued and growing minority protest, and, as the chosen leader of the American people, he represented their interests in the world when the United States was, by all tests, the determining power. Roosevelt by act and word determined in large measure the state of the world in which Americans live ten years after his death. In fact, as well as in legend, Franklin Roosevelt will rank as the most powerful of American Presidents.

Yet, as leader when he came to power in 1933, he was not placed there, as were Washington, Jackson, and Grant, because of a personal record that the people approved. Nor did he win a place as leader of the minds of men as did Jefferson, Lincoln, and Wilson. Nor did he come to his supreme opportunity, as did Herbert Hoover, because of the conviction of an overwhelming majority of voters that in his conception of the power of the individual citizen there might be a New Day for all mankind in a world of science, invention, and co-operation.

Roosevelt emerges, even now, as a leader identified with the aspirations of the common man and the hopes of democracy—as Americans have known it. He expressed the desires of a great popular movement in the United States which had been a half-century in the making. He expressed the weaknesses in the movement. In the end he symbolized the frustrations of all popular rule.

Throughout the years of majority support, there was opposed to Mr. Roosevelt a great minority who were convinced of his inadequacy in office,

From the book *The Roosevelt Leadership: 1933–1945,* by Edgar Eugene Robinson. Copyright 1954 by Edgar Eugene Robinson. Reprinted by permission of J. B. Lippincott Company.

of the unsoundness of his program, and of the vital necessity of blocking him at every possible opportunity.

When he ceased to lead, the effect of his years in power was manifested in a weakened Constitutional system, in imperiled national security, in diminished national morale, in deteriorated political morality, and in an overburdened economy. Powerful beyond comprehension, because of the power of the American people, President Roosevelt had an important part in destroying dictators representing the entrenched totalitarianism of the few, only to leave his nation exposed at home and abroad to a totalitarianism of the masses more terrible than any foe yet faced by a free people.

If Americans are to see Mr. Roosevelt in the perspective of history, it must be first of all in an acceptance of the fact of his wide acclaim. But it is vital to honest thought that the legend of accomplishment be measured against the facts that explain continued support. We should examine in detail the development of this theme in the dozen fateful years in which President Roosevelt dominated the American scene.

Franklin Roosevelt prepared himself for the Presidency in ways quite unlike those used by contemporaries who were aspirants for the office. He acquired an extensive knowledge of the intricate machinery not only of politics as practiced in the United States, but also of government as operated by politicians. More than Jackson, Cleveland, or Wilson, Roosevelt embodied in his leadership the diverse elements that enter into the Democratic party. To millions his political personality came to mean superlative leadership. Facing the crisis of depression, he was affirmative in his program. Its immediate success seemed to justify the course taken.

In lands beyond the seas, this American figure became in his lifetime the symbol of hope to millions. This hope has come to be a legend. Franklin Roosevelt remains in world history the great champion of the masses. Identified by word and deed with compassion for all who were in need, this patrician—who had shared in all the opportunities that the United States had to offer—was hailed as their leader by those whose lives were less fortunate.

Thus, in a world in the throes of profound social and economic change, Mr. Roosevelt from the outset of his Presidency was thought of by many as a leader in a revolution. It might be his particular kind of revolution, but it was seen as a revolt against the *status quo*. And it seemed to the informed somehow inevitable, for the United States was itself the product of continuous change for the betterment of the common man.

To millions of people, at home and abroad, the historic figure of Franklin Roosevelt is one of undiminished brilliance. His voice, his smile, his gestures have been immortalized in recording, film, and photograph. His utterances have come to be a part of the American heritage. His actions, as he appeared among the great of the earth, are vividly portrayed. His influence transcends all bounds of over-emphasis. What manner of man was he? What is legend, and how much is fact?

Those who seek a full explanation of human conduct and of national destiny dare not accept the "history" of the Roosevelt years as prepared by the supporters of Mr. Roosevelt. Led by Mr. Roosevelt himself and his group of immediate aides in preparation of the personal record, the participants have presented the narrative of these years countless times in the frame of reference prepared by themselves. In the decade since Mr. Roosevelt's death, this pattern has not changed in any marked degree.

It must be said that the majority of the American people have tended to accept this pattern inasmuch as they feel themselves, as was so often asserted by Mr. Roosevelt, to have had a very important part in the making of the story. But it is not the whole truth as posterity will find it. Nor is it the full record that the interested citizen can find, even today.

A realization that the Roosevelt followers have not told the whole story has led to an outpouring of highly critical works. These reflect the intensity of feeling of many who were opponents of the President during his lifetime. Few of them have attempted to present or pretend to present a rounded picture. Their purpose has been to correct the record, and this has given them the appearance of extreme partisanship, and has tended to put them constantly on the defensive in that they were attacking a record already made.

Now the truth that we seek is not to be found in a minute examination of the record for its flaws and errors and falsehoods. Of course they are there, and it will take a generation or more to sift them out and to make sure what does stand the test of careful examination. But the primary task is that of dealing with the existent pattern of Roosevelt's leadership and it must be done now.

The task is this: To provide a frame of reference that expresses exactly and without partisanship the basic problems faced by the people of the United States in these twelve years. Upon these problems Mr. Roosevelt took action and gave his opinion, and his opponents did likewise. Of primary concern to us is the question of the relation of these problems to the daily life of the people as they tried to determine their national future.

The basic problems were those of *livelihood*, *co-operation*, and *defense*. On each of these the President was called upon to take a stand.

His position from the outset was that the livelihood of the citizen was the concern of the government. Upon this he built a vast structure of public works and of social security—each of these to protect the citizen.

Likewise, co-operation was called for repeatedly by the President. It was a co-operation of citizens forced by necessity, not by conviction, nor by belief in a basic philosophy. It was the essence of social democracy as envisaged by followers of the President.

And a people dedicated to the support of all and the co-operation of all must defend itself at home and abroad from those forces that denied these fundamentals. Herein lay dramatic foundation for leaders who as a matter of daily life were satisfied with generalizations and who lived in a world of desirable objectives.

What then gave Roosevelt the transcendent power he undoubtedly had —in utterance and in action—in leading his fellow Americans? It must be concluded that he represented fairly well the level of conception, understanding, and purpose that characterized the mass of the American people of his time. In him there was a happy combination of elements that gave highest place to aspiration, compelling regard for simplicity of statement, and an abiding faith in the judgment of the common man.

This kind of democratic appeal fitted the mood of the time—and it had deep roots in American history. Franklin Roosevelt built upon the work of innumerable rebels that preceded him. This is true. But more important than the legacy of these earlier reformers is the heritage of the masses of Americans who have always been radical in outlook and aspiration, though infrequently in action. They have, however, wanted practical results. These Franklin Roosevelt could provide them, for a time, because of the crisis in which he first appeared, and because of the unusual combination of radical elements that repeatedly returned him to power.

When, in due time, the American people and their leaders realize that the hard realities of a mechanized world demand economics and politics of a superior order, it will be found that the record of these years is as barren of real understanding and accomplishment as it is rich in expressions of the promises that have always made America the hope of the world.

The significance of the twelve-year debate with former President Hoover was not realized by the American people because Mr. Hoover was a private citizen at the time. Yet there is every reason to accept R. G. Tugwell's phrase descriptive of Roosevelt and Hoover: "protagonists in an epic struggle of ideas."

We shall see that in these years there were other "revolutionaries" at work. Roosevelt's leadership was the façade behind which a less understanding but profoundly convinced revolutionary leadership was provided in the Congress, in administrative departments, in the press, on the radio, and in the colleges and schools. It was rarely a leadership pledged to doctrines alien to American soil.

Indeed, this other leadership arose directly from American experience, and many Americans found it to their liking for that reason. It was a revolutionary leadership in the sense that it was the work of fairly small groups dedicated to making over American society. And it used the slogans that found ready response in the hearts of Americans, in particular those associated with freedom of thought and expression. Eventually these advocates of fundamental change found their counterparts in other nations, and America was plunged into a world conflict of ideas, as well as of armies.

Franklin Roosevelt, possessing indomitable courage and will power, won the allegiance of innumerable enthusiasts, and by an incomparable sense of timing, he won continuing support of a huge body of voters.

This gave him control of a nation, and direction of the greatest striking force in the world. For a time he was the most powerful leader of the twentieth century, and in fact the most powerful in the history of mankind. A man of good intention cast in the role of hero, he was overwhelmed by the inexorable forces of his time. This was his tragedy, the tragedy of his people, and the tragedy of the world.

What was the political situation out of which such continued leadership arose? What were the methods by which President Roosevelt retained that leadership in peace and in war? What was the status of the United States, and what was the outlook of the American people when he gave up this power at the time of his death in April, 1945?

Answers to these questions must be found if we are to evaluate the nature and significance of Franklin Roosevelt's leadership, and to pass judgment upon the interests and skills of American citizens in maintaining self-government in a world of war, revolution, and uneasy peace.

Roosevelt: The Liberal Myth

Howard Zinn

Almost from its inception the New Deal elicited a wide range of criticism, much of which continues to be reflected in historians' accounts. Critics on the extreme right were alarmed at what they considered the marked leftist tendencies of the era; critics on the extreme left, including many of the in-house "planners," argued that the government was not taking sufficient advantage of the economic crisis to move the country to the left. Howard Zinn, Professor of Government at Boston University, represents what has been termed the "new left" approach to the New Deal. While generally ignoring the conservatives, Professor Zinn labels as myth the views of liberal, pro-New Deal scholars who see the phenomenon as sound, innovative, and far-reaching. While they respect the spirit of FDR and the New Deal, Professor Zinn and other "new leftists" seem to regret opportunities lost—to see the thrust of the era as simply righting the ship of state, the restoration of traditional America.

When we compel the past to speak, we want neither the gibberish of total recall nor the nostalgia of fond memories; we would like the past to speak wisely to our present needs. And so we have a good reason for trying to recapture some of the lost dialogue of the New Deal years—that which was carried on, with varying degrees of tension, inside and outside the Roosevelt circle.

The New Dealers themselves were articulate, humane, and on occasion profound. Among them were the "brains trust"* (Adolf A. Berle, Raymond Moley, Rexford Guy Tugwell), the cabinet members (Henry Wallace, Frances Perkins, Harold Ickes, and others), the administrators of the alphabetic agencies (Harry Hopkins, David Lilienthal, and others), the Congressional spokesmen (Robert F. Wagner, Hugo Black, and others). And above them all was Franklin D. Roosevelt himself. They had no clearly defined set of goals, beyond that of extricating the nation from the depression of 1929–1932. In the course of easing the crisis, however, they found themselves—pushed partly by the cries of alarm on all sides, partly by inner humanitarian impulses—creating new laws and institutions like the Tennessee Valley Authority, the social security system, farm subsidies, minimum wage standards, the National Labor Relations Board, and public housing.

*Moley and Tugwell both insist that the proper name is "brains trust," as originally used by James Kieran, a *New York Times* reporter, although the term became popular as "brain trust."

These accomplishments were considerable enough to give many Americans the feeling they were going through a revolution, while they successfully evaded any one of a number of totalitarian abysses into which they might have fallen. So it is not surprising that the New Deal left a glow of enthusiasm, even adoration, in the nation at large.

Yet, when it was over, the fundamental problem remained—and still remains—unsolved: how to bring the blessings of immense natural wealth and staggering productive potential to every person in the land. Also unsolved was the political corollary of that problem: how to organize ordinary people to convey to national leadership something more subtle than the wail of crisis (which speaks for itself); how to communicate the day-to-day pains felt, between emergencies, in garbage-strewn slums, crowded schools, grimy bus stations, inadequate hospital wards, Negro ghettos, and rural shacks— the environment of millions of Americans clawing for subsistence in the richest country in the world.

When the reform energies of the New Deal began to wane around 1939 and the depression was over, the nation was back to its normal state: a permanent army of unemployed; twenty or thirty million poverty-ridden people effectively blocked from public view by a huge, prosperous, and fervently consuming middle class; a tremendously efficient yet wasteful productive apparatus that was efficient because it could produce limitless supplies of what it decided to produce, and wasteful because what it decided to produce was not based on what was most needed by society but on what was most profitable to business.[1]

What the New Deal did was to refurbish middle-class America, which had taken a dizzying fall in the depression, to restore jobs to half the jobless, and to give just enough to the lowest classes (a layer of public housing, a minimum of social security) to create an aura of good will. Through it all, the New Dealers moved in an atmosphere thick with suggestions, but they accepted only enough of these to get the traditional social mechanism moving again, plus just enough more to give a taste of what a truly far-reaching reconstruction might be.

This harsh estimate of New Deal achievements derives from the belief that the historian discussing the past is always commenting—whether he realizes it or not—on the present; and that because he is part of a morally responsible public, his commentary should consider present needs at the expense, if necessary, of old attachments. It is fruitless today to debate "interpretations" of the New Deal. We can no longer vote for or against Roosevelt. We can only affect the world around us. And although this is the 1960's, not the 1930's, some among us live very high, and some live very low, and a chronic malaise of lost opportunities and wasted wealth pervades the economic air.[2]

It is for today, then, that we turn to the thinking of the New Deal period. Although the New Deal gave us only fragments of solutions, it did leave us—perhaps because those were desperate years, and desperation stimulates innovation—with a public discussion more intense and more sweeping than any we have had before or since. People outside the New Deal entourage, invited or not, joined that discussion and extended the boundaries of political and economic imagination beyond those of the New Dealers—sometimes to the left, sometimes to the right, sometimes in directions hard to plot.

Among these were philosophers, writers, critics, lawyers, poets, college professors, journalists, dissident politicians, or commentators without special portfolio. Their names are still known today: John Dewey, Charles Beard, Reinhold Niebuhr, Paul Douglas, Stuart Chase, John Maynard Keynes, Norman Thomas, Oswald Garrison Villard, Heywood Broun, Max Lerner, Morris Cohen, Walter White, Edmund Wilson, Felix Frankfurter, John Steinbeck, John L. Lewis, Upton Sinclair.

Their thinking does not give us facile solutions, but if history has uses beyond that of reminiscence, one of them is to nourish lean ideological times with the nectars of other years. And although the present shape of the world was hardly discernible in 1939, certain crucial social issues persist in both eras. Somehow, in the interaction between the ideas of the New Dealers themselves and those of social critics who gathered in various stances and at various distances around the Roosevelt fire, we may find suggestions or approaches that are relevant today.

The word "pragmatic" has been used, more often perhaps than any other, to describe the thinking of the New Dealers.[3] It refers to the experimental method of the Roosevelt administration, the improvisation from one step to the next, the lack of system or long-range program or theoretical commitment. Richard Hofstadter, in fact, says that the only important contribution to political theory to come out of the Roosevelt administration was made by Thurman Arnold, particularly in his two books, *The Symbols of Government* and *The Folklore of Capitalism*. Hofstadter describes Arnold's writing as "the theoretical equivalent of FDR's opportunistic virtuosity in practical politics —a theory that attacks theories."[4] As the chief expression of Roosevelt's "ideology," Arnold's work deserves some attention.

All through both his books, in a style of cool irony, Arnold cuts away at "preconceived faiths," "preconceived principles," "theories and symbols of government," "high-sounding prejudices," "traditional ideals," "moral ideals," "permanent cures." In the last paragraphs of *The Symbols of Government*, he writes:

> So long as the public holds preconceived faiths about the fundamental principles of government, they will persecute and denounce new ideas in that science, and orators will prevail over technicians. So long as preconceived principles are considered more important than practical results, the practical alleviation of human distress and the distribution of available comforts will be paralyzed. . . . The writer has faith that a

new public attitude toward the ideals of law and economics is slowly appearing to create an atmosphere where the fanatical alignments between opposing political principles may disappear and a competent, practical, opportunistic governing class may rise to power. . . .[5]

Because the Roosevelt administration did, in fact, experiment and improvise without a total plan, FDR's "pragmatism" has come, for many, to be the most important statement about the thinking of the New Dealers. This emphasis on the method rather than on the substance of that thinking tends to obscure what may be its greatest significance.[6]

Most statesmen experiment: Tsar Nicholas instituted a Duma, Lenin encouraged private enterprise for several years, Bismarck sponsored social welfare measures, Mao Tse-tung introduced back-yard steel furnaces, and George Washington supported a national bank. These examples show that experimentation can be linked to a variety of social ideals. Some statesmen engage in more experiments than others, and in a time of crisis one who is willing to undertake a vast number of them deserves commendation, as Roosevelt does. The truly important question that can be asked about the thinking of any government is: in what direction, and how far, is it willing to experiment? What goals, what ideals, what expectations direct that experimentation?

Thurman Arnold himself contributed to this misplaced emphasis on method rather than substance. He was so anxious to demolish old myths that stood in the way of the welfare measures of the New Deal that mythology itself became his chief concern. He was so intent on sweeping away old debris, that he became obsessed, ironically, with a folklore of his own, in which the idea of debris-clearing crowded out the concept of what he wanted to plant in the cleared area.

Examining Arnold's *The Symbols of Government*, one sees that what started him on a crusade against myths was that he sought to expose the symbolism that stood in the way of bringing cheap electric power to people and of instituting relief, public works, social security.[7] His strongest expression on social justice was his statement that: "Those who rule our great industrial feudalism still believe inalterably the old axioms that man works efficiently only for personal profit; that humanitarian ideals are unworkable as the principal aim of government or business organization; that control of national resources, elimination of waste, and a planned distribution of goods would destroy both freedom and efficiency."[8]

As was true of his associate, Thurman Arnold, FDR's experimentalism and iconoclasm were not devoid of standards and ideals. They had a certain direction, which was toward governmental intervention in the economy to prevent depression, to help the poor, and to curb ruthless practices in big business. Roosevelt's speeches had the flavor of a moral crusade. Accepting the nomination at the Democratic Convention of 1932, he said that "the Federal Government has always had and still has a continuing responsibility for the broader public welfare," and pledged "a new deal for the American people." In a campaign speech that year at the Commonwealth Club in San Francisco, he said: "Our government . . . owes to every one an avenue to possess himself of a portion of that plenty sufficient for his needs, through his own work." In his 1936 speech accepting the nomination, he spoke of the power of the "economic royalists" and said: "Our allegiance to American institutions requires the overthrow of this kind of power."

But FDR's ideas did not have enough clarity to avoid stumbling from one approach to another: from constant promises to balance the budget, to large-scale spending in emergencies; from an attempt to reconcile big business interests and labor interests (as in the National Recovery Act), to belated support for a pro-labor National Labor Relations Act; from special concern for the tenant farmer (in the Resettlement Administration), to a stress on generous price supports for the large commercial farmer (in the Agricultural Adjustment Act of 1938).

His ideas on political leadership showed the same indecision, the same constriction of boundaries, as did his ideas about economic reform. Roosevelt was cautious about supporting the kind of candidates in 1934 (Socialist Upton Sinclair in California, Progressive Gifford Pinchot in Pennsylvania) who represented bold approaches to economic and social change; and when he did decide to take vigorous action against conservative Congressional candidates in 1938, he did so too late and too timorously. He often attempted to lead Congress in a forceful way to support his economic program; yet his leadership was confined to working with the existing Congressional leadership, including many Southern conservatives who ruled important committees. Roosevelt's political daring did not extend to building new political forces among the poor, the unemployed, the tenant farmers, and other disadvantaged groups, with whose support he might have given the country a bolder economic program.

The circle of men around Roosevelt, the cabinet members and administrators, was an odd mixture of liberals and conservatives who often worked at cross-purposes. Rexford Guy Tugwell, a bold advocate of national planning to help the lower-income groups, was close to Roosevelt for several years; but so was Raymond Moley, who believed in a kind of planning more beneficial to business interests. Even the liberal New Dealers, with rare exceptions, hesitated to carry their general concern for the underprivileged too far. Frances Perkins, the Secretary of Labor, had the humanitarian instincts of a first-rate social worker, but she seemed often to be trailing behind the labor movement, rather than helping to give it direction. (The most advanced piece of New Deal labor legislation was the Wagner Act, but Secretary Perkins wrote later: "I myself, had very little sympathy with the bill.") Progressive Secretary of the Interior Harold Ickes was offset by conservative Secretary of Commerce Daniel Roper. And although Roper was succeeded in 1939 by Harry Hopkins, there remained in the cabinet a powerful force for fiscal conservatism and budget-balancing—Secretary of the Treasury Henry Morgen-thau.

The experimentalism of the New Deal, in short, had its limits: up to these limits, Roosevelt's social concern was genuinely warm, his political courage huge, his humanitarian spirit unfailing; beyond them, his driving force weakened. Thus, by 1938, with the nation out of the worst of the depression, with a skeletal structure of social reform in the statute books, and with that year's Congressional elections showing a sudden waning of political approbation, the Roosevelt program began to bog down. As it slid to its close, it left behind a mountain of accomplishment, and ahead, mountains still unclimbed. Many millions—businessmen, professionals, unionized workingmen, commercial farmers—had been given substantial help. Many millions more—sharecroppers, slum-dwellers, Negroes of North and South, the unemployed—still awaited a genuine "new deal." . . .

For our view of the New Deal as a particularly energetic gyroscopic motion putting the traditional structure aright again, we have what the natural scientists might call a set of "controls"—a way of checking up on the hypothesis—one in the area of race relations, another in the experience of war.

In the field of racial equality, where there was no crisis as in economics, where the gyroscope did not confront a sharply titled mechanism, there was no "new deal." The special encumbrances of the depression were lifted for Negroes as for many other Americans, but the *permanent* caste structure re-mained unaltered by the kind of innovations that at least threatened the traditional edifice in economics. The white South was left, as it had been since the Compromise of 1877, to deal with Negroes as it chose—by murder, by beatings, by ruthless exclusion from political and economic life; the Four-teenth Amendment waited as fruitlessly for executive enforcement as it had in all earlier administrations since Grant. Washington, D.C., itself remained a tightly segregated city. And the Harlems of the North continued as great symbols of national failure.

The warm belief in equal rights held by Eleanor Roosevelt, as well as by FDR himself, the appointments of Mary McLeod Bethune, Robert Weaver, and others to important secondary posts in the government, even the wide distribution of relief and WPA jobs, were not enough to alter the fundamen-tal injustice attached to being a Negro in the United States. The disposition of the New Deal to experiment could have led to important accomplishments, but the clear goal of ending segregation, as with comparable objectives in economics, was never established.

With the coming of World War II, economic and social experimentation blossomed under Roosevelt's leadership and involved a good measure of national planning, jobs for everyone, and a vast system of postwar educa-tional benefits to eighteen million veterans. There was little inhibition; new, radically different national goals were not required for the traditional objective of winning at war. With such an aim, policy could be fearless and far-reaching.

Some coming generation perhaps, while paying proper respects to the spirit of the New Deal, may find, as William James put it, "the moral equivalent of war"—in new social goals, new expectations, with imaginative, undoctrinaire experimentation to attain them. If, in such an adventure, the thought of the past can help, it should be put to work.

Notes

1. In *The Affluent Society* (Boston: Houghton Mifflin Company, 1958), John Kenneth Galbraith has pointed eloquently to the American economy's emphasis on private rather than public needs. Michael Harrington's *The Other America* (New York: The Macmillan Company, 1963), and Leon Keyserling's *Poverty and Deprivation in the United States* (Washington, D.C.: Conference on Economic Progress, 1962) testify to continuing large blocs of poverty thirty years after the New Deal.

2. David Bazelon, in *The Paper Economy* (New York: Random House, Inc., 1963), and Robert Theobald, in *Free Men and Free Markets* (New York: C. N. Potter, 1963), give trenchant critiques of the American economy in the 1960's.

3. A representative statement is Arthur M. Schlesinger, Jr.'s, in *The Politics of Upheaval* (Boston: Houghton Mifflin Company, 1960), p. 649. "For Roosevelt, the technique of liberal government was pragmatic. . . . Nothing attracted Roosevelt less than rigid intellectual systems."

4. Richard Hofstadter, *The Age of Reform* (New York: Alfred A. Knopf, Inc., 1955), p. 317.

5. Thurman Arnold, *The Symbols of Government* (New Haven: Yale University Press, 1935), pp. 270–271.

6. A notable exception is William E. Leuchtenburg, *Franklin D. Roosevelt and the New Deal* (New York: Harper & Row, 1963), pp. 344–346.

7. *The Symbols of Government*, pp. 16, 110–111, 120. Hofstadter, in *The Age of Reform*, p. 318, analyzes the words that recur frequently in Arnold's books to show his movement away from the Progressivist moralism. Yet even to make this point he finds he must include the word "humanitarian" because it appears so frequently.

8. *The Symbols of Government*, pp. 259–260. Arnold was so reluctant to admit he possessed a set of values that Sidney Hook, reviewing *The Folklore of Capitalism*, took him at his word (or rather at his emphasized words), and described him as one who believed "all standards and ideals are nonsense." *University of Chicago Law Review*, V (April 1938), 341–357.

American Entry into World War II:
A Historiographical Appraisal

Wayne S. Cole

The crisis of a war experience seems to have the peculiar quality of heightening a society's ever-present inclination to passion and preju-dice, while simultaneously clouding the sensibilities and intellectual precision of historians. To Wayne S. Cole of the University of Mary-land, this merging of image and emotion is particularly character-istic of the volatile circumstances surrounding American involvement in World War II. Through a discussion of the various and diverse "schools" of historical thought concerning American entry into the war, Cole suggests the limitations of historical interpretation and the inherent difficulty in determining what constitutes historical "truth."

The aggressive expansion of the Axis powers in Europe and Asia in the 1930's aroused an impassioned debate on American foreign policy. "Isola-tionists" contended with "interventionists" over the policies adopted by the Roosevelt administration. Though few, if any, of the so-called isolationists wanted literally to isolate the United States from the rest of the world, they joined in opposition to what seemed the major trend in foreign affairs under President Roosevelt. A second phase in the dispute over policy was inaugu-rated by the attack on Pearl Harbor on December 7, 1941, for with that event the old quarrels became academic. But the policies of the Roosevelt adminis-tration continued as the core of dispute between two schools of historians who launched their own war of words over the background of America's entry into war. In the years after 1941 the "internationalist" writers were met by the "revisionists"—the latter term now used almost universally to describe the historians who have written critically of Roosevelt's pre-Pearl Harbor foreign policies and of American entry into World War II. Since the controversy is a continuing one, and because the books and articles on the subject have grown to confusing proportions, some orientation is necessary both for the reader who must work his way through the published historical materials and for those attracted to the problem as a field for further research and writing.

Histories of American entry into World War II published during the war defended the pre-Pearl Harbor policies of the Roosevelt administration. Forrest Davis and Ernest K. Lindley had close ties with the administration

From "American Entry into World War II: A Historiographical Appraisal," by Wayne S. Cole. *Mississippi Valley Historical Review* (March 1957). Reprinted by permission of the publisher.

which enabled them to obtain important data for their volume, *How War Came*. Walter Johnson's book, *The Battle against Isolation*, published in 1944, was a study of the most powerful interventionist pressure groups before Pearl Harbor. Johnson, unlike some later writers, based his study upon previously unused manuscripts—principally the William Allen White papers. In the same year Dexter Perkins provided a concise survey in *America and Two Wars*. The authors of these books shared and endorsed most of the assumptions and convictions of the interventionists and the Roosevelt administration on foreign affairs. The emotional atmosphere of the war years, the necessity for unity in the prosecution of the war, and the inadequacy of available source materials combined to prevent any serious challenge to the pro-Roosevelt interpretation during the war. Pamphlets by John T. Flynn, published in 1944 and 1945, advanced the revisionist point of view, but they received relatively little attention.

During and since World War II growing quantities of raw materials for historical research and interpretation on the subject have been published and made available to scholars. The United States government published special sets of documents related to American entry into the war, beginning with the publication in 1943 of *Peace and War: United States Foreign Policy, 1931–1941*. In addition, the regular *Foreign Relations* series is now being brought close to Pearl Harbor. Military leaders and civilians associated with the Roosevelt administration published personal accounts. Among Americans whose memoirs or letters have been published in full or in part are Raymond Moley, William E. Dodd, Joseph E. Davies, Sumner Welles, Frances Perkins, John G. Winant, Henry Morgenthau, Jr., Henry L. Stimson, Cordell Hull, James A. Farley, Sherman Miles, Eleanor Roosevelt, William D. Leahy, Samuel I. Rosenman, Joseph C. Grew, Ernest J. King, Harold L. Ickes, Husband E. Kimmel, and Jay P. Moffat. Several key figures thus far have not published memoirs—including George C. Marshall, Harold R. Stark, Walter C. Short, Frank Knox, and President Roosevelt. Edited volumes of Roosevelt's speeches, press conferences, and personal letters, however, have been published. Documents, testimony, and reports of the several Pearl Harbor investigations were made available with the publication in 1946 of a total of forty volumes covering the work of the Joint Congressional Committee on the Investigation of the Pearl Harbor Attack. The war crimes trials in Nuremberg and the Far East added pertinent documents and testimony. Documents on British and German foreign policy before the war have been published. Memoirs of leaders of European states were printed, containing much information of value for an understanding and analysis of American policies. The volumes by Winston Churchill and Count Ciano's diaries are two important examples. And gradually in recent years historians have obtained increased opportunities for research in unpublished manuscripts.

Most of the histories published from 1947 to 1950 on American entry into World War II were based almost exclusively on published sources—

particularly on the volumes growing out of the Pearl Harbor investigations and on the memoirs of Hull, Stimson, and others. Most of these early books followed the lead of either the majority (pro-Roosevelt) or the minority (anti-Roosevelt) report of the congressional investigation committee. Among the volumes of this sort defending Roosevelt's foreign policies were *This Is Pearl*, by Walter Millis, and *Roosevelt, from Munich to Pearl Harbor*, by Basil Rauch. Revisionist volumes, based largely on published sources, included *Pearl Harbor*, by George Morgenstern; *President Roosevelt and the Coming of the War, 1941*, by Charles A. Beard; *America's Second Crusade*, by William Henry Chamberlin; *Design for War*, by Frederic R. Sanborn, published in 1951; and *The Final Secret of Pearl Harbor*, by Robert A. Theobald, published in 1954.

Gradually in the late 1940's and early 1950's scholars began to expand into new frontiers by research in unpublished manuscripts. Most of this group wrote from points of view sympathetic with the policies followed by the American government before Pearl Harbor. Robert E. Sherwood used the files of Harry Hopkins as the basis for his Pulitzer-prize-winning *Roosevelt and Hopkins*, published in 1948. *The Battle of the Atlantic* and *The Rising Sun in the Pacific*, by Samuel Eliot Morison, traced the naval side of the background of American entry into the war. *Chief of Staff: Prewar Plans and Preparations*, by Mark S. Watson, analyzed the role of the Army. Herbert Feis' study of American relations with Japan, entitled *The Road to Pearl Harbor*, was based on more extensive research than earlier volumes on that subject. The culmination of the internationalist interpretation came with the publication in 1952 and 1953 of the two-volume work by William L. Langer and S. Everett Gleason under the general title of *The World Crisis and American Foreign Policy*. This massive study, covering the years from 1937 to 1941, was sponsored and financed by the Council on Foreign Relations and the Rockefeller Foundation. These volumes were based not only on published materials but also on extensive research in the records of the Department of State and in the material at the Franklin D. Roosevelt Library at Hyde Park. Since the publication of the Langer-Gleason work, the most recent book written from this same general point of view is *The Passing of American Neutrality, 1937-1941*, by Donald F. Drummond, published in 1955. On the revisionist side, Charles Callan Tansill, after research comparable to that of Langer and Gleason, published his *Back Door to War* in 1952. Harry Elmer Barnes, who had published several pamphlets on the subject earlier, edited a volume called *Perpetual War for Perpetual Peace* that included essays written by most major revisionists. Richard N. Current's critical study, *Secretary Stimson*, was published in 1954. In addition, other books and numerous articles have appeared, particularly since 1950, on specialized aspects of the subject.

The interpretative controversies among historians concerning American entry into World War II are in part a direct extension of the pre-Pearl Harbor debate between interventionists and non-interventionists. Writers of history have not only dealt with the same basic subject and issues, but have also used the same arguments, made the same fundamental assumptions, and advanced similar hypotheses. For most major hypotheses advanced by postwar historians, counterparts could be found in the writings and speeches of prewar interventionists and non-interventionists. Furthermore, the debate among historians aroused some of the same emotional heat, the same ideological dogmatism, the same intolerance of conflicting views, and the same black-and-white portraits—on both sides—as were aroused in the "Great Debate" before Pearl Harbor. There are exceptions, of course, but there were also exceptions before Pearl Harbor.

In many instances the individuals who have written scholarly histories on the subject were involved directly (sometimes prominently) in the pre-Pearl Harbor foreign policy debate—and on the same side that they are now defending in their histories. There is no evidence that any of these writers was persuaded to change his basic point of view as the result of historical research after the war. It is true, of course, that Walter Millis' *Road to War*, published in 1935, was a major revisionist interpretation of American entry into World War I. Millis, however, was on the editorial staff of the interventionist New York *Herald Tribune*, and by 1939 he publicly endorsed the interventionist position. In June, 1940, he signed a petition urging an American declaration of war on Nazi Germany. In 1941 he was a sponsor of the Fight for Freedom Committee—a major pressure group advocating full United States participation in the war against the Axis. Robert E. Sherwood's Pulitzer-prize-winning play, *Idiot's Delight*, with its arraignment of war and war passions, undoubtedly aroused pacifist and non-interventionist emotions. By 1939–1941, however, Sherwood was an interventionist. He actively and prominently supported William Allen White's Committee to Defend America by Aiding the Allies. Harry Hopkins assured himself of the vigor of Sherwood's interventionist views before he added the playwright to President Roosevelt's speech-writing staff in 1940.

Barnes and Tansill refer to the internationalist writers as "Court Historians." One need not endorse the sinister implications of this sobriquet. Many internationalist writers, however, did have sympathetic personal ties and friendships with key figures in the events they described in their histories. Several of them have held important government positions in the administration whose foreign policies they were analyzing and evaluating. Ernest K. Lindley's personal friendship with President Roosevelt and other key administration figures enabled him to obtain special interviews and inside information for the preparation of his sympathetic volume. Robert E. Sherwood assisted President Roosevelt with the writing of his speeches from 1940 until the President's death in 1945. Herbert Feis was an economic adviser in the Department of State from 1931 to 1943 and was special consultant to the Secretary of War from 1944 to 1946. William L. Langer from 1941 to 1946 held various positions in the Office of Coordinator of Information, the Office of Strategic Services, and the Department of State. He served the Central Intelligence Agency in 1950–1951. S. Everett Gleason was with the Office of Strategic Services from 1943 to 1945 and the Department of State in 1945. He has served as deputy executive secretary to the National Security Council since 1950. Samuel Eliot Morison was commissioned in the naval reserve with the sole duty of preparing the history of United States naval operations in World War II. He rose to the rank of rear admiral by the time he retired in 1951. Mark S. Watson's book is a part of the official history of the Army in World War II. None of the major revisionist writers, on the contrary, held important administrative positions under either President Roosevelt or President Truman.

All revisionists for whom specific evidence is available adhered to the non-interventionist position before Pearl Harbor. Charles A. Beard's prewar "Continentalism" as expressed in such books as *The Open Door at Home* and *A Foreign Policy for America* is well known. He publicly endorsed (but did not join) the America First Committee, the leading non-interventionist pressure group before Pearl Harbor. He also testified against Lend-Lease before the Senate Foreign Relations Committee. Harry Elmer Barnes, one of the leading and more uncompromising revisionists regarding the origins of World War I, spoke at meetings of the America First Committee in 1941. Charles C. Tansill in 1938 published the best of the revisionist studies of American entry into World War I. George Morgenstern joined the editorial staff of the non-interventionist Chicago *Tribune* in 1941. For revisionist as well as internationalist it is possible to discern a continuity in viewpoint, extending from the pre- to the post-Pearl Harbor period.

Any brief summaries of the revisionist and internationalist interpretations of American entry into World War II can at best be no more than simplified versions of detailed and complicated accounts. It is necessary in presenting such a summary to pass over countless important details and individual variations in interpretation. There is, nevertheless, a wide area of agreement among writers on each side of the interpretative controversy.

Internationalist writers, looking back to the days before Pearl Harbor, view the Axis powers as extremely serious threats to American security and interests. They point to the strength and speed of the Axis forces which by the middle of 1940 had rolled over Austria, Czechoslovakia, Poland, Denmark, Norway, the Netherlands, Luxemburg, Belgium, and France. Britain alone was successfully resisting Nazi assaults on her home islands. By May, 1941, Hitler was in control of the Balkan Peninsula and was threatening the Middle East. Most authorities at the time expected the Soviet Union to fall quickly after Hitler's *Blitzkrieg* was turned against Russia on June 22, 1941. Axis successes in North Africa raised fears that control of that continent might prove a steppingstone to the Western Hemisphere. In the meantime

Japan took advantage of the European crises to step up her aggressive campaigns in Asia.

According to the internationalist interpretation, President Roosevelt believed the United States could most effectively increase the possibility of peace in the 1930's by using its power to discourage potential aggressors from provoking war. In this aim, however, he was handicapped by the "isolationist" attitude of the American people and particularly by the powerful opposition in Congress. After war began in Asia and in Europe, according to this interpretation, the President hoped to prevent the United States from becoming involved in the hostilities—providing that could be accomplished without sacrificing American security, vital interests, and principles.

President Roosevelt and his major advisers believed that aggression by Germany and Italy in Europe constituted a more serious threat to American security than did Japanese actions in the Far East. In general, internationalist writers follow the administration view that the defeat of Nazi Germany and Fascist Italy was essential to American peace and security. Like the Roosevelt administration, most of these writers tend to rule out a negotiated peace as a possible acceptable alternative in Europe—particularly after the fall of France. President Roosevelt hoped that his policy of extending aid short of war to the victims of Axis aggression in Europe would prevent the defeat of Great Britain, contribute to the essential defeat of the Axis powers, and thereby enable the United States to maintain both its peace and its security. Among the many steps taken by the Roosevelt administration to aid the victims of aggression in Europe were repeal of the arms embargo, the destroyer deal, Lend-Lease, the Atlantic patrol system, occupation of Iceland, the shoot-on-sight policy, arming of American merchant ships, and permitting the use of those ships to transport goods directly to England.

According to the internationalist interpretation, Roosevelt and Hull wanted to prevent war between the United States and Japan—in part because such a war would interfere with the main task of defeating Hitler. They believed that the best way to preserve American peace and security in the Pacific was to take steps short of war to check Japanese aggression. Among American actions of this sort were the "moral embargo," the termination of the commercial treaty with Japan, various forms of aid to Chiang Kai-shek, keeping the American fleet at Pearl Harbor, and freezing Japanese assets in the United States. The United States was eager to seek a peaceful settlement with Japan—providing such a settlement would not jeopardize American security and principles, and providing it would not require the United States to abandon China, Britain, France, and the Netherlands in the Pacific. As it became increasingly apparent that compromise was impossible on terms acceptable to both countries, the Roosevelt administration tried to delay war to gain time for military preparations.

With regard to the European theater as well as the Pacific, there were distinct variations in the views of administration leaders before Pearl Harbor about implementing American policies and presenting them to the American people. Cordell Hull, hoping to avoid war and fearful of non-interventionist opposition, generally advised caution. He favored limiting action to steps short of war and he explained each step in terms of peace, security, and international morality. Henry L. Stimson, Frank Knox, Henry Morgenthau, Jr., and others were critical of this indirect and step-at-a-time approach. They early came to believe that aid short of war would not be sufficient to insure the defeat of the Axis and they urged the President to take more vigorous action against the aggressors. Stimson believed the American people would support the President in a declaration of war even before Pearl Harbor. Of a different temperament, President Roosevelt, like Hull, was fearful of arousing effective public opposition to his policies and adhered to the step-at-a-time, short-of-war approach.

Internationalist interpretations tend to reflect these variations in attitudes among prewar interventionists. Feis treats Hull with considerable respect. Rauch's interpretation is similar to that advanced by Hull, though the hero in Rauch's book is definitely President Roosevelt. A number of writers, like Davis, Lindley, Millis, and Sherwood, generally feel that in view of conditions then existing President Roosevelt's decisions and methods on foreign policy matters were wise and sound at most crucial points before Pearl Harbor. Dexter Perkins has emphasized that Roosevelt's actions to check the Axis in Europe short of war reflected and expressed the desires of the majority of the American people. Langer and Gleason are sympathetic with the more direct and vigorous approach urged by Stimson—particularly as applied to the European theater. They believe that Roosevelt overestimated the strength of the opposition to his policies among the American people.

Writers of the internationalist school find the fundamental causes for American involvement in the war in developments in other parts of the world —beyond the American power to control by 1941. They do not find the explanation within the United States—except in so far as non-interventionist opposition inhibited administration actions that might have prevented the war from beginning or from reaching such a critical stage. Nearly all internationalist histories are highly critical of the opponents of Roosevelt's foreign policies. Needless to say, they all deny that President Roosevelt wanted to get the United States into war. They are convinced that the Japanese attack on Pearl Harbor was a genuine surprise to the members of the Roosevelt administration. These leaders knew that Japanese armed forces were under way and that war was imminent, but they expected the blows to fall in the southwest Pacific. In that event, administration leaders believed the United States would have to fight—though they were worried about the reaction of the American people to a declaration of war on Japan if American territory were not attacked. In so far as there was any American responsibility for the disaster at Pearl Harbor most internationalist writers blame the military commanders in Hawaii—Admiral Husband E. Kimmel and General Walter C.

Short. None of them believe that there were any alternatives available to President Roosevelt by 1940–1941 which could have prevented American involvement in World War II without sacrificing American security and principles.

Revisionists have formed an entirely different estimate of Roosevelt's role and policies. Most of the revisionist interpretation can be summarized under four major headings. First, revisionists believe the Axis powers did not (or, need not—if the United States had followed wiser policies) constitute a serious threat to American security and vital interests. Second, they contend that President Roosevelt followed policies that he knew (or should have known) would lead to war in Asia and Europe and would involve the United States in those wars. Third, while leading the nation to war, the President deceived the American people by telling them he was working for peace. And fourth, revisionists maintain that American policies before and during World War II contributed to the rise of a much more serious threat to peace and security—Communist Russia and her satellites.

In striking contrast to the internationalist interpretation, the revisionists minimize or reject the idea that the Axis powers constituted a threat to American security. They point out that Hitler had no concrete plans for attacking the Western Hemisphere. They portray the Japanese attack on Pearl Harbor as an action provoked by American restrictions that threatened Japanese security and vital interests. In so far as revisionists concede the reality of an Axis threat to the United States, they believe it was caused largely by American shortsighted and provocative policies. Like non-interventionists before Pearl Harbor, the revisionists maintain that the issue was not primarily security but instead was war or peace. And revisionists hold that the United States government had the power to choose for itself whether it would or would not enter the war. Thus, in contrast to internationalists, the revisionists find the explanation for American entry into World War II primarily within the United States rather than in the actions of nations in other parts of the world. In seeking the explanation within the United States, they focus their attention almost exclusively upon administration and military leaders—and particularly upon President Roosevelt.

Some revisionist historians believe that the Roosevelt foreign policies helped to provoke and prolong war in Asia and Europe. They interpret Roosevelt's steps to aid Britain short of war as actually steps *to* war. Opinions of revisionists vary on the question of whether Roosevelt deliberately meant these as steps to war. In any event, they contend, these actions did not provoke Hitler into war against the United States; and the shooting incidents that occurred in the Atlantic did not arouse American enthusiasm for entering the European war.

Instead, according to most revisionist writers, the Roosevelt administration got the United States into war through the Asiatic "back door" by provoking the Japanese attack on Pearl Harbor. This was accomplished by increasing pressures on Japan while refusing any compromise that the Japanese could accept. The decisive economic pressure in 1941 was exerted through the curtailment of oil shipments, and the key issue on which compromise proved impossible was China. The freezing of Japanese assets in the United States on July 26, 1941, accompanied by parallel action by the British and Dutch, virtually terminated American trade with Japan. This was particularly serious in cutting Japan off from her essential oil supplies. On August 17, 1941, at the suggestion of Churchill, President Roosevelt presented a formal and vigorous warning to the Japanese against further expansion. The President then rejected Premier Konoye's proposal for a personal meeting between the two leaders. Then, Secretary of State Hull, after objections from China and Britain, abandoned the idea of proposing a *modus vivendi*. Instead, on November 26, Hull (though aware that time was running out) submitted a ten-point program to Japan—including the demand that the Japanese withdraw from China and Indo-China. This proposal (which revisionists generally call an "ultimatum") was so extreme that Hull knew in advance that Japan would not accept it. According to most revisionists these and other actions by the Roosevelt administration (out of either design or blunder) provoked war with Japan. The United States confronted Japan with the alternatives of backing down or fighting. With oil reserves falling dangerously low, and believing that their vital interests and security were at stake, the Japanese chose to fight.

Through all of this, according to the revisionists, President Roosevelt deceived the American people concerning his policies and objectives in foreign affairs. Revisionists maintain that Roosevelt publicly committed his administration to a policy of peace while secretly leading the nation to war— a war that these writers consider contrary to national interests and contrary to the desires of 80 percent of the American people. The most famous expression of this thesis is in Beard's last book and particularly in his final chapter.

Most revisionists maintain that administration and military leaders in Washington gave inadequate, ambiguous, and belated warnings to the commanders in Hawaii and withheld essential information from them. According to their contention, officials in Washington had sufficient information—including that obtained by breaking the Japanese secret diplomatic code—to anticipate an early Japanese attack. Furthermore, most of the revisionists believe that data at the disposal of leaders in Washington were sufficient (if properly analyzed) to have warned of a possible attack on Pearl Harbor. After Pearl Harbor, they say, the administration attempted unjustly to make General Short and Admiral Kimmel, the commanders in Hawaii, scapegoats for the tragedy. Instead of blaming the commanders in Hawaii, the revisionists place the main responsibility upon civilian and military leaders in Washington—including Marshall, Stark, Stimson, Knox, and particularly President Roosevelt. Tansill phrased the idea of Washington responsibility for the war most starkly when he wrote: "It seems quite possible that the Far Eastern

Military Tribunal brought to trial the wrong persons. It might have been better if the tribunal had held its sessions in Washington." On this, as on other phases of the subject, some revisionists, including Beard, Current, and William L. Neumann, write in more restrained and qualified terms than either Tansill or Barnes.

Finally, the revisionists insist that the Roosevelt foreign policies failed to serve American national interests. If, as Roosevelt and Hull contended, American aid to the victims of aggression was designed to keep America out of war, these policies obviously failed. If the Roosevelt policies were designed to protect American security, they were, according to revisionists, of questionable success. By helping to crush Germany and Japan the United States removed two major barriers to Soviet expansion and created power vacuums and chaos which contributed to the rise of the Soviet Union to world power and to the resultant explosive Cold War situation. China, which was considered too vital to compromise in 1941, is now in Communist hands—in part, some revisionists say, because of Roosevelt's policies before and during World War II. Revisionists maintain in general that American involvement left the United States less secure, more burdened by debts and taxes, more laden with the necessity of maintaining huge armed forces than ever before in American history. Some revisionists predict that unless the United States returns to a policy of "continentalism" the nation may be headed for the nightmare described by George Orwell in *Nineteen Eighty-Four*, and toward World War III.

It is probable that the reception accorded the revisionist or the internationalist interpretation has been affected as much by the climate of thought and the international developments since Pearl Harbor as by the specific evidence and reasoning relied upon by historians. Emotional, ideological, political, economic, and military conditions from 1942 to 1950 contributed to a widespread acceptance of the internationalist interpretation. The historian who conformed to prevailing modes of thought in the profession did not seriously question the pro-Roosevelt interpretation of American entry into World War II. Revisionist hypotheses were viewed for the most part as biased and unsound. Critical references to the Beard group were in vogue.

With the breakdown of bipartisanship around 1950, the beginning of a new "Great Debate," the development of neo-isolationism of the Hoover-Taft-Knowland variety, and the Republican campaign of 1952, revisionist interpretations found a somewhat more receptive environment. The Cold War tensions and insecurity encouraged the conviction that American entry into World War II had some aftereffects dangerous to American security. These developments were supplemented by a growth of political, economic, and intellectual conservatism that encouraged a more critical attitude toward Roosevelt's prewar domestic policies as well as his actions in foreign affairs. Revisionist volumes and articles were published in increasing numbers. Although most historians continued to express themselves sympathetically toward Roosevelt's foreign policies before Pearl Harbor, there was a more widespread inclination to question specific features of the internationalist interpretation. Internationalist historians, such as Feis, or Langer and Gleason, phrased their accounts in moderate, restrained, and qualified terms. At the same time some revisionist historians became less defensive and more positive in their phrasing. But the neo-isolationism of the early 1950's did not win the dominant position in popular thought or national policies. And revisionist interpretations still failed to gain a really large following among American historians. It well may be that the future attitudes of many historians and of the American people toward American entry into World War II will be shaped as much by the future course of the United States as by the evidence uncovered by historical research.

Historians need not speak disparagingly, however, of the results of their inquiries during a period of only fifteen years on the subject of American entry into World War II. A prodigious amount of research has been accomplished. The diplomatic and military phases have been examined with striking thoroughness within the limits of available sources. Important beginnings have been made in the study of other aspects of the subject. Both revisionist and internationalist writers have advanced provocative and stimulating interpretations and have buttressed them with impressive documentation.

Despite these major accomplishments, there are important deficiencies and much work remains. Individuals will vary widely in their evaluations of what has been done and what remains to be done, but many of the criticisms of existing studies (criticisms which suggest possible directions for future efforts) may be analyzed under two major headings. In the first place, the narrow focus of most publications has left major areas almost untouched by serious historical research. Secondly—though the problem is probably incapable of final solution—there is need for a serious re-examination of the role and limitations of historical interpretation.

When measured by the standards of the "actualities" of pre-Pearl Harbor events, the scope and depth of available publications on American entry into World War II have been quite narrow in terms of time covered, subject matter, and source materials. Only a few books dealing specifically with this subject put it in the time context of the two World Wars. The volumes by Perkins, Chamberlin, Tansill, and Barnes all have this merit. Most studies of American entry into World War II, however, begin with 1940 or 1937. This point of departure is defensible if the scholar remains sensitively aware that he is examining only a tiny segment of the path that led to Pearl Harbor. Many historians, however, write almost as though the years from 1937 through 1941 were separated from and uninfluenced by earlier developments. For example, from a study of most available volumes a reader would not learn that these years were preceded by a devastating world depression with jolting economic, social, ideological, emotional, political, and power consequences that influenced the course of nations to December 7, 1941. Despite many important volumes and articles now available, there is much need for substantial research on foreign affairs in the years from 1921 to 1937. And a more meaningful perspective might be obtained if the subject were put in the broader context of the long-term but changing power relationships, industrialization of the world, the rise of the common man, and the development of secular ideologies designed to explain the mysteries of social, economic, and political changes whose ultimate form can only be dimly and imperfectly perceived.

Most published volumes are concerned largely with diplomatic, military, and some political aspects of the subject. The authors trace in intricate detail the policy planning, the minutiae of diplomatic exchanges, and the reactions of statesmen to the developments abroad. These phases are of major importance. They do not, however, constitute the whole story nor necessarily the most meaningful part. Economic, social, psychological, ethnic, religious, and political conditions that help to give direction and meaning to the diplomacy have been inadequately and imprecisely studied.

Political influences have been given much attention. Even the political analyses, however, often leave much to be desired when the subject is American entry into World War II. A good many historians on both sides have followed the almost standard procedure of charging individuals whose foreign policy views they do not like with partisan political motives. Writers on both sides often seem blind to political influences among those with whom they sympathize. Political analysts also have directed their attention largely to the top administration, military, and diplomatic officials. There has been relatively little serious study of the influence of individual congressmen and of state political organizations on the nation's foreign policies before Pearl Harbor. Furthermore, most references to political figures—even the prominent administration leaders—are of a two-dimensional variety. There is need for thorough biographies of scores of individuals. Frank Freidel's excellent biography of Franklin D. Roosevelt, now being published, suggests the sort of work needed on countless other figures in the story. Some important beginnings have been made, too, in studying sectional variations, but this subject has by no means been exhausted.

One need not be an economic determinist to be disturbed by the neglect of economic influences in existing histories of American entry into World War II. How did foreign policies affect those groups of persons who shared a particular economic interest? How did such effects influence the attitude of those groups toward foreign policy? What influence did those groups exert on policy making? Articles by John W. Masland and Roland N. Stromberg provide important beginnings on this phase of the subject, but much more remains to be done.

Samuel Lubell and John Norman have published studies on the foreign policy attitudes of German-Americans and Italian-Americans. There is need, however, for additional research on the role of numerous ethnic and religious groups in the history of American foreign affairs before Pearl Harbor. Volumes have been published on such pressure groups as the Committee to Defend America by Aiding the Allies, the Fight for Freedom Committee, the America First Committee, and the American Legion. But studies are needed on the attitudes and influence of countless other organized pressure groups of all sorts on American foreign policies before Pearl Harbor. Several books and articles have analyzed the non-interventionists and interventionists— but neither of these groups has by any means been exhausted as a field for constructive historical research.

There has been almost no serious research on the influence of psychological and emotional factors. Both revisionists and internationalists write almost as though the actions of the key figures could all be explained in intellectual and rational terms. It is conceivable that historians could learn as much about American entry into World War II by studying the psychological and emotional make-up of the individuals involved, as by studying the phrasing of the diplomatic dispatches and state papers. Ralph K. White, Harold Lavine, and James Wechsler have published suggestive studies on the role of propaganda in pre-Pearl Harbor developments, but for the most part the role of psychological influences on the attitudes of the American people and of American statesmen has scarcely been touched.

Results of the limited research on these non-diplomatic influences have seldom been integrated into the major works. Thomas A. Bailey's interpretative survey, *The Man in the Street,* contains more data on these phases of the subject than do any of the major volumes on American entry into World War II. But his study is suggestive rather than definitive.

In addition to the narrowness of approach with regard to time span and subject matter, there has been a narrowness in terms of the source materials used. If the focus of the subject matter is to be broadened as suggested in this article, historians will have to demonstrate a high degree of ingenuity in tapping additional source materials—including manuscripts in private hands. This appeal for greater breadth and depth is not meant to disparage the work thus far completed. But much of great importance remains to be done by scholars on the subject of American involvement in the war.

Montaigne's assertion that "nothing is so firmly believed as what we least know" suggests a second deficiency in most major volumes on American entry into World War II. The most heated controversies among historians do not center on those matters for which the facts and truth can be determined with greatest certainty. The interpretative controversies, on the contrary, rage over questions about which the historian is least able to determine truth. Despite the thousands of documents and tons of manuscripts, the written record and the physical remains constitute only a tiny fraction of the reality of America's course toward World War II—and these remains do not necessarily represent the "truth."

With the relatively inexact methods and incomplete data at his command, even the finest historian can often make only semi-informed guesses concerning motives, causes, and wisdom of pre-Pearl Harbor decisions. As

Herbert Butterfield phrased it, the historian "can never quite carry his enquiries to that innermost region where the final play of motive and the point of responsibility can be decided. . . . He does not study human nature, therefore, in the way that an omniscient deity might observe it, with an eye that pierces our unspoken intentions, our thick folds of insincerity and the motives that we hardly avow to ourselves." The historian can determine that certain events preceded American entry into World War II and he may find circumstantial evidence suggesting possible causal relationships. But he cannot conduct controlled experiments to measure with any degree of certainty the causal significance of antecedent developments and incidents. Furthermore, these various interpretations of individual historians are based upon different opinions concerning the wisdom of possible pre-Pearl Harbor policies as judged in terms of certain criteria, such as world peace and security, American peace and security, economic order and prosperity, and freedom and democracy. As Sumner Welles phrased it, "The wisdom of any foreign policy can generally be determined only by its results." But in order to measure this wisdom, the results of policies that were actually followed would have to be compared with the results of possible alternative policies that were not followed. It is, of course, impossible to run controlled experiments to determine what would have happened if alternative policies had been followed. Furthermore, the possible alternatives were not necessarily of the simple "either/or" variety. The path to Pearl Harbor was filled with millions of decisions, great and small, each based upon other decisions which preceded it. There were countless forks in the road that led to Pearl Harbor. And no historian can know for certain what lay at the end of the paths that were not followed.

Writers on both sides, of course, are conscious of limitations inherent in historical interpretation. All of them qualify their generalizations with references to the inadequacy of their sources. But they recognize the limitations more clearly when referring to interpretations with which they do not agree. Sanborn, a revisionist, wrote that the internationalists' "first line of defense has always rested and still rests upon a foundation blended of faith, emotion, and hypothesis." Dexter Perkins, on the other side, has written that revisionism is "shot through with passion and prejudice. . . . It also rests upon hypotheses which . . . cannot be demonstrated." To a certain extent both Sanborn and Perkins are correct. But their generalizations apply in varying degree to books on *both* sides in the interpretative controversy.

Probably no one would want the historian to refrain from interpreting the course of events simply because he cannot scientifically prove the truth of his interpretations. The historian could not avoid some degree of interpretation even if he tried. Inadequate though his analyses may be, who is better qualified to perform the function? Both revisionist and internationalist historians have a responsibility to attempt to explain American entry into World War II as they understand it.

Nevertheless, considering the incompleteness and inexactness of their knowledge and understanding, historians do not seem justified in the cavalier, dogmatic tone that they so frequently use. They base their interpretations in part on a personal faith in the wisdom of the policies they support. Like devout believers in less secular faiths, writers on both sides tend to be intolerant of conflicting beliefs. This may not be true of all writers on the subject, but it does apply in varying degree to many on both sides. Historians need to emphasize the limits of their knowledge as well as the expansiveness of it. There is need for more awareness of the tentative nature of human inquiry, for self-criticism and the humility of an Albert Einstein, rather than the positive, dogmatic, self-righteousness of the propagandist. Perhaps in the furious twentieth-century struggle for men's minds there can be no real place for moderation and restraint—even in historical interpretation. Numerous critics, however, both here and abroad, are fearful of the immaturity of American attitudes toward international affairs. If the historian is sensitive to the many-sided complexities of issues and demonstrates intellectual humility and ideological tolerance, perhaps others, influenced by his example, may be less inclined to grasp at simplified, crusading, utopian theories regarding contemporary international affairs.

The Liberals, Truman, and FDR as Symbol and Myth

Alonzo L. Hamby

Alonzo L. Hamby of Ohio University notes the important mythical qualities that conditioned Democratic politics as America witnessed the passing of the hero-President Franklin D. Roosevelt and the assumption of presidential power by his successor Harry S. Truman. The tradition bequeathed from the Roosevelt to the Truman administration, says Professor Hamby, was one replete with symbol and myth. The unique charisma of FDR, as transformed into an equally unique source of inspiration by American liberals, cast a mythic shadow of skepticism over Truman's first administration. As Hamby perceives it: "... the FDR mythology ... added an emotional and subjective element to the liberal attitude." In the end, Truman's redemption would only be finally achieved via his upset victory over Thomas E. Dewey in the presidential election of 1948.

> We cannot think of President Roosevelt as one who is gone. He is here. Every hope, yes, the peace of the world, requires his constant spiritual presence. . . .
>
> How we miss him. Hardly a domestic problem or an international situation today but what we say 'Oh, if F.D.R. were only here.'
>
> *Fiorello La Guardia*
> *January 26, 1947*
> *WJZ radio script*

With these words, spoken twenty-one months after Franklin D. Roosevelt's death, Fiorello La Guardia eloquently demonstrated a sense of loss and aimlessness which many liberals felt. The liberals, those middle-class reformers often described as "intellectuals," were held together by a body of well-articulated principles—equal opportunity, economic security, racial equality, international economic development, and the support of democratic forces abroad—but their sense of identity, as is the case with any social movement, depended also upon a mythology which gave inner inspiration, provided symbols for outer persuasion, and did much to determine their perceptions of reality. In the years immediately after World War II, the liberal mythology was built around the memory of Franklin D. Roosevelt and the New Deal.

His death left the liberal movement in a state of crisis. His personality had given the liberals unity as well as inspiration; Harry S. Truman could

From "The Liberals, Truman, and FDR as Symbol and Myth," by Alonzo L. Hamby, in *Journal of American History* (March 1970). Reprinted by permission of the publisher.

provide neither. Moreover, the ambiguity of FDR's legacy in foreign affairs left no sure guidelines in a chaotic and swiftly changing international situation. What followed was a period of demoralization and division among liberals, which is entirely understandable only if one grasps the importance of the myths and symbols that developed out of the memory of FDR.

Truman's lack of Rooseveltian qualities almost immediately distressed liberals. FDR had been sophisticated and cosmopolitan; Truman came from the small-town, Midwestern middle class. His cultural heritage, the *New Republic* commented, was not "too well attuned to the future of a world in depression, war, and revolution." FDR, the liberals believed, had been essentially an independent reformer; Truman was a party regular who had been associated with the notorious Pendergast machine. The liberals, somewhat mistakenly, thought of Franklin D. Roosevelt as an overpowering mass leader who could put a reform program through Congress by mobilizing public opinion. In contrast, Truman seemed weak and ineffective. The nation, commented *New Republic* columnist "T.R.B." in the spring of 1946, was "listening for a clarion call, but maybe the man who could give it is dead."

At least as disturbing as Truman's personal qualities was the steady departure from the administration of men who had been associated with the New Deal years and their displacement by the mediocre "cronies," whom the President seemed to find congenial. Truman had been in office only six weeks when a California liberal commented privately: "You get this stuff every place you turn: 'Truman is a nice man, but no superman; he is surrounded by a bunch of "regular" party hacks who are going to drive every decent person out of important administrative positions.' "

In 1945 and 1946, one New Dealer after another left the government, some voluntarily, some in anger. William H. Davis, head of the Office of Economic Stabilization, was arbitrarily fired. Robert Nathan, the deputy director of the Office of War Mobilization and Reconversion, resigned after he found himself unable to work or even communicate with his new chief, Truman's close friend, John Snyder. Samuel I. Rosenman, Franklin D. Roosevelt's close lieutenant, returned to private law practice. Harold Ickes, Secretary of the Interior, stormed out of the administration, outraged by Truman's effort to appoint Edwin Pauley, a California oil company executive, as undersecretary of the navy. Chester Bowles, the foremost champion of price controls, resigned in mid-1946 after, though not because of, policy disagreements with Snyder. And, in September 1946, Truman fired the most important of all the New Dealers, Henry Wallace, after a fundamental foreign-policy disagreement.

With each departure or dispute apprehension among liberals increased. "I have kept my confidence in [Truman's] integrity of purpose," Californian Bartley Crum wrote to Rosenman. "You can understand, however, that each resignation—top-side—makes the task of convincing others more difficult. It makes, in brief, for dissolution of the coalition of progressive forces."

By the time Wallace was fired, the Chicago *Sun* felt that, "the New Deal, as a driving force, is dead within the Truman administration."

There also was talk of a massive exodus of liberals from the government. "Hundreds on the lower levels have slipped out unnoticed . . . ," wrote labor journalist Henry Zon, "and thousands of others are eyeing the door." Zon was probably exaggerating, but many did leave Washington. The "Truman climate" was not congenial to the bright, idealistic young lawyers who had come into the Roosevelt administration. As Zon remarked, it seemed more important to have a connection with Truman's old army outfit than with Felix Frankfurter. "Who wants to work in a set-up where you have to go through this forward-wall of politicians?" asked a disillusioned liberal within the administration, adding that: "Even FDR's bad appointments were first-team." By late 1946, the New York *Post* was attributing the administration defeat in the congressional elections to the fact that: "The men who gave the New Deal its vitality have been brushed out of Washington."

Actually, many who left government service in 1945 and 1946—including Harry Hopkins, Rosenman, and Bowles—had no desire to repudiate Truman. They simply were physically and financially exhausted by arduous wartime jobs. Yet, as the astute journalist Cabell Phillips observed, they were more willing to leave an administration headed by Truman. Franklin D. Roosevelt had been a "spiritual anchor" holding them to their positions; Truman could play no such role.

Nor could Truman replace FDR as a source of inspiration who could unify the liberals. The fate of liberalism had been bound up to a remarkable extent with Franklin D. Roosevelt's personal fortunes. His talent as a political leader and manipulator had made it largely unnecessary for the liberals to do much of the day-to-day work of politics—the vital jobs of organizing and campaigning. His death left the liberal movement in disarray.

During World War II, the liberals had groped toward the objective of establishing a power base independent of the Roosevelt charisma. In 1941, some founded the Union for Democratic Action (UDA); but, despite the prestige of such leaders as Reinhold Niebuhr and Eleanor Roosevelt, it remained a weak little group tottering on the edge of bankruptcy. In 1944, the Congress of Industrial Organizations, as part of its ambitious political program, set up the National Citizens Political Action Committee; and at about the same time an impressive group of writers, artists, actors, directors, producers, and scientists formed the Independent Citizens Committee of the Arts, Sciences, and Professions. These organizations worked primarily for a common objective—the support of FDR—but it is questionable that many of their members looked beyond the Roosevelt era. Only a few liberals, most notably James Loeb, Jr., of UDA, sought to establish the attitudes and organizational base which would allow the liberal movement to transcend its dependence upon FDR. Franklin D. Roosevelt's sudden death cut their efforts short.

In 1946, as disillusion with Truman deepened and as the liberal movement suffered repeated defeats, many liberals felt that the memory of Franklin D. Roosevelt presented the best hope for the revival of their cause. John L. Nichols, a transportation consultant with an interest in Democratic politics, proposed an elaborate system of National Roosevelt Clubs in order to resuscitate the spirit of the New Deal and identify it with the Democratic party. Some important liberal politicians—Claude Pepper, Bowles, and Oscar Chapman—planned a national pressure group tentatively called the Roosevelt Forum. Both schemes proceeded from the assumption that Truman had rejected the New Deal. A memorandum outlining the ambitious plans for the Roosevelt Forum asserted that popular dissatisfaction with the Truman administration stemmed from "the fact that the leadership of the Democratic Party has turned away from the Roosevelt program and policies." Neither plan reached fruition because of the hostility of the Democratic National Committee and the intense activity underway on other fronts to rebuild the liberal movement.

At the end of 1946, the National Citizens Political Action Committee and the Independent Citizens Committee of the Arts, Sciences, and Professions merged to become the Progressive Citizens of America (PCA), which was under Wallace's informal leadership. Just a few days later, a greatly expanded Union for Democratic Action became the Americans for Democratic Action (ADA). It soon was apparent that these two new liberal organizations were involved in an irreconcilable conflict, despite the fact that both passionately identified with FDR. The struggle between PCA and ADA was the result of an argument among liberals about the nature of the Cold War. The argument demonstrated that, in some respects, the Roosevelt legacy was too hazy and ambiguous to serve as a sure guide for liberals and that it could not serve as a basis for liberal unity.

As the wartime alliance began to disintegrate, virtually all liberals assumed that FDR had developed the correct formula for dealing with the Soviet Union, but they differed in their interpretations of that formula. One group—probably a majority of the liberals until the announcement of the Marshall Plan and the shock of the Communist coup in Czechoslovakia—felt that FDR, by one means or another, would have preserved Big Three unity and that the Truman administration had junked FDR's foreign policies just as it had abandoned the Roosevelt heritage in domestic politics.

As early as December 1945, the Independent Citizens Committee, at a New York "crisis meeting," adopted a resolution asserting that the Truman administration was "departing from the tested and successful foreign policy of the late President Roosevelt." A few months later, the Win-the-Peace Conference, a gathering of diverse liberals and leftists reminiscent of the Popular Front, met in Washington and reasserted this position. Speakers combined criticism of Truman with eulogies of Franklin D. Roosevelt; FDR's picture was on the front page of the program; and large portraits of him dominated the meeting hall.

At about the same time, the first anniversary of Franklin D. Roosevelt's death, the widely read liberal columnist Samuel Grafton insisted that FDR could have prevented the Cold War:

> [I]t is because he is gone that the West, squealing legalisms, is now forlornly on the defensive, whereas if he had lived, blessed bad lawyer that he was, we might now be trying for a new level of international understanding.
>
> For he, more than any other, was the coalition, he, who could deal with Mr. Churchill as a country squire, and with Mr. Stalin as a commoner. Somehow, in him, the two currents had met, but not in a whirlpool; and the fact that these two contrary streams could produce a man so much at peace with himself and at ease with his world, made hope feasible for others.

In mid-1946, Elliott Roosevelt's *As He Saw It* seemed to confirm this viewpoint. Depicting his father as a determined opponent of British imperialism and a dedicated believer in Soviet-American friendship, Elliott Roosevelt asserted that FDR had forged a successful relationship with Joseph Stalin in the joint battle against fascism and reaction. FDR had listened to both sides and had established himself as an honest broker. But now the United States was blindly backing the British imperialists, and, "a small group of willful men in London and Washington are anxious to create and foster an atmosphere of war hatred against the Russians. . . ."

Jonathan Daniels, a liberal southerner who had served as a presidential assistant throughout the war, expressed his agreement: "Nothing is so obvious as that the warm, human, smiling, face-to-face dealings Roosevelt made famous and effective have disappeared." Truman was a man of good intentions, but he had been pushed toward a break with FDR's foreign policies by state department reactionaries, conservative publishers, "Irish politicians and Claghorn senators." "He was—and I believe is—eager to fulfill the hopes Roosevelt delivered to him. But Mr. Truman is not Roosevelt."

In the fall of 1946, a wide and representative assembly of liberals, the Conference of Progressives, met in Chicago. Its foreign policy resolutions urged "a swift return to the progressive global thinking of Franklin Roosevelt," specifically the "recapture" of the Big Three unity which FDR had forged. The Conference also adopted a resolution of greeting to Wallace, who had just been ejected from the cabinet: "Carry on with confidence that you have the support of the millions upon millions of Americans who believe in the program of Franklin Delano Roosevelt."

Wallace himself constantly invoked the name of FDR and the symbols connected with it. Under his direction, the *New Republic* began a series of articles calling for "A New Deal With Russia." "Where are the millions who supported Roosevelt's ideals?" he asked, as he attempted to rally the liberal movement behind him. As he traveled around the country, large crowds actually paid admission to hear him, a phenomenon which the New York

Post reluctantly conceded was "an eloquent demonstration of the widespread thirst for affirmative idealism in public life; a thirst which has been virtually unslaked since the death of President Franklin Delano Roosevelt."

Wallace's liberal opponents, however, drew upon their own version of the Roosevelt mythology and were equally convinced that they represented the Roosevelt heritage. Important policy differences were involved in the liberal split, but they were differences which could exist largely because the Roosevelt legacy in foreign policy was so vague. The argument, therefore, was also a dispute over which side could rightly invoke the name and symbolism of FDR. Adolf A. Berle, Jr., the old New Dealer and a leader of the New York Liberal party, asserted, for example, not that FDR had been wrong or unrealistic in his attitudes toward the Russians, but rather that Elliott Roosevelt had reported these attitudes incorrectly—"a passionate perversion of the truth," he wrote indignantly. ADA stressed its connections with Rooseveltian symbols. Many of ADA's leading members had come to prominence under the New Deal and men like Leon Henderson, Bowles, Paul Porter, William Davis, Isador Lubin, Benjamin V. Cohen, and Elmer Davis, among others laid claim to the FDR aura. Moreover, Franklin D. Roosevelt, Jr., then a dynamic young politician of considerable ability, was, no doubt because of the memory of his father, ADA's foremost attraction as a speaker. Even more valuable was the membership of Eleanor Roosevelt. She was an asset so great that, shortly after ADA was established, Wallace attempted to minimize her affiliation, and ADA leadership responded with a sharp rebuke. After such an incident, an uninformed observer might well have wondered whether the liberal debate was about questions of substance and national interest or simply an argument over which side possessed the best claim to the memory of FDR.

There was, of course, more to liberal politics in the early postwar years than the memory of FDR, but liberal rhetoric and political perceptions were dominated to a remarkable extent by symbol and myth. Criticisms of Truman, for example, were almost invariably expressed in terms of a comparison with Franklin D. Roosevelt. The implication seemed to be that if Truman "departed" from a "Roosevelt policy," the departure had to be bad. If Truman's style was unlike Roosevelt's, then Truman could not be a liberal leader. Truman's policies might be discussed rationally; the FDR mythology, however, added an emotional and subjective element to the liberal attitude. Criticism became alienation. By 1948, there was little substantive policy difference between Truman and ADA liberals; yet ADA led a vain effort to replace the President with either Dwight D. Eisenhower or William O. Douglas. One reason was the belief that Truman would be a weak candidate, but also important was a quest for Rooseveltian charisma. Douglas, a vigorous New Dealer, was the special favorite of the liberals, although few of them believed that he could win the election. As one ADA member put it, "we would rather lose with Douglas than lose with Truman."

Moreover, it is difficult to imagine a major split among liberals on foreign policy had FDR lived. As it was, both factions argued that they were following the guidelines he had left. They seemed to assume that his course necessarily would have been the right one and that the conduct of foreign relations was primarily a matter of somehow discovering what he would have done. If both sides drew inspiration from their identification with him, they also had demonstrated that his memory could not serve as the unifying force which the liberals needed.

In 1947 and 1948, Truman at least partially provided leadership for the liberals by making the Marshall Plan the keystone of American foreign policy, vetoing the Taft-Hartley bill, advocating a comprehensive civil rights program, and striking blow after blow at the reactionary Eightieth Congress. As the presidential campaign began, an editorial cartoon in the New York *Star* depicted Truman as a battered but undefeated figure holding aloft the flickering "Liberal Torch of F.D.R."

Truman's unexpected victory largely resolved the liberal division on foreign policy and won him a large degree of acceptance within the liberal movement. "This election clearly is a victory for the progressive principles and policies of Franklin D. Roosevelt," noted the St. Louis *Post-Dispatch.* "The New Deal and the Democratic Party did not die with their great champion," observed the New York *Post.* Truman, said Elmer Davis, "made a New Deal campaign and won a New Deal victory; at this moment he has made himself the successor to Roosevelt." Truman had not eclipsed the memory of FDR; he had succeeded in identifying himself with it. As a result, for the first time since April 1945, a majority of the liberals could feel that they had a leader in the White House.

J.F.K.: The Stained-Glass Image

Andy Logan

The assassination of President John F. Kennedy and the distinct
aura of its aftermath provide the historian with a ready example of
the interrelationships of political reality and social myth. The circumstances of his death, combined with the "Kennedy mystique,"
have worked much to the advantage of the mythmakers and falsifiers
of history. Numerous exercises in "instant history" have created a
mythical residue as to John F. Kennedy's proper place in history.
Andy Logan, a staff writer for the *New Yorker*, finds the results unfortunate. Through undue sentimentalism, and a compromising of
objectivity reminiscent of the Lincoln legend, the myth and the
reality of the Kennedy era have proven difficult to distinguish.

In mid-November, 1963, according to all the major best-seller lists, by far
the most popular nonfiction publication in America was a book that portrayed Jack Kennedy as "immature," "arrogant," "snobbish," "glib,"
"slick," "calculating," "hard as nails," "mealymouthed," "opportunistic,"
"Machiavellian," "intellectually shallow," "spiritually rootless," "morally
pusillanimous," "passionless," "vain," "shifty-eyed," and, for every good
reason, nicknamed "Jack the Knife." The book, of course, was *J.F.K.: The
Man and the Myth,* by Victor Lasky. By the end of the same month there
burned above the grave of the very same man an eternal flame, more often
reserved in the protocol of his religion for saints of the first order. Whatever
their religious or political persuasion, few Americans were protesting this
instant canonization. In the horror, grief, and guilt that overwhelmed the
nation following the assassination, the minor Kennedy myth that Lasky
had contended against—the fine-liberal-fellow image—had expanded un-
countable times, been transformed and purified, burst all mortal bonds, and
soared toward the realm of the supernatural. As after the death of Lincoln
nearly a hundred years earlier, the common thought of Americans was "How
are the fallen mighty!" and John F. Kennedy was on his way to becoming
the legendary national hero of his century.

"It is difficult now to comprehend the wave of hero-worship which
swept over the country after Lincoln's assassination," Roy P. Basler wrote
a generation ago in *The Lincoln Legend.* "Lincoln was suddenly lifted into
the sky as the folk-hero, the deliverer, and the martyr who had come to save

his people and to die for them . . . the folk mind was enraptured with the stories of how Lincoln had suffered, prayed, dreamed, and loved mankind and conquered his enemies. How he had doubted, despaired, cunningly schemed, and contrived to effect his ends, no one wanted to hear." Thousands of Americans were soon seriously arguing that Lincoln was of divine origin. (After all, in his own words he was the son of an "angel mother"; his father-of-record was a poor carpenter; and he was shot on Good Friday.) This conclusion would have astonished Lincoln only a little more than, in the view of Arthur Krock and some of John Kennedy's other friends, the lighting of the eternal flame would have embarrassed Kennedy nearly a century later. But neither man was by this time making history. It was being made for him.

Until 1872 Lincoln biography was entirely in the hands of spiritual and stylistic descendants of Parson Weems, rather than of men who had known him as he was. Then a book appeared by Ward Hill Lamon, a jovial crony of Lincoln's who had ridden the backwoods legal circuit with him in central Illinois. Lamon was "pre-eminently the Good Fellow," writes Sandburg, and the President's more punctilious associates regarded the long Lincoln–Lamon alliance as evidence of "a certain degree of . . . obtuseness" on Lincoln's part. "Sing me a little song," he often said to Lamon, who would then make him smile with some such nonsensical ballad as "Cousin Sally Downard." "I want you with me, I must have you," Lincoln told his old friend when he was about to leave for Washington, and he arranged to have Lamon appointed a city marshal at the capital. Lamon's biography of Lincoln, pulled together by a ghostwriter, was based largely on material gathered by Lincoln's onetime law partner, William H. Herndon. A bald account of the late President's political opportunism and his often indecorous life during his western years, it was denounced as "shameless." "Want of delicacy and even decency," wrote a more worshipful biographer, made its appearance "something close to a national misfortune." The book did not even reap the traditional reward of publications charged with indecency; it was a financial failure. In the first years after the assassination Herndon had delivered several lectures based on the material he had made available to Lamon, but it wasn't until 1889 that he published his own biography, *Herndon's Lincoln,* in which Lincoln emerged as an earthy, moody, irreligious frontier hero, unrecognizable as the saintly Christian martyr of prevailing legend. ("Why, Lamon," wrote Herndon, "if you and I had not told the exact truth about Lincoln he would have been a myth in a hundred years after 1865.") The Herndon book, which, of course, launched myths of its own, such as the Ann Rutledge love story so infuriating to Mary Todd Lincoln, brought Herndon less than five hundred dollars in royalties in the next eight years. Their tedious, circumspect *Abraham Lincoln: A History* proved to be a more profitable venture for Lincoln's two private secretaries, John G. Nicolay and John Hay. Authorized by Robert Todd Lincoln, the President's surviving son (Nicolay and Hay, gibed Herndon, were "afraid of Bob; he gives them materials and they in their turn play *hush"*), the widely admired biography appeared in serial form in the *Century Magazine* during the eighties but was not published as a book until 1890, a quarter of a century after Lincoln's death.

The colleagues of our twentieth-century presidential martyr did not wait so long to be heard from. As we all know, among the nearly two hundred books on Kennedy issued in the thirty-six months after his death (including *The Mind of JFK, The Faith of JFK, The Kennedy Wit, More Kennedy Wit,* and other striking signs of publishers' faith in the selling power of the newly sacred name) were reports by his special counsel (Theodore Sorensen's *Kennedy*), by one of his special assistants (Arthur Schlesinger, Jr.'s *A Thousand Days*), by his chief of press relations (Pierre Salinger's *With Kennedy*), by his private secretary (Evelyn Lincoln's *My Twelve Years with John F. Kennedy*), and by his children's nurse (Maud Shaw's *White House Nannie*). Besides these, there was *The Pleasure of His Company*, by Paul B. "Red" Fay, Jr., Kennedy's old friend from PT-boat days whom he called "Grand Old Lovable," who could always make him laugh with his uninhibited rendition of "Hooray for Hollywood!" and whom Kennedy brought to Washington by arranging his appointment as Under Secretary of the Navy.

None of these posthumous best sellers was authorized by the surviving Kennedys, of course, in the same sense that they authorized the Manchester account of the assassination. Indeed, the family tried to prevent publication of *White House Nannie*. After the attempt failed, however, they censored only a few paragraphs since it turned out to be in the inane tradition of inside stories by refined nannies who wouldn't dream of telling all ("[Mrs. Kennedy] never likes to put other people out, even the tiniest bit"). *The Pleasure of His Company* is on the family Index, although Fay submitted it for clearance and has said that he deleted 90,000 of about 180,000 words at Mrs. Kennedy's request. His publisher thinks it was not so many. He balked, he said, at removing another 30,000, which would have reduced it to a third of its original length and might have rendered it unpublishable, an outcome the Kennedys may have had in mind. No *passim* cuts could remedy its pervading indiscretion—the evidence throughout the book that Kennedy, the symbol of intellect and culture come to the White House, had chosen to spend a large share of his leisure time during the last twenty years of his life with a good-hearted end man whose mother tongue is Kiwanis Club slang and who cheerfully admits he had to be clued in on Renoir and Cézanne. ("If you have to ask a question like that, do it in a whisper," Kennedy told him. "We're trying to give this administration a semblance of class.") Rejecting Fay's three-thousand-dollar gift to the Kennedy Library, Mrs. Kennedy—for whom those long, recurrent weekends *en famille* with the Fays may have been somewhat of a trial—wrote that she regarded the contribution as "hypocritical." Of all the diarists of the Kennedy era to date, Fay, best man at the Kennedy wedding, had been closest to the Hyannisport-Hickory Hill contingent. Since the appearance of his fond but inelegant view of life with their martyred brother, he and the Kennedys have been, as the columnists say, don't-invite-'ems.

Schlesinger, Sorensen, and Salinger—the S-men—remain decidedly *grata* in the compound, however, nor have diplomatic relations apparently been severed with Mrs. Lincoln, in whose adoring book the Kennedys made no changes. She had relied almost entirely on her personal diary and her trusty notebook; but the long, intensively documented accounts of the Kennedy administration by Sorensen and Schlesinger—and, to an extent perhaps, Salinger's specialized report of those years as seen from the White House press office—could not have been written without access to information and records in Kennedy control. Only nonbelievers would suggest that the authors played "hush" in any respect just because someone named Bob gave them materials. But even before their books were stamped with approval, these men were part of the privy council, sworn to serve the clan that the same nonbelievers have charged with assuming the prerogatives of an American royal family in temporary exile. Members of the council (William Manchester must now be inclined to refer to it as another "tong," the epithet that, in *Death of a President*, he applies to Johnson's Texas followers) are pledged to rally around during all Kennedy campaigns, to run general interference in off-election years, to squire the widow about on occasion, and to help the family maintain its dominion over all insiders' published recollections of the Kennedy era— or so it appears to gawkers on the sidelines. Of course, in the years since the White House was their second home, they have all made other lucrative professional commitments, but there doesn't seem to be much doubt about where the priorities would lie if a footman should arrive with a summons from Jackie.

During Kennedy's term of office his staff was accused of trying to manage the news. Now, of course, the charge on several fronts is that of managing history. Kennedy himself during his drive for the presidency had no qualms about attempting to control what appeared in books written about him. In the late fifties he saw to it that some of his father's anti-Semitic remarks were removed from a biography of the family, and at about the same time, according to Sorensen, he "waged an intensive effort with his contacts in the publishing world to prevent a projected biography by a writer inaccurately representing himself to potential publishers as a Kennedy intimate—a man whom Senator Kennedy in fact regarded as uninformed, unobjective and unsound."

The authors of the certified chronicles do not pretend to be objective. Salinger notes that his inability to continue to work for Lyndon Johnson was no fault of Johnson's, whom he liked. He simply came to realize that "the memory of J.F.K. was too overpowering." "Our faith in him and in what he was trying to do was absolute," he writes of Kennedy's cadre of White House assistants, and, in retrospect, Sorensen is moved by their sense of common challenge and dedication to their leader's cause to quote Henry V at Agincourt:

... we ... shall be remembered—
We few, we happy few, we band of brothers. . . .
And gentlemen . . . now abed
Shall think themselves accurs'd they were not here.

Kennedy once joked with his staff about Evelyn Lincoln's blind devotion to him. "If I had said just now, 'Mrs. Lincoln, I have cut off Jackie's head, would you please send over a box?' she still would have replied, 'That's wonderful, Mr. President, I'll send it right away. . . . Did you get your nap?' " Often, in these approved histories, when a head has been cut off, Schlesinger and company, though they don't run for a box, seem to suggest that somebody else did the dirty deed or anyhow talked Kennedy into it, or that, even if their leader did it himself, it was all, in the long run, for the best—especially if he got his nap. For example, they cite every pragmatic political excuse for Kennedy's trepid record on McCarthyism, and Sorensen himself takes full blame for not pairing him against McCarthy in the Senate vote on censure. (Since Kennedy was incommunicado in the hospital and had not heard the final debate, says his loyal assistant, Sorensen felt it would be in violation of due process to record his vote.) Kennedy, having assailed Eisenhower for failing to issue an executive order forbidding racial discrimination in federally financed housing, then sat on the same order for nearly two years after he took office, but *his* delay is treated as an instance of his shrewd sense of values—even grace under pressure—since the controversial edict would have endangered the rest of his legislative program. The excuse is not extended retroactively to his predecessor.

The band of brothers combines to portray Mrs. Roosevelt as a villainess, as indeed she appeared to Kennedy in the pre-nomination days when she held him in deep distrust and maneuvered her forces in favor of Stevenson and Humphrey. And although Kennedy did once telephone the *New York Times* and suggest a vacation for David Halberstam, whose Vietnam dispatches were rankling, he made the call, argues Salinger, knowing full well that its effect would be to insure Halberstam's continued presence in Southeast Asia. As for the Cuban invasion, some of the press at the time noted that while Kennedy at his own desk was manfully taking entire responsibility for the disaster, his staff in the outer office was plying newspapermen with evidence that the debacle was really the fault of the C.I.A., the Joint Chiefs of Staff, and the previous administration. In their books they are still at it. But then, as Sorensen writes: "This is not . . . a neutral account. An impassioned participant cannot be an objective observer."

Still, if we should not be surprised to find Kennedy's friends giving him the best of it, it's all right, perhaps, to be taken aback when Schlesinger in the *Life* serialization of *A Thousand Days* has the President crying in his wife's arms after the Cuban setback and then removes the scene from his published book, announcing that "it sounded sob-sisterish" and "didn't come off." Apparently where John Kennedy is concerned, the previous winner of the Bancroft, Parkman, and Pulitzer prizes for history thinks of historic material as something that may be tried this way, turned around and tried that way, and balled up and discarded if it doesn't seem entirely becoming to the subject. And then there is the matter of the style sheet that probably didn't need to be sent to these prospective authors since they knew the house rules. Among its apparent proscriptions:

Don't call Bobby "Bobby," as everybody else does. Salinger, Sorensen, Fay, and Mrs. Lincoln dutifully make it "Bob." Schlesinger prefers "Robert Kennedy," even in describing the celebrated occasion when, fully clothed, he jumped or fell into Robert's swimming pool. There are a few exceptions, almost unavoidable since the books are full of remarks by their President in which he used the politically awkward diminutive. Schlesinger breaks ranks all the way on the few pages that cover the events at the 1960 convention after Kennedy offered Johnson the vice-presidential nomination and, apparently to his astonishment, was accepted, and his brother then appeared in the Johnson hotel suite on what Johnson interpreted as a campaign to talk him out of it. In the farrago that followed, right out of the second act of *Three Men on a Horse*, the cast of characters included another Bobby, last name Baker. Possibly Schlesinger won a special dispensation, arguing that to play fair and also call the latter "Robert" struck him as a bit much. However, in the account of the same melee by Sorensen, now quite a formal fellow for a born-and-bred Nebraskan, it is "Robert Baker."

Pretend you always called the President's wife "Mrs. Kennedy" or "Jacqueline," not *"Jackie,"* as the whole world knows her. Although he complies, this stipulation must have been a particular drag to Paul Fay, a highly informal type whose own wife the President always referred to as "the Bride," who knew Kennedy for many years as "Shafty Boy," and who shared with him a fraternity of pals called, in middle age as in their youthful Navy days, by such nicknames as Bitter Bill, Dirty John, and Jim Jam Jumping Jim.

The President's father is not to be called "Joe," "Old Joe," or "Big Joe." *Refer to him as Mr. Joseph P. Kennedy or "the Ambassador"—and always respectfully.* ("I would like to see Red Fay write this story if my father was not ill—I think it is an outrage," runs a notation on the Fay manuscript beside an anecdote about Kennedy, Sr., that did not appear in the book.)

Rules having to do with nomenclature need not signify much. Yet anyone reading a biography of Jack Kennedy that leaves out characters called "Jackie," "Bobby," and "Big Joe" may be entitled to wonder what else has been omitted to suit his survivors. The only matters suppressed in his book, says Sorensen, are those absent "for reasons of security or propriety." One of the men delegated by Mrs. Kennedy to help blue-pencil the Fay as well as the Salinger efforts is J. Kenneth Galbraith (who once wrote an essay on the general topic of the political build-up, which he defined as "synthesizing a public reputation as a matter of deliberate design"). Most of the deletions that were eventually made in the books in question, he wrote recently, "involved the elimination of language or anecdotes which, out of context, cast reflection on the dignity of the office of President or which might, without purpose, have injured the feelings of personal friends of President Kennedy"—a patriotic and benevolent censorship policy with built-in conveniences. Mrs. Kennedy, he added, insisted on protecting more feelings—that is, removing more material—than he thought strictly necessary. One noticeable excision from all the books, just for openers: the name of any woman Kennedy ever had the slightest interest in other than his wife, unless you count Mrs. Lincoln's passing reference to a few anonymous girls so unimportant to Kennedy in his premarital years that he usually took them to the movies once apiece and had his secretary set up the dates at that. One of Fay's unforgiven transgressions, according to rumor, is his casual mention of the presence at the inaugural festivities, presumably with Kennedy's approval, of a young actress the President is said to have admired. Other evidence in the Fay book makes it obvious that Grand Old Lovable saw a great deal of his old Navy friend in the decade between the PT-boat episode and Kennedy's marriage at the rather advanced age of thirty-six, but virtually everything that went on in that unencumbered time is apparently among the thousands of words that Fay was persuaded to sacrifice in the vain hope of staying in the family favor. His book was published by Harper and Row, which had brought out *Profiles in Courage* and at the time was hoping to publish Manchester's *Death of a President* without legal incident. Clearly, if the present keepers of the eternal flame can prevent it, there will be no Ann Rutledge chapter in the Kennedy legend.

Lincoln once found a life of Edmund Burke "so lavish in praise of his every act that one is almost driven to believe that Burke never made a mistake or a failure in his life." Most biographies, he grumbled, "commemorate a lie, and cheat posterity out of the truth." Kennedy had a similar complaint after reading the first volume of Eisenhower's autobiography. "Apparently Ike never did anything wrong," he said. "When we come to writing the memoirs of this administration, we'll do it differently." Whatever blocking tactics Kennedy tried to use on books about himself during his long campaign for the Presidency, once that was won and then irrevocably lost, it was his remark about biography and infallibility that his personal historians tried to keep in mind. Despite all their excuses for him *vis-à-vis* McCarthy, they felt free to conclude that in many respects he was "insensitive" and "wrong" on this issue. After all the many alibis for the Bay of Pigs, his performance there is labelled essentially "stupid"—and, as is often the case in these books, the harsh judgment is his own.

Kennedy's part in the Vietnam war is not glossed over: it was "his great failure in foreign policy." The influence of his humor and instinct for self-mockery is consistently present, as when Sorensen points out that in his chapter on the 1960 fight for the nomination he finds that he has referred to powerful Kennedy supporters as "political leaders" while those in the opposition camp are "bosses," who are then converted to "political leaders" when they come over to the right side. And though Ambassador Kennedy gets the specified respectful treatment, his son Jack made a telling remark that is also available for balance. It came after a Georgia court had sent Dr. Martin Luther King, Jr., to jail and Kennedy had made a sympathy call to King's pregnant wife. On learning of the call, King's father announced that it had persuaded him to support Kennedy, whom he had planned to vote against on strictly religious grounds. The candidate's comment was, "Imagine Martin Luther King having a bigot for a father. . . . Well, we all have fathers, don't we?"

Soon after he took office, Kennedy directed the Voice of America to broadcast the nation's story "with all our blemishes and warts, all those things about us that may not be so immediately attractive." If certain of his own blemishes are still considered unmentionable, the authorized accounts are not without authorized warts. They don't hesitate to mention his crankiness, his scorching sarcasm and quick temper, his lack of consideration for those working for him, and his impatience with anyone, no matter how worthy, who bored him. Although only an infrequent "son of a bitch" or "kicked in the can" is quoted, there is no pretense that his language in private was in keeping with his posthumous saintlike image. Even the White House nannie tells of an occasion when Caroline left behind in Kennedy's office a large doll whose special accomplishment was that it would repeat whatever was said to it. The feat involved a tape recorder, and the next day when Caroline retrieved the doll and pressed the proper button, there emerged from its rosebud plastic lips Daddy's angriest voice, using, said Miss Shaw, "a very naughty word." Not knowing how to erase the tape, she hastily called a Secret Service agent to perform a disembowelment.*

The books by Kennedy's three White House assistants are, of course, the memoirs that will be of serious interest to future historians. Of these the gracefully written *A Thousand Days* is much the best job. After all, Schlesinger has been arranging presidential crises into orderly chapters for two decades. Moreover, most of his White House years were spent not in Kennedy's West Wing wheelhouse but in the East Wing writing voluminous memos, from which task he would be summoned now and then for advice or for a bit of political legwork. His engagement in Kennedy's program was not the roll-call-by-roll-call affair that it was to Sorensen and Salinger, and

*Curiously, Miss Shaw's account of the day of the assassination omits Caroline's harrowing ride through the Washington streets with a Secret Service man just after the news from Dallas began to come in, the episode that *Death of a President* relates in such detail. Caroline and John, she says, had just had lunch at the White House with Teddy Kennedy's children and were about to be put down for their naps when the word came. Thus, as in so many aspects of the Kennedy saga, historians are reminded of how variable is the human memory of events even so soon after the fact.

he was able to view it with some perspective against a background of what had gone before and what was happening elsewhere and was thus able to write a book that is more the history of an exhilarating national interval than the biography of one man. Sorensen's *Kennedy* is shorter than the Schlesinger book (758 pages *vs.* 1,031) but it gives the impression of being far longer, since it covers in dense detail the last eleven years of Kennedy's life (Schlesinger was involved only in the last four) from a vantage point rarely more than a centimeter from Kennedy's elbow. Salinger's *With Kennedy* is a slighter book than either of these; yet it has a certain long-range interest, especially in its accounts of the vast preparations for total war in October, 1962, the problems confronting the American press during the two Cuban crises, and his own comparative intimacy with individual Russians, including Khrushchev.

Before joining Kennedy's staff, reports Schlesinger, he was warned that he would be plunging into "a ruthless scramble for access and power." He found instead that "the Kennedy White House remained to the end remarkably free of the rancor which has so often welled up in Presidential households." Although the three members of the brotherhood whose memories of Kennedy are now in print often deal with the same event, in which each played some part, little jockeying for historical position clutters their books. Their put-downs and waspish digs are generally reserved for others, usually those not wearing a PT-boat tie clasp. Here also the influence of Kennedy as editor-*in-absentia* is apparent. "Nor would he tolerate from his staff the slightest disparagement of the Vice President," notes Schlesinger, and although it may have taken some self-control, there are no swipes at the Vice President by these witnesses. All three, in fact, write with sympathy of Johnson's understandable discomfort in his diminished role. Kennedy's biographers feel freer to let their disparagement show, however, in reporting the 1960 convention when the two politicians were sworn enemies and, as Schlesinger puts it with historical detachment, Johnson was "laying about with heavy saber strokes, Kennedy mastering him with an urbane and deadly rapier." As for Rusk, since Kennedy's commitment to him was no longer total by 1963, Sorensen and Schlesinger permit themselves to write of him with less than total Saint Crispin's Day loyalty. He was "almost too amiably cautious," "bland," "colorless," "Buddha-like," and so circumspect that during any given crisis "no one knew quite where he stood."

There have been complaints, of course, that it was unseemly for Kennedy confidants to rush into print—and then off to the bank—with their versions of events that were so recent and that in some cases involved men still in office. But some historians will presumably be grateful that these reports were published while the memories of the impassioned participants were fresh and feisty rather than, like the biography by Lincoln's secretaries, written decades later when the excitements of the age were measured from a stately distance. As for their lack of neutrality and occasional discreet excision, perhaps their degree of candor should be compared to that of accounts of the Eisenhower administration that Sherman Adams or George Humphrey might have written if *their* President had died in office—whether or not the testimonials had been cleared with his survivors.

History, like the news, has always been subject to some management, but the stage directions should be out of earshot. The question is how far the Kennedys and company propose to carry their by now conspicuous presumption. Only three of Kennedy's ten White House assistants and none of his Cabinet have so far been heard from. But nearly all of them, it now appears, scurried directly home from the West Wing each night to write in their diaries, and the next wave of memoirs should start rolling from the type-writers soon. The planned collaboration by the Irish Mafia—Ken O'Donnell, Dave Powers, and Larry O'Brien—will apparently be a mere tandem affair. O'Brien, unlike the rest of the old gang, is still welcomed in the redecorated West Wing where augmenting the J.F.K. mythology is not politically healthy. But doubtless O'Brien's version will not be permanently withheld from us.

Will the heirs and tenders of the Kennedy mystique continue to assert editorial rights over each new volume, and will the authors acknowledge their eminent domain? No doubt it will depend on whether the authors firmly believe that a new Saint Crispin's Day lies ahead and care to keep their place among the happy brotherhood around the new Henry V. If so, they will probably see the merit of not tampering with the legend. After all, the saintly-Lincoln myth that flourished after 1865 was of prodigious value to the then-new Republican party, whose dubious political caracoles in the next decades often took place behind a blown-up poster image of a much-loved President dead by an assassin's hand.

Kennedy's inaugural message was written after Sorensen, at the President-elect's direction, made a searching study of the Gettysburg Address, try-ing to discover its magic formula for immortality. To White House gratifica-tion, Sam Rayburn announced after hearing the result of this effort that Kennedy was "better than Lincoln" ("I think—I really think—he's a man of destiny"). But in *Portrait of a President*, his first book on Kennedy, published before he became a true, genuflecting believer, William Manchester wrote: "Certainly John Kennedy is not as lovable as Abe. He has a weaker grasp on the nation's heartstrings, and the reason isn't that he hasn't been shot." It was, of course, after he was shot that the two names began to be linked in an incessant litany. (The other two assassinated Presidents, Garfield and McKinley, were way out of it.) Reams were written about their common vein of humor, their similar fatalism about the danger of assassination, their century-apart (and equally gingerly) enlistment of the authority of the Presidency to help the Negro cause. Jim Bishop, who had written *The Day Lincoln Was Shot* and was soon making plans to give the same treatment to November 22, 1963, played a macabre game in the Hearst papers, listing numerous other similarities—from the fact that both men were succeeded by Vice Presidents named Johnson to the discovery that the names John Wilkes Booth and Lee Harvey Oswald had fifteen letters each. And right after the murder, Bill Mauldin's cartoon in the Chicago *Sun-Times* showed the statue in the Lincoln Memorial covering its face with its hands.

"Find out how Lincoln was buried," were Jacqueline Kennedy's words to Chief of Protocol Angier Biddle Duke a few moments after Air Force One landed at the Washington airport on the tragic flight from Dallas. It was not a precedent that was desirable to follow in all details. After the Washington rites, Lincoln's body was borne on a dead march through a dozen cities before finally being laid to rest in Springfield on May 4, nearly three harrowing weeks after the murder. The Lincoln funeral arrangements were in the hands of Secretary of War Stanton, the widow being bedfast and only half-lucid. Fortunately for the nation, Mrs. Kennedy was of a different mettle. Indeed it seems probable that the memory of her strength and heartbreaking dignity and the part she played in getting the American people through that terrible weekend will make it impossible for most of them to find serious fault with anything she does for the rest of her days (unless, as she herself shrewdly put it three years later, "I do something silly like run away with Eddie Fisher"). At her direction, Kennedy's coffin, like Lincoln's, stood in the candlelit East Room of the White House beneath chandeliers draped in black, and then in the great rotunda of the Capitol on the same catafalque, covered in black velvet, that had held Lincoln's coffin. Following the ninety-eight-year-old scenario, six gray horses drew it down Pennsylvania Avenue to the same muffled roll of drums. Behind the wooden caisson walked, as in 1865, a riderless gelding with boots reversed in the stirrups, the military symbol of the fallen warrior. Two weeks later when Mrs. Kennedy and her children left the White House, the new tenants found that, in case anyone had missed the point, the names of the two murdered Presidents were now permanently linked in stone. The words "In this room lived John Fitzgerald Kennedy with his wife Jacqueline during the two years, ten months, and two days he was President of the United States, January 20, 1961–November 22, 1963" had been carved in the white marble fireplace of what had been Kennedy's bedroom, directly below those that had long read: "In this room Abraham Lincoln slept during his occupancy of the White House as President of the United States, March 4, 1861–April 13, 1865." It is doubtful if A. Philip Randolph, who a few days earlier had said that Kennedy's "place in history will be next to Abraham Lincoln," expected his words to be followed so literally, or so soon. But what seems most remarkable of all is that Abraham Lincoln found his place—in history, graven in stone, enshrined in legend—although at the time of his death his widow was the kind of woman no one paid any attention to, and he hadn't a father, mother, sister, or brother to his name.

America as Peaceful Belligerent:
A Myth Revisited

J. William Fulbright

History suggests the tendency of great nations to equate power with
virtue, and world responsibility with universal mission. Certainly
America qualifies in this regard; if she has not always claimed the
mandate of God for her sometimes intemperate posture in foreign
affairs, certainly her "arrogance of power" has been solidly based
upon her mythical sense of destiny. Grasping these qualities of ambiguity and paradox in the American past, J. William Fulbright, U.S.
Senator and former President of the University of Arkansas, isolates
two major, opposing threads in American foreign policy: the tradition
of Abraham Lincoln–Adlai Stevenson, and the tradition of Theodore
Roosevelt; the former humane, the latter belligerent. In her international conduct, America has too often followed the Roosevelt tradition
—unfortunate indeed, for it has been a tradition nurtured by myth.

America is the most fortunate of nations—fortunate in her rich territory,
fortunate in having had a century of relative peace in which to develop that
territory, fortunate in her diverse and talented population, fortunate in the
institutions devised by the founding fathers and in the wisdom of those who
have adapted those institutions to a changing world.

For the most part America has made good use of her blessings, especially
in her internal life but also in her foreign relations. Having done so much and
succeeded so well, America is now at that historical point at which a great
nation is in danger of losing its perspective on what exactly is within the
realm of its power and what is beyond it. Other great nations, reaching this
critical juncture, have aspired to too much, and by overextension of effort
have declined and then fallen.

The causes of the malady are not entirely clear, but its recurrence is one
of the uniformities of history: power tends to confuse itself with virtue and
a great nation is peculiarly susceptible to the idea that its power is a sign of
God's favor, conferring upon it a special responsibility for other nations—
to make them richer and happier and wiser, to remake them, that is, in its
own shining image. Power confuses itself with virtue and tends also to take
itself for omnipotence. Once imbued with the idea of a mission, a great
nation easily assumes that it has the means as well as the duty to do God's
work. The Lord, after all, surely would not choose you as His agent and then

deny you the sword with which to work His will. German soldiers in the First World War wore belt buckles imprinted with the words *"Gott mit uns."* It was approximately under this kind of infatuation—an exaggerated sense of power and an imaginary sense of mission—that the Athenians attacked Syracuse and Napoleon and then Hitler invaded Russia. In plain words, they overextended their commitments and they came to grief.

I do not think for a moment that America, with her deeply rooted democratic traditions, is likely to embark upon a campaign to dominate the world in the manner of a Hitler or Napoleon. What I do fear is that she may be drifting into commitments which, though generous and benevolent in intent, are so far-reaching as to exceed even America's great capacities. At the same time, it is my hope—and I emphasize it because it underlies all of the criticisms and proposals to be made in these pages—that America will escape those fatal temptations of power which have ruined other great nations and will instead confine herself to doing only that good in the world which she *can* do, both by direct effort and by the force of her own example.

The stakes are high indeed: they include not only America's continued greatness but nothing less than the survival of the human race in an era when, for the first time in human history, a living generation has the power of veto over the survival of the next.

When the abstractions and subtleties of political science have been exhausted, there remain the most basic unanswered questions about war and peace and why nations contest the issues they contest and why they even care about them. As Aldous Huxley has written:

> There may be arguments about the best way of raising wheat in a cold climate or of re-afforesting a denuded mountain. But such arguments never lead to organized slaughter. Organized slaughter is the result of arguments about such questions as the following: Which is the best nation? The best religion? The best political theory? The best form of government? Why are other people so stupid and wicked? Why can't they see how good and intelligent *we* are? Why do they resist our beneficent efforts to bring them under our control and make them like ourselves?[1]

Many of the wars fought by man—I am tempted to say most—have been fought over such abstractions. The more I puzzle over the great wars of history, the more I am inclined to the view that the causes attributed to them—territory, markets, resources, the defense or perpetuation of great principles—were not the root causes at all but rather explanations or excuses for certain unfathomable drives of human nature. For lack of a clear and precise understanding of exactly what these motives are, I refer to them as the "arrogance of power"—as a psychological need that nations seem to have in order to prove that they are bigger, better, or stronger than other nations. Implicit in this drive is the assumption, even on the part of normally peaceful nations, that force is the ultimate proof of superiority—that when a nation shows that it has the stronger army, it is also proving that it has better people, better institutions, better principles, and, in general, a better civilization.

Evidence for my proposition is found in the remarkable discrepancy between the apparent and hidden causes of some modern wars and the discrepancy between their causes and ultimate consequences.

The precipitating cause of the Franco-Prussian War of 1870, for example, was a dispute over the succession to the Spanish throne, and the ostensible "underlying" cause was French resistance to the unification of Germany. The war was followed by the completion of German unification—which probably could have been achieved without war—but it was also followed by the loss of Alsace-Lorraine, the humiliation of France, and the emergence of Germany as the greatest power in Europe, which could not have been achieved without war. The peace treaty, incidentally, said nothing about the Spanish throne, which everyone apparently had forgotten. One wonders to what extent the Germans were motivated simply by the desire to cut those haughty Frenchmen down to size and have a good excuse to build another monument in Berlin.

The United States went to war in 1898 for the stated purpose of liberating Cuba from Spanish tyranny, but after winning the war—a war which Spain had been willing to pay a high price to avoid—the United States brought the liberated Cubans under an American protectorate and incidentally annexed the Philippines, because, according to President McKinley, the Lord told him it was America's duty "to educate the Filipinos, and uplift and civilize and Christianize them, and by God's grace do the very best we could by them, as our fellowmen for whom Christ also died."[2]

Isn't it interesting that the voice was the voice of the Lord but the words were those of Theodore Roosevelt, Henry Cabot Lodge, and Admiral Mahan, those "imperialists of 1898" who wanted America to have an empire just because a big, powerful country like the United States *ought* to have an empire? The spirit of the times was expressed by Albert Beveridge, soon thereafter to be elected to the United States Senate, who proclaimed Americans to be "a conquering race": "We must obey our blood and occupy new markets and if necessary new lands," he said, because "In the Almighty's infinite plan . . . debased civilizations and decaying races" must disappear "before the higher civilization of the nobler and more virile types of man."[3]

In 1914 all Europe went to war, ostensibly because the heir to the Austrian throne had been assassinated at Sarajevo, but really because that murder became the symbolic focus of the incredibly delicate sensibilities of the great nations of Europe. The events of the summer of 1914 were a melodrama of abnormal psychology: Austria had to humiliate Serbia in order not to be humiliated herself but Austria's effort at recovering self-esteem was profoundly humiliating to Russia; Russia was allied to France, who had been feeling generally humiliated since 1871, and Austria in turn was allied to Germany, whose pride required that she support Austria no matter how insanely Austria behaved and who may in any case have felt that it would be fun to give the German Army another swing down the Champs-Elysées. For these ennobling reasons the world was plunged into a war which took tens of millions of lives, precipitated the Russian Revolution, and set in motion the events that led to another world war, a war which took tens of millions more lives and precipitated the worldwide revolutions of our time, revolutions whose consequences are beyond the foresight of any of us now alive.

The causes and consequences of war may have more to do with pathology than with politics, more to do with irrational pressures of pride and pain than with rational calculations of advantage and profit. There is a Washington story, perhaps apocryphal, that the military intellectuals in the Pentagon conducted an experiment in which they fed data derived from the events of the summer of 1914 into a computer and that, after weighing and digesting the evidence, the machine assured its users that there was no danger of war. What this "proves," if anything, is that computers are more rational than men; it also suggests that if there is a root cause of human conflict and of the power drive of nations, it lies not in economic aspirations, historical forces, or the workings of the balance of power, but in the ordinary hopes and fears of the human mind.

It has been said that buried in every woman's secret soul is a drum majorette; it might also be said that in all of our souls there is a bit of the missionary. We all like telling people what to do, which is perfectly all right except that most people do not like being told what to do. I have given my wife some splendid suggestions on household management but she has been so consistently ungrateful for my advice that I have stopped offering it. The phenomenon is explained by the Canadian psychiatrist and former Director-General of the World Health Organization, Brock Chisholm, who writes:

> ... Man's method of dealing with difficulties in the past has always been to tell everyone else how they should behave. We've all been doing that for centuries.
> It should be clear by now that this no longer does any good. Everybody has by now been told by everybody else how he should behave. ... The criticism is not effective; it never has been, and it never is going to be. ... [4]

Ineffective though it has been, the giving—and enforcement—of all this unsolicited advice has at least until recently been compatible with the survival of the human race. Man is now, however, for the first time, in a situation in which the survival of his species is in jeopardy. Other forms of life have been endangered and many destroyed by changes in their natural environment; man is menaced by a change of environment which he himself has wrought by the invention of nuclear weapons and ballistic missiles. Our power to kill has become universal, creating a radically new situation which, if we are to survive, requires us to adopt some radically new attitudes about the giving and enforcement of advice and in general about human and international relations.

The enormity of the danger of extinction of our species is dulled by the frequency with which it is stated, as if a familiar threat of catastrophe were no threat at all. We seem to feel somehow that because the hydrogen bomb has not killed us yet, it is never going to kill us. This is a dangerous assumption because it encourages the retention of traditional attitudes about world politics when our responsibility, in Dr. Chisholm's words, is nothing less than "to re-examine all of the attitudes of our ancestors and to select from those attitudes things which we, on our own authority in these present circumstances, with our knowledge, recognize as still valid in this new kind of world. . . ."[5]

The attitude above all others which I feel sure is no longer valid is the arrogance of power, the tendency of great nations to equate power with virtue and major responsibilities with a universal mission. The dilemmas involved are pre-eminently American dilemmas, not because America has weaknesses that others do not have but because America is powerful as no nation has ever been before, and the discrepancy between her power and the power of others appears to be increasing. One may hope that America, with her vast resources and democratic traditions, with her diverse and creative population, will find the wisdom to match her power; but one can hardly be confident because the wisdom required is greater wisdom than any great nation has ever shown before. It must be rooted, as Dr. Chisholm says, in the re-examination of "all of the attitudes of our ancestors." . . .

There are two Americas. One is the America of Lincoln and Adlai Stevenson; the other is the America of Teddy Roosevelt and the modern superpatriots. One is generous and humane, the other narrowly egotistical; one is self-critical, the other self-righteous; one is sensible, the other romantic; one is good-humored, the other solemn; one is inquiring, the other pontificating; one is moderate, the other filled with passionate intensity; one is judicious and the other arrogant in the use of great power.

We have tended in the years of our great power to puzzle the world by presenting to it now the one face of America, now the other, and sometimes both at once. Many people all over the world have come to regard America as being capable of magnanimity and farsightedness but no less capable of pettiness and spite. The result is an inability to anticipate American actions which in turn makes for apprehension and a lack of confidence in American aims.

The inconstancy of American foreign policy is not an accident but an expression of two distinct sides of the American character. Both are characterized by a kind of moralism, but one is the morality of decent instincts tempered by the knowledge of human imperfection and the other is the morality of absolute self-assurance fired by the crusading spirit. The one is exemplified by Lincoln, who found it strange, in the words of his second Inaugural Address, "that any man should dare to ask for a just God's assistance in wringing their bread from the sweat of other men's faces," but then added: "let us judge not, that we be not judged." The other is exemplified by Theodore Roosevelt, who in his December 6, 1904, Annual Message to Congress, without question or doubt as to his own and his country's capacity to judge right and wrong, proclaimed the duty of the United States to exercise an "internal police power" in the hemisphere on the ground that "Chronic wrongdoing, or an impotence which results in a general loosening of the ties of civilized society, may in America ... ultimately require intervention by some civilized nation...." Roosevelt of course never questioned that the "wrongdoing" would be done by our Latin neighbors and we of course were the "civilized nation" with the duty to set things right.

After twenty-five years of world power the United States must decide which of the two sides of its national character is to predominate—the humanism of Lincoln or the arrogance of those who would make America the world's policeman. One or the other will help shape the spirit of the age—unless of course we refuse to choose, in which case America may come to play a less important role in the world, leaving the great decisions to others.

The current tendency is toward a more strident and aggressive American foreign policy, which is to say, toward a policy closer to the spirit of Theodore Roosevelt than of Lincoln. We are still trying to build bridges to the communist countries and we are still, in a small way, helping the poorer nations to make a better life for their people; but we are also involved in a growing war against Asian communism, a war which began and might have ended as a civil war if American intervention had not turned it into a contest of ideologies, a war whose fallout is disrupting our internal life and complicating our relations with most of the world.

Our national vocabulary has changed with our policies. A few years ago we were talking of détente and building bridges, of five-year plans in India and Pakistan, or agricultural cooperatives in the Dominican Republic, and land and tax reform all over Latin America. Today these subjects are still discussed in a half-hearted and desultory way but the focus of power and interest has shifted to the politics of war. Diplomacy has become largely image-making, and instead of emphasizing plans for social change, the policy-planners and political scientists are conjuring up "scenarios" of escalation and nuclear confrontation and "models" of insurgency and counterinsurgency.

The change in words and values is no less important than the change in policy, because words *are* deeds and style *is* substance insofar as they influence men's minds and behavior. What seems to be happening, as Archibald MacLeish has put it, is that "the feel of America in the world's mind" has begun to change and faith in "the idea of America" has been shaken for the world and, what is more important, for our own people. MacLeish is suggesting—and I think he is right—that much of the idealism and inspiration is disappearing from American policy, but he also points out that they are not yet gone and by no means are they irretrievable:

> . . . if you look closely and listen well, there is a human warmth, a human meaning which nothing has killed in almost twenty years and which nothing is likely to kill. . . . What has always held this country together is an idea—a dream if you will—a large and abstract thought of the sort the realistic and the sophisticated may reject but mankind can hold to.[6]

The foremost need of American foreign policy is a renewal of dedication to an "idea that mankind can hold to"—not a missionary idea full of pretensions about being the world's policemen but a Lincolnian idea expressing that powerful strand of decency and humanity which is the true source of America's greatness. . . .

For my own part, I prefer the America of Lincoln and Adlai Stevenson. I prefer to have my country the friend rather than the enemy of demands for social justice; I prefer to have the communists treated as human beings, with all the human capacity for good and bad, for wisdom and folly, rather than as embodiments of an evil abstraction; and I prefer to see my country in the role of sympathetic friend to humanity rather than its stern and prideful schoolmaster.

There are many respects in which America, if she can bring herself to act with the magnanimity and the empathy which are appropriate to her size and power, can be an intelligent example to the world. We have the opportunity to set an example of generous understanding in our relations with China, of practical cooperation for peace in our relations with Russia, of reliable and respectful partnership in our relations with Western Europe, of material helpfulness without moral presumption in our relations with developing nations, of abstention from the temptations of hegemony in our relations with Latin America, and of the all-around advantages of minding one's own business in our relations with everybody. Most of all, we have the opportunity to serve as an example of democracy to the world by the way in which we run our own society. America, in the words of John Quincy Adams, should be "the well-wisher to the freedom and independence of all" but "the champion and vindicator only of her own."[7]

If we can bring ourselves so to act, we will have overcome the dangers of the arrogance of power. It would involve, no doubt, the loss of certain glories, but that seems a price worth paying for the probable rewards, which are the happiness of America and the peace of the world.

Notes

1. Aldous Huxley, "The Politics of Ecology" (Santa Barbara: Center for the Study of Democratic Institutions, 1963), p. 6.
2. Quoted in Samuel Flagg Bemis, *A Diplomatic History of the United States* (New York: Henry Holt, 1955), p. 472.
3. Quoted in Barbara Tuchman, *The Proud Tower* (New York: Macmillan, 1966), p. 153.
4. Brock Chisholm, *Prescription for Survival* (New York: Columbia University Press, 1957), p. 54.
5. *Ibid.*, p. 9.
6. Archibald MacLeish, Address to the Congress of the International Publishers Association, May 31, 1965.
7. John Quincy Adams, July 4, 1821, Washington, D.C. Reported in *The National Intelligencer*, July 11, 1821.

Image and Reality in Indochina

Harrison E. Salisbury

The idea of myth implies that it is instructive to study the differences between reality and men's view of reality. In the judgement
of Harrison E. Salisbury, Assistant Managing Editor of the *New
York Times*, such a frame of reference is viable as regards the
nature and goals of the U.S. policy in Indochina. The interplay between myth and reality as it has affected America's Vietnam policy,
Mr. Salisbury advises, began even before our entry into the Second
World War. It has continued unabated ever since. A dimension of
complexity has been added, however, in that the mythical images
have undergone constant change, and that they have become common to all parties concerned. In this instance, the past could well
prove to be prologue; the distortions that have plagued the Indochina question in the past are likely to continue in the future.

Re-examining the thirty and more years since Indochina entered the agenda
of world problems one is struck constantly by the curious mirages, the dis-
cordance between image and reality which seem to persist not only in
American perceptions of Indochina but in the evaluations by other great
powers and the Indochinese themselves of the actual nature and goals of
U.S. policy.

We are all familiar with the "mirror image" phenomenon in which two
rival powers tend to see each other in somewhat similar turns of threat, each
mirroring the other's fears and expectations, thus often giving rise to self-
fulfilling prophecies. The Indochina phenomenon is different. It lies in a
distortion of perception in which one, two or more powers see a different
sequence of events as being in progress, each one of these images having
little or no resemblance to reality or to the image in the consciousness of the
other powers. It strikingly reminds one of the classic Japanese story of
Rashomon. An event, a series of events takes place. But exactly what were
these events? To each participant it seems that a different thing has happened.
We see the tragedy through the eyes of one participant after the other. Each
vision is so different, so contradictory, that in the end we can never be
certain of what it is that has actually transpired.

So it is with Indochina. I think that it is this diverse interplay of myth
and reality, this inability at almost any given moment to find common understanding not only of motivation but of the nature of current evolutions which

From "Image and Reality in Indochina," by Harrison E. Salisbury. Reprinted by
permission from *Foreign Affairs*, April 1971.

has placed resolution of the Indochina problem almost beyond the reach of even the most skillful diplomats.

For the United States this process began long, long ago. Even before our entry into World War II, President Roosevelt was expressing to Admiral Leahy, our ambassador to Vichy, the essence of what came to be an *idée fixe* —that French colonial policy in Indochina (and to a lesser extent that of the Dutch in the East Indies and the British in Southeast Asia) was "responsible" for the aggressions of the Japanese. Indeed, later, FDR went so far as to blame the whole war in the Pacific on the colonial powers and, specifically, on the French. He advised Leahy on July 29, 1941, that "if Japan wins Japan gets Indochina—if the Allies win *we* would" take it over. It is not likely that he contemplated an actual "U.S. takeover." More probably, he had in mind some kind of international supervision in which the United States would play a leading role.

It was the President's confused view that France and French policy in Indochina were "responsible" for Japan's aggression and that France must therefore be penalized, and specifically, that for this reason Indochina must never go back to the French. The President's position hardened with the years. He advanced it at the wartime meetings with Churchill and Stalin, winning mild, *pro forma* support from Stalin (who never displayed the slightest interest in this portion of the world) and indignation on the part of Churchill, who was always aroused by Roosevelt's stubborn desire to liquidate colonial empires.

Probably the acme of Rooseveltian schemes for Indochina (of course, by this time under the vicious occupation of the Japanese) was a proposal conveyed to Chiang Kai-shek through Vice President Wallace during his 1944 mission to Chungking in which he offered China a "trusteeship" over Indochina on the grounds that, after all, the Indochinese and the Chinese were "the same kind of people."

If Mr. Roosevelt's thesis that French conduct in Indochina put the Japanese on the road to Pearl Harbor was dubious, his assumption of communality between the peoples of Indochina and those of China displayed an even more profound distortion of reality, both ethnic and historic. Probably the most striking fact about the Indochinese (be they Vietnamese, Cambodians, Laotians or Montagnards) is their ethnic differentiation from the Han Chinese, the two thousand years of intermittent war and struggle between the Indochinese and the Chinese and the implacable hostility and fear with which most Indochinese regard the Chinese. It is no accident that the first visit of every foreigner coming to Hanoi is to the Museum of the Revolution where he is shown the historic record of the endless wars with the Chinese, combat that started at a time when the Vietnamese occupied areas of what is now South China, and is made acquainted with the national and folk heroes of Vietnam, all of them winning their fame in victories over the hated Chinese.

Fortunately, Chiang Kai-shek possessed a keener grasp of reality than FDR. He rejected Roosevelt's offer. There is no record as to what he thought the American motive might be but it would have been natural for him to think that the President was trying to stir up trouble for China in Southeast Asia.

Thus the situation stood at the time of FDR's death in April 1945. Because of his repeated insistence, the French were not permitted to participate in the liberation of Indochina. Under plans made before the President's death the Chinese accepted the Japanese surrender in the north and the British in the south.

This early episode makes plain that major illusions as to the nature of Indochina lay largely on the American side, that is, specifically, in President Roosevelt's mind. But another small yet significant episode involving Indochina and the United States was in the process of taking shape. A close and increasingly warm and friendly liaison had been established in Indochina between special U.S. forces (specifically, OSS teams) and the Vietminh, the nationalist Vietnamese movement, then led by Ho Chi Minh. These relations have sometimes been characterized in recent years in a rather sentimental way, as if they were compounded simply of goodwill and good feeling between the OSS team, on the one hand, and Ho, on the other. That genuine mutual regard existed on both sides there can be no doubt. When Ho in September 1945 proclaimed the new Republic of Vietnam he modelled his declaration on the U. S. Declaration of Independence, actually requesting of the OSS men a copy of the Declaration in order to copy its language in his draft. None of the OSS officers possessed a copy. None the less, the Vietnamese declaration begins: "All men are created equal. They are endowed by their Creator with certain inalienable rights, among these are Life, Liberty and the Pursuit of Happiness. . . ." At about the same time a delegation of Vietminh ladies called at the OSS Mission in Hanoi, asking to be put in touch with their sister American organization, the Daughters of the American Revolution. There is no record as to what, if anything, resulted from this bizarre effort.

The Americans saw in these relations a "natural" affinity between themselves and Ho's Vietminh. What did Ho see? Did he and his associates feel a kinship between their movement, their independence, their revolution and that of America? There was some such feeling, and even in his last years when deeply engaged in warfare with the United States Ho occasionally spoke with nostalgia of the Statue of Liberty (which he had seen as a young seaman) and of the principles of the American Constitution. But underlying this was something, of course, far more fundamental, as Ho's policy clearly revealed. In 1945 Ho had three major antagonists: the Japanese, who were being expelled from Indochina and who, presumably, would not soon again endanger the region; the French, who were only too eager to resume their colonial overlordship; and the Chinese, whom geography and history had made Indochina's traditional enemy.

What more natural, then, that Ho hoped to get a distant and presumably disinterested but important power involved as Indochina's chief protector? This would prevent the return of France and would hold the Chinese at bay. This was the classic policy of the weak power. It was the device which Turkey employed during its long years as "the sick man of Europe."

That, in fact, Ho was actually following the policy of the "lesser evil" quickly became apparent. When, after Roosevelt's death, U.S. policy changed, and the way was opened for France's return, Ho did not turn to the Chinese as a "protecting power" (as FDR might have expected). Rather, he sought to make a deal with the French and successfully concluded one which the French promptly violated. Anything, thus, rather than be thrust into the nearby Asian but dangerous arms of the Chinese. Even as the war with the French quickened Ho did not turn to China. The Vietminh fought on their own. Only after the emergence of Mao's communist régime, that is after—considerably after—1949, did Ho approach China and even then on a carefully limited and circumscribed basis.

This ancient history is useful as a benchmark in analyzing later development of great-power policy *vis-à-vis* Indochina. It shows the United States frequently misjudging the reality in Indochina. It shows Indochina misjudging the United States as well. It also shows marked realism—and antagonism—between Indochina and China and profound lack of interest in the whole region on the part of the Soviet Union.

Between 1945 and 1950 France was the principal outside power engaged in Indochina. U.S. interest was minimal. So was that of the Soviet Union. China, wracked by the great struggle of nationalists versus communists, had neither time nor inclination for affairs beyond its frontiers.

It was the success of the communist Chinese Revolution and the steadily deteriorating position of the French which finally brought Indochina back into American focus—but a focus which was probably more distorted than it had ever been before or was likely to be in the future.

From 1949 onward the official American perception of Indochina cannot be separated from the U.S. overview of the communist world and, specifically, of the Chinese Revolution. Mao's success was seen initially as a Chinese victory in a Chinese civil war. But this image quickly was to change. The signature of the Sino-Soviet Alliance, February 14, 1950, after a long visit to Moscow by Mao, was widely interpreted in and out of the U.S. government as primary evidence that the Kremlin had "put over" the Chinese Revolution and now dominated Peking.

As Senator McCarthy said on March 30, 1950: "It was not Chinese democracy under Mao that conquered China as Acheson, Lattimore and Jessup contended. Soviet Russia conquered China, and an important ally of this conqueror was the small left-wing element in our Department of State."

Or as Dean Rusk put it a year later, May 18, 1951: "We do not recognize the authorities in Peiping for what they pretend to be. The Peiping régime may be a colonial Russian government—a Slavic Manchukuo on a larger scale. It is not the Government of China. It does not pass the first test. It is not Chinese."

It was not necessary for Dean Acheson and President Truman to share this view in toto (although they may have moved very far in this direction by mid-spring 1950) for them to agree on May 8, 1950, to advance $10,000,-000 in credits to France for the support of the Bao Dai régime which was opposing Ho's Vietminh. By this time Acheson had been persuaded that the Kremlin was directing the Vietminh operations in Indochina.

The date of May 8, 1950, is an important one. Ordinarily it is assumed that the U.S. involvement in Vietnam occurred *after* Korea, that is in June 1950. In reality we had already begun to edge into Indochina *before* Korea under the perceived image of a united, powerful communist challenge, directed in Moscow and remarkably reinforced by the "puppet" régime in Peking.

What was the reality of China and the communist world at that moment?

We now know it was far, far different. Mao Tse-tung arrived in Moscow in early December 1949, having officially proclaimed his régime on October 1, 1949. The treaty with Stalin was signed nearly two months later, February 14, 1950. There was much evidence at that time (and even earlier) suggesting that Sino-Soviet relations were neither so close nor so warm as each party sought to indicate. But it was only after the open breach of the two powers and the polemics beginning in 1961 that Nikita Khrushchev revealed the reality—that China and Russia almost came to a parting of the ways in the very period when the world, and America in particular, concluded they were almost one and the same thing. Mao was so outraged by Stalin's "great power chauvinism," his insistence upon quasi-colonial agreements for the exploitation of China's natural resources, his determination to regain Russia's traditional economic and military posture in North China and Manchuria (and especially, the Dairen and Port Arthur bases) that Mao almost broke off talks. The two powers were held together only by their perception of the overwhelming danger of U.S. aggression.

The inference is clear that had President Truman and Secretary Acheson persisted in the policy which was almost surely their intention in the autumn of 1949, after Mao's October 1 proclamation and before his arrival in Moscow in December—that is, to move toward the recognition of the new Peking régime—this act alone would have been sufficient to derail the alliance of the two communist states and set China on the path of a far different course in world affairs.

Thus, by mid-spring 1950 America perceived a singular unity and direction of a Muscovite communist menace in Asia (which, in fact, did not exist) and the two communist powers perceived a unified aggressive U.S. policy (which, in fact, did not exist). What of the perceptions in Peking of Russia and in Moscow of Peking?

There is substantial evidence to indicate that Stalin, at least, envisaged Mao as much more of an immediate and direct threat than, perhaps, Mao saw Stalin. I support that conclusion with what I readily confess is a somewhat unorthodox hypothesis concerning the cause and origin of the Korean War. I believe the war was instigated by Stalin but that his target was not, as is supposed, the United States but actually communist China.

In general terms, we know that Stalin placed very little confidence in any foreign communist leaders, including those he had named himself. The long record of hostile relations between the Chinese Party and Stalin and the emergence of Mao with a program and a strategy almost diametrically opposed to Stalin's (Mao, of course, was repeatedly reprimanded and even expelled from the Central Committee and the party for his deviations) in itself would be strong evidence for Stalinist hostility. The years 1949 and 1950 were those of extreme paranoia on Stalin's part, so far as foreign parties were concerned, touched off by Tito's defiant break. These were the years when Stalin and his secret police put in motion the purges of the East European parties, eliminating the old wheelhorses and replacing them with even more handpicked police nominees. There was nothing in the emergence and success of Mao and his movement calculated to quiet Stalin's nerves. In Moscow he purged at least two suspected Maoists, Mikhail Borodin and Anna Louise Strong.

Moreover, there is compelling evidence that even before Mao proclaimed his régime Stalin had secretly begun to construct an apparatus in China, to be used for his own purposes when the time came. His vehicle was a Chinese party official named Kao Kang who emerged in early 1949 as the leader of the special Northeastern Autonomous region. As early as June and July of 1949 Kao Kang had been to Moscow and had signed special direct economic and other agreements. His relations with Moscow were extremely close, quite independent of Peking, and he was the virtual master of the most important industrial area of China. After Stalin's death convincing evidence came to light that Kao Kang was, in fact, Stalin's agent. He committed suicide and was charged by the Chinese with having been a traitor and with having plotted to turn Manchuria into a separate "kingdom." No public mention of whom he may have plotted with. The only plausible partner, of course, was Stalin, with whom he had so often conferred.

Premier Tsedenbal of Outer Mongolia has told me that one of Mao's first acts on coming to power was a request to Stalin for the return to Chinese suzerainty of Outer Mongolia. Stalin refused this request and tightened his control of this strategic area with its 1,500-mile frontier on China under his most reliable ally, the then party chief Choibalsan. He also improved Soviet military positions in Manchuria and North China by the terms of the 1950 treaty.

In the reality of the Soviet position *vis-à-vis* China the Korean venture assumes a radically new light. Acheson on January 12, 1950, speaking to the National Press Club in Washington, had drawn the U.S. defense line in the Pacific from Alaska and the Aleutians to Japan to the Ryukyus (Okinawa) and south to the Philippines. He did not mention Korea in this context. There were other similar statements (including one the year before by Mac-Arthur), but the Acheson declaration was the most important. It was specific, detailed, calculated. There could be no reason for the omission of Korea (although Acheson continues to argue otherwise), except that it was not, in fact, on the U.S. defense perimeter.

The United States and Russia had withdrawn their occupation forces from South and North Korea respectively. I think it is reasonable to assume that Stalin felt he could take Washington's word—that we did not feel obligated to rise to the defense of South Korea.

This, then, unexpectedly presented him with a tempting possibility: if he could overrun all of Korea he would, in fact (although Mao, ignorant of the secret Stalin-Kao Kang relationship, could not be aware of this) be able to dominate Peking from positions in Mongolia, Manchuria and Korea. He would possess the power to deal with Mao as he once said he would with Tito ("I'll shake my little finger and Tito will fall").

Khrushchev in his new volume of reminiscences depicts Kim Il-sung as coming to Moscow and asking permission to attack the South—permission which Stalin gave. If this hypothesis is correct, Stalin triggered the Korean War on the basis of a mistaken image of the U.S. position. He anticipated noninterference. He got, instead, massive intervention under the auspices of the United Nations.

But if Stalin's image of the U.S. position was distorted, the U.S. image of Korea, Russia and China was equally distorted. Whatever the inner convictions of President Truman and Secretary Acheson may have been regarding the instigator of the conflict they treated it as one, basically, of Chinese aggression. Moscow was asked to use its good offices in Pyongyang and Peking to persuade Kim Il-sung to withdraw. The U.S. response, outside of Korea, was entirely directed against the image of imminent Chinese aggression. The President not only ordered General MacArthur to take up Korea's defense. He gave Chiang Kai-shek the pledge specifically denied him in October 1949, an immediate defense blanket. He sent the Seventh Fleet into the Formosa Straits to bar an attack by communist China. He rushed military aid to the Philippines and sent (fateful move!) a military mission to aid the beleaguered French in Indochina.

Now, as can quite readily be determined today, there was no Chinese connection whatever with the Korean attack. There is every indication that Peking was as startled as Washington. The North Korean forces were armed and trained by the Russians. The Chinese had no part in that whatever. Kim Il-sung was a chosen Soviet agent for North Korea, trained by and devoted to Moscow. While the Soviet armed forces had left Korea in January 1949, Soviet specialists remained in all branches of the Korean military and government. The Chinese did not even send a diplomatic mission to North Korea until August 1950, two months after the attack occurred.

Of course, the hypothesis may be mistaken. Stalin may have given Mao some warning. But Mao's attention was deeply occupied at that time with the consolidation of his régime. He was busy with the absorption of Tibet and myriad other problems. His principal forward objective was Formosa, not Korea, and the Korean attack effectively put Formosa beyond his reach by the interposition of the U.S. fleet.

It is likely that Mao regarded the Korean move as a reckless Soviet gamble which confronted China with critical problems and serious dangers. If so, his analysis would have been fairly accurate, as the events of September and October 1950, the threat to the Yalu and the massive Chinese intervention, were to show. By this time, Stalin could see that his perception of U.S. policy had been grossly distorted and was probably quite willing to settle for as deep and complex an entanglement between the United States and China as could be produced. If his gambit for getting a stranglehold around Peking had failed, at least he had succeeded in embroiling two of his major antagonists.

However the Chinese may have perceived Soviet motivations in 1950, they have in recent years on several occasions informally cited the Korean War as a deliberate Soviet provocation, designed to embroil them with the United States. Certainly by the time that MacArthur approached the Yalu the Chinese had concluded that the American operations in Korea were only a springboard for an assault upon China and a reopening of the U.S. intervention which had come to a close with the departure of Chiang Kai-shek from the mainland.

Here, to be sure, the Chinese deluded themselves. While there clearly was MacArthurian enthusiasm for going into China, President Truman dramatically demonstrated a bit later that he had absolutely no intention of broadening the Korean engagement into a continental war with China.

What of events in Indochina?

Here again reality was quite different from the perceptions of most of the participants. Ho had appealed for recognition of his régime on January 14, 1950. The Chinese granted recognition January 18, the Russians not until January 30. But neither of the major communist powers sent any formal missions to North Vietnam until after the 1954 ceasefire. Nor, in the opinion of the late Bernard Fall, did any direct connections exist with the Soviet Union until that time. Indeed, in his opinion Hanoi's principal communist party link up to 1954 was with the French Communist Party, not the Russian, not the Chinese, further evidence of the cautious effort of the Vietnamese to avoid falling under domination of a force which might control them.

In contrast to this reality there is abundant evidence that Secretary of State Dulles fully shared the perception of President Truman and Secretary

Acheson (from June 1950 onwards) that Indochina was, in essence, merely the southern sector of a common front against China which extended from North Korea southward in a long curving arc. The truce in Korea did not shake the Dulles concept nor, in fact, did the Geneva agreement of 1954 which was designed to end the Indochina fighting. It is true that by this time, and particularly in the preparations of the Dien Bien Phu trap sprung against the French, Ho and General Giap were receiving a measure of cooperation from the Chinese, particularly in the form of rice to feed the besieging forces and the arms which were transported, broken down into loads carried by men and mules, some 1,500 miles from China.

But neither then nor later was it true, as Dulles and many U.S. policy-makers supposed, that Ho was a "puppet" of Peking or that Peking was a "puppet" of Moscow. Khrushchev's remembrances cast some, not necessarily clarifying, light on this relationship. He asserts that the Chinese believed that Ho's jig was up at the time of Dien Bien Phu, that the Vietminh had come to the end of the road—an analysis which would indicate that the Chinese were not in close touch with the real situation and the Russians in even less touch. He also recalls telling his colleagues on his return from his first visit with Mao in Peking in November 1954 that "conflict is inevitable" with the Chinese.

Perhaps at no time did distortion and misperception over Indochina rise higher than in the 1965–66 period when U.S. air and ground action was constantly escalating to heights undreamed of earlier. By this time, to be sure, Hanoi had established close relationships with both Moscow and Peking. An estimated one billion dollars in aid had flowed into North Vietnam by the time of the Sino-Soviet break, roughly two-thirds Chinese and one-third Russian. In the subsequent years the totals were carefully balanced and probably the net contribution of the Soviet Union plus that of her East European allies more than equalled that of China. None the less, as anyone in a position to observe Hanoi closely could testify, North Vietnam had in no sense fallen under the domination of either of the great communist powers. In fact, Hanoi's role was one of constant, careful balancing between the two because hostility between Russia and China was so intense that the slightest act of favoritism was magnified and could—indeed, often did—result in reprisals by the affronted power, usually China.

It is not possible to reconstruct a unified American image of Vietnam at that time. Sometimes, Washington seemed to regard Hanoi as an instrument of Chinese policy, sometimes (particularly when trying to get Moscow to intercede in our behalf) as an instrument of Soviet policy, sometimes—ignoring the obvious evidence of Sino-Soviet hostility—as an instrument of the "international communist conspiracy" and even, occasionally, as an intransigent native communist movement seeking to "humiliate" the United States.

The view of the United States held in Hanoi at this time, as I was able to establish in conversations with Hanoi officials in December 1966 and

January 1967, was much more in the image of the French than of the American reality. It was generally asserted and assumed that the United States simply wished to replace France as the exploiting colonial power in Indochina and that we had mounted the huge war effort for the benefit of capitalists who wished to exploit the enormous natural resources of Vietnam. When I rejoined that there was really nothing in the way of assets or resources in Vietnam which the United States coveted, my comment was regarded as both unfriendly and naive.

The Chinese image of the United States at that time was entirely different. The Chinese (as they told me) saw the U.S. escalation as the opening move in preparation for an all-out assault on China itself, an operation in which the United States was said to be collaborating closely with Moscow. Indochina was merely needed as a *place d'armes*, a springboard for the U.S. attack. It was expected that we would use nuclear arms, and a frequent justification given for the Red Guard and cultural revolution movement which was launched in mid–1966 was that it was designed to prepare, harden and "blood" the youth of China for the tremendous hardships of war with the United States which lay just ahead.

Peking's fear that Moscow was conniving with the United States in Vietnam was matched by fears expressed in Moscow that the Chinese, in some manner, would turn the Vietnamese war in a direction which would embroil the United States and the Soviet Union. It was fear of such possibilities which spurred Moscow, occasionally, to lend some assistance to the United States in exploring possible ways toward peace in Vietnam.

By 1969, it should be noted, the Chinese had moved away from their image of Vietnam as an American springboard for attack on China and, indeed, gradually were tending to abandon the theory of U.S.–U.S.S.R. collaboration against Peking. By this time both China and the Soviet Union tended to view Vietnam not so much in terms of U.S.–Vietnamese confrontation but as a "front" in their own ever-widening confrontation. Thus, China had opposed negotiations between the United States and Hanoi which finally opened in Paris in January 1969, to a substantial extent because of fear that this might move the United States and the U.S.S.R. closer to détente. Moscow generally favored negotiations because the end of the war in Indochina would be a blow to the Chinese communist propaganda line, directed toward Asian communist movements, of a continuous and constantly widening revolutionary movement of backward countries against more advanced ones.

The wide difference between the image of Indochina as viewed by Peking and by Moscow was spectacularly demonstrated in the Cambodian events of 1970. Peking seized upon the coup against Sihanouk to sponsor a summit meeting of Indochinese movements—Sihanouk for Cambodia, Prince Souphanouvong for Laos, Premier Pham Van Dong of North Vietnam and representatives of the Provisional Revolutionary Government of South Vietnam. With Chinese sponsorship, all the forces opposed to the United States in

Indochina formed a "united front," dedicated to the principle of a common struggle and unified peace negotiation. The Russians, excluded from the China-sponsored meeting, studiously snubbed Sihanouk, maintained relations with the Lon Nol government (and insisted that their satellites do the same) and blamed the Chinese for the U.S. action in Cambodia (and in Vietnam) on the grounds that China had refused to form a "united front" against U.S. aggression.

I think enough instances have been presented (although there are many more which might be noted) to establish the thesis that the image of Indochina not only varies widely from one power to another but also from one period to another. The same is true of the images which the involved powers have of each other's actions and motivations. Rarely at any time do these perceptions coincide; almost equally rarely do they coincide with what, in retrospect, the objective truth is seen to be.

What does this imply for the future? I fear the distortion between image and reality has by no means run its course. We are far advanced in a program of "Vietnamization" which envisages a day when the Saigon government will be able to undertake virtually full military and diplomatic responsibility, supported only by some minimum technical presence of the U.S. forces—air, communications, supplies. This implies a belief in a more or less permanent shift in the balance of force so pervasive, so striking that the North and its southern allies will be dissuaded from an effective military or political challenge to the Saigon régime. On the other hand, by widening the war into Laos, the American-supported South Vietnamese forces may have enlarged the field of battle in a manner which General Giap has always claimed would serve the revolutionary interest.

Let us leave to one side the question (which I believe is arguable) as to whether such an image of a competent, secure and confident Saigon government is realistic. Does the concept of a subdued, resigned, low-posture Hanoi and National Liberation Front forces, or Provisional Revolutionary Government as it now calls itself, seem likely to be borne out in real life? It does not fit the pattern of policy and conduct characteristic of the communist side, going all the way back to its Vietminh origins. The pattern, rather, has been one of struggle, struggle, struggle, regardless of odds, of the changing enemy and his tactics. Hanoi has always matched its tactics and strategy to the image it perceives of the enemy, holding back until a moment of opposition weakness, a development which tips the advantage to its side.

Is it not more realistic to assume that Hanoi will deliberately lie low as the American pullout continues, concentrating on recuperation of strength at home and rebuilding the infrastructure in the South? Then, when U.S. force levels are really low and when, perhaps, a moment of internal political crisis arises in Saigon, suddenly striking with utmost force in the belief (which may or may not be realistic) that once American forces are drawn down to a minimum no U.S. government will reëscalate—or indeed have time for such reëscalation unless it is prepared to employ air power on a more massive scale than ever before or even invoke nuclear power. The image which Hanoi may develop of U.S. options may be distorted. The image we may be in the process of drawing for ourselves may also be distorted. But this is in the grand pattern of Indochina, the pattern which has been marked from the very beginning.

If we are to avoid such a critical turn as is here suggested it would seem that an initial requisite must be a persistent and stubborn effort by all concerned parties—and particularly by ourselves—to arrive at some common approximation of both our own role and goal and those of Hanoi—and the great communist powers which back Hanoi. Without such understanding the future is likely to be as illusory as the past. And perhaps one of the greatest of illusions is the American belief that Hanoi, having been, as it feels, cheated both in the French settlement of 1945 and the Geneva settlement of 1954, is likely to put much credence in any end of the war which is not achieved by tilting the military balance in its favor.

Suggested Further Reading for Chapter 4

Thurman Arnold, *The Folklore of Capitalism* (New Haven: Yale University Press, 1937).

John M. Blum, " 'That Kind of a Liberal': F.D.R. After Twenty-five Years," *Yale Review*, 60 (1970).

Paul Conkin, *The New Deal* (New York: Thomas Y. Crowell Company, 1967).

J. W. Fulbright, *Old Myths and New Realities: And Other Commentaries* (New York: Vintage Books, 1964).

Eric Goldman, *The Crucial Decade—And After: America, 1945–1960* (New York: Vintage Books, 1960).

Eric Goldman, *Rendezvous with Destiny: A History of Modern American Reform* (New York: Vintage Books, 1952).

Otis Graham (ed.), *The New Deal: The Critical Issues* (Boston: Little, Brown, and Company, 1971).

George Kennan, *American Diplomacy, 1900–1950* (Chicago: University of Chicago Press, 1967).

Robert E. Osgood, *Ideals and Self-Interest in America's Foreign Relations: The Great Transformation of the Twentieth Century* (Chicago: University of Chicago Press, 1953).

Edgar Robinson, *The Roosevelt Leadership* (Philadelphia: J. B. Lippincott Co., 1955).

Athan G. Theoharis, *The Yalta Myths: An Issue in U.S. Politics, 1945–1955* (Columbia, Mo.: University of Missouri Press, 1970).

William Appleman Williams, *The Tragedy of American Diplomacy* (New York: Dell Publishing Co., 1962).

Mythology—the body of a primitive people's beliefs concerning its origin, early history, heroes, deities and so forth, as distinguished from the true accounts which it invents later.

Ambrose Bierce
The Devil's Dictionary

5

AND THE MYTHS CONTINUE...

The Historical Roots of Our Ecologic Crisis
Lynn White, Jr.

The Myth of Middle America
Richard Parker

Revolution without Ideology: The Changing Place of Women in America
Carl N. Degler

Black History, or Black Mythology?
Peter Chew

The Uses of Violence in American History
Michael Wallace

Room at the Top? The Blueing of America
Peter L. Berger and Brigitte Berger

Sport: If You Want to Build Character, Try Something Else
Bruce Ogilvie and Thomas A. Tutko

American Indians: People without a Future
Ralph Nader

TIP TOP WEEKLY

Issued Weekly—By Subscription $2.50 per year.   Entered as Second Class Matter at the N. Y. Post Office by STREET & SMITH.

July 31, 1897.   Vol. 1. No. 68.   Price Five Cents

FRANK MERRIWELL'S COMBINATION
OR
THE ALL ROUND ATHLETES

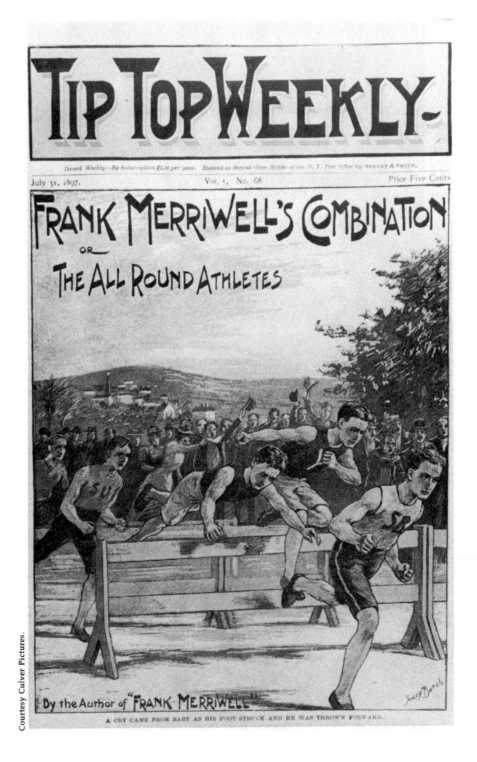

By the Author of "FRANK MERRIWELL"

A CRY CAME FROM BART AS HIS FOOT STRUCK AND HE WAS THROWN FORWARD.

341

Introduction

To assure the intellectual integrity of one's society it is necessary continually to think anew. The familiar must be reexamined in the interest of achieving greater dimensions of clarity and understanding. Accepting this, and the axiom that the time for historical reinterpretation is always *now*, historians have continually renewed their inquiry into the nuances of the American past. As we hope the previous chapters have demonstrated, they have concluded that myth is an important ingredient of the American experience. Accordingly, a growing consensus seems to suggest that America can no longer find historical sanction for either the enchantment that surrounds much of her past, or the heroic stature enjoyed by many of its participants. Ironically, the previous selections have sought to argue that myth supplies much of the inner logic of American history.

At this juncture, it would be well to keep in mind the warning of American historian Carl Becker, who in his essay "Everyman His Own Historian," observed: "We are apt to think of the past as dead, the future as nonexistent, the present alone as real." Of course no such easy distinction can be made. The past is prologue; it underscores the present, and conditions the future. Therefore, we might be wise to become attuned to the continuation of myth within our present social and political context.

The dominant theme and perspective of this book—the idea of myth in American history—seems especially logical and appropriate when juxtaposed with some relevant features of America's present condition. Convinced that important mythical discrepancies existed in our past historical experience, we might more easily come to see that present American attitudes toward ecology, minorities, violence, sports, and the place of women in our society are, at least in some degree, shaped in accordance with myth. Myth is today an ongoing enterprise of the American mind, as prolific as the current issues of a dynamic society.

Myth, then, has decided importance to contemporary American society, for men individually and societies collectively are selective in what they wish to remember concerning their past. Even though myth operates universally and diversely, Americans seem to have found the material for their myths nearer at hand than have older and more traditional societies. Thus do we continue to base our behavior and policies on distorted facts and, hence, questionable conclusions.

An awareness of myth, however, does not imply its successful eradication—assuming that were desirable. The literary critic Mark Shorer argued this point when he contended:

Myths are the instruments by which we continually struggle to make our experience intelligible to ourselves. A myth is a large controlling image that gives philosophical meaning to the facts of ordinary life.

Paradoxically, as an important dimension of human existence, myth is at once the process by which man orders his world and that which serves to perpetuate his grandest illusions. As the American poet Robert Penn Warren once pointedly observed: "The dream is a lie, but the dreaming is true." Thus, the question remains valid for historians and Becker's "Everyman" alike: *What is myth and what is reality—yesterday, today, and in the future?*

The Historical Roots of
Our Ecologic Crisis

Lynn White, Jr.

The clouds of myth and insensitivity concerning the problems of ecology in America have only recently begun to be dispelled. Lynn White, Jr., former President of Mills College, founder and Director of the Center for Medieval and Renaissance Studies, and Professor of History at U.C.L.A., strikes at one of the more subtle and sophisticated levels of ecology-related mythology: that found in the religious attitudes of American society. Placing his subject within the broader context of Western civilization as a whole, White argues that religious mythology—specifically the Judeo-Christian axiom of "arrogance toward nature"—is at the core of our ecologic crisis. Part of the solution to that crisis, White says, lies in re-thinking our all-too-basic religious notion that nature has no reason for existence save to serve man.

A conversation with Aldous Huxley not infrequently put one at the receiving end of an unforgettable monologue. About a year before his lamented death he was discoursing on a favorite topic: man's unnatural treatment of nature and its sad results. To illustrate his point he told how, during the previous summer, he had returned to a little valley in England where he had spent many happy months as a child. Once it had been composed of delightful grassy glades; now it was becoming overgrown with unsightly brush because the rabbits that formerly kept such growth under control had largely succumbed to a disease, myxomatosis, that was deliberately introduced by the local farmers to reduce the rabbits' destruction of crops. Being something of a Philistine, I could be silent no longer, even in the interests of great rhetoric. I interrupted to point out that the rabbit itself had been brought as a domestic animal to England in 1176, presumably to improve the protein diet of the peasantry.

All forms of life modify their contexts. The most spectacular and benign instance is doubtless the coral polyp. By serving its own ends, it has created a vast undersea world favorable to thousands of other kinds of animals and plants. Ever since man became a numerous species he has affected his environment notably. The hypothesis that his fire-drive method of hunting created the world's great grasslands and helped to exterminate the monster mammals of the Pleistocene from much of the globe is plausible, if not proved.

For six millennia at least, the banks of the lower Nile have been a human artifact rather than the swampy African jungle which nature, apart from man, would have made it. The Aswan Dam, flooding 5000 square miles, is only the latest stage in a long process. In many regions terracing or irrigation, over-grazing, the cutting of forests by Romans to build ships to fight Carthaginians or by Crusaders to solve the logistics problems of their expeditions have profoundly changed some ecologies. Observation that the French landscape falls into two basic types, the open fields of the north and the *bocage* of the south and west, inspired Marc Bloch to undertake his classic study of medieval agricultural methods. Quite unintentionally, changes in human ways often affect nonhuman nature. It has been noted, for example, that the advent of the automobile eliminated huge flocks of sparrows that once fed on the horse manure littering every street.

The history of ecologic change is still so rudimentary that we know little about what really happened, or what the results were. The extinction of the European aurochs as late as 1627 would seem to have been a simple case of overenthusiastic hunting. On more intricate matters it often is impossible to find solid information. For a thousand years or more the Frisians and Hollanders have been pushing back the North Sea, and the process is culminating in our own time in the reclamation of the Zuider Zee. What, if any, species of animals, birds, fish, shore life, or plants have died out in the process? In their epic combat with Neptune have the Netherlanders overlooked ecological values in such a way that the quality of human life in the Netherlands has suffered? I cannot discover that the questions have ever been asked, much less answered.

People, then, have often been a dynamic element in their own environment, but in the present state of historical scholarship we usually do not know exactly when, where, or with what effects man-induced changes came. As we enter the last third of the twentieth century, however, concern for the problem of ecologic backlash is mounting feverishly. Natural science, conceived as the effort to understand the nature of things, had flourished in several eras and among several peoples. Similarly, there had been an age-old accumulation of technological skills, sometimes growing rapidly, sometimes slowly. But it was not until about four generations ago that Western Europe and North America arranged a marriage between science and technology, a union of the theoretical and the empirical approaches to our natural environment. The emergence in widespread practice of the Baconian creed that scientific knowledge means technological power over nature can scarcely be dated before about 1850, save in the chemical industries, where it is anticipated in the eighteenth century. Its acceptance as a normal pattern of action may mark the greatest event in human history since the invention of agriculture, and perhaps in nonhuman terrestrial history as well.

Almost at once the new situation forced the crystallization of the novel concept of ecology; indeed, the word *ecology* first appeared in the English language in 1873. Today, less than a century later, the impact of our race upon the environment has so increased in force that it has changed in essence. When the first cannons were fired, in the early fourteenth century, they affected ecology by sending workers scrambling to the forests and mountains for more potash, sulfur, iron ore, and charcoal, with some resulting erosion and deforestation. Hydrogen bombs are of a different order: a war fought with them might alter the genetics of all life on this planet. By 1285 London had a smog problem arising from the burning of soft coal, but our present combustion of fossil fuels threatens to change the chemistry of the globe's atmosphere as a whole, with consequences which we are only beginning to guess. With the population explosion, the carcinoma of planless urbanism, the now geological deposits of sewage and garbage, surely no creature other than man has ever managed to foul its nest in such short order.

There are many calls to action, but specific proposals, however worthy as individual items, seem too partial, palliative, negative: ban the bomb, tear down the billboards, give the Hindus contraceptives and tell them to eat their sacred cows. The simplest solution to any suspect change is, of course, to stop it, or, better yet, to revert to a romanticized past: make those ugly gasoline stations look like Anne Hathaway's cottage or (in the Far West) like ghost-town saloons. The "wilderness area" mentality invariably advocates deep-freezing an ecology, whether San Gimignano or the High Sierra, as it was before the first Kleenex was dropped. But neither atavism nor prettification will cope with the ecologic crisis of our time.

What shall we do? No one yet knows. Unless we think about fundamentals, our specific measures may produce new backlashes more serious than those they are designed to remedy.

As a beginning we should try to clarify our thinking by looking, in some historical depth, at the presuppositions that underlie modern technology and science. Science was traditionally aristocratic, speculative, intellectual in intent; technology was lower-class, empirical, action-oriented. The quite sudden fusion of these two toward the middle of the nineteenth century is surely related to the slightly prior and contemporary democratic revolutions which, by reducing social barriers, tended to assert a functional unity of brain and hand. Our ecologic crisis is the product of an emerging, entirely novel, democratic culture. The issue is whether a democratized world can survive its own implications. Presumably we cannot unless we rethink our axioms.

One thing is so certain that it seems stupid to verbalize it: both modern technology and modern science are distinctively *Occidental*. Our technology has absorbed elements from all over the world, notably from China; yet everywhere today, whether in Japan or in Nigeria, successful technology is Western. Our science is the heir to all the sciences of the past, especially perhaps to the work of the great Islamic scientists of the Middle Ages, who so often outdid the ancient Greeks in skill and perspicacity: ibn-al-Haytham in optics, for example; or Omar Khayyám in mathematics. Indeed, not a few works of such geniuses seem to have vanished in the original Arabic and to

346

survive only in medieval Latin translations that helped to lay the foundation for later Western developments. Today, around the globe, all significant science is Western in style and method, whatever the pigmentation or language of the scientists.

A second pair of facts is less well recognized because they result from quite recent historical scholarship. The leadership of the West, both in technology and in science, is far older than the so-called Scientific Revolution of the seventeenth century or the so-called Industrial Revolution of the eighteenth century. These terms are in fact outmoded and obscure the true nature of what they try to describe—significant stages in two long and separate developments. By 1000 A.D. at the latest—and perhaps, feebly, as much as two hundred years earlier—the West began to apply water power to industrial processes other than milling grain. This was followed in the late twelfth century by the harnessing of wind power. . . . From simple beginnings, but with remarkable consistency of style, the West rapidly expanded its skills in the development of power machinery, labor-saving devices, and automation. Not in craftsmanship but in basic technological capacity, the Latin West of the later Middle Ages far outstripped its elaborate, sophisticated, and aesthetically magnificent sister cultures, Byzantium and Islam. In 1444 a great Greek ecclesiastic, Bessarion, who had gone to Italy, wrote a letter to a prince in Greece. He is amazed. by the superiority of Western ships, arms, textiles, glass. But above all he is astonished by the spectacle of water wheels sawing timbers and pumping the bellows of blast furnaces. Clearly, he had seen nothing of the sort in the Near East.

By the end of the fifteenth century the technological superiority of Europe was such that its small, mutually hostile nations could spill out over all the rest of the world, conquering, looting, and colonizing. The symbol of this technological superiority is the fact that Portugal, one of the weakest states of the Occident, was able to become, and to remain for a century, mistress of the East Indies. And we must remember that the technology of Vasco da Gama and Albuquerque was built by pure empiricism, drawing remarkably little support or inspiration from science.

In the present-day vernacular understanding, modern science is supposed to have begun in 1543, when both Copernicus and Vesalius published their great works. It is no derogation of their accomplishments, however, to point out that such structures as the *Fabrica* and the *De revolutionibus* do not appear overnight. The distinctive Western tradition of science, in fact, began in the late eleventh century with a massive movement of translation of Arabic and Greek scientific works into Latin. A few notable books—Theophrastus, for example—escaped the West's avid new appetite for science, but within less than two hundred years effectively the entire corpus of Greek and Muslim science was available in Latin, and was being eagerly read and criticized in the new European universities. Out of criticism arose new observation, speculation, and increasing distrust of ancient authorities. By the late thirteenth century Europe had seized global scientific leadership from the faltering hands of Islam. It would be as absurd to deny the profound originality of Newton, Galileo, or Copernicus as to deny that of the fourteenth-century scholastic scientists like Buridan or Oresme on whose work they built. Before the eleventh century, science scarcely existed in the Latin West, even in Roman times. From the eleventh century onward, the scientific sector of Occidental culture has increased in a steady crescendo.

Since both our technological and our scientific movements got their start, acquired their character, and achieved world dominance in the Middle Ages, it would seem that we cannot understand their nature or their present impact upon ecology without examining fundamental medieval assumptions and developments.

Until recently, agriculture has been the chief occupation even in "advanced" societies; hence, any change in methods of tillage has much importance. Early plows, drawn by two oxen, did not normally turn the sod but merely scratched it. Thus, cross-plowing was needed, and fields tended to be squarish. In the fairly light soils and semi-arid climates of the Near East and Mediterranean, this worked well. But such a plow was inappropriate to the wet climate and often sticky soils of Northern Europe. By the latter part of the seventh century after Christ, however, following obscure beginnings, certain Northern peasants were using an entirely new kind of plow, equipped with a vertical knife to cut the line of the furrow, a horizontal share to slice under the sod, and a moldboard to turn it over. The friction of this plow with the soil was so great that it normally required not two but eight oxen. It attacked the land with such violence that cross-plowing was not needed, and fields tended to be shaped in long strips.

In the days of the scratch plow, fields were distributed generally in units capable of supporting a single family. Subsistence farming was the presupposition. But no peasant owned eight oxen: to use the new and more efficient plow, peasants pooled their oxen to form large plow teams, originally receiving (it would appear) plowed strips in proportion to their contribution. Thus, distribution of land was based no longer on the needs of a family but, rather, on the capacity of a power machine to till the earth. Man's relation to the soil was profoundly changed. Formerly man had been part of nature; now he was the exploiter of nature. Nowhere else in the world did farmers develop any analogous agricultural implement. Is it coincidence that modern technology, with its ruthlessness toward nature, has so largely been produced by descendants of these peasants of Northern Europe?

This same exploitive attitude appears slightly before 830 A.D. in Western illustrated calendars. In older calendars the months were shown as passive personifications. The new Frankish calendars, which set the style for the Middle Ages, are very different: they show men coercing the world around them—plowing, harvesting, chopping trees, butchering pigs. Man and nature are two things, and man is master.

These novelties seem to be in harmony with larger intellectual patterns. What people do about their ecology depends on what they think about themselves in relation to things around them. Human ecology is deeply conditioned by beliefs about our nature and destiny—that is, by religion. To Western eyes this is very evident in, say, India or Ceylon. It is equally true of ourselves and of our medieval ancestors.

The victory of Christianity over paganism was the greatest psychic revolution in the history of our culture. It has become fashionable today to say that for better or worse we live in "the post-Christian age." Certainly the forms of our thinking and language have largely ceased to be Christian, but to my eye the substance often remains amazingly akin to that of the past. Our daily habits of action, for example, are dominated by an implicit faith in perpetual progress which was unknown either to Greco-Roman Antiquity or to the Orient. It is rooted in, and is indefensible apart from, Judeo-Christian teleology. The fact that Communists share it merely helps to show what can be demonstrated on many other grounds: that Marxism, like Islam, is a Judeo-Christian heresy. We continue today to live, as we have lived for about 1700 years, very largely in a context of Christian axioms.

What did Christianity tell people about their relations with the environment?

While many of the world's mythologies provide stories of creation, Greco-Roman mythology was singularly incoherent in this respect. Like Aristotle, the intellectuals of the ancient West denied that the visible world had had a beginning. Indeed, the idea of a beginning was impossible in the framework of their cyclical notion of time. In sharp contrast, Christianity inherited from Judaism not only a concept of time as nonrepetitive and linear but also a striking story of creation. By gradual stages a loving and all-powerful God had created light and darkness, the heavenly bodies, the earth and all its plants, animals, birds, and fishes. Finally, God had created Adam and, as an afterthought, Eve to keep man from being lonely. Man named all the animals, thus establishing his dominance over them. God planned all of this explicitly for man's benefit and rule: no item in the physical creation had any purpose save to serve man's purposes. And, although man's body is made of clay, he is not simply part of nature: he is made in God's image.

Especially in its Western form, Christianity is the most anthropocentric religion the world has seen. As early as the second century both Tertullian and St. Irenaeus of Lyons were insisting that when God shaped Adam he was foreshadowing the image of the incarnate Christ, the Second Adam. Man shares, in great measure, God's transcendence of nature. Christianity, in absolute contrast to ancient paganism and Asia's religions (except, perhaps, Zoroastrianism), not only established a dualism of man and nature but also insisted that it is God's will that man exploit nature for his proper ends.

At the level of the common people this worked out in an interesting way. In Antiquity every tree, every spring, every stream, every hill had its own *genius loci*, its guardian spirit. These spirits were accessible to men, but were very unlike men; centaurs, fauns, and mermaids show their ambivalence. Before one cut a tree, mined a mountain, or dammed a brook, it was important to placate the spirit in charge of that particular situation, and to keep it placated. By destroying pagan animism, Christianity made it possible to exploit nature in a mood of indifference to the feelings of natural objects.

It is often said that for animism the Church substituted the cult of saints. True; but the cult of saints is functionally quite different from animism. The saint is not *in* natural objects; he may have special shrines, but his citizenship is in heaven. Moreover, a saint is entirely a man; he can be approached in human terms. In addition to saints, Christianity of course also had angels and demons inherited from Judaism and perhaps, at one remove, from Zoroastrianism. But these were all as mobile as the saints themselves. The spirits *in* natural objects, which formerly had protected nature from man, evaporated. Man's effective monopoly on spirit in this world was confirmed, and the old inhibitions to the exploitation of nature crumbled.

When one speaks in such sweeping terms, a note of caution is in order. Christianity is a complex faith, and its consequences differ in differing contexts. What I have said may well apply to the medieval West, where in fact technology made spectacular advances. But the Greek East, a highly civilized realm of equal Christian devotion, seems to have produced no marked technological innovation after the late seventh century, when Greek fire was invented. The key to the contrast may perhaps be found in a difference in the tonality of piety and thought which students of comparative theology find between the Greek and the Latin Churches. The Greeks believed that sin was intellectual blindness, and that salvation was found in illumination, orthodoxy—that is, clear thinking. The Latins, on the other hand, felt that sin was moral evil, and that salvation was to be found in right conduct. Eastern theology has been intellectualist. Western theology has been voluntarist. The Greek saint contemplates; the Western saint acts. The implications of Christianity for the conquest of nature would emerge more easily in the Western atmosphere.

The Christian Dogma of creation, which is found in the first clause of the Creeds, has another meaning for our comprehension of today's ecologic crisis. By revelation, God had given man the Bible, the Book of Scripture. But since God had made nature, nature also must reveal the divine mentality. The religious study of nature for the better understanding of God was known as natural theology. In the early Church, and always in the Greek East, nature was conceived primarily as a symbolic system through which God speaks to men: the ant is a sermon to sluggards; rising flames are the symbol of the soul's aspiration. This view of nature was essentially artistic rather than scientific. While Byzantium preserved and copied great numbers of ancient Greek scientific texts, science as we conceive it could scarcely flourish in such an ambience.

However, in the Latin West by the early thirteenth century natural theology was following a very different bent. It was ceasing to be the decoding of the physical symbols of God's communication with man and was becoming the effort to understand God's mind by discovering how his creation operates.

The rainbow was no longer simply a symbol of hope first sent to Noah after the Deluge: Robert Grosseteste, Friar Roger Bacon, and Theodoric of Freiberg produced startlingly sophisticated work on the optics of the rainbow, but they did it as a venture in religious understanding. From the thirteenth century onward into the eighteenth, every major scientist, in effect, explained his motivations in religious terms. Indeed, if Galileo had not been so expert an amateur theologian he would have got into far less trouble: the professionals resented his intrusion. It was not until the late eighteenth century that the hypothesis of God became unnecessary to many scientists.

It is often hard for the historian to judge, when men explain why they are doing what they want to do, whether they are offering real reasons or merely culturally acceptable reasons. The consistency with which scientists during the long formative centuries of Western science said that the task and the reward of the scientist were "to think God's thoughts after him" leads one to believe that this was their real motivation. If so, then modern Western science was cast in a matrix of Christian theology. The dynamism of religious devotion, shaped by the Judeo-Christian dogma of creation, gave it impetus.

We would seem to be headed toward conclusions unpalatable to many Christians. Since both *science* and *technology* are blessed words in our contemporary vocabulary, some may be happy at the notions, first, that, viewed historically, modern science is an extrapolation of natural theology and, second, that modern technology is at least partly to be explained as an Occidental, voluntarist realization of the Christian dogma of man's transcendence of, and rightful mastery over, nature. But, as we now recognize, somewhat over a century ago science and technology, hitherto quite separate activities, joined to give mankind powers which, to judge by many of the ecologic effects, are out of control. If so, Christianity bears a huge burden of guilt.

I personally doubt that disastrous ecologic backlash can be avoided simply by applying to our problems more science and more technology. Our science and technology have grown out of Christian attitudes toward man's relation to nature which are almost universally held not only by Christians and neo-Christians but also by those who fondly regard themselves as post-Christians. Despite Copernicus, all the cosmos rotates around our little globe. Despite Darwin, we are *not*, in our hearts, part of the natural process. We are superior to nature, contemptuous of it, willing to use it for our slightest whim. A governor of California, like myself a churchman but less troubled than I, spoke for the Christian tradition when he said (as is alleged), "When you've seen one redwood tree, you've seen them all." To a Christian a tree can be no more than a physical fact. The whole concept of the sacred grove is alien to Christianity and to the ethos of the West. For nearly two millennia Christian missionaries have been chopping down sacred groves, which are idolatrous because they assume spirit in nature.

What we do about ecology depends on our ideas of the man-nature relationship. More science and more technology are not going to get us out of the present ecologic crisis until we find a new religion, or rethink our old one. The beatniks and hippies, who are the basic revolutionaries of our time, show a sound instinct in their affinity for Zen Buddhism and Hinduism, which conceive of the man-nature relationship as very nearly the mirror image of the Christian view. These faiths, however, are as deeply conditioned by Asian history as Christianity is by the experience of the West, and I am dubious of their viability among us.

Possibly we should ponder the greatest radical in Christian history since Christ: St. Francis of Assisi. The prime miracle of St. Francis is the fact that he did not end at the stake, as many of his left-wing followers did. He was so clearly heretical that a General of the Franciscan Order, St. Bonaventura, a great and perceptive Christian, tried to suppress the early accounts of Franciscanism. The key to an understanding of Francis is his belief in the virtue of humility, not merely for the individual but for man as a species. Francis tried to depose man from his monarchy over creation and set up a democracy of all God's creatures. With him the ant is no longer simply a homily for the lazy, flames a sign of the thrust of the soul toward union with God; now they are Brother Ant and Sister Fire, praising the Creator in their own ways as Brother Man does in his.

Later commentators have said that Francis preached to the birds as a rebuke to men who would not listen. The records do not read so; he urged the little birds to praise God, and in spiritual ecstasy they flapped their wings and chirped rejoicing. Legends of saints, especially the Irish saints, had long told of their dealings with animals but always, I believe, to show their human dominance over creatures. With Francis it is different. The land around Gubbio in the Apennines was being ravaged by a fierce wolf. St. Francis, says the legend, talked to the wolf and persuaded him of the error of his ways. The wolf repented, died in the odor of sanctity, and was buried in consecrated ground.

What Sir Steven Runciman calls "the Franciscan doctrine of the animal soul" was quickly stamped out. Quite possibly it was in part inspired, consciously or unconsciously, by the belief in reincarnation held by the Cathar heretics who at that time teemed in Italy and southern France, and who presumably had got it originally from India. It is significant that at just the same moment, about 1200, traces of metempsychosis are found also in Western Judaism, in the Provençal *Cabbala*. But Francis held neither to transmigration of souls nor to pantheism. His view of nature and of man rested on a unique sort of pan-psychism of all things animate and inanimate, designed for the glorification of their transcendent Creator, who, in the ultimate gesture of cosmic humility, assumed flesh, lay helpless in a manger, and hung dying on a scaffold.

I am not suggesting that many contemporary Americans who are concerned about our ecologic crisis will be either able or willing to counsel with wolves or exhort birds. However, the present increasing disruption of the global environment is the product of a dynamic technology and science which were originating in the Western medieval world and against which St. Francis was rebelling in so original a way. Their growth cannot be understood historically apart from distinctive attitudes toward nature which are deeply grounded in Christian dogma. The fact that most people do not think of these attitudes as Christian is irrelevant. No new set of basic values has been accepted in our society to displace those of Christianity. Hence we shall continue to have a worsening ecologic crisis until we reject the Christian axiom that nature has no reason for existence save to serve man.

The greatest spiritual revolutionary in Western history, St. Francis, proposed what he thought was an alternative Christian view of nature and man's relation to it: he tried to substitute the idea of the equality of all creatures, including man, for the idea of man's limitless rule of creation. He failed. Both our present science and our present technology are so tinctured with orthodox Christian arrogance toward nature that no solution for our ecologic crisis can be expected from them alone. Since the roots of our trouble are so largely religious, the remedy must also be essentially religious, whether we call it that or not. We must rethink and refeel our nature and destiny. The profoundly religious, but heretical, sense of the primitive Franciscans for the spiritual autonomy of all parts of nature may point a direction. I propose Francis as a patron saint for ecologists.

The Myth of Middle America

Richard Parker

A recurrent theme in American history has been the "rediscovery of poverty." Each historical generation discovers anew that the Promise of American Life is not shared by all—that the "economic millennium" has not yet arrived. In scrutinizing the "myth of the New Affluence," Richard Parker, a Junior Fellow at the Center for the Study of Democratic Institutions, attempts to describe the reality of income distribution in America. In provocative fashion, Parker supplies data testifying to the existence of a "myth of middle America."

It was a tenet of both liberal and conservative dogmas following World War II that, economically, life in America was getting better all the time. Aside from the political flurry of McCarthyism in the early nineteen-fifties, the economy was everyone's favorite topic of discussion. After economists had predicted a major postwar recession, the American economy fooled them and began what seemed like a skyrocket burst. Between 1945 and 1965, the Gross National Product quadrupled, and disposable personal income increased two-and-a-half-fold. Postulating a "trickle-down" theory of income distribution, economists assumed that it was only a question of time before poverty was eliminated in America.

Suckled on the Horatio Alger myth and teethed on depression and war, the American public was glad to hear the news. Madison Avenue blared the New Affluence across front pages, and invited all of us to join the feast of consumption. The new symbol of America was the suburb, the grassy, tree-shaded Eden of responsible Americans. There a family was safe and happy with its two cars, two children, dog, and barbeque pit. Social science and the academy in general took over the affluence myth virtually *in toto,* declaring the end of scarcity, and with it the end of ideology, and the dawn of a new technocratic age where abundance, rather than scarcity, would be our bane. A Gallup Poll would most likely have found wide acceptance of David Lilienthal's views that "one finds the physical benefits of our society distributed widely, to almost everyone, with scant regard to status, class, or origin of the individual."

But the myth of the New Affluence was a cruel distortion of reality. Composed of half-truths, it closed our eyes, cut us off from a recognition of America, and blocked off political and social alternatives. Today, poverty in the midst of prosperity seems almost characteristic of mature capitalism.

From "The Myth of Middle America," by Richard Parker. Reprinted, with permission, from March 1970 issue of *The Center Magazine,* a publication of the Center for the Study of Democratic Institutions in Santa Barbara, California.

Moreover, deprivation also seems characteristic and, together with poverty, describes the living conditions of nearly half the American people. What once appeared to be a New Affluence, I contend, is in fact an expansion of the economy which has disproportionately benefited the upper and upper-middle classes, while it has left the poor and the deprived to gather what crumbs fall from the table.

Marx contended in *Das Kapital* and elsewhere that poverty was a normal condition of capitalism even in the best of times. He argued that even if workers' actual wages rose, the differential between their wages and the income of the rich would continue to increase. The issue was settled to the satisfaction of most American economists by the performance of their own economy after the Second World War. A number of them had their faith in capitalism shaken by the Depression, but the postwar boom quickly allayed most of their doubts. The original Marxian criticism that wages might rise but differentials between classes grow larger was lost sight of in the general euphoria of the nineteen-fifties.

The euphoria, moreover, was not limited to the traditional, or laissez-faire, economists. Liberal interventionists and Keynesians alike joined with conservatives to announce the death of poverty in mature capitalism. John Kenneth Galbraith, for example, claimed that by the late fifties American poverty was limited to "the insular poor" and "the case poor." The former were the inhabitants of areas like Appalachia and the rural South, where shifting employment patterns were causing "painful, but temporary hardship." The "case poor" were the alcoholics, invalids, and elderly who could not, or would not, get ahead. Keynes himself (like Marx) had, of course, foreseen no such amelioration, even in Keynesian capitalism. As Paul Mattick notes in his book *Marx and Keynes*, "Keynesian interventions in the economy necessarily adjust production and consumption in favor of investments. Such adjustments cannot end the paradox of poverty in the midst of plenty, and are not designed to do so." The problem of economists was to explain *why* poverty was disappearing at such a rapid rate. Census statistics indicated that families with incomes below three thousand dollars had declined from twenty-eight to fourteen percent between 1947 and 1966. But why? Obviously prosperity in general, and unionization in particular, had improved the lot of the workingman. But raw data, as well as a few highly sophisticated studies, indicated not only that the economic pie was getting bigger but that a significant reallocation was taking place. It appeared that, for some poorly understood reasons, a real change was taking place in the economy. Arthur Burns, then an Eisenhower adviser, rejoiced: "The transformation in the distribution of our national income . . . may already be counted as one of the great social revolutions of history." Paul Samuelson spoke for the liberals when he said, "The American income pyramid is becoming less unequal."

Though still lacking an explanation, the economists' statistical foundations seemed eminently solid. Simon Kuznets' massive study, *Shares of Upper Income Groups in Income and Savings*, indicated a major decline in the percentage of personal income controlled by the upper strata of the society, a decline that "would continue." The late Selma Goldsmith and her associates showed that the share of personal income received by the top five percent declined from thirty percent in 1929 to 26.5 percent in 1936–37, and to 20.7 percent by 1944. Similarly, she showed that the share of the top twenty percent declined from 54.4 to 51.7 to 45.8 percent in the same periods. At the other end of the spectrum, the bottom twenty percent began to show some, if sizably smaller, gains.

Using these data, plus rawer data collected by the Bureau of the Census and other government agencies, economists postulated a theory for income distribution. According to the theory, income was slowly but irreversibly "trickling down" the income scale from the rich to the poor, to result finally in Samuelson's "flattened pyramid." It was presumed to be only a question of time before the last vestiges of poverty would disappear entirely; by the late fifties, Galbraith declared calmly, poverty in America was no longer "a massive affliction but more nearly an afterthought."

As a consequence, the study of income distribution as an economic discipline rapidly declined throughout the fifties. The university, like the nation at large, mesmerized by the new Affluent Society, was content to rest its discussions of poverty on clichés and rudimentary data. In economics, the new interest was in "value-free" econometrics; in the popular consciousness, it was in *The Organization Man* and *The Man in the Gray Flannel Suit*. Affluence was the presumed condition of almost all, and discussion centered on suburbia, Martinis, and psychoanalysis. Maladies were the result of too much rather than too little.

The "rediscovery" of poverty in America, then, came as a rude awakening to most. Michael Harrington's *The Other America*, which got widespread attention in the early sixties, provided graphic portrayals of the personal impact as well as the extent of poverty. It inspired a major re-examination of the country's goals. Harrington's estimation that one-quarter of the American people lived in poverty shattered not only national pride but also the sublime self-confidence of the economics establishment. To them, his words were heresy.

Discomfiture was not limited to economists. It spread through the social sciences. Two sociologists, S. M. Miller and Martin Rein, looking back on their colleagues' embarrassing mistakes, described the general theory that had governed sociological thinking in the fifties: "The expansion of production and productivity resulted in a much greater economic pie. The graduated income tax, expanded welfare services, and education were more equitably distributing this larger pie. Continued increase in aggregate economic wealth would invariably filter down, more or less equitably, to all income groupings. Marginal economic groups, it was assumed, would in time 'gracefully succumb' to continued economic growth and that small residual group not covered by expanded welfare and social security programs would be handily cared for by the public dole."

But even after Harrington pricked the popular balloon, air leaked out with surprising slowness. Those running the federal government's War on Poverty (and many social scientists) agreed to define as poor only those families with annual incomes below three thousand dollars. This swift bit of statistical legerdemain immediately shrank Harrington's one-quarter to a less frightening one-fifth. The effect was not only to minimize the poverty in America but to ignore the basic contradictions in the myth of prosperity.

A re-evaluation of postwar prosperity leads to major second thoughts about "trickle down" theories of income distribution. As early as 1957, Robert Lampman, of the University of Michigan, noted that initial gains by the poor to increase their share of the wealth had not only stopped but were reversing. By the early sixties, the rich were again increasing their control of the lion's share of personal income.

The premature optimism of economists like Burns lay in statistics that took no official notice of their unusual circumstances. During the war and shortly thereafter, the income of laborers and service workers increased almost twice as fast as that of professionals and managerial workers. But this was due chiefly to war-related factors that would be unlikely in a peacetime economy, such as full employment mixed with a shortage of non-skilled labor. By the late fifties, the lower categories no longer showed high-rate gains: laborers' and service workers' income increased only forty-eight percent while managerial income increased seventy-five percent. Joseph Pechman concluded in 1969 that "the distribution of income in the nineteen-fifties period may not have been very different from what it was in the early nineteen-twenties."

These gross figures, some would argue, are misleading because of shifts in the labor market. Thus the small gains for laborers might be offset by the diminishing number of common laborers, or the high incidence of poverty among farmers offset by decreasing numbers of farmers. But Herman Miller, an economist with the Census Bureau, disagreed. Writing in a Bureau monograph, *Income Distribution in the United States*, he concluded that shifts in job distribution did not substantially affect patterns of income distribution. "Of course it could still be argued that the over-all stability of income distribution for the urban population masks important changes which have taken place for various subgroups within the population. But this hypothesis . . . does not appear to be supported by the facts. Income distribution within the urban population has not shifted even when that population is further classified by labor force status of wife, age of head, or size of family."

Miller, however, does underline one important trend: the increasing number of families in which both husband and wife work. "It should be noted that incomes are much more equally distributed among families where the wife is working than where she is not working; the sizable increase in the proportion of families with working wives has therefore tended to decrease income inequality during the past decade." Moreover, Census projections show that the proportion of women in the labor force will continue to grow over the next two decades.

Yet even the increased family income provided by a second earner was unable to offset the gains by upper and upper-middle classes in control of personal income. Using Census data as well as studies by various economic agencies, Joseph Pechman acknowledged that the rich, but not the poor, had prospered in the postwar era. He pointed out that the simplest Census tables, those most often cited, exclude capital gains and therefore grossly misrepresent income trends in the upper fifth of the economy. For example, the following table shows the standard before-tax income shares of the rich, according to Census data:

Year	Top 5% of Families	Top 20% of Families
1952	18%	42%
1957	16	40
1962	16	42
1967	15	41

What this table indicates obviously is confirmation of Burns' "great revolution." But are the figures accurate?

Tax data are needed to push the analysis further. These data are more useful because they show the realized capital gains of these families and net income after federal taxes. The salient observation here is that, contrary to another popular myth now also on the wane, the federal income tax is *not* progressive in its effect. Computing total disposable (i.e. after-tax) income, we find the following:

Year	Tax Units Top 5%	Tax Units Top 15%
1952	16%	30%
1963	17	33
1967	17	34

However, this table itself can only be considered an estimate that falls to the low side. Since the Second World War, innumerable tax benefits and payment forms have grown up which benefit only the rich. Pechman names tax-exempt interest and depletion allowances as sources of income, then adds: "During World War II, methods of compensation were devised to funnel income to business executives in non-taxable forms. The devices used are well known: deferred compensation and pension plans, stock option arrangements, and direct payment of personal consumption expenditures through expense accounts." Having listed these varieties of unreported income, he prefers caution, and concludes, "Little is known about the impact on the distribution of income."

Gabriel Kolko is not so timorous. In *Wealth and Power in America*, Kolko announced that "the impact of the federal income tax on the actual distribution of income has been minimal, if not negligible." Drawing on a number of sources for his data, he deduced that adding the uncomputed income of the upper classes would raise their total disposable income two or three percentage points above Pechman's own figures. (Thus the top five percent received about twenty percent of the personal income, and the top one percent about ten percent of that income.) Since 1952, the effective federal tax rate on the upper one percent of the population has *dropped* from thirty-three to twenty-six percent.

What may be said of the federal tax structure can be repeated *ad nauseam* for state and local tax structures. The impact of property and sales taxes is clearly regressive, and, as one economist put it, this is "disturbing because the state-local tax system is the growing element of the national system." Federal tax revenues have remained fairly constant as a proportion of Gross National Product, hovering around twenty percent since 1951. State and local taxes, by contrast, have risen from 7.1 percent of the Gross National Product in 1951 to 11.9 percent in 1968. "Assuming that state-local taxes respond more or less proportionately to the rise in the national product . . . the state and local governments must have increased rates by sixty-eight percent in these seventeen years to push up their tax yields to current levels." The motivation is obviously not simple greed, but a reflection of increased demand on public services and increasing population concentration in metropolitan areas. Nonetheless, the burden of these social changes falls most heavily on those least able to pay.

The Economic Report of the President, 1969 shows the following:

Income Classes	State and Local Taxes (Percentage of Income)
Under $2,000	25%
2,000–4,000	11
4,000–6,000	10
6,000–8,000	9
8,000–10,000	9
10,000–15,000	9
15,000 and over	7

Analysis of income alone, in the case of the rich, obviously also misrepresents the actual concentration of economic well-being in the country. Affluence for the rich, unlike income for the middle and lower classes, is rarely limited to wages and salaries. Rents, dividends, interest, all go into the total wealth of the upper class. James D. Smith, of the Office of Economic Opportunity, in analyzing data of persons with gross assets in excess of sixty thousand dollars, found a highly concentrated wealth structure. This group, representing the top 1.5 percent of the wealth-holders in the country, received the following amounts of income:

Type	Billions	Percent of Total (Each Type)
Wages and salaries	$25.9	10.8%
Dividends	8.0	74.8
Interest	3.1	27.9
Rent	6.4	52.5
Capital gains	57.6	71.4

Furthermore, this table is an understatement of concentration. It excludes $1.7 billion in dividends paid to trust funds and non-profit foundations; it assumes only average yields on assets, rather than optimum figures to be obtained through the advice of investment counselors; finally, its data are for 1958, and all subsequent information shows increasing pyramiding of the wealth structure.

Gabriel Kolko also contributes significant figures on the concentration of total wealth in the upper brackets which supplement Smith's own research. For example, in 1960 the top ten percent controlled two-thirds of all liquid assets, while fifty-one percent of the spending units headed by unskilled or service workers had no assets. Other, more shocking data suggest that between .2 and .3 of one percent of the population control twenty-two percent of the personal wealth and sixty to seventy percent of all privately held corporate wealth.

What in fact was the condition of the poor through the fifties and into the sixties? First of all, we must have a definition of poverty. The federal government has chosen the income-line method, with all families falling below three thousand dollars (now thirty-seven hundred, because of inflation) defined as poor, and therefore eligible for charitable assistance. Before 1962, little was known about this group; since then, a veritable anti-poverty industry has dredged up quantities of information about these people, from their illiteracy rates to their reproduction out of wedlock.

Given all this information, what have we learned? First of all, the income-line method is misleading. It fails to account for assets, temporary impoverishment, and several other factors. Second, and more important, the three thousand dollars has been recognized as ridiculously, if not criminally, low.

How in fact was the government's poverty budget originally arrived at? Politically, several factors interacted; methodologically, the explanation is simple. An annual food budget was prepared, and then that figure was tripled. The budget followed Department of Agriculture guidelines that included the notion that food occupies about one-third of normal expenditures. But simple methodology belied the gross underestimation of need. Oscar Ornati, in *Poverty Amid Affluence*, summarized a typical 1960 "adequate minimum" budget for a family of four:

"It provides for simple clothing to protect against the weather and maintain cleanliness. A woman's coat, for instance, must last five years. Leftover food must be retrieved. A cup of flour spilled means no thickening that week; a blown bulb, no light for that month; and a chair broken in anger cannot be replaced for a year. The meat budget allows for stewing lamb, beef liver, or heart, picnic shoulder, fillet of haddock, or perhaps a boned veal roast. No frozen foods are provided for. It allows nothing for an occasional glass of beer, tobacco, or telephone calls. The budget assumes a small rented five-room flat. The family living room might have two chairs. A mattress and spring on legs may serve as a couch, a dropleaf table for eating; two straight chairs may also be there. Linoleum may cover the floor, and there can be a lamp or two. An electric refrigerator and iron are allowed. The family may listen to the radio an hour a day, but television is not included in the budget. There will be money to buy aspirin but none for 'miracle' drugs. The husband may get a haircut once a month, and the wife a home permanent once a year. She can use a self-service launderette. There will be no money to buy the children candy or ice cream, or to go to the movies, or to offer a visitor a cup of coffee."

The government's budget is unrealistic on other scores. It fails to take account of the overpricing and shoddy quality of food in poor areas, as documented in books like David Caplovitz' *The Poor Pay More*. It ignores the high cost of other items such as housing and furniture, etc. (usually ten to twenty-five percent overpriced, according to one Bureau of the Census economist) that drives up maintenance costs in the other two-thirds of its budget. In farm areas, it still relies heavily on the presumption that the rural families produce much of their own food, although as a percentage of the total food consumed, home-grown items have fallen from seventy to thirty-six percent in the past twenty years. It makes no allowances for the higher education of the children, unless one presumes they will receive full scholarship aid, which is highly unlikely. Finally, it assumes no major medical expenses in the family, although over half of the poor are not covered by medical insurance.

The actual meals upon which the entire budget is based inspire greater disbelief. The words of the Census that "assuming the homemaker is a good manager and has the time and skill to shop wisely, she may prepare nutritious, palatable meals . . . for herself, a husband, and two young children" on a budget of seventy cents per day per person inspired one pundit to comment that "Betty Crocker herself would starve." A statistician for H.E.W. describes how a housewife must spend her money:

"For a meal all four of them ate together, she could spend on the average only ninety-five cents, and to stay within her budget she must allow no more a day than a pound of meat, poultry, or fish altogether, barely enough for one small serving for each family member at one of the three meals. Eggs could fill out her family fare only to a limited degree because the plan allows less than two dozen a week for all uses in cooking and at the table, not even one to a person a day. And any food extras, such as milk at school for the children or the coffee her husband might buy to supplement the lunch he carries to work, have to come out of the same food money or compete with the limited funds available for rent, clothing, medical care, and all other expenses. Studies indicate that, on the average, family members eating a meal away from home spend twice as much as the homemaker would spend for preparing one for them at home. The twenty-five cents allowed for a meal at home in the economy plan would not buy much even in the way of supplementation."

Despite the obvious sub-minimal character of this "minimum budget," some optimism has been generated by the War on Poverty and a booming economy, inducing people to believe that the poor are "disappearing." But this optimism needs closer scrutiny. First of all, a three-thousand-dollar limit is a ridiculously low level separating the poor from the non-poor. Second, the government has continued to play games with its own figures ever since the War on Poverty began. For example, the cutoff limit of poverty is measured by pre-tax income figures, although the poverty budget was constructed on an after-tax basis. Third, politics has taken a heavy toll on the poor. According to the McGovern Committee: "In 1968, government statisticians estimated there were between twenty-two and twenty-seven million Americans living in poverty." But at the beginning of 1969 "the higher of these two figures was dropped without explanation" and the twenty-two million used as the official estimate. Finally, government economists have consistently underestimated the effect of taxes and inflation on the poor, or so say a group of non-government economists (writing in *Life*, August 15, 1969). Since fixture of the three-thousand-dollar figure in 1960–61 dollars, inflation and taxes have required a gain of forty-one percent in actual income to maintain a real income equivalent. This would require a present definition of the poverty level at $4,240, or $540 more than the government now allows. Such an adjustment would add several million more families to the rolls of the poor.

For the extremely poor, times are now even harder. As the Southern Rural Research Project reported: "The poor and the hungry had their brief moment in the sun: America may lionize its victims, but the vogue of compassion passes quickly on; the hungry have now become somewhat passé. Americans seem to take it for granted that once such alarming conditions are publicly known, the appropriate authorities will automatically step in and clear the matter up." Dr. Arnold Schaefer, who headed the Public Health

Service's National Nutrition Survey, had been among the first to document malnutrition in sample counties in Texas and Louisiana; now the survey has been discontinued, and Dr. Schaefer has passed quietly from the scene. One wonders if the fifteen million malnourished have disappeared as quietly.

The Nixon Administration's response to the crisis of poverty remains to be seen, since its proposed revamping of the welfare system has yet to pass Congress. The central feature of minimum income is an advance over existing programs, since it recognizes working as well as non-working poor; but its own ceilings of aid are so low as to offset the extension in coverage. His proposals to tie Social Security to cost-of-living indices also seem designed to benefit one segment of the poor, but this was rejected in favor of a one-shot fifteen-percent bonus.

The central fallacy, or perhaps the central design, in the government's designation of the poor is its narrowness. Given the present definition of the poor, we avoid the larger contours of our social reality. Compared with the wealthy or near-wealthy, the gains of the poor have been almost immaterial. In 1946, the bottom twenty percent of all families (the government estimate of the "poor" hovers around sixteen percent) received five percent of the income; by 1967, the same fifth—now forty million people—received 5.4 percent. In other words, the intonations of "trickle down" by economists of the fifties now sound hollow indeed.

Crucial to the isolation of the poor is not only the government's action, but the basic American myth. We are people of the *middle* class, bourgeois, home folks, people who still like Norman Rockwell and live decent, unextravagant lives. De Tocqueville did not instigate the myth, but *Democracy in America* certainly strengthened it. His comments on the "tendencies toward the equalization of the conditions of life" set the pattern for all later social scientists and historians who sought to capture the fundamental character of the country. Louis Hartz, as recently as the middle nineteen-fifties, still wrote of "irrational Lockeanism" as the controlling factor in American political life, and saw this as a reflection of the dominant "middle class."

The belief in progress has always caused Americans to see their past in an ambivalent light. They have viewed the past romantically, choosing to see our problems as smaller and our victories larger than life. What is imperialism to some has been Manifest Destiny in America. What for some was genocide directed toward the Indian was only "resettlement" of the natives. Even when we made mistakes, there was seldom an accusation of guile or willfulness on our part. The Spanish-American War was "misguided," but it was fought with the best of intentions.

By this kind of logic, our poor today are still better off than ninety percent of the world, and certainly in a better state than they were fifty years ago. The discomfort that greeted disclosures by the muckrakers and writers of the naturalist school at the turn of the century has been replaced today by a comfortable agreement that "things were bad then, but just look at them now." After all, the middle class has always been America's strength and salvation. If we do have poor, well, either they are lazy and inefficient (the conservative view) or they are victimized minorities—blacks, the old, unwed welfare mothers (the liberal view). In any case, nobody opposes welfare anymore—Nixon is pushing the guaranteed income—and besides, as liberal economist Alan Batchelder has assured us, "the poor will continue to disappear as the economy expands."

The fundamental misdirection of all this is away from analysis of the "middle class" to a blind invocation of the myth itself. As recently as October, 1969, *Newsweek*, for example, ran an otherwise perceptive article entitled simplistically: *The Troubled American—A Special Report on the White Majority*. Studded with references to "America's vast white middle-class majority," it intoned the familiar lauds: "America has always been the most middle class of nations, the most generous and the most optimistic." But what in fact the article showed most clearly is that for an enormous proportion of the "middle class," embourgeoisement has been a half-filled dream, a set of unsatisfied hopes. These are the people Leon Keyserling has called not the poor but "the deprived Americans"—"above poverty but short of the minimum requirements for a modestly comfortable level of living." In 1964, Keyserling estimated their number at seventy-seven million men, women, and children.

Keyserling's distinction between a family income of thirty-five hundred dollars ("poverty") and forty-five hundred ("deprivation") should be clear to an economist: the "deprived" all work. Unlike the poor, whose ranks are swelled by the elderly, the infirm, and the blacks, the "deprived" cannot be dismissed as victims of "non-market forces." The "deprived" are functioning, productive members of our economic system: the manual laborers, the clerks, the launderers, the hospital workers of our society. They may have their own home, but it is heavily mortgaged; they may have a late-model car, but it has been financed at steep rates. Their savings, which form a family's cushion against disaster, are marginal: forty percent are either in debt or have savings of less than one hundred dollars. Liquid assets show even less room for error: twenty percent of all families own no assets, and forty-eight percent own less than five hundred dollars' worth. Yet, as Kolko rightly points out: "Liquid assets—such as checking and savings accounts, shares in savings-and-loan associations and credit unions, and government savings bonds—are of decisive importance to low- and even middle-income families exposed to layoffs, unemployment, or medical and other emergencies. Often they represent the entire margin between security and the relief rolls."

The myth of the middle class serves as a permanent leash on the deprived. Lacking the income, they are still expected to provide their families with the amenities that advertising, television, and the academic mythmakers have told them the "middle class" enjoys. Constantly under pressure, they retain all the old American virtues as a desperate bulwark against the encroachment of the "shiftless poor." They, like the poor, bear a heavy burden of the taxation because of regressive tax structures. They aspire to better education for their children, their own home, and more leisure. Yet, in a great many cases, both father and mother must work simply to maintain their present condition.

The disparities within the "middle class" and the number of the "deprived" are brought out most clearly when one examines the data of income growth over the past half-century. The accompanying table shows control of the income shares by population tenths since 1910. Omitting the top tenth as "upper class" and the bottom two-tenths as "poor," analysis of the remaining "middle class" yields striking results.

PERCENTAGE OF NATIONAL PERSONAL INCOME, BEFORE TAXES,
RECEIVED BY EACH INCOME-TENTH*

	Highest Tenth	2nd	3rd	4th	5th	6th	7th	8th	9th	Lowest Tenth
1910	33.9	12.3	10.2	8.8	8.0	7.0	6.0	5.5	4.9	3.4
1918	34.5	12.9	9.6	8.7	7.7	7.2	6.9	5.7	4.4	2.4
1921	38.2	12.8	10.5	8.9	7.4	6.5	5.9	4.6	3.2	2.0
1929	39.0	12.3	9.8	9.0	7.9	6.5	5.5	4.6	3.6	1.8
1934	33.6	13.1	11.0	9.4	8.2	7.3	6.2	5.3	3.8	2.1
1937	34.4	14.1	11.7	10.1	8.5	7.2	6.0	4.4	2.6	1.0
1941	34.0	16.0	12.0	10.0	9.0	7.0	5.0	4.0	2.0	1.0
1945	29.0	16.0	13.0	11.0	9.0	7.0	6.0	5.0	3.0	1.0
1946	32.0	15.0	12.0	10.0	9.0	7.0	6.0	5.0	3.0	1.0
1947	33.5	14.8	11.7	9.9	8.5	7.1	5.8	4.4	3.1	1.2
1948	30.9	14.7	11.9	10.1	8.8	7.5	6.3	5.0	3.3	1.4
1949	29.8	15.5	12.5	10.6	9.1	7.7	6.2	4.7	3.1	0.8
1950	28.7	15.4	12.7	10.8	9.3	7.8	6.3	4.9	3.2	0.9
1951	30.9	15.0	12.3	10.6	8.9	7.6	6.3	4.7	2.9	0.8
1952	29.5	15.3	12.4	10.6	9.1	7.7	6.4	4.9	3.1	1.0
1953	31.4	14.8	11.9	10.3	8.9	7.6	6.2	4.7	3.0	1.2
1954	29.3	15.3	12.4	10.7	9.1	7.7	6.4	4.8	3.1	1.2
1955	29.7	15.7	12.7	10.8	9.1	7.7	6.1	4.5	2.7	1.0
1956	30.6	15.3	12.3	10.5	9.0	7.6	6.1	4.5	2.8	1.3
1957	29.4	15.5	12.7	10.8	9.2	7.7	6.1	4.5	2.9	1.3
1958	27.1	16.3	13.2	11.0	9.4	7.8	6.2	4.6	3.1	1.3
1959	28.9	15.8	12.7	10.7	9.2	7.8	6.3	4.6	2.9	1.1

*In terms of "recipients" for 1910-37 and "spending units" for 1941-59.
Source: Data for 1910-37 are from National Industrial Conference Board, *Studies in Enterprise and Social Progress* (New York: National Industrial Conference Board, 1939), p. 125. Data for 1941-59 were calculated by the Survey Research Center. Figures for 1941-46 are available in rounded form only.

The most interesting observation is that there are two distinct strata in the "middle class," the upper of the two having gained markedly greater control of income. Between 1910 and 1959, the second, third, and fourth deciles increased their percentage of the total income more than one-quarter, while the fifth, sixth, seventh, and eighth deciles were able to advance only from 26.5 percent to 27.9 percent in the same period.

This information sheds light on much of the writing over the past two decades on the Affluent Society. The "middle class," as a homogeneous group, has done well; but closer examination reveals that that success becomes smaller and smaller as one moves down the income scale within that class. The astigmatic concern of the social scientists for suburbia, executive anomy, and the crises of "the abundant society" has proceeded from myths that now seem badly worn—from the myth of the New Affluence, from the myth of "trickle-down" income and wealth redistribution and the omnipotence of Keynes, and from the capstone myth of them all—the myth of the American middle class.

As a matter of fact, the "middle class" may have escaped the grasp of more than the poor and the deprived. If by "middle class" one means a decent, modest standard of living, it seems that perhaps sixty to seventy percent of the country have difficulty in reaching it. In 1966, the Bureau of Labor Statistics announced that the average urban family required $9,191 per year to live comfortably; yet the median income that same year was fourteen hundred dollars less than that figure.

At this point, it seems wise to stop and make two observations: the first an estimation of some present and possibly future realities; the second, an historical speculation.

The first observation is about the "unmentioned middle class," the professional, technical élite and its immediate support structure. These people are the true beneficiaries of the Affluent Society, and are the class which has sought to reshape the American myths in its image. College-educated, employed as lawyers, engineers, advertisers, and real-estate dealers, these people are the upper strata of the middle class that experienced the greatest gains in postwar years. The suburban crises of the fifties were *their* crises, the suburban malaise was drowned in *their* Martini glasses. If one were to seek a paradigm for their group, one would find it during the Kennedy era, in the bright young men around the seat of power; but one could also find it in the older and younger men, in corporations and universities. They are those whom Daniel Bell described as the "technocratic élite."

An attack on this group here is not immediately relevant. The Vietnam war has already prompted a number of incisive critiques of them, particularly on the university level. However, critique and solution are not synonymous. It seems likely that the import of young people's radicalism will be diffused and co-opted back into electoral party politics, and the thrust of radical restructuring lost, as it was in the New Deal. Already the "beautiful people" seem to be emerging as the new archetype of this social caste . . . human beings who span Establishment and anti-Establishment factionalism, who work for corporations by day, yet smoke dope by night.

The problem is that their amorality is more difficult to detect because it so often hides behind a veil of rhetorical concern. Unlike the industrial captains of the last century, their contemporary lieutenants feign not indifference but impotence. After all, they *are* concerned, God knows, but they are only vice-presidents or mere managers. They may give occasionally to the political *outré* or talk of "repressive tolerance" at cocktail parties, but those gestures mark the boundaries of their social concern.

One index of that social indifference emerges in an ironic place: Michael Harrington in January had an article in *The Atlantic* entitled "The Betrayal of the Poor." The irony is that *The Atlantic*, for all its enlightenment, is still an organ of that upper-middle class who have not so much resisted, as they have ignored, social change.

The article begins: "For all the rhetoric of recent years about the war on poverty, the poor in America are almost as numerous as ever. . . . Unless the government makes immensely greater commitments of resources and planning, the country is doomed to a social explosion in the seventies that will make the turbulent sixties seem tranquil by comparison." The article, like articles on the malnourished, on housing conditions, on the quality of education in the ghetto, will be read and then lost in the comfortable notion that once federal programs are established, everything will be taken care of. Enter the New Deal, Phase II.

The error in this remains the presumption of the liberal upper-middle class since the first decade of this century: that social legislation by the federal government will cure what ails us. Jane Addams suggested it; Ralph Hunter, one of the nation's first social welfare workers, endorsed it; the New Deal itself put the seal of approval on it; and now even Republicans have begun to see merit in the idea. Unfortunately, the theory has never worked.

The critical assumption behind liberal optimism about coalition between the federal government and corporate capitalism has been that things keep getting better all the time. There are more cars, more homes, better schools, etc., than ever before and, in the midst of this prosperity, the distribution of all this largesse has been getting better as well.

Taking the first half of this claim—that the total quantity of goods has increased—there is no dispute. But one *can* make some comparisons between the United States and other industrialized nations. Fifteen nations have higher literacy rates. Ten nations have lower infant mortality rates. To my knowledge, the United States is the only industrialized nation that does not offer comprehensive medical insurance for all its people. It offers perhaps the worst unemployment protection and the worst welfare system among the developed countries. It has fifteen million malnourished. It has thirty million poor. It has seventy-seven million deprived. Few other nations can claim such tawdry conditions amid such phenomenal growth.

On the second half of the comfortable liberal optimism—that distribution has been getting better and better—there is a fundamental error in the assumption. Since the Second World War, the only significant redistribution of income in the United States has been between the upper and the upper-middle classes. Overall, distribution has remained essentially stable not only over the past twenty years but over the entire twentieth century.

There are three sources for this statement. The first is the chart on income distribution (see p. 363) that shows the limits of change. The second is from Joseph Pechman, a conventionally liberal economist, writing in *The Public Interest*, who states: "The year 1929 must have been the high point of inequality during the nineteen-twenties, so that distribution of income in the more recent period may not have been very different from what it was in the early twenties if account is taken of undistributed profits." The third is a much earlier source. Published in 1904, Robert Hunter's *Poverty* is probably the first attempt made to estimate the number of poor in America. Highly sympathetic to the poor, it uses the data of state and private welfare agencies (since federal data were nonexistent). While emphasizing the wretched conditions of the poor, Hunter limits their number to only twelve percent of the population. Today economic historians agree that Hunter's estimate was off the mark by six percent, thus leaving at the turn of the century a minority poor of eighteen percent. Yet eighteen percent was the government's estimate of the poor sixty years later!

None of these three estimates is perfect (none ever can be, because crucial data are lacking); but they can give a newer and perhaps more accurate contour of poverty and affluence in America. We are, as De Toqueville said, and as American social scientists have reaffirmed ever since, "a people of the middle class." But to be middle class is both a social-psychological and economic problem. Among those who call themselves "middle class," perhaps a majority have always lacked the money to be in fact what they believe they are. Not only are the poor still with us, but they have been there for years. Michael Harrington's announcement that our poor are the "first minority poor in history" has been misunderstood; the poor have always been a minority in America, but a stubborn minority that refuses to decrease and disappear. The rich in America just keep getting richer. All the talk of income distribution, of flattening pyramids, and of peaceful economic revolutions has been nonsense, fabricated in part out of optimism, in part out of a myopia in the professional classes who themselves gained so rapidly after the Second World War.

At the end of an account such as this, it is usually expected that the author will offer remedies, specific reforms such as tax legislation or welfare payments—or at least see reason for hope on the horizon. I cannot. First, because "reform" has become the province of politicians and electoral platforms, and deals with our needs about as realistically as someone using a

Band-Aid on a compound fracture. Yet, even liberals accept reformism, as they did when they quietly applauded the Nixon proposal of a guaranteed annual income for the poor, despite the dire (and probably accurate) warning of Michael Harrington that "a guaranteed annual income could be a way to institutionalize poverty at the subsistence level in the United States."

Second, and more important, I do not seek "reform" because, at age twenty-three, I have lost faith in the willingness of America to "reform." I have lived with the poor, eaten their food, slept in their beds, and taught their children, in Alabama, in Vermont, in Watts. I know their bitterness, and I share it. John Kenneth Galbraith observed recently that "liberalism has been excessively tender toward the rich." A surprise to liberals, but a fact of life for the poor. Attempts at reform have delivered to the poor nothing but promises. They have watched the War on Poverty beaten into ineffectual irrelevance. They have listened to America's liberal politicians promise food as they stare at empty plates. They know the sham of reform.

Revolution without Ideology:
The Changing Place of
Women in America

Carl N. Degler

According to the leadership of the Women's Liberation Movement in
America, the bastions of male supremacy are no longer safe in the
Republic. Myths concerning the role of women in our society—
based as they are on sexual attitudes, social roles, and cultural
mores—are indeed being challenged with much vigor. In an attempt
to deal with the historical reality of the place of women in America,
however, Carl N. Degler (who spent a considerable portion of his academic career teaching at Vassar) seeks to demonstrate that basic
conditions in American society have often worked to a feminist advantage. What could be called the "Playboy Syndrome," speaks to
only a small portion of women's historical experience. In Degler's
view, factors such as the frontier, industrialism, and war have from
the beginning created an uncommon feminine bias in America.

If feminism is defined as the belief that women are human beings and entitled
to the same opportunities for self-expression as men, then America has har-
bored a feminist bias from the beginning. In both the eighteenth and nineteenth centuries foreign travelers remarked on the freedom for women in
America. "A paradise for women," one eighteenth-century German called
America, and toward the close of the nineteenth century Lord Bryce wrote
that in the United States "it is easier for women to find a career, to obtain
work of an intellectual as of a commercial kind, than in any part of Europe."

Certainly the long history of a frontier in America helps to account for
this feminist bias. In a society being carved out of a wilderness, women were
active and important contributors to the process of settlement and civilization.
Moreover, because women have been scarce in America they have been highly
valued. During almost the whole of the colonial period men outnumbered
women, and even in the nineteenth century women remained scarce in the
West. As late as 1865, for example, there were three men for each woman in
California; in Colorado the ratio was as high as 20 to 1. Such disparities in
the sex ratio undoubtedly account for the West's favorable attitude toward
women, as in an Oregon law of 1850 that granted land to single women and,
even more significant for the time, to married women; or in the willingness
of western territories like Wyoming (1869) and Utah (1870) to grant the

From "Revolution without Ideology: The Changing Place of Women in America,"
by Carl N. Degler. Reprinted by permission of *Daedalus*, Journal of the American
Academy of Arts and Sciences, Boston, Massachusetts, Spring 1964, *The Women
in America*.

suffrage to women long before other regions where the sex ratio was more nearly equal.

Another measure of women's high esteem in American society was the rapidity with which the doors of higher education opened to women. Even without counting forerunners like Oberlin College, which admitted women in 1837, the bars against women came down faster and earlier in America than anywhere. The breakthrough came during the Civil War era, when women's colleges like Elmira, Vassar and Smith were founded, and universities like Michigan and Cornell became coeducational. The process was later and slower in Europe. Girton College, Cambridge, for example, which opened in 1869, was the sole English institution of higher education available to women until London University accorded women full privileges in 1879. Heidelberg, which was the first German university to accept women, did not do so until 1900. More striking was the fact that at its opening Girton provided six places for young women; Vassar alone, when it opened in 1865, counted some 350 students in residence. Another indication of the American feminist bias was that at the end of the century girls outnumbered boys among high school graduates.

But if the frontier experience of America helped to create a vague feminist bias that accorded women more privileges than in settled Europe, the really potent force changing women's place had little to do with the frontier or the newness of the country. It was the industrial revolution that provided the impetus to women's aspirations for equality of opportunity; it was the industrial revolution that carried through the first stage in the changing position of women—the removal of legal and customary barriers to women's full participation in the activities of the world.

Today it is axiomatic that men work outside the home. But before the industrial revolution of the nineteenth century, the great majority of men and women were co-workers on the land and in the home. Women worked in the fields when the chores of the home and child-rearing permitted, so that there was not only close association between work and home for both sexes, but even a certain amount of overlap in the sexual division of labor. The coming of machine production changed all that. For a time, it is true, many unmarried women and children—the surplus labor of the day—were the mainstay of the new factory system, but that was only temporary. By the middle of the nineteenth century the bulk of industrial labor was male. The coming of the factory and the city thus wholly changed the nature of men's work. For the first time in history, work for most men was something done outside the family, psychologically as well as physically separated from the home.

The same industrial process that separated work and home also provided the opportunities for women to follow men out of the home. For that reason the feminist movement, both socially and intellectually, was a direct consequence of the industrial changes of the nineteenth century. Furthermore, just as the new industrial system was reshaping the rural men who came under its influence, so it reshaped the nature of women.

The process began with the home, which, in the early years of industrialization, was still the site of most women's work. Because of high land values, the city home was smaller than the farm house, and with less work for children, the size of the urban family was smaller than the rural. Moreover, in the city work in the home changed. Machines in factories now performed many of the tasks that had long been women's. In truth, the feminist movement began not when women felt a desire for men's jobs, but when men in factories began to take away women's traditional work. Factory-produced clothing, commercial laundries, prepared foods (e.g., prepared cereals, canned vegetables, condensed milk, bakery bread) were already available in the years after the Civil War. Toward the end of the century an advanced feminist like Charlotte Perkins Gilman, impressed by the accelerating exodus of women's chores from the middle-class home, predicted that the whole kitchen would soon be gone. She was wrong there, but even today the flight continues with pre-cooked and frozen foods, TV dinners, cake mixes, special packaging for easy disposal, diaper services and the like.

Middle-class women were the main beneficiaries of the lightening of the chores of the home; few working-class or immigrant women could as yet take advantage of the new services and products. These middle-class women became the bone and sinew of the feminist movement, which was almost entirely an urban affair. They joined the women's clubs, organized the temperance crusades and marched in the suffrage parades. With an increasing amount of time available to them in the city, and imbued with the historic American value of work, they sought to do good. And there was much to be done in the raw, sometimes savage, urban environment of the late nineteenth century. For example, public playgrounds in the United States began in Boston only in the 1880's, when two public-spirited middle-class women caused a cartload of sand to be piled on an empty lot and set the neighborhood children loose upon it. Many a city and small town at the turn of the century owed its public library or its park to the dedicated work of women's clubs. The venerable giant redwood trees of northern California survive today because clubwomen of San Francisco and nearby towns successfully campaigned in 1900 to save them from being cut down for lumber. The saloon and prostitution were two other prevalent urban blights that prompted study and action by women's organizations.

More important than women's opposition to social evils was the widening of women's knowledge and concerns that inevitably accompanied it. What began as a simple effort to rid the community of a threat to its purity often turned into a discovery of the economic exploitation that drove young working girls into brothels and harried working men into saloons. Frances Willard, for example, while head of the Women's Christian Temperance Union, broadened the WCTU's reform interests far beyond the liquor question, causing it to advocate protective legislation for working women, kindergartens and training programs for young working girls. Jane Addams, at Hull-House in Chicago's slums, quickly learned what historians have only recently discovered, that it was the urban boss's undeniable services to the immigrants that were the true sources of his great political power and the real secret of his successful survival of municipal reform campaigns.

The most direct way in which industrialization altered the social function of women was by providing work for women outside the home. Production by machine, of course, widened enormously the uses to which women's labor could be put once physical strength was no longer a consideration. And toward the end of the century, as business enterprises grew and record-keeping, communications and public relations expanded, new opportunities for women opened up in business offices. The telephone operator, the typist, the clerical worker and the stenographer now took places beside the seamstress, the cotton mill operator and the teacher.

As workers outside the home, women buried the Victorian stereotype of the lady under a mountain of reality. After all, it was difficult to argue that women as a sex were weak, timid, incompetent, fragile vessels of spirituality when thousands of them could be seen trudging to work in the early hours of the day in any city of the nation. Nor could a girl who worked in a factory or office help but become more worldly. A young woman new to a shop might have been embarrassed to ask a male foreman for the ladies' room, as some working girls' autobiographies report, but such maidenly reticence could hardly survive very long. Even gentle, naïve farm girls soon found out how to handle the inevitable, improper advances of foremen. They also learned the discipline of the clock, the managing of their own money, the excitement of life outside the home, the exhilaration of financial independence along with the drudgery of machine labor. Having learned something of the ways of the world, women could not be treated then, nor later in marriage, as the hopeless dependents Victorian ideals prescribed.

In time work transformed the outer woman, too. First to go were the hobbling, trailing skirts, which in a factory were a hazard and a nuisance. Even before the Civil War, Amelia Bloomer and other feminists had pointed out that women, if they were to work in the world as human beings, needed looser and lighter garments than those then in fashion. Until working women were numbered in the millions, no change took place. After 1890 women's skirts gradually crept up from the floor, and the neat and simple shirtwaist became the uniform of the working girl. A costume very like the original bloomer was widely worn by women factory workers during the First World War. Later the overall and the coverall continued the adaptation of women's clothes to the machine.

The most dramatic alteration in the image of woman came after the First World War, when there was a new upsurge in women's employment. The twenties witnessed the emergence of the white-collar class, and women were a large part of it. Over twice as many women entered the labor force that decade as in the previous one; the number of typists alone in 1930 was three-quarters of a million, a tenfold increase since 1900. And woman's appearance reflected the requirements of work. Except for some of the extreme flapper fashions, which were transient, the contemporary woman still dresses much as the woman of the 1920's did. In the 1920's women threw out the corset and the numerous petticoats in favor of light undergarments, a single slip, silk or rayon stockings, short skirts and bobbed hair. So rapid and widespread was the change that an investigation in the 1920's revealed that even most working-class girls no longer wore corsets, and the new interest in bobbed hair resulted between 1920 and 1930 in an increase of 400 percent in the number of women hair dressers.

The physical freedom of dress that women acquired during the 1920's was but the superficial mark of a new social equality. The social forces behind this new equality are several. Some of these forces, like the growing number of college-trained women and the increasing number of women in the working force, go back far into the past; others, like the impact of the war and the arduous campaign for women's suffrage, were more recent. But whatever the causes, the consequences were obvious. Indeed, what is generally spoken of as the revolution in morals of the 1920's is more accurately a revolution in the position of women. Within a few short years a spectrum of taboos was shed. For the first time women began to smoke and drink in public; cigarette manufacturers discovered and exploited in advertising a virtually untouched market. As recently as 1918 it was considered daring for a New York hotel to permit women to sit at a bar. In the twenties, despite prohibition, both sexes drank in public.

Perhaps most significant, as well as symbolic, of the new stage in the position of women was their new sexual freedom. The twenties have long been associated with the discovery of Freud and a fresh, publicly acknowledged interest in sex. But insofar as these attitudes were new they represented changes in women, particularly those of the middle and upper classes. Premarital and extramarital sexuality by men had never been severely criticized, and discussion of sexual matters was commonplace wherever men gathered. Now, though, middle-class women also enjoyed that freedom. For the first time, it has been said, middle-class men carried on their extramarital affairs with women of their own social class instead of with cooks, maids and prostitutes.

An easier sexuality outside of marriage was only the most sensational side of the revolution in morals; more important, if only because more broadly based, was a new, informal, equal relationship between the sexes, culminating in a new conception of marriage. The day was long since past when Jennie June Croly could be barred, as she was in 1868, from a dinner in honor of Charles Dickens at a men's club even though her husband was a member and she was a professional writer. (Indeed, so thoroughly has such separation of the sexes been abandoned that the New Princeton Club in New York City has closed all but one of its public rooms to any man who is not accompanied by a woman!) And at least in the gatherings of the educated middle class, talk between the sexes was often free, frank and wide-ranging. The same mutual acceptance of the sexes was visible in the prevalent talk about the "new marriage," in which the woman was a partner and a companion, not simply a mother, social convenience and a housekeeper.

The reality of the new conception of marriage was reflected in the sharp increase in the divorce rate. Because marriage, legally as well as socially, in the nineteenth century was more confining for women than for men, the early feminists had often advocated more liberal divorce laws. And even though divorce in the nineteenth century was more common in the United States than in any European country, the divorce rate in the 1920's shot up 50 percent over what it had been only ten years before. One sign that women in the 1920's were seeking freedom from marriage if they could not secure equality in marriage was that two thirds of the divorces in that decade were instituted by women.

By the close of the twenties the ordinary woman in America was closer to a man in the social behavior expected of her, in the economic opportunities open to her and in the intellectual freedom enjoyed by her than at any time in history. To be sure there still was a double standard, but now its existence was neither taken for granted nor confidently asserted by men.

In truth, the years since the twenties have witnessed few alterations in the position of women that were not first evident in that crucial decade. The changes have penetrated more deeply and spread more widely through the social structure, but their central tendency was then already spelled out. Even the upsurge in women's employment, which was so striking in the twenties, continued in subsequent years. Each decade thereafter has counted a larger number of working women than the previous one. During the depression decade of the 1930's, even, half a million more women entered the labor force than in the prosperous twenties. By 1960 some 38 percent of all women of working age—almost two out of five women—were employed outside the home.

The movement of women out of the home into remunerative work, however, has been neither steady nor unopposed. Undoubtedly one of the underlying conditions is an expanding economy's need for labor. But something more than that is needed to break society's traditional habits of mind about the proper work for women. Certainly here the feminist demands for equality for women played a part. But a social factor of equal importance was war. By their very disruption of the steady pulse of everyday living, wars break the cake of custom, shake up society and compel people to look afresh at old habits and attitudes. It is not accidental, for instance, that women's suffrage in England, Russia and Germany, as well as the United States, was achieved immediately after the First World War and in France and Italy after the Second.

At the very least, by making large and new demands upon the established work force, war draws hitherto unused labor into the economic process. During the Civil War, for example, young women assumed new roles in the economy as workers in metal and munitions factories, as clerks in the expanded bureaucracy in Washington and as nurses in war hospitals. Moreover, when the war was over women had permanently replaced men as the dominant sex in the teaching profession. Furthermore, since many women found a new usefulness in the Sanitary Fairs and other volunteer work, the end of hostilities left many women unwilling to slip back into the seclusion of the Victorian home. It is not simply coincidental that the women's club movement began very soon after the war.

When the First World War came to the United States, feminist leaders, perhaps recalling the gains of the Civil War, anticipated new and broad advances for their sex. And the demand for labor, especially after the United States entered the war, did open many jobs to women, just as it was doing in contemporary Great Britain and Germany. All over the United States during the war customary and legal restrictions on the employment of women fell away. Women could be seen doing everything from laying railroad ties to working in airplane factories. The war also brought to a successful climax the struggle for the suffrage. Pointedly women had argued that a war for democracy abroad should at least remedy the deficiencies of democracy at home.

If politically the war was a boon to women, economically it failed to live up to feminist anticipations. The First World War, unlike the Civil War, did not result in a large permanent increase in the number of working women. Indeed, by 1920 there were only 800,000 more women working than in 1910. But as a result of wartime demands, women did get permanent places in new job categories, like elevator operators and theater ushers. (But women street car conductors disappeared soon after the armistice.) Certain traditional professions for women, like music teaching, lost members between 1910 and 1920, while professions that required more training and provided steadier income, like library and social work and college teaching, doubled or tripled their numbers in the same period.

The Second World War, with its even more massive demands for labor and skills, brought almost four million new women workers into the nation's factories and offices. Once again jobs usually not filled by women were opened to them. For example, the number of women bank officers rose 40 percent during the four years of the war and the number of women employees in finance has continued to rise ever since. Furthermore, unlike the situation after the First World War, the female work force after 1945 not only stayed up but then went higher.

Measured in the number of women working, the changes in the economic position of women add up to a feminist success. Twenty-four million working women cannot be ignored. But weighed in the scales of quality instead of quantity, the change in women's economic status is not so striking.

It is true that women now work in virtually every job listed by the Bureau of the Census. Moreover, the popular press repeatedly tells of the inroads women are making into what used to be thought of as men's jobs. Three years ago, for example, a woman won a prize as the mutual fund salesman of the year. Women are widely represented in advertising and in real estate, and even women taxicab drivers are no longer rare. Yet the fact remains that the occupations in which the vast majority of women actually engage are remarkably similar to those historically held by women. In 1950 almost three quarters of all employed women fell into twenty occupational categories, of which the largest was stenographers, typists and secretaries—a category that first became prominent as a woman's occupation over a half century ago. Other occupations which have traditionally been women's, like domestic service, teaching, clerical work, nursing and telephone service, are also conspicuous among the twenty categories. Further than that, the great majority of women are employed in occupations in which they predominate. This sexual division of labor is clearly evident in the professions, even though women are only a small proportion of total professional workers. Two thirds of all professional women are either nurses or teachers; and even in teaching there is a division between the sexes. Most women teach in the primary grades; most men teach in high school. Women are notoriously underrepresented in the top professions like law, medicine, engineering and scientific research. No more than 7 percent of all professional women in 1950 were in the four of these categories together. Only 6 percent of medical doctors and 4 percent of lawyers and judges were women. In contrast, almost three quarters of medical doctors are women in the Soviet Union; in England the figure is 16 percent. In both France and Sweden women make up a high proportion of pharmacists and dentists; neither of those professions attracts many women in the United States.

One consequence as well as manifestation of the sexual division of labor in the United States has been the differences in pay for men and women. That difference has been a historical complaint of feminist leaders. In 1900 one study found women's wages to be, on the average, only 53 percent of men's. The reason was, of course, that women were concentrated in the poorer paying jobs and industries of the economy. The disparity in pay between the sexes has been somewhat reduced today, but not very much. In 1955 among full-time women workers of all types the median wage was about two thirds of that for men. In short, women are still supplying the low-paid labor in the economy just as they were in the last century. (In substance, women workers and Negroes of both sexes perform a similar function in the economy.) The willingness of women to supply cheap labor may well account for their getting the large number of jobs they do; men often will not work for the wages that women will accept.

Today, there does not seem to be very much disparity between men's and women's wages for the same work, though the sexual division of labor is so nearly complete that it is difficult to find comparable jobs of the two sexes to make a definitive study.

There has been no improvement in women's position in higher education; indeed, it can be argued that women have failed to maintain the place reached much earlier. As we have seen, the United States led the world in opening higher education to women. This country also led in broadening the social base of education for women. No other country educated such a large proportion of women in its universities and colleges as did the United States. At the close of the nineteenth century, one third of American college students were women; by 1937 women made up almost 40 percent of the students in American institutions of higher learning. In Germany, just before Hitler took power, no more than one out of ten university students was a woman; in Swedish universities in 1937 only 17 percent of the students were women; in British universities the ratio was 22 percent.

But since the Second World War the gap between American and European proportions of women in higher education has narrowed considerably. In 1952–1953 women constituted only 35 percent of the American college population, while France counted women as 36 percent of its university students and Sweden 26 percent. The *number* of women in American colleges, of course, is considerably greater than it was in the 1920's and 1930's, but in proportion to men, women have lost ground in America while gaining in Europe.

A further sign of the regression in the educational position of women in the United States is that in the early 1950's women earned about 10 percent of the doctoral degrees in this country as compared with almost 15 percent in the 1920's.

How is one to explain this uneven, almost contradictory record of women in America? How does it happen that a country with a kind of built-in feminism from the frontier falls behind more traditional countries in its training of college women; that a country with one of the highest proportions of working women in the world ends up with such a small proportion of its women in medicine, in law and in the sciences? Perhaps the correct answer is that the question should not be asked—at least not by Americans. For like so much else in American society, such contradictions are a manifestation of the national avoidance of any ideological principle, whether it be in feminist reform or in anything else. To be sure there has been no lack of feminist argument or rationale for women's work outside the home, for women's education and for other activities by women. But American women, like American society in general, have been more concerned with individual practice than with a consistent feminist ideology. If women have entered the labor force or taken jobs during a war they have done so for reasons related to the immediate individual or social circumstances and not for reasons of feminist ideology. The women who have been concerned about showing that women's capabilities can match men's have been the exception. As the limited, and low-paying, kinds of jobs women occupy demonstrate, there is not now and never has been any strong feminist push behind the massive and continuing movement of women into jobs. Most American women have been interested in jobs, not careers. To say, as many feminists have, that men have opposed and resisted the opening of opportunities to women is to utter only a half truth. The whole truth is that American society in general, which includes women, shuns like a disease any feminist ideology.

Another way of showing that the historical changes in the status of women in America bear little relation to a feminist ideology is to examine one of those rare instances when women did effect a social improvement through an appeal to ideology, for instance, the struggle for the suffrage. By the early twentieth century the feminist demand for the vote overrode every other feminist goal. Once women achieved the vote, it was argued, the evils of society would be routed, for women, because of their peculiar attributes, would bring a fresh, needed and wholesome element into political life. In form, and in the minds of many women leaders, the arguments for the suffrage came close to being a full-blown ideology of feminism.

In point of fact, of course, the Nineteenth Amendment ushered in no millennium. But that fact is of less importance than the reason why it did not. When American women obtained the vote they simply did not use it ideologically; they voted not as women but as individuals. Evidence of this was the failure of many women to vote at all. At the end of the first decade of national suffrage women still did not exercise the franchise to the extent that men did. Nor did many women run for or hold political offices. The first woman to serve in Congress was elected in 1916; in 1920, the first year of national women's suffrage, four women were elected to Congress, but until 1940 no more than nine women served at one time in the House of Representatives and the Senate together. That we are here observing an American and not simply a sexual phenomenon is shown by a comparison with European countries. In nonfeminist Germany, where the ballot came to women at about the same time as in the United States, the first Reichstag after suffrage counted forty-one women as members. In 1951 seventeen women sat in the British House of Commons as compared with ten in the United States House of Representatives. Twice the number of women have served as cabinet ministers in Britain between 1928 and 1951 as have served in the United States down to the present.

Another instance in which social change was effected by feminist ideology was prohibition. The achievement of national prohibition ran second only to the suffrage movement as a prime goal of the organized women's movement; the Eighteenth Amendment was as much a product of feminist ideology as the Nineteenth. Yet like the suffrage movement, prohibition, despite its feminist backing, failed to receive the support of women. It was *after* prohibition was enacted, after all, that women drank in public.

In the cases of both suffrage and prohibition, women acted as individuals, not as members of a sex. And so they have continued to act. It is not without relevance that the women's political organization that is most

379

respected—the League of Women Voters—is not only nonpartisan but studiously avoids questions pertaining only to women. To do otherwise would be feminist and therefore ideological.

One further conclusion might be drawn from this examination of the non-ideological character of American women. That the changes that have come to the position of women have been devoid of ideological intent may well explain why there has been so little opposition to them. The most successful of American reforms have always been those of an impromptu and practical nature. The great revolution of the New Deal is a classic example. The American people, like FDR himself, simply tried one thing after another, looking for something—anything—that would get the nation out of the depression. If lasting reforms took place too, so much the better. On the other hand, reforms that have been justified by an elaborate rationale or ideology, like abolition, have aroused strong and long-drawn-out opposition. By the same token, when women became ideological in support of suffrage and prohibition, they faced their greatest opposition and scored their most disappointing triumphs.

The achievement of the suffrage in 1920 is a convenient date for marking the end of the first phase in the changing position of women, for by then women were accorded virtually the same rights as men even if they did not always exercise them. The second phase began at about the same time. It was the participation of married women in the work force. During the nineteenth century few married women worked; when they did it was because they were childless or because their husbands were inadequate providers. Even among the poor, married women normally did not work. A survey of the slum districts in five large cities in 1893 revealed that no more than 5 percent of the wives were employed. Only Negro wives in the South and immigrant wives in big northern cities provided any significant exceptions to this generalization.

Before the First World War, the movement of wives into the working force was barely noticeable. During the 1920's there was an acceleration, but as late as 1940 less than 17 percent of all married women were working. Among working women in 1940, 48 percent were single and only 31 percent were married. The Second World War dramatically reversed these proportions —another instance of the influence of war on the position of women. By 1950 the proportion of married women living with their husbands had risen to 48 percent of all working women while that of single women had fallen to 32 percent. In 1960 the Census reported that almost 32 percent of all married women were employed outside the home and that they comprised 54 percent of all working women. No industrial country of Europe, with the exception of the Soviet Union, counted such a high proportion. Today, married women are the greatest source of new labor in the American economy. Between 1949 and 1959, for example, over four million married women entered the labor force, some 60 percent of *all* additions, male and female.

Such a massive movement of married women out of the home was a development few of the early feminists could have anticipated. That it has taken place is at once a sign and a yardstick of the enormous change in women's position in society and in the family. In the nineteenth century work outside the home was unthinkable for the married woman. Not only were there children to care for, but there were objections from husbands and society to consider. That is why the convinced feminist of the nineteenth century often spurned marriage. Indeed, it is often forgotten that the feminist movement was a form of revolt against marriage. For it was through marriage, with the legal and social dominance of the husband, that women were most obviously denied opportunities for self-expression. Even after the legal superiority of the husband had been largely eliminated from the law, middle-class social conventions could still scarcely accommodate the working wife. To the woman interested in realizing her human capabilities, marriage in the nineteenth century was not an opportunity but a dead end. And it was indeed a minor scandal of the time that many of the "new women" did in fact reject marriage. The tendency was most pronounced, as was to be expected, among highly educated women, many of whom felt strongly their obligation to serve society through careers. Around 1900 more than one fourth of women who graduated from college never married; more than half of the women medical doctors in 1890 were single.

Like other changes in the position of women, the movement of married women into the work force—the reconciliation of marriage and work—must be related to the social changes of the last three decades. One of these social changes was the increase in contraceptive knowledge, for until married women could limit their families they could not become steady and reliable industrial workers. Information about contraceptive techniques which had been known for a generation or more to educated middle-class women did not seep down to the working class until the years of the Great Depression. In 1931, for instance, there were only 81 clinics disseminating birth control information in the United States; in 1943 there were 549, of which 166 were under public auspices. As the number of public clinics suggest, by the end of the 1930's birth control was both socially and religiously acceptable, at least among Protestants. And a method was also available then to Roman Catholics, since it was in the same decade that the rhythm method, the only one acceptable to the Roman Catholic Church, was first brought to popular attention with the approval of ecclesiastical authorities.

Another social force underlying the movement of wives and mothers in the work force was the growing affluence of an industrial society, especially after 1940. Higher health standards, enlarged incomes of husbands and a better standard of living in general permitted a marked alteration in the temporal cycle of women's lives. Women now lived longer, stayed in school later and married earlier. In 1890 half the girls left school at 14 or before— that is, when they finished grammar school; in 1957 the median age was 18

—after graduation from high school. The girl of 1890, typically, did not marry until she was 22; the age of her counterpart in 1957 was 20, leaving no more than two years for work between the end of school and marriage. Among other things this fact explains the fall in the proportion of single women in the work force in the United States as compared with other industrial societies. Few other countries have such an early median age of marriage for girls.

Early marriages for women produce another effect. With knowledge of contraceptive techniques providing a measure of control over child-bearing, women are now having their children early and rapidly. When this tendency is combined with a younger age of marriage, the result is an early end to child-bearing. In 1890 the median age of a mother when her last child was born was 32; in 1957 it was 26. A modern mother thus has her children off to school by the time she is in her middle thirties, leaving her as much as thirty-five years free for work outside the home. And the fact is that almost half of working women today are over forty years of age. Put another way, 34 percent of married women between the ages of thirty-five and forty-four years are gainfully employed.

Unquestionably, as the practical character of the woman's movement would lead us to expect, an important force behind the influx of married women into the work force is economic need. But simple poverty is not the only force. Several studies, for example, have documented the conclusion that many women who work are married to men who earn salaries in the upper income brackets, suggesting that poverty is not the controlling factor in the wife's decision to work. A similar conclusion is to be drawn from the positive correlation between education and work for married women. The more education a wife has (and therefore the better salary her husband is likely to earn) the more likely she is to be working herself. Many of these women work undoubtedly in order to raise an adequate standard of living to a comfortable one. Many others work probably because they want to realize their potentialities in the world. But that women are so poorly represented in the professions and other careers suggests that most married women who work are realizing their full capabilities neither for themselves nor for society.

Over sixty years ago, in *Women and Economics*, the feminist Charlotte Perkins Gilman cogently traced the connection between work and the fulfillment of women as human beings. In subsequent writings she grappled with the problem of how this aim might be realized for married women. As a mother herself, raising a child under the trying circumstances of divorce, Gilman knew first hand that work outside the home and child-rearing constituted *two* full-time jobs. No man, she knew, was expected or required to shoulder such a double burden. Gilman's remedies of professional domestic service and kitchenless apartments never received much of a hearing, and considering the utopian if not bizarre character of her solutions, that is not

382

surprising. Yet the problem she raised remained without any solution other than the eminently individualistic and inadequate one of permitting a woman to assume the double burden if she was so minded. Meanwhile, as the economy has grown, the problem has entered the lives of an ever increasing number of women. Unlike most of her feminist contemporaries, who were mainly concerned with the suffrage and the final elimination of legal and customary barriers to women's opportunities, Gilman recognized that the logic of feminism led unavoidably to the working mother as the typical woman. For if women were to be free to express themselves, then they should be able to marry as well as to work. Women should not have to make a choice any more than men. To make that possible, though, would require that some way be found to mitigate the double burden which biology and society had combined to place only on women.

As women moved into the second stage of their development—the reconciliation of work and marriage—the problem which Gilman saw so early was increasingly recognized as the central issue. Virginia Collier, for example, in a book *Marriage and Careers*, published in 1926, wrote that since so many married women were working, "The question therefore is no longer should women combine marriage with careers, but how do they manage it and how does it work." Interestingly enough, her study shows that what today Betty Friedan, in *The Feminine Mystique*, has called the "problem that has no name," was already apparent in the 1920's. One working wife explained her reasons for taking a job in these words, "I am burning up with energy and it is rather hard on the family to use it up in angry frustration." Another said, "I had done everything for Polly for six years. Suddenly she was in school all day and I had nothing to do. My engine was running just as hard as ever, but my car was standing still." A year after Collier's book appeared, President William A. Neilson of Smith College observed "that the outstanding problem confronting women is how to reconcile a normal life of marriage and motherhood with intellectual activity such as her college education has fitted her for." That the issue was taken seriously is attested by an action of the Board of Trustees of Barnard College in 1932. The board voted to grant six months' maternity leave with pay to members of the staff and faculty. In announcing the decision, Dean Virginia Gildersleeve clearly voiced its import. "Neither the men nor the women of our staff," she said, "should be forced into celibacy, and cut off from that great source of experience of joy, sorrow and wisdom which marriage and parenthood offer."

With one out of three married women working today, the problem of reconciling marriage and work for women is of a social dimension considerably larger than in the days of Charlotte Gilman or even in the 1930's. But the fundamental issue is still the same: how to make it possible, as Dean Gildersleeve said, to pursue a career or hold a job while enjoying the "experience . . . joy, sorrow and wisdom" of marriage and parenthood. The practical solutions to this central problem of the second stage in the changing position of women seem mainly collective or governmental, not individual. Child-care centers, efficient and readily available house-keeping services, and emergency child-care service such as the Swedes have instituted are obviously a minimal requirement if women are to have the double burdens of homemaking and employment lightened. The individual working woman cannot be expected to compensate for the temporary disabilities consequent upon her role as mother any more than the individual farmer or industrial worker can be expected single-handedly to overcome the imbalance between himself and the market. Today both farmers and workers have government and their own organizations to assist them in righting the balance.

But as the history of farmers and industrial labor makes evident, to enact legislation or to change mores requires persuasion of those who do not appreciate the necessity for change. Those who would do so must organize the like-minded and mobilize power, which is to say they need a rationale, an ideology. And here is the rub; in pragmatic America, as we have seen, any ideology must leap high hurdles. And one in support of working wives is additionally handicapped because women themselves, despite the profound changes in their status in the last century, do not acknowledge such an ideology. Most American women simply do not want work outside the home to be justified as a normal activity for married women. Despite the counter-argument of overwhelming numbers of working wives, they like to think of it as special and exceptional. And so long as they do not advance such an ideology, American society surely will not do so, though other societies, like Israel's and the Soviet Union's, which are more ideological than ours, obviously have.

Perhaps the kind of gradual, piecemeal advance toward a feminist ideology that Mrs. Rossi proposes in other pages of this book [*Daedalus* 93 (1964)] may contain the seeds of change. But a reading of the past reminds us forcefully that in America the soil is thin and the climate uncongenial for the growth of any seedlings of ideology.

Black History, or Black Mythology

Peter Chew

A strong current of change has lately gripped the academic world
with demand for inclusion of Black history and Black Studies programs. Truly, the Black past has constituted the "underside" of
American history—seldom seen and little discussed. In an incisive
critique of the directions in which the new Black curriculums appear to be developing, Peter Chew, a staff writer for the *National
Observer*, warns that "Black" historians must be wary of overcom-
pensation and myth-building. The essence of the Black experience,
according to Chew, is that Blacks have traditionally been faced with
a white America that has not allowed them a historical past. In short,
the absence of Blacks in American history is ample commentary
upon America's successful suppression of the Black minority. It does
little good, says Chew, to lionize the obscure and the questionable
and inflate the Black contribution, for this does little but compromise historical accuracy. Since history must prove to be more than
a tale told by moralists, one must beware of new purveyors of myth.

Bored with spoofing Governor Ronald Reagan and the Establishment, a group
of young "with it" players known as the San Francisco Mime Troupe have
concocted a skit designed to outrage the liberals in their audience. The scene
is Boston's King Street on the frosty night of March 5, 1770. A crowd of
patriots merrily toss paving stones, jagged chunks of ice, and oyster shells
at Captain Thomas Preston's redcoats standing guard before the Custom
House; they taunt the soldiers with cries of "lobsterback"—the eighteenth-
century equivalent of "pig." Upstage, on the fringe of the crowd, a Negro
street cleaner sweeps the gutter, ignoring the hubbub. Suddenly the crack of
musketry is heard. Five men fall, including the Negro sweeper.

"*That* was the role played by Crispus Attucks in the American Revolution," says the narrator.

The lights fade; the scene changes.

Professor Hugh Davis Graham, associate director of the Institute of
Southern History at Johns Hopkins University, likes to cite the Attucks skit
as a reaction to a problem that contemporary American schools and universities are being forced to confront: the demands by students for an exclusive
focus on Negro history and culture.

Like most white teachers of American history today, Graham concedes
that the substantial contributions of the American Negro have often been

ignored, or "at best, minimized"; that much of the writing of American history up until the last twenty-five years or so was rooted in a condescension that presupposed the basic inferiority of the black man. But Graham and other leaders in the profession are sometimes appalled by the blatant myth-making now in progress, by the diet of just plain bad history being served up, as often as not for political or therapeutic purposes; served up, sometimes, under the threat of violence by black revolutionaries on the rampage in high schools and universities. Afro-American history has become terribly fashionable. It sells. And to meet the demands, a great many philosophical descendants of Parson Weems are abroad in the land, hard at work on separate but equal black fables to match such stories as the one about George Washington and the cherry tree. What we are witnessing, says a distinguished American historian, is "a frantic rummaging in the file-drawers of history for Negro men of accomplishment—any kind of accomplishment." Crispus Attucks is a case in point. History reveals practically nothing about the man beyond the fact that an individual of that name was among the five Boston citizens killed by Captain Preston's soldiers in the "Boston Massacre," five years before the outbreak of the American Revolution. Although one historian says there is strong evidence to suggest that Attucks was a full-blooded Natick Indian, the consensus seems to be that he was a middle-aged mulatto seaman. Certainly he was no street cleaner; in fact John Adams, who successfully defended the British soldiers in the trial that followed, declared that it was to Attucks's "mad behavior" that "in all probability, the dreadful carnage of that night is chiefly to be ascribed." That doesn't make him a hero. Many historians, attempting to evaluate the character of the so-called massacre, consider it little more than an incident of street hooliganism. But Samuel Adams, the Lenin of the American Revolution, turned it to his propagandistic purposes; he did all he could to make Preston appear a practitioner of "police brutality."

Today we are being told, over and over again, that Attucks, a runaway slave, was the first black American to lay down his life in the cause of freedom. Even the most respected Negro historians are inclined to support this myth. John Hope Franklin of the University of Chicago declared in *From Slavery to Freedom*: "Here was a fugitive slave who, with his bare hands, was willing to resist England to the point of giving his life." Last year, Mayor Hugh Addonizio of Newark, New Jersey, proclaimed a public school holiday in honor of the black martyr; this year, Plainfield and Paterson followed suit. When the demands of black students for Crispus Attucks holidays elsewhere in the country have been denied by school principals and local mayors, trouble has ensued.

Across the nation Negroes press for monuments to their race. Tenants in a Harlem housing development named for composer Stephen Foster persuade the city to rename the buildings for Dr. Martin Luther King, Jr. In Brooklyn, the black citizenry agitates to rename a park for Marcus Garvey, the flamboyant "Black Moses" who led an abortive back-to-Africa movement. State legislatures, feeling the pressure, rush through laws requiring the teaching of Afro history and culture—leaving it up to harried teachers to determine just what Afro courses ought to consist of. A bill has been introduced in Congress to establish a National Commission on Negro History, at a cost of $1,000,000, to determine how that subject can best be "integrated into the mainstream of American education and life." In some cities, slum children struggle with the Swahili language, taught by black nationalists in flowing daishiki robes who tell them that English is the language of their colonial oppressors. Some high-school bands, under pressure from Negro students, have stopped playing "Dixie" because it was originally composed as a blackface minstrel song.

This is not just nonsense. Certain aspects of the drive to elevate black history and the Negro's "sense of identity" are disturbing—quite aside from the question of accuracy *vs.* mythmaking. Shortly after the murder of Dr. King in April, 1968, the Washington, D.C., Teacher's Union distributed "a relevant lesson plan" suggesting, among other things, that the arson and looting by Negroes that ensued in Washington, Chicago, Detroit, and other cities be likened to the Boston Tea Party. Thus, revised history is related to a current revolutionary trend that may become increasingly violent as time goes by. "You must have a cultural revolution before the violent revolution," says Ronald Everett, better known as Ron Karenga (*karenga* being a Swahili word meaning "keeper of the tradition"). A leading theoretician of the Black Power movement, he foresees black-*vs.*-white guerrilla warfare breaking out in the early 1970's, once the present black generation has been sufficiently indoctrinated.

Undoubtedly this is an extreme view, but it is akin to a more widespread emphasis in recent efforts to galvanize Negro history—the gravitation toward black separatism. This was evident in an eighteen-week television series put on by CBS and Columbia University early this year. The program, "Black Heritage," drew immediate fire from a prominent Negro leader, Roy Wilkins, executive director of the National Association for the Advancement of Colored People. "Judging by the first two programs, and especially by the official syllabus, the presentation is hopelessly flawed," said Mr. Wilkins. "It is quite clear that 'Black Heritage' will not be a history of Afro-Americans, but an interpretation of history from a single point of view: the contemporary left-of-center black militant minority view, liberally garnished with the thrust for a new apartheid."

In a dramatic statement a few days after his remarks about the television series, Mr. Wilkins opposed the demands of militant black students that universities establish all-black studies programs. Black history courses, he said, were fine, as long as they were part of the general curriculum; but it would be "simple suicide" for the black minority to talk seriously of apartheid, of going it alone:

> If some white Americans, torn and confused by today's clamor of some black students, should accede officially to the call for separate dormitories and autonomous racial schools within colleges and universities, there will be court action to determine anyone's right to use public tax funds to set up what are, patently, Jim Crow schools. . . . We have suffered too many heartaches and shed too many tears and too much blood in fighting the evil of racial segregation to return in 1969 to the lonely and dispiriting confines of its demeaning prison.

Nevertheless, just such study programs as Wilkins denounced are being considered on scores of American college campuses, and some have already been put into operation. At the University of Wisconsin last spring, an aggressive black-student organization clamored for an independent black-studies department: authorized to grant degrees, staffed by black teachers only, teaching its own curriculum, and *open only to black students*. At Antioch College, an Ohio school that has long prided itself on an experimental approach to education, a program meeting all of those stipulations is already in effect—and, as Mr. Wilkins predicted, it is being investigated by the federal government to determine whether, by a preposterous irony, it violates the civil rights laws passed to guarantee the Negro in America an equal education. Similar courses of study have been demanded, often to the accompaniment of rioting and destruction, and always with provocative arrogance, at such institutions as Duke University, Wesleyan (in Connecticut), Brandeis, and San Francisco State. Blacks also complain about "quotas," even though unprecedented numbers of their race are being sought out, admitted, and supported financially at colleges all over the country—and with entrance requirements often conveniently lowered.

Nor have the Ivy League universities been exempt from the push to give a place in the sun to the study of black history and culture. Harvard and Yale will both begin degree-granting programs in Afro-American studies this fall. So far, however, these bastions of academic freedom are resisting any attempts to organize such programs outside the regular curriculum: they hope to hire only the best-qualified teachers, regardless of color, and the courses will be open to all. "We are dealing with 25,000,000 of our own people with a special history, culture, and range of problems," says a Harvard faculty report. "It can hardly be doubted that the study of black men in America is a legitimate and urgent academic endeavor."

This cognizance, it seems, may not be enough to satisfy the militants. Already, in a course in Negro history taught at Harvard by historian Frank Freidel, there have been disruptive attacks from black students who insist that the professor's views are inevitably "white-oriented" and therefore "irrelevant" to their needs. From their point of view, apparently, almost any Negro scholar, regardless of his other qualifications, would be better fitted to teach black history than the most learned white man. That this is racism of the crudest variety seems to be lost upon the aspiring militants. It also suggests what many academic leaders fear: that black history, taught by blacks to blacks, will be in constant danger of departing from historical objectivity and degenerating into mere anti-Establishment propaganda.

Some Negro historians counter this suggestion with the claim that American white-controlled universities have been dishing out anti-Negro propaganda for several hundred years. "You can say all you want on behalf of normal academic procedure and academic objectivity," observes Professor Vincent Harding of Atlanta's Spelman College; "but the fact is that normal academic procedure has done nothing to stop the destruction of Negro lives in this country for 400 years. Rather, the universities have served to support the main theses of American society, which have included the dispensing of injustice toward the black man." Supposing this to be true, the proper rejoinder, presumably, is that two streams of propaganda will never make one truth.

At any rate, a pertinent fact, often ignored, is that there are today few Negro scholars thoroughly trained in black history. Professor August Meier of Ohio's Kent State University, a consultant on Negro history to a large publishing firm, explains it thus:

> Negro historians who took their Ph.D.'s in the 1950's tended to avoid Negro history, and this occurred at a time when a small but growing number of white scholars was becoming increasingly interested in the subject. Both phenomena reflected the growing tendency toward integration in intellectual and academic circles.

The extent to which the trend toward black-white integration in the field of history has reversed itself in recent years became apparent in the debate over the merits of William Styron's novel, The Confessions of Nat Turner. Most white historians see the fictionalized story as historically sound. In a book entitled William Styron's Nat Turner: Ten Black Writers Respond, some blacks charge that Styron has portrayed Nat as a stereotypic "Sambo" figure when he was, in historical fact, "virile, commanding, courageous."

The battle was joined in two spirited reviews of Ten Black Writers Respond, one in the New York Review of Books by Professor Eugene Genovese of Sir George Williams University in Montreal; the other by Princeton's Professor Martin Duberman in the New York Times Book Review. Both reviewers said in effect that it was obvious that the blacks' heroes must all be straight-arrow, devoid of self-doubts, and larger-than-life, or the blacks won't play. Genovese wrote:

> William Styron's Nat Turner: Ten Black Writers Respond shows the extent to which the American intelligentsia is splitting along racial rather than ideological lines. As such, the book needs to be taken with alarmed seriousness, no matter how absurd most of the contributions are. . . . It is clear that the black intelligentsia faces a serious crisis. Its political affinities lie with the black power movement which increasingly demands conformity, mythmaking, and historical fabrication.

Duberman took issue with the black writers' contention—first put forward by Marxist historian Herbert Aptheker twenty-five years ago—that the American slaves were an angry proletariat, seething with revolt, and that Nat Turner's rebellion was but one of hundreds.

> By insisting that all slaves "craved freedom," the essayists force themselves into a bizarre view of the institution of slavery. For slavery could not have been as barbaric as they otherwise insist if it inculcated self-love and masculine assertion in the slaves, rather than the self-hate and loss of identity more usually taken to be its products.
>
> Only when slavery is viewed as an essentially benign institution . . . can it follow that it left no deep personality scars on its victims. But the weight of historical evidence and opinion suggests that American slavery was harsh enough to produce serious character disorders in many slaves.

The question of the total effect of slavery on the human personality goes to the heart of the Negro history dilemma. A subjugated people, reduced to and held in a condition little better than that of domestic animals, is not likely to make much history. Many blacks today are highly sensitive on this point, and most white historians are therefore rather gingerly in the way they approach it. What they say, nevertheless, is this: the Negro has only recently become intrigued with his American heritage because he has only recently been able to take part in history. He was brought here in chains from West Africa, and until his freedom was achieved after the Civil War, the black man was not *allowed* by the white man to make history, except in the mass. As uneducated slaves, blacks were obviously in no position to lead noteworthy careers: they could not become doctors, lawyers, military leaders, architects, engineers, statesmen.

It is true, as *Ebony* magazine said movingly in a recent issue devoted to Negro history, that the black man has had to fight even for the right to die in the service of this country in all its wars.

> A hostage to fate and a warrior against fate, the black soldier has fought for some 300 years on the front lines of ambiguity. Never sure of the real identity of *his* enemy, or the precise location of *his* battlefield, never completely accepted by his comrades in arms or his white neighbors at home, the black soldier has willingly and repeatedly offered himself as witness in war to the truths America refuses to recognize in war or peace.

Yet the harsh fact remains that, through no fault of his own, the Negro fought—at least until the Korean War—as a spear-carrier in the ranks. In the main he fought, and he died, in the mass; a segregated mass.

With the exception of a few enormously courageous and talented individuals like Frederick Douglass, it cannot be said that the Negro took part in the public affairs of this country until after the Civil War. And in antebellum America, notes Professor Graham, whites had "a near-monopoly on wealth and education, and the levers of economic and political power, if not on the reservoir of native intelligence. No amount of romanticizing about Frederick Douglass or Nat Turner and incipient slave revolts can modify that essential fact."

In his introduction to *From Slavery to Freedom*, which, despite vagaries like the passage on Crispus Attucks, is perhaps the best and most objective treatment of the subject, Franklin says: ". . . the history of the Negro in America is essentially the story of the strivings of the nameless millions who have sought adjustment in a new and sometimes hostile world."

To put it more bluntly: the history of the Negro in this country is the history of the white man's resistance to his aspirations. This is a tragic fact, and it is understandable that Negroes look for something less depressing and more inspiring in their new evaluation of their past. Perhaps, indeed, it is inevitable. White historian Eric Goldman sees the writing of American history as having gone through a number of ethnic cycles, with the accent on the Afro-American as just one more swing of the pendulum:

> Back in the 1880's and 90's, most American history was written by conservative white Anglo-Saxon Protestants who tended to glorify free enterprise and the WASP businessman, and to ignore the despised Negroes, Italians, Irish, and the other poor. Early in the twentieth century, Charles Beard brought in the farmers and the workers and made *them* the good guys. Then some of the immigrant boys grew up and began writing history, and the immigrants came into their own—the Jews, for instance. Now the civil rights drive has brought the Negro forward for special attention.

In Goldman's view, it is too much to expect cool, objective history from underprivileged groups that have begun to achieve equality: "The Jews play up the Einsteins in their midst, not the slumlords. The Irish-Americans don't emphasize their record as saloonkeepers. The Negroes, of course, want the same kind of favorably selective history."

Nevertheless, it is disheartening to examine some of the material that has recently been dug up or contrived and offered as legitimate documentation for black history. There is a commercial angle, of course: money is being made out of the urgent demand for books, pamphlets, records, and film strips that can be used as the basis for courses in Afro history. Otherwise respectable companies become surprisingly involved: the *New York Times*, for example, formed Arno Press to reprint a list of "Forty-Five Books America Forgot," edited by William Loren Katz, author of *Eyewitness: The Negro in American History*. (Arno's staff, incidentally, is white by six to one.) Sure enough, Crispus Attucks turns up in ads for the set (price, $485) as evidence that "the Negro past has for the most part been suppressed, neglected, or distorted"; Attucks died, according to Arno Press, "leading the patriots." Although many of the individual books are worthy selections, like Carter G. Woodson's *The Education of the Negro Prior to 1861*, and George W. Williams' classic *History of the Negro Race in America from 1619 to 1880*, there are also some dubious members. *American Slavery As It Is*, for instance, an antislavery propaganda tract compiled in 1839 by the Grimké sisters and Theodore Dwight Weld, is presented as if it were straight history; and *The Life and Adventures of Nat Love*, better known as Deadwood Dick, the black cowboy who integrated gun fighting in the Wild West of yesteryear, is offered without apology. As J. Frank Dobie has written, there were many black cowboys in the old West, and fine cowboys they were. Deadwood, however, operated mostly on the far side of the law, and was an inveterate teller of tall tales: the truth was not in him. He also comes through as something of a bigot; he enjoyed killing "painted savages" and "dirty Mexicans." In an anticlimax that must not greatly please today's black militants, Deadwood sold out, ending his days in comfortable circumstances as a Pullman porter.

Enterprising amateurs have also jumped into the black history field. Henry Dabbs, a talented young Negro artist who works for a New York advertising firm, has designed an *Afro-American History Fact Pack* that includes a book, sketches by Dabbs of Negro heroes, a phonograph record, and slides, tracing the history of the black man from the time of Creation. The *Fact Pack* sells for $80, and Mr. Dabbs says it is being snapped up by public school systems as fast as his Afro-American Heritage House publishing company can produce it.

Mr. Dabbs's approach is unabashedly chauvinistic. He has come up with a black Civil War martyr who he claims was the first casualty on the Union side.

> As a member of the First Volunteers from Schuylkill County, Pennsylvania, responding to President Lincoln's call to save the White House from secessionists, Nicholas Biddle became the first man to shed his blood for the cause of the Union in the Civil War. The date: April 18, 1861.

The *Fact Pack* also implies strongly that the black man was the father of the human race.

> Recent fossil findings by world famous paleontologist Dr. Louis S. B. Leakey and his wife in Olduvai Gorge, Tanganyika Territory, East Africa, unquestionably establish the African as the first man on earth. The fossils date back 1,750,000 years, older by as much as half a million years than all previous fossil findings!

The question of whether these fossils were once covered with bare skin or with fur, and what color it may have been in either case, is not raised.

Yet despite mythmaking, despite black separatism with its destructive tendency to confuse history and propaganda, despite the relative meagerness of genuine Negro history, and despite more or less meretricious attempts to satisfy the clamor for Afro material with shoddy products, it seems that there ought to be a respectable way out of the dilemma of black history.

"The solution is to tell it like it was, tell it like it is, and tell why it wasn't told before," said a report issued last year by a group of educators and civil rights officials under the sponsorship of the President's Commission for the Observance of Human Rights. "The real story of the degradation of black people by white, the history of prejudice and the account of the nature of prejudice is a more powerful instrument for building the ego of Negroes and the social understanding of all people than any fictional history could be."

Along this line, explicit recognition has recently been given to the failure, especially in school textbooks, to treat Negro history with an even hand. Professor James M. McPherson of Princeton University's history department cites the extensive influence of the southern historian Ulrich B. Phillips, whose *American Negro Slavery* was published in 1918. Phillips was a leading promoter of the thesis, still popular in the South, that most slaves were happy on the plantation and were lucky to be introduced by their kind masters to the rudiments of civilization: "On the whole, the plantations were the best schools yet invented for the mass training of that sort of inert and backward people which the bulk of American Negroes represented." Comments McPherson:

> This interpretation was consciously or subconsciously a bulwark of white supremacy and segregation. It taught white children that they were superior to Negroes, that second-class citizenship . . . was right for the Negro; that he was a carefree, irresponsible human being, satisfied with his place in American life just as he had once been satisfied with slavery.

The view of most historians today is that the research that underlay Phillips's "plantation legend" was seriously flawed: in the main it was based on the personal records of the larger southern slave-owners, and he paid little heed to observations of travellers through the South, to authentic memoirs by ex-slaves, or to the newspapers of the period. Yet the extent to which Phillips's views colored the interpretations of writers of textbooks in both the North and the South can be inferred from this astonishing passage in early editions of *The Growth of the American Republic,* by Samuel Eliot Morison and Henry Steele Commager, neither of whom is generally thought of as a white supremacist:

> As for "Sambo," whose wrongs moved the abolitionists to wrath and tears, there is some reason to believe that he suffered less than any other class in the South for its "Peculiar Institution." . . . Although brought to America by force, the incurably optimistic Negro soon became attached to the country, and devoted to his white folks.

When that passage first appeared, in 1930, Negro civil rights leaders protested; and Morison (who wrote it) and Commager agreed to remove it. Apparently communication broke down, however, since the offending words were not actually taken out until the 1962 edition of the book.

Another legitimate facet of the effort to "tell it like it was" is the growing interest today in the history of Africa's black civilizations before the coming of European colonization. It is true that much of this history lies in the preliterate past. Yet modern scholarship is making advances in this field, and it is now clear that well-developed political states and even empires existed in sub-Sahara Africa many centuries ago. The ancient kingdom of Ghana, for example, reached high levels of wealth and cultivation in the eleventh century under the black king Tenkamenin.

As for well-researched studies of American Negro history, there has actually been much more produced than many of the black chauvinists and revolutionaries seem to be aware of, busy as they are with their repeated "confrontations" and their long lists of demands. Representative of many excellent works by both white and black historians are such books as Kenneth M. Stampp's *The Peculiar Institution* (1956), C. Vann Woodward's *The Strange Career of Jim Crow* (1955), Gilbert Osofsky's *The Burden of Race* (1967), and Leon F. Litwack's *North of Slavery* (1961), as well as the books by Franklin and by Woodson.

Surely, in this connection, special honor is due to those Negro historians who have striven valiantly for objectivity while themselves incessantly subject to the painful discriminations of a segregated society. The career of one of the most brilliant of them, W. E. B. Du Bois, is illustrative. "I write," he said in *Black Reconstruction* (1935), "in a field devastated by passion. . . . But . . . I want to be fair, objective, and judicial; to let no searing of the memory by intolerable insult and cruelty make me fail to sympathize with human frailties and contradiction, in the eternal paradox of good and evil. But armed and warned by all this, and fortified by long study of the facts, I stand at the end of this writing, literally aghast at what American historians have done in this field." In the end, Du Bois was unable to contemplate longer the slow and stumbling pace of the American people toward the fulfillment of their pledge as a nation "indivisible, with liberty and justice for all." He died in 1963, in Accra, Ghana, an embittered expatriate and a member of the Communist party.

Unhappily, the sober conclusions of real historians, whether white or black, do not seem to filter down very rapidly into grade school and high school textbooks—nor to fill the bill for Afro courses when they do. Not long ago I visited the Robert A. Waller High School in Chicago. A predominantly Negro school, it had been in turmoil for many months, with black students presenting countless grievances, and I wanted to observe their reactions to the supplemental black history course introduced there.

How, I wondered, do you conduct a course that focuses upon the cruelties of slavery, on the fact that Negroes were literally written out of the Declaration of Independence; on the fact that once freed they were disfranchised, lynched, held back, and degraded—and not have the Negro students wind up hating Whitey the more? It is one thing to teach them about Frederick Douglass, and poetess Phyllis Wheatley, and Harriet Tubman of the Underground Railroad, and Matthew Henson, who was with Peary at the Pole, and Benjamin Banneker, who helped plan the city of Washington, D.C., and other remarkable black men and women who overcame incredible obstacles to achieve what they did; but what are the side effects? If Waller High is typical, and I believe it is, they are disturbing.

For one thing, much concomitant debunking of traditional white heroes seems to take place. And in some schools, where black militants are doing the teaching, traditional black heroes are also debunked, and contemporary revolutionaries of dubious accomplishment are thrust forward. ("They must drop George Washington and Benjamin Franklin and Thomas Jefferson, those mothers," exclaims Jimmy Garrett, chairman of the Black Studies Program of the new Federal City College in Washington, D.C., speaking of his teachers. "They must make Malcolm X, Elijah Muhammed, Huey Newton, and LeRoi Jones real heroes.")

The over-all situation, at this writing, does not look very encouraging at either the school or university level. After a night of violence at Harvard last spring the faculty voted to allow students a voice in choosing teachers for the new black studies program—a decision that, as President Nathan M. Pusey observed, "is going to create quite a few difficulties in trying to get the kind of program we want"—that is, one taught objectively by genuine historians. At Cornell, despite an elaborate effort to install an Afro studies curriculum conforming to black demands, dissatisfaction led to an episode that jarred the entire country when black students were photographed occupying a campus building with rifles in their hands and bandoleers of bullets over their shoulders.

I was talking about all this one afternoon in the quiet study of Professor C. Vann Woodward of Yale University, a shy southerner who appears to have the confidence and affection of both black and white historians. He turned to the words of George Washington Williams, the first great Negro historian. "Not as a blind panegyrist for my race," wrote Williams, "nor as the partisan apologist, but from a love for the 'truth of history,' I have striven to record the truth."

The correction of bias and distortion in Negro history, said Woodward, would not be brought about by eulogy and apology and panegyrics, but "rather by the spirit that informed the work of George Williams."

But the evidence of that spirit seems faint in many sectors, and meanwhile the shadow of Crispus Attucks lengthens across the land.

The Uses of Violence in
American History

Michael Wallace

Americans like to think of their past as "homogenized." We believe
that ours is a history of consensus rather than conflict. In short, as
regards our violent past, Americans suffer from an acute case of
"historical amnesia." As Michael Wallace of Franconia College in
New Hampshire sees it, violence is truly an American social trait.
The American acceptance of the Horatio Alger myth—our continued belief that ours is an open and fluid society in which all eventually have a stake in the existing order—has allowed us to conclude
that violence has seldom been necessary in the "land of the free."
Despite our desire to forget this dimension of our past, violence
related to racial, ethnic, and economic conflict has been an important historical reality in America.

Students of European collective violence once agreed that it was irrational.
Recently, scholars like George Rudé, Eric Hobsbawm, E. P. Thompson and
Charles Tilly have argued that it was in fact purposive, a technique of protest,
a demand for change. In this country we have experienced no such debate,
partly because we have developed, as has been said, a case of "historical
amnesia." We have not argued about the nature of our violent past because
we have forgotten we had one. True, when we do consider instances of violence it is assumed that they are pointless and irrational, as the McCone
Commission did in its interpretation of the Watts uprising. But this attitude
has never inspired an interpretive school or the formation of a revisionist
critique.

But *why* have we forgotten about our violence? Two answers seem important here: first, Americans have accepted the Horatio Alger myth, never
doubting that ours was a society in which all groups had the opportunity to
advance and prosper peacefully. For a variety of reasons—abundance of
resources, a frontier safety valve, absence of feudal institutions or class
divisions, the two-party system—ours was an open, fluid system. Rising
groups easily entered the great middle class; ethnic differences softened and
ran together in the great melting pot. The outs had no need for revolutionary
violence; the ins, no need for forceful repression. Thus when violence did
appear, it had to be dismissed as an inexplicable aberration. Second, with
the exception of the Civil War and Reconstruction, only a tiny fraction of

From "The Uses of Violence in American History," by Michael Wallace. Reprinted
from *The American Scholar*, Volume 40, Number 1, Winter 1970–71. Copyright
© 1970, by the United Chapters of Phi Beta Kappa. Reprinted by permission of the
publishers.

our violence has been directed against the state. Perhaps because we have been conditioned by the European experience to consider only antistate violence truly significant, we have been prone to dismiss the American varieties.

But if we shift our focus on violence and look at its place in relations between groups rather than in relation to the state, violence assumes a much larger significance in our history. It has been one of the widely employed methods used by groups competing for places in the structure of power. Americans have often eschewed the normal electoral processes and have taken their quarrels into the streets. In the main, violence has been used most frequently and effectively by dominant groups seeking to preserve their power and less frequently and less effectively by subordinate groups seeking to protest or improve their situation. The great bulk of our violence, at least until the 1960s, has been *repressive*, rather than expressive or insurrectionary. Much of our violence has also been informal and private, committed by citizens against other citizens. The state was often not a participant, and when it did become intimately involved in the struggles of groups, as in our economic history, it usually played a secondary, assisting role; thus it aroused relatively little violence against itself.

The pattern of violent encounter in three areas—racial, economic and ethnic—supports these propositions. We find in our racial history the violent suppression of blacks by whites; in our economic history, the violent suppression of labor by capital; and in our ethnic history, the violent suppression of recent immigrant groups by more established ones.

Let us begin with racial violence in general and slavery in particular. Violence was a basic device used to change or preserve the system. Blacks used it in full-scale revolts, in individual breaks for freedom, or in attacks on hated masters. Whites used it to repress real or imagined threats to their supremacy. Compared to some other slave societies, slave-initiated violence was relatively slight. The great bulk of the violence came from the masters.

When slaves used violence, they were rigorously dealt with. In reprisal for an uprising in New York City in 1712, eighteen of the rebels were put to death: some were hanged, some were burned at the stake, and one was sentenced to be "burned with a slow fire that he may continue in torment for eight or ten hours, and continue burning in the said fire until he be dead and consumed to ashes." In 1811 five hundred slaves marched on New Orleans, burning plantations, but they were routed, and the heads of sixteen leaders were cut off and stuck up on poles at intervals along the Mississippi. In 1831 Nat Turner and his followers killed at least fifty-seven whites, but were immediately the victims of a countermassacre by roving bands of militia and vigilante groups in which at least one hundred blacks were killed. Twenty others went to the gallows. Thus were the perils of resistance made clear.

It was not necessary for blacks actually to use violence to bring on murderous repression. Although the Vesey conspiracy left whites unharmed in

1822, mass executions quickly followed. Twenty-two blacks were hanged on one day, their bodies left to dangle for hours; dozens more were scheduled for execution but the court stopped when thirty-five were dead, explaining that "the terror of example we thought would be sufficiently operative by the number of criminals sentenced to death." In 1860 some fires in Texas towns produced rumors of an uprising. In Fort Worth, two lists of "black Republicans, abolitionists or higher law men of every class" were prepared: "List no. 1, all suspected persons; no. 2, black list, to be exterminated by immediate hanging." Extermination proceeded through the summer, and an estimated seventy-five were killed, most of them blacks.

This violence is not surprising: under slavery, a system for subordinating and exploiting black people, the use of violence to terrorize and repress was logical. In the North, egalitarian pretensions made repression hypocritical but did not prevent it. Segments of the white communities which felt threatened by the growth and progress of blacks often resorted to violence to contain such advances. Most large cities in the Northeast—Philadelphia, New York, Providence and others—experienced race riots before the Civil War. The riots in Columbia, Pennsylvania, in 1834, although not notably violent, offer an example of how ends not easily achieved within the political process were achieved outside it. The black population of the town had grown with the influx of runaway slaves; many were employed in the lumber yards and several had amassed considerable property; black institutions were established and flourishing. In August of 1834, a recession year and a time of antiblack violence throughout the country, a crowd of whites assaulted the black district, breaking up houses and beating blacks. A few days later the working men of the town met and resolved that

> the practice of others in employing Negroes to do that labor which was formerly done entirely by whites, we consider deserving our severest animadversions; . . . Must the poor honest citizens that so long have maintained their families by their labor, fly from their native place that a band of disorderly Negroes may revel with the money that ought to support the white man and his family?

The whites boycotted those who employed blacks and petitioned the town "to devise some means to prevent the further influx of colored persons to this place." These efforts were unavailing and were again supplemented with violence: two more riots saw black homes destroyed and blacks beaten.

This pattern prevailed in the Northwest as well: the frontier, far from liberalizing race relations, worsened them. In Cincinnati, when black population and enterprise grew, upper- and lower-class whites demanded that the local government "take measures to prevent the increase of negro population." In 1829, blacks were given several weeks to leave town or to post a five-hundred-dollar bond for good behavior as required under a dormant law; when these measures proved ineffective, hundreds of whites descended on the black district, beating and destroying, and over a thousand blacks fled the city for Canada.

Racial violence in this period culminated in a wave of wartime draft riots, the worst of which occurred in New York in 1863. These were complicated affairs, involving class and political antagonisms, but a critical aspect was racial. White workers feared the potential challenge of the liberated slaves and resented the continued competition of native blacks in key occupations. During the New York riots blacks were stomped, clubbed, shot or hanged; longshoremen and hotel workers were prime targets. The violence was successful: many blacks were fired by terrified employers, and the black population of the city dropped twenty percent between 1860 and 1865.

The next major period of racial upheaval—Reconstruction—was the most violent period of civil disorder in American history, and violence was fundamental to its outcome. The Northern armies had shattered the Southern social structure and undermined the ruling group, the white plantation owners. Had the North fostered an alliance between the black freedman and the lower-class white by expropriating the plantation owners' land, a social revolution might have been realized. For a multitude of reasons this was not done, but the critical one for our purposes is that the lower-class whites identified with their caste, not their class. In matters of race, after all, they belonged to a dominant group, not a subordinate one. But emancipation had endangered the caste system itself. The story of Reconstruction, then, is the use of violence by normally dominant whites of all classes to repress the challenge of the black freedman, and the use of force by Northern armies, for a time, to protect them. We may take as the Southern whites' rallying cry the demand of an Alabama newspaper that "We must render this either a white man's government, or convert the land into a negro man's cemetery."

White violence in the counterrevolutionary campaign took several forms. The commonest, numbering perhaps in the thousands, involved small-scale assaults against individual blacks who refused to accept the traditionally subordinate role. Black militia leaders, voters, Republicans, Union League organizers, school teachers, pupils, blacks who married whites, quit jobs, or simply were known as local leaders of their race, were systematically terrorized or killed. Somewhat less frequently, guerrilla operations became massive attacks on whole groups of blacks. Thus, in New Orleans in 1866, radicals challenged the 1864 Constitution, which restricted suffrage to whites, by reconvening the Convention. The city's whites, led by the police, mounted a furious assault on the convention hall, firing at the blacks and their white allies within. By the time federal troops arrived, at least thirty-eight were dead and a hundred and forty-six wounded. In Memphis, in 1866, white mobs led by local officials and police burned down black schools, churches and homes, raped and sexually humiliated black women, and shot down black men on sight. Forty-six blacks died and seventy-five to a hundred were wounded. At Laurens, South Carolina, in October, 1870, thirteen were killed and over a hundred wounded; in Texas it was estimated that over a thousand were killed during 1868–70. In Louisiana, General Philip Sheridan estimated that between 1866 and 1875, thirty-five hundred were killed and wounded, mostly blacks. Twenty-five to thirty were killed in 1871 in Meridian, Mississippi, fifty to eighty died at Ellenton, South Carolina, and an estimated eighty perished in the 1875 riots in and around Yazoo City, Mississippi.

Southern blacks did not sit passively while they were slaughtered. They organized in militia companies at the behest of Reconstruction governors and often were employed at election time to intimidate whites or to protect black and Republican voters. Otis Singletary tells us that "Republicans were victorious directly in proportion to their military preparedness." But there were many inherent weaknesses in the militia, and the white radical governors never really dared to employ them fully. They cited the danger of race war, although race war was going on all around them. Had they realized clearly the necessity of relying on armed blacks and mobilized accordingly, the story of Reconstruction might have been different.

Blacks also organized informally to defend themselves, but the odds in weapons and military experience were against them, and resistance often led to slaughter. In Millican, Texas, in 1868, for example, blacks, hearing that a comrade had been lynched, marched on the town in armed formation, led by a black preacher, and attempted to hang the guilty white. Other whites came to his rescue and, in the ensuing shoot-out, twenty blacks and four whites died and at least seventy-five were wounded.

As Reconstruction moved toward an end, whites resorted more and more to insurrectionary violence and directly attacked the Reconstruction states. In September, 1874, in New Orleans, the White League, a paramilitary organization of over twenty-five thousand men, including the largest property holders of the state, demanded that radical Governor William Kellogg resign. He refused and ordered his Adjutant General, James A. Longstreet of Confederate fame, to rally the militia, largely black, and join with the police to defend the government; he then took refuge in the federal Customs House. The White League forces put up barricades in the street, captured city hall and the telegraph office, routed Longstreet's forces, took the state house and effected a *coup d'état*; total casualties were twenty-seven dead and over a hundred wounded. But President Grant supported Kellogg, and federal troops put down the insurrection peacefully, for the insurgents declined to resist federal force. Although the insurgents were temporarily repulsed, this was the beginning of the end for the Reconstruction government. In 1877, when the national government refused to use force to underwrite the regime, it collapsed.

The struggle to preserve the caste system did not end with the overthrow of Reconstruction. In the years of the Populist movement in the late 1880s and 1890s when the whites did split along class lines, blacks were able to participate in coalition governments and to hold public office again. In addition, a new generation of black people had arisen, the first born out of slavery and free of whatever internalized restraints slavery created. Whites met the challenge of the blacks with repressive violence.

To some extent it was large-scale. The whites of Wilmington, North Carolina, for example, infuriated by office-holding blacks, announced in 1898, "we will not live under these intolerable conditions. . . . We intend to change it, if we have to choke the current of Cape Fear River with negro carcasses!" The whites rioted, murdered blacks, and effected a *coup d'état*. Increasingly, however, lynching became the preferred form of repressive violence. Between 1882 and 1927, about five thousand persons were lynched in the United States, seventy percent of them black. Many lynchings were by summary hanging or shooting, but many, in keeping with the desire to terrorize blacks into subordination, were spectacles of sadism. In 1899, at Palmetto, Georgia, excursion trains brought thousands on a Sunday afternoon to see a black man burned alive, but only after his ears, toes and fingers were cut off and passed to the crowd, his eyes gouged, his tongue torn out, and his flesh cut in strips with knives; afterward, his heart was cut out and slices of it were sold for souvenirs. In May, 1911, a black charged with murder was taken to the local opera house in Livermore, Kentucky, and tied on stage to a stake. Tickets were sold, and orchestra seats entitled men to empty their revolvers into the victim. Gallery seats gave them one shot apiece. In 1918 there was a five-day orgy of killing in Georgia, in which eight blacks died, one pregnant woman was slowly roasted alive, and her baby cut out and trampled. The charges on which such atrocities were based ranged from murder and rape to such offenses against the racial system as striking or talking back to whites, testifying against whites, making boastful remarks, or using offensive language.

With the coming of the twentieth century, lynching began its slow decline, and race riots became the main form of conflict between the dominant and subordinate groups. Increasingly, most outbreaks occurred in the North because blacks, spurred by the employment opportunities of two world wars, had migrated in enormous numbers to the North. Their coming posed a tremendous challenge to those whites in the lower rungs of the economy who had to confront increased competition for jobs, housing and recreational facilities. The challenge was sharpened by the increasing refusal of blacks, many of them veterans, to accept discrimination. A common white response was massive violent assaults on black communities.

At East St. Louis in 1917 employers broke strikes by hiring migrant blacks, and the fury and frustration of white laborers grew and was fanned by politicians. After a small riot failed to terrorize blacks into leaving, the whites resorted to all-out violence in July. Streetcars were stopped, blacks were pulled off, stoned, clubbed, kicked, shot, stomped and knifed. Mobs, thousands strong, roamed the streets chanting, "Get a nigger, get another."

Most blacks were terrified into passivity, although at one point a hundred barricaded themselves in a building and shot it out with the mob. Nine whites and thirty-nine blacks were killed. In Chicago, the black population had doubled between 1916 and 1919. Beatings, bombings and murders marked the boundary line between white and expanding black territories. Then, on July 27, a black youth swimming in Lake Michigan floated past the imaginary boundary line separating white from black beach. He was stoned by whites and drowned. Blacks demanded that the police arrest the whites. Instead they arrested the complainants, touching off a riot that after seven days found twenty blacks and fifteen whites dead, over five hundred and thirty-seven injured, and about a thousand homeless. In 1921, in Tulsa, Oklahoma, blacks armed to protect an accused black rapist from the usual lynch mob. They clashed with police, and the white community, infuriated, organized a small army, led by American Legionnaires, that invaded the black district, burning and shooting. The entire area, one mile square, was burnt to the ground. Perhaps as many as a hundred and fifty men, women and children perished.

The 1940s brought another transformation in racial violence. With the exception of wartime riots in Detroit and Los Angeles, massive confrontations between black and white citizens ceased. Huge black ghettos developed, peopled with much more militant blacks. It was no longer safe to attempt forays into fortresses like Harlem. Whites themselves increasingly moved to suburban strongholds isolated from contact with blacks. Postwar prosperity alleviated many of the economic pressures on whites that had made them vulnerable to black advances. The burden of containing subordinate groups was left to one specialized segment of the white community: the police.*

Police violence is not "police brutality," a misleading term that implies that violent acts are aberrant phenomena, the product of a few sadists. Police violence in this instance is an outgrowth of the task that police have been assigned by the white community: to patrol the borders of the ghetto. The police treat blacks as a deviant or criminal group like, say, prostitutes, to be restricted to certain territories, black light districts if you will. By such procedures as "aggressive preventative patrols," roving task forces conduct intensive and indiscriminate stops and searches, obtaining dossiers on sizeable portions of the community; by using violence against blacks who in any way challenge their authority, they keep the subordinate group in line. James Baldwin summed up the system neatly when he said that the police

---

*There are two general exceptions to this. First is the white bombing campaign of the 1950s against blacks who tried to follow them to the suburbs. Second is the violent campaign against the civil rights movement of the 1950s and 1960s in which dozens were killed and hundreds injured. Much of this violence was by private terrorist groups or individuals but, in line with the newer trend, much was by southern law enforcement agents; indeed, the two groups often had overlapping memberships.

represent the force of the white world, and that world's real intentions are, simply, for that world's criminal profit and ease, to keep the black man corraled up here, in his place. The badge, the gun in the holster, and the swinging club make vivid what will happen should his rebellion become overt.

Lest anyone should assume that police violence is limited to southern sheriffs, let us remember that, at the time of this writing, twenty-eight members of the Black Panther party have met violent death at police hands. Thus are the perils of resistance made clear.

As the pattern of white repression changed, so did that of black resistance. A utilization of violence as protest developed in a fashion reminiscent of the European crowd violence that Rudé and Hobsbawm analyzed. The new style occurred first in Harlem in 1935. Ghetto conditions, aggravated by the Depression, brought organized protest, but attempts at producing change via the political process failed. A Jobs for Negroes campaign, which boycotted Harlem stores refusing to employ blacks, was broken by injunctions, and police violence against demonstrations was a commonplace. Harlemites finally erupted on hearing rumors of an incident of police violence. Policemen, symbols of white authority, were assaulted, and those stores that had been picketed unsuccessfully before were now burned to the ground. The commission that investigated the riot dismissed charges of Communist instigation and insisted that the riot was a protest against discrimination, unemployment and police violence. But the message failed to get through. Although there were some positive responses to the Harlem 1935 riot and to the hundreds that followed it in the 1960s, the basic situation of America's subordinate racial group has not changed; and a disturbingly characteristic response of dominant whites has been to develop more effective means of violent suppression.

We move now from racial violence to economic violence, from considerations of caste to considerations of class. Economic violence encompasses far more than the industrial violence that we usually associate with it. We have had, for example, food riots, bank riots, tollgate riots, Luddite violence, anti-rent disturbances, agrarian land riots, squatters' riots and anti-eviction riots. But considerations of space force me to restrict my focus to the more familiar field of relations between capital and labor.

Labor's challenge to capital began early in the nineteenth century. Workers were unable to better their conditions peacefully because the formation of unions was defined as criminal. Wildcat strikes, often accompanied by violence, were common. Outbursts against superintendents, business property or strikebreakers occurred in enterprises like railroads, canals, waterworks and mills. Ethnic communities, particularly Irish ones, provided the organizational basis. Thus canal workers rioted near Harrisburg in 1828, Irish workers on the Baltimore and Ohio Railroad beat up contractors and demolished their homes in 1829, and there were violent outbreaks on the Croton waterworks in 1840. These early communal outbursts were replaced by the more disciplined efforts of trade unions; when this happened, labor-initiated violence dropped sharply.

A major response of American capitalism to the challenge of labor, peaceful or not, was violence. Recently Philip Taft and Philip Ross found the pervasiveness of violence in American labor disputes "paradoxical" in light of the nonideological nature of our working class and their rejection of force as a method of achieving change. The "paradox" comes from looking in the wrong direction. The point is that the most moderate labor demands have called forth ferocious resistance; our "labor violence," in fact, might be more aptly renamed "capitalist violence."

From the first manifestations of unrest much effort went into developing effective means of repression. Increasingly, capitalists gained the assistance of the state. From the 1850s to the 1870s, according to a study in progress by Dennis Van Essendelft, militia units evolved from the traditional citizens' army into mobile compact forces that could deal with the rising disorders of urbanizing, industrializing America. Until 1877, the militia was supplemented by the Regular Army; as one Congressman found in 1878: "Generals commanding military departments, north, south and east, report the employment, hundreds of times, of hundreds of detachments of the standing army in the suppression of strikes." After the Great Strike of 1877, emphasis returned to the militia: William Riker has found that states spent money on expanding the militia in direct proportion to the amount of strike activity the state experienced. Armories sprouted in American cities to defend the better classes against the dangerous classes. New York, for example, constructed armories in forty districts at a cost of twenty million dollars.

American capitalists did not put all their eggs in the government's basket, however. They developed private resources of violence: economic Hessians like the Pinkertons, Baldwin-Felts, the Coal and Iron Police. Often the line between public and private means of violence, already largely meaningless, was effaced completely: employers' hired guns were transformed into a public force by having compliant sheriffs or marshals deputize them, instantly cloaking them with the privileges and immunities of the law.

The catalog of industrial violence is staggering. Many of the bloodiest incidents occurred in the extractive industries, in the small coal towns or silver mines, where the absence of limiting institutions led to straight-out warfare. The spectacular affairs that took place in isolated mountain communities like Ludlow, Cripple Creek and Coeur D'Alene are well known. But how many have heard of the violence at, say, Morewood Mine, Pennsylvania, where in 1891 sheriffs' deputies shot and killed eleven Hungarian coal miners and wounded more than fifty of them? Or at Latimer, Pennsylvania, where over twenty died and over ninety were wounded; or the thirty deaths at Mucklow, West Virginia, when Baldwin-Felts and militiamen used armored trains to attack strikers?

Violence came to the cities as well. Some incidents are well known, like the crushing of the 1877 railroad strike in which scores of workers were killed, or the suppression of the 1919 strike against U.S. Steel, in which the owners mobilized over twenty-five thousand armed men. But there were hundreds of other incidents, such as transit strikes like the one in Chicago in 1905, in which fourteen strikers were killed, hundreds wounded and over fifteen hundred arrested; or that in Denver in 1920 where federal troops broke a strike at a cost of seven dead and eighty-one wounded. There were strikes in the clothing industry, like Chicago's of 1910, in which forty thousand walked out, and private guards killed seven and wounded many more.

Violence came to the fields. In the South, where much of the rural labor force was black, violence was particularly vicious—and effective. In 1887 nine thousand blacks working the Louisiana sugar plantations, together with a thousand whites, struck for one dollar a day. The planters persuaded the governor to send in the militia, which shot into a crowd of strikers at Pattersonville, killing several. Strike leaders were lynched. Finally, at Thibodaux, the "most prominent citizens" organized a private vigilante force, massacred thirty-five strikers, and broke the strike. In 1919, when black Arkansas sharecroppers formed a union, their meetings were shot up; when the blacks fired back and killed some attackers, whites went on a week-long rampage, hunting out blacks in the countryside and killing them. Estimates of the murdered run from fifty to over two hundred.

Not all the violence was directed against organized labor or strikers. During depressions, when unemployed victims of the business cycle, either spontaneously or led by radical organizations, demanded bread and work, they were swiftly beaten into quiescence. In 1874, club-swinging police dispersed a mass meeting of seven thousand men, women and children gathered in Tompkins Square Park in New York City to back demands for a program of public works. The press enthusiastically commended repression of the unemployed, denounced their spirit as "communistic," and urged the authorities, should a similar spirit emerge, to "club it to death at the hands of the police or shoot it to death at the hands of the militia." In the depression of the 1890s, police tangled with the tramps and industrial (non-violent) armies and urban unemployed spawned by the hard times. In 1932, when unemployed workers organized by the Communist party marched on Henry Ford's Dearborn plant with a list of demands, the mayor, a relative of Ford's, told the chief of police, a former security chief of Ford's, to disperse them; this was done, with firehoses, pistols and a machine gun, killing four and wounding more.

Labor fought back when not hopelessly outmatched, or accepted defeat and tried again. But they seldom initiated violence against employers, except to destroy their property. Dynamite was a popular counterweapon at certain periods: in the 1880s, a virtual cult developed around it as the great equalizer. But the bulk of labor violence was directed against members of their own class. As workers climbed the economic ladder, they reacted violently against real or imagined threats to their hard-won positions. Massacres of scabs were all too common occurrences, often made easier by racial or ethnic antagonisms.

Probably the worst campaign of labor violence was that directed against the Chinese. Many incidents did not involve actual scabbing by the Orientals; rather, workers detested these men who worked for low wages, rejected American culture, and were hired in bulk in a fashion reminiscent of slavery. White workers responded with a blend of political action, leading to the legal restriction of Chinese immigration, and direct terrorism. The first major outburst came in Los Angeles in 1871, when eighteen Chinese, some children, were shot or hanged. Waves of riots and raids drove Chinese out of towns all over California in the 1870s; homes were destroyed, many persons were killed. This period was capped by riots in San Francisco and Chico in 1877. Even after the exclusion law was passed, anti-Chinese violence continued, particularly during depressions or periods of large-scale organizing. In 1885, members of a fledgling Knights of Labor local at Rocksprings, Wyoming, furious because the Union Pacific hired Chinese to ward off strikes, killed twenty-eight Orientals in a gruesome massacre.

The massive series of violent confrontations between capital and labor continued for about sixty years and amounted to an industrial war. A truce was called in the 1930s, when labor's strength had grown to such proportions that violence became too expensive and counterproductive and the state withdrew from its role of arms supplier. But for three score years the use of violence was a commonplace in the struggle for economic power in America.

When we turn to ethnic conflict, we find a similar pattern of violent clashes. There are innumerable instances of armed encounters between ethnic groups to establish or contest control of territory; in the nineteenth century the formation of armed, ethnic self-defense groups was a commonplace. But the history of ethnic conflict differs significantly from the pattern of economic or racial violence. While the bulk of ethnic violence was repressive, as dominant, established immigrant groups resisted newcomers, the wavelike character of the migrations and the multiplicity of groups prevented the formation of a rigid ethnic hierarchy; that is, there was never an overwhelmingly predominant group for very long. Ethnic conflicts were thus seldom as lopsided as economic or racial clashes.

Another consequence of this relative balance of power was that no single ethnic group controlled the state in the way that whites and capitalists did. The state came close to being what it was supposed to be in theory: open to control by any group mustering sufficient electoral strength. And it was a prize worth competing for. It could enforce the cultural norms of any group by legislative fiat. Much ethnic violence resulted from such state action, as when Germans in Chicago rioted in 1855 over the closing of beer halls on Sundays or when, in 1844, the decision of Philadelphia authorities to allow the use of non-Protestant bibles in public schools so aroused the native population that two riots against Irish Catholics ensued, in which dozens were killed.

In addition to direct ecological warfare, and reactions to state policies, there was a third type of ethnic violence, the election riot, in which groups fought to gain control of the state. This extraordinary phenomenon was a blend of constitutionalism and insurrectionary violence that may have been peculiarly American. Ethnic groups—too constitutional to resort to ethnic coups, and too eager to limit themselves to constitutional methods—hit on the procedure of keeping opponents away from the polls. They did so by force, by terror or by murder. Yet no matter how violent the election, the outcome was considered valid. Groups fought to control the polls at least as early as the Bloody Election of 1742 in Philadelphia, but the election riot reached its peak as immigrants packed into the cities in the 1840s and 1850s. Scores were killed in riots at Louisville, New Orleans, Cincinnati, New York and Philadelphia. Marines were called out in 1857 to put down an attempted nativist seizure of the Washington polls by groups carrying blacksmith sledges, revolvers, bowie knives, slingshots and cannon.

But the art was raised to its highest in Baltimore where innumerable ethnic street gangs became politicized after 1854 and turned out en masse on election day. They devised a whole panoply of methods for eliminating opponents. The Blood Tubs, for example, threw venturesome Irishmen into tubs of blood obtained from local butchers, then chased them down the street with knives. This was a most potent deterrent to would-be voters. Another strategy was to strap sharp shoemakers' awls to knees and gouge holes in persistent opponents. These tactics inevitably provoked retaliation, and full-scale street warfare would begin. The Know Nothing groups in Maryland, representing the established Protestants, were spectacularly successful, winning local and state contests and, in 1856, the presidential election; in many districts, not a single immigrant managed to cast a ballot.

Such riots did not end in the 1850s. They were common during Reconstruction, when they served a racial function, and they were characteristic of the South long after the 1870s. Catholics and Protestants fought on election days in the heyday of the American Protective Association in the 1890s, and the Klan and its opponents occasionally struggled for control of the polls in the 1920s. In sum, election riots were one of the primary ways in which ethnic groups battled for hegemony.

Much of America's violence, then, has been between groups struggling for power: conflicts have repeatedly skidded out of the normal political processes. Much of the violence took the form of direct confrontation, although in many instances the state did aid one of the contending sides, almost always the dominant one. And American violence has been characteristically repressive: the great bulk of it was used by dominant groups defending their positions of privilege. Strikes have been crushed, slave revolts put down, peaceful growth of black communities blocked, abolitionists mobbed or killed, civil rights workers beaten or killed, thousands of blacks lynched, ethnic newcomers mobbed and kept from the polls, and radical labor organizations broken up.

This is not to deny a tradition of violence by the oppressed in our history. We have had slave revolts, agrarian rebellions (particularly in the colonial period when even *formal* opposition was considered illegitimate), and labor violence like that of the Molly Maguires. But three things are striking about such violence: its relative scarcity (our bread riots and Luddite violence were faint echoes of vigorous European traditions, for example); its characteristically low level (subordinate groups have engaged far more often in acts of force than of violence, and even their violence has been primarily directed against property rather than persons); its lack of challenge to the legitimacy of the state (such revolutionary violence as has occurred has come from the *right*, from displaced dominant groups, as during Reconstruction and the Civil War).

But this poses an important question. Why has there been so little expressive or revolutionary violence by subordinate groups throughout our history? I do not presume to have a simple explanation, but I offer a series of suggestions. It is best to start with the most obvious. To be subordinate is not automatically to be rebellious. I think that, on a gross level, Louis Hartz's notion of a Lockean consensus is largely correct: most groups at the bottom of the social and economic scale have not raised *fundamental* objections to the nature of bourgeois, capitalist America. They have attempted to become part of it, to get "more," in Samuel Gompers' words. Violence, therefore, would have been a most inappropriate tactic. Those who do not want to overthrow, but to be admitted, generally avoid violence. Still, there has been no lack of dissatisfied, angry groups who might readily have turned to violence to better their lot, so this explanation is not sufficient.

One reason why the anger was not turned against the *state* grows out of the peculiar nature of our repressive violence: the informal, nongovernmental nature of much of it. Subordinate groups have often suffered more violence from dominant groups than from the state. In race riots, lynchings, strike-smashing by private armies, massacres of scabs and Chinese by laborers, ethnic clashes, election riots, actions against civil rights workers, and vigilante terrorism, the state was simply not responsible for the bloodshed. It could not, therefore, be easily blamed, or become the focus for violent response. But often the state did actively engage in violence without producing lasting resentment against itself. Why was this so? Why were workers who were crushed by troops not turned into potential revolutionaries? Again there are many explanations, including the realities of power, the ethnic and racial divisions among the working class, and the vitiating effects of bourgeois ideology, but perhaps one explanation is that the state was considered to be a satellite, firmly within the orbit of some dominant social group. This may partly account for why it was seldom held directly and primarily responsible.

This dismissal of the state is a deeply ingrained American trait. It is the essence of the vigilante tradition that when there is serious work to be done, the community does it itself: it "takes the law into its own hands." Partly this attitude is a product of the weakness of the early American state, particularly on the frontier, but also in urban areas, where police forces were slow to develop. Partly it is due to the fragmentation of the American state into nation, state, county, town and city governments, many of them often at odds with one another. More directly, the dismissal of the state is related to the way decisions have been made in this country. A large number of critical decisions about the allocation of power and privilege have been in private arenas. Determinations about control of the economy, ethnic hegemony and racial power have often been made not in legislatures, but in the marketplace, if you will. Subordinate groups have not been accustomed to looking at the *laissez-faire* national state as a potential source of remedial action. Labor, for example, organized not parties to influence the state, but unions to confront capitalists directly. Perhaps anti-state violence has also seemed irrelevant to subordinate groups accustomed to thinking of the state as amorphous and secondary.*

Two traditional explanations for nonviolence by the discontented I have space only to mention. There is the important fact that the bulk of the white male population was integrated into the *formal* political process quite early in the nation's history. We had a voting proletariat before we had an organized proletariat. Secondly, individuals belonging to a discontented subordinate group in, say, an economic capacity might belong to a dominant racial group, and thus feel represented by the state in at least some manner. Both these facts would lessen the likelihood of anti-state violence.

A final, seemingly simple explanation for the relative nonviolence of the oppressed is that our subordinate groups have been *minorities*. They have been outnumbered. They have been outgunned. The relatively pacific history of Afro-Americans, for example, can most readily be explained in terms of the realities of power. They have been only ten or fifteen percent of the population. And while blacks occasionally did resort to violence against great odds, particularly during slavery, they have consistently avoided *revolutionary* action, and with good reason. Even if they successfully overthrew the government they would only have to rule the other hostile eighty-five or

---

*Perhaps, also, this is changing, as blacks and radicals now clearly perceive the national state as a source of both oppression and possible relief. Perhaps the assumption by the state of the task of repressing blacks that was previously performed by masses of whites might yet elicit an even more direct antistate response than the antipolice violence of the rebellions of the 1960s.

ninety percent. The direction that angry blacks have taken is either emigration, or the formation of some kind of autonomous structure within the larger community, in which they would be, at the least, a clear majority.

The question of numbers cuts deeper than mere tactical considerations, however: it goes to the root of the nature of our violence. America is peculiar in that our dominant groups have been, for the most part, *majorities*. American history has been a great success story (in purely material terms) for a large proportion of the population. Because the majority of the people (and "majority" includes *élites* as well as *masses*) has benefited from the economic structure of the nation, they have been conservative, determined to hold what they have. They have repeatedly seen attempts to partake of that success by those excluded—the poor, the blacks, the ethnic minorities, the unions—as imperiling their own position. They repeatedly repressed such challenges. And because they were majorities, in a nation that exalted the power of the majority and placed only feeble restrictions in its path, there was little to stop them from resorting to violence if they chose to; and little to keep even that violence within "civilized" boundaries, once employed.

I would like to suggest the relevance here of the worn idea that tyranny is a product of unchecked power, and particularly of Tocqueville's application of that dictum to majorities. Listen to his fears voiced more than a hundred and thirty years ago, and apply them to the plight of the black man, of that day or this:

> When an individual or a party is wronged in the United States, to whom can he apply for redress? If to public opinion, public opinion constitutes the majority; if to the legislature, it represents the majority and implicitly obeys it; if to the executive power, it is appointed by the majority and serves as a passive tool in its hands. The public force consists of the majority under arms; the jury is the majority invested with the right of hearing judicial cases; and in certain states even the judges are elected by the majority. However iniquitous or absurd the measure of which you complain, you must submit to it as well as you can.

What has much of our violence been but the ultimate form of the tyranny of the majority? Certainly this has been true of our racial history. The vigilante impulse has been central to the white American mind.

Our industrial violence is more complicated. It is true that union members, and even the poor, have been a minority in this country, but industrialists have been numerically even fewer than workers. The crucial fact is that the values of the capitalists were accepted by a majority of the country: a sufficiently monolithic consensus existed to ensure that the interests of the economic élite would be respected. The widespread diffusion of property, and the Horatio Alger mythology (which assured those who did not have a stake in the existing order that they eventually would), bolstered the power of the industrialists. They were able to transmute a defense of privilege into a defense of something more abstract, more acceptable to the majority: the defense of law, order and property. Unions, particularly when largely composed of aliens, were branded as dangers to the existing order; labeling them anarchist or Communist helped isolate them. As a consequence, the majority did not check, but indeed acquiesced in, the resort to repressive violence by the economic élite.

The absence of restraint is a critical factor. Here again the work of Louis Hartz is illuminating when he speaks of the absence in America of powerful institutions that were Europe's inheritance from feudalism. Stanley Elkins applied this insight to the nature of American slavery, arguing that the absence of institutional checks on profit-oriented masters produced a particularly harsh system. We need not agree with all of Elkins' thesis to suspect that the idea is important for the character of American industrial capitalism. For its growth was essentially unchecked, certainly unchecked by a state that for much of our history accepted the principle of *laissez-faire* when it came to regulating business, but that, when it came to assisting it, became so integrated with the economy as to be almost indistinguishable from it. Industrialists developed a logical ruthlessness, and a disregard for human life that is perhaps the inevitable outgrowth of virtually unchecked power.

I am aware that I have passed over a host of ambiguities and subtleties. I am convinced, however, that when they are all taken into account, the pattern I have sketched, at this level of generalization, remains unchanged. It may be objected, for example, that the groups I have discussed are far from monolithic. Of course, there are many varieties of capitalists: industrialists, merchants, financiers and so on; and divisions among them are important in determining the time, intensity, duration and nature of violent episodes. But capitalists are capitalists; their differences often dissolve in the face of a common enemy. For all practical purposes, on the broad question of dealing with labor during the industrial war, they were in substantial agreement; dissenters didn't affect the course of events significantly. It may be objected that there are difficulties in measuring intentions and purposiveness, particularly when dealing with crowds. But to avoid generalizations because in specific cases we lack direct evidence of the mind of participants is to be unnecessarily fastidious. We are dealing, after all, with *patterns* of events, as the lynching of blacks by whites, thousands of times, often in a public ritual fashion, for transgressions against the caste system. Granting that many crowd (or élite) actions are undisciplined, and at times partake of the psychopathological, the overall pattern clearly bespeaks social intentionality. Crowds are not irrational herds, nor are they mechanistic bodies reacting reflexively to stimuli like "relative deprivation": they are acting politically— with passion perhaps, but usually with a clear sense of what they are about.

Finally, if it be objected that I have not discussed many other types of purposive violence, I would agree. We are just beginning to probe this area.

There are many kinds of domestic violence to be considered: vigilantism; the repression of antiwar groups, political and cultural radicals, and abolitionists; crime; our own war of national liberation, the greatest single incident of purposive violence, the Civil War. I have not discussed our use of violence against other people: the Indian and Mexican wars, by which we gained our continent, the wars by which we gained our empire, or the interventions all over the world, including Vietnam, by which we seek to maintain it. There are intriguing questions about the *interaction* between our domestic and exported violence that have been passed over. Why is it, for example, that almost without exception the greatest outbreaks of racial violence in our history have come in wartime—in 1863, 1917–19, 1943, 1964–68, with lesser outbreaks in other war periods, like 1740 and 1898? Conversely, how has America's pervasive racism and readiness to use violence against Indians and blacks affected our imperialist ventures? In our repression of the Philippine insurrection, our rationalization for violence was that the Filipinos were an inferior race that we had a duty to civilize. (It is noteworthy that in those lynching days our troops, including officers, habitually referred to the Filipinos whom they killed and tortured, and whose huts they burned, as "niggers.") And when all these aspects of our violence have been explored, it will remain to be seen how our history compares with that of other countries, but it is not too early to suggest that the use of violence has been a fundamental and grim characteristic of the American past.

Room at the Top?
The Blueing of America

Peter L. Berger and Brigitte Berger

It was with no small measure of insight that English poet and social wit Oscar Wilde observed in 1893: "The youth of America is their oldest tradition. It has been going on for three hundred years." Wilde's observation, though originally applied to the American nation generally, has the added value of highlighting the myths surrounding today's "counterculture." Talk of a contemporary "children's crusade" and a cultural "greening of America" is not without historical precedents that flirt with the realm of fantasy. The youth cult, which sees the current generation as the saving element of society, is anything but an original or unique phenomenon. Youth has always sought to provide its society with a new cultural texture and horizon of expectation. Peter and Brigitte Berger, professors of sociology at Rutgers and Long Island University respectively, note the lessons that both history and sociological insight provide in this regard. Excursions into a "utopia of childhood" merely give others more in tune with the actualities of class and power in America "the possibilities of engineering reality."

A sizable segment of the American intelligentsia has been on a kick of revolution talk for the last few years. Only very recently this talk was carried on in a predominantly Left mood, generating fantasies of political revolution colored red or black. The mood appears to have shifted somewhat. Now the talk has shifted to cultural revolution. Gentle grass is pushing up through the cement. It is "the kids," hair and all, who will be our salvation. But what the two types of revolution talk have in common is a sovereign disregard for the realities of technological society in general, and for the realities of class and power in America.

Only the most religious readers of leftist publications could ever believe that a political revolution from the Left had the slightest prospects in America. The so-called black revolution is at a dividing fork, of which we shall speak in a moment. But as to the putatively green revolution, we think that the following will be its most probable result: It will accelerate social mobility in America, giving new opportunities for upward movement of lower-middle-class and working-class people, and in the process will change the ethnic and religious composition of the higher classes. Put differently: far from "greening" America, the alleged cultural revolution will serve to strengthen the vitality of the technological society against which it is directed, and will further the interests of precisely those social strata that are least touched by its currently celebrated transformations of consciousness.

The cultural revolution is not taking place in a social vacuum, but has a specific location in a society that is organized in terms of classes. The cadres of the revolution, not exclusively but predominantly, are the college-educated children of the upper-middle class. Ethnically, they tend to be Wasps and Jews. Religiously, the former tend to belong to the main-line Protestant denominations, rather than to the more fundamentalist or sectarian groups. The natural focus of the revolution is the campus (more precisely, the type of campus attended by this population), and such satellite communities as have been springing up on its fringes. In other words, the revolution is taking place, or minimally has its center, in a subculture of upper-middle-class youth.

The revolution has not created this subculture. Youth, as we know it today, is a product of technological and economic forces intimately tied to the dynamics of modern industrialism, as is the educational system within which the bulk of contemporary youth is concentrated for ever-longer periods of life. What is true in the current interpretations is that some quite dramatic transformations of consciousness have been taking place in this sociocultural ambience. These changes are too recent, and too much affected by distortive mass-media coverage, to allow for definitive description. It is difficult to say which manifestations are only transitory and which are intrinsic features likely to persist over time. Drugs are a case in point. So is the remarkable upsurge of interest in religion and the occult. However, one statement can be made with fair assurance: the cultural revolution has defined itself in diametric opposition to some of the basic values of bourgeois society, those values that since Max Weber have commonly been referred to as the "Protestant ethic"—discipline, achievement and faith in the onward-and-upward thrust of technological society. These same values are now perceived as "repression" and "hypocrisy," and the very promises of technological society are rejected as illusionary or downright immoral. A hedonistic ethic is proclaimed in opposition to the "Protestant" one, designed to "liberate" the individual from the bourgeois inhibitions in all areas of life, from sexuality through aesthetic experience to the manner in which careers are planned. Achievement is perceived as futility and "alienation," its ethos as "uptight" and, in the final analysis, inimical to life. Implied in all this is a radical aversion to capitalism and the class society that it has engendered, thus rendering the subculture open to leftist ideology of one kind or another.

Its radicalism, though, is much more far-reaching than that of ordinary, politically defined leftism. It is not simply in opposition to the particular form of technological society embodied in bourgeois capitalism but to the very idea of technological society. The rhetoric is Rousseauean rather than Jacobin, the imagery of salvation is intensely bucolic, the troops of the revolution are not the toiling masses of the Marxist prophecy but naked children of nature dancing to the tune of primitive drums.

When people produce a utopia of childhood it is a good idea to ask what their own childhood has been like. In this instance, the answer is not difficult. As Philippe Ariès has brilliantly shown, one of the major cultural accomplishments of the bourgeoisie has been the dramatic transformation of the structure of childhood, in theory as well as in practice. Coupled with the steep decline in child mortality and morbidity that has been brought about by modern medicine and nutrition, this transformation is one of the fundamental facts of modern society. A new childhood has come into being, probably happier than any previous one in human society. Its impact, however, must be seen in conjunction with another fundamental fact of modern society—namely, the increasing bureaucratization of all areas of social life. We would see the turmoil of youth today as being rooted in the clash between these two facts —paraphrasing Max Weber, in the clash between the new "spirit of childhood" and the "spirit of bureaucracy." However one may wish to judge the merits of either fact, both are probably here to stay. Logically enough, the clash almost invariably erupts when the graduates of the new childhood first encounter bureaucracy in their own life—to wit, in the educational system.

We cannot develop this explanation any further here, though we would like to point out that it is almost exactly the opposite of the Freudian interpretations of the same clash provided, for example, by Lewis Feuer or Bruno Bettelheim: Rebellious youth is not fighting against any fathers; on the contrary, it is outraged by the *absence* of parental figures and familial warmth in the bureaucratic institutions that envelop it. The point to stress, though, is that the transformation of childhood, born of the bourgeoisie, today affects nearly all classes in American society—*but it does not affect them equally.* As, for example, the work of John Seeley and Herbert Gans has demonstrated, there exist far-reaching differences between the childrearing practices of different classes. The transformation, and with it the new "spirit of childhood," developed most fully and most dramatically in the upper-middle class—that is, in the same social context that is presently evincing the manifestations of "greening."

To say this is in no way to engage in value judgments. If value judgments are called for, we would suggest calibrated ones. Very few human cultures (or subcultures) are either wholly admirable or wholly execrable, and the intellectuals who extoll this particular one are as much *terribles simplificateurs* as the politicians who anathematize it. In any case, our present purpose is to inquire into the probable consequences of the cultural changes in question.

The matrix of the green revolution has been a class-specific youth culture. By definition, this constitutes a biographical way station. Long-haired or not, *everyone*, alas, gets older. This indubitable biological fact has been used by exasperated over-thirty observers to support their hope that the new youth culture may be but a noisier version of the old American pattern of sowing wild oats. Very probably this is true for many young rebels, especially those who indulge in the external paraphernalia and gestures of the youth culture without fully entering into its new consciousness. But there is evidence that for an as yet unknown number, the way station is becoming a place of permanent settlement. For an apparently growing number there is a movement *from youth culture to counter-culture*. These are the ones who drop out permanently. For yet others, passage through the youth culture leaves, at any rate, certain permanent effects, not only in their private lives but in their occupational careers. As with the Puritanism that gave birth to the bourgeois culture of America, this movement too has its fully accredited saints and those who only venture upon a *halfway covenant*. The former, in grim righteousness, become sandal makers in Isla Vista. The latter at least repudiate the more obviously devilish careers within "the system"—namely, those in scientific technology, business and government that lead to positions of status and privilege in the society. They do not drop out, but at least they shift their majors—in the main, to the humanities and the social sciences, as we have recently seen in academic statistics.

The overall effects of all this will, obviously, depend on the magnitude of these changes. To gauge the effects, however, one will have to relate them to the class and occupational structures of the society. For those who become permanent residents of the counter-culture, and most probably for their children, the effect is one of downward social mobility. This need not be the case for the halfway greeners (at least as long as the society is ready to subsidize, in one way or another, poets, T-group leaders and humanistic sociologists). But they too will have been deflected from those occupational careers (in business, government, technology and science) that continue to lead to the higher positions in a modern society.

What we must keep in mind is that whatever cultural changes may be going on in this or that group, the personnel requirements of a technological society not only continue but actually expand. The notion that as a result of automation fewer and fewer people will be required to keep the technological society going, thus allowing the others to do their own thing and nevertheless enjoy the blessings of electricity, is in contradiction to all the known facts. Automation has resulted in changes in the occupational structure, displacing various categories of lower-skilled labor, but it has in no way reduced the number of people required to keep the society going. On the contrary, it has increased the requirements for scientific, technological and (last but not least) bureaucratic personnel. (The recent decline in science and engineering jobs is due to recession, and does not affect the long-term needs of the society.) The positions disdained by the aforementioned upper-middle-class individuals will therefore have to be filled by someone else. The upshot is simple: *There will be new "room at the top."*

Who is most likely to benefit from this sociological windfall? It will be the newly college-educated children of the lower-middle and working classes. To say this, we need not assume that they remain untouched by their contact with the youth culture during their school years. Their sexual mores, their aesthetic tastes, even their political opinions might become permanently altered as compared with those of their parents. We do assume, though, that they will, now as before, reject the anti-achievement ethos of the cultural revolution. They may take positions in intercourse that are frowned upon by Thomas Aquinas, they may continue to listen to hard rock on their hi-fi's and they may have fewer racial prejudices. But all these cultural acquisitions are, as it were, functionally irrelevant to making it in the technocracy. Very few of them will become sandal makers or farmers on communes in Vermont. We suspect that not too many more will become humanistic sociologists.

Precisely those classes that remain most untouched by what is considered to be the revolutionary tide in contemporary America face *new prospects of upward social mobility.* Thus, the "revolution" (hardly the word) is not at all where it seems to be, which should not surprise anyone. The very word *avant-garde* suggests that one ought to look behind it for what is to follow—and there is no point asking the *avant-gardistes,* whose eyes are steadfastly looking forward. Not even the Jacobins paid attention to the grubby tradesmen waiting to climb up over their shoulders. A technological society, given a climate of reasonable tolerance (mainly a function of affluence), can afford a sizable number of sandal makers. Its "knowledge industry" (to use Fritz Machlup's term) has a large "software" division, which can employ considerable quantities of English majors. And, of course, the educational system provides a major source of employment for nontechnocratic personnel. To this may be added the expanding fields of entertainment and therapy, in all their forms. All the same, quite different people are needed to occupy the society's command posts and to keep its engines running. These people will have to retain the essentials of the old "Protestant ethic"—discipline, achievement orientation, and also a measure of freedom from gnawing self-doubt. If such people are no longer available in one population reservoir, another reservoir will have to be tapped.

There is no reason to think that "the system" will be unable to make the necessary accommodations. If Yale should become hopelessly greened, Wall Street will get used to recruits from Fordham or Wichita State. Italians will have no trouble running the RAND Corporation, Baptists the space program. Political personnel will change in the wake of social mobility. It is quite possible that the White House may soon have its first Polish occupant (or, for that matter, its first Greek). Far from weakening the class system, these changes will greatly strengthen it, moving new talent upward and preventing rigidity at the top (though, probably, having little effect at the *very* top). Nor will either the mechanics or the rewards of social mobility change in any significant degree. A name on the door will still rate a Bigelow on the floor; only there will be fewer Wasp and fewer Jewish names. Whatever other troubles "the system" may face, from pollution to Russian ICBMS, it will not have to worry about its being brought to a standstill by the cultural revolution.

It is, of course, possible to conceive of such economic or political shocks to "the system" that technological society, as we have known it in America, might collapse, or at least seriously deteriorate. Ecological catastrophe on a broad scale, massive malfunction of the capitalist economy, or an escalation of terrorism and counter-terror would be cases in point. Despite the currently fashionable prophecies of doom for American society, we regard these eventualities as very unlikely. If any of them should take place after all, it goes without saying that the class system would stop operating in its present form. But whatever else would then be happening in America, it would *not* be the green revolution. In the even remoter eventuality of a socialist society in this country, we would know where to look for our greeners—in "rehabilitation camps," along the lines of Castro's Isle of Pines.

We have been assuming that the children of the lower-middle and working classes remain relatively unbitten by the "greening" bug—at least sufficiently unbitten so as not to interfere with their aspirations of mobility. If they too should drop out, there would be literally no one left to mind the technological store. But it is not very easy to envisage this. America falling back to the status of an underdeveloped society? Grass growing over the computers? A totalitarian society, in which the few remaining "uptight" people run the technocracy, while the rest just groove? Or could it be Mongolian ponies grazing on the White House lawn? Even if the great bulk of Americans were to become "beautiful people," however, the rest of the world is most unlikely to follow suit. So far in history, the uglies have regularly won out over the "beautiful people." They probably would again this time.

The evidence does not point in this direction. The data we have on the dynamics of class in a number of European countries would suggest that the American case may not be all that unique. Both England and western Germany have been undergoing changes in their class structures very similar to those projected by us, with new reservoirs of lower-middle-class and working-class populations supplying the personnel requirements of a technological society no longer served adequately by the old élites.

What we have described as a plausible scenario is not terribly dramatic, at least compared with the revolutionary visions that intellectuals so often thrive on. Nor are we dealing with a process unique in history. Vilfredo Pareto called this type of process the "circulation of élites." Pareto emphasized (rightly, we think) that such circulation is essential if a society is going to survive. In a Paretian perspective, much of the green revolution would have to be seen in terms of decadence (which, let us remark in passing, is not necessarily a value judgment—some very impressive flowerings of human creativity have been decadent in the same sociological sense).

But even Marx may, in a paradoxical manner, be proven right in the end. It may be the blue-collar masses that are, at last, coming into their own. "Power to the people!"—nothing less than that. The "class struggle" may be approaching a new phase, with the children of the working class victorious. These days we can see their banner all over the place. It is the American flag. In that perspective, the peace emblem is the old bourgeoisie, declining in the face of a more robust adversary. Robustness here refers, above all, to consciousness—not only to a continuing achievement ethos, but to a self-confidence not unduly worried by unending self-examination and by a basically intact faith in the possibilities of engineering reality. Again, it would not be the first time in history that a declining class leaned toward pacifism, as to the "beautiful things" of aesthetic experience. Seen by that class, of course, the blue-collar masses moving in suffer from considerable aesthetic deficiencies.

"Revolutionary" America? Perhaps, in a way. We may be on the eve of its blueing.

Sport: If You Want to Build Character, Try Something Else

Bruce Ogilvie and Thomas A. Tutko

The practice and ritual of athletics have become central to American popular culture today. Many see competitive sports as the essence of the "American way." Some have gone so far as to suggest that it is to sports that America owes her greatness. A former football coach at the University of Notre Dame is purported to have said that America succeeded in World War II because it had the T-formation and the Germans did not. The American emphasis on sport, and the widely-held notion that athletics builds character, are the subjects of the selection that follows. Bruce Ogilvie and Thomas A. Tutko, psychologists at San José State College in California, challenge "the last stronghold of the American myth—the locker room."

The cultural revolution has penetrated the last stronghold of the American myth—the locker room. Young athletes, having scaled new levels of consciousness, now challenge a long-standing article of faith—the belief that competition has intrinsic value. They enter sports in search of particular esthetic experience, essentially personal in nature. They no longer accept the authoritarian structure of sports, nor do they accept the supreme emphasis on winning. Outside critics who see in the sports world a metaphor for the moral deficiencies of American society add to the pressure in the once-sacred precincts.

Coaches and administrators defend organized sport with traditional claims that competition builds character and toughens the young for life in the real world. Coaches in particular don't want to listen to the requests of the young. The stereotype of the ideal athlete is fading fast. Long-haired radicals with life-styles and political beliefs unheard of a few years ago people the uncomfortable dreams of coaches.

In the midst of the controversy psychologists find themselves being asked what personal, social or psychological significance can be attributed to organized sport. For the past eight years we have been studying the effects of competition on personality. Our research began with the counseling of problem athletes, but it soon expanded to include athletes from every sport, at every level from the high-school gym to the professional arena. On the evidence gathered in this study, we can make some broad-range value judgments. We found no empirical support for the tradition that sport builds character. Indeed, there is evidence that athletic competition limits growth in some areas. It seems that the personality of the ideal athlete is not the result of any molding process, but comes out of the ruthless selection process that occurs at all levels of sport. Athletic competition has no more beneficial effects than intense endeavor in any other field. Horatio Alger success—in sport or elsewhere—comes only to those who already are mentally fit, resilient and strong.

The problem athletes who made up our original sample displayed such severe emotional reactions to stress that we had serious doubts about the basic value of athletic competition. The problems associated with sport covered a wide spectrum of behavior, but we were able to isolate major syndromes: the con-man athlete, the hyperanxious athlete, the athlete who resists coaching, the success-phobic athlete, the injury-prone athlete and the depression-prone athlete.

When we confronted such cases, it became more and more difficult for us to make positive clinical interpretations on the effects of competition. In 1963, we established the Institute for the Study of Athletic Motivation to start research aimed at helping athletes reach their potentials. We wanted to examine normal players as well as problem athletes. To identify sport-specific personality traits, we and Lee Lyon developed the Athletic Motivation Inventory (AMI), which measures eleven traits common to most successful sports figures. We have since administered the AMI to approximately 15,000 athletes. The results of these tests indicate that general sports personalities do exist.

Athletes who survive the high attrition rate associated with sports competition are characterized by all or most of the following traits:

(1) They have great need for achievement and tend to set high but realistic goals for themselves and others.

(2) They are highly organized, orderly, respectful of authority and dominant.

(3) They have large capacity for trust, great psychological endurance, self-control, low-resting levels of anxiety and slightly greater ability to express aggression.

Most athletes indicate low interest in receiving support and concern from others, low need to take care of others, and low need for affiliation. Such a personality seems necessary to achieve victory over others. There is some question whether these trends are temporary character traits—changing when the athlete gets out of sport—or permanent ones. Using men coaches and women physical educators as reference groups, we would predict that these character trends remain highly stable.

We discovered subgroupings within the athletic personality. For example, outstanding women competitors show a greater tendency toward introversion, greater autonomy needs, and a combination of qualities suggesting that they are more creative than their male counterparts. They show less need for sensitive and understanding involvement with others. Women competitors are more reserved and cool, more experimental, more independent than male. Interestingly, we found that among women there was far less trait variation from one sport to another than there was among men. (Exceptions were women fencers, gymnasts and parachutists.) We attribute this to cultural repression of women—to succeed in *any* field, a woman has to be able to stand up and spit in the eye of those in charge.

In addition to sex differences, we were able to distinguish a team-sports personality from an individual-sports personality. Persons in individual competition tend more toward healthy introversion. They are less affiliative than team players, have a higher level of aggression and tend to be more creative.

For some sports we could even distinguish a particular personality type. For example, the data strongly distinguish a race-driver personality. More than participants in any other sport, drivers are tough-minded, hard-headed realists. They are reserved and cool. They override their feelings and are not fanciful. They do not show anxiety or tension and are self-sufficient. They are tremendously achievement-oriented, far more than the average athlete.

Our original hypothesis about the ill effects of high-level competition turned out to be unfounded. When we completed tests on the original teams, we discovered no negative relation between athletic achievement and emotional maturity or control. On the contrary, the higher the achievement, the greater the probability the athlete would have emotional maturity or control. Sport is like most other activities—those who survive tend to have stronger personalities.

The competitive-sport experience is unique in the way it compresses the selection process into a compact time and space. There are few areas of human endeavor that can match the Olympic trials or a professional training camp for intensity of human stress. A young athlete often must face in hours or days the kind of pressure that occurs in the life of the achievement-oriented man over several years. The potential for laying bare the personality structure of the individual is considerable. When the athlete's ego is deeply invested in sports achievement, very few of the neurotic protective mechanisms provide adequate or sustaining cover. Basically, each must face his moment of truth and live with the consequences. The pro rookie usually gets only three or four chances to demonstrate ability before he is sent home. What sort of personality structure supports the person who can face this blunt reinforcement of reality?

And beyond brutally rapid and clear evaluation of competence is the stress from the neglect of basic human needs that may accompany athletic success. Take the case of a high draft-choice football player; after tearing up the camp the first few days, he turned morose and sullen. He was experiencing what often happens to men who excel in any area—the withdrawal of emotional support from those outside his field. Persons who were close to this gifted young man had pulled away, assuming that they were no longer important in his life, that he had outgrown his need for them. They anticipated rejection, but rather than live with this threat they retreated at the first opportunity. Quite often an athlete's wife experiences this reaction. Threatened by her husband's new acclaim, she may withhold love and support from him. When the tension between his success on the field and his crumbling home life gets unbearable, the athlete sometimes manages to get a mild injury. Rare is the man who can make it in sport without the support of his wife.

Under such intense pressure, with threats from so many different directions, personality flaws manifest themselves quickly. We found that personal reactions to the stress of competition remain fairly constant across the sports. Depression, combined with failure due to unconscious fear of success, hyper-anxiety (the athlete who burns himself out before the competition begins), and exaggerated sensitivity to failure or criticism accounted for more than half of our referrals. The same telescoping of time and space that uncovers personality deficiencies with such rapidity, however, provides a splendid laboratory for experimentation with self-change. The rapidity and clarity of feedback in competitive sport provides a fine opportunity for the individual athlete who knows which traits he wants to change and who has the motivation to do so.

By showing the athlete that certain habitual ways of behaving or thinking keep him from reaching his potential, we open a collaborative approach between coach and athlete that may solve the problem. Obviously the motive to change depends on a number of variables, including the extent to which the ego is invested in sports. When we sit down with a young man who has just signed a contract for $250,000 and tell him that on the basis of his test scores he doesn't measure up to his fellow pros in certain traits, he makes only one comment: "How do I change that, Doc?" But the high-school athlete has a motivational conflict of another order when he has to decide whether he will work to support his car so that he can keep his girl friend or spend his time excelling in his sport.

Though we can identify the common traits of successful athletes and counsel a highly motivated youth on how to strengthen particular traits, we cannot tell how much these traits actually contribute to athletic success. Competition doesn't seem to build character and it is possible that competition doesn't even *require* much more than a minimally integrated personality.

Innate physical ability is always a contaminating factor when we attempt to make statements about the relationship between character and success. Even using a sample of Olympic competitors and professionals, we find that independent judges' ratings of ability in any given athlete fluctuate considerably. At best, judges can agree on the relative ability of athletes in the top and bottom six to twelve percent.

We are similarly unable to determine the extent to which character contributes to coaching success. In this case the uncontrolled factor is the degree to which the coach is master of his science. We found that there is no way to compensate for lack of knowledge in one's field, but we do not know the degree to which this skill must be augmented by strong character traits.

We know from our work hundreds of outstanding competitors who possess strong character formation that complements high motor skill. But we found others who possessed so few strong character traits that it was difficult on the basis of personality to account for their success. There were gold-medal Olympic winners in Mexico and Japan whom we would classify as overcompensatory greats. Only magnificent physical gifts enabled them to overcome constant tension, anxiety and self-doubt. They are unhappy, and when the talent ages and fades, they become derelicts, while someone like Roosevelt Grier just goes on to bigger mountains. We often wonder how much higher some of these great performers might have gone if they had, say, the strong personality structure that characterized our women's Olympic fencing team.

A certain minimum personality development is essential. We once encountered a long-distance runner who was so gifted that, late one night, running in total darkness with only pacers and timers, he broke the NCAA record for his event. The mark would have survived for the next four years. But upon achieving this goal, he quit the team, never to compete again. He later explained that he did it to get even with his coach; but our data suggest a different interpretation. It seems that grave personal doubts about his worth as a person impaired his capacity to support the burden of success. He preferred to protect his fragile ego by showing bursts of superior performance then retreating to mediocrity so that others would not depend on him.

We have also seen some indications that there may be an *upper* limit on the character development needed for success in sport. Sometimes we find players who have good physical skills coupled with immense character strengths who don't make it in sports. They seem to be so well put together emotionally that there is no neurotic tie to sport. The rewards of sport aren't enough for them any more, and they turn away voluntarily to other, more challenging fields. This is singularly frustrating to their coaches.

We quickly discovered that the coach was the crucial factor—whether we were trying to modify a disturbed athlete's behavior, or measure the influence of competition on the successful athlete's personality. Consequently, we made special efforts to identify the personality traits of coaches. We found that there was indeed a coach personality. It was similar to the competitor's, but the traits tended to be intensified, as with race drivers.

We found that our test data provided a more reliable personality model of athletes than the coaches' observations, that the tests gave better insights into individual differences and allowed for better gauging of individual limitations as well as strengths. Coaches are most reliable in their perception of personality tendencies that are a significant part of their own character structure. They prove to be most reliable in identifying the traits of dominance, psychological endurance and athletic drive, but are unable to recognize such traits as emotional control, self-confidence, trust, conscience, self-abasement, or tenderness. We also found that coaches tend to be blind to deficiencies in gifted athletes.

We find most coaches uncertain and anxious about the changes taking place in sport. They have shown an overwhelming positive response to our efforts to bring the tools of psychology into their careers. They're crying for new methods, new information. They know that they are not fully prepared for their tasks.

Many of the changes run counter to values deeply rooted in the coach personality. Athletes who ask the basic question—"Is winning all that worthwhile?"—deny the coach's life's work, and his very existence. Most coaches go by the Vince Lombardi dictum that "winning isn't everything—it's the only thing."

Conflict over values manifests itself in struggles over discipline. Hair length comes to mind. The coach sees hair as a problem of authority; he orders the athlete to get it cut and expects his order to be obeyed. In contrast, the athlete sees discipline as a peripheral, frivolous issue compared with his own struggle to find identity in the hair styles of his peers. Coach and hirsute athlete talk past each other. Value changes that involve drugs and politics put the coach under strain. Most coaches believe that a truly good athlete is also, by definition, a red-blooded, clean-living, truth-telling, prepared patriot. A top-notch competitor who disagrees with national policy is a heavy thing for a coach who undoubtedly believes that the wars of England were indeed won on the playing fields of Eton.

Many coaches won't be able to stand the strain. Eventually, the world of sport is going to take the emphasis off winning-at-any-cost. The new direction will be toward helping athletes make personally chosen modifications in behavior; toward the joyous pursuit of esthetic experience; toward wide variety of personality types and values. Inevitably these changes are going to force the least flexible coaches out of the business—perhaps as many as a third of them.

American Indians:
People without a Future

Ralph Nader

By way of footnote to the pervasiveness and continuance of myth, perhaps a final comment is in order as to its continued impact upon the first Americans. Except for the short period of grace, during which he functioned as Noble Savage, the Indian has suffered the fate of "centuries of dishonor" at the collective hands of White America. Consumer advocate Ralph Nader, a person not unaccustomed to dealing with myths related to the American Dream, here strikes at the perversions of the "histories of the conqueror"—the mythical contention sustained by "white" history that the American Indian contributed little to "American" institutions and traditions. Like his fellow Black American, the American Indian has stood witness to a society bent on denying him a historical and cultural past. Despite "buried legacy" and "grotesque stereotype," the American Indian has always had a past of significant stature. Mr. Nader suggests that the best way to assure the Indian a future is to refund him his past.

> "We are people who are better known for what we were not than what we were, for what we are not than for what we are."
>
> *A Crow Indian, 1955*

American historical and fictional writings have instilled in the American public a misinformed and highly inaccurate view of the American Indian.

What our forefathers conquered, according to the writers, was an almost empty land whose tranquility was disturbed by a few scattered groupings of wild savages whose chief vocations were scalp-collecting, pottery-making and dancing. These primitives, so the myth goes, steadily receded before the onrush of "civilization" and have now become the "Vanishing American" of novel and poem.

There developed a voluminous history of the American idea of the Indian as a savage, a concept indispensable to a righteous and ethnocentric people appropriating a continent. Even today, on the screen and in cheap fiction, the "bloodthirsty Indian" has too often been used as an ugly background against which the virtues of our pioneers may be projected.

In more recent times a more refined concept of the "savage" Indian performs another function. It provides a readily-available rationalization for those who covet Indian lands and resources. Bureaucrats promote programs

From "American Indians: People without a Future," by Ralph Nader, *Harvard Law Record* (April 5, 1956). Reprinted by permission of the *Harvard Law School Record Corporation*.

to "liberate" the Indian under the mistaken notion that Indian culture and misery go together.

There is also a strain running through our literary heritage which has depicted the "noble" side of the aborigine. At times this noble savage theme has done the Indian more harm than good.

Countering the common belief, Jack Schaefer, author of "Shane," wrote: "These natives, on the whole, were not as savage as the Europeans who called them savages. They had a distinct and in some respects highly developed civilization. . . . In the fundamentals of human decency, the simple amenities of daily life, in the relationships between man and man and between man and his God, they were easily as refined as the Europeans. But from the conquerors' point of view they were guilty to two sins: They were different; they were in the way. So they were called savages."

Our historians have been almost exclusively concerned with influences emanating from Europe. A comprehensive study of the impact of Indian culture on American society would reveal some important insights into the contributing cultural elements that make America what it is today. The material and institutional impact of Indian culture remains inadequately understood and largely underestimated. Space limitations necessarily require only a superficial statement of such contributions.

The changes that American Indians wrought in the life of our pioneers were far more impressive and less destructive than any changes "white" teachers have yet brought to Indian life. Early settlers recognized that Indian modes and methods were functionally adapted to their physical environment. Four-sevenths of our national farm produce consists of plants domesticated by Indian botanists of pre-Columbian times. Indian agricultural products also had a tremendous impact on the European economy. The story of the potato in Europe need not be retold. Methods of planting, irrigation, cultivation, storage and utilization were also acquired by settlers from the Indians.

In medicine, as in the production of food and textiles, the conventional picture of the Indian as an ignorant savage is far removed from the truth. Cocaine, quinine, cascara, sagrada, ipecac, arnica and other drugs were developed and used by the Indian before Columbus landed. In the four hundred years that physicians and botanists have been examining and analyzing the flora of America, they have not yet discovered a medicinal herb unknown to the Indians. The social significance of such material contributions is impressive.

As is being illustrated in "underdeveloped" countries today, a change in material living standard inevitably influences, destroys, and creates institutional patterns and modes of behavior. The impact of Indian material culture undoubtedly has had important repercussions on our society from our economy to the homestead system, and in land use, athletics, our boy scout movement and our national worship of sun, air, and water.

But the Indian gave more in the realm of the intangible. The distinctive political ideals of young America owed much to a rich Indian democratic tradition—a debt often recognized by statements of our leading colonists. The pattern of states within a state that we call federalism, the habit of treating chiefs as servants of the people instead of masters, the insistence that the community must respect the diversity of men and their dreams—all these things were part of the American way of life before 1492.

Franklin carried his admiration for the great Iroquois Confederacy to the Albany Congress, and Jefferson made numerous references to the freedom and democracy of Indian society which achieved the maximum degree of order with the minimum degree of coercion. The late Felix Cohen, noted legal scholar and Indian authority, remarked: "those accustomed to the histories of the conqueror will hardly be convinced, though example be piled on example, that American democracy, freedom and tolerance are more American than European, and have deep aboriginal roots in our land."

At this point the reader may well ask: "Of what relevance is this buried legacy to the present and future?" First, there is still much that the Indian can contribute to our cultural enrichment. Indian ingenuity in agriculture, government, medicine, sports, education and craftsmanship is not at an end.

Let a few examples do for many. Not long ago, the rediscovery of an old Indian dish, toasted corn flakes, revolutionized the breakfast routine of American families. A classic study of Cheyenne law by the anthropologist E. Adamson Hoebel and Prof. Karl Llewellyn provided insights into our own jurisprudence. Indian methods of child training have caught the attention of psychiatrists and pediatricians, who are now comparing these methods with the rigid schedules and formulas that have molded our antiseptic babies of recent decades.

Second, recognition by legislators, administrators and the American public of the true nature of our Indian heritage has great importance in freeing the Indian from a contemptuous and grotesque stereotype. It also may diminish the persistent themes of pity, superiority and the white man's burden, which have been twisted into a vicious weapon against Indian culture and landholdings. Respect for different cultures may bring about a reasoned and humane policy which will fulfill Indian desires to achieve a higher living standard and still maintain his ethnic identity.

Suggested Further Reading for Chapter 5

Carl Becker, "Everyman His Own Historian," *American Historical Review*, 37 (1932).

Tom Christofell *et al.* (eds.), *Up Against the American Myth: A Radical Critique of Corporate Capitalism* (New York: Holt, Rinehart & Winston, 1970).

Malcolm Cowley, "American Myths Old and New," *Saturday Review*, 45 (1962).

H. D. Graham, "Paradox of American Violence: A Historical Appraisal," *Annals of The American Academy*, 391 (1970).

Richard C. Gregory, *No More Lies: The Myth and the Reality of American History* (New York: Harper & Row, Publishers, 1971).

Aileen S. Kraditor (ed.), *Up From the Pedestal: Selected Writings in the History of American Feminism* (Chicago: Quadrangle Books, 1970).

Dwight McDonald, "Our Invisible Poor," *The New Yorker*, 39 (1963).

Roger L. Nichols and George R. Adams (eds.), *The American Indian: Past and Present* (Waltham, Mass.: Xerox College Publishing, 1971).

Richard L. Rapson (ed.), *Individualism and Conformity in the American Character* (Lexington, Mass.: D.C. Heath & Co., 1967).

Richard L. Rapson (ed.), *The Cult of Youth in Middle-Class America* (Lexington, Mass.: D. C. Heath & Co., 1971).

Charles Reich, *The Greening of America* (New York: Random House, Inc., 1970).

Peter Schrag, "The Age of Willie Mays," *Saturday Review*, 54 (1971).

Peter Schrag, "The Negro in Modern American History Textbooks," *Saturday Review*, 50 (1967).

Page Smith, *Daughters of the Promised Land: Women in American History* (Boston: Little, Brown and Company, 1970).

Michael Wallace and Richard Hofstadter (eds.), *American Violence: A Documentary History* (New York: Alfred A. Knopf, Inc., 1970).

John William Ward, "The Ideal of Individualism and the Reality of Organization," in *Red, White, and Blue: Men, Books, and Ideas in American Culture* (New York: Oxford University Press, 1969).